AF887515

NCERT EXEMPLAR

Problems - Solutions

Mathematics 9th

BEST Solution
Guaranteed •••

NCERT EXEMPLAR
Problems - Solutions
Mathematics 9th

Author
Rakesh Pandey
Hewanti Kushwaha

arihant
SUCCESS AND NOTHING LESS

Fully Updated as per Latest **Rationalized NCERT**

arihant
SUCCESS AND NOTHING LESS

ARIHANT PRAKASHAN (Series), MEERUT

卐 **Administrative & Production Offices**

Regd. Office

'Ramchhaya' 4577/15, Agarwal Road, Darya Ganj, New Delhi -110002
Tele: 011- 47630600, 43518550

卐 **Head Office**

Kalindi, TP Nagar, Meerut (UP) - 250002
Tel: 0121-7156203, 7156204

卐 **Sales & Support Offices**

Agra, Ahmedabad, Bengaluru, Bareilly, Chennai, Delhi, Guwahati, Hyderabad, Jaipur, Jhansi, Kolkata, Lucknow, Nagpur & Pune.

卐 **PRICE** ₹275.00

卐 **PO No :** TXT-XX-XXXXXXX-X-XX

Published by Arihant Publications (India) Ltd.

For further information about the books published by Arihant, log on to www.arihantbooks.com or e-mail at info@arihantbooks.com

Follow us on

PREFACE

NCERT Exemplar Problems, published by the NCERT, are designed to provide students with a diverse range of quality questions in formats such as Multiple Choice Questions, Short Answer Type Questions with Reasoning, Short Answer Type Questions and Long Answer Type Questions, catering to varying levels of difficulty.

These problems are essential for success in school and board exams, as well as competitive exams like engineering and medical entrances. Regular practice with these problems prepares students to tackle challenging questions effectively.

This book, **NCERT Exemplar Problems-Solutions Mathematics 9th**, offers precise and detailed solutions to all the questions in the NCERT Exemplar Mathematics textbook. Each solution is complemented by explanatory notes and authentic explanations, enabling students to deepen their conceptual understanding and enhance their analytical skills.

Key features

- **Thinking Process** Provides simple steps to approach and solve the question, clearing up any confusion.
- **Concept Insight** Explains the main ideas and concepts needed to answer the questions correctly.
- **Mistake Alert!** Points out common mistakes students might make and helps them avoid these errors.

We hope this book proves to be a valuable resource, aiding students in their academic journey and leading them to great success.

Authors

CONTENTS

1.	Number Systems	1-28
2.	Polynomials	29-53
3.	Coordinate Geometry	54-71
4.	Linear Equation in Two Variables	72-88
5.	Introduction to Euclid's Geometry	89-99
6.	Lines and Angles	100-117
7.	Triangles	118-146
8.	Quadrilaterals	147-176
9.	Area of Parallelograms and Triangles*	177-198
10.	Circles	199-232
11.	Construction*	233-245
12.	Heron's Formula	246-270
13.	Surface Area and Volumes	271-287
14.	Statistics and Probability*	288-326

Note (*) *These Chapters and topic Probability have been deleted from Latest NCERT.*

Chapter

01 Number Systems

Multiple Choice Questions (MCQs)

Choose the correct answer from the given four options in the following questions:

Q.1 Every rational number is

(a) a natural number (b) an integer
(c) a real number (d) a whole number

Ans. *(c)* Since, real numbers are the combination of rational and irrational numbers. Hence, every rational number is a real number.

Q.2 Between two rational numbers

(a) there is no rational number
(b) there is exactly one rational number
(c) there are infinitely many rational numbers
(d) there are only rational numbers and no irrational numbers

Ans. *(c)* Between two rational numbers, there are infinitely many rational numbers.
e.g., If $\frac{3}{5}$ and $\frac{4}{5}$ are two rational numbers, then $\frac{31}{50}, \frac{32}{50}, \frac{33}{50}, \frac{34}{50}, \frac{35}{50}, \ldots$ are infinite rational numbers between them.

Q.3 Decimal representation of a rational number cannot be

(a) terminating (b) non-terminating
(c) non-terminating repeating (d) non-terminating non-repeating

Ans. *(d)* Decimal representation of a rational number cannot be non-terminating non-repeating because the decimal expansion of rational number is either terminating or non-terminating recurring (repeating).

Q.4 The product of any two irrational numbers is

(a) always an irrational number
(b) always a rational number
(c) always an integer
(d) sometimes rational, sometimes irrational

Ans. *(d)* We know that the product of any two irrational numbers is sometimes rational and sometimes irrational.
e.g., $\sqrt{2} \times \sqrt{2} = 2$ (rational) and $\sqrt{2} \times \sqrt{3} = \sqrt{6}$ (irrational)

Q.5 The decimal expansion of the number $\sqrt{2}$ is

(a) a finite decimal (b) 1.41421
(c) non-terminating recurring (d) non-terminating non-recurring

Ans. *(d)* The decimal expansion of the number $\sqrt{2}$ is 1.41421 ..., which is non-terminating non-recurring. Because $\sqrt{2}$ is an irrational number. And as we know that an irrational number is non-terminating and non-recurring.

Q.6 Which of the following is irrational?

(a) $\sqrt{\frac{4}{9}}$ (b) $\frac{\sqrt{12}}{\sqrt{3}}$ (c) $\sqrt{7}$ (d) $\sqrt{81}$

- **Concept Insight** An irrational number cannot be expressed as a fraction. It cannot be represented terminating or repeating decimals.

Ans. *(c)* ∵

$$\sqrt{\frac{4}{9}} = \frac{2}{3} \text{ (rational)},$$

$$\frac{\sqrt{12}}{\sqrt{3}} = \frac{2\sqrt{3}}{\sqrt{3}} = 2 \text{ (rational)},$$

$$\sqrt{81} = 9 \text{ (rational)}$$

but $\sqrt{7} = 2.645751$ ... (irrational).

Hence, $\sqrt{7}$ is an irrational number.

Q.7 Which of the following is irrational?

(a) 0.14 (b) $0.14\overline{16}$ (c) $0.\overline{1416}$ (d) 0.4014001400014

Ans. *(d)* An irrational number is non-terminating and non-recurring which is 0.4014001400014....

Here, 0.14 is terminating and $0.14\overline{16}, 0.\overline{1416}$ are non-terminating recurring decimal. Hence, it can not be an irrational number.

Q.8 A rational number between $\sqrt{2}$ and $\sqrt{3}$ is

(a) $\frac{\sqrt{2}+\sqrt{3}}{2}$ (b) $\frac{\sqrt{2}\cdot\sqrt{3}}{2}$ (c) 1.5 (d) 1.8

Ans. *(c)* We know that $\sqrt{2} = 1.414$ ... and $\sqrt{3} = 1.732$ ... .

(a) $\frac{\sqrt{2}+\sqrt{3}}{2}$, which is an irrational number, so it is not a solution.

(b) $\frac{\sqrt{2}\cdot\sqrt{3}}{2} = \frac{\sqrt{6}}{2}$, which is an irrational number, so it is not a solution.

Now, 1.5 and 1.8 both are the rational numbers but only 1.5 lies between 1.414 and 1. 732.

Q.9 The value of 1.999... in the form of $\frac{p}{q}$, where p and q are integers and $q \neq 0$, is

(a) $\frac{19}{10}$ (b) $\frac{1999}{1000}$ (c) 2 (d) $\frac{1}{9}$

Ans. *(c)* Let $x = 1.999...$ ...(i)

Now, $10x = 19.999...$ ...(ii)

On subtracting Eq. (i) from Eq. (ii), we get

$$10x - x = (19.999...) - (1.9999...)$$

$\Rightarrow$ $9x = 18$

$\therefore$ $x = \frac{18}{9} = 2$

Q.10 $2\sqrt{3} + \sqrt{3}$ is equal to

(a) $2\sqrt{6}$ (b) 6 (c) $3\sqrt{3}$ (d) $4\sqrt{6}$

Ans. *(c)* We have, $2\sqrt{3} + \sqrt{3} = \sqrt{3}(2 + 1) = 3\sqrt{3}$

Q.11 $\sqrt{10} \times \sqrt{15}$ is equal to

(a) $6\sqrt{5}$ (b) $5\sqrt{6}$ (c) $\sqrt{25}$ (d) $10\sqrt{5}$

Ans. *(b)* We have, $\sqrt{10} \times \sqrt{15} = \sqrt{2 \times 5} \times \sqrt{3 \times 5} = \sqrt{2} \times \sqrt{5} \times \sqrt{3} \times \sqrt{5}$

$$= (\sqrt{2} \times \sqrt{3})(\sqrt{5} \times \sqrt{5}) = \sqrt{6} \times 5 = 5\sqrt{6}$$

Q.12 The number obtained on rationalising the denominator of $\frac{1}{\sqrt{7} - 2}$ is

(a) $\frac{\sqrt{7} + 2}{3}$ (b) $\frac{\sqrt{7} - 2}{3}$ (c) $\frac{\sqrt{7} + 2}{5}$ (d) $\frac{\sqrt{7} + 2}{45}$

Ans. *(a)* We have, $\frac{1}{\sqrt{7} - 2} = \frac{1}{\sqrt{7} - 2} \times \frac{\sqrt{7} + 2}{\sqrt{7} + 2}$

[on multiplying numerator and denominator by $\sqrt{7} + 2$]

$$= \frac{\sqrt{7} + 2}{(\sqrt{7})^2 - (2)^2}$$

$$= \frac{\sqrt{7} + 2}{7 - 4} = \frac{\sqrt{7} + 2}{3}$$ [$\because (a - b)(a + b) = a^2 - b^2$]

Q.13 $\frac{1}{\sqrt{9} - \sqrt{8}}$ is equal to

(a) $\frac{1}{2}(3 - 2\sqrt{2})$ (b) $\frac{1}{3 + 2\sqrt{2}}$

(c) $3 - 2\sqrt{2}$ (d) $3 + 2\sqrt{2}$

Ans. *(d)* We have, $\frac{1}{\sqrt{9} - \sqrt{8}} = \frac{1}{3 - 2\sqrt{2}} = \frac{1}{3 - 2\sqrt{2}} \times \frac{3 + 2\sqrt{2}}{3 + 2\sqrt{2}}$ [$\because \sqrt{8} = \sqrt{2 \times 2 \times 2} = 2\sqrt{2}$]

[on multiplying numerator and denominator by $3 + 2\sqrt{2}$]

$$= \frac{3 + 2\sqrt{2}}{9 - (2\sqrt{2})^2}$$ [$\because (a - b)(a + b) = a^2 - b^2$]

$$= \frac{3 + 2\sqrt{2}}{9 - 8} = 3 + 2\sqrt{2}$$

Q.14 After rationalising the denominator of $\frac{7}{3\sqrt{3}-2\sqrt{2}}$, we get the denominator as

(a) 13 (b) 19 (c) 5 (d) 35

Ans. *(b)* We have, $\frac{7}{3\sqrt{3}-2\sqrt{2}} = \frac{7}{3\sqrt{3}-2\sqrt{2}} \times \frac{3\sqrt{3}+2\sqrt{2}}{3\sqrt{3}+2\sqrt{2}}$

[on multiplying numerator and denominator by $3\sqrt{3}+2\sqrt{2}$]

$= \frac{7(3\sqrt{3}+2\sqrt{2})}{(3\sqrt{3})^2-(2\sqrt{2})^2}$ $[\because (a-b)(a+b)=a^2-b^2]$

$= \frac{7(3\sqrt{3}+2\sqrt{2})}{27-8} = \frac{7(3\sqrt{3}+2\sqrt{2})}{19}$

Hence, after rationalising the denominator of $\frac{7}{3\sqrt{3}-2\sqrt{2}}$, we get the denominator as 19.

Q.15 The value of $\frac{\sqrt{32}+\sqrt{48}}{\sqrt{8}+\sqrt{12}}$ is

(a) $\sqrt{2}$ (b) 2 (c) 4 (d) 8

Ans. *(b)* We have, $\frac{\sqrt{32}+\sqrt{48}}{\sqrt{8}+\sqrt{12}} = \frac{\sqrt{16\times 2}+\sqrt{16\times 3}}{\sqrt{4\times 2}+\sqrt{4\times 3}} = \frac{4\sqrt{2}+4\sqrt{3}}{2\sqrt{2}+2\sqrt{3}} = \frac{4(\sqrt{2}+\sqrt{3})}{2(\sqrt{2}+\sqrt{3})} = 2$

Q.16 If $\sqrt{2}=1.4142$, then $\sqrt{\frac{\sqrt{2}-1}{\sqrt{2}+1}}$ is equal to

(a) 2.4142 (b) 5.8282
(c) 0.4142 (d) 0.1718

Ans. *(c)* We have, $\sqrt{\frac{\sqrt{2}-1}{\sqrt{2}+1}} = \sqrt{\frac{\sqrt{2}-1}{\sqrt{2}+1} \times \frac{\sqrt{2}-1}{\sqrt{2}-1}}$

[inside the root, multiplying numerator and denominator by $(\sqrt{2}-1)$]

$= \sqrt{\frac{(\sqrt{2}-1)^2}{(\sqrt{2})^2-(1)^2}}$ $[\because (a-b)(a+b)=a^2-b^2]$

$= \sqrt{\frac{(\sqrt{2}-1)^2}{2-1}} = \sqrt{2}-1 = 1.4142-1 = 0.4142$

Q.17 $\sqrt[4]{\sqrt[3]{2^2}}$ equals to

(a) $2^{-\frac{1}{6}}$ (b) 2^{-6} (c) $2^{\frac{1}{6}}$ (d) 2^6

Ans. *(c)* We have, $\sqrt[4]{\sqrt[3]{2^2}} = [\sqrt[3]{2^2}]^{1/4} = [(2^2)^{1/3}]^{1/4}$ $[\because \sqrt[n]{a} = a^{1/n}]$

$= [2^{2/3}]^{1/4} = 2^{\frac{2}{3}\times\frac{1}{4}} = 2^{\frac{1}{6}}$ $[\because (a^m)^n = a^{mn}]$

Q.18 The product $\sqrt[3]{2}\cdot\sqrt[4]{2}\cdot\sqrt[12]{32}$ equals to

(a) $\sqrt{2}$ (b) 2 (c) $\sqrt[12]{2}$ (d) $\sqrt[12]{32}$

Ans. *(b)* We have, $\sqrt[3]{2}\cdot\sqrt[4]{2}\cdot\sqrt[12]{32} = (2)^{\frac{1}{3}}\cdot(2)^{\frac{1}{4}}\cdot(2^5)^{\frac{1}{12}}$ $[\because \sqrt[m]{a} = (a)^{1/m}]$

$= (2)^{1/3}\cdot(2)^{1/4}\,(2)^{5/12}$

$= (2)^{\frac{1}{3}+\frac{1}{4}+\frac{5}{12}} = (2)^{\frac{4+3+5}{12}} = (2)^{\frac{12}{12}} = 2$

Q.19 Value of $\sqrt[4]{(81)^{-2}}$ is

(a) $\frac{1}{9}$ (b) $\frac{1}{3}$ (c) 9 (d) $\frac{1}{81}$

Ans. *(a)* We have, $\sqrt[4]{(81)^{-2}} = \sqrt[4]{\frac{1}{(81)^2}} = \frac{1}{(81)^{2/4}} = \frac{1}{(81)^{1/2}}$ $[\because \sqrt[m]{a^n} = a^{n/m}]$

$= \frac{1}{(9^2)^{1/2}} = \frac{1}{9^{2/2}} = \frac{1}{9}$ $[\because (a^m)^n = a^{mn}]$

Q.20 Value of $(256)^{0.16}\times(256)^{0.09}$ is

(a) 4 (b) 16 (c) 64 (d) 256.25

Ans. *(a)* We have, $(256)^{0.16}\times(256)^{0.09} = (256)^{\frac{16}{100}}\times(256)^{\frac{9}{100}} = (256)^{\frac{16}{100}+\frac{9}{100}}$ $[\because x^a\cdot x^b = x^{a+b}]$

$= (256)^{\frac{25}{100}} = (256)^{\frac{1}{4}} = (4^4)^{\frac{1}{4}} = 4$ $[\because (a^m)^n = a^{mn}]$

Q.21 Which of the following is equal to x?

(a) $x^{\frac{12}{7}} - x^{\frac{5}{7}}$ (b) $\sqrt[12]{(x^4)^{\frac{1}{3}}}$ (c) $(\sqrt{x^3})^{\frac{2}{3}}$ (d) $x^{\frac{12}{7}}\times x^{\frac{7}{12}}$

Ans. *(c)* (a) $x^{\frac{12}{7}} - x^{\frac{5}{7}} = x^{\frac{5}{7}+1} - x^{\frac{5}{7}}$

$= x^{\frac{5}{7}}.x - x^{\frac{5}{7}} = x^{\frac{5}{7}}(x-1) \neq x$ $[\because a^{m+n} = a^m a^n]$

(b) $\sqrt[12]{(x^4)^{\frac{1}{3}}} = \left((x^4)^{\frac{1}{3}}\right)^{\frac{1}{12}}$ $[\because \sqrt[m]{a} = a^{1/m}]$

$= x^{4\times\frac{1}{3}\times\frac{1}{12}} = x^{\frac{1}{9}}$ $[\because \{(x^m)^n\}^p = x^{mnp}]$

$\neq x$

(c) $(\sqrt{x^3})^{\frac{2}{3}} = (x^{\frac{3}{2}})^{\frac{2}{3}} = x^{\frac{3}{2}\times\frac{2}{3}}$ $[\because (a^m)^n = a^{mn}]$

$= x$

(d) $x^{\frac{12}{7}}\times x^{\frac{7}{12}} = x^{\frac{12}{7}+\frac{7}{12}}$ $[\because a^m\cdot a^n = a^{m+n}]$

$= x^{\frac{144+49}{84}} = x^{\frac{193}{84}} \neq x$

Hence, option (c) is correct.

Short Answer Questions with Reasoning

Q.1 Let x and y be rational and irrational numbers, respectively. Is $x + y$ necessarily an irrational number? Give an example in support of your answer.

Ans. *Yes,* $(x + y)$ is necessarily an irrational number.

e.g., Let $x = 2, y = \sqrt{3}$

Then, $x + y = 2 + \sqrt{3}$

Let $x + y = 2 + \sqrt{3}$ be a rational number.

Again let, $a = 2 + \sqrt{3}$

On squaring both sides, we get

$$a^2 = (2 + \sqrt{3})^2 \qquad [\because (a + b)^2 = a^2 + b^2 + 2ab]$$

$$\Rightarrow \quad a^2 = 2^2 + (\sqrt{3})^2 + 2(2)(\sqrt{3})$$

$$\Rightarrow \quad a^2 = 4 + 3 + 4\sqrt{3} \Rightarrow \frac{a^2 - 7}{4} = \sqrt{3}$$

Thus, a is rational $\Rightarrow \frac{a^2 - 7}{4}$ is rational $\Rightarrow \sqrt{3}$ is rational.

But, this contradicts the fact that $\sqrt{3}$ is an irrational number. Thus, our assumption is wrong.

Hence, $x + y$ is an irrational number.

Q.2 Let x be rational and y be irrational. Is xy necessarily irrational? Justify your answer by an example.

Ans. *No,* xy is necessarily an irrational only when $x \neq 0$.

Let x be a non-zero rational and y be an irrational. Then, we have to show that xy be an irrational. Let xy be a rational number. Since, quotient of two non-zero rational number is a rational number.

So, $\left(\frac{xy}{x}\right)$ is a rational number.

$\Rightarrow$ y is a rational number.

But, this contradicts the fact that y is an irrational number. Thus, our assumption is wrong.

Hence, xy is an irrational number. Let $x = 0$ is a rational number and $y = \sqrt{3}$ is a irrational number. Then, $xy = 0 \times \sqrt{3} = 0$, which is a rational number. Therefore, xy is not necessarily are irrational number.

Q.3 State whether the following statements are true or false? Justify your answer.

(i) $\frac{\sqrt{2}}{3}$ is a rational number.

(ii) There are infinitely many integers between any two integers.

(iii) Number of rational numbers between 15 and 18 is finite.

(iv) There are numbers which cannot be written in the form $\frac{p}{q}, q \neq 0, p, q$ both are integers.

(v) The square of an irrational number is always rational.

(vi) $\frac{\sqrt{12}}{\sqrt{3}}$ is not a rational number as $\sqrt{12}$ and $\sqrt{3}$ are not integers.

(vii) $\frac{\sqrt{15}}{\sqrt{3}}$ is written in the form $\frac{p}{q}$, $q \neq 0$ and so it is a rational number.

Ans. (i) *False,* here $\sqrt{2}$ is an irrational number and 3 is a rational number, we know that when we divide irrational number by non-zero rational number it will always give an irrational number.

(ii) *False,* because between two consecutive integers *e.g.,* 1 and 2, there does not exist any other integer.

(iii) *False,* because between any two rational numbers there exist infinitely many rational numbers.

(iv) *True,* because there are infinitely many numbers which cannot be written in the form $\frac{p}{q}$, $q \neq 0$, p, q both are integers and these numbers are called irrational numbers.

(v) *False, e.g.,* let the irrational numbers be $\sqrt{2}$ and $\sqrt[4]{2}$

(a) $(\sqrt{2})^2 = 2$, which is a rational number.

(b) $(\sqrt[4]{2})^2 = \sqrt{2}$, which is not a rational number.

Hence, the square of an irrational number is not always a rational number.

(vi) *False,* $\frac{\sqrt{12}}{\sqrt{3}} = \frac{\sqrt{4 \times 3}}{\sqrt{3}} = \frac{\sqrt{4} \times \sqrt{3}}{\sqrt{3}} = 2 \times 1 = 2$, which is a rational number.

(vii) *False,* $\frac{\sqrt{15}}{\sqrt{3}} = \frac{\sqrt{5 \times 3}}{\sqrt{3}} = \frac{\sqrt{5} \times \sqrt{3}}{\sqrt{3}} = \sqrt{5}$, which is an irrational number.

Q.4 Classify the following numbers as rational or irrational with justification

(i) $\sqrt{196}$

(ii) $3\sqrt{18}$

(iii) $\sqrt{\frac{9}{27}}$

(iv) $\frac{\sqrt{28}}{\sqrt{343}}$

(v) $-\sqrt{0.4}$

(vi) $\frac{\sqrt{12}}{\sqrt{75}}$

(vii) 0.5918

(viii) $(1 + \sqrt{5}) - (4 + \sqrt{5})$

(ix) 10.124124...

(x) 1.010010001...

● **Concept Insight** Use the definition, a rational number is in the form of $\frac{p}{q}$, where p and q are integers and $q \neq 0$ and otherwise it is an irrational number.

Ans. (i) $\sqrt{196} = \sqrt{(14)^2} = 14$

Hence, it is a rational number.

(ii) $3\sqrt{18} = 3\sqrt{(3)^2 \times 2} = 3 \times 3\sqrt{2} = 9\sqrt{2}$

Hence, it is an irrational number. because $\sqrt{2}$ is an irrational number.

(iii) $\sqrt{\frac{9}{27}} = \sqrt{\frac{9}{9 \times 3}} = \frac{1}{\sqrt{3}}$

Hence, it is an irrational number, because $\sqrt{3}$ is an irrational number.

(iv) $\frac{\sqrt{28}}{\sqrt{343}} = \frac{\sqrt{2 \times 2 \times 7}}{\sqrt{7 \times 7 \times 7}} = \frac{2\sqrt{7}}{7\sqrt{7}} = \frac{2}{7}.$

Hence, it is a rational number.

(v) $-\sqrt{0.4} = -\sqrt{\frac{4}{10}} = -\frac{2}{\sqrt{10}}.$

Hence, it is the quotient of a rational and an irrational number, so it is an irrational number.

(vi) $\frac{\sqrt{12}}{\sqrt{75}} = \frac{\sqrt{4 \times 3}}{\sqrt{25 \times 3}} = \frac{\sqrt{4}\sqrt{3}}{\sqrt{25}\sqrt{3}} = \frac{2}{5}.$ Hence, it is a rational number.

(vii) 0.5918, it is a number with terminating decimal, so it can be written in the form of $\frac{p}{q}$, where $q \neq 0$, p and q are integers. Hence, it is a rational number.

(viii) $(1+\sqrt{5}) - (4+\sqrt{5}) = 1 - 4 + \sqrt{5} - \sqrt{5} = -3$, which is an integer.

Hence, it is a rational number.

(ix) 10.124124 ......, is a number with non-terminating recurring decimal expansion.

Hence, it is a rational number.

(x) 1.010010001 ...., is a number with non-terminating non-recurring decimal expansion.

Hence, it is a irrational number.

Short Answer Type Questions

Q.1 Find which of the variables x, y, z and u represent rational numbers and which irrational numbers.

(i) $x^2 = 5$ (ii) $y^2 = 9$

(iii) $z^2 = 0.04$ (iv) $u^2 = \frac{17}{4}$

Ans. (i) Given, $x^2 = 5$

On taking square root both sides, we get

$x = \pm\sqrt{5}$ [irrational number]

(ii) Given, $y^2 = 9$

On taking square root both sides, we get

$y = \pm\sqrt{9} = \pm 3$ [rational number]

(iii) Given, $z^2 = 0.04$

On taking square root both sides, we get

$z = \sqrt{0.04} = \sqrt{\frac{4}{100}} = \frac{2}{10}$ [rational number]

$\left[\because \frac{p}{q} \text{ form, } q \neq 0, p \text{ and } q \text{ are integers}\right]$

(iv) Given, $u^2 = \frac{17}{4}$

On taking square root both sides, we get

$$u = \pm\sqrt{\frac{17}{4}} = \pm\frac{\sqrt{17}}{2}$$

[irrational number because numerator is an irrational]

Mistake Alert! *Student may assume $\sqrt{0.04}$ as an irrational number, instead of rational number.*

Q.2 Find three rational numbers between

(i) −1 and −2 (ii) 0.1 and 0.11

(iii) $\frac{5}{7}$ and $\frac{6}{7}$ (iv) $\frac{1}{4}$ and $\frac{1}{5}$

- **Concept Insight** There exist infinitely many rational numbers between the two given numbers. So, student's answers might vary.

Ans. (i) Write −1 and −2 as rational numbers with denominator 4 = 3 + 1

i.e., $-1 = \frac{-4}{4}$ and $-2 = \frac{-8}{4}$

∴ Rational numbers between −1 and −2 are $\frac{-5}{4}, \frac{-6}{4}, \frac{-7}{4}$.

Alternate Method

Let $x = -1$ and $y = -2$

We know, a rational number between x and $y = \frac{x+y}{2}$

∴ A rational number between −1 and − 2 $= \frac{-1-2}{2} = -\frac{3}{2}$

and a rational number between −1 and $-\frac{3}{2} = \frac{-1-\frac{3}{2}}{2} = \frac{-2-3}{4} = -\frac{5}{4}$

Similarly, $-\frac{11}{8}$ is a rational number between $-\frac{3}{2}$ and $-\frac{5}{4}$

∴ Required rational numbers between −1 and −2 are $\frac{-3}{2}, \frac{-5}{4}, \frac{-11}{8}$.

(ii) Write 0.100 and 0.110 as rational numbers with denominator 4 (= 3 + 1) [∵ 0.1 = 0.100]

i.e., $0.100 = \frac{0.400}{4}$ and $0.110 = \frac{0.440}{4}$

∴ Rational numbers between 0.100 and 0.110 are $\frac{0.410}{4}, \frac{0.420}{4}, \frac{0.430}{4}$.

i.e., 0.1025, 0.105, 0.1075

Alternate Method

Here, $x = 0.1$, $y = 0.110$

We know, a rational number between x and $y = \frac{x+y}{2}$.

$\therefore$ A rational number between 0.1 and 0.110 $= \frac{0.1 + 0.110}{2} = 0.105$

and, a rational number between 0.1 and 0.105 $= \frac{0.1 + 0.105}{2} = 0.1025$

Similarly, a rational number between 0.105 and 0.110 = 0.1075

(iii) Given numbers are $\frac{5}{7}$ and $\frac{6}{7}$.

Multiply the numerator and denominator by 4 (= 3 + 1)

i.e., $\frac{5}{7} = \frac{5 \times 4}{7 \times 4} = \frac{20}{28}$ and $\frac{6}{7} = \frac{6 \times 4}{7 \times 4} = \frac{24}{28}$

$\therefore$ Rational numbers between $\frac{5}{7}$ and $\frac{6}{7}$ are $\frac{21}{28}, \frac{22}{28}, \frac{23}{28}$.

Alternate Method

Let $x = \frac{5}{7}$ and $y = \frac{6}{7}$

We know, a rational number between x and $y = \frac{x+y}{2}$

$\therefore$ A rational number between $\frac{5}{7}$ and $\frac{6}{7} = \frac{\frac{5}{7} + \frac{6}{7}}{2} = \frac{13}{14}$

and a rational number between $\frac{5}{7}$ and $\frac{13}{14} = \frac{\frac{5}{7} + \frac{13}{14}}{2} = \frac{23}{28}$

Similarly, a rational number between $\frac{13}{14}$ and $\frac{6}{7} = \frac{\frac{13}{14} + \frac{6}{7}}{2} = \frac{25}{28}$

$\therefore$ Rational numbers between $\frac{5}{7}$ and $\frac{6}{7}$ are $\frac{13}{14}, \frac{23}{28}, \frac{25}{28}$.

(iv) Firstly, make the denominators of rational number equal.

i.e., $\frac{1}{4} \times \frac{5}{5} = \frac{5}{20}$ and $\frac{1}{5} \times \frac{4}{4} = \frac{4}{20}$

Now, multiply both numerator and denominator by 4 (= 3 + 1)

i.e., $\frac{5}{20} = \frac{5 \times 4}{20 \times 4} = \frac{20}{80}$

And $\frac{4}{20} = \frac{4 \times 4}{20 \times 4} = \frac{16}{80}$

$\therefore$ Rational numbers between $\frac{1}{4}$ and $\frac{1}{5}$ are $\frac{17}{80}, \frac{18}{80}, \frac{19}{80}$.

Alternate Method

Let $x = \frac{1}{4}$ and $y = \frac{1}{5}$

So, a rational number between x and $y = \frac{x+y}{2}$

$\therefore$ A rational number between $\frac{1}{4}$ and $\frac{1}{5} = \frac{\frac{1}{4}+\frac{1}{5}}{2} = \frac{\frac{5+4}{20}}{2}$

$= \frac{9}{2 \times 20} = \frac{9}{40}$

Again, a rational number between $\frac{1}{4}$ and $\frac{9}{40} = \frac{\frac{1}{4}+\frac{9}{40}}{2} = \frac{\frac{10+9}{40}}{2} = \frac{19}{2 \times 40} = \frac{19}{80}$

Again, a rational number between $\frac{1}{5}$ and $\frac{9}{40} = \frac{\frac{1}{5}+\frac{9}{40}}{2} = \frac{\frac{8+9}{40}}{2} = \frac{\frac{17}{40}}{2} = \frac{17}{40 \times 2} = \frac{17}{80}$

Hence, three rational numbers between $\frac{1}{4}$ and $\frac{1}{5}$ are $\frac{9}{40}, \frac{19}{80}, \frac{17}{80}$.

Q.3 Insert a rational number and an irrational number between the following

(i) 2 and 3 (ii) 0 and 0.1

(iii) $\frac{1}{3}$ and $\frac{1}{2}$ (iv) $\frac{-2}{5}$ and $\frac{1}{2}$

(v) 0.15 and 0.16 (vi) $\sqrt{2}$ and $\sqrt{3}$

(vii) 2.357 and 3.121 (viii) .0001 and .001

(ix) 3.623623 and 0.484848 (x) 6.375289 and 6.375738

Ans. We know that there are infinitely many rational and irrational numbers between any two numbers.

(i) A rational number between 2 and 3 is 2.5.

To find an irrational number between 2 and 3, we will find a number which is non-terminating and non-recurring lying between them.

$\therefore$ Such number is 2.040040004.........

(ii) A rational number between 0 and 0.1 is 0.05.

An irrational number between 0 and 0.1 is 0.007000700007.........

(iii) A rational number between $\frac{1}{3}$ and $\frac{1}{2}$ is $\frac{5}{12}$. An irrational number between $\frac{1}{3}$ and $\frac{1}{2}$ *i.e.*, between $0 \cdot \bar{3}$ and 0.5 is 0.4141141114.........

(iv) A rational number between $\frac{-2}{5}$ and $\frac{1}{2}$ is 0. An irrational number between $\frac{-2}{5}$ and $\frac{1}{2}$ *i.e.*, between – 0.4 and 0.5 is 0.151151115.........

(v) A rational number between 0.15 and 0.16 is 0.151. An irrational number between 0.15 and 0.16 is 0.1515515551.........

(vi) A rational number between $\sqrt{2}$ and $\sqrt{3}$ *i.e.*, between 1.4142, ... and 1.7320 .... is 1.5. An irrational number between $\sqrt{2}$ and $\sqrt{3}$ is 1.585585558.........

(vii) A rational number between 2.357 and 3.121 is 3. An irrational number between 2.357 and 3.121 is 3.101101110.........

(viii) A rational number between 0.0001 and 0.001 is 0.00011. An irrational number between 0.0001 and 0.001 is 0.0001131331333.........

(ix) A rational number between 3.623623 and 0.484848 is 1. An irrational number between 3.623623 and 0.484848 is 1.909009000.........

(x) A rational number between 6.375289 and 6.375738 is 6.3753. An irrational number between 6.375289 and 6.375738 is 6.375414114111.........

*** Q.4** Represent the following numbers on the number line 7, 7.2, $-\frac{3}{2}$ and $-\frac{12}{5}$.

Ans. Firstly, we draw a number line whose mid-point is 0. Mark positive numbers on right hand side of 0 and negative numbers on left hand side of 0.

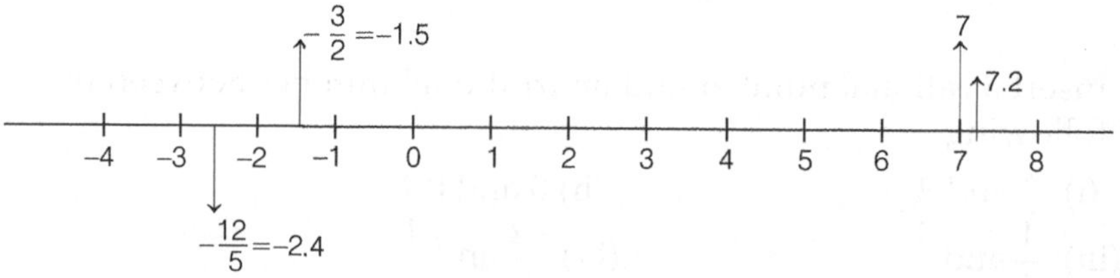

(i) Number 7 is a positive number. So we mark a number 7 on the right hand side of 0, which is at a distance of 7 units from zero.

(ii) Number 7.2 is a positive number. So, we mark a number 7.2 on the right hand side of 0, which is at a distance of 7.2 units from zero.

(iii) Number $-\frac{3}{2}$ or -1.5 is a negative number. So, we mark a number 1.5 on the left hand side of 0, which is at a distance of 1.5 units from zero.

(iv) Number $-\frac{12}{5}$ or -2.4 is a negative number. So, we mark a number 2.4 on the left hand side of 0, which is at a distance of 2.4 units from zero.

Q.5 Locate $\sqrt{5}$, $\sqrt{10}$ and $\sqrt{17}$ on the number line.

Thinking Process Try to express the given number as the sum of the squares of two numbers.

i.e., $(\sqrt{5})^2 = (2)^2 + (1)^2; (\sqrt{10})^2 = (3)^2 + (1)^2$

and $(\sqrt{17})^2 = (4)^2 + (1)^2$

It becomes easier to represent a number on the number line.

(*) Topics related to these question have been removed from latest NCERT.

Ans. (i) Here, $(\sqrt{5})^2 = 2^2 + 1^2$

So, draw a right angled ΔOAB, in which $OA = 2$ units and $AB = 1$ unit and $\angle OAB = 90°$

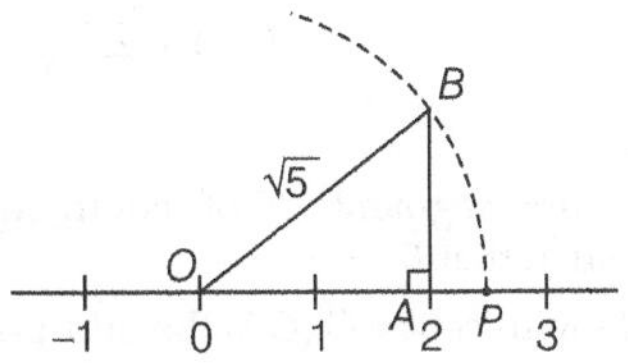

By using Pythagoras theorem, we get

$$OB = \sqrt{OA^2 + AB^2} = \sqrt{2^2 + 1^2} = \sqrt{4 + 1} = \sqrt{5}$$

Now, take $OB = \sqrt{5}$ as radius and point O as centre, draw an arc which meets the number line at point P on the positive side of it.

Hence, it is clear that point P represents $\sqrt{5}$ on the number line.

(ii) Here, $(\sqrt{10})^2 = 3^2 + 1^2$

So, draw a right angled ΔOAB, in which $OA = 3$ units and $AB = 1$ unit and $\angle OAB = 90°$.

By using Pythagoras theorem, we get

$$OB = \sqrt{OA^2 + AB^2} = \sqrt{3^2 + 1^2} = \sqrt{9 + 1} = \sqrt{10}$$

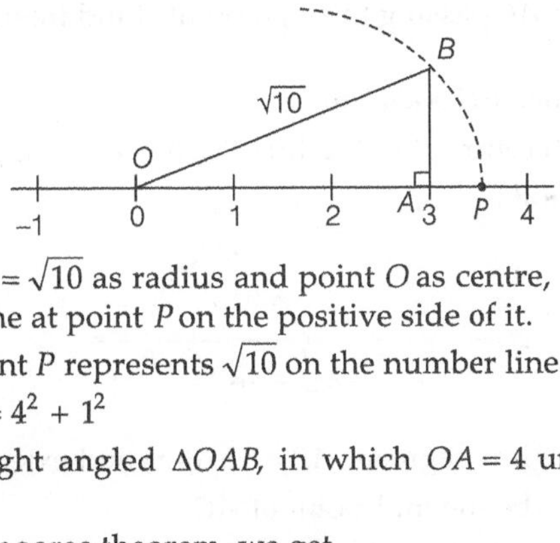

Now, take $OB = \sqrt{10}$ as radius and point O as centre, draw an arc which meets the number line at point P on the positive side of it.

Therefore, point P represents $\sqrt{10}$ on the number line.

(iii) Here, $(\sqrt{17})^2 = 4^2 + 1^2$

So, draw a right angled ΔOAB, in which $OA = 4$ units and $AB = 1$ unit and $\angle OAB = 90°$

By using Pythagoras theorem, we get

$$OB = \sqrt{OA^2 + AB^2} = \sqrt{4^2 + 1^2} = \sqrt{16 + 1} = \sqrt{17}$$

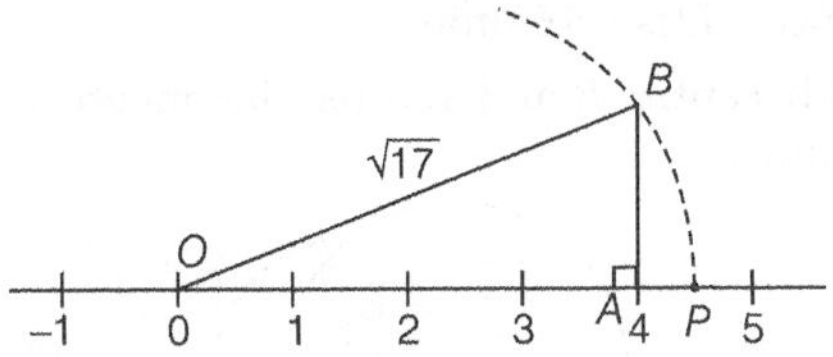

Now, take $OB = \sqrt{17}$ as radius and point O as centre, draw an arc which meets the number line at point P on the positive side of it.

Therefore, point P represents $\sqrt{17}$ on the number line.

Q.6 Represent geometrically the following numbers on the number line

(i) $\sqrt{4.5}$ (ii) $\sqrt{5.6}$

(iii) $\sqrt{8.1}$ (iv) $\sqrt{2.3}$

Thinking Process

(i) Firstly, we draw a line segment AB of length equal to the number inside the root and extend it to C such that $BC = 1$.

(ii) Draw a semi-circle with centre O (O is the mid-point of AC) and radius OA.

(iii) Now, draw a perpendicular line to AC passing through a point B and intersecting the semi-circle at a point D.

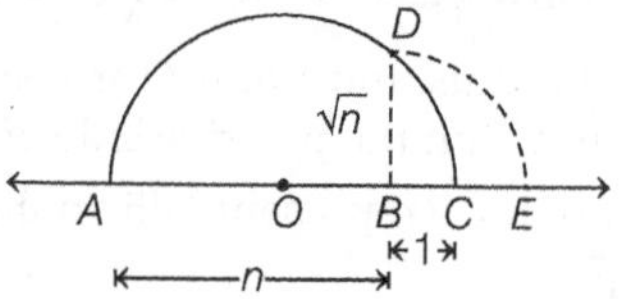

(iv) Further, draw an arc with centre B and radius BD, meeting AC produced at E.

Ans. (i) Firstly, we draw a line segment $AB = 4.5$ units and extend it to C such that $BC = 1$ unit. Let O be the mid-point of AC.

Now, draw a semi-circle with centre O and radius OA. Let us draw a line BD, perpendicular to AC passing through point B and intersecting the semi-circle at point D.

Hence, the distance BD is $\sqrt{4.5}$ units.

Draw an arc with centre B and radius BD, meeting AC produced at E, then $BE = BD = \sqrt{4.5}$ units

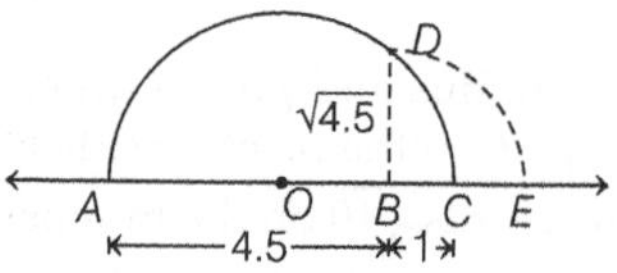

(ii) Firstly, we draw a line segment $AB = 5.6$ units and extend it to C such that $BC = 1$ unit. Let O be the mid-point of AC.

Now, draw a semi-circle with centre O and radius OA. Let us draw a line BD, perpendicular to AC passing through point B and intersecting the semi-circle at point D.

Hence, the distance BD is $\sqrt{5.6}$ units.

Draw an arc with centre B and radius BD, meeting AC produced at E, then $BE = BD = \sqrt{5.6}$ units.

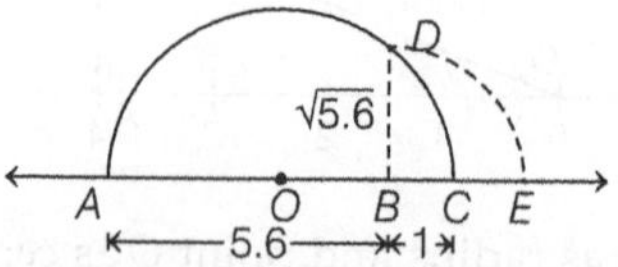

(iii) Firstly, we draw a line segment $AB = 8.1$ units and extend it to C such that $BC = 1$ unit. Let O be the mid-point of AC.

Now, draw a semi-circle with centre O and radius OA. Let us draw a line BD perpendicular to AC passing through point B intersecting the semi-circle at point D.

Hence, the distance BD is $\sqrt{8.1}$ units

Draw an arc with centre B and radius BD, meeting AC produced at E, then $BE = BD = \sqrt{8.1}$ units

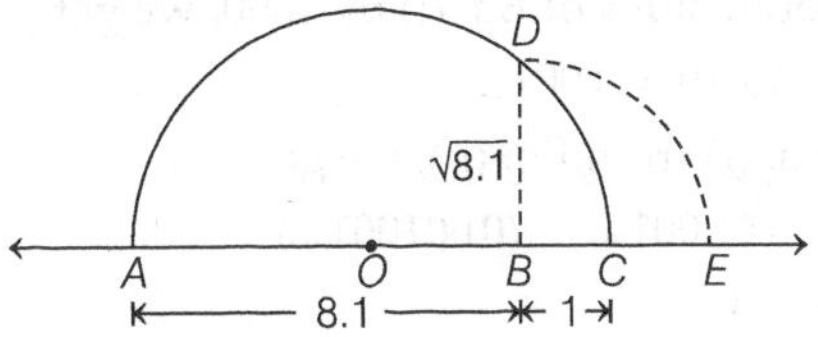

(iv) Firstly, we draw a line segment $AB = 2.3$ units and extend it to C such that $BC = 1$ unit. Let O be the mid-point of AC.

Now, draw a semi-circle with centre O and radius OA. Let us draw a line BD perpendicular to AC passing through point B and intersecting the semi-circle at point D.

Hence, the distance BD is $\sqrt{2.3}$ units.

Draw an arc with centre B and radius BD, meeting AC produced at E, then

$BE = BD = \sqrt{2.3}$ units.

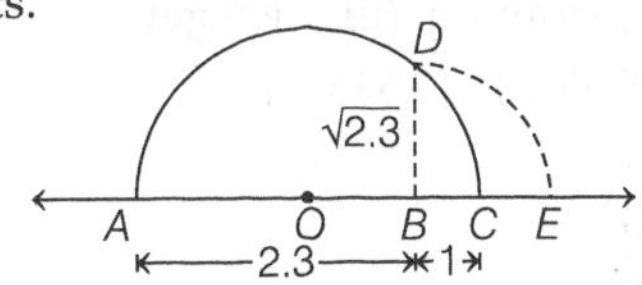

Q.7 Express the following in the form $\frac{p}{q}$, where p and q are integers and $q \neq 0$.

(i) 0.2	(ii) 0.888...
(iii) $5.\overline{2}$	(iv) $0.\overline{001}$
(v) 0.2555...	(vi) $0.1\overline{34}$
(vii) 0.00323232...	(viii) 0.404040...

Ans. (i) Let $\qquad x = 0.2 = \frac{2}{10} = \frac{1}{5}$

(ii) Let $\qquad x = 0.888.........$ $\qquad$ ...(i)

On multiplying both sides of Eq.(i) by 10, we get

$10x = 8.888.........$ $\qquad$ ...(ii)

On subtracting Eq. (i) from Eq. (ii), we get

$$10x - x = (8.88.....) - (0.888\ ......) \Rightarrow 9x = 8$$

$\therefore \qquad x = \frac{8}{9}$

(iii) Let $\qquad x = 5.\overline{2} = 5.222..$ $\qquad$ ...(i)

On multiplying both sides of Eq. (i) by 10, we get

$$10x = 52.222........ \qquad ...(ii)$$

On subtracting Eq. (i) from Eq. (ii), we get

$$10x - x = (52.222...) - (5.222...) \Rightarrow 9x = 47$$

$\therefore \qquad x = \frac{47}{9}$

(iv) Let $x = 0.\overline{001}$

$\Rightarrow$ $x = 0.\overline{001} = 0.001001........$ ...(i)

On multiplying both sides of Eq. (i) by 1000, we get

$1000x = 1.001......$ ...(ii)

On subtracting Eq. (i) from Eq. (ii), we get

$1000x - x = (1.001...) - (0.001001...)$

$\Rightarrow$ $999x = 1$

$\therefore$ $x = \frac{1}{999}$

(v) Let $x = 0.2555.........$ ...(i)

On multiplying both sides of Eq. (i) by 10, we get

$10x = 2.555.........$ ...(ii)

On multiplying both sides of Eq. (ii) by 10, we get

$100x = 25.55.........$ ...(iii)

On subtracting Eq. (ii) from Eq. (iii), we get

$100x - 10x = (25.55...) - (2.555...)$

$\Rightarrow$ $90x = 23$

$\therefore$ $x = \frac{23}{90}$

(vi) Let $x = 0.1\overline{34}$

$\Rightarrow$ $x = 0.1\overline{34} = 0.13434.........$ ...(i)

On multiplying both sides of Eq. (i) by 10, we get

$10x = 1.3434........$ ...(ii)

On multiplying both sides of Eq. (ii) by 100, we get

$1000x = 134.3434.........$ ...(iii)

On subtracting Eq. (ii) from Eq. (iii), we get

$1000x - 10x = (134.34) - (1.3434...)$

$\Rightarrow$ $990x = 133$

$\therefore$ $x = \frac{133}{990}$

(vii) Let $x = 0.00323232........$ ...(i)

On multiplying both sides of Eq. (i) by 100 we get

$100x = 0.3232.........$ ...(ii)

On multiplying both sides of Eq. (ii) by 100, we get

$10000x = 32.3232.........$ ...(iii)

On subtracting Eq. (ii) from Eq. (iii), we get

$10000x - 100x = (32.32...) - (0.3232...)$

$\Rightarrow$ $9900x = 32$

$\therefore$ $x = \frac{32}{9900} = \frac{8}{2475}$ [divide numerator and denominator by 4]

(viii) Let $x = 0.404040...$ ...(i)

On multiplying both sides of Eq. (i) by 100, we get

$$100x = 40.4040\ldots \quad ...(ii)$$

On subtracting Eq. (i) from Eq. (ii), we get

$$100x - x = (40.4040\ldots) - (0.404040\ldots)$$

$$\Rightarrow \quad 99x = 40$$

$$\therefore \quad x = \frac{40}{99}$$

Q.8 Show that $0.142857142857... = \frac{1}{7}$.

Ans. Let $x = 0.142857142857\ldots$ ...(i)

On multiplying both sides of Eq. (i) by 1000000, we get

$$1000000\,x = 142857.142857... \quad ...(ii)$$

On subtracting Eq. (i) from Eq. (ii), we get

$$1000000\,x - x = (142857.142857...) - (0.142857...)$$

$$\Rightarrow \quad 999999\,x = 142857$$

$$\therefore \quad x = \frac{142857}{999999} = \frac{1}{7}$$

Hence proved.

Q.9 Simplify the following

(i) $\sqrt{45} - 3\sqrt{20} + 4\sqrt{5}$ (ii) $\frac{\sqrt{24}}{8} + \frac{\sqrt{54}}{9}$

(iii) $\sqrt[4]{12} \times \sqrt[7]{6}$ (iv) $4\sqrt{28} \div 3\sqrt{7} \div \sqrt[3]{7}$

(v) $3\sqrt{3} + 2\sqrt{27} + \frac{7}{\sqrt{3}}$ (vi) $(\sqrt{3} - \sqrt{2})^2$

(vii) $\sqrt[4]{81} - 8\sqrt[3]{216} + 15\sqrt[5]{32} + \sqrt{225}$

(viii) $\frac{3}{\sqrt{8}} + \frac{1}{\sqrt{2}}$ (ix) $\frac{2\sqrt{3}}{3} - \frac{\sqrt{3}}{6}$

Ans. (i) We have, $\sqrt{45} - 3\sqrt{20} + 4\sqrt{5} = \sqrt{3 \times 3 \times 5} - 3\sqrt{2 \times 2 \times 5} + 4\sqrt{5}$

$$= 3\sqrt{5} - 3 \times 2\sqrt{5} + 4\sqrt{5} = 3\sqrt{5} - 6\sqrt{5} + 4\sqrt{5} = \sqrt{5}$$

(ii) We have, $\frac{\sqrt{24}}{8} + \frac{\sqrt{54}}{9} = \frac{\sqrt{2 \times 2 \times 2 \times 3}}{8} + \frac{\sqrt{3 \times 3 \times 3 \times 2}}{9}$

$$= \frac{2\sqrt{6}}{8} + \frac{3\sqrt{6}}{9} = \frac{\sqrt{6}}{4} + \frac{\sqrt{6}}{3} = \frac{3\sqrt{6} + 4\sqrt{6}}{12} = \frac{7\sqrt{6}}{12}$$

(iii) We have, $\sqrt[4]{12} \times \sqrt[7]{6} = (12)^{1/4} \times (6)^{1/7}$ $[\because \sqrt[n]{a} = a^{1/n}]$

$$= (2 \times 2 \times 3)^{1/4} \times (2 \times 3)^{1/7} = 2^{1/4} \times 2^{1/4} \times 3^{1/4} \times 2^{1/7} \times 3^{1/7}$$

$$= (2)^{\frac{1}{4}+\frac{1}{4}+\frac{1}{7}} \times (3)^{\frac{1}{4}+\frac{1}{7}} \quad [\because x^m \cdot x^n = x^{m+n}]$$

$$= 2^{9/14} \times 3^{11/28} = \sqrt[14]{2^9}\ \sqrt[28]{3^{11}} \quad \left[\because a^{\frac{m}{n}} = \sqrt[n]{a^m}\right]$$

$$= \sqrt[28]{2^{18}}\ \sqrt[28]{3^{11}} = \sqrt[28]{2^{18} \times 3^{11}} \quad [\because \sqrt[m]{a} = \sqrt[mn]{a^n}]$$

(iv) We have, $4\sqrt{28} \div 3\sqrt{7} \div \sqrt[3]{7} = (4\sqrt{4 \times 7} \div 3\sqrt{7}) \div \sqrt[3]{7} = \left(\frac{8\sqrt{7}}{3\sqrt{7}}\right) \div (7)^{\frac{1}{3}}$ $\quad [\because \sqrt[n]{a} = a^{1/n}]$

$$= \frac{8}{3} \div 7^{\frac{1}{3}} = \frac{8}{3\sqrt[3]{7}}$$

(v) We have, $3\sqrt{3} + 2\sqrt{27} + \frac{7}{\sqrt{3}} = 3\sqrt{3} + 2\sqrt{3 \times 3 \times 3} + \frac{7}{\sqrt{3}} \times \frac{\sqrt{3}}{\sqrt{3}}$

$$= 3\sqrt{3} + 6\sqrt{3} + \frac{7\sqrt{3}}{3} = 9\sqrt{3} + \frac{7\sqrt{3}}{3}$$

$$= \frac{27\sqrt{3} + 7\sqrt{3}}{3} = \frac{34\sqrt{3}}{3}$$

(vi) We have, $(\sqrt{3} - \sqrt{2})^2 = (\sqrt{3})^2 + (\sqrt{2})^2 - 2\sqrt{3} \times \sqrt{2}$

$[\because (a - b)^2 = a^2 + b^2 - 2ab]$

$$= 3 + 2 - 2\sqrt{3 \times 2} = 5 - 2\sqrt{6}$$

(vii) We have, $\sqrt[4]{81} - 8\sqrt[3]{216} + 15\sqrt[5]{32} + \sqrt{225}$

$$= (81)^{\frac{1}{4}} - 8 \times (216)^{\frac{1}{3}} + 15 \times (32)^{\frac{1}{5}} + \sqrt{(15)^2} \quad [\because \sqrt[m]{a} = a^{1/m}]$$

$$= (3^4)^{\frac{1}{4}} - 8 \times (6^3)^{\frac{1}{3}} + 15 \times (2^5)^{\frac{1}{5}} + 15$$

$$= (3)^{4 \times \frac{1}{4}} - 8 \times (6)^{3 \times \frac{1}{3}} + 15 \times (2)^{5 \times \frac{1}{5}} + 15 \quad [\because (a^m)^n = a^{mn}]$$

$$= 3^1 - 8 \times 6^1 + 15 \times 2^1 + 15$$

$$= 3 - 48 + 30 + 15 = 48 - 48 = 0$$

(viii) We have, $\frac{3}{\sqrt{8}} + \frac{1}{\sqrt{2}} = \frac{3}{\sqrt{2 \times 2 \times 2}} + \frac{1}{\sqrt{2}} = \frac{3}{2\sqrt{2}} + \frac{1}{\sqrt{2}} = \frac{3 + 2}{2\sqrt{2}} = \frac{5}{2\sqrt{2}} \times \frac{\sqrt{2}}{\sqrt{2}}$

[on multiplying numerator and denominator by $\sqrt{2}$]

$$= \frac{5\sqrt{2}}{2 \times 2} = \frac{5\sqrt{2}}{4}$$

(ix) We have, $\frac{2\sqrt{3}}{3} - \frac{\sqrt{3}}{6} = \frac{4\sqrt{3} - \sqrt{3}}{6} = \frac{3\sqrt{3}}{6} = \frac{\sqrt{3}}{2}$

Q.10 Rationalise the denominator of the following

(i) $\frac{2}{3\sqrt{3}}$

(ii) $\frac{\sqrt{40}}{\sqrt{3}}$

(iii) $\frac{3 + \sqrt{2}}{4\sqrt{2}}$

(iv) $\frac{16}{\sqrt{41} - 5}$

(v) $\frac{2 + \sqrt{3}}{2 - \sqrt{3}}$

(vi) $\frac{\sqrt{6}}{\sqrt{2} + \sqrt{3}}$

(vii) $\frac{\sqrt{3} + \sqrt{2}}{\sqrt{3} - \sqrt{2}}$

(viii) $\frac{3\sqrt{5} + \sqrt{3}}{\sqrt{5} - \sqrt{3}}$

(ix) $\frac{4\sqrt{3} + 5\sqrt{2}}{\sqrt{48} + \sqrt{18}}$

Thinking Process

(i) If the denominator has only one term, i.e. in the form of $\sqrt{a}$ then multiply both numerator and denominator by the same irrational number.

(ii) If the denominator is in the form $(\sqrt{a}+\sqrt{b})$, then multiply the both numerator and denominator by $\sqrt{a}-\sqrt{b}$ and *vice-versa.*

Ans. (i) Let $E=\frac{2}{3\sqrt{3}}$

For rationalising the denominator, multiplying numerator and denominator by $\sqrt{3}$,

$$E=\frac{2}{3\sqrt{3}}\times\frac{\sqrt{3}}{\sqrt{3}}=\frac{2\sqrt{3}}{3\times 3}=\frac{2\sqrt{3}}{9}$$

(ii) Let $E=\frac{\sqrt{40}}{\sqrt{3}}$

For rationalising the denominator, multiplying numerator and denominator by $\sqrt{3}$,

$$E=\frac{\sqrt{40}}{\sqrt{3}}\times\frac{\sqrt{3}}{\sqrt{3}}=\frac{\sqrt{40\times 3}}{(\sqrt{3})^2}=\frac{\sqrt{120}}{3}=\frac{\sqrt{2\times2\times2\times5\times3}}{3}=\frac{2}{3}\sqrt{30}$$

(iii) Let $E=\frac{3+\sqrt{2}}{4\sqrt{2}}$

For rationalising the denominator, multiplying numerator and denominator by $\sqrt{2}$,

$$E=\frac{3+\sqrt{2}}{4\sqrt{2}}\times\frac{\sqrt{2}}{\sqrt{2}}=\frac{3\sqrt{2}+(\sqrt{2})^2}{4(\sqrt{2})^2}=\frac{3\sqrt{2}+2}{4\times 2}=\frac{3\sqrt{2}+2}{8}$$

(iv) Let $E=\frac{16}{\sqrt{41}-5}$

For rationalising the denominator, multiplying numerator and denominator by $\sqrt{41}+5$,

$$E=\frac{16}{\sqrt{41}-5}\times\frac{\sqrt{41}+5}{\sqrt{41}+5}=\frac{16(\sqrt{41}+5)}{(\sqrt{41})^2-(5)^2}\qquad[\because (a-b)(a+b)=a^2-b^2]$$

$$=\frac{16(\sqrt{41}+5)}{41-25}=\frac{16(\sqrt{41}+5)}{16}=\sqrt{41}+5$$

(v) Let $E=\frac{2+\sqrt{3}}{2-\sqrt{3}}$

For rationalising the denominator, multiplying numerator and denominator by $2+\sqrt{3}$,

$$E=\frac{2+\sqrt{3}}{2-\sqrt{3}}\times\frac{2+\sqrt{3}}{2+\sqrt{3}}=\frac{(2+\sqrt{3})^2}{(2)^2-(\sqrt{3})^2}\qquad[\because (a-b)(a+b)=a^2-b^2]$$

$$=\frac{2^2+(\sqrt{3})^2+2\times2\times\sqrt{3}}{4-3}\qquad[\because (a+b)^2=a^2+2ab+b^2]$$

$$=4+3+4\sqrt{3}=7+4\sqrt{3}$$

(vi) Let $E = \dfrac{\sqrt{6}}{\sqrt{2}+\sqrt{3}}$

For rationalising the denominator, multiplying numerator and denominator by $\sqrt{2}-\sqrt{3}$,

$$E = \frac{\sqrt{6}}{\sqrt{2}+\sqrt{3}} \times \frac{\sqrt{2}-\sqrt{3}}{\sqrt{2}-\sqrt{3}} = \frac{\sqrt{6}(\sqrt{2}-\sqrt{3})}{(\sqrt{2})^2-(\sqrt{3})^2}$$

$[\because (a-b)(a+b) = a^2 - b^2]$

$$= \frac{\sqrt{6}(\sqrt{2}-\sqrt{3})}{2-3} = \frac{\sqrt{6}(\sqrt{2}-\sqrt{3})}{-1} = \sqrt{6}(\sqrt{3}-\sqrt{2})$$

$$= \sqrt{18} - \sqrt{12} = \sqrt{9\times 2} - \sqrt{4\times 3} = 3\sqrt{2} - 2\sqrt{3}.$$

(vii) Let $E = \dfrac{\sqrt{3}+\sqrt{2}}{\sqrt{3}-\sqrt{2}}$

For rationalising the denominator, multiplying numerator and denominator by $\sqrt{3}+\sqrt{2}$,

$$E = \frac{\sqrt{3}+\sqrt{2}}{\sqrt{3}-\sqrt{2}} \times \frac{\sqrt{3}+\sqrt{2}}{\sqrt{3}+\sqrt{2}} = \frac{(\sqrt{3}+\sqrt{2})^2}{(\sqrt{3})^2-(\sqrt{2})^2}$$

$[\because (a-b)(a+b) = a^2 - b^2]$

$$= \frac{(\sqrt{3})^2 + (\sqrt{2})^2 + 2\sqrt{3}\sqrt{2}}{3-2} \qquad [\because (a+b)^2 = a^2 + b^2 + 2ab]$$

$$= 3 + 2 + 2\sqrt{6} = 5 + 2\sqrt{6}$$

(viii) Let $E = \dfrac{3\sqrt{5}+\sqrt{3}}{\sqrt{5}-\sqrt{3}}$

For rationalising the denominator, multiplying numerator and denominator by $\sqrt{5}+\sqrt{3}$,

$$E = \frac{3\sqrt{5}+\sqrt{3}}{\sqrt{5}-\sqrt{3}} \times \frac{\sqrt{5}+\sqrt{3}}{\sqrt{5}+\sqrt{3}} = \frac{3\sqrt{5}(\sqrt{5}+\sqrt{3}) + \sqrt{3}(\sqrt{5}+\sqrt{3})}{(\sqrt{5})^2-(\sqrt{3})^2}$$

$[\because (a+b)(a-b) = a^2 - b^2]$

$$= \frac{15 + 3\sqrt{15} + \sqrt{15} + 3}{5-3} = \frac{18 + 4\sqrt{15}}{2} = 9 + 2\sqrt{15}$$

(ix) Let $E = \dfrac{4\sqrt{3}+5\sqrt{2}}{\sqrt{48}+\sqrt{18}} = \dfrac{4\sqrt{3}+5\sqrt{2}}{\sqrt{16\times 3}+\sqrt{9\times 2}} = \dfrac{4\sqrt{3}+5\sqrt{2}}{4\sqrt{3}+3\sqrt{2}}$

For rationalising the denominator, multiplying numerator and denominator by $4\sqrt{3}-3\sqrt{2}$,

$$= \frac{4\sqrt{3}+5\sqrt{2}}{4\sqrt{3}+3\sqrt{2}} \times \frac{(4\sqrt{3}-3\sqrt{2})}{(4\sqrt{3}-3\sqrt{2})} = \frac{4\sqrt{3}(4\sqrt{3}-3\sqrt{2}) + 5\sqrt{2}(4\sqrt{3}-3\sqrt{2})}{(4\sqrt{3})^2-(3\sqrt{2})^2}$$

$[\because (a+b)(a-b) = a^2 - b^2]$

$$= \frac{48 - 12\sqrt{6} + 20\sqrt{6} - 30}{30}$$

$$= \frac{18 + 8\sqrt{6}}{30} = \frac{9 + 4\sqrt{6}}{15}$$

Q.11 Find the values of a and b in each of the following

(i) $\dfrac{5+2\sqrt{3}}{7+4\sqrt{3}} = a - 6\sqrt{3}$ (ii) $\dfrac{3-\sqrt{5}}{3+2\sqrt{5}} = a\sqrt{5} - \dfrac{19}{11}$

(iii) $\dfrac{\sqrt{2}+\sqrt{3}}{3\sqrt{2}-2\sqrt{3}} = 2 - b\sqrt{6}$ (iv) $\dfrac{7+\sqrt{5}}{7-\sqrt{5}} - \dfrac{7-\sqrt{5}}{7+\sqrt{5}} = a + \dfrac{7}{11}\sqrt{5}b$

Ans. (i) We have, $\dfrac{5+2\sqrt{3}}{7+4\sqrt{3}} = a - 6\sqrt{3}$

On rationalising the denominator of LHS, we get

$$\frac{5+2\sqrt{3}}{7+4\sqrt{3}} \times \frac{7-4\sqrt{3}}{7-4\sqrt{3}} = a - 6\sqrt{3}$$

$$\Rightarrow \frac{5(7-4\sqrt{3})+2\sqrt{3}(7-4\sqrt{3})}{7^2-(4\sqrt{3})^2} = a - 6\sqrt{3} \quad [\because (a+b)(a-b) = a^2 - b^2]$$

$$\Rightarrow \frac{35-20\sqrt{3}+14\sqrt{3}-24}{49-48} = a - 6\sqrt{3}$$

$$\Rightarrow 11 - 6\sqrt{3} = a - 6\sqrt{3} \Rightarrow a = 11$$

(ii) We have, $\dfrac{3-\sqrt{5}}{3+2\sqrt{5}} = a\sqrt{5} - \dfrac{19}{11}$

On rationalising the denominator of LHS, we get

$$\frac{(3-\sqrt{5})}{3+2\sqrt{5}} \times \frac{3-2\sqrt{5}}{3-2\sqrt{5}} = a\sqrt{5} - \frac{19}{11}$$

$$\Rightarrow \frac{3(3-2\sqrt{5})-\sqrt{5}(3-2\sqrt{5})}{(3)^2-(2\sqrt{5})^2} = a\sqrt{5} - \frac{19}{11} \quad [\because (a-b)(a+b) = a^2 - b^2]$$

$$\Rightarrow \frac{9-6\sqrt{5}-3\sqrt{5}+10}{9-4\times 5} = a\sqrt{5} - \frac{19}{11}$$

$$\Rightarrow \frac{19-9\sqrt{5}}{9-20} = a\sqrt{5} - \frac{19}{11} \Rightarrow \frac{19-9\sqrt{5}}{-11} = a\sqrt{5} - \frac{19}{11}$$

$$\Rightarrow \frac{9\sqrt{5}}{11} - \frac{19}{11} = a\sqrt{5} - \frac{19}{11} \Rightarrow \frac{9\sqrt{5}}{11} = a\sqrt{5}$$

$$\therefore \quad a = \frac{9}{11}$$

(iii) We have, $\dfrac{\sqrt{2}+\sqrt{3}}{3\sqrt{2}-2\sqrt{3}} = 2 - b\sqrt{6}$

On rationalising the denominator of LHS, we get

$$\frac{\sqrt{2}+\sqrt{3}}{3\sqrt{2}-2\sqrt{3}} \times \frac{3\sqrt{2}+2\sqrt{3}}{3\sqrt{2}+2\sqrt{3}} = 2 - b\sqrt{6}$$

$$\Rightarrow \frac{\sqrt{2}(3\sqrt{2}+2\sqrt{3})+\sqrt{3}(3\sqrt{2}+2\sqrt{3})}{(3\sqrt{2})^2-(2\sqrt{3})^2} = 2 - b\sqrt{6}$$

$[\because (a-b)(a+b) = a^2 - b^2]$

$$\Rightarrow \quad \frac{6+2\sqrt{6}+3\sqrt{6}+6}{18-12} = 2-b\sqrt{6} \Rightarrow \frac{12+5\sqrt{6}}{6} = 2-b\sqrt{6}$$

$$\Rightarrow \quad 2+\frac{5\sqrt{6}}{6} = 2-b\sqrt{6} \Rightarrow b\sqrt{6} = -\frac{5\sqrt{6}}{6}$$

$$\Rightarrow \quad b = -\frac{5}{6}$$

(iv) We have, $\frac{7+\sqrt{5}}{7-\sqrt{5}} - \frac{7-\sqrt{5}}{7+\sqrt{5}} = a + \frac{7}{11}\sqrt{5}b$

$$\Rightarrow \quad \frac{(7+\sqrt{5})^2-(7-\sqrt{5})^2}{(7-\sqrt{5})(7+\sqrt{5})} = a+\frac{7}{11}\sqrt{5}b$$

$$\Rightarrow \quad \frac{[7^2+(\sqrt{5})^2+2\times7\times\sqrt{5}]-[7^2+(\sqrt{5})^2-2\times7\times\sqrt{5}]}{7^2-(\sqrt{5})^2} = a+\frac{7}{11}\sqrt{5}b$$

$$\left[\begin{array}{l}\because (a+b)^2 = a^2+2ab+b^2,\\ (a-b)^2 = a^2-2ab+b^2\\ \text{and} \quad (a-b)(a+b) = a^2-b^2\end{array}\right]$$

$$\Rightarrow \quad \frac{49+5+14\sqrt{5}-49-5+14\sqrt{5}}{49-5} = a+\frac{7}{11}\sqrt{5}b \Rightarrow \frac{28\sqrt{5}}{44} = a+\frac{7}{11}\sqrt{5}b$$

$$\Rightarrow \quad \frac{7}{11}\sqrt{5} = a+\frac{7}{11}\sqrt{5}b$$

$$\Rightarrow \quad 0+\frac{7}{11}\sqrt{5} = a+\frac{7}{11}\sqrt{5}b$$

On comparing both sides, we get

$$a = 0 \text{ and } b = 1$$

Q.12 If $a = 2+\sqrt{3}$, then find the value of $\left(a-\frac{1}{a}\right)$.

Ans. We have, $a = 2+\sqrt{3}$

Then, $\frac{1}{a} = \frac{1}{2+\sqrt{3}} \times \frac{2-\sqrt{3}}{2-\sqrt{3}}$

[on multiplying numerator and denominator by $(2-\sqrt{3})$]

$$= \frac{2-\sqrt{3}}{(2)^2-(\sqrt{3})^2} = \frac{2-\sqrt{3}}{4-3} = 2-\sqrt{3}$$

$[\because (a+b)(a-b) = a^2-b^2]$

$$\Rightarrow \quad \frac{1}{a} = 2-\sqrt{3}$$

$$\therefore \quad a-\frac{1}{a} = (2+\sqrt{3})-(2-\sqrt{3}) = 2+\sqrt{3}-2+\sqrt{3} = 2\sqrt{3}$$

Mistake Alert! *Students may take the rationalising factor with the same sign as the given denominator i.e.,* $\frac{1}{2+\sqrt{3}} \times \frac{2+\sqrt{3}}{2+\sqrt{3}}$.

Q.13 Rationalise the denominator in each of the following and hence evaluate by taking $\sqrt{2} = 1.414$, $\sqrt{3} = 1.732$ and $\sqrt{5} = 2.236$ upto three places of decimal.

(i) $\dfrac{4}{\sqrt{3}}$ (ii) $\dfrac{6}{\sqrt{6}}$ (iii) $\dfrac{\sqrt{10}-\sqrt{5}}{2}$

(iv) $\dfrac{\sqrt{2}}{2+\sqrt{2}}$ (v) $\dfrac{1}{\sqrt{3}+\sqrt{2}}$

Ans. (i) Let $E = \dfrac{4}{\sqrt{3}}$

For rationalising the denominator, multiplying numerator and denominator by $\sqrt{3}$, we get

$$E = \frac{4}{\sqrt{3}} \times \frac{\sqrt{3}}{\sqrt{3}} = \frac{4\sqrt{3}}{3} = \frac{4}{3} \times 1.732 = \frac{6.928}{3} = 2.309 \text{ (approx)} \quad [\text{put } \sqrt{3} = 1.732]$$

(ii) Let $E = \dfrac{6}{\sqrt{6}}$

For rationalising the denominator, multiplying numerator and denominator by $\sqrt{6}$, we get

$$E = \frac{6}{\sqrt{6}} \times \frac{\sqrt{6}}{\sqrt{6}} = \frac{6\sqrt{6}}{6} = \sqrt{6}$$

$$= \sqrt{2} \times \sqrt{3}$$

$$= 1.414 \times 1.732 = 2.449 \text{ (approx)} \quad [\text{put } \sqrt{2} = 1.414 \text{ and } \sqrt{3} = 1.732]$$

(iii) Let $E = \dfrac{\sqrt{10}-\sqrt{5}}{2} = \dfrac{\sqrt{5}\,\sqrt{2}-\sqrt{5}}{2} = \dfrac{\sqrt{5}\,(\sqrt{2}-1)}{2}$ $\quad [\because \sqrt{10} = \sqrt{2} \times \sqrt{5}]$

$$= \frac{2.236\,(1.414-1)}{2} = 1.118 \times 0.414 = 0.46285 \approx 0.463 \text{ (approx)}$$

(iv) Let $E = \dfrac{\sqrt{2}}{2+\sqrt{2}}$

For rationalising the denominator, multiplying numerator and denominator by $2-\sqrt{2}$, we get

$$= \frac{\sqrt{2}}{2+\sqrt{2}} \times \frac{2-\sqrt{2}}{2-\sqrt{2}} = \frac{\sqrt{2}\,(2-\sqrt{2})}{(2)^2-(\sqrt{2})^2} \quad [\because (a-b)(a+b) = a^2-b^2]$$

$$= \frac{\sqrt{2} \times \sqrt{2}\,(\sqrt{2}-1)}{4-2} = \frac{2\,(\sqrt{2}-1)}{2}$$

$$= \sqrt{2}-1 = 1.414-1 = 0.414 \quad [\text{put } \sqrt{2} = 1.414]$$

(v) Let $E = \dfrac{1}{\sqrt{3}+\sqrt{2}}$

For rationalising the denominator, multiplying numerator and denominator by $\sqrt{3}-\sqrt{2}$, we get

$$E = \frac{1}{\sqrt{3}+\sqrt{2}} \times \frac{\sqrt{3}-\sqrt{2}}{\sqrt{3}-\sqrt{2}} = \frac{\sqrt{3}-\sqrt{2}}{(\sqrt{3})^2-(\sqrt{2})^2} \quad [\because (a-b)(a+b) = a^2-b^2]$$

$$= \frac{\sqrt{3}-\sqrt{2}}{3-2} = \sqrt{3}-\sqrt{2} = 1.732-1.414 = 0.318 \quad [\text{put } \sqrt{3} = 1.732 \text{ and } \sqrt{2} = 1.414]$$

Q.14 Simplify

(i) $(1^3+2^3+3^3)^{\frac{1}{2}}$ (ii) $\left(\frac{3}{5}\right)^4\left(\frac{8}{5}\right)^{-12}\left(\frac{32}{5}\right)^6$ (iii) $\left(\frac{1}{27}\right)^{\frac{-2}{3}}$

(iv) $\left[\left((625)^{-\frac{1}{2}}\right)^{-\frac{1}{4}}\right]^2$ (v) $\dfrac{9^{\frac{1}{3}}\times 27^{-\frac{1}{2}}}{3^{\frac{1}{6}}\times 3^{-\frac{2}{3}}}$ (vi) $64^{-\frac{1}{3}}\left[64^{\frac{1}{3}}-64^{\frac{2}{3}}\right]$

(vii) $\dfrac{8^{\frac{1}{3}}\times 16^{\frac{1}{3}}}{32^{-\frac{1}{3}}}$

Ans. (i) We have, $(1^3+2^3+3^3)^{\frac{1}{2}}=(1+8+27)^{\frac{1}{2}}$

$$=(36)^{\frac{1}{2}}=(6^2)^{\frac{1}{2}}=6^{2\times\frac{1}{2}}=6 \qquad [\because (a^m)^n=a^{mn}]$$

(ii) We have, $\left(\frac{3}{5}\right)^4\left(\frac{8}{5}\right)^{-12}\left(\frac{32}{5}\right)^6=\frac{3^4}{5^4}\times\left(\frac{5}{2^3}\right)^{12}\times\left(\frac{2^5}{5}\right)^6$ $\left(\because a^{-1}=\frac{1}{a}\right)$

$$=\frac{3^4}{5^4}\times\frac{5^{12}}{2^{36}}\times\frac{2^{30}}{5^6} \qquad [\because (a^m)^n=a^{mn}]$$

$$=\frac{3^4\times 5^{12-4-6}}{2^{36-30}} \qquad \left[\because \frac{a^m}{a^n}=a^{m-n}\right]$$

$$=\frac{3^4}{2^6}\times 5^2=\frac{81\times 25}{64}=\frac{2025}{64}$$

(iii) We have, $\left(\frac{1}{27}\right)^{-2/3}=\left(\frac{1}{3^3}\right)^{-2/3}=(3^{-3})^{-2/3}$ $\left[\because \frac{1}{a}=a^{-1}\right]$

$$=3^{(-3)\times\left(-\frac{2}{3}\right)}=3^2=9 \qquad [\because (a^m)^n=a^{mn}]$$

(iv) We have, $\left[\left((625)^{-\frac{1}{2}}\right)^{\frac{-1}{4}}\right]^2=\left[\left((25^2)^{-\frac{1}{2}}\right)^{-\frac{1}{4}}\right]^2=(25^{-1})^{-\frac{1}{4}\times 2}=[(5^2)^{-1}]^{-\frac{1}{4}\times 2}$

$[\because (a^m)^n=a^{mn}]$

$$=5^{-2\times-\frac{1}{4}\times 2}=5^1=5$$

(v) We have, $\dfrac{9^{\frac{1}{3}}\times 27^{-\frac{1}{2}}}{3^{\frac{1}{6}}\times 3^{-\frac{2}{3}}}=\dfrac{(3^2)^{\frac{1}{3}}\times(3^3)^{-\frac{1}{2}}}{3^{\frac{1}{6}}\times 3^{-\frac{2}{3}}}$ $[\because (a^m)^n=a^{mn}]$

$$=\frac{3^{\frac{2}{3}}\times 3^{-\frac{3}{2}}}{3^{\frac{1}{6}}\times 3^{-\frac{2}{3}}}=\frac{3^{\frac{2}{3}-\frac{3}{2}}}{3^{\frac{1}{6}-\frac{2}{3}}} \qquad [\because a^m\times a^n=a^{m+n}]$$

$$=\frac{3^{\frac{4-9}{6}}}{3^{\frac{1-4}{6}}}=\frac{3^{-\frac{5}{6}}}{3^{-\frac{3}{6}}}=3^{-\frac{5}{6}+\frac{3}{6}}=3^{-\frac{2}{6}}=3^{-\frac{1}{3}} \qquad \left[\because \frac{a^m}{a^n}=a^{m-n}\right]$$

(vi) We have, $64^{-\frac{1}{3}}\left[64^{\frac{1}{3}} - 64^{\frac{2}{3}}\right] = (4^3)^{-\frac{1}{3}}\left[(4^3)^{\frac{1}{3}} - (4^3)^{\frac{2}{3}}\right]$

$$= 4^{3\times\left(-\frac{1}{3}\right)}\left(4^{3\times\frac{1}{3}} - 4^{3\times\frac{2}{3}}\right) = 4^{-1}(4-4^2) \qquad [\because (a^m)^n = a^{mn}]$$

$$= \frac{1}{4}(4-16) = -\frac{12}{4} = -3$$

(vii) We have, $\dfrac{8^{\frac{1}{3}} \times 16^{\frac{1}{3}}}{32^{-\frac{1}{3}}} = \dfrac{(2^3)^{\frac{1}{3}} \times (2^4)^{\frac{1}{3}}}{(2^5)^{-\frac{1}{3}}} = \dfrac{2^{3\times\frac{1}{3}} \times 2^{4\times\frac{1}{3}}}{2^{5\times-\frac{1}{3}}}$ $\qquad [\because (a^m)^n = a^{mn}]$

$$= \frac{2^{\frac{3}{3}+\frac{4}{3}}}{2^{-\frac{5}{3}}} = \frac{2^{\frac{7}{3}}}{2^{-\frac{5}{3}}} = 2^{\frac{7}{3}+\frac{5}{3}} = 2^{\frac{12}{3}} = 2^4 = 16 \qquad \left[\because \frac{a^m}{a^n} = a^{m-n}\right]$$

Long Answer Type Questions

Q.1 Express $0.6 + 0.\overline{7} + 0.4\overline{7}$ in the form $\frac{p}{q}$, where p and q are integers and $q \neq 0$.

Ans. Let $\qquad x = 0.\overline{7} = 0.777\ldots\ldots \qquad \ldots(i)$

On multiplying both sides of Eq. (i) by 10, we get

$$10x = 7.77\ldots\ldots \qquad \ldots(ii)$$

On subtracting Eq. (i) from Eq. (ii), we get

$$10x - x = (7.77\ldots) - (0.77\ldots)$$

$\Rightarrow \qquad 9x = 7$

$\therefore \qquad x = \frac{7}{9}$

Now, let $\qquad y = 0.4\overline{7} = 0.4777\ldots \qquad \ldots(iii)$

On multiplying both sides of Eq. (iii) by 10, we get

$$10y = 4.777\ldots \qquad \ldots(iv)$$

On multiplying both sides, Eq. (iv) by 10, we get

$$100y = 47.777\ldots \qquad \ldots(v)$$

On subtracting Eq. (iv) from Eq. (v), we get

$$(100y - 10y) = (47.777\ldots) - (4.777\ldots)$$

$\Rightarrow \qquad 90y = 43 = \frac{43}{90} \Rightarrow y = \frac{43}{90}$

$\therefore \qquad 0.6 + 0.\overline{7} + 0.4\overline{7} = \frac{6}{10} + \frac{7}{9} + \frac{43}{90}$

$$= \frac{54 + 70 + 43}{90} = \frac{167}{90}$$

Q.2 Simplify $\dfrac{7\sqrt{3}}{\sqrt{10}+\sqrt{3}}-\dfrac{2\sqrt{5}}{\sqrt{6}+\sqrt{5}}-\dfrac{3\sqrt{2}}{\sqrt{15}+3\sqrt{2}}$.

Ans. We have, $\dfrac{7\sqrt{3}}{\sqrt{10}+\sqrt{3}}-\dfrac{2\sqrt{5}}{\sqrt{6}+\sqrt{5}}-\dfrac{3\sqrt{2}}{\sqrt{15}+3\sqrt{2}}$

Now, $\dfrac{7\sqrt{3}}{\sqrt{10}+\sqrt{3}}\times\dfrac{\sqrt{10}-\sqrt{3}}{\sqrt{10}-\sqrt{3}}=\dfrac{7\sqrt{30}-21}{(\sqrt{10})^2-(\sqrt{3})^2}$ [by rationalisation]

[$\because (a-b)(a+b)=a^2-b^2$]

$=\dfrac{7\sqrt{30}-21}{10-3}=\dfrac{7(\sqrt{30}-3)}{7}=\sqrt{30}-3$ ...(i)

$\dfrac{2\sqrt{5}}{\sqrt{6}+\sqrt{5}}=\dfrac{2\sqrt{5}}{(\sqrt{6}+\sqrt{5})}\times\dfrac{(\sqrt{6}-\sqrt{5})}{(\sqrt{6}-\sqrt{5})}$ [by rationalisation]

$=\dfrac{2\sqrt{30}-10}{(\sqrt{6})^2-(\sqrt{5})^2}$ [$\because (a-b)(a+b)=a^2-b^2$]

$=\dfrac{2\sqrt{30}-10}{6-5}=2\sqrt{30}-10$ ...(ii)

and $\dfrac{3\sqrt{2}}{\sqrt{15}+3\sqrt{2}}=\dfrac{3\sqrt{2}}{\sqrt{15}+3\sqrt{2}}\times\dfrac{\sqrt{15}-3\sqrt{2}}{\sqrt{15}-3\sqrt{2}}$ [by rationalisation]

$=\dfrac{3\sqrt{30}-18}{(\sqrt{15})^2-(3\sqrt{2})^2}$ [$\because (a-b)(a+b)=a^2-b^2$]

$=\dfrac{3(\sqrt{30}-6)}{15-18}=\dfrac{3(\sqrt{30}-6)}{-3}=6-\sqrt{30}$ ...(iii)

$\therefore$ $\dfrac{7\sqrt{3}}{\sqrt{10}+\sqrt{3}}-\dfrac{2\sqrt{5}}{\sqrt{6}+\sqrt{5}}-\dfrac{3\sqrt{2}}{\sqrt{15}+3\sqrt{2}}$

$=(\sqrt{30}-3)-(2\sqrt{30}-10)-(6-\sqrt{30})$ [from Eqs. (i), (ii) and (iii)]

$=\sqrt{30}-3-2\sqrt{30}+10-6+\sqrt{30}=2\sqrt{30}-2\sqrt{30}+10-9=1$

Q.3 If $\sqrt{2}=1.414$ and $\sqrt{3}=1.732$, then find the value of $\dfrac{4}{3\sqrt{3}-2\sqrt{2}}+\dfrac{3}{3\sqrt{3}+2\sqrt{2}}$.

Ans. We have, $\dfrac{4}{3\sqrt{3}-2\sqrt{2}}+\dfrac{3}{3\sqrt{3}+2\sqrt{2}}$

$=\dfrac{4(3\sqrt{3}+2\sqrt{2})+3(3\sqrt{3}-2\sqrt{2})}{(3\sqrt{3}-2\sqrt{2})(3\sqrt{3}+2\sqrt{2})}$

$=\dfrac{12\sqrt{3}+8\sqrt{2}+9\sqrt{3}-6\sqrt{2}}{(3\sqrt{3})^2-(2\sqrt{2})^2}$ [$\because (a+b)(a-b)=a^2-b^2$]

$=\dfrac{21\sqrt{3}+2\sqrt{2}}{27-8}=\dfrac{21\sqrt{3}+2\sqrt{2}}{19}$

$=\dfrac{21\times1.732+2\times1.414}{19}$ [put $\sqrt{2}=1.414$ and $\sqrt{3}=1.732$]

$=\dfrac{36.372+2.828}{19}=\dfrac{39.2}{19}=2.06316\approx2.063$ (approx)

Q.4 If $a=\dfrac{3+\sqrt{5}}{2}$, then find the value of $a^2+\dfrac{1}{a^2}$.

Ans. Given, $$a=\frac{3+\sqrt{5}}{2} \quad ...(i)$$

Now, $$\frac{1}{a}=\frac{2}{3+\sqrt{5}}=\frac{2}{3+\sqrt{5}}\times\frac{3-\sqrt{5}}{3-\sqrt{5}}$$ [rationalise the denominator]

$$=\frac{6-2\sqrt{5}}{3^2-(\sqrt{5})^2}$$ [$\because (a-b)(a+b)=a^2-b^2$]

$$=\frac{6-2\sqrt{5}}{9-5}=\frac{6-2\sqrt{5}}{4}$$

$\Rightarrow$ $$\frac{1}{a}=\frac{2(3-\sqrt{5})}{4}=\frac{3-\sqrt{5}}{2} \quad ...(ii)$$

$\therefore$ $$a^2+\frac{1}{a^2}=a^2+\frac{1}{a^2}+2-2=\left(a+\frac{1}{a}\right)^2-2$$ [add and substract 2]

[$\because (a+b)^2=a^2+b^2+2ab$]

$$=\left(\frac{3+\sqrt{5}}{2}+\frac{3-\sqrt{5}}{2}\right)^2-2$$ [from Eqs. (i) and (ii)]

$$=\left(\frac{6}{2}\right)^2-2=(3)^2-2=9-2=7$$

Hence, the value of $a^2+\dfrac{1}{a^2}$ is equal to 7.

Q.5 If $x=\dfrac{\sqrt{3}+\sqrt{2}}{\sqrt{3}-\sqrt{2}}$ and $y=\dfrac{\sqrt{3}-\sqrt{2}}{\sqrt{3}+\sqrt{2}}$, then find the value of x^2+y^2?

Ans. Given, $$x=\frac{\sqrt{3}+\sqrt{2}}{\sqrt{3}-\sqrt{2}}\times\frac{\sqrt{3}+\sqrt{2}}{\sqrt{3}+\sqrt{2}}$$ [rationalise the denominator]

$$=\frac{(\sqrt{3}+\sqrt{2})^2}{(\sqrt{3})^2-(\sqrt{2})^2}$$ [$\because (a+b)(a-b)=a^2-b^2$]

$$=\frac{(\sqrt{3})^2+(\sqrt{2})^2+2\times\sqrt{3}\times\sqrt{2}}{3-2}$$ [$\because (a+b)^2=a^2+b^2+2ab$]

$$=\frac{3+2+2\sqrt{6}}{1}$$

$\therefore$ $$x=5+2\sqrt{6} \quad ...(i)$$

On squaring both sides, we get

$$x^2=(5+2\sqrt{6})^2=(5)^2+(2\sqrt{6})^2+2\times5\times2\sqrt{6}$$ [$\because (a+b)^2=a^2+b^2+2ab$]

$$=25+24+20\sqrt{6}$$

$\Rightarrow$ $$x^2=49+20\sqrt{6} \quad ...(ii)$$

$\therefore$ $$y=\frac{\sqrt{3}-\sqrt{2}}{\sqrt{3}+\sqrt{2}}=\frac{1}{x}=\frac{1}{5+2\sqrt{6}}$$ [from Eq. (i)]

$$= \frac{1}{5+2\sqrt{6}} \times \frac{5-2\sqrt{6}}{5-2\sqrt{6}}$$ [rationalise the denominator]

$$= \frac{5-2\sqrt{6}}{(5)^2-(2\sqrt{6})^2} = \frac{5-2\sqrt{6}}{25-24} = \frac{5-2\sqrt{6}}{1}$$ $[\because (a-b)(a+b) = a^2 - b^2]$

$\Rightarrow \quad y = 5 - 2\sqrt{6}$

On squaring both sides, we get

$y^2 = (5-2\sqrt{6})^2$

$\Rightarrow \quad y^2 = (5)^2 + (2\sqrt{6})^2 - 2 \times 5 \times 2\sqrt{6}$

$[\because (a-b)^2 = a^2 + b^2 - 2ab]$

$\Rightarrow \quad y^2 = 25 + 24 - 20\sqrt{6}$

$\Rightarrow \quad y^2 = 49 - 20\sqrt{6}$ ...(iii)

On adding Eqs. (ii) and (iii), we get

$$x^2 + y^2 = 49 + 20\sqrt{6} + 49 - 20\sqrt{6} = 98$$

Q.6 Simplify $(256)^{-\left(4^{-\frac{3}{2}}\right)}$.

Ans. We have, $(256)^{-\left(4^{-\frac{3}{2}}\right)} = (256)^{-(4)^{-\frac{3}{2}}} = (256)^{-(2^2)^{-\frac{3}{2}}}$

$$= (256)^{-\left(2^{2\times -\frac{3}{2}}\right)} = (256)^{-(2^{-3})}$$ $[\because b^{(a^m)^n} = b^{a^{mn}}]$

$$= (2^8)^{-\left(\frac{1}{2^3}\right)} = (2^8)^{-\frac{1}{8}}$$

$\left[\because a^{-m} = \frac{1}{a^m}\right]$ $$= 2^{8\times -\frac{1}{8}} = 2^{-1} = \frac{1}{2}$$

Q.7 Find the value of $\dfrac{4}{(216)^{-\frac{2}{3}}} + \dfrac{1}{(256)^{-\frac{3}{4}}} + \dfrac{2}{(243)^{-\frac{1}{5}}}$.

Ans. We have, $\dfrac{4}{(216)^{-\frac{2}{3}}} + \dfrac{1}{(256)^{-\frac{3}{4}}} + \dfrac{2}{(243)^{-\frac{1}{5}}} = \dfrac{4}{(6^3)^{-\frac{2}{3}}} + \dfrac{1}{(4^4)^{-\frac{3}{4}}} + \dfrac{2}{(3^5)^{-\frac{1}{5}}}$

$$= \frac{4}{6^{3\times\left(-\frac{2}{3}\right)}} + \frac{1}{4^{4\times\left(\frac{-3}{4}\right)}} + \frac{2}{3^{5\times\left(-\frac{1}{5}\right)}}$$ $[\because (a^m)^n = a^{mn}]$

$$= \frac{4}{6^{-2}} + \frac{1}{4^{-3}} + \frac{2}{3^{-1}}$$

$$= 4 \times 6^2 + 4^3 + 2 \times 3^1$$ $\left[\because \frac{1}{a} = a^{-1}\right]$

$$= 144 + 64 + 6 = 214$$

Chapter

02

Polynomials

Multiple Choice Questions (MCQs)

Choose the correct answer from the given four options in the following questions:

Q.1 Which one of the following is a polynomial?

(a) $\frac{x^2}{2}-\frac{2}{x^2}$ (b) $\sqrt{2x}-1$ (c) $x^2+\frac{3x^{3/2}}{\sqrt{x}}$ (d) $\frac{x-1}{x+1}$

Ans. ***(c)*** (a) We have, $\frac{x^2}{2}-\frac{2}{x^2}=\frac{x^2}{2}-2x^{-2}$, it is not a polynomial, because the exponent of x^{-2} is –2 which is not a whole number.

(b) We have, $\sqrt{2x}-1=\sqrt{2}x^{1/2}-1$, it is not a polynomial, because the exponent of $x^{1/2}$ is $\frac{1}{2}$ which is not a whole number.

(c) We have, $x^2+\frac{3x^{3/2}}{\sqrt{x}}=x^2+3x^{\frac{3}{2}-\frac{1}{2}}=x^2+3x^{\frac{2}{2}}=x^2+3x$, it is a polynomial, because each exponent of x is a whole number.

(d) $\frac{x-1}{x+1}$, it is not a standard form of a polynomial because it is a rational function.

Hence, option (c) is correct.

Q.2 $\sqrt{2}$ is a polynomial of degree

(a) 2 (b) 0 (c) 1 (d) $\frac{1}{2}$

Ans. ***(b)*** $\sqrt{2}=\sqrt{2}x^0$. Hence, $\sqrt{2}$ is a polynomial of degree 0, becaucse exponent of x is 0.

Q.3 Degree of the polynomial $4x^4+0x^3+0x^5+5x+7$ is

(a) 4 (b) 5 (c) 3 (d) 7

Ans. ***(a)*** We know that the degree of $4x^4+0x^3+0x^5+5x+7$ is equal to the highest power of variable x. Here, the highest power of x is 4 that has a non-zero coefficient. Hence, the degree of the given polynomial is 4.

Q.4 Degree of the zero polynomial is

(a) 0 (b) 1

(c) any natural number (d) not defined

Ans. ***(d)*** The degree of zero polynomial is not defined, because in zero polynomial, the coefficient of any variable is zero *i.e.*, $0x^2$ or $0x^5$ etc.

Hence, we cannot exactly determine the degree of variable.

Q.5 If $p(x) = x^2 - 2\sqrt{2}x + 1$, then $p(2\sqrt{2})$ is equal to

(a) 0 (b) 1 (c) $4\sqrt{2}$ (d) $8\sqrt{2} + 1$

Ans. *(b)* Given, $p(x) = x^2 - 2\sqrt{2}x + 1$ ...(i)

On putting $x = 2\sqrt{2}$ in Eq. (i), we get

$$p(2\sqrt{2}) = (2\sqrt{2})^2 - (2\sqrt{2})(2\sqrt{2}) + 1$$
$$= 8 - 8 + 1 = 1$$

Q.6 The value of the polynomial $5x - 4x^2 + 3$, when $x = -1$ is

(a) -6 (b) 6 (c) 2 (d) -2

Ans. *(a)* Let $p(x) = 5x - 4x^2 + 3$ ...(i)

On putting $x = -1$ in Eq. (i), we get

$$p(-1) = 5(-1) - 4(-1)^2 + 3 = -5 - 4 + 3 = -6$$

Q.7 If $p(x) = x + 3$, then $p(x) + p(-x)$ is equal to

(a) 3 (b) $2x$ (c) 0 (d) 6

Ans. *(d)* Given, $p(x) = x + 3$.... ...(i)

$$p(-x) = -x + 3$$

Now, $p(x) + P(-x) = x + 3 - x + 3 = 6$

Q.8 Zero of the zero polynomial is

(a) 0 (b) 1

(c) any real number (d) not defined

Ans. *(c)* Let us consider zero polynomial be $0(x-k)$, where k is a real number.

For determining the zero, put $x - k = 0 \Rightarrow x = k$

Hence, zero of the zero polynomial is any real number.

Q.9 Zero of the polynomial $p(x) = 2x + 5$ is

(a) $-\frac{2}{5}$ (b) $-\frac{5}{2}$ (c) $\frac{2}{5}$ (d) $\frac{5}{2}$

Ans. *(b)* Given, $p(x) = 2x + 5$

For zero of the polynomial, put $p(x) = 0$

$\therefore$ $2x + 5 = 0$

$\Rightarrow$ $x = -\frac{5}{2}$

Hence, zero of the polynomial $p(x)$ is $\frac{-5}{2}$.

Q.10 One of the zeroes of the polynomial $2x^2 + 7x - 4$ is

(a) 2 (b) $\frac{1}{2}$ (c) $-\frac{1}{2}$ (d) -2

Thinking Process

(i) Firstly, determine the factor by using splitting method.

(ii) Further, put the factors equals to zero, then determine the values of x.

Ans. *(b)* Let $p(x) = 2x^2 + 7x - 4$

$= 2x^2 + 8x - x - 4$ [by splitting middle term]

$= 2x(x+4) - 1(x+4)$

$= (2x-1)(x+4)$

For zeroes of $p(x)$, put $p(x) = 0$

$\therefore \quad (2x-1)(x+4) = 0$

$\Rightarrow \quad 2x - 1 = 0$ and $x + 4 = 0$

$\Rightarrow \quad x = \frac{1}{2}$ and $x = -4$

Hence, one of the zeroes of the polynomial $p(x)$ is $\frac{1}{2}$.

***Q.11** If $x^{51} + 51$ is divided by $x + 1$, then the remainder is

(a) 0 (b) 1 (c) 49 (d) 50

Ans. *(d)* Let $p(x) = x^{51} + 51$ ...(i)

We know that, when we divide $p(x)$ by $x + 1$, then the remainder is $p(-1)$.

[by remainder theorem]

On putting $x = -1$ in Eq. (i), we get

$p(-1) = (-1)^{51} + 51 = -1 + 51 = 50$

Hence, the remainder is 50.

Q.12 If $x + 1$ is a factor of the polynomial $2x^2 + kx$, then the value of k is

(a) – 3 (b) 4 (c) 2 (d) – 2

- **Concept Insight** If $(x + a)$ is a factor of polynomial $p(x)$, then $p(-a) = 0$.

Ans. *(c)* Let $p(x) = 2x^2 + kx$

Since, $(x + 1)$ is a factor of $p(x)$, then

$p(-1) = 0$

$\therefore \quad 2(-1)^2 + k(-1) = 0$

$\Rightarrow \quad 2 - k = 0 \Rightarrow k = 2$

Hence, the value of k is 2.

Q.13 $x + 1$ is a factor of the polynomial

(a) $x^3 + x^2 - x + 1$ (b) $x^3 + x^2 + x + 1$

(c) $x^4 + x^3 + x^2 + 1$ (d) $x^4 + 3x^3 + 3x^2 + x + 1$

Ans. *(b)* Let $(x + 1)$ is a factor of the polynomial $x^3 + x^2 + x + 1$.

So, $x = -1$ is a zero of $x^3 + x^2 + x + 1$

$\therefore \quad (-1)^3 + (-1)^2 + (-1) + 1 = 0$

$\Rightarrow \quad -1 + 1 - 1 + 1 = 0 \Rightarrow 0 = 0$

Hence, our assumption is true.

Q.14 One of the factors of $(25x^2 - 1) + (1 + 5x)^2$ is

(a) $5 + x$ (b) $5 - x$

(c) $5x - 1$ (d) $10x$

(*) Topics related to these question have been removed from latest NCERT.

Ans. *(d)* We have, $(25x^2 - 1) + (1 + 5x)^2$

$= 25x^2 - 1 + 1 + 25x^2 + 10x$ $\quad [\because (a+b)^2 = a^2 + b^2 + 2ab]$

$= 50x^2 + 10x = 10x(5x + 1)$

Hence, one of the factor of given polynomial is $10x$.

Q.15 The value of $249^2 - 248^2$ is

(a) 1^2 (b) 477 (c) 487 (d) 497

Ans. *(d)* We have, $249^2 - 248^2$

$= (249 + 248)(249 - 248)$ $\quad [\because a^2 - b^2 = (a-b)(a+b)]$

$= 497 \times 1 = 497$

Q.16 The factorisation of $4x^2 + 8x + 3$ is

(a) $(x + 1)(x + 3)$ (b) $(2x + 1)(2x + 3)$ (c) $(2x + 2)(2x + 5)$ (d) $(2x - 1)(2x - 3)$

Ans. *(b)* We have, $4x^2 + 8x + 3 = 4x^2 + 6x + 2x + 3$ [by splitting middle term]

$= 2x(2x + 3) + 1(2x + 3)$

$= (2x + 3)(2x + 1)$

Q.17 Which of the following is a factor of $(x + y)^3 - (x^3 + y^3)$?

(a) $x^2 + y^2 + 2xy$ (b) $x^2 + y^2 - xy$ (c) xy^2 (d) $3xy$

Ans. *(d)* We have, $(x + y)^3 - (x^3 + y^3) = (x + y)^3 - (x + y)(x^2 - xy + y^2)$

$[\because a^3 + b^3 = (a + b)(a^2 - ab + b^2)]$

$= (x + y)[(x + y)^2 - (x^2 - xy + y^2)]$

$= (x + y)(x^2 + y^2 + 2xy - x^2 + xy - y^2)$

$[\because (a + b)^2 = a^2 + b^2 + 2ab)]$

$= (x + y)(3xy)$

Hence, one of the factor of given polynomial is $3xy$.

Mistake Alert! *Students may incorrectly apply the identity as $a^3 + b^3 = (a + b)(a^2 + ab + b^2)$ instead of $a^3 + b^3 = (a + b)(a^2 - ab + b^2)$.*

Q.18 The coefficient of x in the expansion of $(x + 3)^3$ is

(a) 1 (b) 9 (c) 18 (d) 27

Thinking Process In this question, we will use the identity, $(a + b)^3 = a^3 + b^3 + 3ab(a + b)$.

Ans. *(d)* We have, $(x + 3)^3 = x^3 + 3^3 + 3x(3)(x + 3)$

$[\because (a + b)^3 = a^3 + b^3 + 3ab(a + b)]$

$= x^3 + 27 + 9x(x + 3)$

$= x^3 + 27 + 9x^2 + 27x$

Hence, the coefficient of x in $(x + 3)^3$ is 27.

Q.19 If $\frac{x}{y} + \frac{y}{x} = -1$ (where $x, y \neq 0$), retain this part value of $x^3 - y^3$ is

(a) 1 (b) -1 (c) 0 (d) $\frac{1}{2}$

Ans. *(c)* Given, $\frac{x}{y}+\frac{y}{x}=-1$

$\Rightarrow \quad \frac{x^2+y^2}{xy}=-1 \Rightarrow x^2+y^2=-xy$

$\Rightarrow \quad x^2+y^2+xy=0$ ...(i)

Now, $x^3-y^3=(x-y)(x^2+xy+y^2)$

$[\because a^3-b^3=(a-b)(a^2+ab+b^2)]$

$=(x-y)\times 0=0$ [from Eq. (i)]

Q.20 If $49x^2-b=\left(7x+\frac{1}{2}\right)\left(7x-\frac{1}{2}\right)$, then the value of b is

(a) 0 (b) $\frac{1}{\sqrt{2}}$ (c) $\frac{1}{4}$ (d) $\frac{1}{2}$

● **Concept Insight** In this question, we will use the identity, $a^2-b^2=(a+b)(a-b)$.

Ans. *(c)* Given, $(49x^2-b)=\left(7x+\frac{1}{2}\right)\left(7x-\frac{1}{2}\right)$

$\Rightarrow \quad [49x^2-(\sqrt{b})^2]=\left[(7x)^2-\left(\frac{1}{2}\right)^2\right]$ $[\because (a+b)(a-b)=a^2-b^2]$

$\Rightarrow \quad 49x^2-(\sqrt{b})^2=49x^2-\left(\frac{1}{2}\right)^2 \Rightarrow -(\sqrt{b})^2=-\left(\frac{1}{2}\right)^2$

$\Rightarrow \quad (\sqrt{b})^2=\left(\frac{1}{2}\right)^2$ [multiplying both sides by −1]

$\therefore \quad b=\frac{1}{4}$

Q.21 If $a+b+c=0$, then $a^3+b^3+c^3$ is equal to

(a) 0 (b) abc (c) $3abc$ (d) $2abc$

Ans. *(c)* Given, $a+b+c=0$ ...(i)

Now, $a^3+b^3+c^3=(a+b+c)(a^2+b^2+c^2-ab-bc-ca)+3abc$

$[\because a^3+b^3+c^3-3abc=(a+b+c)(a^2+b^2+c^2-ab-bc-ca]$

$=0\times(a^2+b^2+c^2-ab-bc-ca)+3abc$ [from Eq. (ii)]

$\therefore \quad a^3+b^3+c^3=3abc$

Short Answer Type Questions with Reasoning

Q.1 Which of the following expressions are polynomials? Justify your answer

(i) 8 (ii) $\sqrt{3}x^2-2x$ (iii) $1-\sqrt{5x}$

(iv) $\frac{1}{5x^{-2}}+5x+7$ (v) $\frac{(x-2)(x-4)}{x}$ (vi) $\frac{1}{x+1}$

(vii) $\frac{1}{7}a^3-\frac{2}{\sqrt{3}}a^2+4a-7$ (viii) $\frac{1}{2x}$

Ans. (i) Polynomial, because the exponent of the variable of 8 or $8x^0$ is 0, which is a whole number.

(ii) Polynomial, because each exponent of the variable of $\sqrt{3}x^2-2x$ is a whole number.

(iii) Not polynomial, because the exponent of the variable of $1-\sqrt{5x}$ or $1-\sqrt{5}x^{\frac{1}{2}}$ is $\frac{1}{2}$, which is not a whole number.

(iv) Polynomial, because each exponent of the variable of $\frac{1}{5x^{-2}}+5x+7$ or $\frac{1}{5}x^2+5x+7$ is a whole number.

(v) Not polynomial, because the exponent of the variable of $\frac{(x-2)(x-4)}{x}=\frac{x^2-6x+8}{x}$ $=x-6+8x^{-1}$ is -1, which is not a whole number.

(vi) Not polynomial, as the polynomial is expressed as $a_0+a_1x+a_2x^2+...+a_nx^n$, where $a_0, a_1, a_2,..., a_n$ are constants. Now, $f(x)=\frac{p(x)}{q(x)}$ is a rational expression where $q(x)\neq 0$, $p(x)$ and $q(x)$ are polynomials. Hence, $\frac{1}{x+1}$ is a rational expression but not a polynomial.

(vii) Polynomial, because each exponent of the variable of $\frac{1}{7}a^3-\frac{2}{\sqrt{3}}a^2+4a-7$ is a whole number.

(viii) Not polynomial, because the exponent of the variable of $\frac{1}{2x}$ or $\frac{1}{2}x^{-1}$ is -1, which is not a whole number.

Q.2 Write whether the following statements are true or false. Justify your answer.

(i) A binomial can have atmost two terms.

(ii) Every polynomial is a binomial.

(iii) A binomial may have degree 5.

(iv) Zero of a polynomial is always 0.

(v) A polynomial cannot have more than one zero.

(vi) The degree of the sum of two polynomials each of degree 5 is always 5.

Ans. (i) *False*, because a binomial has exactly two terms.

(ii) *False*, because every polynomial is not a binomial

e.g., $3x^2+4x+5$ [polynomial but not a binomial]

(iii) *True*, because a binomial is a polynomial whose degree is a whole number which is greater than or equal to one. So, it may have degree 5.

(iv) *False*, because the zeros of a polynomial are the values of the variable that make the polynomial equal to zero.

e.g., let $p(x)=x-2$, then 2 is a zero of polynomial $p(x)$.

(v) *False*, because a polynomial can have any number of zeroes. It depends upon the degree of the polynomial.

e.g., let $p(x)=x^2-2$, as degree of $p(x)$ is 2, so it has two zeroes *i.e.*, $\sqrt{2}$ and $-\sqrt{2}$.

(vi) *False*, because the sum of any two polynomials of same degree is not always same degree.

e.g., let $f(x)=x^5+2$ and $g(x)=-x^5+4x^3+2x$

$\therefore$ Sum of two polynomials,

$$f(x)+g(x)=x^5+2+(-x^5+4x^3+2x)$$
$$=4x^3+2x+2,\text{ which is not a polynomial of degree 5.}$$

Short Answer Type Questions

Q.1 Classify the following polynomials as polynomials in one variable, two variables etc.

(i) $x^2 + x + 1$ (ii) $y^3 - 5y$

(iii) $xy + yz + zx$ (iv) $x^2 - 2xy + y^2 + 1$

Ans. (i) Polynomial $x^2 + x + 1$ is a one variable polynomial, because it contains only one variable *i.e.*, x.

(ii) Polynomial $y^3 - 5y$ is a one variable polynomial, because it contains only one variable *i.e.*, y.

(iii) Polynomial $xy + yz + zx$ is a three variables polynomial, because it contains three variables x, y and z.

(iv) Polynomial $x^2 - 2xy + y^2 + 1$ is a two variables polynomial, because it contains two variables x and y.

Q.2 Determine the degree of each of the following polynomials

(i) $2x - 1$ (ii) -10

(iii) $x^3 - 9x + 3x^5$ (iv) $y^3(1 - y^4)$

Ans. (i) Degree of polynomial $2x - 1$ is one, because the maximum exponent of x is one.

(ii) Degree of polynomial -10 or $-10x^0$ is zero, because the exponent of x is zero.

(iii) Degree of polynomial $x^3 - 9x + 3x^5$ is five, because the maximum exponent of x is five.

(iv) Degree of polynomial $y^3(1 - y^4)$ or $y^3 - y^7$ is seven, because the maximum exponent of y is seven.

Q. 3 For the polynomial $\frac{x^3 + 2x + 1}{5} - \frac{7}{2}x^2 - x^6$, write

(i) the degree of the polynomial (ii) the coefficient of x^3

(iii) the coefficient of x^6 (iv) the constant term

Ans. Given, polynomial $\frac{x^3 + 2x + 1}{5} - \frac{7}{2}x^2 - x^6 = \frac{1}{5}x^3 + \frac{2x}{5} + \frac{1}{5} - \frac{7}{2}x^2 - x^6$

(i) Degree of the polynomial is the highest power of the variable x *i.e.*, 6.

(ii) The coefficient of x^3 in given polynomial is $\frac{1}{5}$.

(iii) The coefficient of x^6 in given polynomial is -1.

(iv) The constant term in given polynomial is $\frac{1}{5}$.

Q.4 Write the coefficient of x^2 in each of the following

(i) $\frac{\pi}{6}x + x^2 - 1$ (ii) $3x - 5$

(iii) $(x - 1)(3x - 4)$ (iv) $(2x - 5)(2x^2 - 3x + 1)$

Ans. (i) The coefficient of x^2 in $\frac{\pi}{6}x + x^2 - 1$ is 1.

(ii) The coefficient of x^2 in $3x - 5$ is 0.

(iii) Let $p(x)=(x-1)(3x-4) = 3x^2-4x-3x+4 = 3x^2-7x+4$

Hence, the coefficient of x^2 in $p(x)$ is 3.

(iv) Let $p(x) = (2x-5)(2x^2-3x+1)$

$= 2x(2x^2-3x+1)-5(2x^2-3x+1)$

$= 4x^3-6x^2+2x-10x^2+15x-5 = 4x^3-16x^2+17x-5$

Hence, the coefficient of x^2 in $p(x)$ is –16.

Q.5 Classify the following as a constant, linear, quadratic and cubic polynomials

(i) $2-x^2+x^3$ (ii) $3x^3$ (iii) $5t-\sqrt{7}$

(iv) $4-5y^2$ (v) 3 (vi) $2+x$

(vii) y^3-y (viii) $1+x+x^2$ (ix) t^2

(x) $\sqrt{2}x-1$

Thinking Process

(i) Firstly determine the maximum exponent of the variable.

(ii) If the maximum exponent of a variable is 0, then it is a constant polynomial.

(iii) If the maximum exponent of a variable is 1, then it is a linear polynomial.

(iv) If the maximum exponent of a variable is 2, then it is a quadratic polynomial.

(v) If the maximum exponent of a variable is 3, then it is a cubic polynomial.

Ans. (i) Polynomial $2-x^2+x^3$ is a cubic polynomial, because maximum exponent of x is 3.

(ii) Polynomial $3x^3$ is a cubic polynomial, because maximum exponent of x is 3.

(iii) Polynomial $5t-\sqrt{7}$ is a linear polynomial, because maximum exponent of t is 1.

(iv) Polynomial $4-5y^2$ is a quadratic polynomial, because maximum exponent of y is 2.

(v) Polynomial 3 is a constant polynomial, because the exponent of variable is 0.

(vi) Polynomial $2+x$ is a linear polynomial, because maximum exponent of x is 1.

(vii) Polynomial y^3-y is a cubic polynomial, because maximum exponent of y is 3.

(viii) Polynomial $1+x+x^2$ is a quadratic polynomial, because maximum exponent of x is 2.

(ix) Polynomial t^2 is a quadratic polynomial, because maximum exponent of t is 2.

(x) Polynomial $\sqrt{2}x-1$ is a linear polynomial, because maximum exponent of x is 1.

Q.6 Give an example of a polynomial, which is

(i) monomial of degree 1. (ii) binomial of degree 20.

(iii) trinomial of degree 2.

Ans. (i) The example of monomial of degree 1 is $5y$ or $10x$.

(ii) The example of binomial of degree 20 is $6x^{20}+x^{11}$ or $x^{20}+1$.

(iii) The example of trinomial of degree 2 is x^2-5x+4 or $2x^2-x-1$.

Q.7 Find the value of the polynomial $3x^3-4x^2+7x-5$, when $x=3$ and also when $x=-3$.

Ans. Let $p(x) = 3x^3-4x^2+7x-5$

At $x=3$, $p(3) = 3(3)^3-4(3)^2+7(3)-5 = 3\times27-4\times9+21-5 = 81-36+21-5$

$\therefore \quad p(3) = 61$

At $x=-3$, $p(-3) = 3(-3)^3-4(-3)^2+7(-3)-5$

$= 3(-27)-4\times9-21-5 = -81-36-21-5 \Rightarrow p(-3) = -143$

Hence, the value of the given polynomial at $x=3$ and $x=-3$ are 61 and –143, respectively.

Q.8 If $p(x) = x^2 - 4x + 3$, evaluate $p(2) - p(-1) + p\left(\frac{1}{2}\right)$.

Ans. Given, $p(x) = x^2 - 4x + 3$

Now, $p(2) = (2)^2 - 4\times2+3 = 4-8+3 = -1$

$p(-1) = (-1)^2 - 4(-1)+3 = 1+4+3 = 8$

And $p\left(\frac{1}{2}\right) = \left(\frac{1}{2}\right)^2 - 4\times\frac{1}{2}+3$

$= \frac{1}{4} - 2 + 3 = \frac{1}{4} + 1 = \frac{5}{4}$

$\therefore \quad p(2) - p(-1) + p\left(\frac{1}{2}\right) = -1 - 8 + \frac{5}{4}$

$= -9 + \frac{5}{4} = \frac{-36+5}{4} = \frac{-31}{4}$

Q.9 Find $p(0)$, $p(1)$ and $p(-2)$ for the following polynomials

(i) $p(x) = 10x - 4x^2 - 3$ (ii) $p(y) = (y+2)(y-2)$

Ans. (i) Given, polynomial $p(x) = 10x - 4x^2 - 3$ ...(i)

On putting $x = 0$, 1 and -2 respectively in Eq. (i), we get

$p(0) = 10(0) - 4(0)^2 - 3$

$= 0 - 0 - 3 = -3$

$p(1) = 10(1) - 4(1)^2 - 3$

$= 10 - 4 - 3 = 10 - 7 = 3$

and $p(-2) = 10(-2) - 4(-2)^2 - 3$

$= -20 - 4\times4 - 3 = -20 - 16 - 3 = -39$

Hence, the values of $p(0)$, $p(1)$ and $p(-2)$ are respectively, -3, 3 and -39.

(ii) Given, polynomial $p(y) = (y+2)(y-2)$ ...(i)

On putting $y = 0$, 1 and -2, respectively in Eq. (i), we get

$p(0) = (0+2)(0-2) = -4$

$p(1) = (1+2)(1-2)$

$= 3\times(-1) = -3$

And $p(-2) = (-2+2)(-2-2)$

$= 0(-4) = 0$

Hence, the values of $p(0)$, $p(1)$ and $p(-2)$ are respectively, -4, -3 and 0.

Q.10 Verify whether the following are true or false.

(i) -3 is a zero of $x - 3$

(ii) $-\frac{1}{3}$ is a zero of $3x + 1$

(iii) $-\frac{4}{5}$ is a zero of $4 - 5y$

(iv) 0 and 2 are the zeroes of $t^2 - 2t$

(v) -3 is a zero of $y^2 + y - 6$

Ans. (i) *False*, because zero of $x - 3$ is 3. [put $x - 3 = 0 \Rightarrow x = 3$]

(ii) *True*, because zero of $3x + 1$ is $-\frac{1}{3}$. $\left[\text{put } 3x + 1 = 0 \Rightarrow x = \frac{-1}{3}\right]$

(iii) *False*, because zero of $4-5y$ is $\frac{4}{5}$. $\left[\text{put } 4-5y=0 \Rightarrow y=\frac{4}{5}\right]$

(iv) *True*, put $t^2-2t=0 \Rightarrow t(t-2)=0$
Hence, zeroes of t^2-2t are 0 and 2.

(v) *True*,
We have, $y^2+y-6=y^2+3y-2y-6$ [by splitting the middle term]
$$= y(y+3)-2(y+3)$$
$$= (y-2)(y+3)$$
Now, put $(y-2)(y+3)=0 \Rightarrow y=2,-3$
Hence, a zero of y^2+y-6 is -3.

Q.11 Find the zeroes of the polynomial in each of the following.

(i) $p(x)=x-4$ (ii) $g(x)=3-6x$
(iii) $q(x)=2x-7$ (iv) $h(y)=2y$

Ans. (i) Given, polynomial $p(x)=x-4$

For zero of polynomial, put $p(x)=0$
$\therefore$ $x-4=0 \Rightarrow x=4$
Hence, zero of polynomial is 4.

(ii) Given, polynomial $g(x)=3-6x$.
For zero of polynomial, put $g(x)=0$
$\therefore$ $3-6x=0 \Rightarrow 6x=3$
$\Rightarrow$ $x=\frac{3}{6}=\frac{1}{2}$

Hence, zero of polynomial is $\frac{1}{2}$.

(iii) Given, polynomial $q(x)=2x-7$
For zero of polynomial, put $q(x)=0$
$\therefore$ $2x-7=0$
$\Rightarrow$ $2x=7$
$\Rightarrow$ $x=\frac{7}{2}$

Hence, zero of polynomial is $\frac{7}{2}$.

(iv) Given polynomial $h(y)=2y$
For zero of polynomial, put $h(y)=0$
$\therefore$ $2y=0 \Rightarrow y=0$
Hence, the zero of polynomial is 0.

Q.12 Find the zeroes of the polynomial $p(x)=(x-2)^2-(x+2)^2$.

Thinking Process First put $p(x)=0$, then find the value of x which is the zero of $p(x)$.

Ans. Given, polynomial $p(x)=(x-2)^2-(x+2)^2$.
For zeroes of polynomial, put $p(x)=0$
$\therefore$ $(x-2)^2-(x+2)^2=0$

$$\Rightarrow \quad (x-2+x+2)(x-2-x-2)=0 \qquad [\because a^2-b^2=(a-b)(a+b)]$$

$$\Rightarrow \quad (2x)(-4)=0$$

$$\Rightarrow \quad -8x=0 \Rightarrow x=0 \qquad [\because -8 \neq 0]$$

Hence, zero of the polynomial $p(x)$ is 0.

***Q.13** By actual division, find the quotient and the remainder when the first polynomial is divided by the second polynomial: $x^4+1;\ x-1$.

Ans. Using long division method,

$$\begin{array}{r|l} x-1 & x^4+1 \ (\ x^3+x^2+x+1 \\ & \underline{\overset{-}{x^4}\ \overset{+}{-x^3}} \\ & \quad x^3+1 \\ & \quad \underline{\overset{-}{x^3}\ \overset{+}{-x^2}} \\ & \qquad x^2+1 \\ & \qquad \underline{\overset{-}{x^2}\ \overset{+}{-x}} \\ & \qquad\quad x+1 \\ & \qquad\quad \underline{\overset{-}{x}\ \overset{+}{-1}} \\ & \qquad\quad\ \ \underline{2} \end{array}$$

Hence, quotient $= x^3+x^2+x+1$ and remainder $= 2$

***Q.14** By remainder theorem find the remainder, when $p(x)$ is divided by $g(x)$, where

(i) $p(x)=x^3-2x^2-4x-1,\ g(x)=x+1$

(ii) $p(x)=x^3-3x^2+4x+50,\ g(x)=x-3$

(iii) $p(x)=4x^3-12x^2+14x-3,\ g(x)=2x-1$

(iv) $p(x)=x^3-6x^2+2x-4,\ g(x)=1-\frac{3}{2}x$

- **Concept Insight** If a polynomial $P(x)$ is divided by a binomial $(x-a)$, then the remainder is $P(a)$.

Ans. (i) Given, $p(x)=x^3-2x^2-4x-1$ and $g(x)=x+1$

Here, zero of $g(x)$ is –1. [put $x+1=0 \Rightarrow x-1$]

By remainder theorem, when we divide $p(x)$ by $g(x)$, then we get the remainder $p(-1)$,

$\therefore \quad p(-1)=(-1)^3-2(-1)^2-4(-1)-1=-1-2+4-1=4-4=0$

Hence, remainder is 0.

(ii) Given, $p(x)=x^3-3x^2+4x+50$ and $g(x)=x-3$

Here, zero of $g(x)$ is 3. [put $x-3=0 \Rightarrow x=3$]

By remainder theorem, when we divide $p(x)$ by $g(x)$, we get the remainder $p(3)$.

$$\therefore \quad p(3)=(3)^3-3(3)^2+4(3)+50$$

$$=27-27+12+50=62$$

Hence, remainder is 62.

(iii) Given, $p(x)=4x^3-12x^2+14x-3$ and $g(x)=2x-1$

Here, zero of $g(x)$ is $\frac{1}{2}$. [put $2x-1=0 \Rightarrow x=\frac{1}{2}$]

(*) Topics related to these question have been removed from latest NCERT.

By remainder theorem, when we divide $p(x)$ by $g(x)$ we get the remainder $p\left(\frac{1}{2}\right)$.

$$\therefore \quad p\left(\frac{1}{2}\right) = 4\left(\frac{1}{2}\right)^3 - 12\left(\frac{1}{2}\right)^2 + 14\left(\frac{1}{2}\right) - 3 = 4\times\frac{1}{8} - 12\times\frac{1}{4} + 14\times\frac{1}{2} - 3$$

$$= \frac{1}{2} - 3 + 7 - 3 = \frac{1}{2} + 1 = \frac{1+2}{2} = \frac{3}{2}$$

Hence, remainder is $\frac{3}{2}$.

(iv) Given, $p(x) = x^3 - 6x^2 + 2x - 4$ and $g(x) = 1 - \frac{3}{2}x$.

Here, zero of $g(x)$ is $\frac{2}{3}$.

By remainder theorem, when we divide $p(x)$ by $g(x)$, we get the remainder $p\left(\frac{2}{3}\right)$.

$$\therefore \quad P\left(\frac{2}{3}\right) = \left(\frac{2}{3}\right)^3 - 6\left(\frac{2}{3}\right)^2 + 2\left(\frac{2}{3}\right) - 4 = \frac{8}{27} - 6\times\frac{4}{9} + 2\times\frac{2}{3} - 4 = \frac{8}{27} - \frac{24}{9} + \frac{4}{3} - 4$$

$$= \frac{8 - 72 + 36 - 108}{27} = \frac{-136}{27}$$

Hence, remainder is $\frac{-136}{27}$.

Q.15 Check whether $p(x)$ is a multiple of $g(x)$ or not

(i) $p(x) = x^3 - 5x^2 + 4x - 3, g(x) = x - 2$.

(ii) $p(x) = 2x^3 - 11x^2 - 4x + 5, g(x) = 2x + 1$

Thinking Process

(i) Firstly, find the zero of $g(x)$ and then put the value of x in $p(x)$ and simplify it.

(ii) If $p(a) = 0$, then $p(x)$ is a multiple of $g(x)$ and if $p(a) \neq 0$, then $p(x)$ is not a multiple of $g(x)$, where 'a' is a zero of $g(x)$.

Ans. (i) Here, $g(x) = x - 2$ [given]

Then, zero of $g(x)$ is 2. [put $x - 2 = 0 \Rightarrow x = 2$]

Now, $p(2) = (2)^3 - 5(2)^2 + 4(2) - 3$ [$\because p(x) = x^3 - 5x^2 + 4x - 3$, given]

$= 8 - 20 + 8 - 3 = -7 \neq 0$

Since, $p(2) \neq 0$, so $p(x)$ is not a multiple of $g(x)$.

(ii) Here, $g(x) = 2x + 1$. [put $2x + 1 = 0 \Rightarrow x = -\frac{1}{2}$]

Then, zero of $g(x)$ is $\frac{-1}{2}$

Now, $p\left(\frac{-1}{2}\right) = 2\left(\frac{-1}{2}\right)^3 - 11\left(\frac{-1}{2}\right)^2 - 4\left(\frac{-1}{2}\right) + 5$ [$\because p(x) = 2x^3 - 11x^2 - 4x + 5$, given]

$$= 2\left(\frac{-1}{8}\right) - 11\left(\frac{1}{4}\right) + 2 + 5 = \frac{-1}{4} - \frac{11}{4} + 7$$

$$= \frac{-1 - 11 + 28}{4} = \frac{16}{4} = 4$$

Since, $p\left(\frac{-1}{2}\right) \neq 0$, so $p(x)$ is not a multiple of $g(x)$.

Q.16 Show that,

(i) $x+3$ is a factor of $69+11x-x^2+x^3$.

(ii) $2x-3$ is a factor of $x+2x^3-9x^2+12$.

Ans. (i) Let $p(x)=x^3-x^2+11x+69$

We have to show that $x+3$ is a factor of $p(x)$

i.e., $p(-3)=0$

Now, $p(-3)=(-3)^3-(-3)^2+11(-3)+69$

$=-27-9-33+69=-69+69=0$

Hence, $(x+3)$ is a factor of $p(x)$.

(ii) Let $p(x)=2x^3-9x^2+x+12$

We have to show that $2x-3$ is a factor of $p(x)$.

i.e., $p\left(\frac{3}{2}\right)=0$

Now, $p\left(\frac{3}{2}\right)=2\left(\frac{3}{2}\right)^3-9\left(\frac{3}{2}\right)^2+\frac{3}{2}+12$

$=2\times\frac{27}{8}-9\times\frac{9}{4}+\frac{3}{2}+12=\frac{27}{4}-\frac{81}{4}+\frac{3}{2}+12$

$=\frac{27-81+6+48}{4}=\frac{81-81}{4}=0$

Hence, $(2x-3)$ is a factor of $p(x)$.

Q.17 Determine which of the following polynomial has $x-2$ a factor

(i) $3x^2+6x-24$ (ii) $4x^2+x-2$

- **Concept Insight** If $(x-a)$ is a factor of the polynomial $p(x)$, then $p(a)=0$.

Ans. (i) Let $p(x)=3x^2+6x-24$ ...(i)

On putting $x=2$ in Eq. (i), we get

$p(2)=3(2)^2+6(2)-24$

$=3\times4+12-24=12-12=0$

Hence, $x-2$ is a factor of $p(x)$.

(ii) Let $p(x)=4x^2+x-2$ ...(i)

On putting $x=2$ in Eq. (i), we get

$p(2)=4(2)^2+2-2=4\times4+0$

$=16\neq0$

Hence, $x-2$ is not a factor of $p(x)$.

Q.18 Show that $p-1$ is a factor of $p^{10}-1$ and also of $p^{11}-1$.

Ans. Let $g(p)=p^{10}-1$ ...(i)

and $h(p)=p^{11}-1$ ...(ii)

On putting $p=1$ in Eq. (i), we get

$g(1)=(1)^{10}-1=1-1=0$

Hence, $p-1$ is a factor of $g(p)$.

Again, putting $p=1$ in Eq. (ii), we get

$h(1)=(1)^{11}-1=1-1=0$

Hence, $p-1$ is a factor of $h(p)$.

***Q.19** For what value of m is $x^3 - 2mx^2 + 16$ divisible by $x + 2$?

Ans. Let $p(x) = x^3 - 2mx^2 + 16$

When, $p(x)$ is divided by $(x+2)$, then the remainder is $p(-2)$. [by remainder theorem]

Since, $p(x)$ is divisible by $(x + 2)$. So remainder = 0 $\Rightarrow$ $p(-2) = 0$

$\Rightarrow \quad (-2)^3 - 2m(-2)^2 + 16 = 0$

$\Rightarrow \quad -8 - 8m + 16 = 0 \Rightarrow 8 = 8m$

$\therefore \quad m = 1$

Hence, the value of m is 1 .

Q.20 If $x + 2a$ is a factor of $x^5 - 4a^2x^3 + 2x + 2a + 3$, find a.

Ans. Let $p(x) = x^5 - 4a^2x^3 + 2x + 2a + 3$

Since, $x + 2a$ is a factor of $p(x)$, then $p(-2a) = 0$

$\therefore \quad (-2a)^5 - 4a^2(-2a)^3 + 2(-2a) + 2a + 3 = 0$

$\Rightarrow \quad -32a^5 + 32a^5 - 4a + 2a + 3 = 0$

$\Rightarrow \quad -2a + 3 = 0$

$\Rightarrow \quad 2a = 3$

$\therefore \quad a = \frac{3}{2}$

Hence, the value of a is $\frac{3}{2}$.

Q.21 Find the value of m, so that $2x - 1$ be a factor of $8x^4 + 4x^3 - 16x^2 + 10x + m$.

Ans. Let $p(x) = 8x^4 + 4x^3 - 16x^2 + 10x + m$

Since, $2x - 1$ is a factor of $p(x)$, then $p\left(\frac{1}{2}\right) = 0$

$\therefore \quad 8\left(\frac{1}{2}\right)^4 + 4\left(\frac{1}{2}\right)^3 - 16\left(\frac{1}{2}\right)^2 + 10\left(\frac{1}{2}\right) + m = 0$

$\Rightarrow \quad 8 \times \frac{1}{16} + 4 \times \frac{1}{8} - 16 \times \frac{1}{4} + 10\left(\frac{1}{2}\right) + m = 0$

$\Rightarrow \quad \frac{1}{2} + \frac{1}{2} - 4 + 5 + m = 0$

$\Rightarrow \quad 1 + 1 + m = 0$

$\therefore \quad m = -2$

Hence, the value of m is -2.

Q.22 If $x + 1$ is a factor of $ax^3 + x^2 - 2x + 4a - 9$, find the value of a.

Ans. Let $p(x) = ax^3 + x^2 - 2x + 4a - 9$

Since, $x+1$ is a factor of $p(x)$, then $p(-1) = 0$

$\therefore \quad a(-1)^3 + (-1)^2 - 2(-1) + 4a - 9 = 0$

$\Rightarrow \quad -a + 1 + 2 + 4a - 9 = 0$

$\Rightarrow \quad 3a - 6 = 0 \Rightarrow 3a = 6$

$\Rightarrow \quad a = \frac{6}{3} = 2$

Hence, the value of a is 2.

(*) Topics related to these question have been removed from latest NCERT.

Q.23 Factorise :

(i) $x^2 + 9x + 18$ (ii) $6x^2 + 7x - 3$

(iii) $2x^2 - 7x - 15$ (iv) $84 - 2r - 2r^2$

Ans. (i) We have, $x^2 + 9x + 18 = x^2 + 6x + 3x + 18$ [by splitting the middle term]

$= x(x+6) + 3(x+6) = (x+3)(x+6)$

(ii) We have, $6x^2 + 7x - 3 = 6x^2 + 9x - 2x - 3$ [by splitting the middle term]

$= 3x(2x+3) - 1(2x+3) = (3x-1)(2x+3)$

(iii) We have, $2x^2 - 7x - 15 = 2x^2 - 10x + 3x - 15$ [by splitting the middle term]

$= 2x(x-5) + 3(x-5) = (2x+3)(x-5)$

(iv) We have, $84 - 2r - 2r^2 = -2(r^2 + r - 42)$

$= -2(r^2 + 7r - 6r - 42)$

$= -2[r(r+7) - 6(r+7)]$

$= -2(r-6)(r+7) = 2(6-r)(r+7)$

Q.24 Factorise :

(i) $2x^3 - 3x^2 - 17x + 30$

(ii) $x^3 - 6x^2 + 11x - 6$

(iii) $x^3 + x^2 - 4x - 4$

(iv) $3x^3 - x^2 - 3x + 1$

Thinking Process

(i) Firstly, find the prime factors of constant term in given polynomial.

(ii) Substitute these factors in place of x in given polynomial and find the minimum factor which satisfies given polynomial and write it in the form of a linear polynomial.

(iii) Now, adjust the given polynomial in such a way that it becomes the product of two factors, one of them is a linear polynomial and other is a quadratic polynomial.

(iv) Further, determine the factor of quadratic polynomial by splitting the middle term.

Ans. (i) Let $p(x) = 2x^3 - 3x^2 - 17x + 30$

Constant term of $p(x) = 30$

$\therefore$ Factors of 30 are $\pm 1, \pm 2, \pm 3, \pm 5, \pm 6, \pm 10, \pm 15, \pm 30$.

By trial, we find that $p(2) = 0$, so $(x-2)$ is a factor of $p(x)$.

[$\because 2(2)^3 - 3(2)^2 - 17(2) + 30 = 16 - 12 - 34 + 30 = 0$]

Now, $2x^3 - 3x^2 - 17x + 30$

$= 2x^3 - 4x^2 + x^2 - 2x - 15x + 30$

$= 2x^2(x-2) + x(x-2) - 15(x-2)$

$= (x-2)(2x^2 + x - 15)$ [taking $(x-2)$ as common factor]

Now, $(2x^2 + x - 15)$ can be factorised by splitting the middle term.

Now, $(2x^2 + x - 15) = 2x^2 + 6x - 5x - 15$ [by splitting the middle term]

$= 2x(x+3) - 5(x+3)$

$= (x+3)(2x-5)$

$\therefore \quad 2x^3 - 3x^2 - 17x + 30 = (x-2)(x+3)(2x-5)$

(ii) Let $p(x) = x^3 - 6x^2 + 11x - 6$

Constant term of $p(x) = -6$

Factors of –6 are $\pm 1, \pm 2, \pm 3, \pm 6$.

By trial, $p(1) = 0$, so $(x - 1)$ is a factor of $p(x)$.

$[\because (1)^3 - 6(1)^2 + 11(1) - 6 = 1 - 6 + 11 - 6 = 0]$

Now, $x^3 - 6x^2 + 11x - 6$

$= x^3 - x^2 - 5x^2 + 5x + 6x - 6$

$= x^2(x-1) - 5x(x-1) + 6(x-1)$

$= (x-1)(x^2 - 5x + 6)$ [taking $(x - 1)$ as common factor]

Now, $(x^2 - 5x + 6) = x^2 - 3x - 2x + 6$ [by splitting the middle term]

$= x(x-3) - 2(x-3) = (x-3)(x-2)$

$\therefore \quad x^3 - 6x^2 + 11x - 6 = (x-1)(x-2)(x-3)$

(iii) Let $p(x) = x^3 + x^2 - 4x - 4$

Constant term of $p(x) = -4$

Factors of –4 are $\pm 1, \pm 2, \pm 4$.

By trial, we find that $p(-1) = 0$, so $(x + 1)$ is a factor of $p(x)$.

$[\because (-1)^3 + (-1)^2 - 4(-1) - 4 = -1 + 1 + 4 - 4 = 0]$

Now, $x^3 + x^2 - 4x - 4 = x^2(x+1) - 4(x+1)$

$= (x+1)(x^2 - 4)$ [taking $(x + 1)$ common factor]

Now, $x^2 - 4 = x^2 - 2^2$

$= (x+2)(x-2)$ $[\because a^2 - b^2 = (a-b)(a+b)]$

$\therefore \quad x^3 + x^2 - 4x - 4 = (x+1)(x-2)(x+2)$

(iv) Let $p(x) = 3x^3 - x^2 - 3x + 1$

Constant term of $p(x) = 1$

Factors of 1 are ± 1.

By trial, we find that $p(1) = 0$, so $(x - 1)$ is a factor of $p(x)$.

$[\because 3(1)^3 - (1)^2 - 3(1) + 1 = 3 - 1 - 3 + 1 = -0]$

Now, $3x^3 - x^2 - 3x + 1$

$= 3x^3 - 3x^2 + 2x^2 - 2x - x + 1$

$= 3x^2(x-1) + 2x(x-1) - 1(x-1)$

$= (x-1)(3x^2 + 2x - 1)$

Now, $(3x^2 + 2x - 1) = 3x^2 + 3x - x - 1$ [by splitting middle term]

$= 3x(x+1) - 1(x+1) = (x+1)(3x-1)$

$\therefore \quad 3x^3 - x^2 - 3x + 1 = (x-1)(x+1)(3x-1)$

Q.25 Using suitable identity, evaluate the following

(i) 103^3 (ii) 101×102 (iii) 999^2

Thinking Process Firstly, adjust the given number into two numbers such that one is a multiple of 10 and use the proper identity.

Ans. (i) We have, $103^3 = (100 + 3)^3$

$= (100)^3 + (3)^3 + 3 \times 100 \times 3 \times (100 + 3)$ $[\because (a+b)^3 = a^3 + b^3 + 3ab(a+b)]$

$= 1000000 + 27 + 900\ (103)$

$= 1000027 + 92700 = 1092727$

(ii) We have, $101 \times 102 = (100 + 1)(100 + 2)$

$= (100)^2 + 100(1+2) + (1 \times 2)$ $[\because (x+a)(x+b) = x^2 + x(a+b) + ab]$

$= 10000 + 300 + 2$

$= 10302$

(iii) We have, $(999)^2 = (1000 - 1)^2$

$= (1000)^2 + (1)^2 - 2 \times 1000 \times 1$ $[\because (a-b)^2 = a^2 + b^2 - 2ab]$

$= 1000000 + 1 - 2000 = 998001$

Q.26 Factorise the following

(i) $4x^2 + 20x + 25$ (ii) $9y^2 - 66yz + 121z^2$

(iii) $\left(2x + \frac{1}{3}\right)^2 - \left(x - \frac{1}{2}\right)^2$

Ans. (i) We have, $4x^2 + 20x + 25 = (2x)^2 + 2 \times 2x \times 5 + (5)^2$

$= (2x + 5)^2$ $[\because a^2 + 2ab + b^2 = (a+b)^2]$

(ii) We have, $9y^2 - 66yz + 121z^2 = (3y)^2 - 2 \times 3y \times 11z + (11z)^2$

$= (3y - 11z)^2$ $[\because a^2 - 2ab + b^2 = (a-b)^2]$

(iii) We have, $\left(2x + \frac{1}{3}\right)^2 - \left(x - \frac{1}{2}\right)^2 = \left[\left(2x + \frac{1}{3}\right) - \left(x - \frac{1}{2}\right)\right]\left[\left(2x + \frac{1}{3}\right) + \left(x - \frac{1}{2}\right)\right]$

$[\because a^2 - b^2 = (a-b)(a+b)]$

$= \left(2x - x + \frac{1}{3} + \frac{1}{2}\right)\left(2x + x + \frac{1}{3} - \frac{1}{2}\right)$

$= \left(x + \frac{2+3}{6}\right)\left(3x + \frac{2-3}{6}\right)$

$= \left(x + \frac{5}{6}\right)\left(3x - \frac{1}{6}\right)$

Q.27 Factorise the following

(i) $9x^2 - 12x + 3$ (ii) $9x^2 - 12x + 4$

Ans. (i) We have, $9x^2 - 12x + 3 = 3(3x^2 - 4x + 1)$ [taking 3 as common factor]

$= 3(3x^2 - 3x - x + 1)$ [by splitting middle term]

$= 3[3x(x-1) - 1(x-1)] = 3(3x-1)(x-1)$

(ii) We have, $9x^2 - 12x + 4 = (3x)^2 - 2 \times 3x \times 2 + (2)^2$

$= (3x - 2)^2$ $[\because (a-b)^2 = a^2 - 2ab + b^2]$

$= (3x-2)(3x-2)$

Q.28 Expand the following

(i) $(4a - b + 2c)^2$ (ii) $(3a - 5b - c)^2$

(iii) $(-x + 2y - 3z)^2$

- **Concept Insight** In this question, we will use the identity, $(a + b + c)^2 = a^2 + b^2 + c^2 + 2ab + 2bc + 2ca$

Ans.(i) We have, $(4a - b + 2c)^2 = (4a)^2 + (-b)^2 + (2c)^2 + 2(4a)(-b) + 2(-b)(2c) + 2(2c)(4a)$

$= 16a^2 + b^2 + 4c^2 - 8ab - 4bc + 16ac$

(ii) We have, $(3a - 5b - c)^2 = (3a)^2 + (-5b)^2 + (-c)^2 + 2(3a)(-5b) + 2(-5b)(-c) + 2(-c)(3a)$

$= 9a^2 + 25b^2 + c^2 - 30ab + 10bc - 6ac$

(iii) We have, $(-x+2y-3z)^2=(-x)^2+(2y)^2+(-3z)^2+2(-x)(2y)+2(2y)(-3z)+2(-3z)(-x)$

$$=x^2+4y^2+9z^2-4xy-12yz+6xz$$

Q.29 Factorise the following

(i) $9x^2+4y^2+16z^2+12xy-16yz-24xz$

(ii) $25x^2+16y^2+4z^2-40xy+16yz-20xz$

(iii) $16x^2+4y^2+9z^2-16xy-12yz+24xz$

Ans.(i) We have, $9x^2+4y^2+16z^2+12xy-16yz-24xz$

$$=(3x)^2+(2y)^2+(-4z)^2+2(3x)(2y)+2(2y)(-4z)+2(-4z)(3x)$$

$$=(3x+2y-4z)^2=(3x+2y-4z)(3x+2y-4z)$$

$[\because (a+b+c)^2=a^2+b^2+c^2+2ab+2bc+2ca]$

(ii) We have, $25x^2+16y^2+4z^2-40xy+16yz-20xz$

$$=(-5x)^2+(4y)^2+(2z)^2+2(-5x)(4y)+2(4y)(2z)+2(2z)(-5x)$$

$$=(-5x+4y+2z)^2=(-5x+4y+2z)(-5x+4y+2z)$$

$[\because (a+b+c)^2=a^2+b^2+c^2+2ab+2bc+2ca]$

(iii) We have, $16x^2+4y^2+9z^2-16xy-12yz+24xz$

$$=(4x)^2+(-2y)^2+(3z)^2+2(4x)(-2y)+2(-2y)(3z)+2(4x)(3z)$$

$$=(4x-2y+3z)^2=(4x-2y+3z)(4x-2y+3z)$$

$[\because (a+b+c)^2=a^2+b^2+c^2+2ab+2bc+2ca]$

Q.30 If $a+b+c=9$ and $ab+bc+ca=26$, find $a^2+b^2+c^2$.

Ans. Given, $a+b+c=9$ and $ab+bc+ca=26$ ...(i)

Now, $a+b+c=9$

On squaring both sides, we get

$$(a+b+c)^2=(9)^2$$

$\Rightarrow$ $a^2+b^2+c^2+2ab+2bc+2ca=81$

$[\because (a+b+c)^2=a^2+b^2+c^2+2ab+2bc+2ca]$

$\Rightarrow$ $a^2+b^2+c^2+2(ab+bc+ca)=81$

$\Rightarrow$ $a^2+b^2+c^2+2(26)=81$ [from Eq. (i)]

$\Rightarrow$ $a^2+b^2+c^2=81-52=29$

Q.31 Expand the following

(i) $(3a-2b)^3$ (ii) $\left(\frac{1}{x}+\frac{y}{3}\right)^3$ (iii) $\left(4-\frac{1}{3x}\right)^3$

Ans. (i) We have, $(3a-2b)^3=(3a)^3+(-2b)^3+3(3a)(-2b)(3a-2b)$

$[\because (a-b)^3=a^3-b^3+3a(-b)(a-b)]$

$$=27a^3-8b^3-18ab(3a-2b)=27a^3-8b^3-54a^2b+36ab^2$$

$$=27a^3-54a^2b+36ab^2-8b^3$$

(ii) We have, $\left(\frac{1}{x}+\frac{y}{3}\right)^3=\left(\frac{1}{x}\right)^3+\left(\frac{y}{3}\right)^3+3\left(\frac{1}{x}\right)\left(\frac{y}{3}\right)\left(\frac{1}{x}+\frac{y}{3}\right)$

$[\because (a+b)^3=a^3+b^3+3ab(a+b)]$

$$=\frac{1}{x^3}+\frac{y^3}{27}+\frac{y}{x}\left(\frac{1}{x}+\frac{y}{3}\right)=\frac{1}{x^3}+\frac{y^3}{27}+\frac{y}{x^2}+\frac{y^2}{3x}=\frac{1}{x^3}+\frac{y}{x^2}+\frac{y^2}{3x}+\frac{y^3}{27}$$

(iii) We have, $\left(4-\frac{1}{3x}\right)^3=(4)^3+\left(-\frac{1}{3x}\right)^3+3(4)\left(-\frac{1}{3x}\right)\left(4-\frac{1}{3x}\right)$

$[\because (a-b)^3=a^3-b^3+3a(-b)(a-b)]$

$$=64-\frac{1}{27x^3}-\frac{4}{x}\left(4-\frac{1}{3x}\right)=64-\frac{1}{27x^3}-\frac{16}{x}+\frac{4}{3x^2}=64-\frac{16}{x}+\frac{4}{3x^2}-\frac{1}{27x^3}$$

Q.32 Factorise the following

(i) $1-64a^3-12a+48a^2$ (ii) $8p^3+\frac{12}{5}p^2+\frac{6}{25}p+\frac{1}{125}$

Ans. (i) We have, $1-64a^3-12a+48a^2=(1)^3-(4a)^3-3\times(1)^2\times 4a+3\times 1\times(4a)^2$

$[\because (a-b)^3=a^3-b^3-3a^2b+3ab^2]$

$$=(1-4a)^3=(1-4a)(1-4a)(1-4a)$$

Mistake Alert! Students may incorrectly apply the identity as $(a-b)^3=a^3-b^3-3a^2b-3ab^2$ instead of $(a-b)^3=a^3-b^3-3a^2b+3ab^2$.

(ii) We have, $8p^3+\frac{12}{5}p^2+\frac{6}{25}p+\frac{1}{125}$

$$=(2p)^3+3\times(2p)^2\times\frac{1}{5}+3\times(2p)\times\left(\frac{1}{5}\right)^2+\left(\frac{1}{5}\right)^3=\left(2p+\frac{1}{5}\right)^3$$

$[\because (a+b)^3=a^3+b^3+3a^2b+3ab^2]$

$$=\left(2p+\frac{1}{5}\right)\left(2p+\frac{1}{5}\right)\left(2p+\frac{1}{5}\right)$$

Q.33 Find the following products

(i) $\left(\frac{x}{2}+2y\right)\left(\frac{x^2}{4}-xy+4y^2\right)$ (ii) $(x^2-1)(x^4+x^2+1)$

Ans.(i) We have, $\left(\frac{x}{2}+2y\right)\left(\frac{x^2}{4}-xy+4y^2\right)=\frac{x}{2}\left(\frac{x^2}{4}-xy+4y^2\right)+2y\left(\frac{x^2}{4}-xy+4y^2\right)$

$$=\frac{x}{2}\left(\frac{x^2}{4}\right)+\frac{x}{2}(-xy)+\frac{x}{2}(4y^2)+2y\left(\frac{x^2}{4}\right)+2y(-xy)+2y(4y^2)$$

$$=\frac{x^3}{8}-\frac{x^2y}{2}+2xy^2+\frac{x^2y}{2}-2xy^2+8y^3=\frac{x^3}{8}+8y^3$$

(ii) We have, $(x^2-1)(x^4+x^2+1)=x^2(x^4+x^2+1)-1(x^4+x^2+1)$

$$=x^2(x^4)+x^2(x^2)+x^2(1)-1(x^4)-1(x^2)-1(1)$$

$$=x^6+x^4+x^2-x^4-x^2-1=x^6-1$$

Q.34 Factorise

(i) $1+64x^3$ (ii) $a^3-2\sqrt{2}b^3$

Thinking Process

(i) Firstly, adjust the given number either in the form of a^3+b^3 or a^3-b^3.

(ii) Further, use any of the identities *i.e.*, $a^3+b^3=(a+b)(a^2+b^2-ab)$ or $a^3-b^3=(a-b)(a^2+b^2+ab)$, then simplify it, to get the factor.

Ans. (i) We have, $1+64x^3=(1)^3+(4x)^3$

$$=(1+4x)[(1)^2-(1)(4x)+(4x)^2]$$ $[\because a^3+b^3=(a+b)(a^2-ab+b^2)]$

$$=(1+4x)(1-4x+16x^2)$$

(ii) We have, $a^3 - 2\sqrt{2}b^3 = (a)^3 - (\sqrt{2}b)^3$

$= (a - \sqrt{2}b)[a^2 + a(\sqrt{2}b) + (\sqrt{2}b)^2]$ $\quad [\because a^3 - b^3 = (a-b)(a^2 + ab + b^2)]$

$= (a - \sqrt{2}b)(a^2 + \sqrt{2}ab + 2b^2)$

Q.35 Find the following product

$(2x - y + 3z)(4x^2 + y^2 + 9z^2 + 2xy + 3yz - 6xz)$

Ans. We have, $(2x - y + 3z)(4x^2 + y^2 + 9z^2 + 2xy + 3yz - 6xz)$

$= (2x - y + 3z)[(2x)^2 + (-y)^2 + (3z)^2 - (2x)(-y) - (-y)(3z) - (2x)(3z)]$

$= (2x)^3 + (-y)^3 + (3z)^3 - 3(2x)(-y)(3z)$

$[\because (a + b + c)(a^2 + b^2 + c^2 - ab - bc - ca) = a^3 + b^3 + c^3 - 3abc]$

$= 8x^3 - y^3 + 27z^3 + 18xyz$

Alternate Method

We have, $(2x - y + 3z)(4x^2 + y^2 + 9z^2 + 2xy + 3yz - 6xz)$

$= 2x(4x^2 + y^2 + 9z^2 + 2xy + 3yz - 6xz) - y(4x^2 + y^2 + 9z^2 + 2xy + 3yz - 6xz) + 3z(4x^2 + y^2 + 9z^2 + 2xy + 3yz - 6xz)$

$= 8x^3 + 2xy^2 + 18xz^2 + 4x^2y + 6xyz - 12x^2z - 4x^2y - y^3 - 9yz^2 - 2xy^2 - 3y^2z + 6xyz + 12x^2z + 3y^2z + 27z^3 + 6xyz + 9yz^2 - 18xz^2$

$= 8x^3 + (2xy^2 - 2xy^2) + (18xz^2 - 18xz^2) + (4x^2y - 4x^2y) + (6xyz + 6xyz + 6xyz) + (-12x^2z + 12x^2z) - y^3 + (-9yz^2 + 9yz^2) + (-3y^2z + 3y^2z) + 27z^3$

$= 8x^3 - y^3 + 27z^3 + 18xyz$

Q.36 Factorise

(i) $a^3 - 8b^3 - 64c^3 - 24abc$

(ii) $2\sqrt{2}a^3 + 8b^3 - 27c^3 + 18\sqrt{2}abc$

Thinking Process In this question, we will use the identity, $a^3 + b^3 + c^3 - 3abc = (a + b + c)(a^2 + b^2 + c^2 - ab - bc - ca)$.

Ans. (i) We have, $a^3 - 8b^3 - 64c^3 - 24abc = (a)^3 + (-2b)^3 + (-4c)^3 - 3 \times (a) \times (-2b) \times (-4c)$

$= (a - 2b - 4c)[(a)^2 + (-2b)^2 + (-4c)^2 - a(-2b) - (-2b)(-4c) - (-4c)(a)]$

$[\because a^3 + b^3 + c^3 - 3abc = (a + b + c)(a^2 + b^2 + c^2 - ab - bc - ca)]$

$= (a - 2b - 4c)(a^2 + 4b^2 + 16c^2 + 2ab - 8bc + 4ac)$

(ii) We have, $2\sqrt{2}a^3 + 8b^3 - 27c^3 + 18\sqrt{2}abc$

$= (\sqrt{2}a)^3 + (2b)^3 + (-3c)^3 - 3(\sqrt{2}a)(2b)(-3c)$

$= (\sqrt{2}a + 2b - 3c)[(\sqrt{2}a)^2 + (2b)^2 + (-3c)^2 - (\sqrt{2}a)(2b) - (2b)(-3c) - (-3c)(\sqrt{2}a)]$

$[\because a^3 + b^3 + c^3 - 3abc = (a + b + c)(a^2 + b^2 + c^2 - ab - bc - ca)]$

$= (\sqrt{2}a + 2b - 3c)[2a^2 + 4b^2 + 9c^2 - 2\sqrt{2}ab + 6bc + 3\sqrt{2}ac]$

Q.37 Without actually calculating the cubes, find the value of

(i) $\left(\frac{1}{2}\right)^3 + \left(\frac{1}{3}\right)^3 - \left(\frac{5}{6}\right)^3$ (ii) $(0.2)^3 - (0.3)^3 + (0.1)^3$

Thinking Process In this question, method firstly check the values of $a + b + c$, then if $a + b + c = 0 \Rightarrow a^3 + b^3 + c^3 = 3abc$.

Ans. (i) Given, $\left(\frac{1}{2}\right)^3+\left(\frac{1}{3}\right)^3-\left(\frac{5}{6}\right)^3$ or $\left(\frac{1}{2}\right)^3+\left(\frac{1}{3}\right)^3+\left(-\frac{5}{6}\right)^3$

Since, $\frac{1}{2}+\frac{1}{3}-\frac{5}{6}=\frac{3+2-5}{6}=\frac{5-5}{6}=0$

$\therefore \quad \left(\frac{1}{2}\right)^3+\left(\frac{1}{3}\right)^3-\left(\frac{5}{6}\right)^3=3\times\frac{1}{2}\times\frac{1}{3}\times\left(\frac{-5}{6}\right)$

[$\because$ if $a+b+c=0$, then $a^3+b^3+c^3=3abc$]

$=-\frac{5}{12}$

(ii) Given, $(0.2)^3-(0.3)^3+(0.1)^3$ or $(0.2)^3+(-0.3)^3+(0.1)^3$

Since, $\quad 0.2-0.3+0.1=0.3-0.3=0$

$\therefore\ (0.2)^3+(-0.3)^3+(0.1)^3=3\times(0.2)\times(-0.3)\times(0.1)$

[$\because$ if $a+b+c=0$, then $a^3+b^3+c^3=3abc$]

$=-0.6\times0.03=-0.018$

Q.38 Without finding the cubes, factorise $(x-2y)^3+(2y-3z)^3+(3z-x)^3$.

- **Concept Insight** If $x+y+z=0$, then $x^3+y^3+z^3=3xyz$.

Ans. We know that, if $a+b+c=0$, then $a^3+b^3+c^3=3abc$

Since, $(x-2y)+(2y-3z)+(3z-x)=0$

$\therefore \quad (x-2y)^3+(2y-3z)^3+(3z-x)^3=3(x-2y)(2y-3z)(3z-x)$

Q.39 Find the value of

(i) $x^3+y^3-12xy+64$, when $x+y=-4$.

(ii) $x^3-8y^3-36xy-216$, when $x=2y+6$.

Ans. (i) Since, $x+y+4=0$

$\therefore \quad x^3+y^3+(4)^3=3xy(4)$ [$\because$ if $a+b+c=0$, then $a^3+b^3+c^3=3abc$]

$=12xy$ ...(i)

Now, $\quad x^3+y^3-12xy+64=x^3+y^3+(4)^3-12xy$

$=12xy-12xy=0$ [from Eq. (i)]

(ii) Since, $x-2y-6=0$

$\therefore \quad x^3+(-2y)^3+(-6)^3=3x(-2y)(-6)$

[$\because$ if $a+b+c=0$, then $a^3+b^3+c^3=3abc$]

$\Rightarrow \quad x^3-8y^3-216=36xy$ ...(i)

Now, $x^3-8y^3-36xy-216$

$=x^3-8y^3-216-36xy$

$=36xy-36xy=0$ [from Eq. (i)]

Q.40 Give possible expression for the length and breadth of the rectangle whose area is given by $4a^2+4a-3$.

Ans. Given, area of rectangle $=4a^2+4a-3$

$=4a^2+6a-2a-3$ [by splitting middle term]

$=2a(2a+3)-1(2a+3)=(2a-1)(2a+3)$

Hence, possible length $=2a+3$ and breadth $=2a-1$

[$\because$ Area of rectangle = length $\times$ breadth]

Long Answer Type Questions

***Q.1** If the polynomials $az^3 + 4z^2 + 3z - 4$ and $z^3 - 4z + a$ leave the same remainder when divided by $z - 3$, find the value of a.

Ans. Let $p_1(z) = az^3 + 4z^2 + 3z - 4$ and $p_2(z) = z^3 - 4z + a$

When we divide $p_1(z)$ by $z - 3$, then we get the remainder $p_1(3)$.

Now, $$p_1(3) = a(3)^3 + 4(3)^2 + 3(3) - 4$$
$$= 27a + 36 + 9 - 4 = 27a + 41$$

When we divide $p_2(z)$ by $z - 3$, then we get the remainder $p_2(3)$.

Now, $$p_2(3) = (3)^3 - 4(3) + a$$
$$= 27 - 12 + a = 15 + a$$

According to the question, both the remainders are same.

i.e., $$p_1(3) = p_2(3)$$
$\therefore$ $$27a + 41 = 15 + a$$
$\Rightarrow$ $$27a - a = 15 - 41$$
$\Rightarrow$ $$26\,a = -26$$
$\therefore$ $$a = -1$$

***Q.2** The polynomial $p(x) = x^4 - 2x^3 + 3x^2 - ax + 3a - 7$ when divided by $x + 1$ leaves the remainder 19. Find the values of a. Also, find the remainder when $p(x)$ is divided by $x + 2$.

Ans. Given, $$p(x) = x^4 - 2x^3 + 3x^2 - ax + 3a - 7$$

By remainder theorem, when we divide $p(x)$ by $x + 1$, then we get the remainder $p(-1)$.

Now, $$p(-1) = (-1)^4 - 2(-1)^3 + 3(-1)^2 - a(-1) + 3a - 7$$
$$= 1 + 2 + 3 + a + 3a - 7 = 4a - 1$$

According to the question, $p(-1) = 19$

$\Rightarrow$ $$4a - 1 = 19 \Rightarrow 4a = 20$$
$\Rightarrow$ $$a = 5$$

$\therefore$ Required polynomial, $p(x) = x^4 - 2x^3 + 3x^2 - 5x + 3(5) - 7$ [put $a = 5$ in $p(x)$]
$$= x^4 - 2x^3 + 3x^2 - 5x + 15 - 7$$
$$= x^4 - 2x^3 + 3x^2 - 5x + 8$$

When we divide $p(x)$ by $x + 2$, then we get the remainder $p(-2)$.

Now, $$p(-2) = (-2)^4 - 2(-2)^3 + 3(-2)^2 - 5(-2) + 8$$
$$= 16 + 16 + 12 + 10 + 8 = 62$$

Hence, the value of a is 5 and remainder is 62.

Q.3 If both $x - 2$ and $x - \frac{1}{2}$ are factors of $px^2 + 5x + r$, show that $p = r$.

Ans. Let $f(x) = px^2 + 5x + r$

Since, $x - 2$ is a factor of $f(x)$, then $f(2) = 0$

$\therefore$ $$p(2)^2 + 5(2) + r = 0$$
$\Rightarrow$ $$4p + 10 + r = 0 \quad \text{...(i)}$$

Since, $x - \frac{1}{2}$ is a factor of $f(x)$, then $f\left(\frac{1}{2}\right) = 0$

(*) Topics related to these question have been removed from latest NCERT.

$\therefore \quad p\left(\frac{1}{2}\right)^2 + 5\left(\frac{1}{2}\right) + r = 0 \Rightarrow p \times \frac{1}{4} + \frac{5}{2} + r = 0$

$\Rightarrow \quad p + 10 + 4r = 0 \quad \text{...(ii)}$

From Eqs. (i) and (ii), we get

$$4p + 10 + r = p + 10 + 4r$$

$\Rightarrow \quad 3p = 3r$

$\Rightarrow \quad p = r$ **Hence proved.**

Q.4 Without actual division, prove that $2x^4 - 5x^3 + 2x^2 - x + 2$ is divisible by $x^2 - 3x + 2$.

Thinking Process

(i) Firstly, determine the factors of quadratic polynomial by splitting middle term.

(ii) The two different values of zeroes put in quadratic polynomial.

(iii) In both the case, if remainder is zero, then biquadratic polynomial is divisible by quadratic polynomial.

Ans. Let $p(x) = 2x^4 - 5x^3 + 2x^2 - x + 2$

Firstly, factorise $x^2 - 3x + 2$.

Now, $x^2 - 3x + 2 = x^2 - 2x - x + 2$ [by splitting the middle term]

$= x(x-2) - 1(x-2) = (x-1)(x-2)$

Hence, zeroes of $x^2 - 3x + 2$ are 1and 2.

We have to prove that $2x^4 - 5x^3 + 2x^2 - x + 2$ is divisible by $x^2 - 3x + 2$

i.e., to prove that $p(1) = 0$ and $p(2) = 0$

Now, $p(1) = 2(1)^4 - 5(1)^3 + 2(1)^2 - 1 + 2$

$= 2 - 5 + 2 - 1 + 2 = 6 - 6 = 0$

and $p(2) = 2(2)^4 - 5(2)^3 + 2(2)^2 - 2 + 2$

$= 2 \times 16 - 5 \times 8 + 2 \times 4 + 0$

$= 32 - 40 + 8 = 40 - 40 = 0$

Hence, $p(x)$ is divisible by $x^2 - 3x + 2$.

Q.5 Simplify $(2x - 5y)^3 - (2x + 5y)^3$.

Ans. We have, $(2x - 5y)^3 - (2x + 5y)^3 = [(2x)^3 - (5y)^3 - 3(2x)(5y)(2x - 5y)]$

$-[(2x)^3 + (5y)^3 + 3(2x)(5y)(2x + 5y)]$

$[\because (a-b)^3 = a^3 - b^3 - 3ab(a-b)$ and $(a+b)^3 = a^3 + b^3 + 3ab(a+b)]$

$= (2x)^3 - (5y)^3 - 30xy(2x - 5y) - (2x)^3 - (5y)^3 - 30xy(2x + 5y)$

$= -2(5y)^3 - 30xy(2x - 5y + 2x + 5y)$

$= -2 \times 125y^3 - 30xy(4x) = -250y^3 - 120x^2y$

Q.6 Multiply $x^2 + 4y^2 + z^2 + 2xy + xz - 2yz$ by $(-z + x - 2y)$.

Ans. We have, $(x - 2y - z)(x^2 + 4y^2 + z^2 + 2xy + xz - 2yz)$

$= (x - 2y - z)[(x)^2 + (-2y)^2 + (-z)^2 - (x)(-2y) - (-2y)(-z) - (x)(-z)]$

$= (x)^3 + (-2y)^3 + (-z)^3 - 3(x)(-2y)(-z)$

[Use the identity, $a^3 + b^3 + c^3 - 3abc = (a + b + c)(a^2 + b^2 + c^2 - ab - bc - ca)$]

$= x^3 - 8y^3 - z^3 - 6xyz$

Alternate Method

We have, $(x^2+4y^2+z^2+2xy+xz-2yz)(-z+x-2y)$

$$= x^2(-z+x-2y)+4y^2(-z+x-2y)+z^2(-z+x-2y)+2xy(-z+x-2y) +xz(-z+x-2y)-2yz(-z+x-2y)$$

$$= -x^2z+x^3-2x^2y-4y^2z+4xy^2-8y^3-z^3+xz^2-2yz^2-2xyz+2x^2y-4xy^2 -xz^2+x^2z-2xyz+2yz^2-2xyz+4y^2z$$

$$= (-x^2z+x^2z)+x^3+(-2x^2y+2x^2y)+(-4y^2z+4y^2z)+(4xy^2-4xy^2)-8y^3 -z^3+(xz^2-xz^2)+(-2yz^2+2yz^2)+(-2xyz-2xyz-2xyz)$$

$$= x^3-8y^3-z^3-6xyz$$

Q.7 If a, b and c are all non-zero and $a+b+c=0$, prove that $\frac{a^2}{bc}+\frac{b^2}{ac}+\frac{c^2}{ab}=3.$

Ans. Given, $a+b+c=0$ ...(i)

We know that $a^3+b^3+c^3-3abc=(a+b+c)(a^2+b^2+c^2-ab-bc-ca)$

$= 0(a^2+b^2+c^2-ab-bc-ca)$ [from Eq. (i)]

$= 0$

$\Rightarrow$ $a^3+b^3+c^3=3abc$

On dividing both sides by abc, we get

$$\frac{a^3}{abc}+\frac{b^3}{abc}+\frac{c^3}{abc}=3$$

$\Rightarrow$ $\frac{a^2}{bc}+\frac{b^2}{ac}+\frac{c^2}{ab}=3$ **Hence proved.**

Q.8 If $a+b+c=5$ and $ab+bc+ca=10$, then prove that $a^3+b^3+c^3-3abc=-25.$

Ans. Given, $a+b+c=5$ ...(i)

And $ab+bc+ca=10$ ...(ii)

On squaring Eq. (i) both sides, we get

$\because$ $(a+b+c)^2=(5)^2$

$\Rightarrow$ $a^2+b^2+c^2+2(ab+bc+ca)=25$

$\Rightarrow$ $a^2+b^2+c^2+2\times 10$ [from Eq. (ii)]

$\Rightarrow$ $a^2+b^2+c^2=25-20$

$\Rightarrow$ $a^2+b^2+c^2=5$ ...(iii)

Now, LHS $= a^3+b^3+c^3-3abc$

$= (a+b+c)(a^2+b^2+c^2-ab-bc-ca)$

$= (5)[5-(ab+bc+ca)]$ [from Eqs. (i) and (iii)]

$= 5(5-10)=5(-5)=-25=$ RHS [from Eq. (ii)] **Hence proved.**

Q.9 Prove that $(a+b+c)^3 - a^3 - b^3 - c^3 = 3(a+b)(b+c)(c+a)$.

Ans. LHS $= [(a+b+c)^3 - a^3] - (b^3 + c^3)$

$$= (a+b+c-a)[(a+b+c)^2 + a^2 + a(a+b+c)] - [(b+c)(b^2+c^2-bc)]$$

$[\because a^3 + b^3 = (a+b)(a^2+b^2-ab)$ and $a^3 - b^3 = (a-b)(a^2+b^2+ab)]$

$$= (b+c)[a^2+b^2+c^2+2ab+2bc+2ca+a^2+a^2+ab+ac] - (b+c)(b^2+c^2-bc)$$

$$= (b+c)[b^2+c^2+3a^2+3ab+3ac-b^2-c^2+3bc]$$

$$= (b+c)[3(a^2+ab+ac+bc)]$$

$$= 3(b+c)[a(a+b)+c(a+b)]$$

$$= 3(b+c)[(a+c)(a+b)]$$

$$= 3(a+b)(b+c)(c+a) = \text{RHS}$$

Hence proved.

Chapter

03 Coordinate Geometry

Multiple Choice Questions (MCQs)

Choose the correct answer from the given four options in the following questions:

Q.1 Point (–3, 5) lies in the

(a) first quadrant
(b) second quadrant
(c) third quadrant
(d) fourth quadrant

Thinking Process

(i) Firstly, check the sign of each coordinate of a point.

(ii) If both x and y coordinates have positive signs *i.e.*, (+, +), then the point lies in first quadrant.

(iii) If x-coordinate has negative sign and y-coordinate has positive sign *i.e.*, (–, +), then the point lies in second quadrant.

(iv) If x and y coordinates both have negative sign, *i.e.*, (–, –), then the point lies in third quadrant.

(v) If x-coordinate has positive sign and y-coordinate has negative sign *i.e.*, (+, –), then the point lies in fourth quadrant.

Ans. *(b)* In point (–3, 5), x-coordinate is negative and y-coordinate is positive. So, the point lies in the second quadrant.

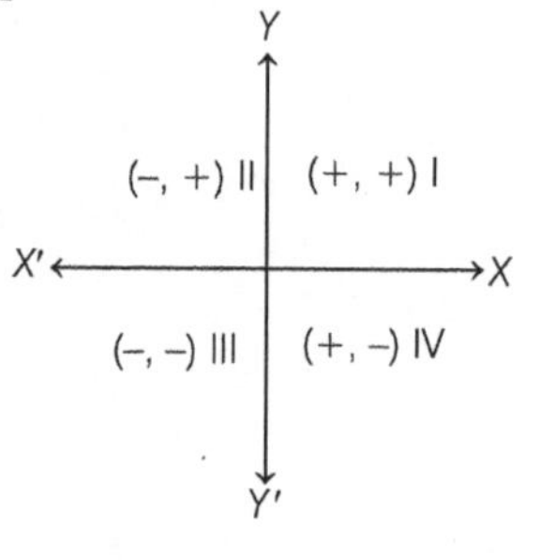

Q.2 Signs of the abscissa and ordinate of a point in the second quadrant are respectively

(a) +, +
(b) –, –
(c) – , +
(d) +, –

Ans. *(c)* In second quadrant, X-axis is negative and Y-axis is positive. So, sign of abscissa (i.e., x-coordinate) of a point is negative and sign of ordinate (i.e. y-coordinate) of a point is positive.

Mistake Alert! *Students may become confused between abscissa and ordinate and may mistake x-coordinate for the ordinate and y-coordinate for the abscissa.*

Q.3 Point (0, − 7) lies

(a) on the X-axis
(b) in the second quadrant
(c) on the Y-axis
(d) in the fourth quadrant

Concept Insight

(i) In this problem, check whether any coordinate of the point is zero.
(a) If x-coordinate is zero and y-coordinate is non-zero, then the point lies on Y-axis.
(b) If y-coordinate is zero and x-coordinate is non-zero, then the point lies on X- axis.
(c) If x and y-coordinates both are zero, then the point lies on origin (or on both the axes).

(ii) If none of the coordinates is zero, then the point lies in any one of the four quadrants

Ans. *(c)* In point (0, −7), x-coordinate is zero, so it lies on Y-axis and y-coordinate is negative, so the point (0, − 7) lies on the Y-axis in the negative direction.

Q.4 Point (− 10, 0) lies

(a) on the negative direction of the X-axis
(b) on the negative direction of the Y-axis
(c) in the third quadrant
(d) in the fourth quadrant

Ans. *(a)* In point (−10, 0), y-coordinate is zero, so it lies on X-axis and its x-coordinate is negative, so the point (−10, 0) lies on the X-axis in the negative direction.

Q.5 Abscissa of all the points on the X-axis is

(a) 0 (b) 1 (c) 2 (d) any number

Ans. *(d)* Abscissa of all the points on the X-axis is any number because X-axis is a number line which contains many real numbers on it.

Q.6 Ordinate of all points on the X-axis is

(a) 0 (b) 1 (c) − 1 (d) any number

Ans. *(a)* Ordinate of all points on the X-axis is zero. Because ordinate or y-coordinate of a point is perpendicular distance of the point from the X-axis measured along the Y-axis. If point lies on X- axis, then the perpendicular distance of the point from X- axis will be zero, so ordinate will be zero.

Q.7 The point at which the two coordinate axes meet is called the

(a) abscissa (b) ordinate (c) origin (d) quadrant

Ans. *(c)* The point at which the two coordinate axes meet is called the origin.

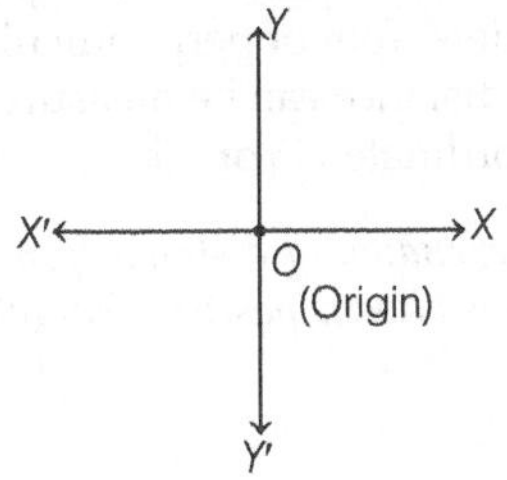

Q.8 A point, both of whose coordinates are negative will lie in

(a) I quadrant (b) II quadrant
(c) III quadrant (d) IV quadrant

Ans. *(c)* A point both of whose coordinates are negative will lie in III quadrant because in III quadrant, x and y-coordinates both are negative.

Q.9 Points $(1, -1), (2, -2), (4, -5)$ and $(-3, -4)$

(a) lie in II quadrant
(b) lie in III quadrant
(c) lie in IV quadrant
(d) do not lie in the same quadrant

Ans. *(d)* In points $(1, -1)$, $(2, -2)$ and $(4, -5)$, x-coordinate is positive and y-coordinate is negative. So, they all lie in IV quadrant. In point $(-3, -4)$, x and y-coordinates both are negative. So, it lies in III quadrant.
So, given points do not lie in the same quadrant.

Q.10 If y-coordinate of a point is zero, then this point always lies

(a) in I quadrant (b) in II quadrant
(c) on X-axis (d) on Y-axis

Ans. *(c)* If y-coordinate of a point is zero, then this point always lies on X-axis. Because the perpendicular distance of the point from X-axis measured along Y-axis is zero.

Q.11 The points $(-5, 2)$ and $(2, -5)$ lie in the

(a) same quadrant
(b) II and III quadrants, respectively
(c) II and IV quadrants, respectively
(d) IV and II quadrants, respectively

Ans. *(c)* In point $(-5, 2)$, x-coordinate is negative and y-coordinate is positive, so it lies in II quadrant and in point $(2, -5)$, x- coordinate is positive and y-coordinate is negative, so it lies in IV quadrant.

Q.12 If the perpendicular distance of a point P from the X-axis is 5 units and the foot of the perpendicular lies on the negative direction of X-axis, then the point P has

(a) x-coordinate $= -5$ (b) y-coordinate $= 5$ only
(c) y-coordinate $= -5$ only (d) y-coordinate $= 5$ or -5

Ans. *(d)* We know that the perpendicular distance of a point from the X-axis gives y-coordinate of that point. Here, foot of perpendicular lies on the negative direction of X-axis, so perpendicular distance can be measure in II quadrant or III quadrant. Hence, the point P has y-coordinate $= 5$ or -5.

Mistake Alert! *When the perpendicular distance from the X- axis is given, students may assume that the y-coordinate is always positive. Forgetting that it could also be negative.*

***Q.13** On plotting the points $O(0, 0)$, $A(3, 0)$, $B(3, 4)$, $C(0, 4)$ and joining OA, AB, BC and CO. Which of the following figure is obtained?

(a) Square (b) Rectangle
(c) Trapezium (d) Rhombus

Ans. ***(b)*** Here, point O (0, 0) is the origin. $A(3, 0)$ lies on the positive direction of X-axis, B (3, 4) lies in Ist quadrant and C (0, 4) lies on the positive direction of Y-axis. On joining OA, AB, BC and CO, the figure obtained is a rectangle.

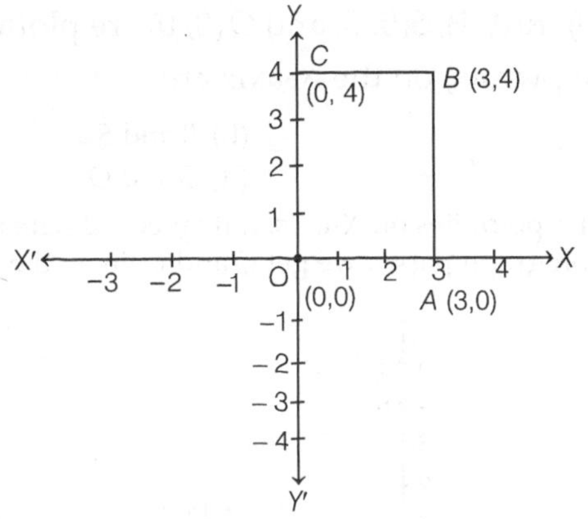

***Q.14** If $P(-1, 1)$, $Q(3, -4)$, $R(1, -1)$, $S(-2, -3)$ and $T(-4, 4)$ are plotted on the graph paper, then the point(s) in the fourth quadrant are

(a) P and T (b) Q and R
(c) Only S (d) P and R

Ans. ***(b)*** In point P (–1, 1), x-coordinate is –1 and y-coordinate is 1. So, it lies in IInd quadrant.

Similarly, we can plot all the points Q (3, – 4), R (1, –1), S (–2, –3) and T (– 4, 4),

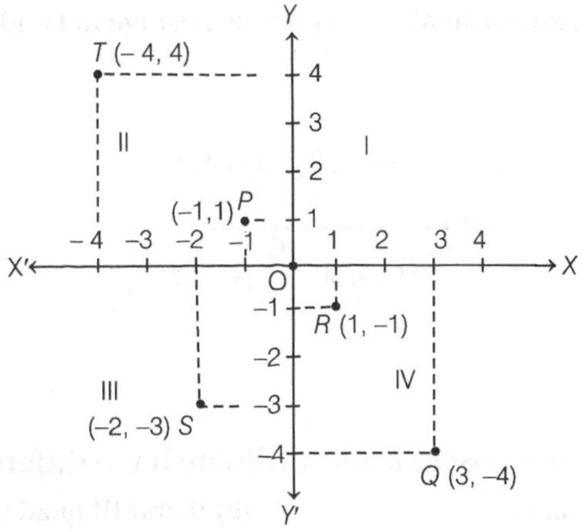

It is clear from the graph that points Q and R lie in fourth quadrant.

(✱) Topics related to these question have been removed from latest NCERT.

Q.15 If the coordinates of the two points are $P(-2, 3)$ and $Q(-3, 5)$, then (Abscissa of P) – (Abscissa of Q) is

(a) – 5 (b) 1 (c) –1 (d) –2

Ans. ***(b)*** We have, points $P(-2, 3)$ and $Q(-3, 5)$.

Here, abscissa of P *i.e.*, x-coordinate of P is –2 and abscissa of Q *i.e.*, x-coordinate of Q is –3. So, (Abscissa of P) – (Abscissa of Q) $= -2-(-3) = -2+3 = 1$

***Q.16** If $P(5, 1)$, $Q(8, 0)$, $R(0, 4)$, $S(0, 5)$ and $O(0, 0)$ are plotted on the graph paper, then the point(s) on the X-axis are

(a) P and R (b) R and S
(c) Only Q (d) Q and O

Ans. ***(d)*** We know that a point lies on X-axis, if its y-coordinate is zero. So, on plotting the given points on graph paper, we get Q and O lie on the X-axis.

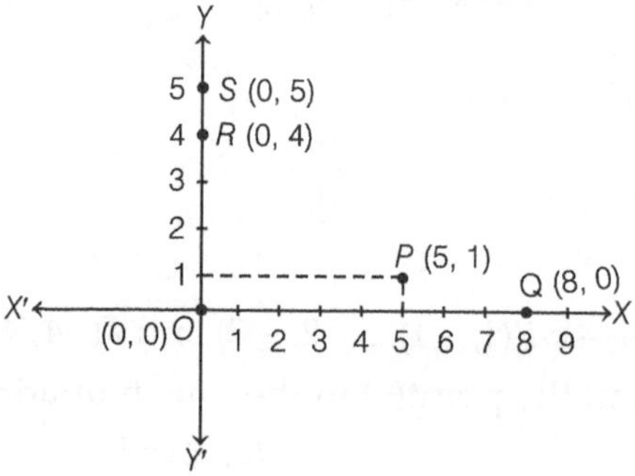

Q.17 Abscissa (i.e. x-coordinate) of a point is positive in

(a) I and II quadrants (b) I and IV quadrants
(c) I quadrant only (d) II quadrant only

Ans. ***(b)*** Abscissa (i.e., x-coordinate) of a point is positive in I and IV quadrants.

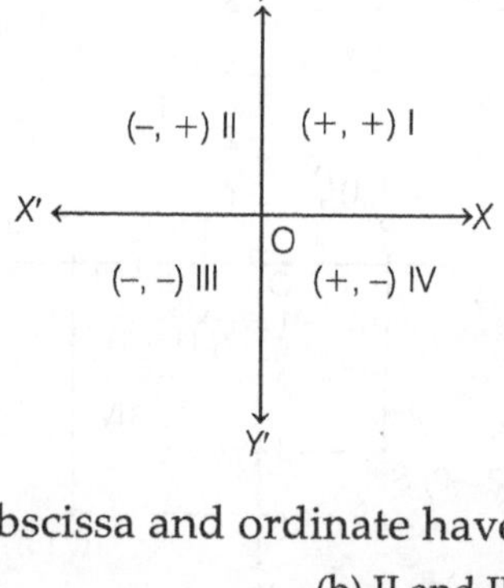

Q.18 The points whose abscissa and ordinate have different signs will lie in

(a) I and II quadrants (b) II and III quadrants
(c) I and III quadrants (d) II and IV quadrants

Ans. ***(d)*** The points whose abscissa and ordinate have different signs will be of the form $(-x, y)$ or $(x, -y)$ and these points will lie in II and IV quadrants.

(*) Topics related to these question have been removed from latest NCERT.

Q.19 In following figure, coordinates of P are

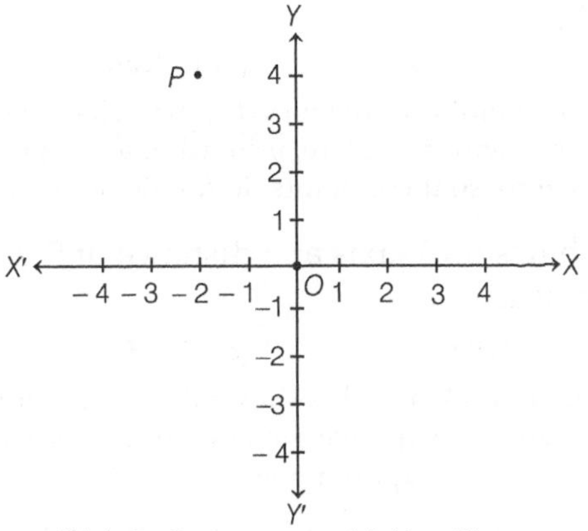

(a) $(-4, 2)$ (b) $(-2, 4)$ (c) $(4, -2)$ (d) $(2, -4)$

Ans. *(b)* Here, given point P lies in II quadrant, so its abscissa will be negative and ordinate will be positive. Also, its perpendicular distance from X-axis is 4 units, so y-coordinate of P is 4 and its perpendicular distance from Y-axis is 2 units, so x-coordinate is -2. Hence, coordinates of P are $(-2, 4)$.

Q.20 In following figure, the point identified by the coordinates $(-5, 3)$ is

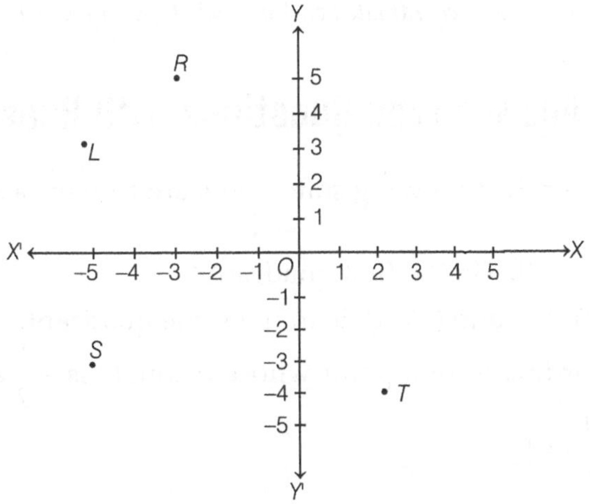

(a) T (b) R

(c) L (d) S

Ans. *(c)* In point $(-5, 3)$, x-coordinate is negative and y-coordinate is positive, so it will lie in II quadrant. Now, we see that perpendicular distance of L from Y-axis is 5 units and from X-axis is 3 units. So, the required point is L.

Q.21 The point whose ordinate is 4 and which lies on Y-axis is

(a) $(4, 0)$ (b) $(0, 4)$

(c) $(1, 4)$ (d) $(4, 2)$

Ans. *(b)* Given that ordinate of the point is 4 and the point lies on Y-axis, so its abscissa is zero. Hence, the required point is $(0, 4)$.

Q.22 Which of the points $P(0, 3)$, $Q(1, 0)$, $R(0, -1)$, $S(-5, 0)$ and $T(1, 2)$ do not lie on the X-axis?

(a) P and R only (b) Q and S only (c) P, R and T (d) Q, S and T

Ans. *(c)* We know that if a point is of the form $(x, 0)$ *i.e.*, its y-coordinate is zero, then it will lie on X-axis otherwise not. Here, y-coordinates of points $P(0, 3)$, $R(0, -1)$ and $T(1, 2)$ are not zero, so these points do not lie on the X-axis.

Q.23 The point which lies on Y-axis at a distance of 5 units in the negative direction of Y-axis is

(a) (0, 5) (b) (5,0) (c) (0, – 5) (d) (–5, 0)

Ans. *(c)* Given the point lies on Y-axis this shows that its x-coordinate is zero. Also, it is at a distance of 5 units in negative direction of Y-axis, so its y-coordinate is negative i.e. – 5. Hence, the required point is (0, – 5).

Q.24 The perpendicular distance of the point $P(3, 4)$ from the Y-axis is

(a) 3 (b) 4 (c) 5 (d) 7

Ans. *(a)* We know that abscissa or the x-coordinate of a point is its perpendicular distance from the Y-axis. So, perpendicular distance of the point $P(3, 4)$ from Y-axis is 3.

Mistake Alert! *Students may incorrectly take the perpendicular distance of the point* (3, 4) *from the Y-axis as y-coordinate i.e.,* 4 *instead of x-coordinate i.e.,* 3.

Short Answer Type Questions with Reasoning

Q.1 Write whether the following statements are true or false? Justify your answer.

(i) Point (3, 0) lies in the first quadrant.

(ii) Points (1, – 1) and (–1, 1) lie in the same quadrant.

(iii) The coordinates of a point whose ordinate is $-\frac{1}{2}$ and abscissa is 1 are $\left(-\frac{1}{2}, 1\right)$.

(iv) A point lies on Y-axis at a distance of 2 units from the X-axis. Its coordinates are (2, 0).

(v) (– 1, 7) is a point in the second quadrant.

Ans. (i) *False,* since the ordinate of the point (3, 0) is zero. So, the point lies on X-axis.

(ii) *False,* because in point (1, – 1), x-coordinate is positive and y-coordinate is negative, so it lies in IV quadrant and in point (–1, 1), x-coordinate is negative and y-coordinate is positive, so it lies in II quadrant.

(iii) *False,* Since, abscissa or x-coordinate of a point is 1 and ordinate or y-coordinate is $-\frac{1}{2}$. Then, the coordinates of the point are $\left(1, -\frac{1}{2}\right)$.

(iv) *False*, because in point (2, 0), ordinate or *y*-coordinate is zero, point (2, 0) lies on X-axis whose distance from Y-axis is 2 units.

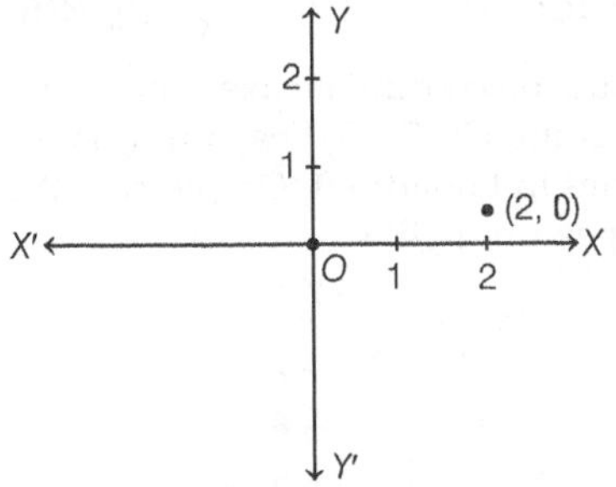

(v) *True*, because in point (–1, 7), abscissa is negative and ordinate is positive.

Short Answer Type Questions

Q.1 Write the coordinates of each of the points *P*, *Q*, *R*, *S*, *T* and *O* from the figure

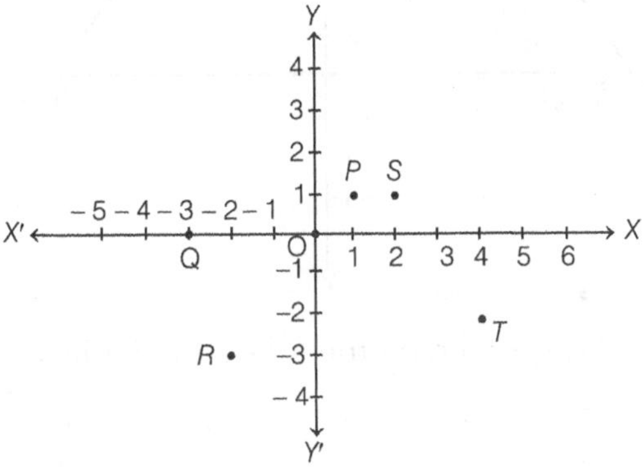

Thinking Process

(i) Firstly, draw the perpendicular lines from the point to the coordinates axes.

(ii) Further, measure the distance from intersecting points to the origin along their signs.

(iii) Finally, write the *x* unit distance and *y* unit distance in the form of a pair.

Ans. Here, points *P* and *S* lie in I quadrant so their both coordinates will be positive. Now, perpendicular distance of *P* from both axes is 1 unit, so coordinates of *P* are (1, 1). Also perpendicular distance of *S* from X-axis is 1 unit and from Y-axis is 2 units, so coordinates of *S* are (2, 1).

Point *Q* lies on X-axis in negative direction, so its *y*-coordinate will be zero and *x*-coordinate will be –3. So, coordinates of *Q* are (–3, 0).

Point *R* lies in III quadrant, so its both coordinate will be negative. Now, its perpendicular distance from X-axis is 3 units and from Y-axis is 2 units, so coordinates of point *R* are (–2, – 3).

Point *T* lies in IV quadrant, so its *x*-coordinate will be positive and *y*-coordinate will be negative. Now its perpendicular distance from X-axis is 2 units and from Y-axis is 4 units, so coordinates of *T* are (4, – 2). Point *O* is the intersection of both axes, so it is the origin and its corrdinates are *O*(0, 0).

***Q.2** Plot the following points and write the name of the figure obtained by joining, them in order : $P(-3, 2)$, $Q(-7, -3)$, $R(6, -3)$, $S(2, 2)$.

Ans. Let $X'OX$ and $Y'OY$ be the coordinate axes and mark points on it. Here, point $P(-3, 2)$ lies in II quadrant, $Q(-7,-3)$ lies in III quadrant, $R(6,-3)$ lies in IV quadrant and $S(2, 2)$ lies in I quadrant. On plotting the points on the graph, the figure obtained is trapezium $PQRS$.

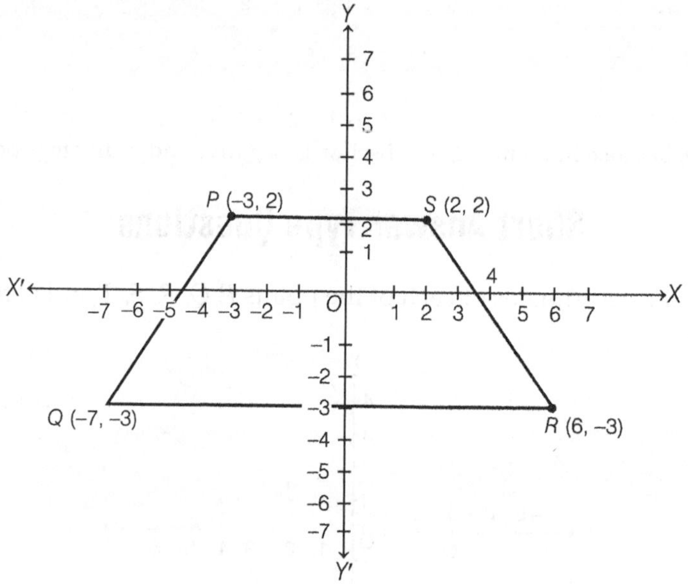

***Q.3** Plot the points (x, y) given by the following table.

x	2	4	–3	–2	3	0
y	4	2	0	5	–3	0

Ans. On plotting the given points on the graph, we get the points $P(2, 4)$. $Q(4, 2)$, $R(-3, 0)$, $S(-2, 5)$, $T(3, -3)$ and $O(0, 0)$.

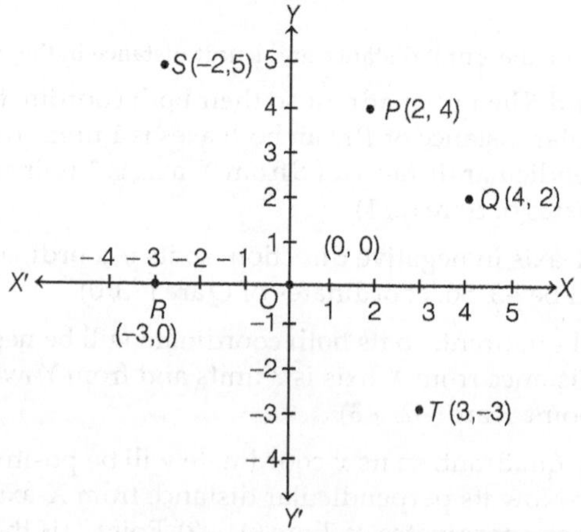

(✱) Topics related to these question have been removed from latest NCERT.

***Q.4** Plot the following points and check whether they are collinear or not

(i) (1, 3), (−1, − 1), (−2, − 3)

(ii) (1, 1), (2, − 3), (−1, − 2)

(iii) (0, 0), (2, 2), (5, 5)

Thinking Process

(i) Firstly, plot all three points on the graph and join them.

(ii) If it is in a straight line , then points are collinear otherwise non-collinear.

Ans. (i) On plotting the points $P(1, 3)$, $Q(-1, -1)$ and $R(-2, -3)$ on the graph and joining these points, we get a straight line. Hence, these points are collinear.

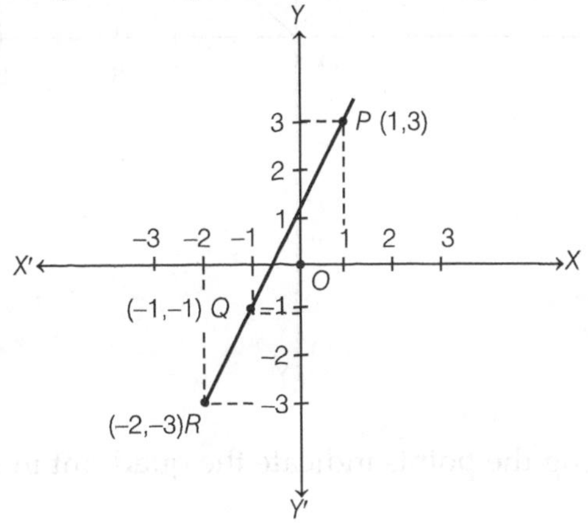

(ii) On plotting the points $P(1, 1)$, $Q(2, -3)$ and $R(-1, -2)$ on the graph and joining these three points, we get three lines *i.e.*, the given points do not lie on the same line. So, these points are not collinear.

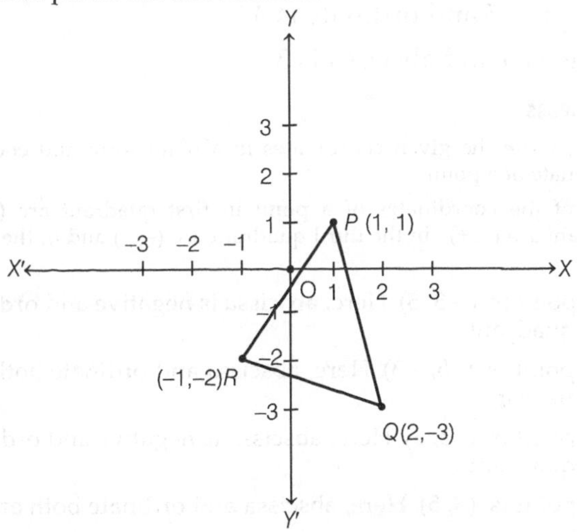

(**✱**) Topics related to these question have been removed from latest NCERT.

(iii) On Plotting the points $O(0, 0)$, $A(2, 2)$ and $B(5, 5)$ on the graph and joining these points, we get a straight line. Hence, these points are collinear.

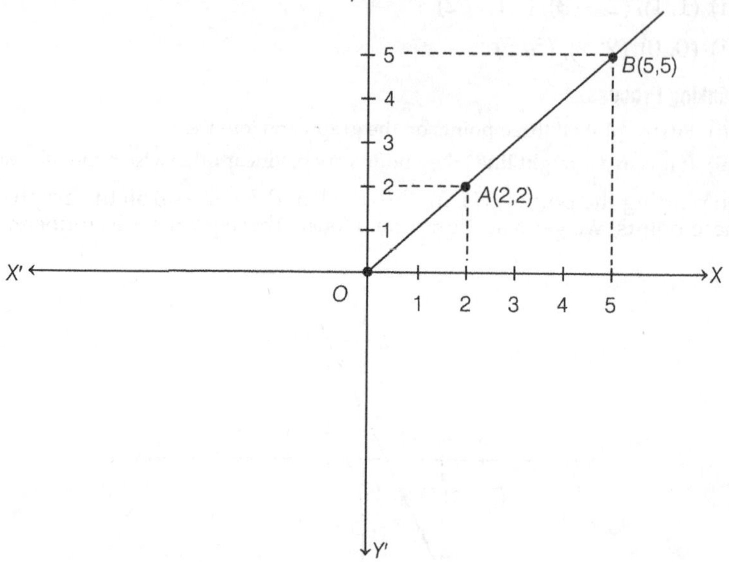

Q.5 Without plotting the points indicate the quadrant in which they will lie, if

(i) ordinate is 5 and abscissa is – 3.

(ii) abscissa is – 5 and ordinate is – 3.

(iii) abscissa is – 5 and ordinate is 3.

(iv) ordinate is 5 and abscissa is 3.

Thinking Process

(i) Firstly, write the given coordinates in a point form and check the sign of each coordinate of a point.

(ii) Signs of the coordinates of a point in first quadrant are (+, +) in the second quadrant are (–, +), in the third quadrant are (–, –) and in the fourth quadrant are (+, –).

Ans. (i) The given point is $(-3, 5)$. Here, abscissa is negative and ordinate is positive, so it lies in II quadrant.

(ii) The given point is $(-5, -3)$. Here, abscissa and ordinate both are negative, so it lies in III quadrant.

(iii) The given point is $(-5, 3)$. Here, abscissa is negative and ordinate is positive, so it lies in II quadrant.

(iv) The given point is $(3, 5)$. Here, abscissa and ordinate both are positive, so it lies in I quadrant.

Q.6 In figure LM is a line parallel to the Y-axis at a distance of 3 units.

(i) What are the coordinates of the points P, R and Q?

(ii) What is the difference between the abscissa of the points L and M?

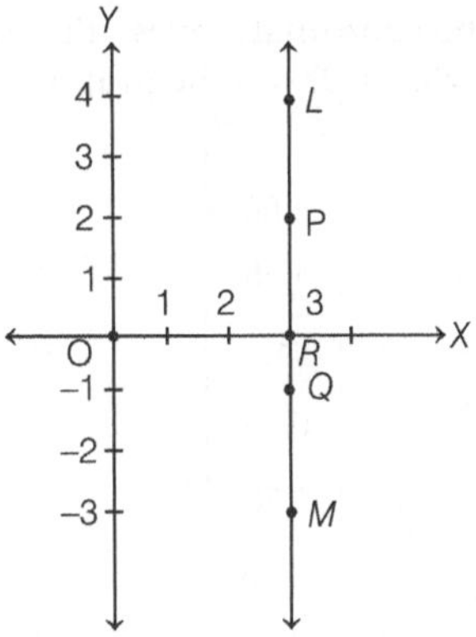

Ans. Given, LM is a line parallel to the Y-axis and its perpendicular distance from Y-axis is 3 units.

(i) Coordinate of point $P = (3, 2)$ [since, its perpendicular distance from X-axis is 2 units in the positive direction of y-axis and its perpendicular distance from y-axis is 3 units in the positive direction of x-axis].

Coordinate of point $Q = (3, -1)$ [since, its perpendicular distance from X-axis is 1 unit in negative direction of Y-axis and its perpendicular distance from y-axis is 3 units in the positive direction of x-axis].

Coordinate of point $R = (3, 0)$ [since its lies on X-axis, so its y-coordinate is zero].

(ii) Abscissa of point $L = 3$, abscissa of point $M = 3$

$\therefore$ Difference between the abscissa of the points L and $M = 3 - 3 = 0$

Q.7 In which quadrant or on which axis each of the following points lie?
$(-3, 5)$, $(4, -1)$, $(2, 0)$, $(2, 2)$, $(-3, -6)$

Ans. (i) In point $(-3, 5)$, x-coordinate is negative and y-coordinate is positive, so it lies in II quadrant.

(ii) In point $(4, -1)$, x-coordinate is positive and y-coordinate is negative, so it lies in IV quadrant.

(iii) In point $(2, 0)$, x-coordinate is positive and y-coordinate is zero, so it lies on X-axis.

(iv) In point $(2, 2)$, x-coordinate and y-coordinate both are positive, so it lies in I quadrant.

(v) In point $(-3, -6)$, x-coordinate and y-coordinate both are negative, so it lies in III quadrant.

Q.8 Which of the following points lies on Y-axis?
$A(1, 1)$, $B(1, 0)$, $C(0, 1)$, $D(0, 0)$, $E(0, -1)$, $F(-1, 0)$, $G(0, 5)$, $H(-7, 0)$ and $I(3, 3)$

● **Concept Insight** The point lies on y-axis means x-coordinate of the point will be zero.

Ans. We know that, a point lies on the Y-axis, if its x-coordinate is zero. Here, x-coordinate of points $C(0, 1)$, $D(0, 0)$, $E(0, -1)$ and $G(0, 5)$ are zero. So, these points lie on Y-axis. Also, $D(0, 0)$ is the intersection point of both the axes, so we can consider that it lies on Y-axis as well as on X-axis.

***Q.9** Plot the points (x, y) given by the following table. Use scale 1 cm = 0.25 units.

x	1.25	0.25	1.5	–1.75
y	–0.5	1	1.5	–0.25

Ans. Let $X'OX$ and $Y'OY$ be the coordinate axes. Plot the given points (1.25, –0.5), (0.25, 1), (1.5, 1.5) and (–1.75, – 0.25) on the graph.

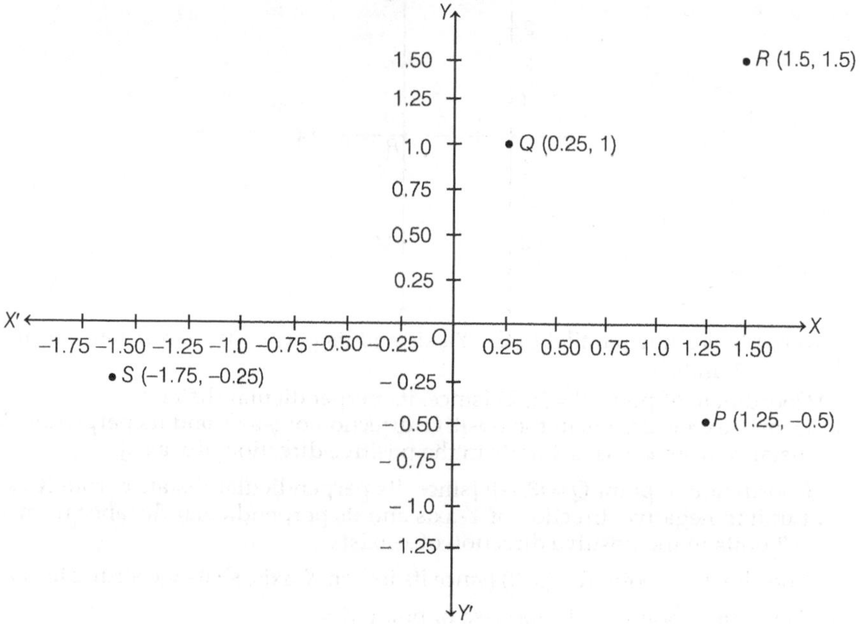

After plotting, we get the points P (1.25, –0.5), Q (0.25, 1), R (1.5, 1.5) and S (–1.75, – 0.25).

Q.10 A point lies on the X-axis at a distance of 7 units from the Y-axis. What are its coordinates? What will be the coordinates if it lies on Y-axis at a distance of –7 units from X-axis?

Ans. Given, point lies on the positive direction of X-axis, so its y-coordinate will be zero and it is at a distance of 7 units from the Y-axis, so its coordinates are (7, 0). If it lies on negative direction of Y-axis, then its x-coordinate will be zero and its distance from X-axis is 7 units in the negative direction of y-axis, so its coordinates are (0, – 7).

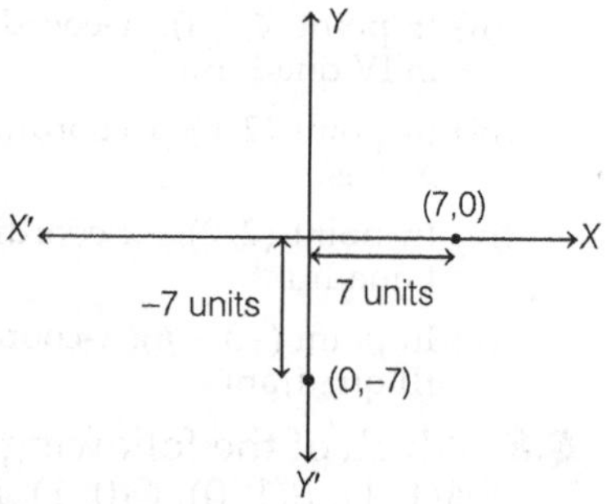

Q.11 Find the coordinates of the point
(i) which lies on X and Y-axes both.
(ii) whose ordinate is – 4 and which lies on Y-axis.
(iii) whose abscissa is 5 and which lies on X-axis.

(*) Topics related to these question have been removed from latest NCERT.

Ans. (i) The point which lies on X and Y-axes both is origin whose coordinates are (0, 0).

(ii) The point whose ordinate is – 4 and which lies on Y-axis *i.e.*, whose x-coordinate is zero, is (0, – 4).

(iii) The point whose abscissa is 5 and which lies on X-axis *i.e.*, whose y-coordinate is zero, is (5, 0).

Mistake Alert ! *Students may become confused about abscissa and ordinate and may incorrectly take the point as* (0, 5) *instead of* (5, 0).

***Q.12** Taking 0.5cm as 1 unit, plot the following points on the graph paper $A(1, 3)$, $B(-3, -1,)$, $C(1, -4)$, $D(-2, 3)$, $E(0, -8)$, $F(1, 0)$.

Ans. Here, in point $A(1, 3)$, x and y-coordinates are positive, so it lies in I quadrant.

In point $B(-3, -1)$, both x and y-coordinates are negative, so it lies in III quadrant.

In point $C(1, -4)$, x-coordinate is positive and y-coordinate is negative, so it lies in IV quadrant.

In point $D(-2, 3)$, x-coordinate is negative and y-coordinate is positive, so it lies in II quadrant.

In point $E(0,-8)$, x-coordinate is zero, so it lies on Y-axis and in point F (1, 0), y-coordinate is zero, so it lies on X-axis. On plotting the given points, we get the following graph.

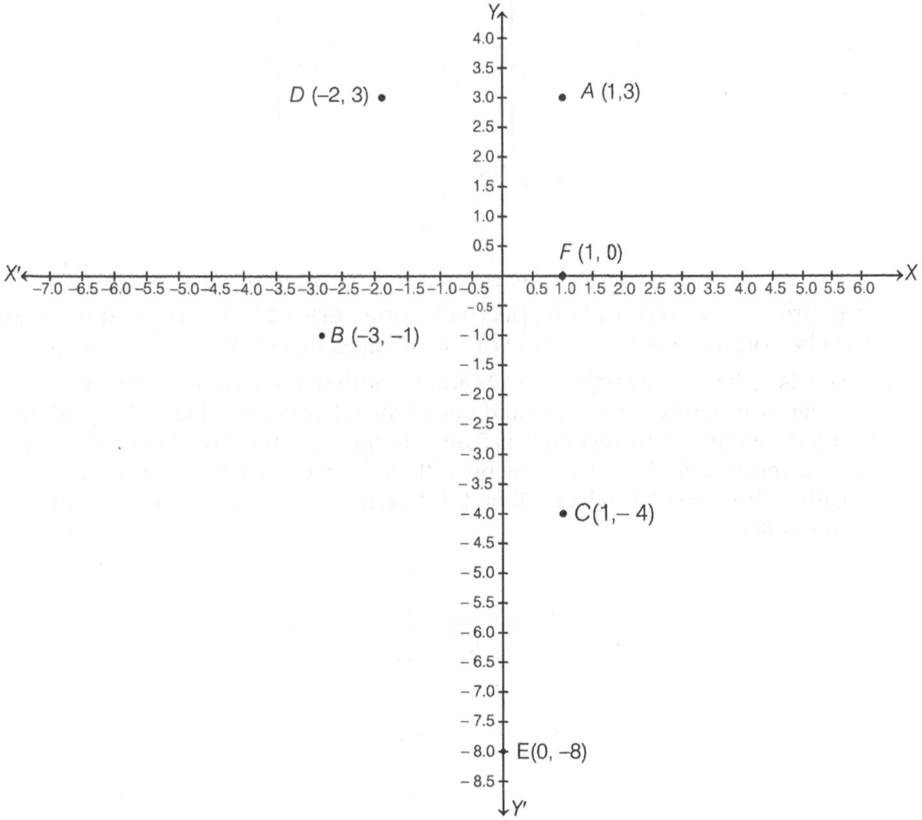

(✱) Topics related to these question have been removed from latest NCERT.

Long Answer Type Questions

***Q.1** Points $A(5, 3)$, $B(-2, 3)$ and $D(5, -4)$ are three vertices of a square $ABCD$. Plot these points on a graph paper and hence, find the coordinates of the vertex C.

Thinking Process

(i) Firstly, plot the given points on the graph and join them.

(ii) Now, we extend a line from point D parallel to X-axis and extend another line from point B parallel to Y-axis, which will meet at point C.

(iii) Further, we measure the distance from coordinate axis C to the point C.

Ans. The graph obtained by plotting the points A, B, C and D is given below. Take a point C on the graph such that $ABCD$ is a square *i.e.*, all sides AB, BC, CD, and AD are equal. So, abscissa of C will be equal to abscissa of B *i.e.*, -2 and ordinate of C will be equal to ordinate of D *i.e.*, -4. Hence, the coordinates of C are $(-2, -4)$.

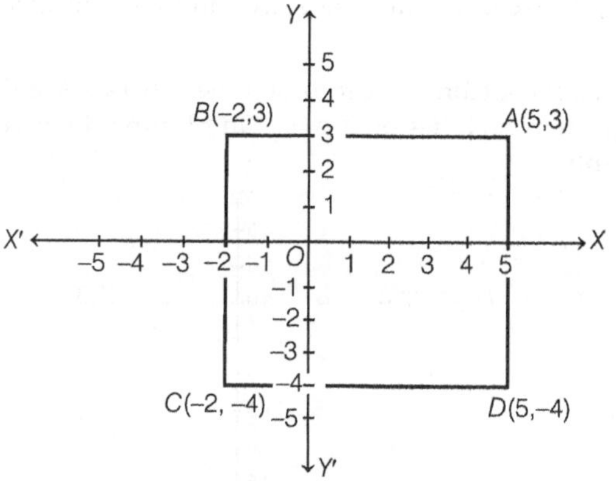

Q.2 Write the coordinates of the vertices of a rectangle whose length and breadth are 5 and 3 units respectively, one vertex at the origin, the longer side lies on the X-axis and one of the vertices lies in the third quadrant.

Ans. Given, length of a rectangle = 5 units and breadth of a rectangle = 3 units.
One vertex is at origin *i.e.*, (0, 0) and one of the other vertices lies in III quadrant. Since, the length of the rectangle is 5 units in the negative direction of X-axis. So, second vertex is $A(-5, 0)$. Also, the breadth of the rectangle is 3 units in the negative direction of Y-axis. So, then third vertex is $C(0, -3)$. Hence, the fourth vertex is $B(-5, -3)$.

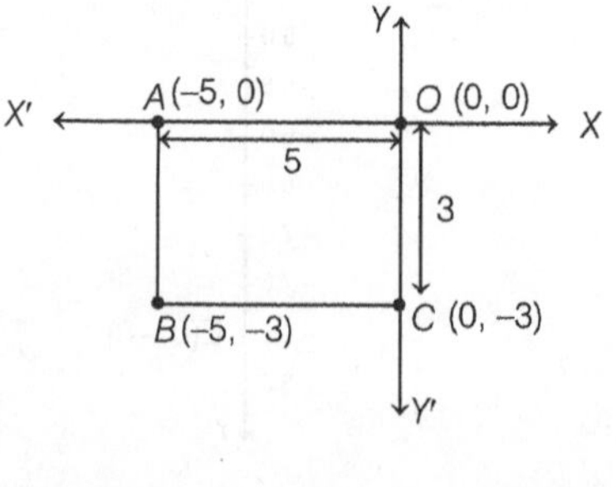

(*****) Topics related to these question have been removed from latest NCERT.

***Q.3** Plot the points $P(1, 0)$, $Q(4, 0)$ and $S(1, 3)$. Find the coordinates of the point R such that $PQRS$ is a square.

- **Concept Insight** The length of all sides of a square are equal.

Ans. In point $P(1, 0)$, y-coordinate is zero, so it lies on X-axis. In point $Q(4, 0)$, y-coordinate is zero, so it lies on X-axis. In point S $(1, 3)$, both coordinates are positive, so it lies in I quadrant.

On plotting these points, we get the following graph.

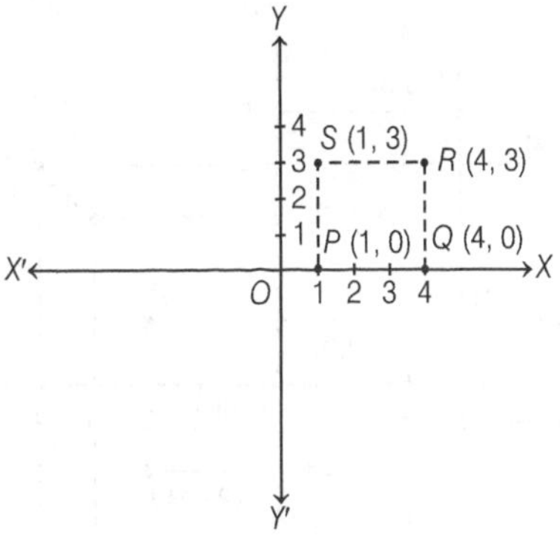

Now, take a point R on the graph such that $PQRS$ is a square. Then, all sides will be equal *i.e.*, $PQ = QR = RS = PS$. So, abscissa of R will be equal to abscissa of Q *i.e.*, 4 and ordinate of R will be equal to ordinate of S *i.e.*, 3. Hence, the coordinates of R are $(4, 3)$.

Q.4 From the given figure, answer the following questions

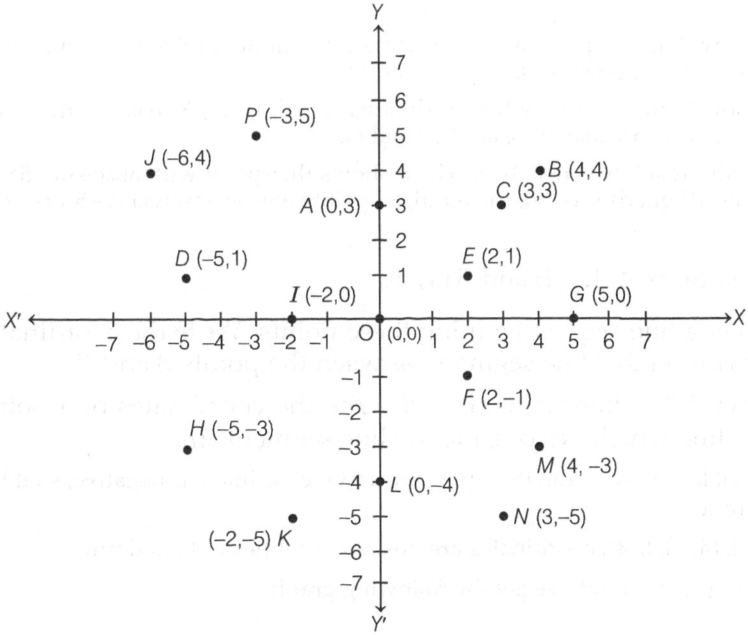

(i) Write the points whose abscissa is 0.
(ii) Write the points whose ordinate is 0.
(iii) Write the points whose abscissa is – 5.

- **Concept Insight** We know that origin O is the intersection point of both axes. So, we can consider it on X-axis as well as on Y-axis.

Ans.

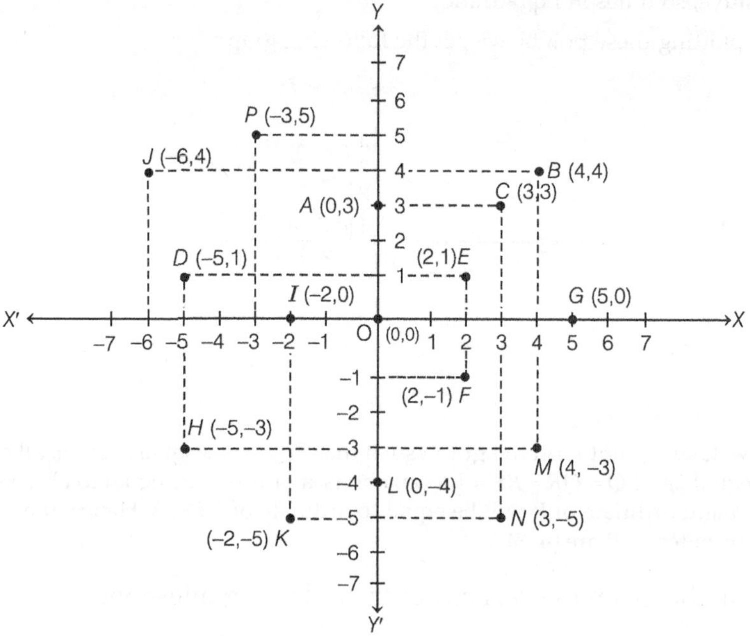

(i) We know that, the point whose abscissa is 0 will lie on *Y*-axis. So, the required points whose abscissa is 0, are *A*, *L* and *O*.

(ii) We know that, the point whose ordinate is 0 will lie on X-axis. So, the required points, whose ordinate is 0, are *G*, *I* and *O*.

(iii) Here, abscissa '–5' is negative, which shows that point with abscissa –5 will lie in II and III quadrants. So, the required points whose abscissa is –5, are *D* and *H*.

***Q.5** Plot the points $A(1, -1)$ and $B(4, 5)$.

(i) Draw a line segment joining these points. Write the coordinates of a point on this line segment between the points *A* and *B*.

(ii) Extend this line segment and write the coordinates of a point on this line which lies outside the line segment *AB*.

Ans. In point $A(1, -1)$, *x*-coordinate is positive and *y*-coordinate is negative, so it lies in IV quadrant.

In point $B(4, 5)$, both coordinates are positive, so it lies in I quadrant.

On plotting these point, we get the following graph.

(*) Topics related to these question have been removed from latest NCERT.

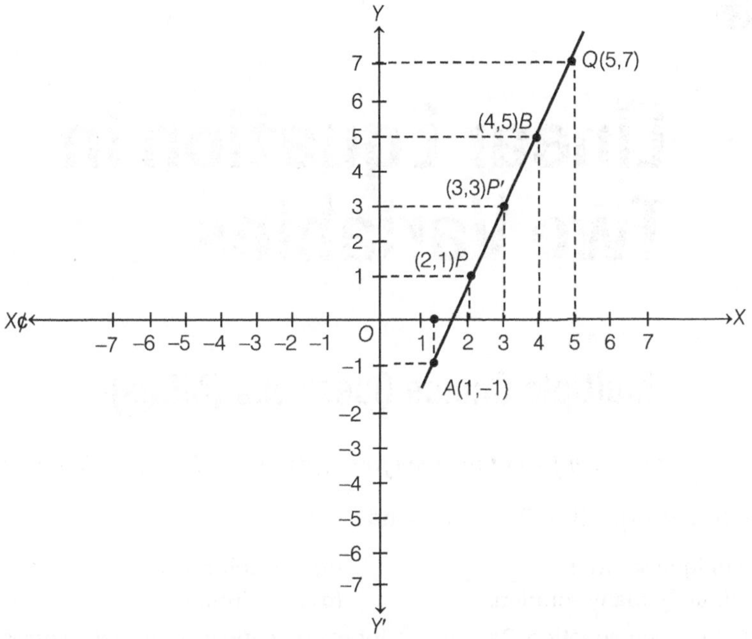

(i) On joining the points A and B, we get the line segment AB. Now, to find the coordinates of a point on this line segment between A and B, draw a perpendicular to X-axis from $x = 2$ and 3. Let it intersect line segment AB at P and P'.

Again, draw a perpendicular to Y-axis from P and P'. Then, it intersect Y-axis at $y = 1$ and 3, respectively. Thus, we get points $P(2, 1)$ and $P(3, 3)$, which lie on line segment AB.

(ii) Extend the line segment AB. Now, draw a perpendicular to X-axis from $x = 5$, let it intersect extended line segment at Q.

Again, draw a perpendicular to Y-axis from Q. Then, it intersects Y-axis at $y = 7$. Thus, we get the point $Q(5, 7)$ which lies outside the line segment AB.

Chapter

04

Linear Equation in Two Variables

Multiple Choice Questions (MCQs)

Choose the correct answer from the given four options in the following questions:

Q.1 The linear equation $2x - 5y = 7$ has

(a) a unique solution (b) two solutions
(c) infinitely many solutions (d) no solution

Ans. *(c)* In the given equation, $2x - 5y = 7$, for every value of x, we get a corresponding value of y and *vice-versa*. Therefore, the linear equation has infinitely many solutions.

Q.2 The equation $2x + 5y = 7$ has a unique solution, if x and y are

(a) Natural numbers (b) Positive real numbers
(c) Real numbers (d) Rational numbers

Ans. *(a)* In natural numbers, there is only one pair *i.e.*, (1, 1) which satisfy the given equation but in positive real numbers, real numbers and rational numbers there are many pairs to satisfy the given linear equation.

Therefore, if x, y are natural numbers, then given equation has a unique solution.

Q.3 If (2, 0) is a solution of the linear equation $2x + 3y = k$, then the value of k is

(a) 4 (b) 6 (c) 5 (d) 2

Ans. *(a)* Since, (2, 0) is a solution of the linear equation $2x + 3y = k$. Then, put $x = 2$ and $y = 0$ in the given equation, we get

$$\therefore \quad 2(2) + 3(0) = k \Rightarrow k = 4$$

Hence, the value of k is 4.

Q.4 Any solution of the linear equation $2x + 0y + 9 = 0$ in two variables is of the form

(a) $\left(-\frac{9}{2}, m\right)$ (b) $\left(n, -\frac{9}{2}\right)$
(c) $\left(0, -\frac{9}{2}\right)$ (d) $(-9, 0)$

Ans. *(a)* The given linear equation is

$$2x + 0y + 9 = 0$$

$\Rightarrow$ $2x + 9 = 0$

$\Rightarrow$ $2x = -9$

$\therefore$ $x = -\frac{9}{2}$ and y can be any real number, say m.

Hence, $\left(-\frac{9}{2}, m\right)$ is the required form of the solution of given linear equation.

***Q.5** The graph of the linear equation $2x + 3y = 6$ cuts the Y-axis at the point

(a) (2, 0) (b) (0, 3) (c) (3, 0) (d) (0, 2)

- **Concept Insight** If the graph of linear equation cuts the Y-axis point (x, y) lies on Y-axis, then $x = 0$

Ans. *(d)* Since, the graph of linear equation $2x + 3y = 6$ cuts the Y-axis.
So, we put $x = 0$ in the equation $2x + 3y = 6$, we get

$$2 \times 0 + 3y = 6$$

$\Rightarrow$ $3y = 6$

$\therefore$ $y = 2$

Hence, the graph of the given linear equation cuts the Y-axis at the point (0, 2).

Q.6 The equation $x = 7$, in two variables can be written as

(a) $1 \cdot x + 1 \cdot y = 7$ (b) $1 \cdot x + 0 \cdot y = 7$ (c) $0 \cdot x + 1 \cdot y = 7$ (d) $0 \cdot x + 0 \cdot y = 7$

Ans. *(b)* Here, the coefficient of 'y' in the given equation $x = 7$ is 0. So, the equation can be written as

$$1 \cdot x + 0 \cdot y = 7$$

Hence, the required equation is $1 \cdot x + 0 \cdot y = 7$.

***Q.7** Any point on the X-axis is of the form

(a) (x, y) (b) $(0, y)$ (c) $(x, 0)$ (d) (x, x)

Ans. *(c)* Every point on the X-axis has its y-coordinate equal to zero.

i.e., $y = 0$

Hence, the general form of every point on X-axis is $(x, 0)$.

Mistake Alert ! *If a point (x, y) lies on X-axis, then students can assume $x = 0$ instead of $y = 0$.*

***Q.8** Any point on the line $y = x$ is of the form

(a) (a, a) (b) $(0, a)$ (c) $(a, 0)$ (d) $(a, -a)$

Ans. *(a)* Every point on the line $y = x$ has same value of x and y-coordinates *i.e.,* $x = a$ and $y = a$.

Hence, (a, a) is the required form of point on the given line.

(*) Topics related to these question have been removed from latest NCERT.

***Q.9** The equation of X-axis is of the form

(a) $x = 0$ (b) $y = 0$ (c) $x + y = 0$ (d) $x = y$

Ans. *(b)* The equation of X-axis is of the form $y = 0$.

***Q.10** The graph of $y = 6$ is a line

(a) parallel to X-axis at a distance 6 units from the origin
(b) parallel to Y-axis at a distance 6 units from the origin
(c) making an intercept 6 on the X-axis
(d) making an intercept 6 on both axes

Ans. *(a)* Given equation of line can be written as, $0 \cdot x + 1 \cdot y = 6$

To draw the graph of above equation, we need atleast two solutions.

When $x = 0$, then $y = 6$

When $x = 2$, then $y = 6$

x	0	2
y	6	6

Here, we get two points A (0, 6) and B (2, 6). So, draw the graph by plotting the points and joining the line AB.

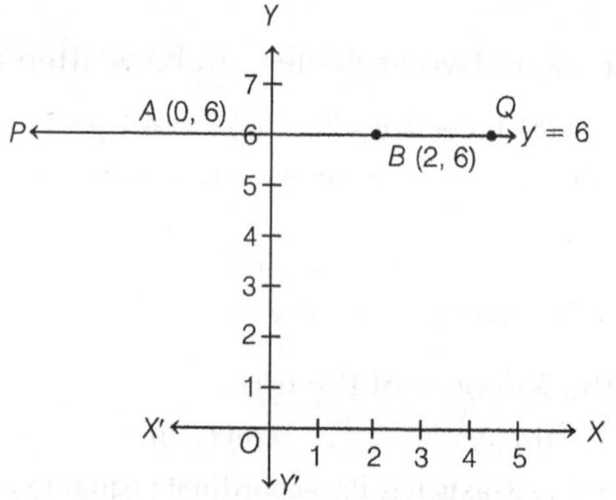

So, the line PQ is parallel to X-axis at a distance 6 units from X-axis is the required graph of $y = 6$.

Q.11 $x = 5, y = 2$ is a solution of the linear equation

(a) $x + 2y = 7$ (b) $5x + 2y = 7$ (c) $x + y = 7$ (d) $5x + y = 7$

Ans. *(c)*

(a) Take $x + 2y$, on putting $x = 5$ and $y = 2$, we get

$$5 + 2(2) = 5 + 4 = 9 \neq 7.$$

So, (5, 2) is not a solution of $x + 2y = 7$

(b) Take $5x + 2y$, on putting $x = 5$ and $y = 2$, we get

$$5 \times 5 + 2 \times 2 = 25 + 4 = 29 \neq 7$$

So, (5, 2) is not a solution of $5x + 2y = 7$.

(*) Topics related to these question have been removed from latest NCERT.

(c) Take $x + y$, on putting $x = 5$ and $y = 2$, we get $5 + 2 = 7$

So, (5, 2) is a solution of $x + y = 7$.

(d) Take $5x + y$, on putting $x = 5$ and $y = 2$, we get

$$5 \times 5 + 2 = 25 + 2 = 27 \neq 7$$

So, (5, 2) is not a solution of $5x + y = 7$.

Q.12 If a linear equation has solutions (–2, 2), (0, 0) and (2, – 2), then it is of the form

(a) $y - x = 0$ (b) $x + y = 0$ (c) $-2x + y = 0$ (d) $-x + 2y = 0$

Ans. *(b)* (a) Take $y - x = 0$, on putting $x = -2$ and $y = 2$, we get

$$(2) - (-2) = 2 + 2 = 4 \neq 0$$

So, (–2, 2) is not a solution of $y - x = 0$

(b) Take $x + y$, on putting $x = -2$ and $y = 2$, we get

$$-2 + 2 = -2 + 2 = 0 = 0$$

Again, on putting $x = 0$ and $y = 0$, we get

$$0 + 0 = 0$$

On putting $x = 2$ and $y = -2$, we get

$$2 + (-2) = 2 - 2 = 0$$

So, (–2, 2), (0, 0) and (2, 2) are the solutions of $x + y = 0$

(c) Take $-2x + y$, on putting $x = -2$ and $y = 2$, we get

$$-2(-2) + 2 = 4 + 2 = 6 \neq 0$$

So, (–2, 2) is not a solution of $-2x + y = 0$

(d) Take $-x + 2y = 0$, on putting $x = -2$ and $y = 2$, we get

$$-(-2) + 2(2) = 2 + 4 = 6 \neq 0$$

So, (–2, 2) is not a solution of $-x + 2y = 0$

Q.13 The positive solutions of the equation $ax + by + c = 0$ always lie in the

(a) Ist quadrant (b) IInd quadrant (c) IIIrd quadrant (d) IVth quadrant

Ans. *(a)* We know that, the co-ordinates of all points in the Ist quadrant are (+, +). Therefore the positive solutions of equation $ax + by + c = 0$ always lie in Ist quadrant.

***Q.14** The graph of the linear equation $2x + 3y = 6$ is a line which meets the X-axis at the point.

(a) (0, 2) (b) (2, 0) (c) (3, 0) (d) (0, 3)

Ans. *(c)* Since, the graph of the linear equation $2x + 3y = 6$ meets the X-axis.

So, we put $y = 0$ in $2x + 3y = 6$, we get

$$2x + 3(0) = 6 \Rightarrow 2x + 0 = 6 \Rightarrow x = \frac{6}{2} \Rightarrow x = 3$$

Hence, the coordinates on X-axis is (3, 0).

Mistake Alert ! *If the graph of the linear equation $ax + by + c = 0$ meets the X-axis, students may incorrectly put $x = 0$ instead of $y = 0$ in the given equation.*

(*) Topics related to these question have been removed from latest NCERT.

***Q.15** The graph of the linear equation $y = x$ passes through the point

(a) $(3/2, -3/2)$ (b) $(0, 3/2)$ (c) $(1,1)$ (d) $\left(-\frac{1}{2}, \frac{1}{2}\right)$

Ans. *(c)* The linear equation $y = x$ has same value of x and y-coordinates. Therefore, the point (1, 1) must lie on the line $y = x$.

Q.16 If we multiply or divide both sides of a linear equation with a non-zero number, then the solution of the linear equation

(a) Changes
(b) Remains the same
(c) Changes in case of multiplication only
(d) Changes in case of division only

Ans. *(b)* We know that, if we multiply or divide both sides of a linear equation with a non-zero number, then the solution of the linear equation remains the same *i.e.*, the solution of the linear equation is remains unchanged.

Q.17 How many linear equations in x and y can be satisfied by $x = 1$ and $y = 2$?

(a) Only one (b) Two
(c) Infinitely many (d) Three

Ans. *(c)* Let the linear equation be $ax + by + c = 0$.
On putting $x = 1$ and $y = 2$ in above equation, we get

$$a + 2b + c = 0, \text{ where } a, b \text{ and } c \text{ are real number}$$

Here, different values of a, b and c satisfy $a + 2b + c = 0$. Hence, infinitely many linear equations in x and y can be satisfied by $x = 1$ and $y = 2$.

***Q.18** The point of the form (a, a) always lies on

(a) X-axis (b) Y-axis
(c) the line $y = x$ (d) the line $x + y = 0$

Ans. *(c)* Since, the given point (a, a) has same value of x and y-coordinates. Therefore, the point (a, a) must be lie on the line $y = x$.

***Q.19** The point of the form $(a, -a)$ always lies on the line

(a) $x = a$ (b) $y = -a$
(c) $y = x$ (d) $x + y = 0$

Ans. *(d)* On taking option (d), $x + y = a + (-a) = a - a = 0$

[since, given point is of the form $(a, -a)$]

Hence, the point $(a, -a)$ always lies on the line $x + y = 0$.

(*) Topics related to these question have been removed from latest NCERT.

Short Answer Questions with Reasoning

Write whether the following statements are Ture or False? Justify your answers:

***Q.1** The point (0, 3) lies on the graph of the linear equation $3x + 4y = 12$.

Ans. *True*

If we put $x = 0$ and $y = 3$ in LHS of the given equation, we get

$$\text{LHS} = 3 \times 0 + 4 \times 3 = 0 + 12 = 12 = \text{RHS}$$

Hence, the point (0, 3) lies on the graph of the linear equation $3x + 4y = 12$

***Q.2** The graph of the linear equation $x + 2y = 7$ passes through the point (0, 7).

Ans. *False,* If we put $x = 0$ and $y = 7$ in LHS of the given equation, we get

$$\text{LHS} = 0 + 2(7) = 0 + 14 = 14 \neq 7 = \text{RHS}$$

Hence, the point (0, 7) does not lie on the line $x + 2y = 7$.

***Q.3** The graph given below represents the linear equation $x + y = 0$.

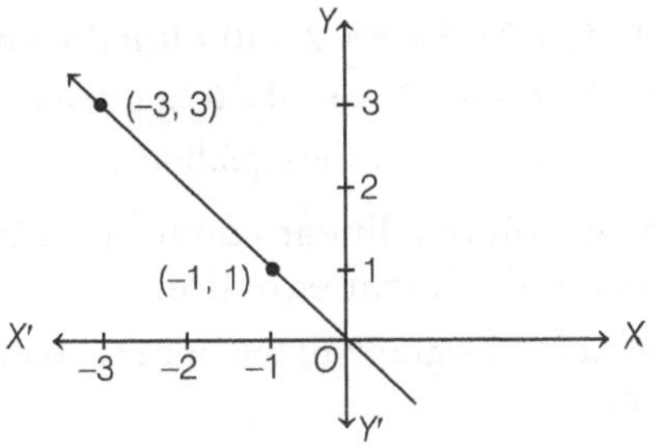

Ans. *True,* If the given points (– 1, 1) and (– 3, 3) lie on the graph of the linear equation $x + y = 0$, then both points will satisfy the equation.

So, at point (–1, 1), we put $x = -1$ and $y = 1$ in LHS of the given equation, we get

$$\text{LHS} = x + y = -1 + 1 = 0 = \text{RHS}$$

Again, at point (– 3, 3), we put $x = -3$ and $y = 3$ in LHS of the given equation, we get

$$\text{LHS} = x + y = -3 + 3 = 0 = \text{RHS}$$

Hence, points (–1, 1) and (–3, 3) both satisfy the given linear equation $x + y = 0$.

***Q.4** The graph given below represents the linear equation $x = 3$.

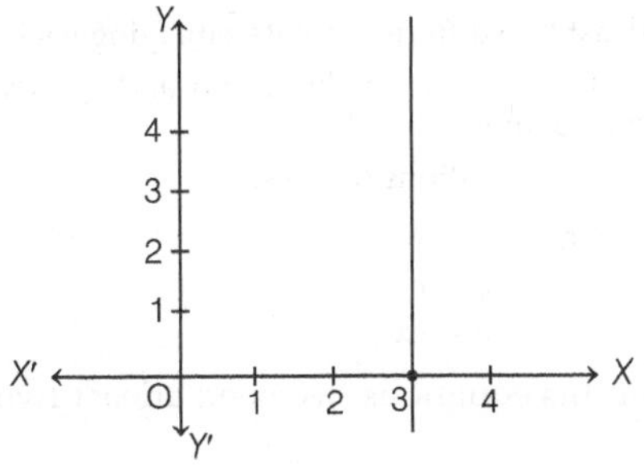

(*) Topics related to these question have been removed from latest NCERT.

Ans. *True*

Since, the given graph is a line parallel to Y-axis at a distance of 3 units to the right of the origin. Hence, it represents a linear equation $x = 3$.

Mistake Alert ! *If a line is parallel to the Y-axis at a distance 'a' units, then students can assume that this represents a linear equation $y = a$ instead of $x = a$.*

Q.5 The coordinates of points in the table

x	0	1	2	3	4
y	2	3	4	–5	6

represent some of the solutions of the equation $x - y + 2 = 0$.

Ans. *False*

The coordinates of points are (0, 2), (1, 3), (2, 4), (3, – 5) and (4, 6).

Given equation is $x - y + 2 = 0$

At point (0, 2), $0 - 2 + 2 = 0 \Rightarrow 0 = 0$, it satisfies.

At point (1, 3), $1 - 3 + 2 = 3 - 3 = 0 \Rightarrow 0 = 0$, it satisfies.

At point (2, 4), $2 - 4 + 2 = 4 - 4 = 0 \Rightarrow 0 = 0$, it satisfies.

At point (3, – 5), $3 - (-5) + 2 = 3 + 5 + 2 = 10 \neq 0$, it does not satisfy.

At point (4, 6), $4 - 6 + 2 = 6 - 6 = 0 \Rightarrow 0 = 0$, it satisfies.

Hence, point (3, – 5) does not satisfy the equation.

***Q.6** Every point on the graph of a linear equation in two variables does not represent a solution of the linear equation.

Ans. *False,* Since, every point on the graph of the linear equation represents a solution of the linear equation.

***Q.7** The graph of every linear equation in two variables need not be a line.

Ans. *False*

Since, the graph of a linear equation in two variables always represent a line.

Short Answer Type Questions

***Q.1** Draw the graphs of linear equations $y = x$ and $y = -x$ on the same cartesian plane. What do you observe?

Thinking Process

(i) Firstly, find atleast two different points satisfying each linear equation.

(ii) Secondly, plot these points on the graph and get two different lines respective after joining their points.

(iii) Further, observe the equations of lines.

Ans. Given linear equations are

$$y = x \quad \ldots(i)$$

and

$$y = -x \quad \ldots(ii)$$

To draw the graph of this equations, we need atleast two points lying on the given line.

(*) Topics related to these question have been removed from latest NCERT.

For $y = x$,

When $x = 1$, then $y = 1$

When $x = 4$, then $y = 4$

x	1	4
y	1	4

Similarly for $y = -x$

When $x = 3, y = -3$

When $x = -4, y = 4$

x	3	-4
y	-3	4

By plotting the points (1, 1) and (4, 4) on the graph paper and joining them by a line, we obtain the graph of $y = x$.

And by plotting the points (3, –3) and (–4, 4) on the graph and joining them by a line, we obtain the graph of $y = -x$.

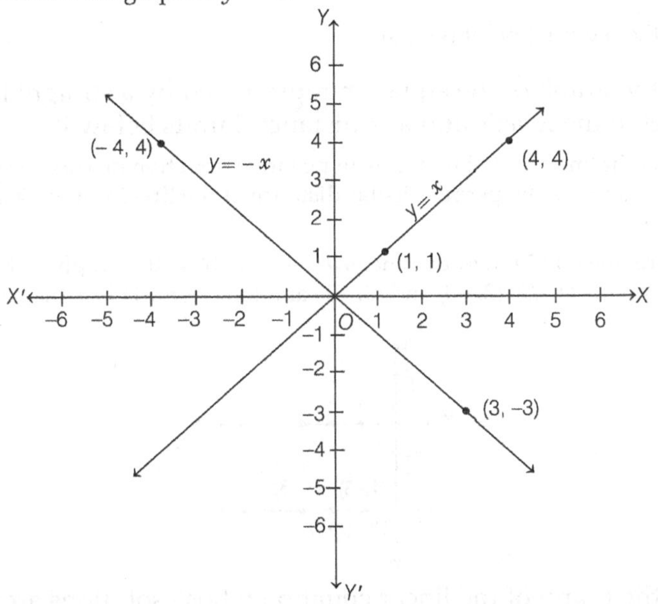

We observe that, the line $y = x$ and $y = -x$ intersect at the point $O(0, 0)$.

***Q.2** Determine the point on the graph of the linear equation $2x + 5y = 19$ whose ordinate is $1\frac{1}{2}$ times its abscissa.

Thinking Process

(i) Firstly, consider abscissa as x and ordinate as y and make a linear equation under the given condition.

(ii) Solving both linear equations to get the values of x and y.

(iii) Further, write the coordinates in a point form.

(*) Topics related to these question have been removed from latest NCERT.

Ans. Let x and y be the abscissa and ordinate respectively of the given line $2x + 5y = 19$, then by given condition,

$$\text{Ordinate} = 1\frac{1}{2} \times \text{Abscissa}$$

$$\Rightarrow \quad y = \frac{3}{2}x \quad \text{...(i)}$$

On putting $y = \frac{3}{2}x$ in given equation, we get

$$2x + 5\left(\frac{3}{2}\right)x = 19 \Rightarrow 4x + 15x = 19 \times 2$$

$$\Rightarrow \quad 19x = 38 \Rightarrow x = \frac{38}{19}$$

$$\therefore \quad x = 2$$

On substituting the value of x in Eq. (i), we get

$$y = \frac{3}{2} \times 2 = 3 \Rightarrow y = 3$$

Hence, the required point is (2, 3).

***Q.3** **Draw the graph of the equation represented by a straight line which is parallel to the X-axis and at a distance 3 units below it.**

Ans. Any straight line parallel to X-axis in negative direction of Y-axis is given by $y = -k$, where k is the perpendicular distance of the line from the X-axis. Here, $k = 3$ units.

Therefore, the equation of the line is $y = -3$. To draw the graph of this equation, plot the points (1,–3), (2, –3) and (3, –3) and join them. This is the required graph.

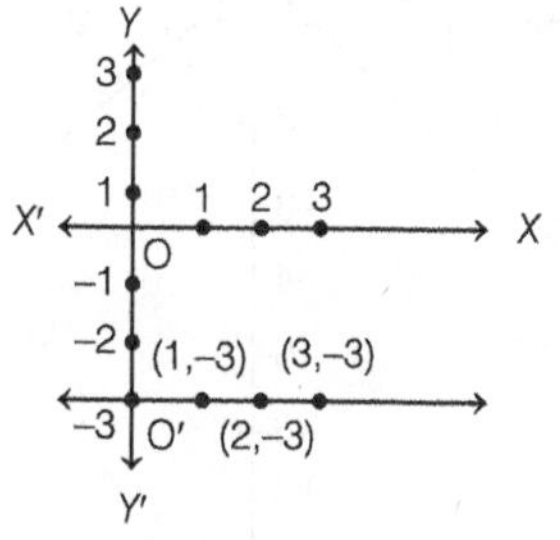

***Q.4** **Draw the graph of the linear equation whose solutions are represented by the points having the sum of the coordinates as 10 units.**

Ans. Given, the sum of the coordinates is 10 units.

Let x and y be two coordinates, then

$$x + y = 10 \quad \text{...(i)}$$

When $x = 5$ then $y = 5$

When $x = 3$ then $y = 7$

x	5	3
y	5	7

(*) Topics related to these question have been removed from latest NCERT.

Now, plotting the points (5, 5) and (3, 7) on the graph and joining them by a line, we get the graph of the linear equation $x + y = 10$

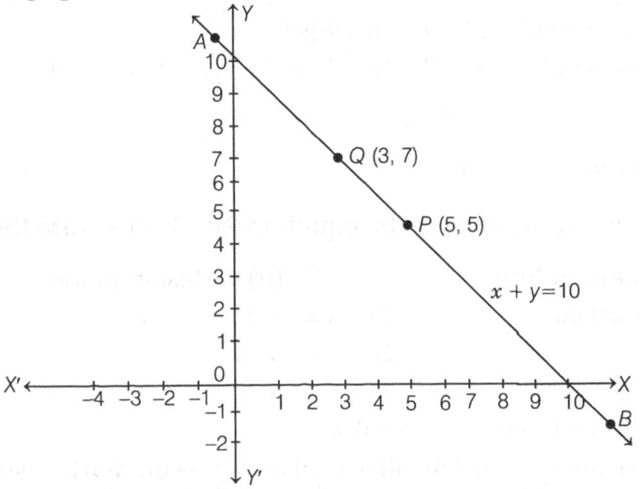

Thus the line AB is the required graph of $x + y = 10$.

***Q.5** Write the linear equation such that each point on its graph has an ordinate 3 times its abscissa.

Ans. Let the abscissa and ordinate of the point be x and y respectively.

According to the question, Ordinate $y = 3 \times$ Abscissa $\Rightarrow$ $y = 3x$

When $x = 1$, then $y = 3 \times 1 = 3$ and when $x = 2$, then $y = 3 \times 2 = 6$

x	1	2
y	3	6

Here, we get two points A (1, 3) and B (2, 6). So, draw the graph by plotting the points and joining the line AB.

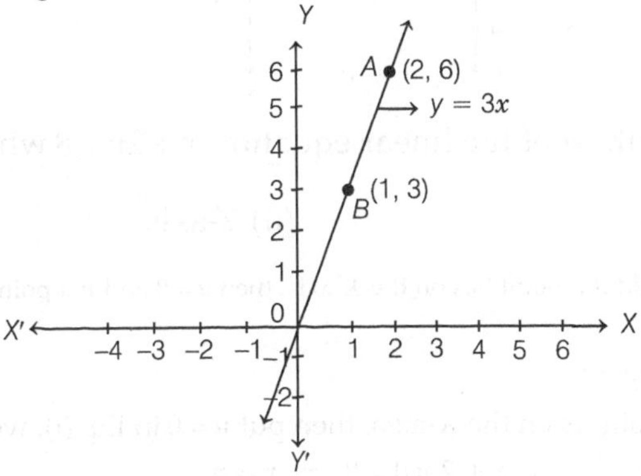

Hence, $y = 3x$ is the required linear equation such that each point on its graph has an ordinate 3 times its abscissa.

***Q.6** If the point (3, 4) lies on the graph of $3y = ax + 7$, then find the value of a.

Ans. Given, equation is $3y = ax + 7$ ...(i)

(*) Topics related to these question have been removed from latest NCERT.

Since, the point (3, 4) lies on the equation $3y = ax + 7$ then the equation will be satisfied by the point.

Now, put $x = 3$ and $y = 4$ in Eq. (i), we get

$$3(4) = a(3) + 7 \Rightarrow 12 = 3a + 7 \Rightarrow 3a = 12 - 7 \Rightarrow 3a = 5$$

$$\therefore \quad a = \frac{5}{3}$$

Hence, the value of a is 5/3.

***Q.7** How many solution(s) of the equation $2x + 1 = x - 3$ are there on the.

(i) number line (ii) cartesian plane

Ans. Given, equation is $2x + 1 = x - 3$

$\Rightarrow \quad 2x - x = -3 - 1$

$\therefore \quad x = -4$

Or it can be written as $1 \cdot x + 0 \cdot y = -4$

(i) Number line represent the all real values of x on the X-axis. Therefore, $x = -4$ is exactly one solution of given equation, which lies on the number line.

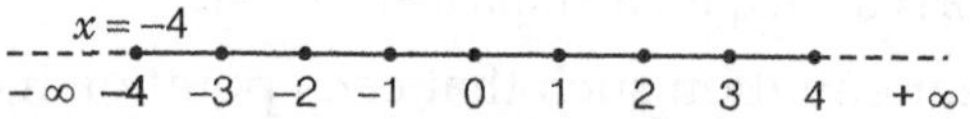

(ii) For $x = -4$, when $y = 1$, $x = -4$, when $y = 2$, $x = -4$

Here, we get two points (– 4, 1) and (– 4, 2). Now, plotting the points on the graph and joining them by a line, we get the graph of the linear equation $x = -4$.

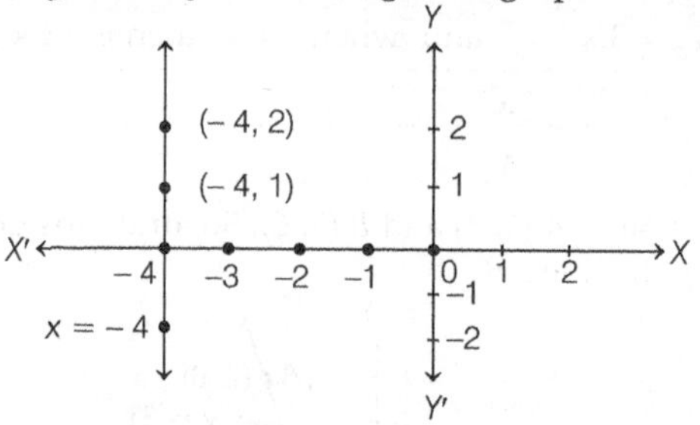

***Q.8** Find the solution of the linear equation $x + 2y = 8$ which represents a point on

(i) X-axis (ii) Y-axis

● **Concept Insight** If a point lies on the X-axis, then $y = 0$ and if a point lies on the Y-axis, then $x = 0$.

Ans. We have, $x + 2y = 8$ ...(i)

(i) When the point is on the X-axis, then put $y = 0$ in Eq. (i), we get

$$x + 2 \times 0 = 8 \Rightarrow x = 8$$

Hence, the required point is (8, 0).

(ii) When the point is on the Y-axis, then put $x = 0$ in Eq. (i), we get

$$0 + 2y = 8 \Rightarrow y = \frac{8}{2} = 4$$

Hence, the required point is (0, 4).

(*) Topics related to these question have been removed from latest NCERT.

Q.9 For what value of c, the linear equation $2x + cy = 8$ has equal values of x and y for its solution?

Ans. We have, $$2x + cy = 8 \quad \ldots(i)$$

Now, by the given condition, x and y-coordinates of given linear equation are same, *i.e.*, $x = y$. On putting $y = x$ in Eq. (i), we get

$$2x + cx = 8 \Rightarrow cx = 8 - 2x \Rightarrow c = \frac{8 - 2x}{x}, x \neq 0$$

Hence, the required value of c is $\frac{8 - 2x}{x}$, $x \neq 0$.

Q.10 Let y varies directly as x. If $y = 12$ when $x = 4$, then write a linear equation. What is value of y when $x = 5$?

Thinking Process

(i) Firstly, write the given condition as $y \propto x$, then remove their proportionality sign by considering arbitrary constant k.

(ii) Secondly, substitute the values of x and y in the obtained equation and determine the value of k.

(iii) Further, substitute the value of k in obtained equation, to get the required equation.

Ans. Given that, y varies directly as x.

i.e., $$y \propto x \Rightarrow y = kx \quad \ldots(i)$$

[where, k is an arbitrary constant]

Given, $$y = 12 \text{ and } x = 4$$

$$12 = 4k \quad \text{[from Eq. (i)]}$$

$$\Rightarrow k = \frac{12}{4}$$

$$\therefore k = 3$$

On putting the value of k in Eq. (i), we get

$$y = 3x \quad \ldots(ii)$$

When $x = 5$, then from Eq. (ii), we get

$$y = 3 \times 5 \Rightarrow y = 15$$

Hence, the value of y is 15.

Long Answer Type Questions

***Q.1** Show that the points A (1, 2), B (–1, – 16) and C (0, –7) lie on the graph of the linear equation $y = 9x - 7$.

Thinking Process

(i) Firstly, make a table of atleast two different points for the given linear equation.

(ii) Secondly, plot the obtained points from the table on a graph and join them to get a straight line.

(iii) Further, we plot the given points on the graph and then find that whether these points we lie on the line.

(*) Topics related to these question have been removed from latest NCERT.

Ans. Given, $y = 9x - 7$

When $x = 2$, then $y = 9 \times 2 - 7 = 18 - 7 = 11$

When $x = -2$, then $y = 9 \times (-2) - 7 = -18 - 7 = -25$

x	2	−2
y	11	−25

Here, we find two points D (2, 11) and E (−2, − 25).

So, draw the graph by plotting the points and joining the line DE.

Now, we plot the given points A (1, 2), B (−1, − 16) and C (0, −7) on the graph paper.

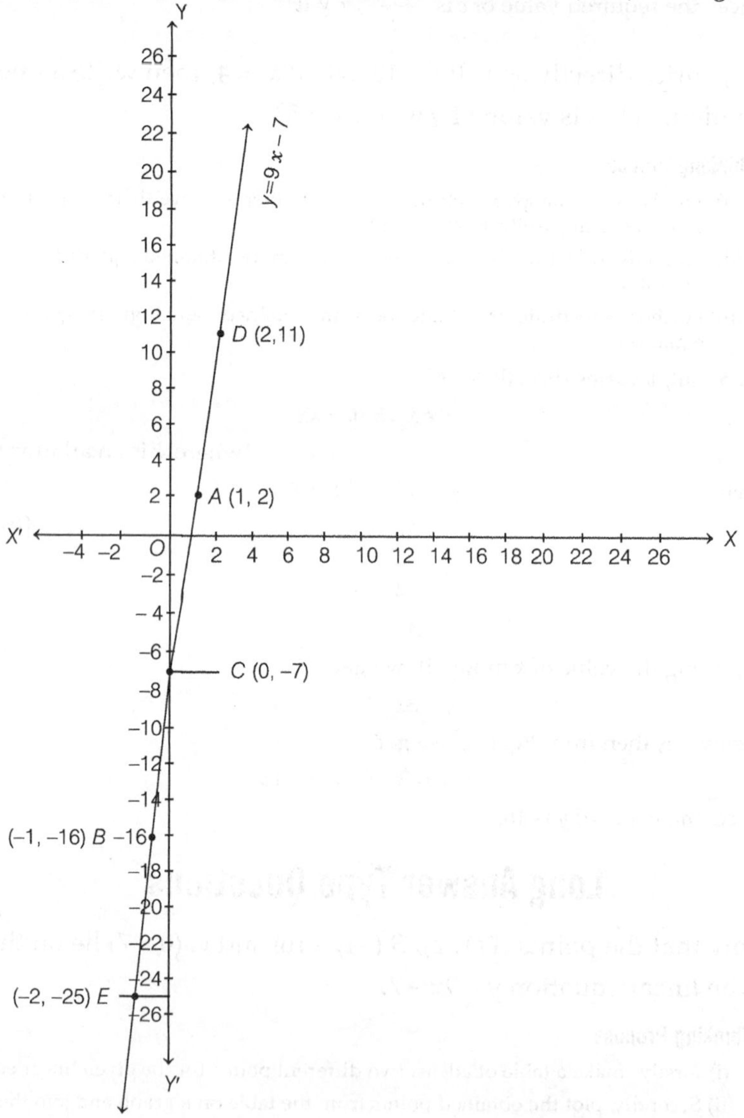

From the graph, we see that all the points lie on line DE.

***Q.2** The following observed values of x and y are thought to satisfy a linear equation. Write the linear equation

x	6	–6
y	–2	6

Draw the graph using the values of x, y as given in the above table.
At what points the graph of the linear equation
(i) cuts the X-axis (ii) cuts the Y- axis

Ans. Given, points are (6, –2) and (–6, 6).

Let the linear equation $y = mx + c$ is satisfied by the points (6, – 2) and (–6, 6).

Then, at point (6, –2),

$$-2 = 6m + c \quad \text{...(i)}$$

And at point (–6, 6), $$6 = -6m + c \quad \text{...(ii)}$$

On subtracting Eq. (ii) from Eq. (i), we get

$$12m = -8 \Rightarrow m = \frac{-8}{12} \Rightarrow m = -\frac{2}{3}$$

On putting the value of m in Eq. (i), we get

$$-2 = 6(-2/3) + c$$

$$\Rightarrow \quad -2 = -4 + c \Rightarrow c = -2 + 4 \Rightarrow c = 2$$

On putting $m = -\frac{2}{3}$ and $c = 2$ in linear equation $y = mx + c$, we get

$$y = -\frac{2}{3}x + 2 \Rightarrow y = \frac{-2x + 6}{3}$$

$$\Rightarrow \quad 3y = -2x + 6 \Rightarrow 3y + 2x = 6$$

(i) When the graph of the linear equation cuts the X-axis.

Then, put $y = 0$ in equation $2x + 3y = 6$, we get

$$2x + 3 \cdot 0 = 6 \Rightarrow 2x = 6$$

$$\therefore \quad x = 3$$

(ii) When the graph of the linear equation cuts the Y-axis.

Then, put $x = 0$ in equation $2x + 3y = 6$, we get

$$\Rightarrow \quad 2 \cdot 0 + 3y = 6 \Rightarrow 3y = 6$$

$$\therefore \quad y = 2$$

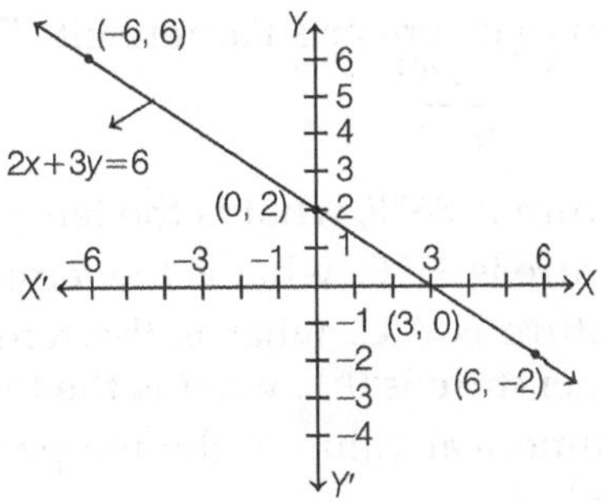

Therefore, the graph of the linear equation $2x + 3y = 6$ cuts the X-axis at the point (3, 0) and the Y-axis at the point (0, 2).

(✱) Topics related to these question have been removed from latest NCERT.

***Q.3** Draw the graph of the linear equation $3x + 4y = 6$. At what points, the graph cuts the X-axis and the Y-axis?

Ans. The given equation is $3x + 4y = 6$. Now, to draw the graph of this equation,we need atleast two points lying on the graph of

$$4y = 6 - 3x \Rightarrow y = \frac{6 - 3x}{4}$$

When $x = 2$, then $y = \frac{6 - 3 \times 2}{4} = \frac{6 - 6}{4} = 0$

When $x = 0$, then $y = \frac{6 - 3 \times 0}{4} = \frac{6}{4} = \frac{3}{2}$

x	2	0
y	0	3/2

Here, we find two points $A\left(0, \frac{3}{2}\right)$ and $B(2, 0)$.

Now, plot the points $A\left(0, \frac{3}{2}\right)$ and $B(2, 0)$ and join them, to get the line AB.

Hence, the line AB is the required graph.

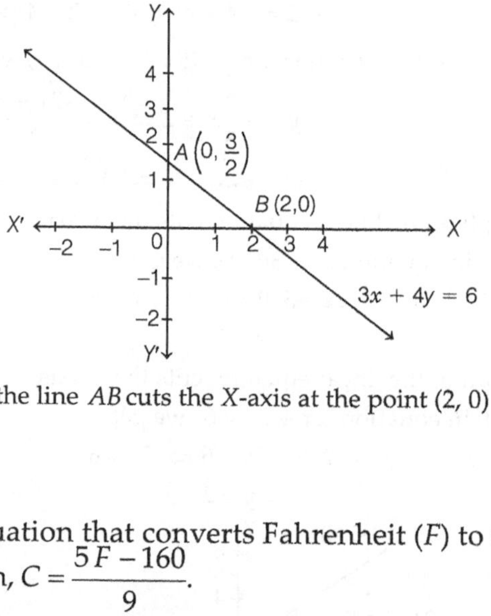

We can see that the line AB cuts the X-axis at the point (2, 0) and the Y-axis at the point $\left(0, \frac{3}{2}\right)$.

***Q.4** The linear equation that converts Fahrenheit (F) to Celsius (C) is given by the relation, $C = \frac{5F - 160}{9}$.

(i) If the temperature is 86°F, what is the temperature in Celsius?

(ii) If the temperature is 35°C, what is the temperature in Fahrenheit?

(iii) If the temperature is 0°C, what is the temperature in Fahrenheit and if the temperature is 0°F, what is the temperature in Celsius?

(iv) What is the numerical value of the temperature which is same in both the scales?

(*****) Topics related to these question have been removed from latest NCERT.

Ans. Given relation is, $$C=\frac{5F-160}{9} \quad ...(i)$$

$$\Rightarrow \quad 9C=5F-160 \Rightarrow 5F=9C+160$$

$$\Rightarrow \quad F=\frac{9C+160}{5} \quad ...(ii)$$

(i) Given, $F = 86°F$, then from Eq. (i), we get

$$C=\frac{5\times 86-160}{9}=\frac{430-160}{9}=\frac{270}{9}=30°C$$

(ii) Given, $C = 35°C$, then from Eq. (ii), we get

$$F=\frac{9\times 35+160}{5}=\frac{315+160}{5}=\frac{475}{5}=95°F$$

(iii) Given, $C = 0°C$, then from Eq. (ii), we get

$$F=\frac{9\times 0+160}{5}=\frac{160}{5}=32°F$$

$F = 0°F$, then from Eq. (i), we get

$$C=\frac{5\times 0-160}{9}=\left(-\frac{160}{9}\right)^{\circ}C$$

(iv) By the given condition, $F = C$

Put this value in Eq. (i), we get

$$C=\frac{5C-160}{9} \Rightarrow 9C=5C-160$$

$$\Rightarrow \quad 9C-5C=-160$$

$$\Rightarrow \quad 4C=-160 \Rightarrow C=\frac{-160}{4} \Rightarrow C=-40=F$$

Thus, the numerical value of the temperature is –40°C or – 40°F.

*** Q.5** If the temperature of a liquid can be measured in Kelvin units as $x°K$ or in fahrenheit units as $y°F$, the relation between the two systems of measurement of temperature is given by the linear equation.

$$Y=\frac{9}{5}(x-273)+32$$

(i) Find the temperature of the liquid in Fahrenheit, if the temperature of the liquid is 313°K.

(ii) If the temperature is 158°F, then find the temperature in kelvin.

Ans. Given relation is $y=\frac{9}{5}(x-273)+32$ ...(i)

(i) Given, $x = 313°K$, then from Eq. (i), we get

$$y=\frac{9}{5}(313-273)+32=\frac{9}{5}\times 40+32=9\times 8+32=72+32=104°F$$

(ii) Given, $y = 158° F$, then from Eq. (i), we get

$$158=\frac{9}{5}(x-273)+32 \Rightarrow 158=\frac{9(x-273)+32\times 5}{5}$$

$$\Rightarrow \quad 158\times 5=9(x-273)+160$$

(✱) Topics related to these question have been removed from latest NCERT.

$$\Rightarrow \quad 790 = 9(x - 273) + 160$$
$$\Rightarrow \quad 790 - 160 = 9(x - 273)$$
$$\Rightarrow \quad 9(x - 273) = 630 \Rightarrow x - 273 = \frac{630}{9} = 70$$
$$\because \quad x = 70 + 273 = 343\,°K$$

***Q.6** The force exerted to pull a cart is directly proportional to the acceleration produced in the body. Express the statement as a linear equation of two variables and draw the graph of the same by taking the constant mass equal to 6 kg. Read from the graph, the force required when the acceleration produced is

(i) 5 ms^{-2} (ii) 6 m/sec^{-2}

Thinking Process

(i) Firstly, make a proportionality equation in terms of force (F) and acceleration (a) *i.e.*, $F \propto a$.

(ii) Secondly, write the proportional equation in linear equation by using arbitrary constant.

(iii) Further, for two different values of a, we get the values of F and write coordinates in a point form. Then, plot these points on the graph and join them to get the line.

Ans. Given that, the force (F) is directly proportional to the acceleration (a).

i.e., $F \propto a$

$\Rightarrow$ $F = ma$ [where, m = arbitrary constant and take value 6 kg of mass]

$\therefore$ $F = 6a$ ...(i)

(i) If $a = 5\ \text{m}/\text{s}^2$, then from Eq. (i), we get

$$F = 6 \times 5 = 30\,\text{N}$$

(ii) If $a = 6\ \text{m}/\text{s}^2$, then from Eq. (i), we get

$$F = 6 \times 6 = 36\,\text{N}$$

Here, we find two points A (5, 30) and B (6, 36). So, draw the graph by plotting the points and join them to get the line AB.

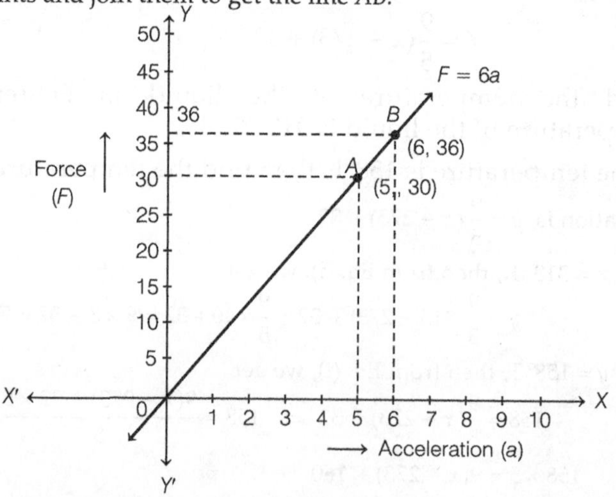

(*****) Topics related to these question have been removed from latest NCERT.

Chapter

05

Introduction to Euclid's Geometry

Multiple Choice Questions (MCQs)

Choose the correct answer from the given four options in the following questions:

Q.1 The three steps from solids to points are

(a) solids-surfaces-lines-points (b) solids-lines-surfaces-points

(c) lines-points-surfaces-solids (d) lines-surfaces-points-solids

Ans. *(a)* The three steps from solids to points are solids-surfaces-lines-points.

Q.2 The number of dimensions, a solid has

(a) 1 (b) 2 (c) 3 (d) 0

Ans. *(c)* A solid has shape, size, position and can be moved from one place to another. So, solid has three dimensions, *e.g.*, Cuboid.

Q.3 The number of dimensions, a surface has

(a) 1 (b) 2 (c) 3 (d) 0

Ans. *(b)* Boundaries of a solid are called surfaces. A surface (plane) has only length and breadth. So, it has two dimensions.

Q.4 The number of dimensions, a point has

(a) 0 (b) 1 (c) 2 (d) 3

Ans. *(a)* A point is that which has no part *i.e.*, no length, no breadth and no height. So, it has no dimension.

Q.5 Euclid divided his famous treatise 'The Elements' into

(a) 13 chapters (b) 12 chapters

(c) 11 chapters (d) 9 chapters

Ans. *(a)* Euclid divided his famous treatise 'The Elements' into 13 chapters.

Q.6 The total number of propositions in 'The Elements' are

(a) 465 (b) 460 (c) 13 (d) 55

Ans. *(a)* The statements that can be proved are called propositions or theorems. Euclid deduced 465 propositions in a logical chain using his axioms, postulates, definitions and theorems.

Q.7 Boundaries of solids are

(a) surfaces (b) curves (c) lines (d) points

Ans. *(a)* Boundaries of solids are called surfaces.

Q.8 Boundaries of surfaces are

(a) surfaces (b) curves (c) lines (d) points

Ans. *(b)* The boundaries of surfaces are curves.

Q.9 In Indus Valley Civilisation (about 3000 BC), the bricks used for construction work were having dimensions in the ratio

(a) 1 : 3 : 4 (b) 4 : 2 : 1 (c) 4 : 4 : 1 (d) 4 : 3 : 2

Ans. *(b)* In Indus Valley Civilisation, the bricks used for construction work were having dimensions in the ratio length: breadth : thickness = 4 : 2 : 1.

Q.10 A pyramid is a solid figure, the base of which is

(a) only a triangle (b) only a square (c) only a rectangle (d) any polygon

Ans. *(d)* A pyramid is a solid figure, the base of which is a triangle or square or some other polygon.

Q.11 The side faces of a pyramid are:

(a) triangles (b) squares (c) polygons (d) trapeziums

Ans. *(a)* The side faces of a pyramid are always triangles.

Q.12 It is known that, if $x + y = 10$, then $x + y + z = 10 + z$. The Euclid's axiom that illustrates this statement is

(a) first axiom (b) second axiom (c) third axiom (d) fourth axiom

Ans. *(b)* The Euclid's axiom that illustrates the given statement is second axiom which states that if equals are added to equals, the wholes are equal.

Q.13 In ancient India, the shapes of altars used for household rituals were

(a) squares and circles (b) triangles and rectangles
(c) trapeziums and pyramids (d) rectangles and squares

Ans. *(a)* In ancient India, the shapes of altares used for house hold rituals were squares and circles.

Q.14 The number of interwoven isosceles triangles in Sriyantra (in the Atharvaveda) is

(a) seven (b) eight (c) nine (d) eleven

Ans. *(c)* The Sriyantra (in the Atharvaveda) consists of nine interwoven isosceles triangles.

Q.15 Greek's emphasised on

(a) inductive reasoning (b) deductive reasoning
(c) Both (a) and (b) (d) practical use of geometry

Ans. *(b)* Greek's emphasised on deductive reasoning.

Q.16 In ancient India, Altars with combination of shapes like rectangles, triangles and trapeziums were used for

(a) public worship (b) household rituals
(c) Both (a) and (b) (d) None of these

Ans. *(a)* In ancient India, Altars whose shapes were combinations of rectangles, triangles and trapeziums were used for public worship.

Q.17 Euclid belongs to the country:

(a) Babylonia (b) Egypt (c) Greece (d) India

Ans. *(c)* Euclid belongs to the country Greece.

Q.18 Thales belongs to the country:

(a) Babylonia (b) Egypt (c) Greece (d) Rome

Ans. *(c)* Thales belongs to the country Greece.

Q.19 Pythagoras was a student of:

(a) Thales (b) Euclid (c) Both (a) and (b) (d) Archimedes

Ans. *(a)* Pythagoras was a student of Thales.

Q.20 Which of the following needs a proof?

(a) Theorems (b) Axiom (c) Definition (d) Postulate

Ans. *(a)* The statements that needs a proof are called propositions or theorems.

Q.21 Euclid stated that all right angles are equal to each other in the form of

(a) an axiom (b) a definition (c) a postulate (d) a proof

Ans. *(c)* Euclid stated that all right angles are equal to each other in the form of a postulate.

Q.22 'Lines are parallel, if they do not intersect' is stated in the form of

(a) an axiom (b) a definition (c) a postulate (d) a proof

Ans. *(b)* 'Lines are parallel, if they do not intersect' is the definition of parallel lines.

Short Answer Questions with Reasoning

Write whether the following statements are True or False? Justify your answer.

Q.1 Euclidean geometry is valid only for curved surfaces.

Ans. *False*

Because Euclidean geometry is valid only for the figures in the plane but on the curved surfaces, it fails.

Q.2 The boundaries of the solids are curves.

Ans. *False*

Because the boundaries of the solids are surfaces.

Q.3 The edges of a surface are curves.

Ans. *False,* Because the edges of surfaces are line.

Q.4 The things which are double of the same thing are equal to one another.

Ans. *True*

Since, it is one of the Euclid's axioms.

Q.5 If a quantity B is a part of another quantity A, then A can be written as the sum of B and some third quantity C.

Ans. *True*

Since, it is one of the Euclid's axioms.

Q.6 The statements that are proved are called axioms.

Ans. *False*

Because the statements that are proved are called theorems.

* **Q.7** "For every line l and for every point P not lying on a given line l, there exists a unique line m passing through P and parallel to l" is known as Playfair's axiom.

Ans. *True*

Because it is an equivalent version of Euclid's fifth postulate and it is known as Playfair's axiom.

*Q.8 Two distinct intersecting lines cannot be parallel to the same line.

Ans. *True*

Because, it is an equivalent version of Euclid's fifth postulate.

* **Q.9** Attempt to prove Euclid's fifth postulate using the other postulates and axioms led to the discovery of several other geometries.

Ans. *True*

All attempts to prove the fifth postulate as a theorem led to a great achievement in the creation of several other geometries. These geometries are quite different from Euclidean geometry and called non-Euclidean geometry.

Short Answer Type Questions

Solve each of the following question using appropriate Euclid's axiom.

Q.1 Two salesmen make equal sales during the month of August. In September, each salesman doubles his sale of the month of August. Compare their sales in September.

- **Concept Insight** Apply the Euclid's axiom, things which are double of the same thing are equal to one another.

(*) Topics related to these question have been removed from latest NCERT.

Ans. Let the equal sales of two salesmen in August be x.
In September, each salesman doubles his sale of August.
Thus, sale of first salesman is $2x$ and sale of second salesman is $2x$.
According to Euclid's axiom, things which are double of the same thing are equal to one another.
So, in September, their sales are again equal.

Q.2 It is known that $x + y = 10$ and that $x = z$. Show that $z + y = 10$.

Thinking Process Apply the Euclid's axiom, if equals are added to equals, the wholes are equal, to show the given result.

Ans. We have, $x + y = 10$ ...(i)
and $x = z$ ...(ii)
According to Euclid's axiom, if equals are added to equals, the wholes are equal.
On adding y both sides of Eq. (ii), we get

$$x + y = z + y \quad \text{...(iii)}$$

From Eqs. (i) and (iii), we get

$$z + y = 10$$

Q.3 Look at the adjoining figure. Show that length $AH >$ sum of lengths of $AB + BC + CD$.

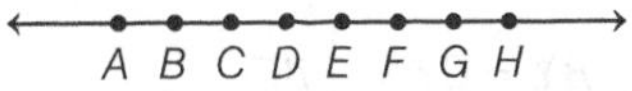

Thinking Process Apply the Euclid's axiom, the whole is greater than the part, to show the given result.

Ans. From the given figure, we have

$$AB + BC + CD = AD \quad \text{...(i)}$$

Here, AD is also the parts of AH. [AB, BC and CD are the parts of AD]
By Euclid's axioms, the whole is greater than the part.
So, $AH > AD$.
i.e., length $AH >$ sum of lengths of $(AB + BC + CD)$. [from Eq. (i)]

Q.4 In the figure, we have $AB = BC$ and $BX = BY$. Show that $AX = CY$.

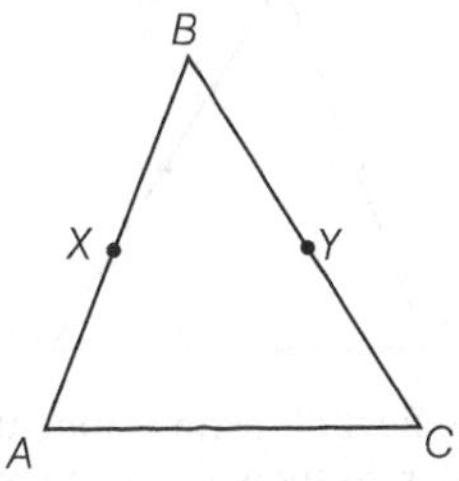

Ans. We have, $AB = BC$ ...(i)
and $BX = BY$ ....(ii)

On subtracting Eq. (ii) from Eq. (i), we get

$$AB - BX = BC - BY$$

[According to Euclid's third axiom, if equals are subtracted from equals, the remainders are equal]

$\Rightarrow$ $AX = CY$ [from figure]

Q.5 In the given figure, we have X and Y are the mid-points of AC and BC and $AX = CY$. Show that $AC = BC$.

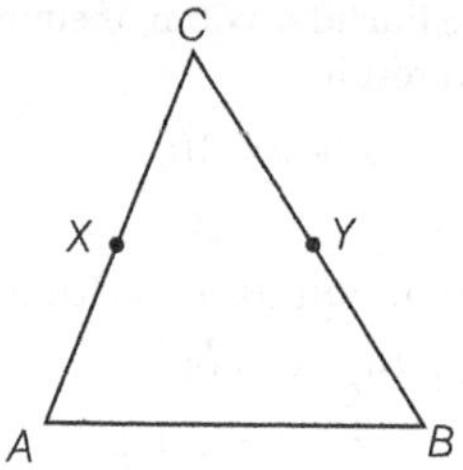

Ans. Given, X is the mid-point of AC.

$\therefore$ $AX = CX = \frac{1}{2} AC$

$\Rightarrow$ $2AX = 2CX = AC$ ...(i)

and Y is the mid-point of BC.

$\therefore$ $BY = CY = \frac{1}{2} BC$

$\Rightarrow$ $2BY = 2CY = BC$ ...(ii)

Also, given $AX = CY$ ...(iii)

According to Euclid's sixth axiom, things which are double of the same thing are equal to one another.

$\Rightarrow$ $2AX = 2CY$ [from Eq. (iii)]

$\Rightarrow$ $AC = BC$ [from Eqs. (i) and (ii)]

Q.6 In the given figure, we have $BX = \frac{1}{2} AB$, $BY = \frac{1}{2} BC$ and $AB = BC$. Show that $BX = BY$.

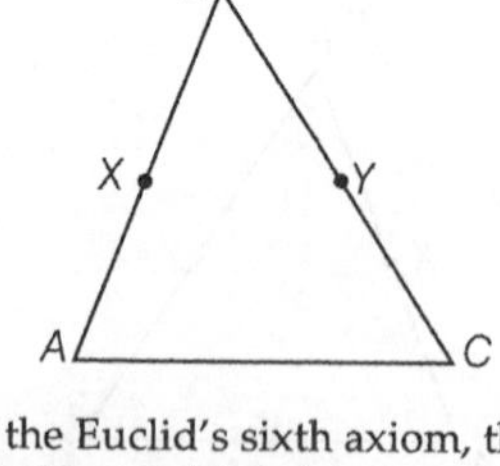

Thinking Process Apply the Euclid's sixth axiom, things which are double of the same thing are equal to one another, to show the given result

Ans. Given, $AB = BC$ ...(i)

$BX = \frac{1}{2} AB$ ...(ii)

$BY = \frac{1}{2} BC$ ...(iii)

According to Euclid's seventh axiom, things which are halves of the same thing are equal to one another.

$\Rightarrow$ $\frac{1}{2}AB = \frac{1}{2}BC$ [from Eq. (i)]

$\Rightarrow$ $BX = BY$ [from Eqs. (ii) and (iii)]

Q.7 In the given figure, we have $\angle 1 = \angle 2$ and $\angle 2 = \angle 3$.

Show that $\angle 1 = \angle 3$.

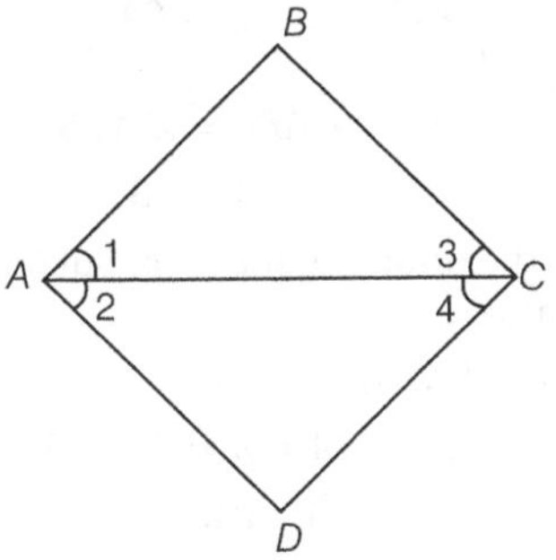

Ans. We have, $\angle 1 = \angle 2$ ...(i)

and $\angle 2 = \angle 3$ ...(ii)

According to Euclid's first axiom, things which are equal to the same thing are equal to one another.

From Eqs. (i) and (ii),

$$\angle 1 = \angle 3$$

Q.8 In the given figure, we have $\angle 1 = \angle 3$ and $\angle 2 = \angle 4$. Show that $\angle A = \angle C$.

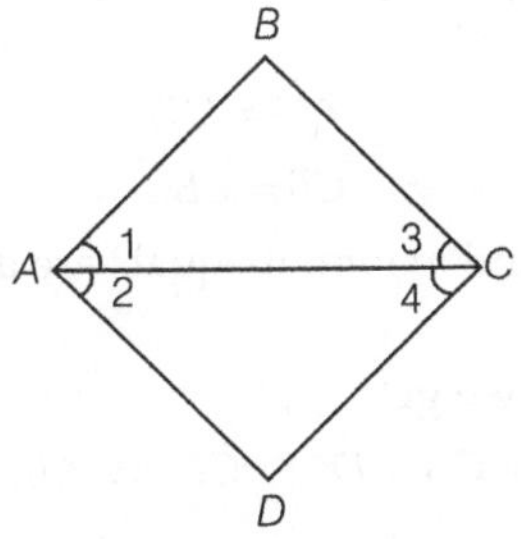

● **Concept Insight** If equals are added to equals, the wholes are equal.

Ans. Given, $\angle 1 = \angle 3$ ...(i)

And $\angle 2 = \angle 4$ ...(ii)

According to Euclid's second axiom, if equals are added to equals, the wholes are equal.

On adding Eqs. (i) and (ii), we get

$$\angle 1 + \angle 2 = \angle 3 + \angle 4$$

$\Rightarrow$ $\angle A = \angle C$

Q.9 In the given figure, we have $\angle ABC = \angle ACB$ and $\angle 3 = \angle 4$. Show that $\angle 1 = \angle 2$.

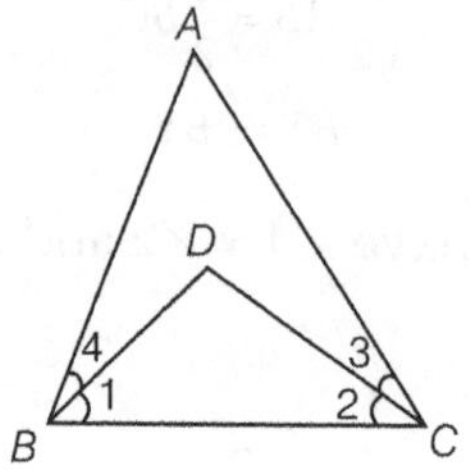

Ans. Given, $\angle ABC = \angle ACB$ ...(i)

and $\angle 4 = \angle 3$ ...(ii)

According to Eulid's third axiom, if equals are subtracted from equals, the remainders are also equal.

On subtracting Eq. (ii) from Eq. (i), we get

$$\angle ABC - \angle 4 = \angle ACB - \angle 3$$

$\Rightarrow$ $\angle 1 = \angle 2$

Mistake Alert! *Students may make the mistake of subtracting the same angle i.e., $\angle 4$ from both sides. Whereas we have to subtract $\angle 4$ from LHS and $\angle 3$ from RHS because $\angle 4 = \angle 3$.*

Q.10 In the figure, we have $AC = DC$ and $CB = CE$. Show that $AB = DE$.

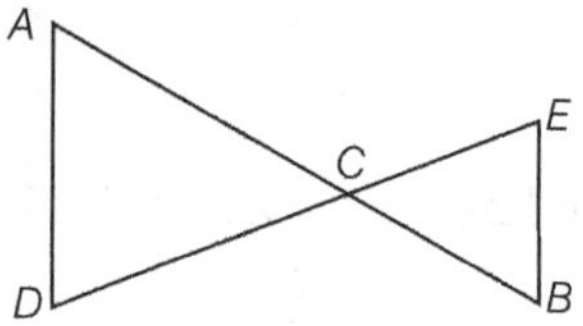

Ans. Given, $AC = DC$ ...(i)

and $CB = CE$ ...(ii)

According to Euclid's second axiom, if equals are added to equals, the wholes are equal.

On adding Eqs.(i) and (ii), we get

$$AC + CB = DC + CE \Rightarrow AB = DE$$

Q.11 In the given figure, if $OX = \frac{1}{2} XY$, $PX = \frac{1}{2} XZ$ and $OX = PX$, show that $XY = XZ$,

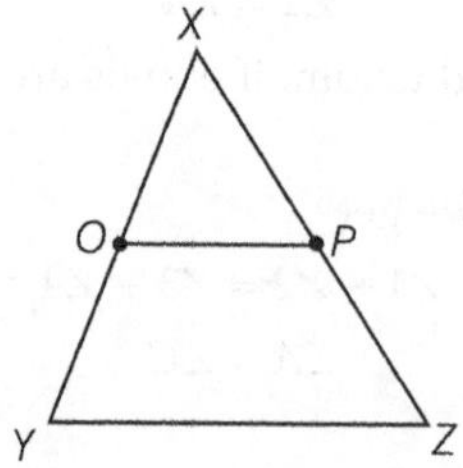

Ans. Given, $OX = \frac{1}{2}XY \Rightarrow 2OX = XY$ ...(i)

$PX = \frac{1}{2}XZ \Rightarrow 2PX = XZ$ ...(ii)

and $OX = PX$ ...(iii)

According to Euclid's sixth axiom, things which are double of the same thing are equal to one another.

$\Rightarrow$ $2OX = 2PX$ [from Eq. (ii)]

$\Rightarrow$ $XY = XZ$ [from Eqs. (i) and (ii)]

Q.12 In the given figure,

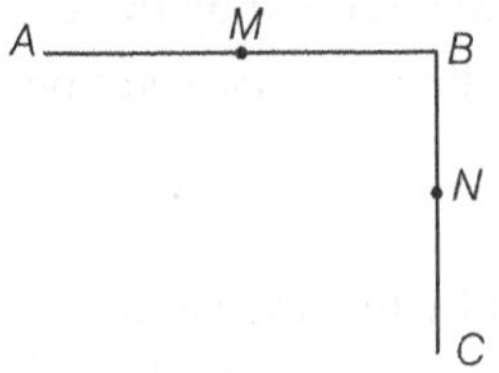

(i) $AB = BC$, M is the mid-point of AB and N is the mid-point of BC. Show that $AM = NC$.

(ii) $BM = BN$, M is the mid-point of AB and N is the mid-point of BC. Show that $AB = BC$.

Ans. (i) Given, $AB = BC$ ... (i)

M is the mid-point of AB.

$\therefore$ $AM = MB = \frac{1}{2}AB$ ...(ii)

and N is the mid-point of BC.

$\therefore$ $BN = NC = \frac{1}{2}BC$ ...(iii)

According to Euclid's axiom 7, things which are halves of the same things are equal to one another.

$\Rightarrow$ $\frac{1}{2}AB = \frac{1}{2}BC$ [from Eq. (i)]

$\Rightarrow$ $AM = NC$ [from Eqs. (ii) and (iii)]

(ii) Given, $BM = BN$ ... (i)

M is the mid-point of AB.

$\therefore$ $AM = BM = \frac{1}{2}AB$

$\Rightarrow$ $2AM = 2BM = AB$ ...(ii)

and N is the mid-point of BC.

$\therefore$ $BN = NC = \frac{1}{2}BC$

$\Rightarrow$ $2BN = 2NC = BC$ ...(iii)

According to Euclid's axiom 6, things which are double of the same thing are equal to one another.

$2BM = 2BN$ [from Eq. (i)]

$\Rightarrow$ $AB = BC$ [using Eqs. (ii) and (iii)]

Long Answer Type Questions

Q.1 Read the following statements

An equilateral triangle is a polygon made up of three line segments out of which two line segments are equal to the third-one and all its angles are 60° each.

Define the terms used in this definition which you feel necessary. Are there any undefined terms in this? Can you justify that all sides and all angles are equal in a equilateral triangle.

Ans. The terms need to be defined are

(i) **Polygon** A closed figure bounded by three or more line segments.

(ii) **Line segment** Part of a line with two end points.

(iii) **Line** Undefined term.

(iv) **Point** Undefined term.

(v) **Angle** A figure formed by two rays with one common initial point.

(vi) **Acute angle** Angle whose measure is between 0° to 90°.

Here, undefined terms are **line** and **point**.

All the angles of equilateral **triangle are 60°** each (given).

Two line segments are equal to the **third** one (given).

Therefore, all three sides of an equilateral triangle are equal, because, according to **Euclid's axiom**, things which are equal to the same thing are equal to one another.

Mistake Alert ! *Students may get confused between line and live regiment.*

***Q.2** Study the following statements

"Two intersecting lines cannot be perpendicular to the same line."
Check whether it is an equivalent version to the Euclid's fifth postulate.

Ans. Two equivalent versions of Euclid's fifth postulate are

(i) For every line l and for every point P not lying on l, there exists a unique line m passing through P and parallel to l.

(ii) Two distinct intersecting lines cannot be parallel to the same line.

From above two statements it is clear that given statement is not an equivalent version to the Euclid's fifth postulate.

Q.3 Read the following statements which are taken as axioms

(i) If a transversal intersects two parallel lines, then corresponding angles are not necessarily equal.

(ii) If a transversal intersect two parallel lines, then alternate interior angles are equal.

Is this system of axioms consistent ? Justify your answer.

Ans. A system of axiom is called consistent, if there is no statement which can be deduced from these axioms such that it contradicts any axiom. We know that, if a transversal intersects two parallel lines, then each pair of corresponding angles are equal, which is a theorem. So, statement (i) is false and not an axiom.

(✱) Topics related to these question have been removed from latest NCERT.

Also, we know that if a transversal intersects two parallel lines, then each pair of alternate interior angles are equal. It is also a theorem. So, statement (ii) is true and an axiom. Thus, in given statements, first is false and second is an axiom. Hence, given system of axioms is not consistent.

Q.4 Read the following two statements which are taken as axioms

(i) If two lines intersect each other, then the vertically opposite angles are not equal.

(ii) If a ray stands on a line, then the sum of two adjacent angles, so formed is equal to 180°.

Is this system of axioms consistent ? Justify your answer.

Ans. We know that if two lines intersect each other, then the vertically opposite angles are equal. It is a theorem. So, given statement (i) is false and not an axiom.

Also, we know that, if a ray stands on a line, then the sum of two adjacent angles so formed is equal to 180°. It is an axiom. So, given statement (ii) is true and an axiom. Thus, in given statements, first is false and second is an axiom. Hence, given system of axioms is not consistent.

Q.5 Read the following axioms

(i) Things which are equal to the same thing are equal to one another.

(ii) If equals are added to equals, the wholes are equal.

(iii) Things which are double of the same things are equal to one another.

Check whether the given system of axioms is consistent or inconsistent.

Thinking Process To check the given system is consistent or inconsistent, we have to find that whether we can deduce a statement from these axioms which contradicts any axiom or not.

Ans. Some of Euclid's axioms are

(i) Things which are equal to the same thing are equal to one another.

(ii) If equals are added to equals, the wholes are equal.

(iii) Things which are double of the same thing are equal to one another.

Thus, given three axioms are Euclid's axioms. So, here we cannot deduce any statement from these axioms which contradicts any axiom. So, given system of axioms is consistent.

Chapter

06 Lines and Angles

Multiple Choice Questions (MCQs)

Choose the correct answer from the given four options in the following questions:

Q.1 In figure, if $AB \parallel CD \parallel EF$, $PQ \parallel RS$, $\angle RQD = 25°$ and $\angle CQP = 60°$, then $\angle QRS$ is equal to

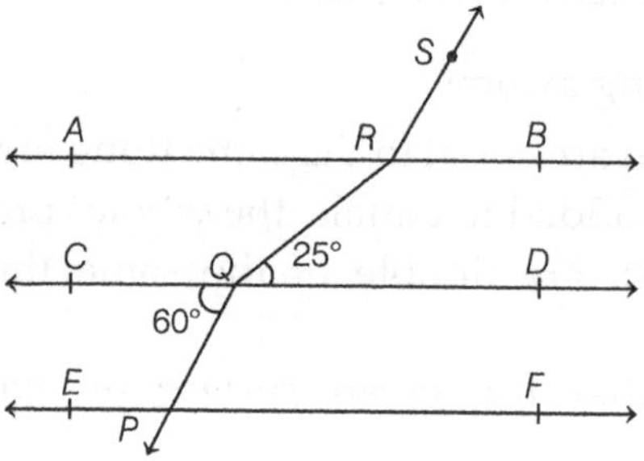

(a) 85° (b) 135° (c) 145° (d) 110°

● **Concept Insight** If a ray stands on a line, then the sum of the two adjacent angles, so formed is 180°.

Ans. ***(c)*** Produced PQ to X which intersect AB at Y.

$\therefore$ $$PQ \parallel RS \Rightarrow PX \parallel RS$$

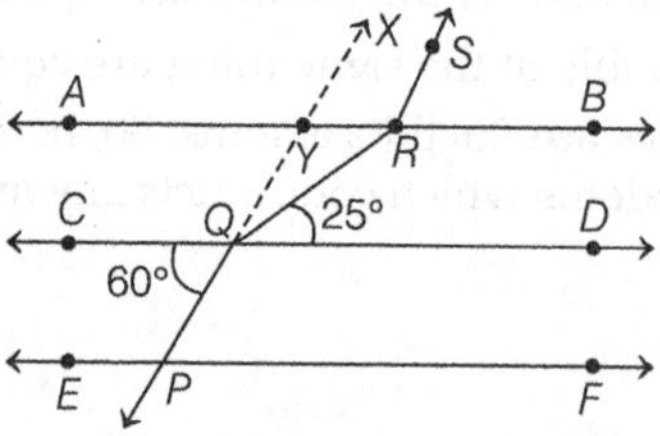

$\because$ $AB \parallel CD$ and PX is transversal

$$\angle CQP + \angle AYX = 180°$$ [Co-exterior angles]

$\Rightarrow$ $$60° + \angle AYX = 180°$$

$\Rightarrow$ $$\angle AYX = 120°$$

$\because$ $PX \parallel RS$ and AB is transversal

$\therefore$ $$\angle YRS = \angle AYX$$ [Corresponding angles]

$\Rightarrow$ $$\angle YRS = 120°$$ ...(i)

and $AB \parallel CD$ and RQ is tranversal

$\therefore \quad \angle YRQ = \angle RQD$ [Alternate interior angles]

$\Rightarrow \quad \angle YRQ = 25^\circ$ ...(ii)

Now, $\angle SRQ = \angle SRY + \angle YRQ$

$\Rightarrow \quad \angle SRQ = 120^\circ + 25^\circ$ [From (i) and (ii)]

$\Rightarrow \quad \angle SRQ = 145^\circ$

***Q.2** If one angle of a triangle is equal to the sum of the other two angles, then the triangle is

(a) an isosceles triangle (b) an obtuse triangle

(c) an equilateral triangle (d) a right triangle

Ans. *(d)* Let the angles of a ΔABC be $\angle A$, $\angle B$ and $\angle C$.

Given, $\angle A = \angle B + \angle C$ ...(i)

In ΔABC, $\angle A + \angle B + \angle C = 180^\circ$

[$\because$ sum of all interior angles of a triangle is 180°] ...(ii)

From Eqs. (i) and (ii),

$$\angle A + \angle A = 180^\circ$$

$$\Rightarrow \quad 2\angle A = 180^\circ$$

$$\Rightarrow \quad \angle A = \frac{180^\circ}{2}$$

$$\therefore \quad \angle A = 90^\circ$$

Hence, the triangle is a right triangle.

***Q.3** An exterior angle of a triangle is 105° and its two interior opposite angles are equal. Each of these equal angles is

(a) $37\frac{1}{2}^\circ$ (b) $52\frac{1}{2}^\circ$ (c) $72\frac{1}{2}^\circ$ (d) 75°

Ans. *(b)* Let one of interior opposite angle of a triangle be x.

$\because$ Sum of two opposite interior angles = Exterior angle

$\therefore \quad x + x = 105^\circ$ [$\because$ exterior angle = 105° (given)]

$\Rightarrow \quad 2x = 105^\circ$

$\therefore \quad x = \frac{105^\circ}{2} \Rightarrow x = 52\frac{1}{2}^\circ$

Hence, each of the interior opposite angle of a triangle is $52\frac{1}{2}^\circ$.

***Q.4** The angles of a triangle are in the ratio 5 : 3 : 7. The triangle is

(a) an acute angled triangle (b) an obtuse angled triangle

(c) a right triangle (d) an isosceles triangle

- **Concept Insight** If all angles of a triangle are less then 90°, then it is an acute angled triangle, if one of the angles of a triangle is greater than 90°, then it is an obtuse angled triangle and if one of the angles of a triangle is 90°, then it is a right angled triangle.

Ans. *(a)* Given, the ratio of angles of a triangle is 5 : 3 : 7.

Let angles of a triangle be $\angle A$, $\angle B$ and $\angle C$.

(*) Topics related to these question have been removed from latest NCERT.

Then, $\angle A = 5x, \angle B = 3x$ and $\angle C = 7x$

In ΔABC, $\angle A + \angle B + \angle C = 180°$

[since, sum of all interior angles of a triangle is 180°]

$\therefore$ $5x + 3x + 7x = 180°$

$\Rightarrow$ $15x = 180° \Rightarrow x = \frac{180°}{15} = 12°$

$\therefore$ $\angle A = 5x = 5 \times 12° = 60°$

$\angle B = 3x = 3 \times 12° = 36°$

and $\angle C = 7x = 7 \times 12° = 84°$

Since, all angles are less than 90°. Hence, the triangle is an acute angled triangle.

***Q.5** If one of the angles of a triangle is 130°, then the angle between the bisectors of the other two angles can be

(a) 50° (b) 65° (c) 145° (d) 155°

Ans. ***(d)*** Let the angles of a triangle be $\angle A$, $\angle B$ and $\angle C$.

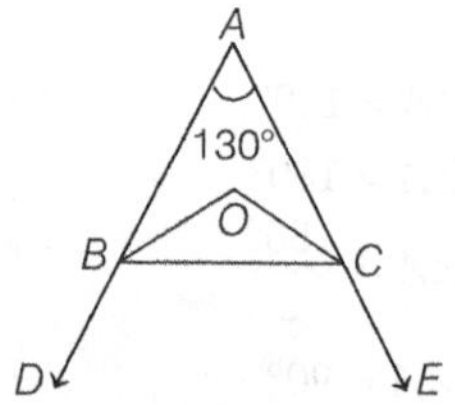

In ΔABC,

$$\angle A + \angle B + \angle C = 180°$$

[sum of all interior angles of a triangle is 180°]

$\Rightarrow$ $\frac{1}{2}\angle A + \frac{1}{2}\angle B + \frac{1}{2}\angle C = \frac{180°}{2} = 90°$ [dividing both sides by 2]

$\Rightarrow$ $\frac{1}{2}\angle B + \frac{1}{2}\angle C = 90° - \frac{1}{2}\angle A$ ...(i)

Now, in ΔOBC,

$$\angle OBC + \angle BCO + \angle COB = 180°$$

$\Rightarrow$ $\frac{\angle B}{2} + \frac{\angle C}{2} + \angle BOC = 180°$ [$\because$ BO and OC are the angle bisectors of $\angle ABC$ and $\angle BCA$, respectively]

$\Rightarrow$ $\frac{\angle B}{2} + \frac{\angle C}{2} = 180° - \angle BOC$

From Eqs. (i) and (ii), we get

$$180° - \angle BOC = 90° - \frac{1}{2}\angle A$$

$\therefore$ $\angle BOC = 180° - 90° + \frac{1}{2}\angle A = 90° + \frac{1}{2}\angle A$

$= 90° + \frac{1}{2} \times 130° = 90° + 65°$ [$\because \angle A = 130°$(given)]

$= 155°$

Hence, the required angle is 155°.

Q.6 In the figure, POQ is a line. The value of x is

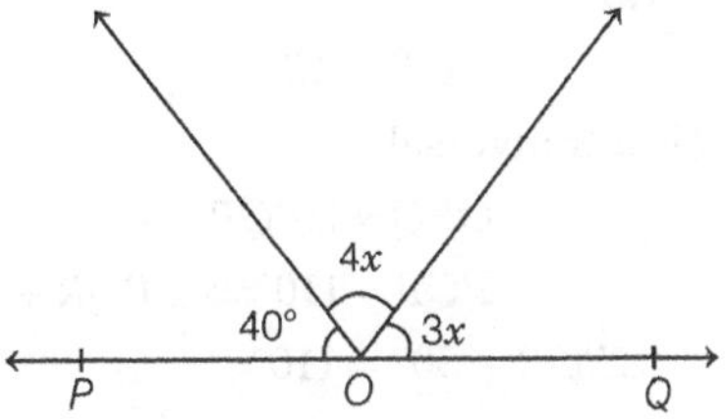

(a) 20° (b) 25° (c) 30° (d) 35°

Thinking Process When two or more rays are initiated from a same point of a line, then the sum of all angles made between the rays and line at the same point is 180°.

Ans. *(a)* The given figure is

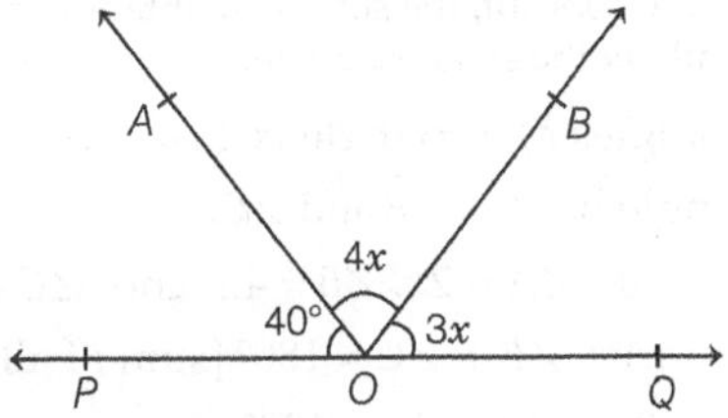

Since, POQ is a line segment.

$\therefore \quad \angle POQ = 180°$

$\Rightarrow \quad \angle POA + \angle AOB + \angle BOQ = 180°$

$\Rightarrow \quad 40° + 4x + 3x = 180°$ [put $\angle POA = 40°$, $\angle AOB = 4x$ and $\angle BOQ = 3x$]

$\Rightarrow \quad 7x = 180° - 40° \Rightarrow 7x = 140°$

$\Rightarrow \quad x = \frac{140°}{7} \Rightarrow x = 20°$

Q.7 In the figure, if $OP \parallel RS$, $\angle OPQ = 110°$ and $\angle QRS = 130°$, then $\angle PQR$ is equal to

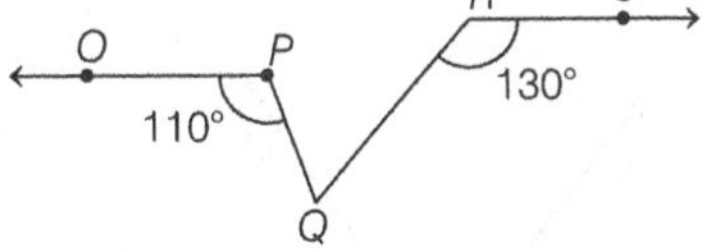

(a) 40° (b) 50° (c) 60° (d) 70°

Ans. *(c)* In the given figure, we draw a line AB parallel to RS thought point Q.

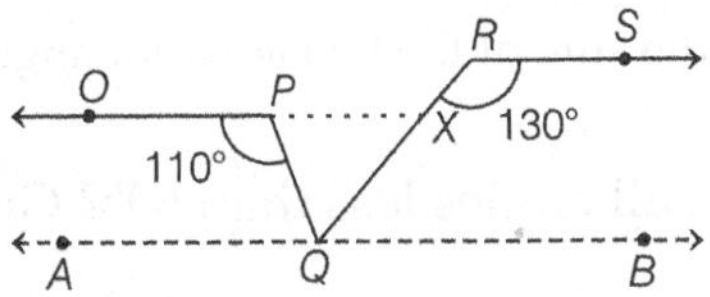

Since, $AB \parallel RS$ and RQ is a transversal.

$\therefore \quad \angle SRQ + \angle RQB = 180°$ [co-interior angles]

$\Rightarrow$ $130° + \angle RQB = 180° \Rightarrow \angle RQB = 180° - 130° = 50°$ ...(i)

Now, $AB \parallel RS$ and $OP \parallel RS$,

$\therefore$ $OP \parallel AB$

Since, $OP \parallel AB$ and PQ is a tranversal.

$\therefore$ $\angle OPQ = \angle PQB$ [alternate interior angles]

$\Rightarrow$ $\angle PQB = 110° \Rightarrow \angle PQR + \angle RQB = 110°$

$\Rightarrow$ $\angle PQR + 50° = 110°$ [from Eq. (i)]

$\Rightarrow$ $\angle PQR = 60°$

***Q.8** Angles of a triangle are in the ratio 2 : 4 : 3. The smallest angle of the triangle is

(a) 60° (b) 40° (c) 80° (d) 20°

Thinking Process Use the concept, the sum of all interior angles in a triangle is 180°. Further, simplify it and get the smallest angle.

Ans. *(b)* Given, the ratio of angles of a triangle is 2 : 4 : 3.

Let the angles of a triangle be $\angle A$, $\angle B$ and $\angle C$.

$\therefore$ $\angle A = 2x$, $\angle B = 4x$ and $\angle C = 3x$

In ΔABC, $\angle A + \angle B + \angle C = 180°$ [sum of all angles of a triangle is 180°]

$\Rightarrow$ $2x + 4x + 3x = 180°$

$\Rightarrow$ $9x = 180° \Rightarrow x = \frac{180°}{9} = 20°$

$\therefore$ $\angle A = 2x = 2 \times 20° = 40°$

$\angle B = 4x = 4 \times 20° = 80°$

And $\angle C = 3x = 3 \times 20° = 60°$

Hence, the smallest angle of a triangle is 40°.

Short Answer Questions with Reasoning

Q.1 For what value of $x + y$ in figure will ABC be a line? Justify your answer.

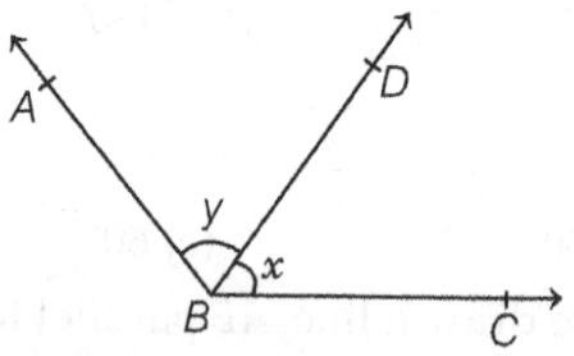

Ans. For ABC to be a line, the sum of the two adjacent angles must be 180° *i.e.*, $x + y = 180°$.

***Q.2** Can a triangle have all angles less than 60°? Give reason for your answer.

Ans. No, a triangle cannot have all angles less than 60°, because if all angles will be less than 60°, then their sum will not be equal to 180°. Hence, it will not be a triangle.

(*) Topics related to these question have been removed from latest NCERT.

***Q.3** Can a triangle have two obtuse angles? Give reason for your answer.

Ans. *No,* because if the triangle have two obtuse angles *i.e.,* more than 90° angle, then the sum of all three angles of a triangle will not be equal to 180°.

***Q.4** How many triangles can be drawn having its angles as 45°, 64° and 72°? Give reason for your answer.

Ans. None, the sum of given angles $= 45° + 64° + 72° = 181° \neq 180°$.

Hence, we see that sum of all three angles is not equal to 180°. So, no triangle can be drawn with the given angles.

***Q.5** How many triangles can be drawn having its angles as 53°, 64° and 63°? Give reason for your answer.

Ans. Infinitely many triangles,

The sum of given angles $= 53° + 64° + 63° = 180°$

Here, we see that sum of all interior angles of triangle is 180°. So, infinitely many triangles can be drawn.

Q.6 In the figure, find the value of x for which the lines l and m are parallel.

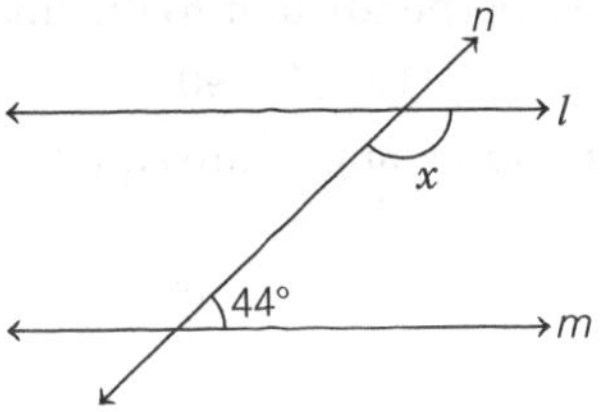

Ans. Let, $l \parallel m$ and we know that if a transversal intersects two parallel lines, then sum of interior angles on the same side of a transversal is supplementary.

$\therefore \quad x + 44° = 180°$ [Co-interior angles]

$\Rightarrow \quad x = 180° - 44° \Rightarrow x = 136°$

Q.7 Two adjacent angles are equal. Is it necessary that each of these angles will be a right angle? Justify your answer.

Ans. *No,* because each of two adjacent angles will be a right angle only when they form a linear pair.

Q.8 If one of the angles formed by two intersecting lines is a right angle, what can you say about the other three angles? Give reason for your answer.

Ans. Let two intersecting lines l and m make a right angle, then it means that lines l and m are perpendicular to each other. By using linear pair axiom, other three angles will be right angles.

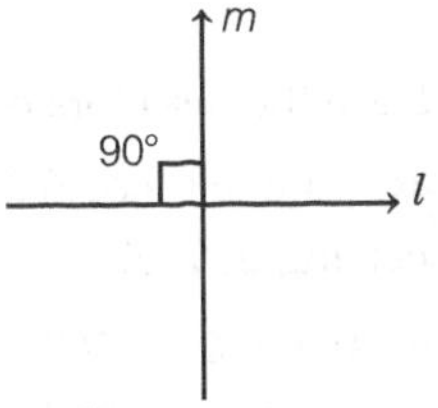

(*) Topics related to these question have been removed from latest NCERT.

Q.9 In the figure, which of the two lines are parallel and why?

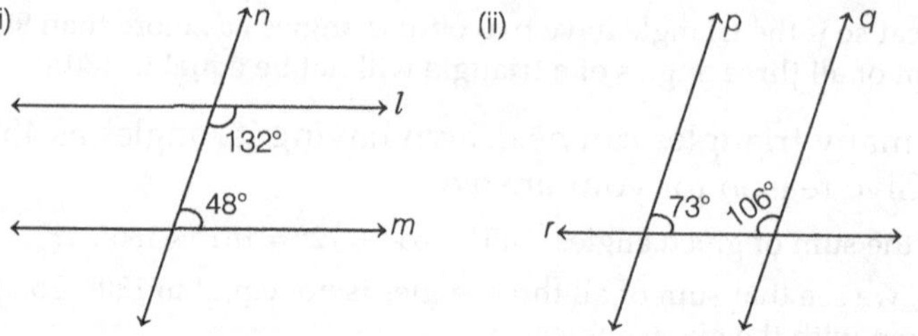

Ans. In Fig. (i) sum of two interior angles 132° + 48° = 180° because the sum of two interior angles on the same side of a transversal line *n* is 180°. Thus, they are the parallel lines.

In Fig. (ii), the sum of two interior angles 73° + 106° = 179° ≠ 180° because the sum of two interior angles on the same side of a transversal line *r* is not equal to 180°. Thus, they are not the parallel lines.

Q.10 Two lines *l* and *m* are perpendicular to the same line *n*. Are *l* and *m* perpendicular to each other? Give reason for your answer.

Ans. No, since, lines *l* and *m* are perpendicular to the line *n*.

$\therefore$ $$\angle 1 = \angle 2 = 90°$$

It implies that the corresponding angles are equal.

Hence, $l \parallel m$.

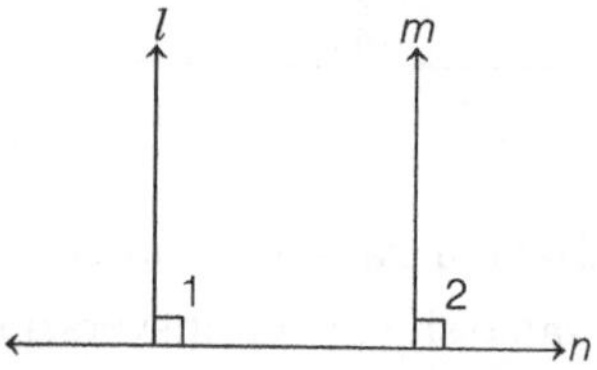

Short Answer Type Questions

Q.1 In the figure, *OD* is the bisector of $\angle AOC$, *OE* is the bisector of $\angle BOC$ and $OD \perp OE$. Show that the points *A*, *O* and *B* are collinear.

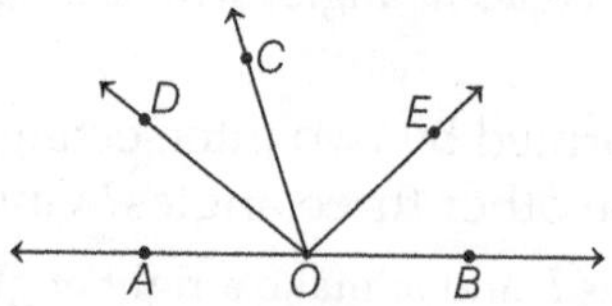

Thinking Process For showing collinearity of *A*, *O* and *B*, we have to show that $\angle AOB = 180°$.

Ans. **Given,** $OD \perp OE$, *OD* and *OE* are the bisectors of $\angle AOC$ and $\angle BOC$, respectively.

To prove Points *A*, *O* and *B* are collinear *i.e.*, *AOB* is a straight line.

Proof Since, *OD* and *OE* bisect angles $\angle AOC$ and $\angle BOC$, respectively.

$\therefore$ $$\angle AOC = 2\angle DOC \quad \text{...(i)}$$

and $$\angle COB = 2\angle COE \quad \text{...(ii)}$$

On adding Eqs. (i) and (ii), we get

$$\angle AOC + \angle COB = 2\angle DOC + 2\angle COE$$

$\Rightarrow$ $$\angle AOC + \angle COB = 2(\angle DOC + \angle COE)$$

$\Rightarrow$ $$\angle AOC + \angle COB = 2\angle DOE$$

$\Rightarrow$ $$\angle AOC + \angle COB = 2 \times 90^\circ \quad [\because OD \perp OE]$$

$\Rightarrow$ $$\angle AOC + \angle COB = 180^\circ$$

$\therefore$ $$\angle AOB = 180^\circ$$

So, $\angle AOC$ and $\angle COB$ form a linear pair.

$\therefore$ AOB is a straight line.

Hence, points A, O and B are collinear. **Hence proved.**

Q.2 In the figure, $\angle 1 = 60^\circ$ and $\angle 6 = 120^\circ$. Show that the lines m and n are parallel.

- **Concept Insight** If the sum of two interior angles on the same side of a transversal is 180°, then the lines are parallel.

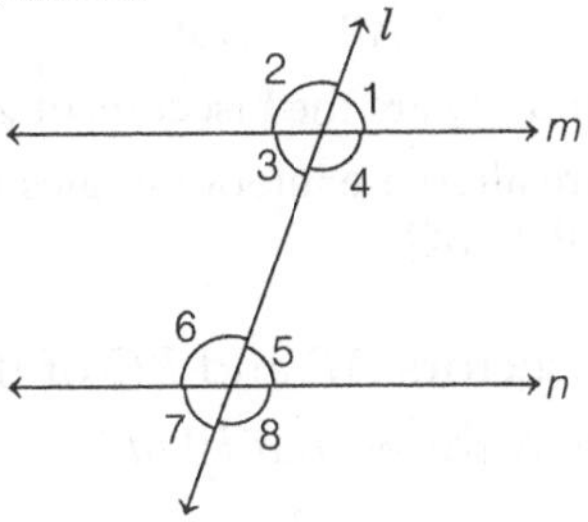

Ans. **Given,** $\angle 1 = 60^\circ$ and $\angle 6 = 120^\circ$

To prove $m \parallel n$

Proof Since, $\angle 1 = 60^\circ$ and $\angle 6 = 120^\circ$

Here, $\angle 1 = \angle 3$ [vertically opposite angles]

$\therefore$ $\angle 3 = \angle 1 = 60^\circ$

Now, $\angle 3 + \angle 6 = 60^\circ + 120^\circ$

$\Rightarrow$ $\angle 3 + \angle 6 = 180^\circ$

We know that if the sum of two interior angles on same side of l is 180°, then lines are parallel. Hence, $m \parallel n$. **Hence proved.**

Q.3 AP and BQ are the bisectors of the two alternate interior angles formed by the intersection of a transversal t with parallel lines l and m (in the given figure). Show that $AP \parallel BQ$.

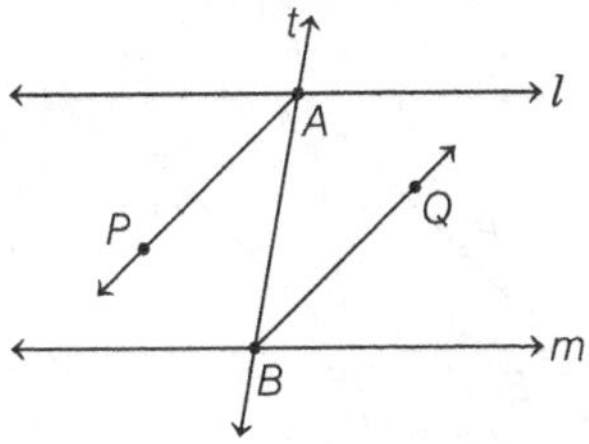

- **Concept Insight** If alternate interior angles are equal, then the lines are parallel.

Ans. **Given** In the figure, $l \parallel m$, AP and BQ are the bisectors of $\angle EAB$ and $\angle ABH$, respectively.

To prove $AP \parallel BQ$

Proof Since, $l \parallel m$ and t is a transversal.

Therefore, $\angle EAB = \angle ABH$ [alternate interior angles]

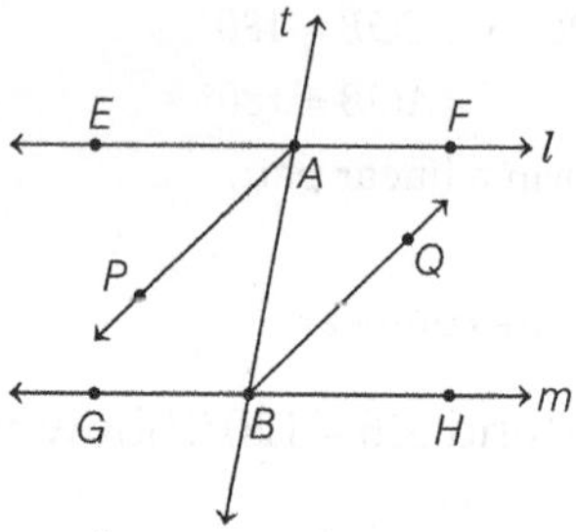

$\Rightarrow$ $\frac{1}{2}\angle EAB = \frac{1}{2}\angle ABH$ [on dividing both sides by 2]

$\Rightarrow$ $\angle PAB = \angle ABQ$

[AP and BQ are the bisectors of $\angle EAB$ and $\angle ABH$, respectively.]

Since, $\angle PAB$ and $\angle ABQ$ are alternate interior angles formed by lines AP, BQ and transversal AB. Hence, $AP \parallel BQ$. **Hence proved.**

Q.4 In the given figure, bisectors AP and BQ of the alternate interior angles are parallel, then show that $l \parallel m$.

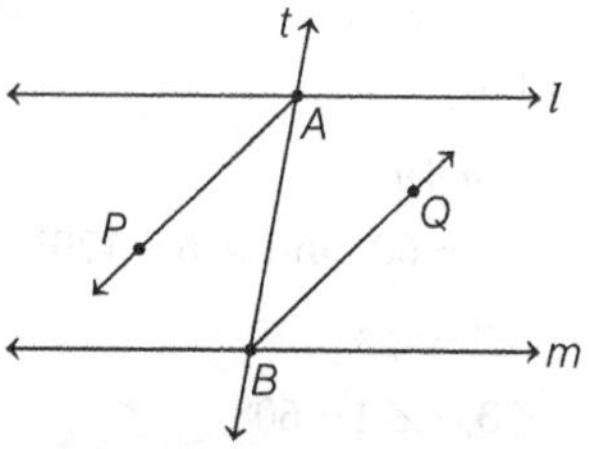

Ans. **Given,** In the figure $AP \parallel BQ$, AP and BQ are the bisectors of alternate interior angles $\angle CAB$ and $\angle ABF$.

To prove $l \parallel m$

Proof Since, $AP \parallel BQ$ and t is a transversal, therefore $\angle PAB = \angle ABQ$

[alternate interior angles]

$\Rightarrow$ $2\angle PAB = 2\angle ABQ$ [on multiplying both sides by 2]

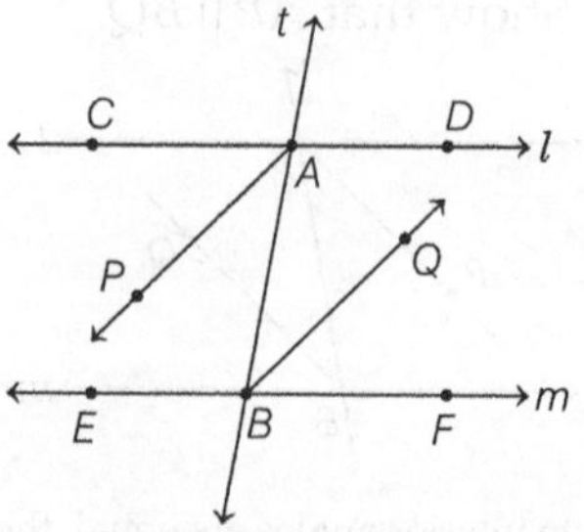

$\Rightarrow \quad \angle CAB = \angle ABF$

[$\because$ AP and BQ are the bisectors of $\angle CAB$ and $\angle ABF$, respectively]

So, alternate interior angles are equal.

We know that if two alternate interior angles are equal, then lines are parallel.

Hence, $l \parallel m$. **Hence proved.**

Q.5 In the figure, $BA \parallel ED$ and $BC \parallel EF$. Show that $\angle ABC = \angle DEF$.

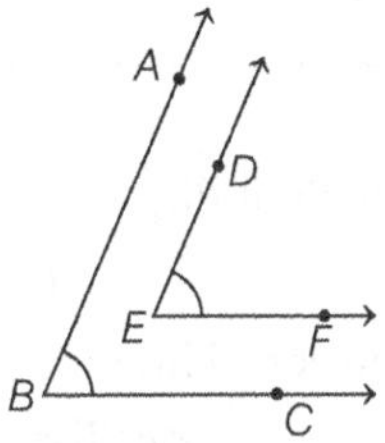

Ans. Given $BA \parallel ED$ and $BC \parallel EF$.

To prove $\angle ABC = \angle DEF$.

Construction Extend the line DE to the point P.

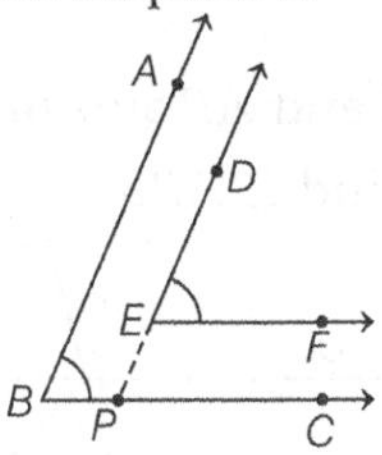

Proof In the figure, $BA \parallel ED$ or $BA \parallel DP$.

$\therefore \quad \angle ABP = \angle EPC$ [corresponding angles]

$\Rightarrow \quad \angle ABC = \angle EPC$ [Common angle] ...(i)

Again, $\quad BC \parallel EF$ or $PC \parallel EF$

$\therefore \quad \angle DEF = \angle EPC$ [corresponding angles] ...(ii)

From Eqs. (i) and (ii), we get

$$\angle ABC = \angle DEF$$

Q.6 In the figure, $BA \parallel ED$ and $BC \parallel EF$. Show that $\angle ABC + \angle DEF = 180°$.

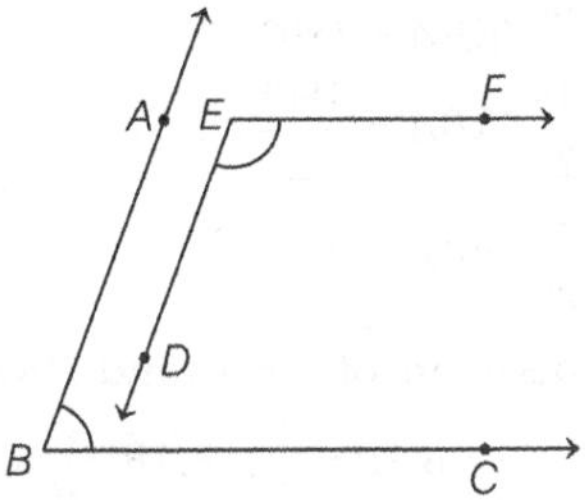

- **Concept Insight** It two parallel lines are cut by a transversal. Then, the sum of co-interior angles is 180°.

Ans. Given $BA \parallel ED$ and $BC \parallel EF$.

To prove $\angle ABC + \angle DEF = 180°$.

Construction Draw a ray PE opposite to ray EF.

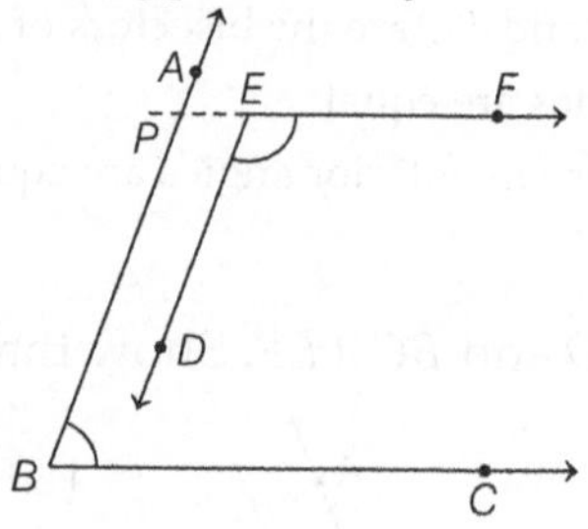

Proof In the figure, $BC \parallel EF$ or $BC \parallel PF$

$\therefore \angle EPB + \angle PBC = 180°$ [sum of co-interior angles is 180°] ...(i)

Now, $AB \parallel ED$ and PE is a transversal line.

$\therefore$ $\angle EPB = \angle DEF$ [corresponding angles] ...(ii)

From Eqs. (i) and (ii), we get $\angle DEF + \angle PBC = 180°$

$\Rightarrow$ $\angle ABC + \angle DEF = 180°$ [$\because \angle PBC = \angle ABC$]

Hence proved.

Q.7 In the figure, $DE \parallel QR$ and AP and BP are bisectors of $\angle EAB$ and $\angle RBA$, respectively. Find $\angle APB$.

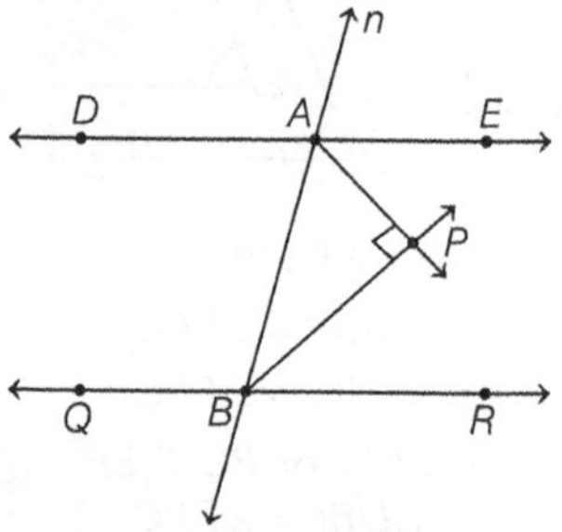

Ans. Given, $DE \parallel QR$ and AP and PB are the bisectors of $\angle EAB$ and $\angle RBA$, respectively.

We know that the interior angles on the same side of a transversal are supplementary.

$\therefore$ $\angle EAB + \angle RBA = 180°$ [co-interior angles]

$\Rightarrow$ $\frac{1}{2}\angle EAB + \frac{1}{2}\angle RBA = \frac{180°}{2}$ [on dividing both sides by 2]

$\Rightarrow$ $\frac{1}{2}\angle EAB + \frac{1}{2}\angle RBA = 90°$ ...(i)

Since, AP and BP are the bisectors of $\angle EAB$ and $\angle RBA$, respectively.

$\therefore$ $\angle BAP = \frac{1}{2}\angle EAB$ ...(ii)

and $\angle ABP = \frac{1}{2}\angle RBA$ ...(iii)

On adding Eqs. (ii) and (iii), we get

$$\angle BAP + \angle ABP = \frac{1}{2}\angle EAB + \frac{1}{2}\angle RBA$$

$\Rightarrow$ $\angle BAP + \angle ABP = 90°$ [from Eq. (i)] ...(iv)

In ΔAPB, $\angle BAP + \angle ABP + \angle APB = 180°$ [$\because$ sum of all angles of a triangle is 180°]

$\Rightarrow$ $90° + \angle APB = 180°$ [from Eq. (iv)]

$\Rightarrow$ $\angle APB = 180° - 90° = 90°$

***Q.8** The angle of a triangle are in the ratio 2 : 3 : 4 Find the angles of the triangle.

● **Concept Insight** The sum of all angles of a triangle is 180°.

Ans. Let the angles of the triangle are $2x, 3x$ and $4x$.

Thus, $2x + 3x + 4x = 180°$

$\Rightarrow$ $9x = 180°$

$\Rightarrow$ $x = 20°$

So, the angles are

$2x = 2 \times 20° = 40°$

$3x = 3 \times 20° = 60°$

and $4x = 4 \times 20° = 80°$

Hence, the angles of a triangle are 40°, 60° and 80°.

***Q.9** A ΔABC is right angled at A. L is a point on BC such that $AL \perp BC$. Prove that $\angle BAL = \angle ACB$.

Ans. **Given** In ΔABC, $\angle A = 90°$ and $AL \perp BC$

To prove $\angle BAL = \angle ACB$

Proof In ΔABC and ΔLAB, $\angle BAC = \angle ALB$ [each 90°] ...(i)

and $\angle ABC = \angle ABL$ [common angle] ...(ii)

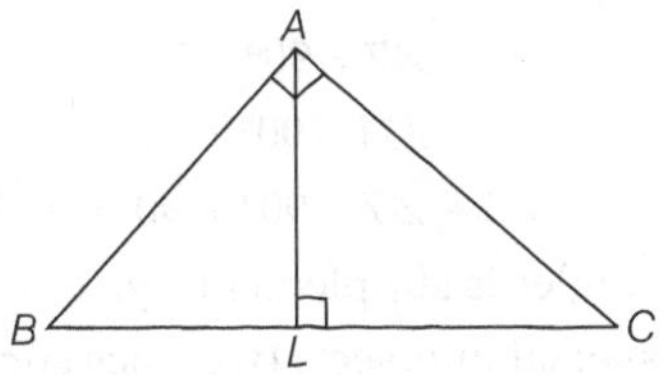

On adding Eqs. (i) and (ii), we get

$$\angle BAC + \angle ABC = \angle ALB + \angle ABL \quad ...(iii)$$

Again, in ΔABC,

$\angle BAC + \angle ACB + \angle ABC = 180°$ [$\because$ sum of all angles of a triangle is 180°]

$\Rightarrow$ $\angle BAC + \angle ABC = 180 - \angle ACB$ ...(iv)

(✱) Topics related to these question have been removed from latest NCERT.

In ΔABL,

$$\angle ABL + \angle ALB + \angle BAL = 180^\circ \quad [\because \text{sum of all angles of a triangle is } 180^\circ]$$

$$\Rightarrow \quad \angle ABL + \angle ALB = 180^\circ - \angle BAL \quad \text{...(v)}$$

On substituting the value from Eqs. (iv) and (v) in Eq. (iii), we get

$$180^\circ - \angle ACB = 180^\circ - \angle BAL$$

$$\Rightarrow \quad \angle ACB = \angle BAL$$

Hence proved.

Q.10 Two lines are respectively perpendicular to two parallel lines. Show that they are parallel to each other.

Ans. **Given** Two lines m and n are parallel and another two lines p and q are respectively perpendicular to m and n.

i.e., $p \perp m,\ p \perp n,\ q \perp m,\ q \perp n$

To prove $p \parallel q$

Proof Since, $m \parallel n$ and p is perpendicular to m and n.

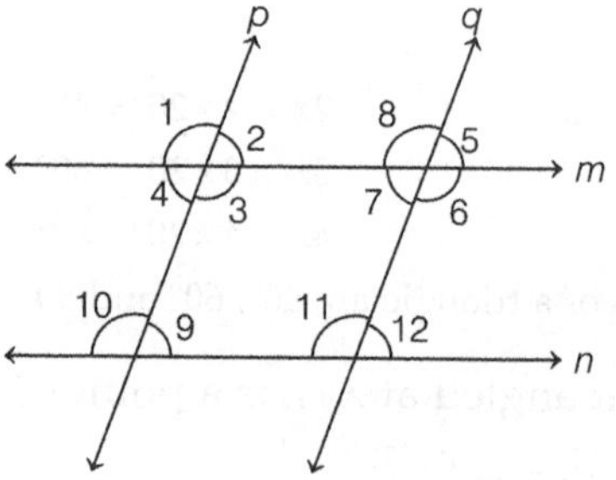

$\therefore$ $\angle 1 = \angle 10 = 90^\circ$ [corresponding angles]

Similarly, $\angle 2 = \angle 9 = 90^\circ$ [corresponding angles]

[$\because p \perp m$ and $p \perp n$]

$\therefore$ $\angle 4 = \angle 9 = 90^\circ$ and $\angle 3 = \angle 10 = 90^\circ$ [alternate interior angles]

Similarly, if $m \parallel n$ and q is perpendicular to m and n.

Then, $\angle 7 = 90^\circ$

and $\angle 11 = 90^\circ$

Now, $\angle 3 + \angle 7 = 90^\circ + 90^\circ = 180^\circ$

So, sum of two interior angles is supplementary.

We know that, if a transversal intersects two lines such that a pair of interior angles on the same side of the transversal is supplementary, then the two lines are parallel.

Hence, $p \parallel q$.

Long Answer Type Questions

Q.1 If two lines intersect, prove that the vertically opposite angles are equal.

Ans. Given Two lines AB and CD intersect at point O.

To prove

(i) $\angle AOC = \angle BOD$

(ii) $\angle AOD = \angle BOC$

Proof

(i) Since, ray OA stands on line CD.

$\therefore \quad \angle AOC + \angle AOD = 180°$ [linear pair axiom]...(i)

Since, ray OD stands on line AB.

$\therefore \quad \angle AOD + \angle BOD = 180°$ [linear pair axiom]...(ii)

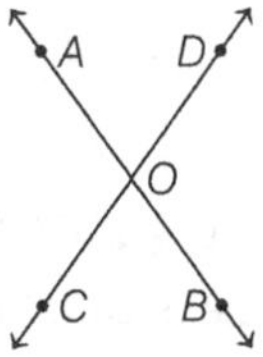

From Eqs. (i) and (ii), we get

$$\angle AOC + \angle AOD = \angle AOD + \angle BOD$$

$$\Rightarrow \quad \angle AOC = \angle BOD$$

(ii) Since, ray OD stands on line AB.

$\therefore \quad \angle AOD + \angle BOD = 180°$ [linear pair axiom] ...(iii)

Since, ray OB stands on line CD.

$\therefore \quad \angle DOB + \angle BOC = 180°$ ...(iv)

From Eqs. (iii) and (iv), we get

$$\angle AOD + \angle BOD = \angle DOB + \angle BOC$$

$$\Rightarrow \quad \angle AOD = \angle BOC$$

Hence, vertically opposite angles are equal. **Hence proved.**

***Q.2** Bisectors of interior $\angle B$ and exterior $\angle ACD$ of a ΔABC intersect at the point T. Prove that $\angle BTC = \frac{1}{2} \angle BAC$.

Thinking Process For obtaining the required result, use the property that the exterior angle of a triangle is equal to the sum of the two opposite angles of triangle.

Ans. Given In ΔABC, produce BC to D and the bisectors of $\angle ABC$ and $\angle ACD$ meet at point T.

To prove $\angle BTC = \frac{1}{2} \angle BAC$

(*) Topics related to these question have been removed from latest NCERT.

Proof

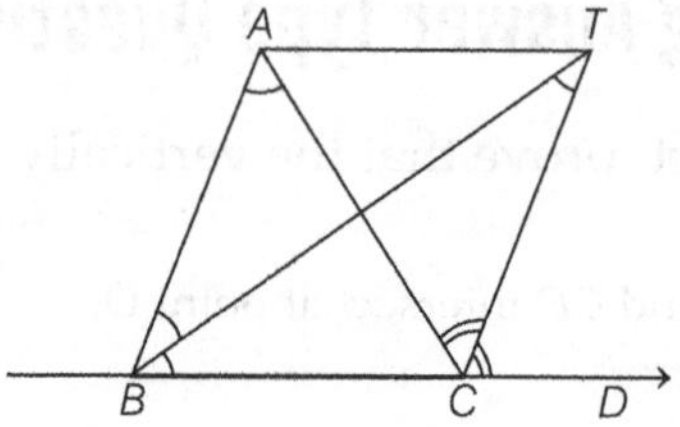

In ΔABC,

$$\angle ACD = \angle ABC + \angle CAB$$

[$\because$ exterior angle of a triangle is equal to the sum of two opposite angles]

$$\Rightarrow \quad \frac{1}{2}\angle ACD = \frac{1}{2}\angle CAB + \frac{1}{2}\angle ABC \text{ [on dividing both sides by 2]}$$

$$\Rightarrow \quad \angle TCD = \frac{1}{2}\angle CAB + \frac{1}{2}\angle ABC \quad \text{...(i)}$$

[$\because$ CT is a bisector of $\angle ACD \Rightarrow \frac{1}{2}\angle ACD = \angle TCD$]

In ΔBTC,

$$\angle TCD = \angle BTC + \angle CBT$$

[$\because$ exterior angle of a triangle is equal to the sum of two opposite interior angles]

$$\Rightarrow \quad \angle TCD = \angle BTC + \frac{1}{2}\angle ABC \quad \text{...(ii)}$$

[$\because$ BT is a bisector of $\angle ABC \Rightarrow \angle CBT = \frac{1}{2}\angle ABC$]

From Eqs. (i) and (ii), we get

$$\frac{1}{2}\angle CAB + \frac{1}{2}\angle ABC = \angle BTC + \frac{1}{2}\angle ABC$$

$$\Rightarrow \quad \angle BTC = \frac{1}{2}\angle CAB$$

$$\Rightarrow \quad \angle BTC = \frac{1}{2}\angle BAC$$

Hence proved.

Q.3 A transversal intersects two parallel lines. Prove that the bisectors of any pair of corresponding angles so formed are parallel.

Ans. **Given** Two lines AB and CD are parallel and intersected by transversal t at P and Q, respectively. Also, EP and FQ are the bisectors of angles $\angle APG$ and $\angle CQP$, respectively.

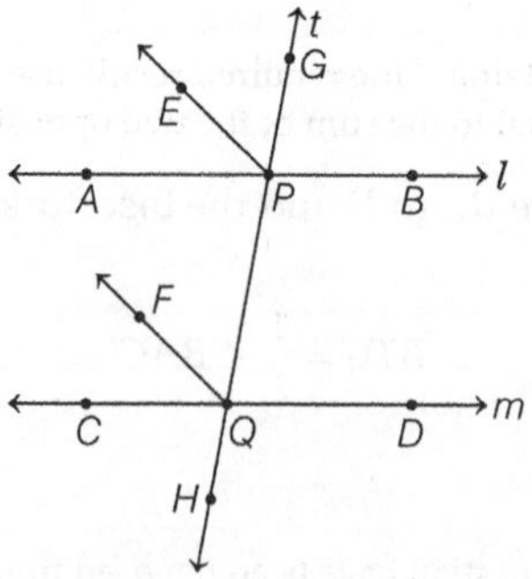

To prove $EP \parallel FQ$

Proof Given, $AB \parallel CD$

$\Rightarrow \quad \angle APG = \angle CQP$ [corresponding angles]

$\Rightarrow \quad \frac{1}{2}\angle APG = \frac{1}{2}\angle CQP$ [on dividing both sides by 2]

$\Rightarrow \quad \angle EPG = \angle FQP$

[$\because$ EP and FQ are the bisectors of $\angle APG$ and $\angle CQP$, respectively]

As these are the corresponding angles made by the lines EP and FQ and on the transversal line t.

$\therefore \quad EP \parallel FQ$ **Hence proved.**

Mistake Alert! *Students may get confused between corresponding angles, alternate interior angles or alternate exterior angles.*

Q.4 Prove that through a given point, we can draw only one perpendicular to a given line.

Ans. Given Consider a line l and a point P.

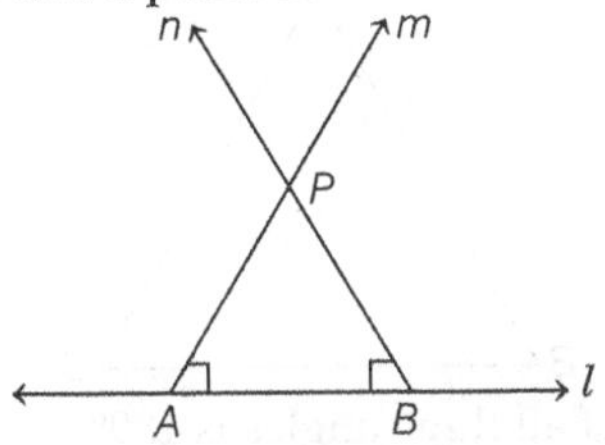

Let m and n are two intersecting lines passing through the point P and which is perpendicular to l at point B and A respectively.

To prove Only one perpendicular line can be drawn through a given point to a given line *i.e.*, to prove $\angle P = 0°$.

Proof In ΔAPB, $\angle A + \angle P + \angle B = 180°$ [by angle sum property of a triangle]

$\Rightarrow \quad 90° + \angle P + 90° = 180°$

$\Rightarrow \quad \angle P = 180° - 180°$

$\therefore \quad \angle P = 0°$

So, lines n and m coincide.

Hence, only one perpendicular line can be drawn through a given point on a given line.

Q.5 Prove that two lines that are respectively perpendicular to two intersecting lines intersect each other.

Ans. Given Let lines l and m are two intersecting lines. Again, let n and p be another two lines which are perpendicular to the intersecting lines meet at point D.

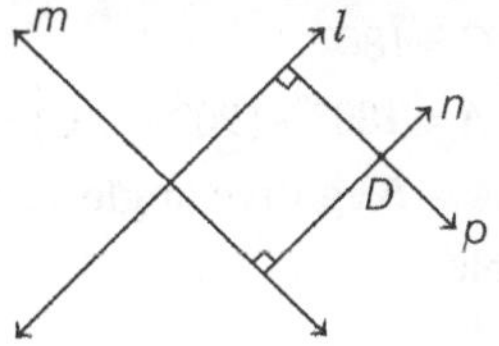

To prove Two lines n and p intersecting at a point.

Proof Let us consider lines n and p are not intersecting that means they are parallel to each other *i.e.*, $n \parallel p$. ...(i)

Since, lines n and p are perpendicular to m and l, respectively.

But from Eq. (i), $n \parallel p$, it implies that $l \parallel m$.

Hence, it is a contradiction.

Thus, our assumption is wrong.

Therefore, lines n and p intersect at a point.

***Q.6** Prove that a triangle must have atleast two acute angles.

Ans. **Given** ΔABC is a triangle.

To prove ΔABC must have two acute angles.

Proof Let us consider the following cases.

***Case* I** When two angles are 90°.

Suppose $\angle B = 90°$ and $\angle C = 90°$

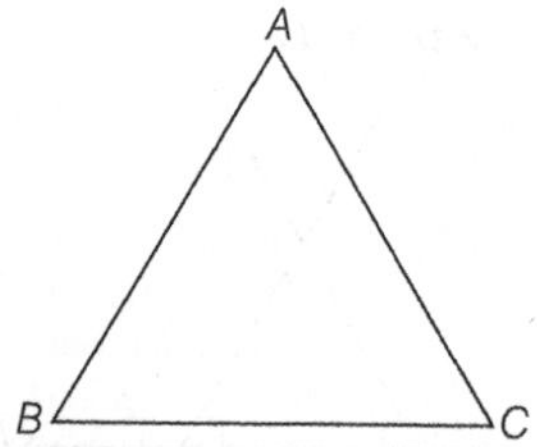

We know that the sum of all three angles is 180°.

$\therefore \quad \angle A + \angle B + \angle C = 180°$ ...(i)

$\therefore \quad \angle A + 90° + 90° = 180°$

$\Rightarrow \quad \angle A = 180° - 180° = 0°$

So, no triangle is possible.

***Case* II** When two angle are obtuse.

Suppose two angles $\angle B$ and $\angle C$ are more than 90°.

From Eq. (i),

$\angle A = 180° - (\angle B + \angle C) = 180° -$ [Angle greater than 180°]

[$\because \angle B + \angle C$ = more than 90° + more than 90° = more than 180°]

$\angle A$ = negative angle, which is not possible.

So, no triangle is possible.

***Case* III** When one angle is 90° and other is obtuse.

Suppose $\angle B = 90°$ and $\angle C$ is obtuse.

From Eq. (i),

$\angle A + \angle B + \angle C = 180°$

$\Rightarrow \quad \angle A = 180° - (90° + \angle C) = 90° - \angle C$

= Negative angle [$\because \angle C$ is obtuse]

Hence, no triangle is possible.

(*) Topics related to these question have been removed from latest NCERT.

Case **IV** When two angles are acute, then sum of two angles is less than 180°, so that the third angle can be an acute or obtuse angle.

Thus, a triangle must have at least two acute angles.

Mistake Alert ! Students may assume that acute angle is greater than 90° and obtuse angle is less than 90°.

****Q.7*** In the given figure, $\angle Q > \angle R$, PA is the bisector of $\angle QPR$ and $PM \perp QR$. Prove that $\angle APM = \frac{1}{2}(\angle Q - \angle R)$.

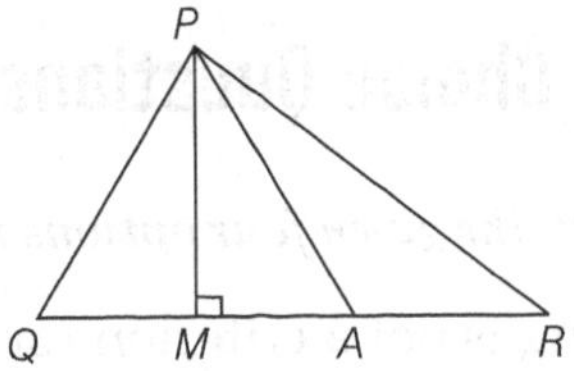

Ans. **Given** In ΔPQR, $\angle Q > \angle R$, PA is the bisector of $\angle QPR$ and $PM \perp QR$.

To prove $\angle APM = \frac{1}{2}(\angle Q - \angle R)$

Proof Since, PA is the bisector of $\angle QPR$.

$\therefore \quad \angle QPA = \angle APR$ ...(i)

In ΔPQM,

$\angle PQM + \angle PMQ + \angle QPM = 180°$ [by angle sum property of a triangle]

$\Rightarrow \quad \angle PQM + 90° + \angle QPM = 180°$ [$\because PM \perp QR \Rightarrow \angle PMQ = 90°$]

$\Rightarrow \quad \angle PQM = 90° - \angle QPM$ ...(ii)

In ΔPMR,

$\angle PMR + \angle PRM + \angle RPM = 180°$ [by angle sum property of a triangle]

$\Rightarrow \quad 90° + \angle PRM + \angle RPM = 180°$ [$\because PM \perp QR \Rightarrow \angle PMR = 90°$]

$\Rightarrow \quad \angle PRM = 180° - 90° - \angle RPM$

$\Rightarrow \quad \angle PRM = 90° - \angle RPM$ ...(iii)

On subtracting Eq. (iii) from Eq. (ii), we get

$\angle Q - \angle R = (90° - \angle QPM) - (90° - \angle RPM)$

[$\because \angle PQM = \angle Q$ and $\angle PRM = \angle R$]

$\Rightarrow \quad \angle Q - \angle R = \angle RPM - \angle QPM$

$\Rightarrow \quad \angle Q - \angle R = [\angle RPA + \angle APM] - [\angle QPA - \angle APM]$ ...(iv)

$\Rightarrow \quad \angle Q - \angle R = \angle QPA + \angle APM - \angle QPA + \angle APM$

[by using Eq. (i)]

$\Rightarrow \quad \angle Q - \angle R = 2\angle APM$

$\therefore \quad \angle APM = \frac{1}{2}(\angle Q - \angle R)$ **Hence proved.**

Mistake Alert ! Students should avoid using $\angle P$ instead of $\angle QPR$, $\angle QPM$ and $\angle QPA$, because more than one angles are formed at point P.

(*) Topics related to these question have been removed from latest NCERT.

Chapter

07

Triangles

Multiple Choice Questions (MCQs)

Choose the correct answer from the given four options in the following questions:

Q.1 Which of the following is not a criterion for congruence of triangles?

(a) SAS (b) ASA (c) SSA (d) SSS

Thinking Process For a triangle to be congruent, it is very important that the equal angles are included between the pairs of equal sides.

Ans. *(c)* We know that two triangles are congruent, if the sides and angles of one triangle are equal to the corresponding sides and angles of the other triangle.

Also, criterion for congruence of triangles are SAS (Side-Angle-Side), ASA (Angle-Side-Angle), AAS (Angle-Angle-Side), SSS (Side-Side-Side) and RHS (right angle-hypotenuse-side).

So, SSA is not a criterion for congruence of triangles.

Q.2 If $AB = QR$, $BC = PR$ and $CA = PQ$, then

(a) $\Delta ABC \cong \Delta PQR$ (b) $\Delta CBA \cong \Delta PRQ$
(c) $\Delta BAC \cong \Delta RPQ$ (d) $\Delta PQR \cong \Delta BCA$

Ans. *(b)* Here, $AB = QR$, $BC = PR$ and $CA = PQ$, which shows that AB covers QR, BC covers PR and CA covers PQ *i.e.*, A correspond to Q, B correspond to R and C correspond to P.

or $$A \leftrightarrow Q,\ B \leftrightarrow R,\ C \leftrightarrow P$$

Under this correspondence,

$\Delta ABC \cong \Delta QRP$, so option (a) is incorrect.

or $\Delta CBA \cong \Delta PRQ$, so option (b) is correct.

or $\Delta BAC \cong \Delta RQP$, so option (c) is incorrect.

or $\Delta BCA \cong \Delta RPQ$, so option (d) is incorrect.

Mistake Alert ! *Students often fail to match corresponding parts correctly.*

Q.3 In ΔABC, if $AB = AC$ and $\angle B = 50°$, then $\angle C$ is equal to

(a) 40° (b) 50° (c) 80° (d) 130°

Concept Insight The angles opposite to equal sides are equal to each other.

Ans. *(b)* Given, ΔABC such that $AB = AC$ and $\angle B = 50°$.

In ΔABC, $AB = AC$ [given]

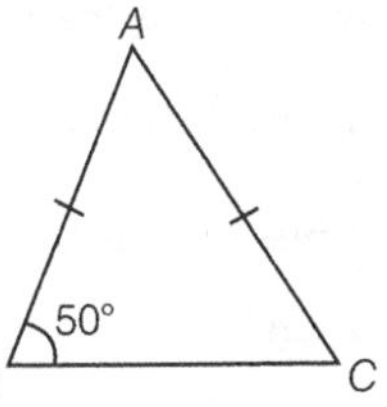

$\Rightarrow$ $\angle C = \angle B$ [$\because$ angles opposite to equal sides are equal]

$\Rightarrow$ $\angle C = 50°$ [$\because$ $\angle B = 50°$ (given)]

Q.4 In ΔABC, if $BC = AB$ and $\angle B = 80°$, then $\angle A$ is equal to

(a) 80° (b) 40° (c) 50° (d) 100°

Ans. *(c)* Given, ΔABC such that $BC = AB$ and $\angle B = 80°$

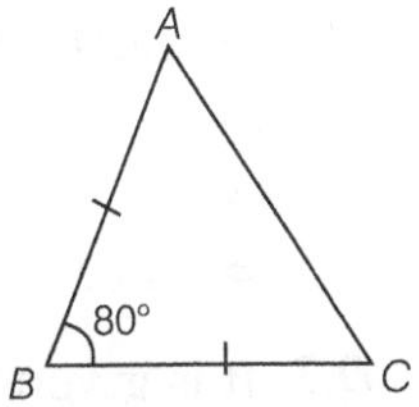

In ΔABC, $AB = BC$

$\Rightarrow$ $\angle C = \angle A$ ...(i)

[$\because$ angles opposite to equal sides are equal]

We know that the sum of all the angles of a triangle is 180°.

$\therefore$ $\angle A + \angle B + \angle C = 180°$

$\Rightarrow$ $\angle A + 80° + \angle A = 180°$ [from Eq. (i)]

$\Rightarrow$ $2\angle A = 180° - 80° = 100°$

$\Rightarrow$ $\angle A = \frac{100°}{2} \Rightarrow \angle A = 50°$

Q.5 In ΔPQR, if $\angle R = \angle P$ and $QR = 4$ cm and $PR = 5$ cm. Then, the length of PQ is

(a) 4 cm (b) 5 cm (c) 2 cm (d) 2.5 cm

Ans. *(a)* Given, ΔPQR such that $\angle R = \angle P$, $QR = 4$ cm and $PR = 5$ cm

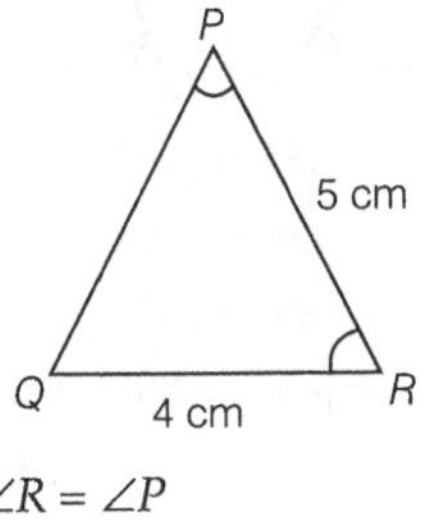

In ΔPQR, $\angle R = \angle P$

$\Rightarrow$ $PQ = QR$ [$\because$ sides opposite to equal angles are equal]

$\Rightarrow$ $PQ = 4$ cm [$\because$ $QR = 4$ cm]

Hence, the length of PQ is 4 cm.

***Q.6** If D is a point on the side BC of a ΔABC such that AD bisects $\angle BAC$. Then,

(a) $BD = CD$ (b) $BA > BD$ (c) $BD > BA$ (d) $CD > CA$

(*) Topics related to these question have been removed from latest NCERT.

Thinking Process

(i) In the given problem we can use the property, exterior angle of a triangle is greater than interior opposite angle.

(ii) Secondly, use the property that in a triangle, the side opposite to the greater angle is longer.

Ans. ***(b)*** Given, ΔABC such that AD bisects $\angle BAC$

$\therefore \quad \angle BAD = \angle CAD \quad$ ...(i)

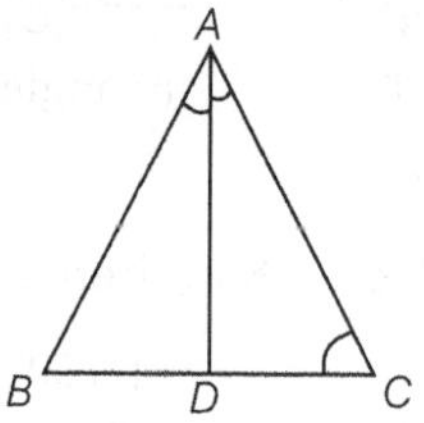

In ΔACD, $\angle BDA$ is an exterior angle.

$\therefore \quad \angle BDA > \angle CAD \quad$ [$\because$ exterior angle > interior opposite angle]

$\Rightarrow \quad \angle BDA > \angle BAD \quad$ [from Eq. (i)]

$\Rightarrow \quad BA > BD \quad$ [$\because$ side opposite to greater angle is longer]

Q.7 It is given that $\Delta ABC \cong \Delta FDE$ and $AB = 5$ cm, $\angle B = 40°$ and $\angle A = 80°$, then which of the following is true?

(a) $DF = 5$ cm, $\angle F = 60°$
(b) $DF = 5$ cm, $\angle E = 60°$
(c) $DE = 5$ cm, $\angle E = 60°$
(d) $DE = 5$ cm, $\angle D = 40°$

Ans. ***(b)*** Given, $\Delta ABC \cong \Delta FDE$ and $AB = 5$ cm, $\angle B = 40°$, $\angle A = 80°$

Since, $\Delta FDE \cong \Delta ABC$

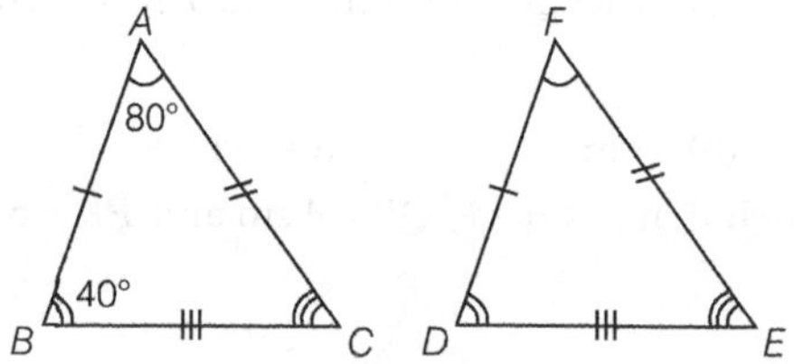

$\therefore \quad DF = AB \quad$ [by CPCT]

$\Rightarrow \quad DF = 5$ cm

and $\quad \angle E = \angle C \quad$ [by CPCT]

$\Rightarrow \quad \angle E = \angle C = 180° - (\angle A + \angle B)$

[by angle sum property in a ΔABC]

$\Rightarrow \quad \angle E = 180° - (80° + 40°) \Rightarrow \angle E = 60°$

Mistake Alert ! Identifying the corresponding sides of angles between two congruent triangles may cause confusion for students.

***Q.8** Two sides of a triangle are of lengths 5 cm and 1.5 cm. The length of third side of the triangle cannot be

(a) 3.6 cm (b) 4.1 cm (c) 3.8 cm (d) 3.4 cm

(*) Topics related to these question have been removed from latest NCERT.

- **Concept Insight** The sum of any two sides of a triangle is greater than third side and difference of any two sides is less than the third side.

Ans. *(d)* Given, the length of two sides of a triangle are 5 cm and 1.5 cm, respectively.

Let sides $AB = 5$ cm and $CA = 1.5$ cm.

We know that a closed figure formed by three intersecting lines (or sides) is called a triangle, if difference of two sides < third side and sum of two sides > third side.

$\therefore \quad 5 - 1.5 < BC$ and $5 + 1.5 > BC$

$\Rightarrow \quad 3.5 < BC$ and $6.5 > BC$

Here, we see that options (a), (b) and (c) satisfy the above inequality but option (d) does not satisfy the above inequality.

***Q.9** In ΔPQR, if $\angle R > \angle Q$, then

(a) $QR > PR$ (b) $PQ > PR$ (c) $PQ < PR$ (d) $QR < PR$

Ans. *(b)* Given, $\angle R > \angle Q$

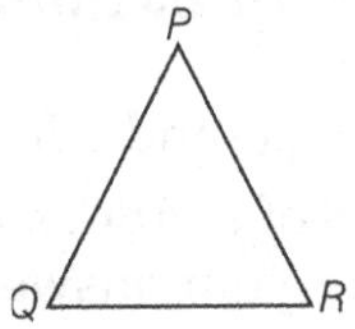

$\Rightarrow \quad PQ > PR$ [$\because$ side opposite to greater angle is longer]

Q.10 In ΔABC and ΔPQR, $AB = AC$, $\angle C = \angle P$ and $\angle B = \angle Q$, then the two triangles are

(a) isosceles but not congruent (b) isosceles and congruent
(c) congruent but not isosceles (d) Neither congruent nor isosceles

Ans. *(a)* In ΔABC, $AB = AC$ [given]

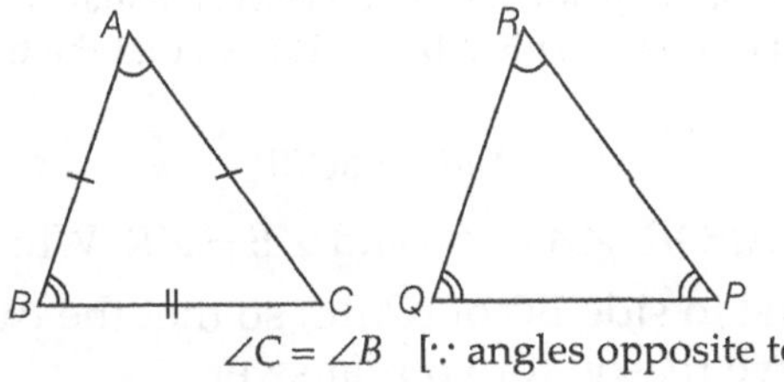

$\Rightarrow \quad \angle C = \angle B$ [$\because$ angles opposite to equal sides are equal]

So, ΔABC is an isosceles triangle.

But it is given that $\angle B = \angle Q \Rightarrow \angle C = \angle P$

$\therefore \quad \angle P = \angle Q$ [$\because \angle C = \angle B$]

$\Rightarrow \quad QR = PR$ [$\because$ sides opposite to equal angles are equal]

So, ΔPQR is also an isosceles triangle.

Therefore, both triangles are isosceles but not congruent. As, we know that AAA is not a criterion for congruence of triangles.

Q.11 In ΔABC and ΔDEF, $AB = FD$ and $\angle A = \angle D$. The two triangles will be congruent by SAS axiom, if

(a) $BC = EF$ (b) $AC = DE$ (c) $AC = EF$ (d) $BC = DE$

(✱) Topics related to these question have been removed from latest NCERT.

Ans. *(b)* We have given

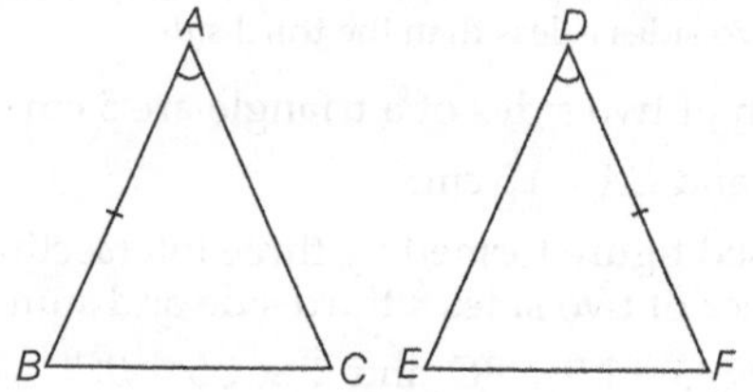

In ΔABC and ΔDEF,

$$AB = FD \text{ and } \angle A = \angle D$$

We know that two triangles will be congruent by *SAS* axiom. If two sides and the included angle of one, triangle are equal to the two sides and the included angle of other triangle.

$$\therefore \quad AC = DE$$

Short Answer Type Questions with Reasoning

Q.1 In ΔABC and ΔPQR, $\angle A = \angle Q$ and $\angle B = \angle R$. Which side of Δ *PQR* should be equal to side *AB* of Δ *ABC*, so that the two triangles are congruent? Give reason for your answer.

Ans. Given, in ΔABC and ΔPQR, $\angle A = \angle Q$ and $\angle B = \angle R$

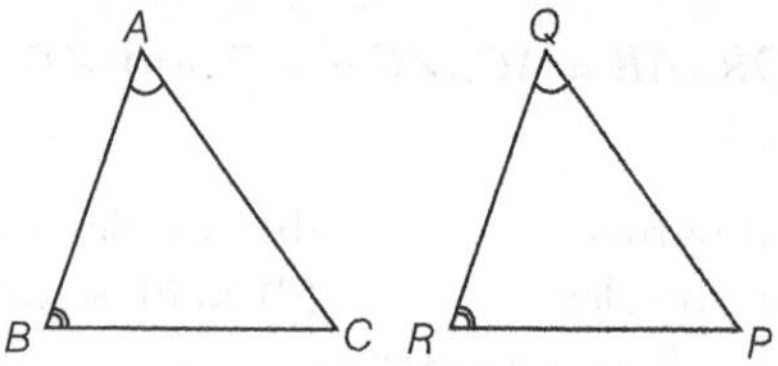

Since, the sides *AB* and *QR* are included between equal angles. Hence, the side *QR* of ΔPQR should be equal to side AB of ΔABC, so that the triangles are congruent by the rule ASA.

Hence, $\Delta aBC \cong \Delta QRP$ [by *ASA* rule]

Q.2 In Δ *ABC* and ΔPQR, $\angle A = \angle Q$ and $\angle B = \angle R$. Which side of ΔPQR should be equal to side *BC* of ΔABC, so that the two triangles are congruent? Give reason for your answer.

Ans. Given, in ΔABC and ΔPQR,

$$\angle A = \angle Q \text{ and } \angle B = \angle R$$

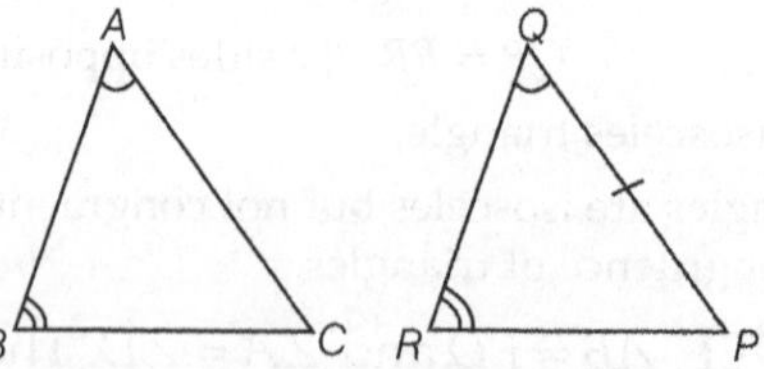

Since, two pairs of angles are equal in two triangles.

We know that two triangles will be congruent by AAS rule, if two angles and the side of one triangle are equal to the two angles and the side of other triangle.

$$\therefore \quad BC = RP$$

Q.3 "If two sides and an angle of one triangle are equal to two sides and an angle of another triangle , then the two triangles must be congruent". Is the statement true? Why?

Ans. *No*, because in the congruent rule, the two sides and the included angle of one triangle are equal to the two sides and the included angle of the other triangle *i.e.*, SAS rule.

Mistake Alert! *Students might assume that if two sides and an angle are given, then they automatically lead to congruency, which is actually wrong as the angle is not the included angle.*

Q.4 "If two angles and a side of one triangle are equal to two angles and a side of another triangle, then the two triangles must be congruent." Is the statement true? Why?

Ans. *No*, because sides must be corresponding sides.

***Q.5** Is it possible to construct a triangle with lengths of its sides as 4 cm, 3 cm and 7 cm? Give reason for your answer.

Ans. *No*, it is not possible to construct a triangle with lengths of its sides as 4 cm, 3 cm and 7 cm because here we see that sum of the lengths of two sides is equal to third side *i.e.*, $4 + 3 = 7$. As we know that, the sum of any two sides of a triangle is greater than its third side, so given statement is not correct.

Q.6 It is given that $\Delta ABC \cong \Delta RPQ$. Is it true to say that $BC = QR$? Why?

- **Concept Insight** Corresponding parts of two congruent triangles are equal.

Ans. *No*, we know that two triangles are congruent, if the sides and angles of one triangle are equal to the corresponding sides and angles of other triangle.

Here, $\Delta ABC \cong \Delta RPQ$

$\therefore$ $AB = RP,\ BC = PQ$ and $AC = RQ$

Hence, it is not true to say that $BC = QR$.

Q.7 If $\Delta PQR \cong \Delta EDF$, then is it true to say that $PR = EF$? Give reason for your answer.

Ans. *Yes*, if $\Delta PQR \cong \Delta EDF$, then it means that corresponding angles and their sides are equal because we know that two triangles are congruent, if the sides and angles of one triangle are equal to the corrosponding sides and angles of other triangle.

Here, $\Delta PQR \cong \Delta EDF$

$\therefore$ $PQ = ED,\ QR = DF$ and $PR = EF$

Hence, it is true to say that $PR = EF$.

***Q.8** In ΔPQR, $\angle P = 70°$ and $\angle R = 30°$. Which side of this triangle is the longest? Give reason for your answer.

Ans. Given, in ΔPQR, $\angle P = 70°$ and $\angle R = 30°$.

We know that sum of all the angles of a triangle is 180°.

$\therefore$ $\angle P + \angle Q + \angle R = 180°$

(✱) Topics related to these question have been removed from latest NCERT.

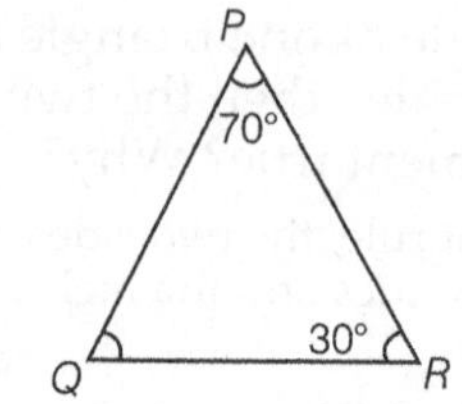

$\therefore \qquad \angle Q = 180° - (70° + 30°)$
$= 80°$

We know that here $\angle Q$ is largest, so side PR is longest.
[$\because$ the side opposite to the largest angle in a triangle is the longest]

***Q.9** AD is a median of the ΔABC. Is it true that $AB + BC + CA > 2AD$? Give reason for your answer.

Ans. *Yes,*

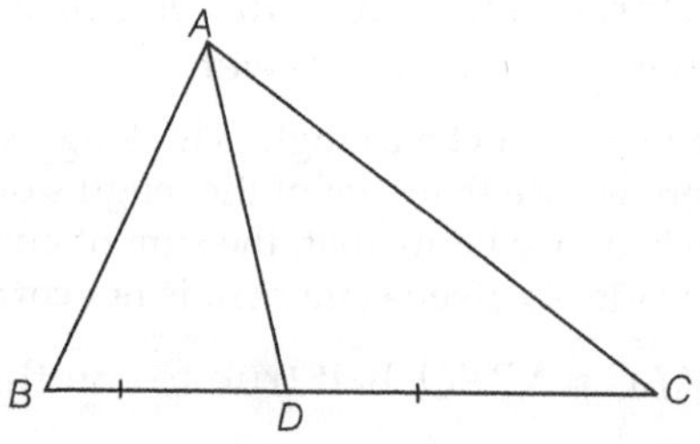

In ΔABD, we have $\quad AB + BD > AD \quad$ ...(i)
[$\because$ sum of any two sides of a triangle is greater than third side]

In ΔACD, we have $\quad AC + CD > AD \quad$ ...(ii)
[$\because$ sum of any two sides of a triangle is greater than third side]

On adding Eqs. (i) and (ii), we get

$$(AB + BD + AC + CD) > 2\,AD$$

$\Rightarrow \qquad (AB + BD + CD + AC) > 2AD$

Hence, $\qquad AB + BC + AC > 2AD \qquad [\because BC = BD + CD]$

Mistake Alert! *Some students might wrongly assume that AD is equal to or greater than the largest sides.*

***Q.10** M is a point on side BC of a triangle ABC such that AM is the bisector of $\angle BAC$. Is it true to say that perimeter of the triangle is greater than $2AM$? Give reason for your answer?

Ans. *Yes,* in ΔABC, M is a point of side BC such that AM is the bisector of $\angle BAC$.

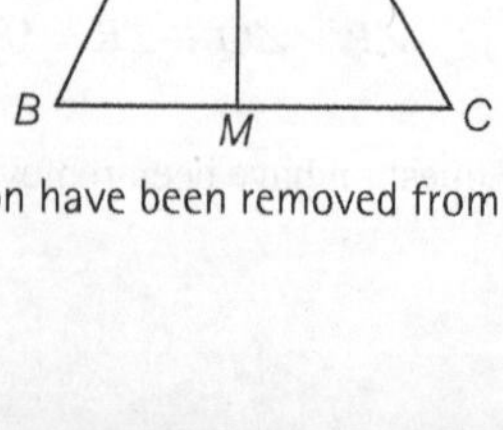

(*) Topics related to these question have been removed from latest NCERT.

In ΔABM, $AB + BM > AM$ ...(i)

[$\because$ sum of two sides of a triangle is greater than the third side]

In ΔACM, $AC + CM > AM$ ...(ii)

[$\because$ sum of two sides of a triangle is greater than the third side]

On adding Eqs. (i) and (ii), we get

$$(AB + BM + AC + CM) > 2AM$$

$$\Rightarrow (AB + BM + MC + AC) > 2AM$$

$$\Rightarrow AB + BC + AC > 2AM \quad [\because BC = BM + MC]$$

$\therefore$ Perimeter of $\Delta ABC > 2AM$

***Q.11** Is it possible to construct a triangle with lengths of its sides as 9 cm, 7 cm and 17 cm? Give reason for your answer.

Ans. *No,* Here, we see that $9 + 7 = 16 < 17$

i.e., the sum of two sides of a triangle is less than the third side.

Hence, it contradicts the property that the sum of two sides of a triangle is greater than the third side. Therefore, it is not possible to construct a triangle with given sides.

***Q.12** Is it possible to construct a triangle with lengths of its sides as 8 cm, 7 cm and 4 cm? Give reason for your answer.

Ans. *Yes,* because in each case the sum of two sides is greater than the third side.

i.e., $7 + 4 > 8,$

$8 + 4 > 7,$

$7 + 8 > 4$

Hence, it is possible to construct a triangle with the given sides.

Short Answer Type Questions

Q.1 ABC is an isosceles triangle with $AB = AC$ and BD and CE are its two medians. Show that $BD = CE$.

● **Concept Insight** Median divides the opposite side of a triangle in two equal parts.

Ans. Given, ΔABC is an isosceles triangle in which $AB = AC$ and BD and CE are its two medians.

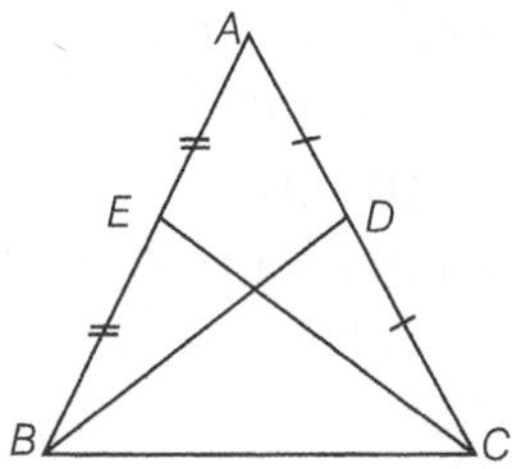

(*) Topics related to these question have been removed from latest NCERT.

In ΔABD and ΔACE, $AB = AC$ [given]

$\angle A = \angle A$ [common angle]

and $AD = AE$

$[\because AB = AC \Rightarrow \frac{1}{2}AB = \frac{1}{2}AC \Rightarrow AE = AD$ as D is the mid-point of AC and E is the mid-point of $AB]$

$\therefore$ $\Delta ABD \cong \Delta ACE$ [by SAS congruence rule]

$\Rightarrow$ $BD = CE$ [by CPCT] **Hence proved.**

Q.2 In figure, D and E are points on side BC of a ΔABC such that $BD = CE$ and $AD = AE$. Show that $\Delta ABD \cong \Delta ACE$.

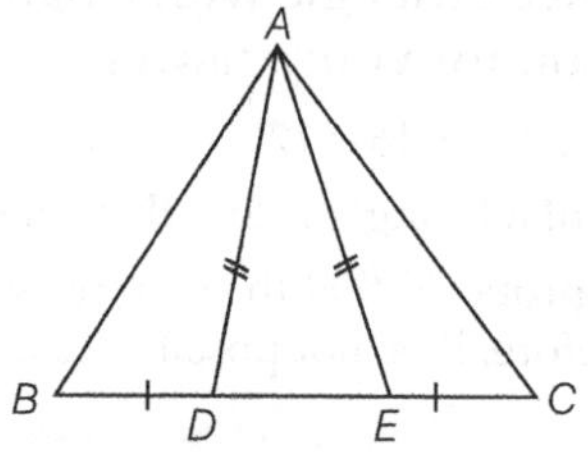

Thinking Process Firstly, use the property, angles opposite to equal sides are equal then use axiom to determine the result of congruency, then prove the congruency of two triangles.

Ans. **Given**, D and E are the points on side BC of a ΔABC such that $BD = CE$ and $AD = AE$.

To prove $\Delta ABD \cong \Delta ACE$

Proof We have, $AD = AE$ [given]

$\Rightarrow$ $\angle ADE = \angle AED$ ...(i)

[$\because$ angles opposite to equal sides are equal]

We have, $\angle ADB + \angle ADE = 180^\circ$ [linear pair axiom]

$\Rightarrow$ $\angle ADB = 180^\circ - \angle ADE$

$= 180^\circ - \angle AED$ [from Eq. (i)]

$= 180^\circ - (180^\circ - \angle AEC)$

$= \angle AFC$

So, $\angle ADB = \angle AEC$

In ΔABD and ΔACE,

$\angle ADB = \angle AEC$

$BD = CE$ [given]

and $AD = AE$ [given]

$\therefore$ $\Delta ABD \cong \Delta ACE$ [by SAS congruence rule]

Hence proved.

Q.3 In the given figure, ΔCDE is an equilateral triangle formed on a side CD of a square $ABCD$. Show that $\Delta ADE \cong \Delta BCE$.

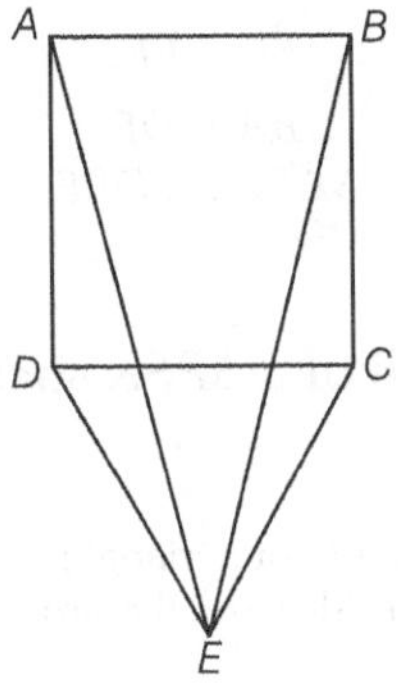

● **Concept Insight** All angles and sides of a regular polygon are equal.

Ans. Given In figure ΔCDE is an equilateral triangle formed on a side CD of a square $ABCD$.

To prove $\Delta ADE \cong \Delta BCE$

Proof In ΔADE and ΔBCE, $DE = CE$ [sides of an equilateral triangle]

$\angle ADE = \angle BCE$

[$\because$ $\angle ADC = \angle BCD = 90°$ (angles of square) and $\angle EDC = \angle ECD = 60°$
$\therefore$ $\angle ADE = \angle ADC + \angle CDE = 90° + 60° = 150°$ and $\angle BCE = \angle BCD + \angle DCE = 90° + 60° = 150°$]

and $AD = BC$ [sides of a square]

$\therefore$ $\Delta ADE \cong \Delta BCE$ [by SAS congruence rule]

Hence proved.

Q.4 In figure, $BA \perp AC$, $DE \perp DF$ such that $BA = DE$ and $BF = EC$. Show that $\Delta ABC \cong \Delta DEF$.

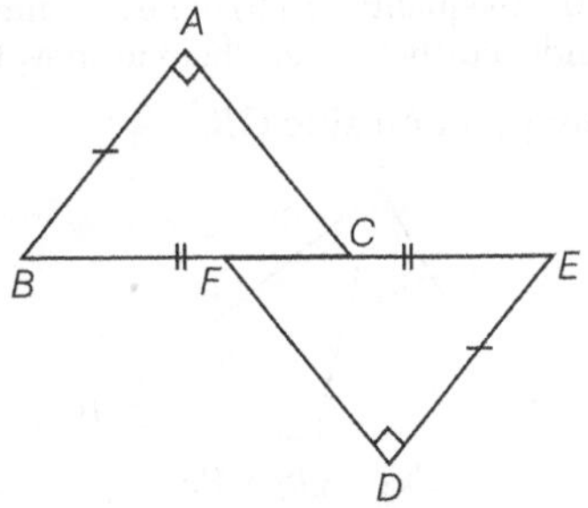

Thinking Process Use the RHS congruence rule to show the given result.

Ans. Given In figure, $BA \perp AC$, $DE \perp DF$ such that $BA = DE$ and $BF = EC$.

To prove $\Delta ABC \cong \Delta DEF$.

Proof Since, $BF = EC$

On adding CF both sides, we get

$$BF + CF = EC + CF$$

$\Rightarrow$	$BC = EF$		...(i)
In ΔABC and ΔDEF,	$\angle A = \angle D = 90°$		[$\because$ $BA \perp AC$ and $DE \perp DF$]
	$BC = EF$		[from Eq. (i)]
and	$BA = DE$		[given]
$\therefore$	$\Delta ABC \cong \Delta DEF$		[by RHS congruence rule]

Hence proved.

***Q.5** Q is a point on the side SR of a ΔPSR such that $PQ = PR$. Prove that $PS > PQ$.

Thinking Process Use the property of a triangle that if two sides are equal then their opposite angles are also equal. Also, use the property that side opposite to greater angle is longer.

Ans. Given, In ΔPSR, Q is a point on the side SR such that $PQ = PR$.

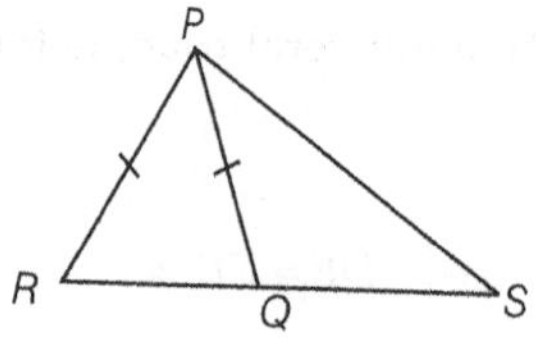

In ΔPRQ, $PQ = PR$ [given]

$\Rightarrow$ $\angle R = \angle PQR$ ...(i)

[angles opposite to equal sides are equal]

But $\angle PQR > \angle S$ ...(ii)

[$\because$ exterior angle of a triangle is greater than each of the opposite interior angle]

From Eqs. (i) and (ii), we get $\angle R > \angle S$

$\Rightarrow$ $PS > PR$ [$\because$ side opposite to greater angle is longer]

$\Rightarrow$ $PS > PQ$ [$\because$ $PQ = PR$] **Hence proved.**

***Q.6** S is any point on side QR of a ΔPQR. Show that $PQ + QR + RP > 2PS$.

Thinking Process Use the inequality of a triangle *i.e.,* sum of two sides of a triangle is greater than the third side. Further, adjust them to show the required result.

Ans. Given, In ΔPQR, S is any point on side QR.

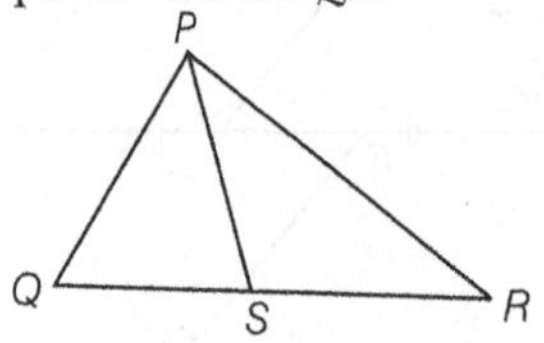

In ΔPQS, $PQ + QS > PS$ ... (i)

[$\because$ sum of two sides of a triangle is greater than the third side]

Similarly, in ΔPRS, $SR + RP > PS$ ...(ii)

[$\because$ sum of two sides of a triangle is greater than the third side]

(✱) Topics related to these question have been removed from latest NCERT.

On adding Eqs. (i) and (ii), we get

$$PQ + QS + SR + RP > 2PS$$

$\Rightarrow$ $PQ + (QS + SR) + RP > 2PS$

$\Rightarrow$ $PQ + QR + RP > 2PS$ [$\because QR = QS + SR$] **Hence proved.**

***Q.7** D is any point on side AC of a ΔABC with $AB = AC$. Show that $CD < BD$.

Ans. Given, In ΔABC, D is any point on side AC such that $AB = AC$.

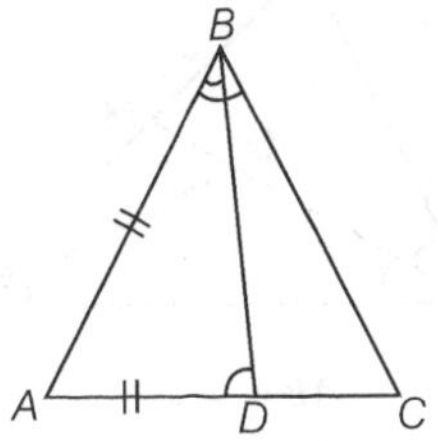

In ΔABC, $AC = AB$ [given]

$\Rightarrow$ $\angle ABC = \angle ACB$ ...(i)

[$\because$ angles opposite to equal sides are equal]

In ΔABC and ΔDBC, $\angle ABC > \angle DBC$ [$\because \angle DBC$ is a internal angle of $\angle B$]

$\Rightarrow$ $\angle ACB > \angle DBC$ [from Eq. (i)]

$\Rightarrow$ $BD > CD$ [side opposite to greater angle is longer]

or $CD < BD$ **Hence proved.**

Q.8 In given figure, $l \parallel m$ and M is the mid-point of a line segment AB. Show that M is also the mid-point of any line segment CD, having its end points on l and m, respectively.

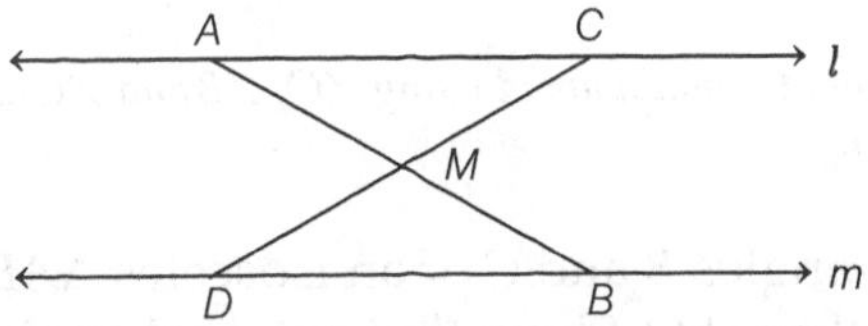

Ans. Given, In the figure, $l \parallel m$ and M is the mid-point of a line segment AB

i.e., $AM = BM$.

$\because$ $l \parallel m$ [given]

$\therefore$ $\angle BAC = \angle ABD$ [alternate interior angles]

And $\angle AMC = \angle BMD$ [vertically opposite angles]

In ΔAMC and ΔBMD, $\angle BAC = \angle ABD$ [proved above]

$AM = BM$ [given]

and $\angle AMC = \angle BMD$ [proved above]

$\therefore$ $\Delta AMC \cong \Delta BMD$ [by ASA congruence rule)

$\Rightarrow$ $MC = MD$ [by CPCT]

Hence, M is the mid-point of line segment CD. **Hence proved.**

(*) Topics related to these question have been removed from latest NCERT.

Q.9 Bisectors of the angles B and C of an isosceles triangle with $AB = AC$ intersect each other at O. BO is produced to a point M. Prove that $\angle MOC = \angle ABC$.

Ans. Given, Lines, OB and OC are the angle bisectors of $\angle B$ and $\angle C$ of an isosceles ΔABC, respectively such that $AB = AC$ which intersect each other at O and BO is produced to M.

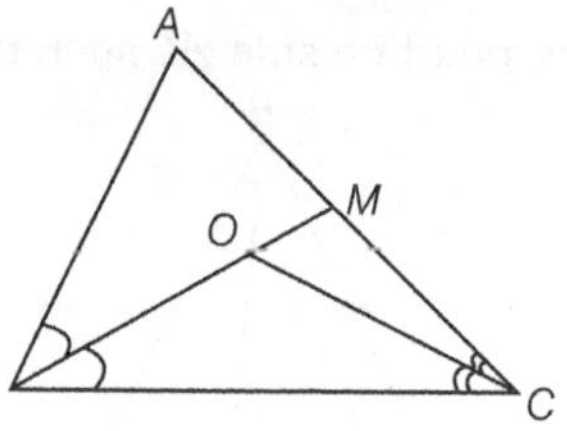

In ΔABC, $AB = AC$ [given]

$\Rightarrow \angle ACB = \angle ABC$ [∵ angles opposite to equal sides are equal]

$\Rightarrow \frac{1}{2}\angle ACB = \frac{1}{2}\angle ABC$ [dividing both sides by 2]

$\Rightarrow \angle OCB = \angle OBC$ ...(i)

[∵ OB and OC are the bisector of $\angle B$ and $\angle C$, respectively]

Now, $\angle MOC = \angle OBC + \angle OCB$

[∵ exterior angle of a triangle is equal to the sum of two interior angles]

$\Rightarrow \angle MOC = \angle OBC + \angle OBC$ [from Eq. (i)]

$\Rightarrow \angle MOC = 2\angle OBC$

$\Rightarrow \angle MOC = \angle ABC$ [∵ OB is the bisector of $\angle B$]

Hence proved.

Mistake Alert! *Students should avoid using $\angle O$, $\angle B$ and $\angle C$ as there are more than one angles at these points.*

Q.10 Bisectors of the angles B and C of an isosceles ΔABC with $AB = AC$ intersect each other at O. Show that external angle adjacent to $\angle ABC$ is equal to $\angle BOC$.

Ans. Given, ΔABC is an isosceles triangle in which $AB = AC$, BO and CO are the bisectors of $\angle ABC$ and $\angle ACB$ respectively, intersect at O.

Extend the line CB to D.

Now, in ΔABC, $AB = AC$ [given]

$\angle ACB = \angle ABC$ [∵ angles opposite to equal sides are equal]

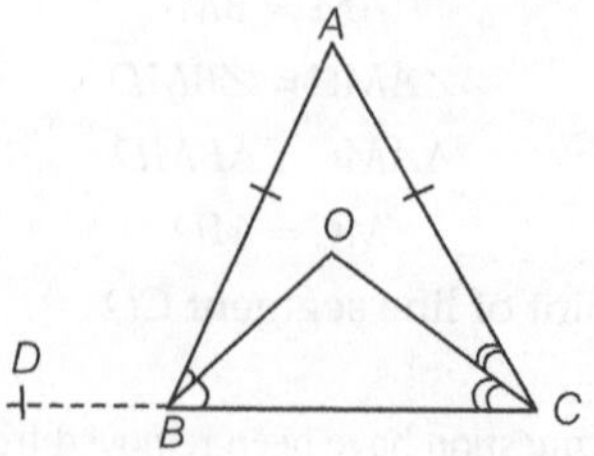

$\Rightarrow \quad \frac{1}{2}\angle ACB = \frac{1}{2}\angle ABC$ [dividing both sides by 2]

$\Rightarrow \quad \angle OCB = \angle OBC$ ...(i)

[∵ *BO* and *CO* are the bisectors of $\angle ABC$ and $\angle ACB$, respectively]

In ΔBOC,

$\angle OBC + \angle OCB + \angle BOC = 180°$ [by angle sum property of a triangle]

$\Rightarrow \quad \angle OBC + \angle OBC + \angle BOC = 180°$ [from Eq. (i)]

$\Rightarrow \quad 2\angle OBC + \angle BOC = 180°$

$\Rightarrow \quad \angle ABC + \angle BOC = 180°$ [∵ *BO* is the bisector of $\angle ABC$]

$\Rightarrow \quad 180° - \angle DBA + \angle BOC = 180°$ [∵ *DBC* is a straight line]

$\Rightarrow \quad -\angle DBA + \angle BOC = 0 \Rightarrow \angle DBA = \angle BOC$

***Q.11** In following figure if *AD* is the bisector of $\angle BAC$, then prove that $AB > BD$.

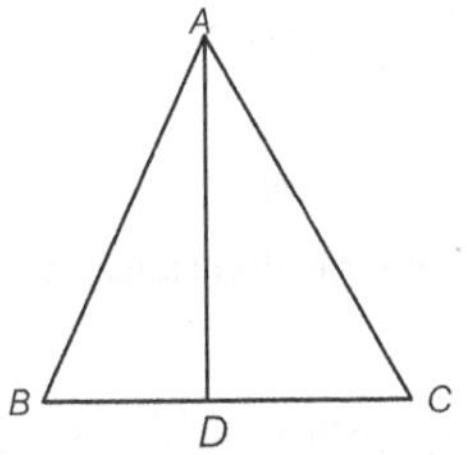

Ans. Given, *ABC* is a triangle such that *AD* is the bisector of $\angle BAC$.

Since, *AD* is the bisector of $\angle BAC$.

$\therefore \quad \angle BAD = \angle CAD$ ...(i)

But $\quad \angle ADB > \angle CAD$

[∵ exterior angle of a triangle is greater than each of the opposite interior angle]

$\therefore \quad \angle ADB > \angle BAD$ [from Eq. (i)]

$\Rightarrow \quad AB > BD$ [∵ side opposite to greater angle is longer] **Hence proved.**

Long Answer Type Questions

Q.1 Find all the angles of an equilateral triangle.

Ans. Let *ABC* be an equilateral triangle such that $AB = BC = CA$.

We have, $\quad AB = AC \Rightarrow \angle C = \angle B$ [∵ angles opposite to equal sides are equal]

Let $\quad \angle C = \angle B = x$ ...(i)

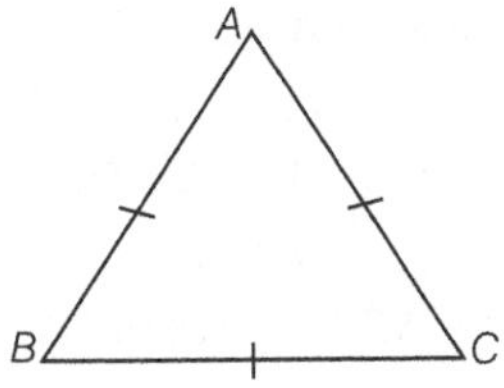

(*) Topics related to these question have been removed from latest NCERT.

Now, $BC = BA$

$\Rightarrow$ $\angle A = \angle C$ ...(ii) [$\because$ angles opposite to equal sides are equal]

From Eqs. (i) and (ii), we get

$$\angle A = \angle B = \angle C = x$$

Now, in ΔABC, $\angle A + \angle B + \angle C = 180°$ [by angle sum property of a triangle]

$\Rightarrow$ $x + x + x = 180° \Rightarrow 3x = 180°$

$\therefore$ $x = 60°$

Hence, $\angle A = \angle B = \angle C = 60°$

Q.2 The image of an object placed at a point A before a plane mirror LM is seen at the point B by an observer at D as shown in figure. Prove that the image is as far behind the mirror as the object is in front of the mirror.

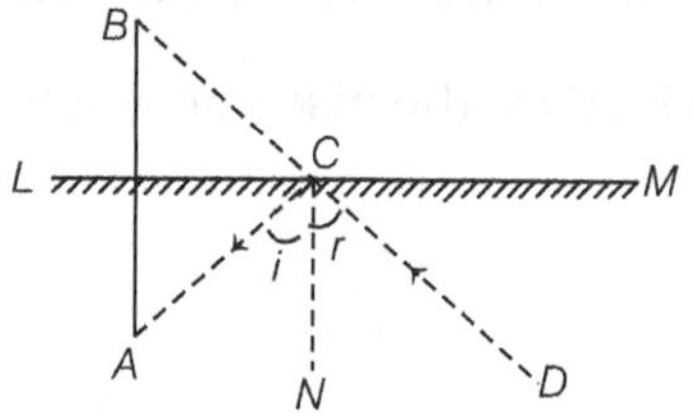

● **Concept Insight** The first law of reflection states that angle of incidence is equal to angle of reflection *i.e.*, $\angle i = \angle r$.

Ans. Let an object OA is placed at a point A, LM be a plane mirror, D be an observer and OB is the image.

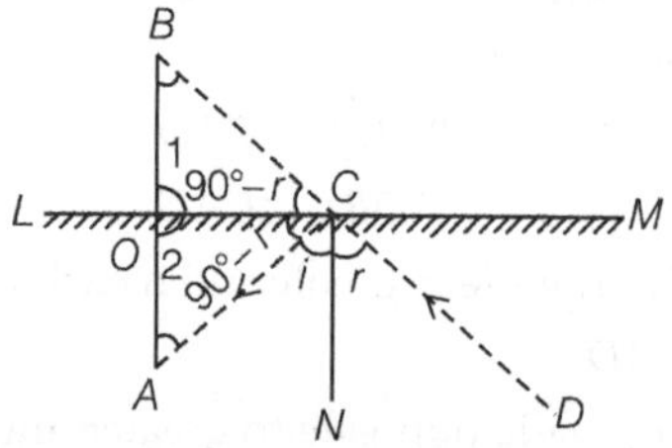

To prove The image is as far behind the mirror as the object is in front of the mirror *i.e.*, $OB = OA$.

Proof $\because$ $CN \perp LM$ and $AB \perp LM$

$\Rightarrow$ $AB \parallel CN$

$\angle A = \angle i$ [alternate interior angles]...(i)

$\angle B = \angle r$ [corresponding angles]...(ii)

Also, $\angle i = \angle r$ [$\because$ incident angle = reflected angle]...(iii)

From Eqs. (i), (ii) and (iii), we get $\angle A = \angle B$

In ΔCOB and ΔCOA, $\angle B = \angle A$ [proved above]

$\angle 1 = \angle 2 = 90°$

and $CO = CO$ [common side]

$\therefore$ $\Delta COB \cong \Delta COA$ [by AAS congruence rule]

$\Rightarrow$ $OB = OA$ [by CPCT] **Hence proved.**

Alternate Method

In ΔOBC and ΔOAC, $\angle 1 = \angle 2$ [each 90°]

Also, $\angle i = \angle r$ [$\because$ incident angle = reflected angle]...(i)

On multiplying both sides of Eq. (i) by −1 and then adding 90° both sides, we get

$$90° - \angle i = 90° - \angle r$$

$\Rightarrow$ $\angle ACO = \angle BCO$

and $OC = OC$ [common side]

$\therefore$ $\Delta OBC \cong \Delta OAC$ [by ASA congruence rule]

$\Rightarrow$ $OB = OA$ [by CPCT]

Hence, the image is as far behind the mirror as the object is in front of the mirror.

Q.3 ABC is an isosceles triangle with $AB = AC$ and D is a point on BC such that $AD \perp BC$ (see figure). To prove that $\angle BAD = \angle CAD$, a student proceeded as follows

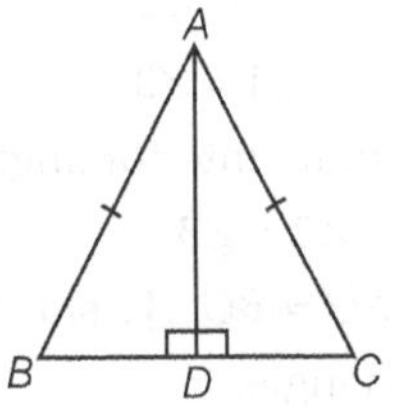

In ΔABD and ΔACD,

$AB = AC$ [given]

$\angle B = \angle C$ [because $AB = AC$]

and $\angle ADB = \angle ADC$

Therefore, $\Delta ABD \cong \Delta ACD$ [by AAS congruence rule]

So, $\angle BAD = \angle CAD$ [by CPCT]

What is the defect in the above arguments?

Ans. We have, In ΔABC, $AB = AC$

$\Rightarrow$ $\angle ACB = \angle ABC$ [$\because$ angles oppsoite to the equal sides are equal]

In ΔABD and ΔACD,

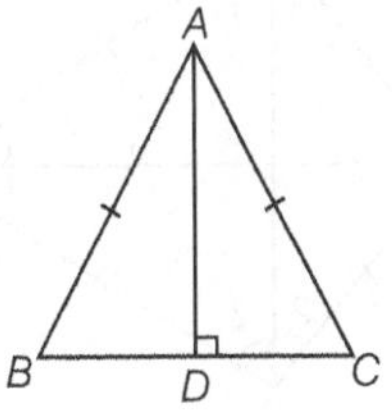

$AB = AC$ [given]

$\angle B = \angle C$ or $\angle ABD = \angle ACD$ [proved above]

$\angle ADB = \angle ADC$ [each 90°]

$\because$ $\Delta ABD \cong \Delta ACD$ [by AAS]

$\therefore$ $\angle BAD = \angle CAD$ [by CPCT]

So, the defect in the given argument is that firstly prove, $\angle ABD = \angle ACD$ or $\angle B = \angle C$

Hence, $\angle ABD = \angle ACD$ is defect. **Hence proved.**

Q.4 P is a point on the bisector of $\angle ABC$. If the line through P, parallel to BA meet BC at Q, prove that BPQ is an isosceles triangle.

Ans. **Given** P is a point on the bisector of $\angle ABC$ and draw the line through P parallel to BA and meet BC at Q.

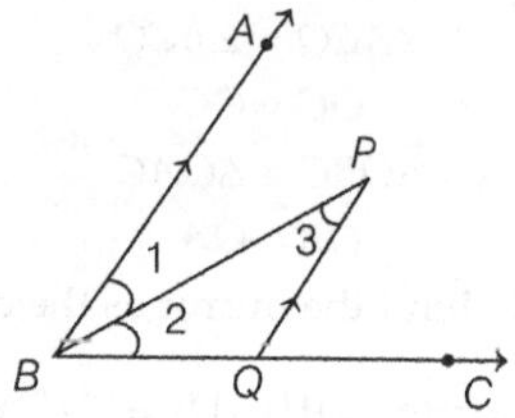

To prove ΔBPQ is an isosceles triangle.

Proof $\angle 1 = \angle 2$ [BP is bisector of $\angle B$] ...(i)

Now, $\angle 1 = \angle 3$ ...(ii)

[alternate interior angles as $PQ \parallel AB$ and PB is transversal]

From Eq (i) and (ii), we get $\angle 2 = \angle 3$

$\Rightarrow$ $PQ = BQ$ [$\because$ sides opposite to equal angles are equal]

Hence, ΔBPQ is an isosceles triangle. **Hence proved.**

Q.5 $ABCD$ is a quadrilateral in which $AB = BC$ and $AD = CD$. Show that BD bisects both the angles ABC and ADC.

Thinking Process Firstly, use the property that if two sides of a triangle are equal, then their opposite angles are equal. Further, show that ΔBAD and ΔBCD are congruent by SAS rule.

Ans. **Given** $ABCD$ is a quadrilateral in which $AB = BC$ and $AD = CD$.

To prove BD bisects both the angles ABC and ADC.

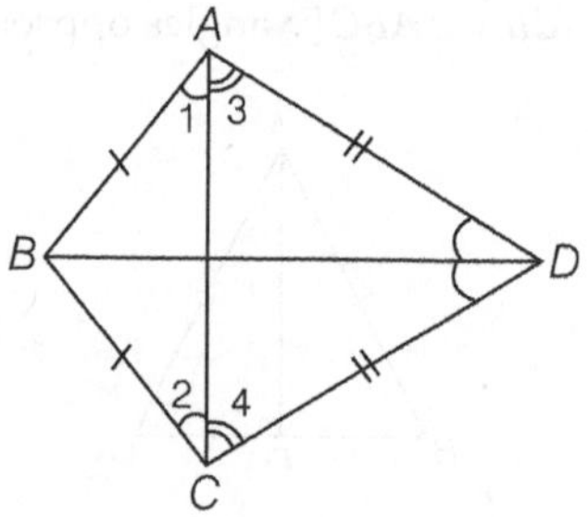

Proof Since, $AB = BC$ [given]

$\therefore$ $\angle 2 = \angle 1$

[$\because$ angles opposite to equal sides are equal] ...(i)

and $AD = CD$ [given]

$\Rightarrow$ $\angle 4 = \angle 3$

[$\because$ angles opposite to equal sides are equal]...(ii)

On adding Eqs. (i) and (ii), we get

$$\angle 2 + \angle 4 = \angle 1 + \angle 3$$

$\Rightarrow \quad \angle BCD = \angle BAD$ ...(iii)

In ΔBAD and ΔBCD,

$AB = BC$ [given]

$\angle BAD = \angle BCD$ [from Eq. (iii)]

and $AD = CD$ [given]

$\therefore \quad \Delta BAD \cong \Delta BCD$ [by SAS congruence rule]

Hence, $\angle ABD = \angle CBD$ and $\angle ADB = \angle CDB$ *i.e.*, BD bisects the angles ABC and ADC. [by CPCT]

Q.6 *ABC* is a right triangle with $AB = AC$. If bisector of $\angle A$ meets BC at D, then prove that $BC = 2AD$.

Ans. Given ΔABC is a right angled triangle with $AB = AC$, AD is the bisector of $\angle A$.

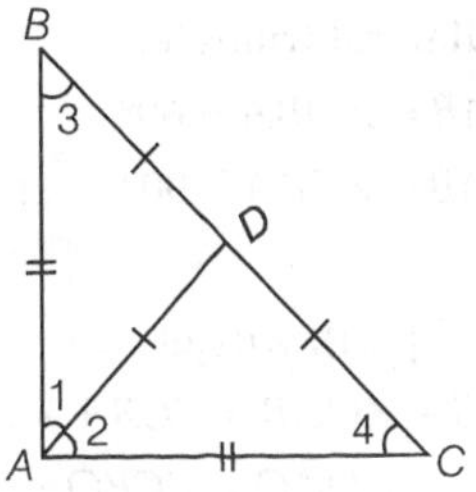

To prove $BC = 2AD$

Proof In ΔABC, $AB = AC$ [given]

$\Rightarrow \quad \angle C = \angle B$ ...(i)

[$\because$ angles opposite to equal sides are equal]

Now, in right angled $\Delta ABC, \angle A + \angle B + \angle C = 180°$

[by angle sum property of a triangle]

$\Rightarrow \quad 90° + \angle B + \angle B = 180°$ [from Eq. (i)]

$\Rightarrow \quad 2\angle B = 90°$

$\Rightarrow \quad \angle B = 45°$

$\Rightarrow \quad \angle B = \angle C = 45°$

or $\quad \angle 3 = \angle 4 = 45°$

Now, $\quad \angle 1 = \angle 2 = 45°$ [$\because$ AD is bisector of $\angle A$]

$\therefore \quad \angle 1 = \angle 3, \angle 2 = \angle 4$

$\Rightarrow \quad BD = AD, \ DC = AD$ ...(ii)

[$\because$ sides opposite to equal angles are equal]

Hence, $\quad BC = BD + CD = AD + AD$

$\Rightarrow \quad BC = 2\ AD$ [from Eq. (ii)]

Hence proved.

Q.7 O is a point in the interior of a square $ABCD$ such that OAB is an equilateral triangle. Show that ΔOCD is an isosceles triangle.

Ans. Given O is a point in the interior of a square $ABCD$ such that ΔOAB is an equilateral triangle.

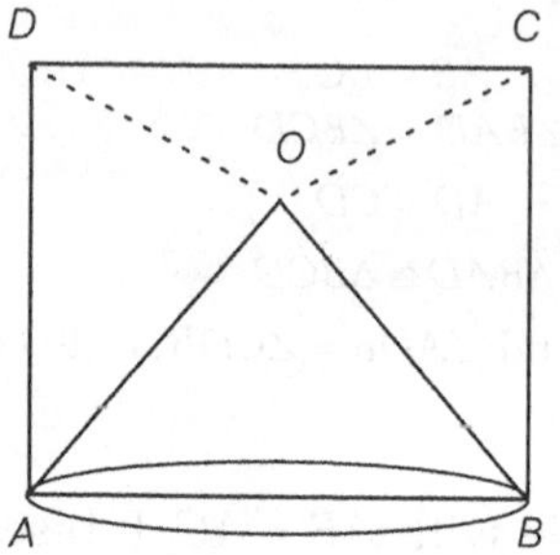

To prove ΔCOD is an isosceles triangle

Construction Let us join OC and OD.

Proof Since, AOB is an equilateral triangle.

$\therefore \quad \angle OAB = \angle OBA = 60°$ ...(i)

Also, $\angle DAB = \angle CBA = 90°$ ...(ii) [∵ each angle of a square is 90°]

[∵ $ABCD$ is a square]

On subtracting Eq. (i) from Eq. (ii), we get

$$\angle DAB - \angle OAB = \angle CBA - \angle OBA = 90° - 60°$$

i.e., $\angle DAO = \angle CBO = 30°$

In ΔAOD and ΔBOC,

$AO = BO$ [given]

[∵ all the sides of an equilateral triangle are equal]

$\angle DAO = \angle CBO$ [proved above]

and $AD = BC$ [sides of a square]

$\therefore \quad \Delta AOD \cong \Delta BOC$ [by SAS congruence rule]

Hence, $OD = OC$ [by CPCT]

In ΔCOD,

$$OC = OD$$

Hence, ΔCOD is an isosceles triangle. **Hence proved.**

Mistake Alert! *Student might assume that BOD and AOC are straight lines, which is actually wrong.*

Q.8 ABC and DBC are two triangles on the same base BC such that A and D lie on the opposite sides of BC, $AB = AC$ and $DB = DC$. Show that AD is the perpendicular bisector of BC.

Ans. Given Two ΔABC and ΔDBC are formed on the same base BC such that A and D lie on the opposite sides of BC such that $AB = AC$ and $DB = DC$. Also, AD intersects BC at O.

To prove AD is the perpendicular bisector of BC *i.e.,* $AD \perp BC$ and AD bisects BC.

Proof In ΔABD and ΔACD,

	$AB = AC$	[given]
	$AD = AD$	[common side]
and	$BD = DC$	[given]
$\therefore$	$\Delta ABD \cong \Delta ACD$	[by SSS congruence rule]
$\Rightarrow$	$\angle BAD = \angle CAD$	[by CPCT]
i.e.,	$\angle BAO = \angle CAO$	

In ΔAOB and ΔAOC,

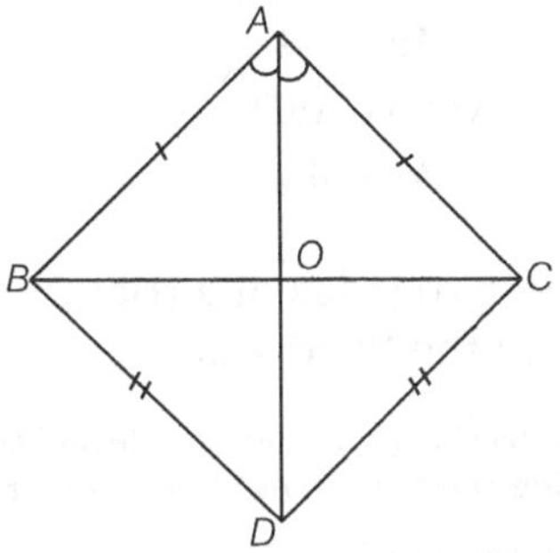

	$AB = AC$	[given]
	$AO = OA$	[common side]
and	$\angle BAO = \angle CAO$	[proved above]
$\therefore$	$\Delta AOB \cong \Delta AOC$	[by SAS congruence rule]
$\Rightarrow$	$BO = OC$	[by CPCT]
and	$\angle AOB = \angle AOC$	[by CPCT]...(i)
But	$\angle AOB + \angle AOC = 180°$	[linear pair axiom]
$\Rightarrow$	$\angle AOB + \angle AOB = 180°$	[from Eq. (i)]
$\Rightarrow$	$2\angle AOB = 180°$	
$\Rightarrow$	$\angle AOB = \frac{180°}{2} = 90°$	

Hence, $AD \perp BC$ and AD bisects BC *i.e.,* AD is the perpendicular bisector of BC.

Hence proved.

Mistake Alert! *While applying the congruence criteria, carefully apply these rules; SSS, SAS, AAS, SAS, CPCT or linear pair axiom.*

Q.9 ABC is an isosceles triangle in which $AC = BC$. AD and BE are respectively two altitudes to sides BC and AC. Prove that $AE = BD$.

Ans. **Given** ΔABC is an isosceles triangle in which $AC = BC$. Also, AD and BE are two altitudes to sides BC and AC, respectively.

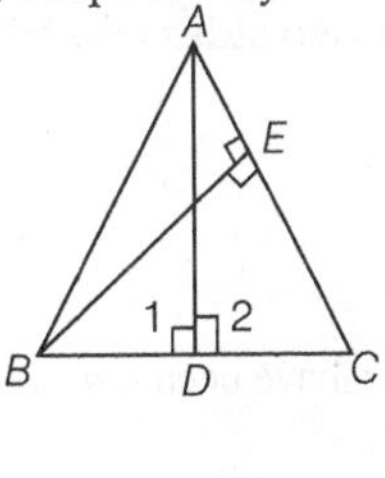

To prove $AE = BD$

Proof In ΔABC, $AC = BC$ [given]

$\angle ABC = \angle CAB$

[$\because$ angles opposite to equal sides are equal]

or $\angle ABD = \angle EAB$ ...(i)

In ΔAEB and ΔBDA,

$\angle AEB = \angle ADB = 90°$ [given, $AD \perp BC$ and $BE \perp AC$]

$\angle EAB = \angle ABD$ [from Eq. (i)]

and $AB = AB$ [common side]

$\therefore$ $\Delta AEB \cong \Delta BDA$ [by AAS congruence rule]

$\Rightarrow$ $AE = BD$ [by CPCT] **Hence proved.**

***Q.10** Prove that sum of any two sides of a triangle is greater than twice the median with respect to the third side.

Thinking process Firstly, use SAS congruence rule and sum of two sides of a triangle is greater than the third side and then show the required result.

Ans. **Given** In ΔABC, AD is a median.

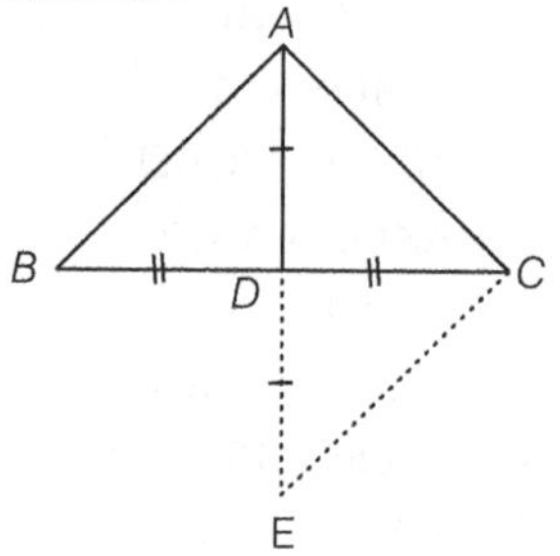

Construction

Let us produce AD to a point E such that $AD = DE$ and join CE.

To prove $AC + AB > 2AD$

Proof In ΔABD and ΔECD,

$AD = DE$ [by construction]

$BD = CD$ [given, AD is the median]

and $\angle ADB = \angle CDE$ [vertically opposite angle]

$\therefore$ $\Delta ABD \cong \Delta ECD$ [by SAS congruence rule]

$\Rightarrow$ $AB = CE$ [by CPCT] ...(i)

Now, in ΔAEC,

$AC + EC > AE$

[$\because$ sum of two sides of a triangle is greater than the third side]

$\therefore$ $AC + AB > 2AD$ [from Eq. (i) and $AD = DE$ (given)]

Hence proved.

(*) Topics related to these question have been removed from latest NCERT.

***Q.11** Show that in a quadrilateral $ABCD$, $AB + BC + CD + DA < 2(BD + AC)$

Thinking Process Firstly, draw a quadrilateral $ABCD$. Further use the property of a triangle that sum of two sides of a triangle is greater than third side and show the required result.

Ans. Given $ABCD$ is a quadrilateral.

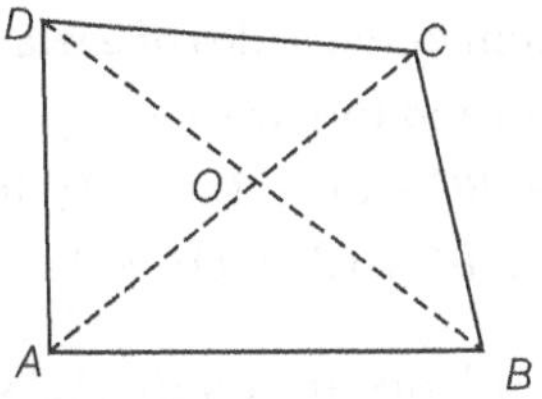

Construction Let us join diagonals AC and BD.

To prove $AB + BC + CD + DA < 2(BD + CA)$

Proof In ΔOAB, $OA + OB > AB$ ...(i)

[$\because$ sum of two sides of a triangle is greater than the third side]

In ΔOBC, $OB + OC > BC$ ...(ii)

[$\because$ sum of two sides of a triangle is greater than the third side]

In ΔOCD, $OC + OD > CD$ ...(iii)

[$\because$ sum of two sides of a triangle is greater than the third side]

In ΔODA, $OD + OA > DA$ ...(iv)

[$\because$ sum of two sides of a triangle is greater than the third side]

On adding Eqs. (i), (ii), (iii) and (iv), we get

$$2[(OA + OB + OC + OD] > AB + BC + CD + DA$$

$\Rightarrow$ $$2[(OA + OC) + (OB + OD)] > AB + BC + CD + DA$$

$\Rightarrow$ $$2(AC + BD) > AB + BC + CD + DA$$

[$\because OA + OC = AC$ and $OB + OD = BD$]

$\Rightarrow$ $$AB + BC + CD + DA < 2(BD + AC)$$ **Hence proved.**

***Q.12** Show that in a quadrilateral $ABCD$, $AB + BC + CD + DA > AC + BD$.

Ans. Given, $ABCD$ is a quadrilateral.

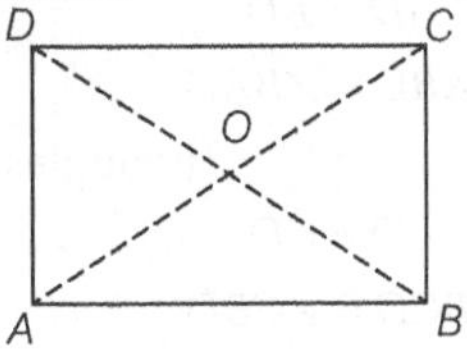

Construction Join diagonals AC and BD.

To prove $AB + BC + CD + DA > AC + BD$

Proof

In ΔABC, $AB + BC > AC$ ...(i)

[$\because$ sum of two sides of a triangle is greater than the third side]

(*) Topics related to these question have been removed from latest NCERT.

In ΔBCD, $BC + CD > BD$ ...(ii)

[$\because$ sum of two sides of a triangle is greater than the third side]

In ΔCDA, $CD + DA > AC$ ...(iii)

[$\because$ sum of two sides of a triangle is greater than the third side]

In ΔDAB, $DA + AB > BD$ ...(iv)

[$\because$ sum of two sides of a triangle is greater than the third side]

On adding Eqs. (i), (ii), (iii) and (iv), we get

$$2(AB + BC + CD + DA) > 2(AC + BD)$$

$\Rightarrow$ $AB + BC + CD + DA > AC + BD$ **Hence proved.**

Q.13 In a $\Delta\ ABC$, D is the mid-point of side AC such that $BD = \frac{1}{2} AC$. Show that $\angle ABC$ is a right angle.

● **Concept Insight** Sum of interior angles of a triangle is 180°.

Ans. Given In ΔABC, D is the mid-point of AC *i.e.*, $AD = CD$ such that $BD = \frac{1}{2} AC$.

To prove $\angle ABC = 90°$

Proof

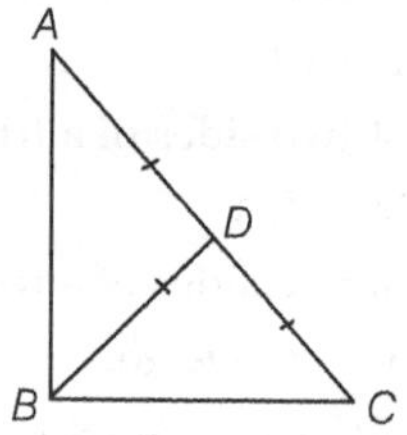

We have, $BD = \frac{1}{2} AC$ ...(i)

Since, D is the mid-point of AC.

$\therefore$ $AD = CD = \frac{1}{2} AC$ ...(ii)

From Eqs. (i) and (ii), we get

$$AD = CD = BD$$

In ΔDAB, $AD = BD$ [proved above]

$\therefore$ $\angle ABD = \angle BAD$ ...(iii)

[$\because$ angles opposite to equal sides are equal]

In ΔDBC, $BD = CD$ [proved above]

$\therefore$ $\angle BCD = \angle CBD$ ...(iv)

[$\because$ angles opposite to equal sides are equal]

In ΔABC, $\angle ABC + \angle BAC + \angle ACB = 180°$ [by angle sum property of a triangle]

$\Rightarrow$ $\angle ABC + \angle BAD + \angle DCB = 180°$

$\Rightarrow$ $\angle ABC + \angle ABD + \angle CBD = 180°$ [from Eqs.(iii) and (iv)]

$\Rightarrow$ $\angle ABC + \angle ABC = 180°$

$\Rightarrow$ $2\angle ABC = 180°$

$\Rightarrow$ $\angle ABC = 90°$ **Hence proved.**

Q.14 In a right triangle, prove that the line-segment joining the mid-point of the hypotenuse to the opposite vertex is half the hypotenuse.

Ans. **Given** In ΔABC, $\angle B = 90°$ and D is the mid-point of AC.

Construction Produce BD to E such that $BD = DE$ and join EC.

To prove $BD = \frac{1}{2} AC$

Proof

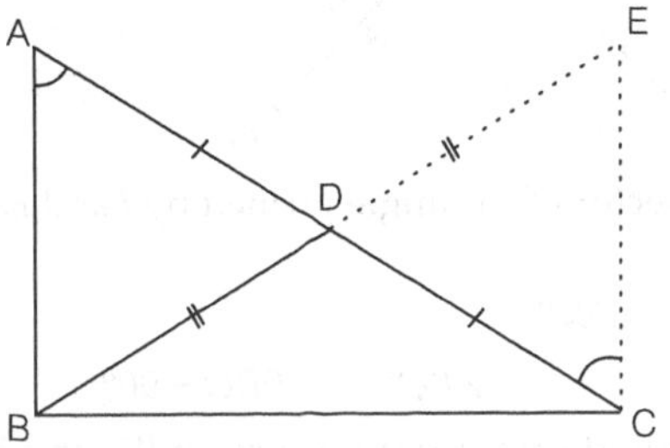

In ΔADB and ΔCDE, $AD = DC$ [$\because$ D is mid-point of AC]

$BD = DE$ [by construction]

and $\angle ADB = \angle CDE$ [vertically opposite angles]

$\therefore$ $\Delta ADB \cong \Delta CDE$ [by SAS congruence rule]

$\Rightarrow$ $AB = EC$ [by CPCT]

and $\angle BAD = \angle DCE$ [by CPCT]

But $\angle BAD$ and $\angle DCE$ are alternate angles.

So, $EC \parallel AB$ and BC is a transversal.

$\therefore$ $\angle ABC + \angle BCE = 180°$ [co-interior angles]

$\Rightarrow$ $90° + \angle BCE = 180°$ [$\because$ $\angle ABC = 90°$, given]

$\Rightarrow$ $\angle BCE = 180° - 90°$

$\Rightarrow$ $\angle BCE = 90°$

In ΔABC and ΔECB, $AB = EC$ [proved above]

$BC = CB$ [common side]

and $\angle ABC = \angle ECB$ [each 90°]

$\therefore$ $\Delta ABC \cong \Delta ECB$ [by SAS congruence rule]

$\Rightarrow$ $AC = EB$ [by CPCT]

$\Rightarrow$ $\frac{1}{2} EB = \frac{1}{2} AC$ [dividing both sides by 2]

$\Rightarrow$ $BD = \frac{1}{2} AC$ **Hence proved.**

Q.15 Two lines l and m intersect at the point O and P is a point on a line n passing through the point O such that P is equidistant from l and m. Prove that n is the bisector of the angle formed by l and m.

- **Concept Insight** If a point is equidistant from two lines, then the the perpendicular lines from that point to both lines are equal in length.

Ans. Given Two lines l and m intersect at the point O and P is a point on a line n passing through O such that P is equidistant from lines l and m. i.e., $PQ = PR$.

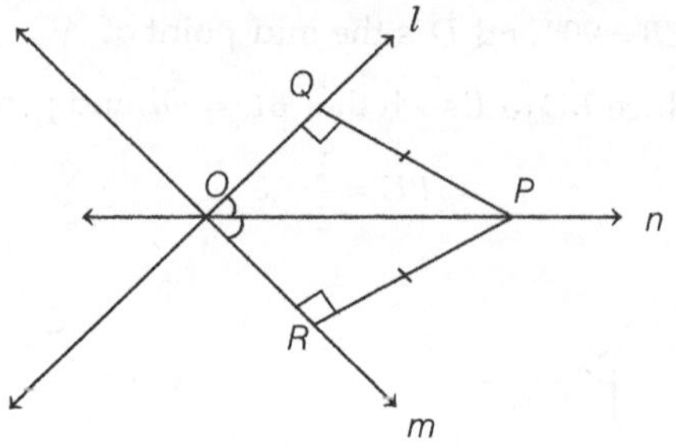

To prove n is the bisector of the angle formed by l and m i.e., n is the bisector of $\angle QOR$.

Proof In ΔOQP and ΔORP,

$$\angle PQO = \angle PRO = 90°$$

[since, P in equidistant from l and m, so PQ and PR will be perpendicular to lines l and m respectively]

$OP = OP$ [common side]

$PQ = PR$ [given]

$\therefore$ $\Delta OQP \cong \Delta ORP$ [by RHS congruence rule]

$\Rightarrow$ $\angle POQ = \angle POR$ [by CPCT]

Hence, n is the bisector of $\angle QOR$. **Hence proved.**

Q.16 Line segment joining the mid-points M and N of parallel sides AB and DC, respectively of a trapezium $ABCD$ is perpendicular to both the sides AB and DC. Prove that $AD = BC$.

Ans. Given In trapezium $ABCD$, points M and N are the mid-points of parallel sides AB and DC, respectively and join MN, which is perpendicular to AB and DC.

To prove $AD = BC$

Proof Since, M is the mid-point of AB.

$\therefore$ $AM = MB$

Now, in ΔAMN and ΔBMN, $AM = MB$ [proved above]

$\angle 3 = \angle 4$ [each 90°]

$MN = MN$ [common side]

$\therefore$ $\Delta AMN \cong \Delta BMN$ [by SAS congruence rule]

$\therefore$ $\angle 1 = \angle 2$ [by CPCT]

On multiplying both sides of above equation by -1 and then adding 90° both sides, we get

$$90° - \angle 1 = 90° - \angle 2$$

$\Rightarrow$ $\angle AND = \angle BNC$ ...(i)

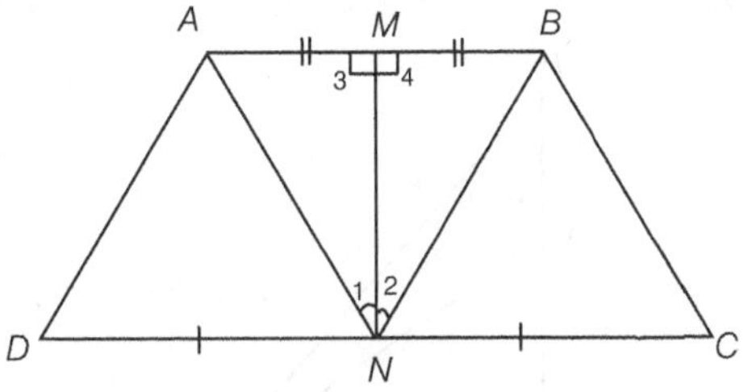

Now, in ΔADN and ΔBCN,

$\angle AND = \angle BNC$ [from Eq. (i)]

$AN = BN$ [$\because \Delta AMN \cong \Delta BMN$]

and $DN = NC$ [$\because N$ is the mid-point of CD (given)]

$\therefore$ $\Delta ADN \cong \Delta BCN$ [by SAS congruence rule]

Hence, $AD = BC$ [by CPCT] **Hence proved.**

Q.17 *ABCD* is a quadrilateral such that diagonal *AC* bisects the angles *A* and *C*. Prove that $AB = AD$ and $CB = CD$.

Ans. Given In a quadrilateral *ABCD*, diagonal *AC* bisects $\angle A$ and $\angle C$.

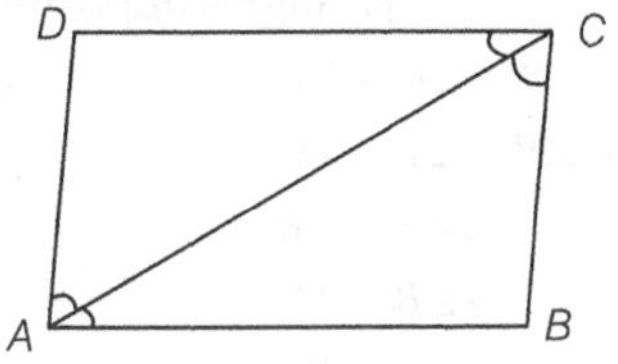

To prove $AB = AD$ and $CB = CD$

Proof In ΔADC and ΔABC,

$\angle DAC = \angle BAC$ [$\because$ *AC* is the bisector of $\angle A$]

$\angle DCA = \angle BCA$ [$\because$ *AC* is the bisector of $\angle C$]

and $AC = AC$ [common side]

$\therefore$ $\Delta ADC \cong \Delta ABC$ [by ASA congruence rule]

$\Rightarrow$ $AD = AB$ [by CPCT]

and $CD = CB$ [by CPCT]

Hence proved.

Q.18 *ABC* is a right angled triangle such that $AB = AC$ and bisector of angle *C* intersects the side *AB* at *D*. prove that $AC + AD = BC$.

Ans. Given In right angled ΔABC, $AB = AC$ and *CD* is the bisector of $\angle C$.

Construction Draw $DE \perp BC$.

To prove $AC + AD = BC$

Proof In right angled ΔABC, $AB = AC$, so *BC* will be a hypotenuse

$\therefore$ $\angle A = 90°$

In ΔDAC and ΔDEC, $\angle A = \angle 3 = 90°$ [by construction]

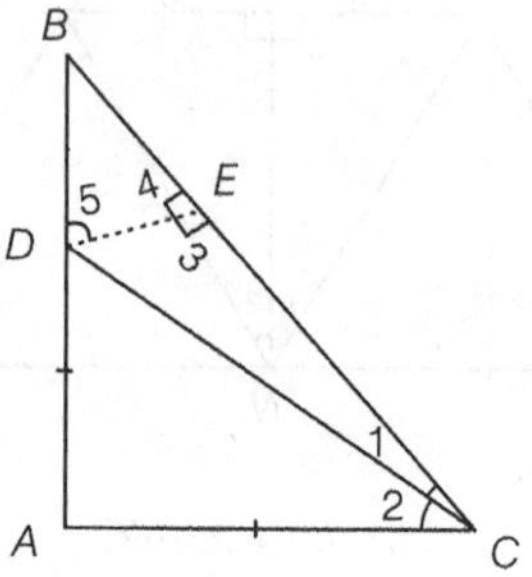

$\angle 1 = \angle 2$ [given, CD is the bisector of $\angle C$]

$DC = DC$ [common sides]

$\therefore$ $\Delta DAC \cong \Delta DEC$ [by AAS congruence rule]

$\Rightarrow$ $DA = DE$ [by CPCT]... (i)

and $AC = EC$ ... (ii)

In ΔABC, $AB = AC$

$\angle C = \angle B$

[$\because$ angles opposite to equal sides are equal] ...(iii)

Again, in ΔABC, $\angle A + \angle B + \angle C = 180°$ [by angle sum property of a triangle]

$\Rightarrow$ $90° + \angle B + \angle B = 180°$ [from Eq. (iii)]

$\Rightarrow$ $2\angle B = 180° - 90°$

$\Rightarrow$ $2\angle B = 90°$

$\Rightarrow$ $\angle B = 45°$

In ΔBED, $\angle 5 = 180° - (\angle B + \angle 4)$

[by angle sum property of a triangle]

$= 180° - (45° + 90°)$

$= 180° - 135° = 45°$

$\therefore$ $\angle B = \angle 5$

$\Rightarrow$ $DE = BE$ [$\because$ sides opposite to equal angles are equal] ...(iv)

From Eqs. (i) and (iv), we get

$DA = DE = BE$ ...(v)

$\because$ $BC = EC + BE$

$= AC + AD$ [from Eqs. (ii) and (v)]

$\therefore$ $AD + AC = BC$ **Hence proved.**

***Q.19** *AB* and *CD* are the smallest and largest sides of a quadrilateral *ABCD*. Out of $\angle B$ and $\angle D$ decide which is greater.

Ans. Given, In quadrilateral *ABCD*, *AB* is the smallest and *CD* is the largest side.

(✱) Topics related to these question have been removed from latest NCERT.

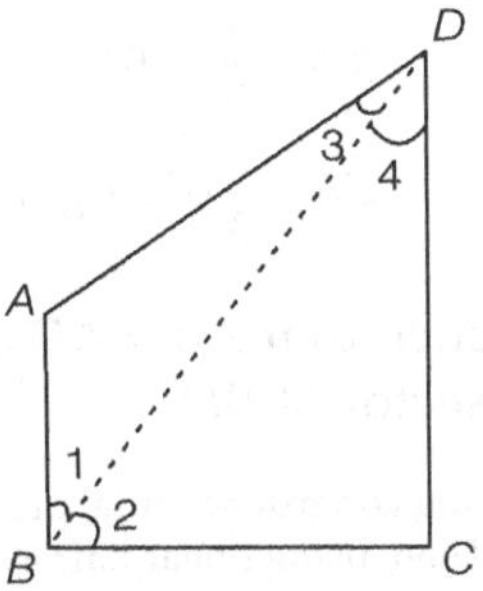

Join BD.

In ΔABD, $AD > AB$ [$\because AB$ is the smallest side in $ABCD$]

$\Rightarrow$ $\angle 1 > \angle 3$ [$\because$ angle opposite to longer side is greater] ...(i)

In ΔBCD, $CD > BC$ [$\because CD$ is the largest side in $ABCD$]

$\Rightarrow$ $\angle 2 > \angle 4$ [$\because$ angle opposite to longer side is greater] ...(ii)

On adding Eqs. (i) and (ii), we get

$$\angle 1 + \angle 2 > \angle 3 + \angle 4$$

$\Rightarrow$ $\angle B > \angle D$

***Q.20** Prove that in a triangle, other than an equilateral triangle, angle opposite the longest side is greater than $\frac{2}{3}$ of a right angle.

Ans. Consider ΔABC in which BC is the longest side.

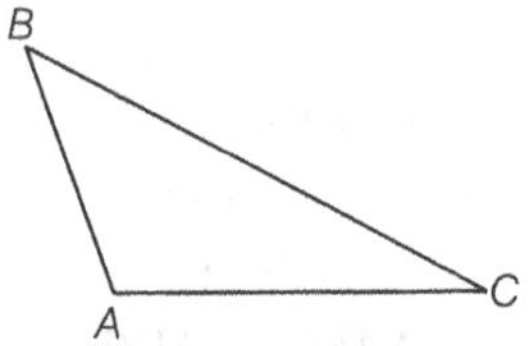

To prove $\angle A = \frac{2}{3}$ of right angle

Proof In ΔABC, $BC > AB$ [consider BC is the largest side]

$\Rightarrow$ $\angle A > \angle C$ ...(i)

[$\because$ angle opposite the longest side is greatest]

and $BC > AC$

$\Rightarrow$ $\angle A > \angle B$ ...(ii)

[$\because$ angle opposite the longest side is greatest]

On adding Eqs. (i) and (ii), we get

$$2\angle A > \angle B + \angle C$$

$\Rightarrow$ $2\angle A + \angle A > \angle A + \angle B + \angle C$ [adding $\angle A$ both sides]

$\Rightarrow$ $3\angle A > \angle A + \angle B + \angle C$

$\Rightarrow$ $3\angle A > 180°$ [$\because$ sum of all the angles of a triangle is 180°]

(*) Topics related to these question have been removed from latest NCERT.

$\Rightarrow \quad \angle A > \frac{2}{3} \times 90°$

i.e., $\quad \angle A > \frac{2}{3}$ of a right angle **Hence proved.**

Q.21 *ABCD* is quadrilateral such that $AB = AD$ and $CB = CD$. prove that *AC* is the perpendicular bisector of *BD*.

Thinking Process Firstly, using congruence rule, prove that the two adjacent angles on the straight line are equal. Then, using linear pair axiom, prove that those two angles are right angle.

Ans. Given In quadrilateral *ABCD*, $AB = AD$ and $CB = CD$.

Construction Join *AC* and *BD*.

To prove *AC* is the perpendicular bisector of *BD*.

Proof

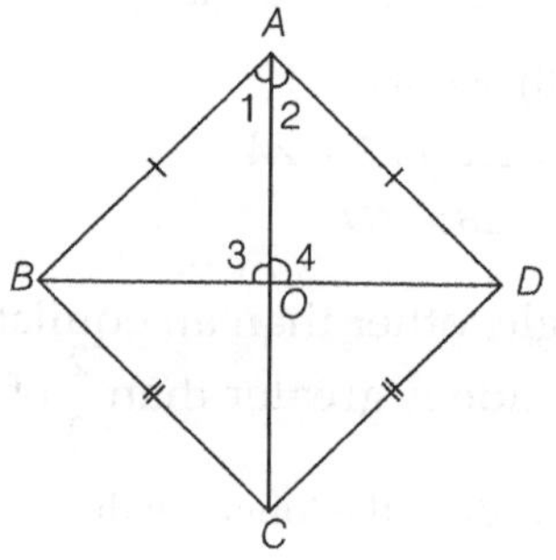

In ΔABC and ΔADC,

	$AB = AD$	[given]
	$BC = CD$	[given]
and	$AC = AC$	[common side]
$\therefore$	$\Delta ABC \cong \Delta ADC$	[by SSS congruence rule]
$\Rightarrow$	$\angle 1 = \angle 2$	[by CPCT]
Now, in ΔAOB and ΔAOD,	$AB = AD$	[given]
$\Rightarrow$	$\angle 1 = \angle 2$	[proved above]
and	$AO = AO$	[common side]
$\therefore$	$\Delta AOB \cong \Delta AOD$	[by SAS congruence rule]
$\Rightarrow$	$BO = DO$	[by CPCT]
and	$\angle 3 = \angle 4$	[by CPCT]...(i)
But	$\angle 3 + \angle 4 = 180°$	[linear pair axiom]
	$\angle 3 + \angle 3 = 180°$	[from Eq. (i)]
$\Rightarrow$	$2\angle 3 = 180° \Rightarrow \angle 3 = \frac{180°}{2}$	
$\therefore$	$\angle 3 = 90°$	

i.e., *AC* is perpendicular bisector of *BD*. **Hence proved.**

Chapter

08

Quadrilaterals

Multiple Choice Questions (MCQs)

Choose the correct answer from the given four options in the following questions:

*** Q.1** Three angles of a quadrilateral are 75°, 90° and 75°, then the fourth angle is

(a) 90° (b) 95° (c) 105° (d) 120°

Ans. ***(d)*** Given, $\angle A = 75°$, $\angle B = 90°$ and $\angle C = 75°$

We know that sum of all the angles of a quadrilateral is 360°.

$$\angle A + \angle B + \angle C + \angle D = 360°$$

$\Rightarrow$ $75° + 90° + 75° + \angle D = 360°$

$\therefore$ $\angle D = 360° - (75° + 90° + 75°) = 360° - 240° = 120°$

Hence, the fourth angle of the quadrilateral is 120°.

Q.2 A diagonal of a rectangle is inclined to one side of the rectangle at 25°. The acute angle between the diagonals is

(a) 55° (b) 50° (c) 40° (d) 25°

● **Concept Insight** Use the concept, the diagonal of parallelogram bisect each other.

Ans. ***(b)*** We know that diagonals of a rectangle are equal in length.

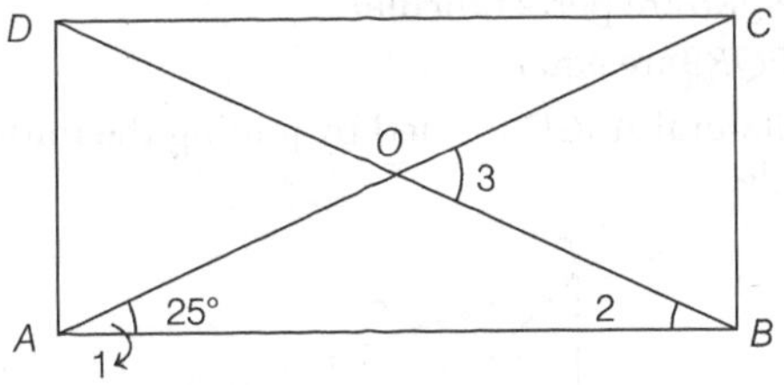

$\therefore$ $AC = BD$

$\Rightarrow$ $\frac{1}{2} AC = \frac{1}{2} BD$ [dividing both sides by 2]

$\Rightarrow$ $OA = OB$ [$\because$ O is the mid-point of AC and BD]

$\Rightarrow$ $\angle 2 = \angle 1$ [$\because$ angles opposite to equal sides are equal]

$= 25°$

$\therefore$ $\angle 3 = \angle 1 + \angle 2$

[$\because$ exterior angle is equal to the sum of two opposite interior angles]

$= 25° + 25° = 50°$

Hence, the acute angle between the diagonals is 50°.

(*) Topics related to these question have been removed from latest NCERT.

Q.3 $ABCD$ is a rhombus such that $\angle ACB = 40°$. Then, $\angle ADB$ is

(a) 40° (b) 45° (c) 50° (d) 60°

Ans. *(c)* Given, $ABCD$ is a rhombus such that $\angle ACB = 40° \Rightarrow \angle OCB = 40°$

Since, $AD \parallel BC$ and AC is transversal

$$\angle DAC = \angle BCA = 40° \quad \text{[alternate interior angles]}$$

Also, $\angle AOD = 90°$

[∵ diagonals of a rhombus are perpendicular to each other]

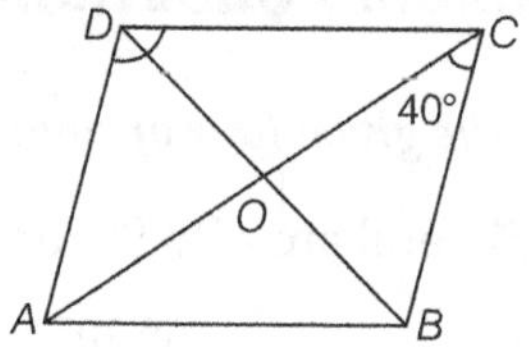

We know that sum of all angles of a triangle is 180°.

Now, in ΔAOD,

$$\angle ADO + \angle DOA + \angle OAD = 180°$$

$$\Rightarrow \quad \angle ADO = 180° - (40° + 90°)$$

$$= 180° - 130° = 50°$$

$$\Rightarrow \quad \angle ADO = 50°$$

$$\therefore \quad \angle ADB = \angle ADO = 50°$$

Q.4 The quadrilateral formed by joining the mid-points of the sides of a quadrilateral $PQRS$, taken in order, is a rectangle, if

(a) $PQRS$ is a rectangle

(b) $PQRS$ is a parallelogram

(c) diagonals of $PQRS$ are perpendicular

(d) diagonals of $PQRS$ are equal

Ans. *(c)* Let the quadrilateral $ABCD$ formed by joining the mid-points of quadrilateral $PQRS$ is a rectangle.

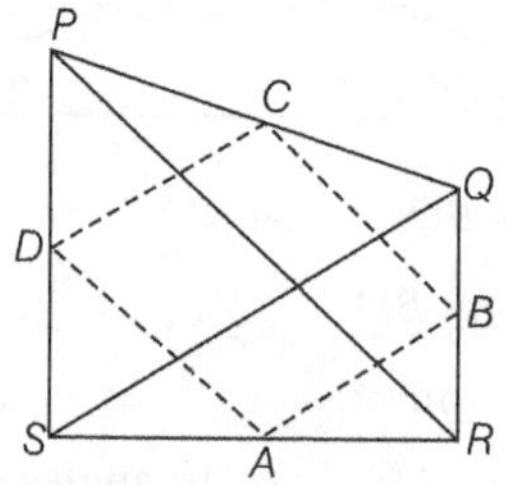

By mid-point theorem in ΔPSR and ΔPSQ,

$$AD \parallel PR \text{ and } CD \parallel SQ$$

Since, $ABCD$ is a rectangle

$$\therefore \quad AD \perp CD$$

So, $PR \perp SQ$

Hence, Diagonals of $PQRS$ are perpendicular.

Q.5 The quadrilateral formed by joining the mid-points of the sides of quadrilateral *PQRS*, taken in order, is a rhombus, if

(a) *PQRS* is a rhombus
(b) *PQRS* is a parallelogram
(c) diagonals of *PQRS* are perpendicular
(d) diagonals of *PQRS* are equal

- **Concept Insight** In this problem, use the mid- point theorem; the line segment joining the mid-points of two sides of a triangle is parallel to the third side.

Ans. *(d)* Given, the quadrilateral *ABCD* is a rhombus.
So, sides *AB, BC, CD* and *AD* are equal.

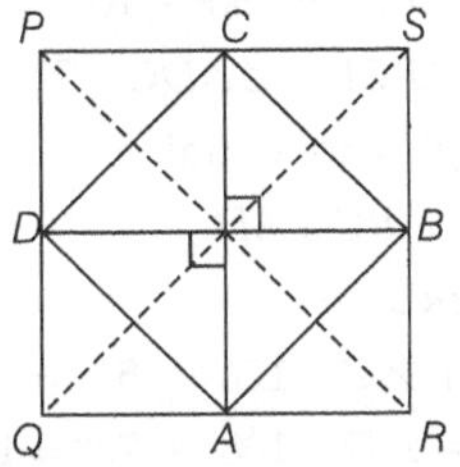

Now, in ΔPQS,
D and *C* are the mid-points of *PQ* and *PS*.

So, $DC = \frac{1}{2}QS$ [by mid-point theorem]...(i)

Similarly, in ΔPSR, $BC = \frac{1}{2}PR$ [by mid-point theorem]...(ii)

As $BC = DC$ [$\because$ *ABCD* is a rhombus]

$\therefore$ $\frac{1}{2}QS = \frac{1}{2}PR$ [from Eqs. (i) and (ii)]

$\Rightarrow$ $QS = PR$

Hence, diagonals of *PQRS* are equal.

***Q.6** If angles *A*, *B*, *C* and *D* of the quadrilateral *ABCD*, taken in order are in the ratio 3:7:6:4, then *ABCD* is a

(a) rhombus
(b) parallelogram
(c) trapezium
(d) kite

Ans. *(c)* Given, ratio of angles of quadrilateral *ABCD* is 3 : 7 : 6 : 4.
Let angles of quadrilateral *ABCD* be 3*x*, 7*x*, 6*x* and 4*x*, respectively.

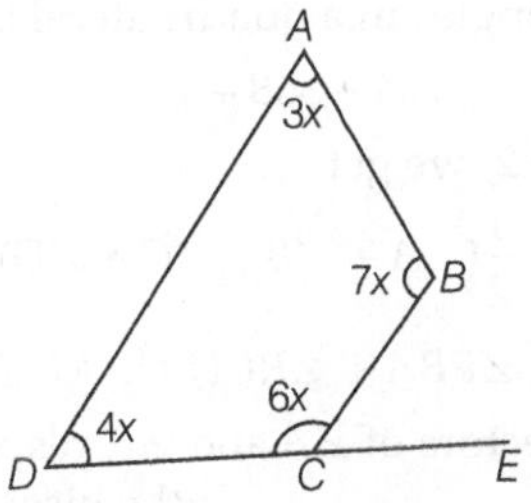

We know that sum of all angles of a quadrilateral is 360°.

$\therefore \quad 3x + 7x + 6x + 4x = 360°$

$\Rightarrow \quad 20x = 360°$

$\Rightarrow \quad x = \frac{360°}{20°} = 18°$

$\therefore$ Angles of the quadrilateral are

$\angle A = 3 \times 18 = 54°$

$\angle B = 7 \times 18 = 126°$

$\angle C = 6 \times 18 = 108°$

and $\angle D = 4 \times 18 = 72°$

From figure, $\angle BCE = 180° - \angle BCD$ [linear pair]

$\Rightarrow \quad \angle BCE = 180° - 108° = 72°$

Here, $\angle BCE = \angle ADC = 72°$

Since, the corresponding angles are equal.

$\therefore \quad BC \parallel AD$

Now, sum of co-interior angles,

$\angle A + \angle B = 126° + 54° = 180°$

and $\angle C + \angle D = 108° + 72° = 180°$

Hence, $ABCD$ is a trapezium.

Q.7 If bisectors of $\angle A$ and $\angle B$ of a quadrilateral $ABCD$ intersect each other at P, of $\angle B$ and $\angle C$ at Q, of $\angle C$ and $\angle D$ at R and of $\angle D$ and $\angle A$ at S, then $PQRS$ is a

(a) rectangle
(b) rhombus
(c) parallelogram
(d) quadrilateral whose opposite angles are supplementary

Ans. ***(d)*** Given, $ABCD$ is a quadrilateral and all angles bisectors form a quadrilateral $PQRS$.

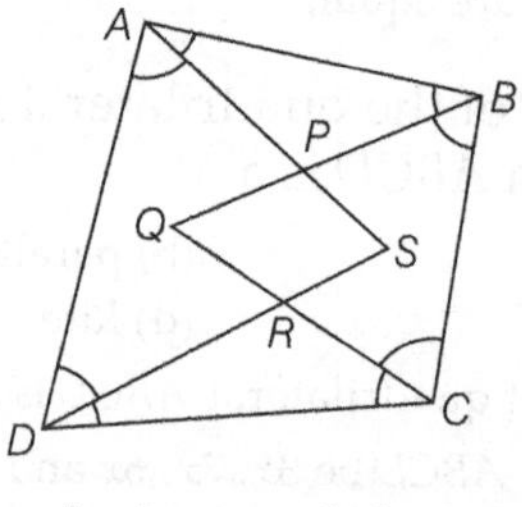

We know that sum of all angles in a quadrilateral is 360°.

$\therefore \quad \angle A + \angle B + \angle C + \angle D = 360°$

On dividing both sides by 2, we get

$$\frac{1}{2}(\angle A + \angle B + \angle C + \angle D) = \frac{360°}{2}$$

$\Rightarrow \quad \angle PAB + \angle PBA + \angle RCD + \angle RDC = 180° \quad \ldots(i)$

[$\because$ AP and PB are the bisectors of $\angle A$ and $\angle B$, respectively and also RC and RD are the bisectors of $\angle C$ and $\angle D$, respectively]

(✱) Topics related to these question have been removed from latest NCERT.

Now, in ΔAPB,

$$\angle PAB + \angle ABP + \angle BPA = 180^\circ \quad \text{[by angle sum property of a triangle]}$$

$$\Rightarrow \quad \angle PAB + \angle ABP = 180^\circ - \angle BPA \quad \text{...(ii)}$$

Similarly in ΔRDC,

$$\angle RDC + \angle DCR + \angle CRD = 180^\circ \quad \text{[by angle sum property of a triangle]}$$

$$\Rightarrow \quad \angle RDC + \angle DCR = 180^\circ - \angle CRD \quad \text{...(iii)}$$

On substituting the value from Eqs. from (ii) and (iii) in Eq. (i), we get

$$180^\circ - \angle BPA + 180^\circ - \angle DRC = 180^\circ$$

$$\Rightarrow \quad \angle BPA + \angle DRC = 180^\circ$$

$$\Rightarrow \quad \angle SPQ + \angle SRQ = 180^\circ$$

[$\because$ $\angle BPA = \angle SPQ$ and $\angle DRC = \angle SRQ$ (vertically opposite angles)]

Hence, $PQRS$ is a quadrilateral whose opposite angles are supplementary.

Q.8 If APB and CQD are two parallel lines, then the bisectors of the angles APQ, BPQ, CQP and PQD form

(a) a square (b) a rhombus

(c) a rectangle (d) any other parallelogram

Ans. *(c)* Given, APB and CQD are two parallel lines.

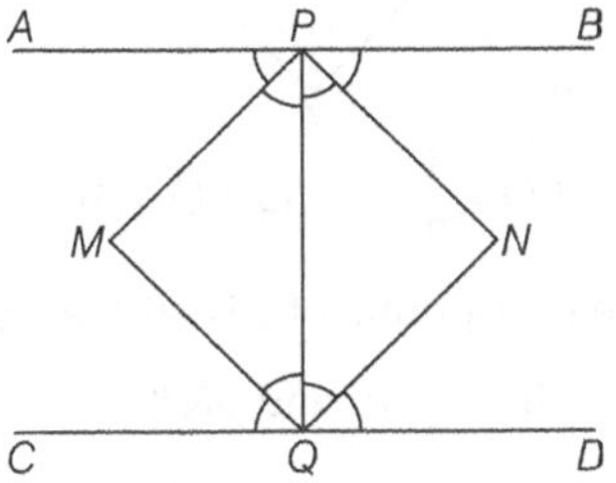

Let the bisectors of angles APQ and CQP meet at a point M and bisectors of angles BPQ and PQD meet at a point N.

Since, $APB \parallel CQD$

Then, $\angle APQ = \angle PQD$ [alternate interior angles]

$$\Rightarrow \quad 2\angle MPQ = 2\angle NQP$$

[$\because$ PM and NQ are the angle bisectors of $\angle APQ$ and $\angle DQP$, respectively]

$$\Rightarrow \quad \angle MPQ = \angle NQP \quad \text{[dividing both sides by 2]}$$

[$\because$ alternate interior angles are equal]

$\therefore$ $PM \parallel QN$

Similarly, $\angle NPQ = \angle MQP$ [alternate interior angles]

$\therefore$ $PN \parallel QM$

So, quadrilateral $PMQN$ is a parallelogram.

$\because$ $\angle CQD = 180^\circ$ [$\because$ CQD is a line]

$$\Rightarrow \quad \angle CQP + \angle DQP = 180^\circ$$

$$\Rightarrow \quad 2\angle MQP + 2\angle NQP = 180^\circ$$

[$\because$ MQ and NQ are the bisectors of the angles CQP and DQP]

$\Rightarrow \quad 2(\angle MQP + \angle NQP) = 180°$

$\Rightarrow \quad \angle MQN = 90°$

Hence, $PMQN$ is a rectangle.

Q.9 The figure obtained by joining the mid-points of the sides of a rhombus, taken in order, is

(a) a rhombus (b) a rectangle
(c) a square (d) any parallelogram

Ans. *(b)* Let $ABCD$ be a rhombus and P, Q, R and S are the mid-points of the sides AB, BC, CD and DA respectively. Join AC.

In ΔABC, P and Q are the mid-points of AB and BC respectively.

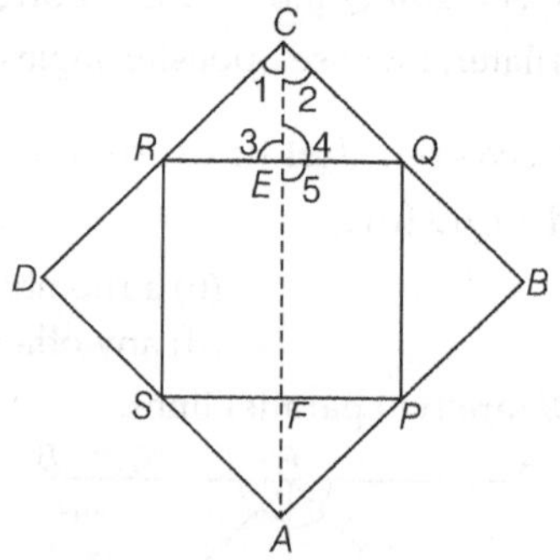

$\therefore \quad PQ = \frac{1}{2} AC$ and $PQ \parallel AC$ [By mid-point theorem] ...(i)

In ΔADC, R and S are the mid-points of CD and DA respectively.

$\therefore \quad SR = \frac{1}{2} AC$ and $SR \parallel AC$ [By mid-point theorem] ...(ii)

From Eqs. (i) and (ii), we get

$$PQ = \frac{1}{2} AC = SR \text{ and } PQ \parallel AC \parallel SR$$

$\Rightarrow \quad PQ = SR$ and $PQ \parallel SR$

$\therefore$ $PQRS$ is a parallelogram. ...(iii)

Now, in ΔERC and ΔEQC,

$\angle 1 = \angle 2$ [$\because$ The diagonals of a rhombus bisects the opposite angles]

$CR = CQ$ $\left[\because \frac{CD}{2} = \frac{BC}{2}\right]$

$CE = CE$ [Common]

$\therefore \quad \Delta ERC \cong \Delta EQC$ [By SAS congruency]

$\Rightarrow \quad \angle 3 = \angle 4$ [By CPCT] ...(iv)

But $\quad \angle 3 = \angle 4 = 180°$ [Linear pair] ...(v)

From Eqs. (iv) and (v), we get

$\Rightarrow \quad \angle 3 + \angle 4 = 90°$

Now, $\angle RQP = 180° - \angle 5$ [$\because$ Co-interior angles for $PQ \parallel AC$ and EQ is transversal]

But $\quad \angle 5 = \angle 3$ [$\because$ Vertically opposite angles are equal]

Q.10 D and E are the mid-points of the sides AB and AC of ΔABC and O is any point on side BC. O is joined to A. If P and Q are the mid-points of OB and OC respectively, then $DEQP$ is

(a) a square (b) a rectangle (c) a rhombus (d) a parallelogram

Thinking Process Use the mid-point theorem *i.e.*, the line segment joining the mid-points of two sides of a triangle is parallel to the third side and is also half of the length of the third side.

Ans. *(d)* In ΔABC, D and E are the mid-points of sides AB and AC, respectively.

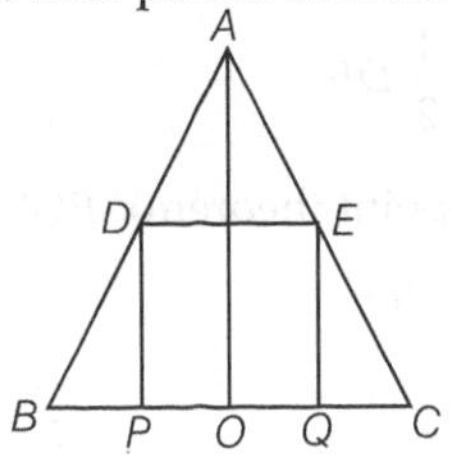

By mid-point theorem,

$$DE \parallel BC$$

and $$DE = \frac{1}{2} BC \qquad \text{...(i)}$$

Then, $$DE = \frac{1}{2}[BP + PO + OQ + QC]$$

$$\Rightarrow \quad DE = \frac{1}{2}[2PO + 2OQ]$$

[$\because$ P and Q are the mid-points of OB and OC, respectively]

$$\Rightarrow \quad DE = PO + OQ$$

$$\Rightarrow \quad DE = PQ \qquad \text{...(ii)}$$

Now, in ΔAOC, Q and E are the mid-points of OC and AC, respectively.

$\therefore$ $EQ \parallel AO$ and $EQ = \frac{1}{2} AO$ [by mid-point theorem]...(iii)

Similarly, in ΔABO, $PD \parallel AO$ and $PD = \frac{1}{2} AO$ [by mid-point theorem] ...(iv)

From Eqs. (iii) and (iv), we get

$$EQ \parallel PD \text{ and } EQ = PD$$

From Eqs. (i) and (ii), we get $DE \parallel PQ$ and $DE = PQ$

Hence, $DEQP$ is a parallelogram.

Q.11 The figure formed by joining the mid-points of the sides of a quadrilateral $ABCD$, taken in order, is a square only, if

(a) $ABCD$ is a rhombus
(b) diagonals of $ABCD$ are equal
(c) diagonals of $ABCD$ are equal and perpendicular
(d) diagonals of $ABCD$ are perpendicular

Ans. *(c)* Given, $ABCD$ is a quadrilateral and P, Q, R and S are the mid-points of sides of AB, BC, CD and DA, respectively. Then, $PQRS$ is a square.

$$\therefore \quad PQ = QR = RS = PS \qquad \text{...(i)}$$

and $PR = SQ$

But $PR = BC = AD$ and $SQ = AB = CD$

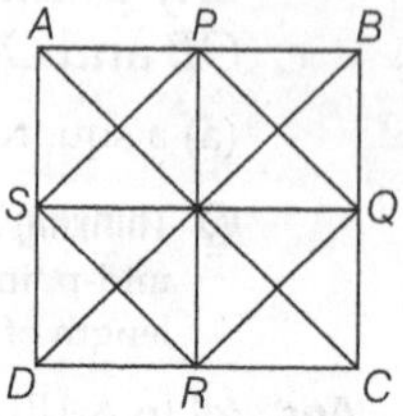

$\therefore$ $AB = BC = CD = AD$

Thus, all the sides of quadrilateral $ABCD$ are equal.

Hence, quadrilateral $ABCD$ is either a square or a rhombus.

Now, in ΔADB, use mid-point theorem

$SP \parallel DB$

and $SP = \frac{1}{2} DB$ ...(ii)

Similarly, in ΔABC (by mid-point theorem), $PQ \parallel AC$ and $PQ = \frac{1}{2} AC$ ...(iii)

From Eq. (i), we get $PS = PQ$

$\Rightarrow$ $\frac{1}{2} DB = \frac{1}{2} AC$ [from Eqs. (ii) and (iii)]

$\Rightarrow$ $DB = AC$

Thus, diagonals of $ABCD$ are equal and therefore quadrilateral $ABCD$ is a square. So, diagonals of quadrilateral are also perpendicular.

Q.12 The diagonals AC and BD of a parallelogram $ABCD$ intersect each other at the point O. If $\angle DAC = 32°$ and $\angle AOB = 70°$, then $\angle DBC$ is equal to

(a) 24° (b) 86° (c) 38° (d) 32°

Ans. *(c)* Given, $\angle AOB = 70°$ and $\angle DAC = 32°$

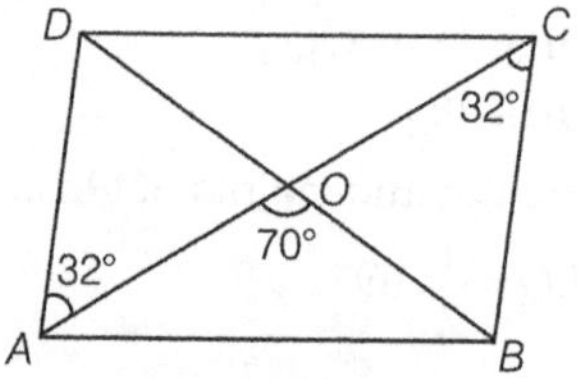

$\therefore$ $\angle ACB = 32°$ [$\because AD \parallel BC$ and AC is transversal]

$\Rightarrow$ $\angle OCB = 32°$

Now, $\angle AOB + \angle BOC = 180°$ [linear pair axiom]

$\Rightarrow$ $\angle BOC = 180° - \angle AOB = 180° - 70° = 110°$

Now, in ΔBOC,

$\angle BOC + \angle OCB + \angle OBC = 180°$ [by angle sum property of a triangle]

$\Rightarrow$ $110° + 32° + \angle OBC = 180°$ [$\because \angle BCO = \angle ACB = 32°$]

$\Rightarrow$ $\angle OBC = 180° - (110° + 32°) = 38°$

$\therefore$ $\angle DBC = \angle OBC = 38°$

Q.13 Which of the following is not true for a parallelogram?

(a) Opposite sides are equal

(b) Opposite angles are equal

(c) Opposite angles are bisected by the diagonals

(d) Diagonals bisect each other

Ans. *(c)* We know that in a parallelogram, opposite sides are equal, opposite angles are equal, opposite angles are not bisected by the diagonals and diagonals bisect each other.

Q.14 D and E are the mid-points of the sides AB and AC respectively of ΔABC. DE is produced to F. To prove that CF is equal and parallel to DA, we need an additional information which is

(a) $\angle DAE = \angle EFC$ (b) $AE = EF$ (c) $DE = EF$ (d) $\angle ADE = \angle ECF$

Ans. *(c)* In ΔADE and ΔCFE, suppose $DE = EF$

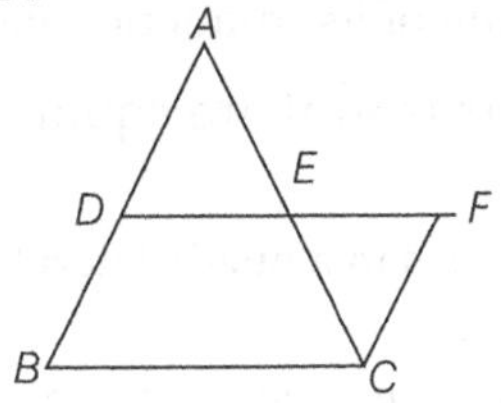

Now,	$AE = CE$	[$\because$ E is the mid-point of AC]
Also,	$DE = EF$	[from Eq. (i)]
and	$\angle AED = \angle FEC$	[vertically opposite angles]
$\therefore$	$\Delta ADE \cong \Delta CFE$	[by SAS congruence rule]
$\therefore$	$AD = CF$	[by CPCT]
and	$\angle ADE = \angle CFE$	[by CPCT]
Hence,	$AD \parallel CF$	[$\because$ alternate interior angles are equal]

Hence, we need an additional information which is $DE = EF$

Short Answer Questions with Reasoning

Q.1 Diagonals AC and BD of a parallelogram $ABCD$ intersect each other at O. If $OA = 3$ cm and $OD = 2$ cm, determine the lengths of AC and BD.

Ans. Given, $ABCD$ is a parallelogram $OA = 3$ cm and $OD = 2$ cm

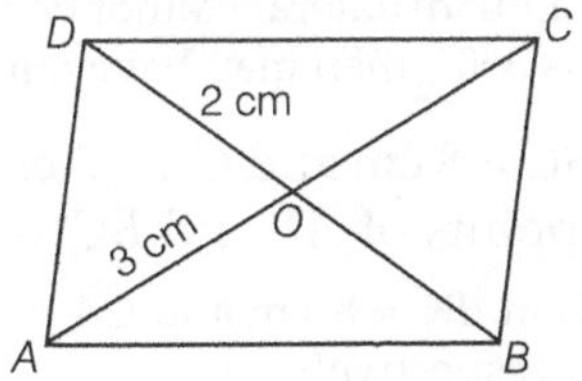

We know that diagonals of a parallelogram bisect each other.

$\therefore$	Diagonal $AC = 2\ OA = 6$ cm	[$\because$ $AO = OC$]
	Diagonal $BD = 2\ OD = 4$ cm	[$\because$ $BO = OD$]

Hence, the length of the diagonals AC and BD are 6 cm and 4 cm, respectively.

Q.2 Diagonals of a parallelogram are perpendicular to each other. Is this statement true? Give reason for your answer.

Ans. *No*, diagonals of a parallelogram are not perpendicular to each other, because they only bisect each other.

***Q.3** Can the angles 110°, 80°, 70° and 95° be the angles of a quadrilateral? Why or why not?

Ans. *No*, we know that sum of all angles of a quadrilateral is 360°.

Here, sum of the angles = 110° + 80° + 70° + 95° = 355° ≠ 360°

So, these angles cannot be the angles of the quadrilateral.

Q.4 In quadrilateral $ABCD$, $\angle A + \angle D = 180°$. What special name can be given to this quadrilateral?

Ans. It is a trapezium because sum of its co-interior angles is 180°.

***Q.5** All the angles of a quadrilateral are equal. What special name is given to this quadrilateral?

Ans. We know that sum of all angles in a quadrilateral is 360°.

If $ABCD$ is a quadrilateral,

$$\angle A + \angle B + \angle C + \angle D = 360° \quad ...(i)$$

But it is given that all angles are equal.

$\therefore$ $\angle A = \angle B = \angle C = \angle D$

From Eq. (i), $\angle A + \angle A + \angle A + \angle A = 360°$

$\Rightarrow$ $4\angle A = 360°$

$\therefore$ $\angle A = 90°$

So, each angle of a quadrilateral is 90°.

Hence, given quadrilateral is a rectangle.

Q.6 Diagonals of a rectangle are equal and perpendicular. Is this statement true? Give reason for your answer.

Ans. *No*, diagonals of a rectangle are equal but not perpendicular because they only bisect each other.

***Q.7** Can all the four angles of a quadrilateral be obtuse angles? Give reason for your answer.

Ans. *No*, all the four angles of a quadrilateral cannot be obtuse. As, the sum of the angles of a quadrilateral is 360°, then may have maximum of three obtuse angles.

Q.8 In ΔABC, $AB = 5$ cm, $BC = 8$ cm and $CA = 7$ cm. If D and E are respectively the mid-points of AB and BC, determine the length of DE.

Ans. In ΔABC, we have $AB = 5$ cm, $BC = 8$ cm and $CA = 7$ cm. Since, D and E are the mid-points of AB and BC, respectively.

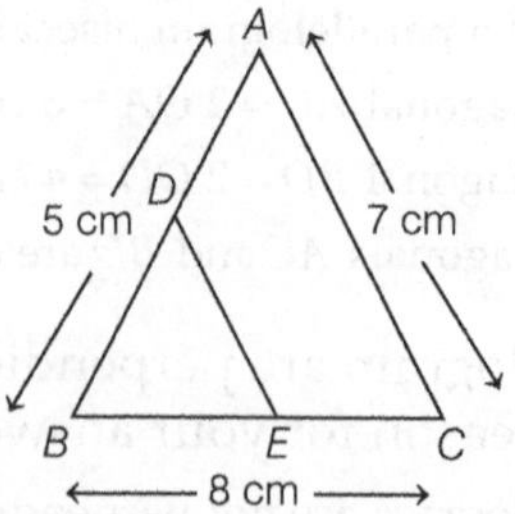

(✱) Topics related to these question have been removed from latest NCERT.

By mid-point theorem, $DE \parallel AC$

and $$DE = \frac{1}{2}AC = \frac{7}{2} = 3.5 \text{ cm}$$

$\therefore$ $$DE = 3.5 \text{ cm}$$

Q.9 In the figure, it is given that $BDEF$ and $FDCE$ are parallelograms. Can you say that $BD = CD$? Why or why not?

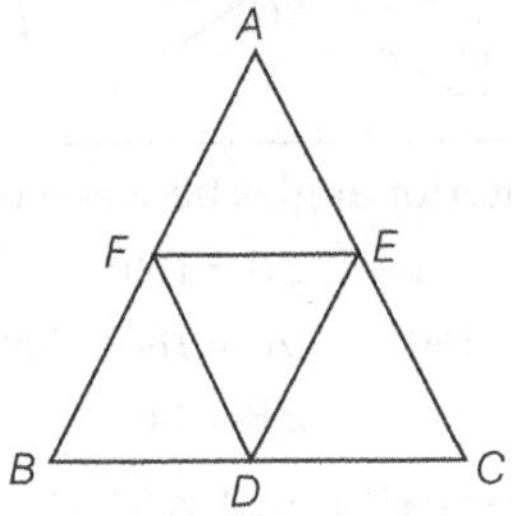

Ans. *Yes,* in the given figure, $BDEF$ is a parallelogram.

$\therefore$ $$BD \parallel EF \text{ and } BD = EF \quad ...(i)$$

Also, $FDCE$ is a parallelogram.

$\therefore$ $$CD \parallel EF$$

and $$CD = EF \quad ...(ii)$$

From Eqs. (i) and (ii), $$BD = CD = EF$$

Q.10 In figure, $ABCD$ and $AEFG$ are two parallelograms. If $\angle C = 55°$, determine $\angle F$.

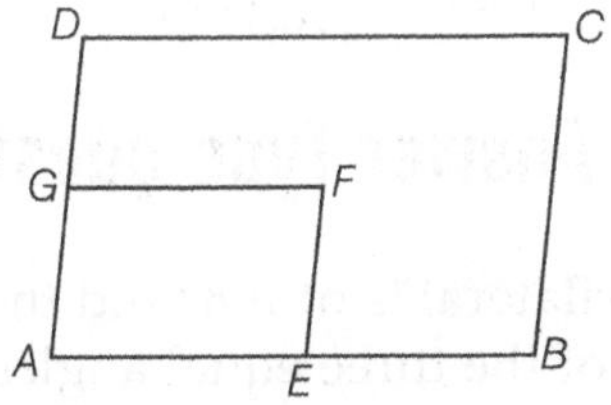

Ans. We have, $ABCD$ and $AEFG$ are two parallelograms and $\angle C = 55°$. Since, $ABCD$ is a parallelogram, then opposite angles of a parallelogram are equal.

$$\angle A = \angle C = 55° \quad ...(i)$$

Also, $AEFG$ is a parallelogram.

$\therefore$ $$\angle A = \angle F = 55° \quad \text{[from Eq. (i)]}$$

***Q.11** Can all the angles of a quadrilateral be acute angles? Give reason for your answer.

Ans. *No,* all the angles of a quadrilateral cannot be acute angles. As, sum of the angles of a quadrilateral is 360. So, maximum of three acute angles will be possible.

***Q.12** Can all the angles of a quadrilateral be right angles? Give reason for your answer.

Ans. *Yes,* all the angles of a quadrilateral can be right angles. In this case, the quadrilateral becomes rectangle or square.

(*) Topics related to these question have been removed from latest NCERT.

Q.13 Diagonals of a quadrilateral $ABCD$ bisect each other. If $\angle A = 35°$, determine $\angle B$.

Ans. Since, diagonals of a quadrilateral bisect each other, so it is a parallelogram.

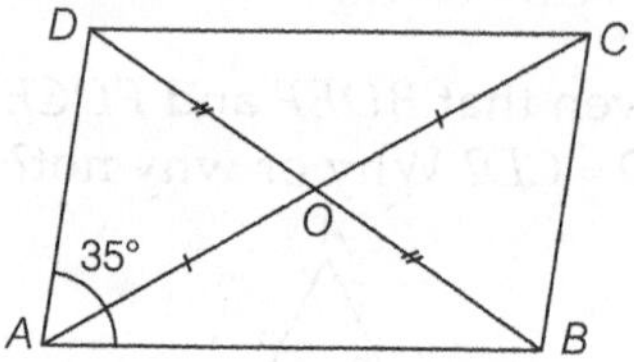

Therefore, the sum of co-interior angles between two parallel lines is 180° *i.e.*,

$$\angle A + \angle B = 180°$$

$\Rightarrow$ $\angle B = 180° - \angle A = 180° - 35°$ [$\angle A = 35°$, given]

$\Rightarrow$ $\angle B = 145°$

Q.14 Opposite angles of a quadrilateral $ABCD$ are equal. If $AB = 4$ cm, determine CD.

Ans. Given, opposite angles of a quadrilateral are equal. So, $ABCD$ is a parallelogram and we know that in a parallelogram, opposite sides are also equal.

$\therefore$ $CD = AB = 4$ cm

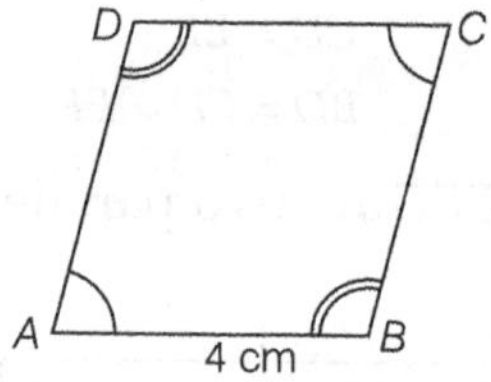

Short Answer Type Questions

***Q.1** One angle of a quadrilateral is of 108° and the remaining three angles are equal. Find each of the three equal angles.

Thinking Process The sum of all the angles in a quadrilateral is 360°, use this result and simplify it.

Ans. Let each of the three equal angles be $x°$.

Now, sum of angles of a quadrilateral = 360°

$\Rightarrow$ $108° + x° + x° + x° = 360° \Rightarrow 3x° = 360° - 108°$

$\Rightarrow$ $x° = \frac{252°}{3}$

$\therefore$ $x° = 84°$

Hence, each of the three equal angles is 84°.

Q.2 $ABCD$ is a trapezium in which $AB \parallel DC$ and $\angle A = \angle B = 45°$. Find angles C and D of the trapezium.

Ans. Given, $ABCD$ is a trapezium and whose parallel sides in the figure are AB and DC. Since, $AB \parallel CD$ and BC is transversal, then sum of two co-interior angles is 180°.

(*) Topics related to these question have been removed from latest NCERT.

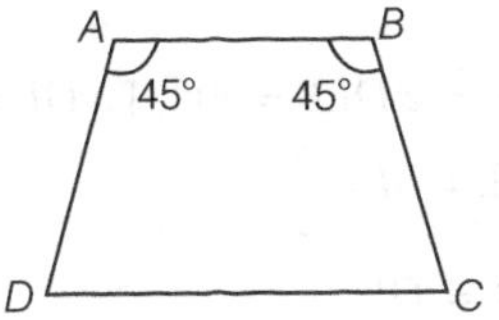

$\therefore$ $\angle B + \angle C = 180^\circ$

$\Rightarrow$ $\angle C = 180^\circ - \angle B = 180^\circ - 45^\circ$ [$\because \angle B = 45^\circ$ (given)]

$\Rightarrow$ $\angle C = 135^\circ$

Similarly, $\angle A + \angle D = 180^\circ$ [$\because$ sum of cointerior angles is 180°]

$\Rightarrow$ $\angle D = 180^\circ - 45^\circ$ [$\because \angle A = 45^\circ$ (given)]

$\Rightarrow$ $\angle D = 135^\circ$

Hence, angles C and D are 135° each.

Q.3 The angle between two altitudes of a parallelogram through the vertex of an obtuse angle of the parallelogram is 60°. Find the angles of the parallelogram.

Ans. Let a parallelogram be $ABCD$, in which $\angle ADC$ and $\angle ABC$ are obtuse angles. Now, DE and DF are two altitudes of parallelogram and angle between them is 60°.

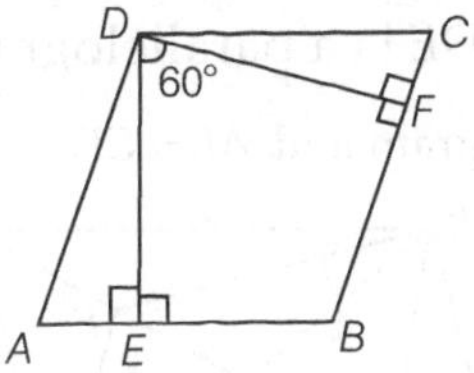

Now, $BEDF$ is a quadrilateral, in which $\angle BED = \angle BFD = 90^\circ$

$\therefore$ $\angle FBE = 360^\circ - (\angle FDE + \angle BED + \angle BFD)$

$= 360^\circ - (60^\circ + 90^\circ + 90^\circ) = 360^\circ - 240^\circ = 120^\circ$

$\Rightarrow$ $\angle FBE = \angle ABC = 120^\circ$

Since, $ABCD$ is a parallelogram.

$\therefore$ $\angle ADC = \angle FBE = 120^\circ$ [opposite angles of *a* parallelogram]

Now, $\angle A + \angle B = 180^\circ$ [$\because$ sum of two co-interior angles is 180°]

$\therefore$ $\angle A = 180^\circ - \angle B$

$\angle A = 180^\circ - 120^\circ$ [$\because \angle FBE = \angle B$]

$\Rightarrow$ $\angle A = 60^\circ$

Also, $\angle C = \angle A = 60^\circ$

Hence, angles of the parallelogram are 60°, 120°, 60° and 120°, respectively.

Q.4 $ABCD$ is a rhombus in which altitude from D to side AB bisects AB. Find the angles of the rhombus.

Ans. Let sides of a rhombus be $AB = BC = CD = DA = x$

Now, join DB.

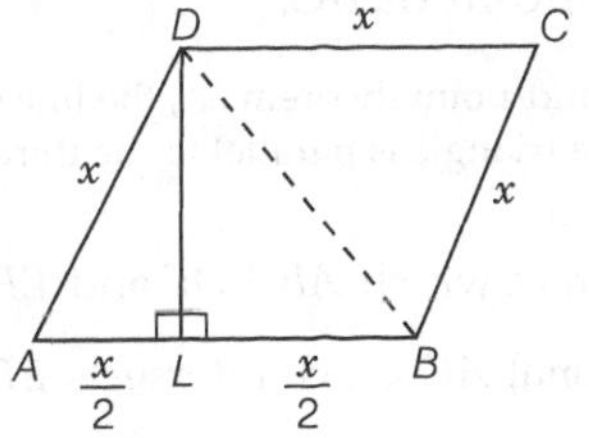

In ΔALD and ΔBLD, $\angle DLA = \angle DLB = 90°$ [$\because$ DL is a perpendicular bisector of AB]

$$AL = BL = \frac{x}{2}$$ [given]

and $DL = DL$ [common side]

$\therefore$ $\Delta ALD \cong \Delta BLD$ [by SAS congruence rule]

$\Rightarrow$ $AD = BD$ [by CPCT]

Now, in ΔADB, $AD = AB = DB = x$

Then, ΔADB is an equilateral triangle.

$\therefore$ $\angle A = \angle ADB = \angle ABD = 60°$

Similarly, ΔDBC is an equilateral triangle.

$\therefore$ $\angle C = \angle BDC = \angle DBC = 60°$

Also, $\angle A = \angle C$

$\therefore$ $\angle D = \angle B = 180° - 60° = 120°$

[$\because$ sum of adjacent angles is 180°]

Q.5 E and F are points on diagonal AC of a parallelogram $ABCD$ such that $AE = CF$. Show that $BFDE$ is a parallelogram.

Ans. **Given** $ABCD$ is a parallelogram and $AE = CF$.

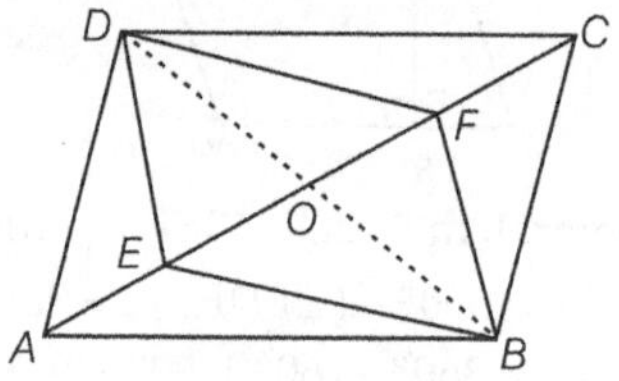

To show $OE = OF$

Construction Join BD, meet AC at point O.

Proof Since, diagonals of a parallelogram bisect each other.

$\therefore$ $OA = OC$

and $OD = OB$

Also, $AE = CF$ [given]

$\Rightarrow$ $OA - AE = OC - CF \Rightarrow OE = OF$

Thus, $BFDE$ is a quadrilateral whose diagonals bisect each other.

Hence, $BFDE$ is a parallelogram. **Hence proved.**

Q.6 E is the mid-point of the side AD of the trapezium $ABCD$ with $AB \parallel DC$. A line through E drawn parallel to AB intersects BC at F. Show that F is the mid-point of BC.

Thinking Process Use the mid-point theorem *i.e.*, the line segment joining the mid-points of two sides of a triangle is parallel to the third side and half of it. Further show the required result.

Ans. **Given** $ABCD$ is a trapezium in which $AB \parallel DC$ and $EF \parallel AB \parallel CD$.

Construction Join the diagonal AC which intersects EF at O.

To show F is the mid-point of BC.

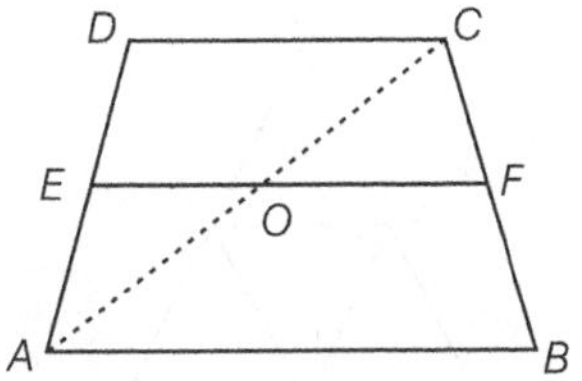

Proof Now, in ΔADC, E is the mid-point of AD and $OE \parallel CD$.

Thus, by converse of mid-point theorem, O is mid-point of AC.

Now, in ΔCBA, O is the mid-point of AC and $OF \parallel AB$.

So, by converse of mid-point theorem, F is the mid-point of BC. **Hence proved.**

Q.7 Through A, B and C, lines RQ, PR and QP have been drawn, respectively parallel to sides BC, CA and AB of a ΔABC as shown in figure. Show that $BC = \frac{1}{2}QR$.

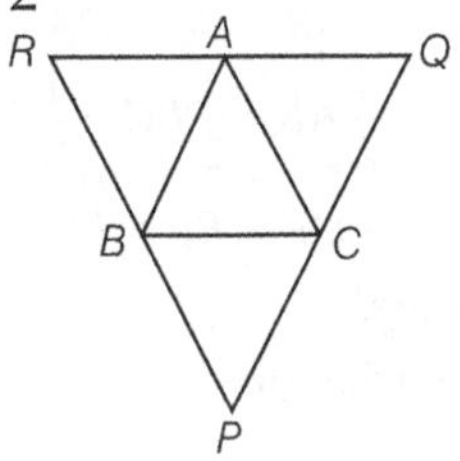

Ans. Given In ΔABC, $PQ \parallel AB$ and $PR \parallel AC$ and $RQ \parallel BC$.

To show $$BC = \frac{1}{2}QR$$

Proof In quadrilateral $BCAR$, $BR \parallel CA$ and $BC \parallel RA$

So, quadrilateral, $BCAR$ is a parallelogram.

$\therefore$ $$BC = AR \quad ...(i)$$

Now, in quadrilateral $BCQA$, $BC \parallel AQ$

and $AB \parallel QC$

So, quadrilateral $BCQA$ is a parallelogram,

$\therefore$ $$BC = AQ \quad ...(ii)$$

On adding Eqs. (i) and (ii), we get

$$2BC = AR + AQ$$

$\Rightarrow$ $$2BC = RQ$$

$\Rightarrow$ $$BC = \frac{1}{2}QR$$ **Hence proved.**

Q.8 D, E and F are the mid-points of the sides BC, CA and AB, respectively of an equilateral ΔABC. Show that ΔDEF is also an equilateral triangle.

Ans. Given In equilateral ΔABC, D, E and F are the mid-points of sides BC, CA and AB, respectively.

To show ΔDEF is an equilateral triangle.

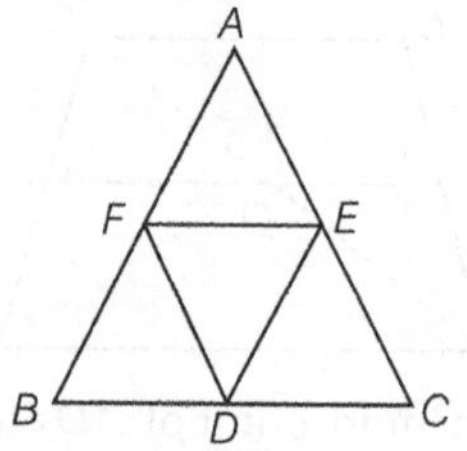

Proof Since, in ΔABC, E and F are the mid-points of AC and AB respectively, then $EF \parallel BC$ and

$$EF = \frac{1}{2} BC \quad \ldots\text{(i)}$$

Similarly, $DF \parallel AC$, $DE \parallel AB$

and $FD = \frac{1}{2} AC$ and $DE = \frac{1}{2} AB$ [by mid-point theorem]...(ii)

Since, ΔABC is an equilateral triangle

$\therefore \quad AB = BC = CA$

$\Rightarrow \quad \frac{1}{2} AB = \frac{1}{2} BC = \frac{1}{2} CA$ [dividing by 2]

$\Rightarrow \quad DE = EF = FD$ [from Eqs. (i) and (ii)]

Thus, all sides of ΔDEF are equal.

Hence, ΔDEF is an equilateral triangle. **Hence proved.**

Q.9 Points P and Q have been taken on opposite sides AB and CD, respectively of a parallelogram $ABCD$ such that $AP = CQ$. Show that AC and PQ bisect each other.

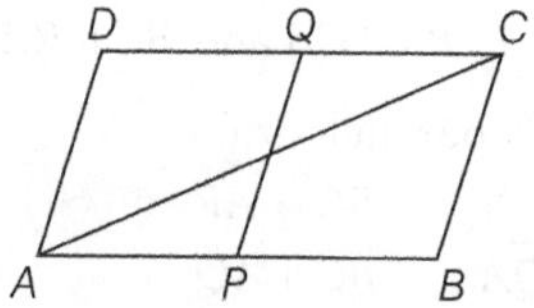

- **Concept Insight**

(i) **ASA congruence rule** Two triangles are congruent if two angles and included side of one triangle are equal to the corresponding two angles and included side of other triangle.

(ii) **CPCT rule** It two triangles are congruent, then their corresponding sides and angles are also congruent.

Ans. **Given** $ABCD$ is a parallelogram and $AP = CQ$

To show AC and PQ bisect each other.

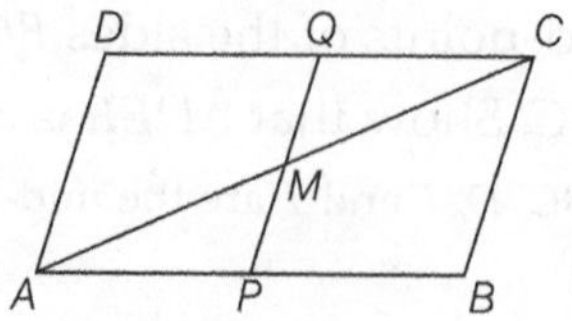

Proof In ΔAMP and ΔCMQ,

$$\angle MAP = \angle MCQ \quad \text{[alternate interior angles]}$$

$$AP = CQ \quad \text{[given]}$$

and $$\angle APM = \angle CQM \quad \text{[alternate interior angles]}$$

$\therefore$ $$\Delta AMP \cong \Delta CMQ \quad \text{[by ASA congruence rule]}$$

$\Rightarrow$ $$AM = CM \quad \text{[by CPCT rule]}$$

and $$PM = MQ \quad \text{[by CPCT rule]}$$

Hence, AC and PQ bisect each other. **Hence proved.**

Q.10 In figure, P is the mid-point of side BC of a parallelogram $ABCD$ such that $\angle BAP = \angle DAP$. Prove that $AD = 2CD$.

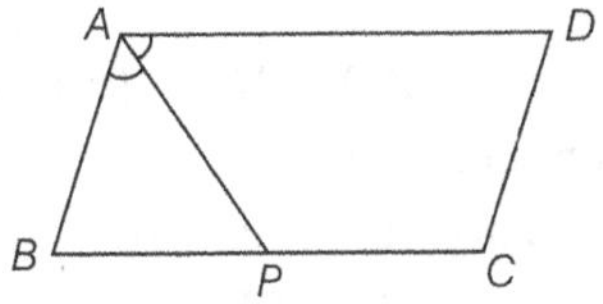

Thinking Process Firstly, use the property that sum of co-interior angles is 180°. Secondly, use the property that sum of all angles in a triangle is 180° and then prove the required result.

Ans. Given In a parallelogram $ABCD$, P is a mid-point of BC such that $\angle BAP = \angle DAP$.

To prove $$AD = 2CD$$

Proof Since, $ABCD$ is a parallelogram.

So, $AD \parallel BC$ and AB is transversal, then

$$\angle A + \angle B = 180° \quad [\because \text{sum of co-interior angles is } 180°]$$

$\Rightarrow$ $$\angle B = 180° - \angle A \quad \text{...(i)}$$

In ΔABP, $$\angle PAB + \angle B + \angle BPA = 180° \quad \text{[by angle sum property of a triangle]}$$

$\Rightarrow$ $$\frac{1}{2}\angle A + 180° - \angle A + \angle BPA = 180° \quad \text{[from Eq. (i), } \angle BAP = \angle DAP \text{ (given)]}$$

$\Rightarrow$ $$\angle BPA - \frac{\angle A}{2} = 0$$

$\Rightarrow$ $$\angle BPA = \frac{\angle A}{2} \quad \text{...(ii)}$$

$\Rightarrow$ $$\angle BPA = \angle BAP$$

$\Rightarrow$ $$AB = BP \quad [\because \text{opposite sides of equal angles are equal}]$$

On multiplying both sides by 2, we get

$$2AB = 2BP$$

$\Rightarrow$ $$2AB = BC \quad [\because P \text{ is the mid-point of } BC]$$

$\Rightarrow$ $$2CD = AD$$

$[\because ABCD$ is a parallelogram, then $AB = CD$ and $BC = AD]$

Hence proved.

Long Answer Type Questions

Q.1 A square is inscribed in an isosceles right triangle, so that the square and the triangle have one angle common. Show that the vertex of the square opposite the vertex of the common angle bisects the hypotenuse.

Ans. Given In isosceles triangle ABC, a square $ADEF$ is inscribed.

To prove $CE = BE$

Proof In an isosceles ΔABC, $\angle A = 90°$

and $AB = AC$ ...(i)

Since, $ADEF$ is a square.

$\therefore$ $AD = AF$ [$\because$ all sides of square are equal] ...(ii)

On subtracting Eq. (ii) from Eq. (i), we get

$$AB - AD = AC - AF$$

$\Rightarrow$ $BD = CF$ ...(iii)

Now, in ΔCFE and ΔBDE,

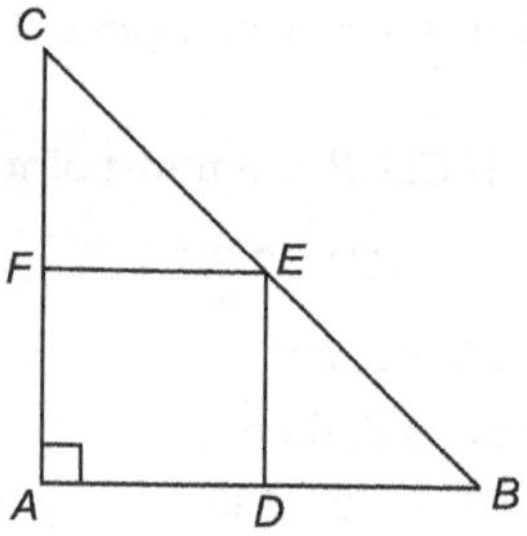

$BD = CF$ [from Eq. (iii)]

$DE = EF$ [sides of a square]

and $\angle CFE = \angle EDB$ [each 90°]

$\Delta CFE \cong \Delta BDE$ [by SAS congruence rule]

$\therefore$ $CE = BE$ [by CPCT]

Hence, vertex E of the square bisects the hypotenuse BC. **Hence proved.**

Q.2 In a parallelogram $ABCD$, $AB = 10$ cm and $AD = 6$ cm. The bisector of $\angle A$ meets DC in E. AE and BC produced meet at F. Find the length of CF.

Thinking Process Firstly, construct AE which is the angle bisector of $\angle A$ and it meets DC at E. Secondly, extend AE to meet BC at F, and draw HF such that HF || AB.

Ans. Given, a parallelogram $ABCD$ in which $AB = 10$ cm and $AD = 6$ cm.

Now, draw a bisector of $\angle A$ meets DC in E and produce it to F and produce BC to meet at F.

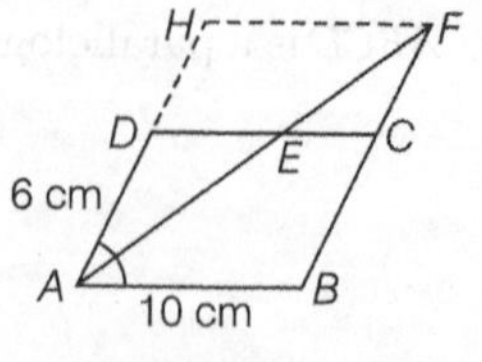

Also, produce AD to H and join HF, so that $ABFH$, is a parallelogram.

Since, $HF \parallel AB$ and AF is a transversal

$\therefore$ $\angle AFH = \angle FAB$ [alternate interior angles]...(i)

and $\angle HAF = \angle FAB$ [$\because$ AF is the bisector of $\angle A$]

$\Rightarrow$ $\angle HAF = \angle AFH$ [from Eq. (i)]

$\Rightarrow$ $HF = AH$

[$\because$ sides opposite to equal angles are equal]

But $HF = AB = 10$ cm

$\therefore$ $AH = HF = 10 \text{ cm} \Rightarrow AD + DH = 10$ cm

$\Rightarrow$ $DH = (10 - 6)$ cm

$\therefore$ $DH = 4$ cm

Since, $CFHD$ is a parallelogram.

Therefore, opposite sides are equal.

Hence, $DH = CF = 4$ cm

Q.3 P, Q, R and S are respectively the mid-points of the sides AB, BC, CD and DA of a quadrilateral $ABCD$ in which $AC = BD$. Prove that $PQRS$ is a rhombus.

Thinking Process Firstly, use the mid-point theorem in various triangles of a quadrilateral. Further, show that the line segments formed by joining the mid-points are equal, which proves the required quadrilateral.

Ans. **Given** In a quadrilateral $ABCD$, P, Q, R and S are the mid-points of sides AB, BC, CD and DA, respectively. Also, $AC = BD$

To prove $PQRS$ is a rhombus.

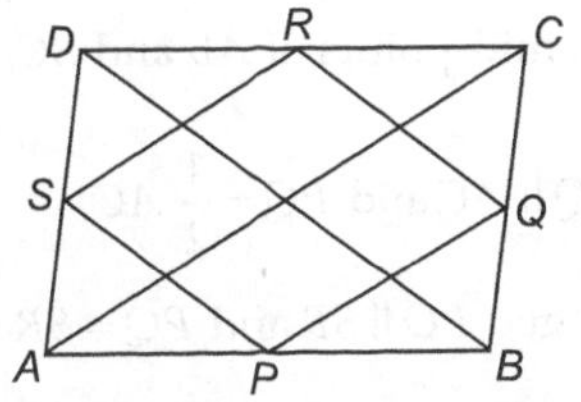

Proof In ΔADC, S and R are the mid-points of AD and DC, respectively. Then, by mid-point theorem.

$$SR \parallel AC \text{ and } SR = \frac{1}{2} AC \quad \text{...(i)}$$

In ΔABC, P and Q are the mid-points of AB and BC, respectively. Then, by mid-point theorem

$$PQ \parallel AC \text{ and } PQ = \frac{1}{2} AC \quad \text{...(ii)}$$

From Eqs. (i) and (ii), we get $SR = PQ = \frac{1}{2} AC$ ...(iii)

Similarly, in ΔBCD, $RQ \parallel BD$ and $RQ = \frac{1}{2} BD$ ...(iv)

And in ΔBAD, $SP \parallel BD$ and $SP = \frac{1}{2} BD$ ...(v)

From Eqs. (iv) and (v), we get $SP = RQ = \frac{1}{2} BD = \frac{1}{2} AC$ [given, $AC = BD$]...(vi)

From Eqs. (iii) and (vi), we get $SR = PQ = SP = RQ$

It shows that all sides of a quadrilateral $PQRS$ are equal.

Hence, $PQRS$ is a rhombus. **Hence proved.**

Q.4 P, Q, R and S are respectively the mid-points of the sides AB, BC, CD and DA of a quadrilateral $ABCD$ such that $AC \perp BD$. Prove that $PQRS$ is a rectangle.

Ans. Given In quadrilateral $ABCD$, P, Q, R and S are the mid-points of the sides AB, BC, CD and DA, respectively.

Also, $AC \perp BD$

To prove $PQRS$ is a rectangle.

Proof Since, $AC \perp BD$

$\therefore$ $\angle COD = \angle AOD = \angle AOB = \angle COB = 90°$

In ΔADC, S and R are the mid-points of AD and DC, respectively, then by mid-point theorem

$$SR \parallel AC \text{ and } SR = \frac{1}{2} AC \quad ...(i)$$

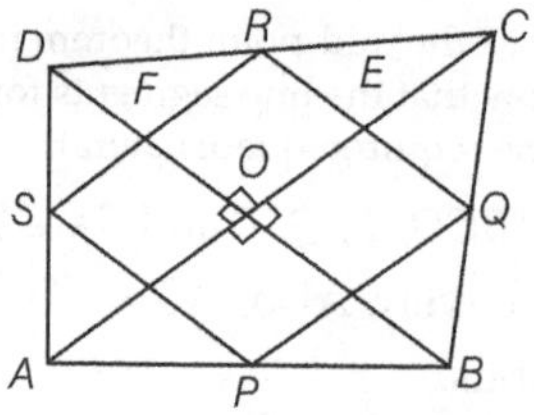

In ΔABC, P and Q are the mid-points of AB and BC, respectively, then by mid-point theorem

$$PQ \parallel AC \text{ and } PQ = \frac{1}{2} AC \quad ...(ii)$$

From Eqs. (i) and (ii), we get $PQ \parallel SR$ and $PQ = SR = \frac{1}{2} AC$ ...(iii)

Similarly, $SP \parallel RQ$ and $SP = RQ = \frac{1}{2} BD$ ...(iv)

Now, in quadrilateral $EOFR$, $OE \parallel FR$, $OF \parallel ER$

$\therefore$ $\angle EOF = \angle ERF = 90°$ ...(v)

[$\because AC \perp BD \Rightarrow \angle DOC = \angle EOF = 90°$ and opposite angles of a parallelogram are equal]

$\therefore$ $PQRS$ is a parallelogram whose angles are of 90°.

So, $PQRS$ is a rectangle. **Hence proved.**

Q.5 P, Q, R and S are respectively the mid-points of sides AB, BC, CD and DA of quadrilateral $ABCD$ in which $AC = BD$ and $AC \perp BD$. Prove that $PQRS$ is a square.

Ans. Given In quadrilateral $ABCD$, P, Q, R and S are the mid-points of the sides AB, BC, CD and DA, respectively.

Also, $AC = BD$ and $AC \perp BD$.

To prove *PQRS* is a square.

Proof In ΔADC, *S* and *R* are the mid-points of the sides *AD* and *DC*, respectively, then by mid-point theorem,

$$SR \parallel AC \text{ and } SR = \frac{1}{2} AC \quad \ldots(i)$$

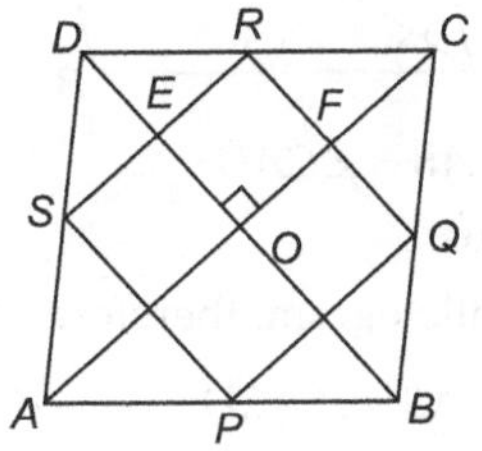

In ΔABC, *P* and *Q* are the mid-points of *AB* and *BC*, then by mid-point theorem,

$$PQ \parallel AC \text{ and } PQ = \frac{1}{2} AC \quad \ldots(ii)$$

From Eqs. (i) and (ii), we get $PQ \parallel SR$ and $PQ = SR = \frac{1}{2} AC$ ...(iii)

Similarly, in ΔABD, by mid-point theorem,

$$SP \parallel BD \text{ and } SP = \frac{1}{2} BD = \frac{1}{2} AC \quad [\text{given, } AC = BD] \ldots(iv)$$

$$\therefore \quad SP = \frac{1}{2} AC$$

and ΔBCD, by mid-point theorem,

$$RQ \parallel BD \text{ and } RQ = \frac{1}{2} BD = \frac{1}{2} AC \quad [\text{given, } BD = AC] \ldots(v)$$

$$\therefore \quad RQ = \frac{1}{2} AC$$

From Eqs. (iv) and (v), we get

$$SP \parallel RQ \text{ and } SP = RQ = \frac{1}{2} AC \quad \ldots(vi)$$

From Eqs. (iii) and (vi), we get

$$PQ = SR = SP = RQ$$

Thus, all four sides are equal.

Now, in quadrilateral *OERF*, $OE \parallel FR$ and $OF \parallel ER$

$$\therefore \quad \angle EOF = \angle ERF = 90^\circ$$

[$\because AC \perp DB \Rightarrow \angle DOC = \angle EOF = 90^\circ$
and opposite angles of a parallelogram are equal]

$$\therefore \quad \angle QRS = 90^\circ$$

Similarly, $\angle RQS = 90^\circ$

So, *PQRS* is a square. **Hence proved.**

Q.6 A diagonal of a parallelogram bisects one of its angles. Show that it is a rhombus.

Ans. Given Let $ABCD$ is a parallelogram and diagonal AC bisects the angle A.

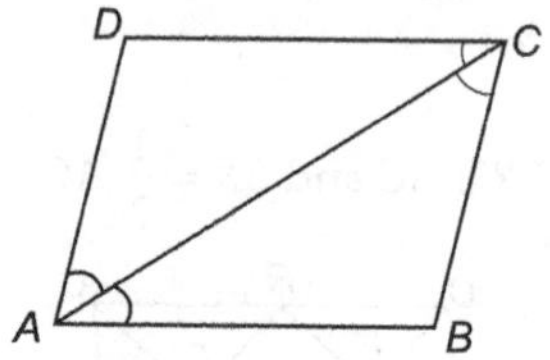

$\therefore \quad \angle CAB = \angle CAD \quad$ ...(i)

To show $ABCD$ is a rhombus.

Proof Since, $ABCD$ is a parallelogram, therefore $AB \parallel CD$ and AC is a transversal.

$\therefore \quad \angle CAB = \angle ACD \quad$ [alternate interior angles]

Again, $AD \parallel BC$ and AC is a transversal.

$\therefore \quad \angle CAD = \angle ACB \quad$ [alternate interior angles]

So, $\quad \angle ACD = \angle ACB \quad$ [$\because \angle CAB = \angle CAD$, given]...(ii)

Also, $\quad \angle A = \angle C \quad$ [$\because$ opposite angles of parallelogram are equal]

$\Rightarrow \quad \frac{1}{2}\angle A = \frac{1}{2}\angle C \quad$ [dividing both sides by 2]

$\Rightarrow \quad \angle DAC = \angle DCA \quad$ [from Eqs. (i) and (ii)]

$\Rightarrow \quad CD = AD \quad$ [$\because$ sides opposite to the equal angles are equal]

Also, $\quad AB = CD$ and $AD = BC$

[$\because$ opposite sides of parallelogram are equal]

$\therefore \quad AB = BC = CD = AD$

Thus, all sides are equal. So, $ABCD$ is a rhombus. **Hence proved.**

Q.7 P and Q are the mid-points of the opposite sides AB and CD of a parallelogram $ABCD$. AQ intersects DP at S and BQ intersects CP at R. Show that $PRQS$ is a parallelogram.

Ans. Given In a parallelogram $ABCD$, P and Q are the mid-points of AB and CD, respectively.

To show $PRQS$ is a parallelogram.

Proof Since, $ABCD$ is a parallelogram.

$AB \parallel CD$

$\Rightarrow \quad AP \parallel QC$

Also, $\quad AB = DC$

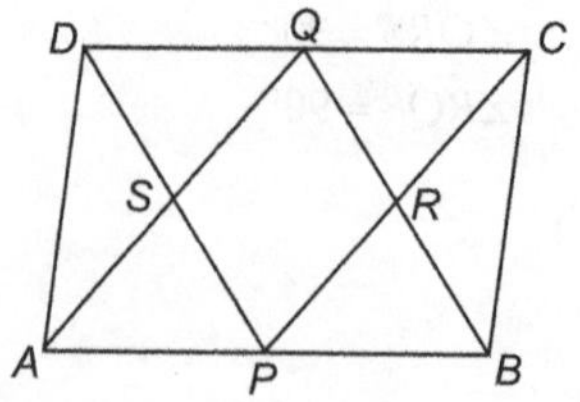

$$\frac{1}{2}AB = \frac{1}{2}DC \quad \text{[dividing both sides by 2]}$$

$\Rightarrow$ $AP = QC$ [$\because$ P and Q are the mid-points of AB and DC]

Now, $AP \parallel QC$ and $AP = QC$

Thus, $APCQ$ is a parallelogram.

$\therefore$ $AQ \parallel PC$ or $SQ \parallel PR$ ...(i)

Again, $AB \parallel DC$ or $BP \parallel DQ$

Also, $AB = DC \Rightarrow \frac{1}{2}AB = \frac{1}{2}DC$ [dividing both sides by 2]

$\Rightarrow$ $BP = QD$

[$\because$ P and Q are the mid-points of AB and DC]

Now, $BP \parallel QD$ and $BP = QD$

So, $BPDQ$ is a parallelogram.

$\therefore$ $PD \parallel BQ$ or $PS \parallel QR$ ...(ii)

From Eqs. (i) and (ii), we get $SQ \parallel RP$ and $PS \parallel QR$

So, $PRQS$ is a parallelogram. **Hence proved.**

Q.8 $ABCD$ is a quadrilateral in which $AB \parallel DC$ and $AD = BC$. Prove that $\angle A = \angle B$ and $\angle C = \angle D$.

Thinking Process Firstly, extend AB to E and draw a line CE parallel to AD. Further, use the concept sum of co-interior angles is 180° and show the required result.

Ans. Given $ABCD$ is a quadrilateral such that $AB \parallel DC$ and $AD = BC$

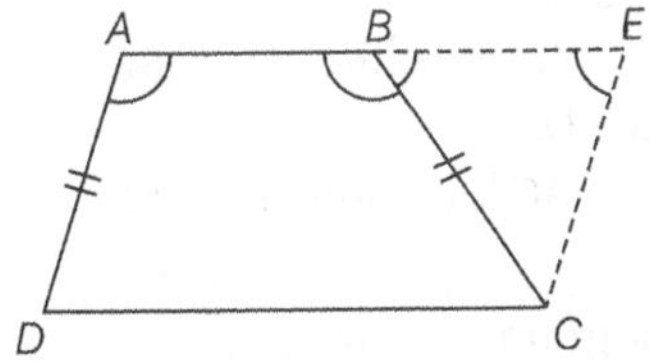

Construction Extend AB to E and draw a line CE parallel to AD.

Proof Since, $AD \parallel CE$ and transversal AE cuts them at A and E, respectively.

$\therefore$ $\angle A + \angle E = 180°$ [$\because$ sum of co-interior angles is 180°]

$\Rightarrow$ $\angle A = 180° - \angle E$ ...(i)

Since, $AB \parallel CD \Rightarrow AE \parallel CD$ and $AD \parallel CE$

So, quadrilateral $AECD$ is a parallelogram.

$\Rightarrow$ $AD = CE \Rightarrow BC = CE$ [$\because$ $AD = BC$, given]

Now, in ΔBCE $CE = BC$ [proved above]

$\Rightarrow$ $\angle CBE = \angle CEB$

[$\because$ opposite angles of equal sides are equal]

Also $180° - \angle B = \angle E$ [$\because$ linear pair]

$\Rightarrow$ $180° - \angle E = \angle B$ ...(ii)

From Eqs. (i) and (ii), we get $\angle A = \angle B$ ...(iii)

Now, $AB \parallel CD$ and AD is a transversal.

Also, $\angle A + \angle D = 180°$

Similarly, $\angle B + \angle C = 180°$ [$\because$ sum of co-interior angles is 180°]

$\therefore$ $\angle A + \angle D = \angle B + \angle C$

$\Rightarrow$ $\angle A + \angle D = \angle A + \angle C$ [from Eq. (iii)]

$\Rightarrow$ $\angle D = \angle C$ **Hence proved.**

Q.9 In figure, $AB \parallel DE$, $AB = DE$, $AC \parallel DF$ and $AC = DF$. Prove that $BC \parallel EF$ and $BC = EF$.

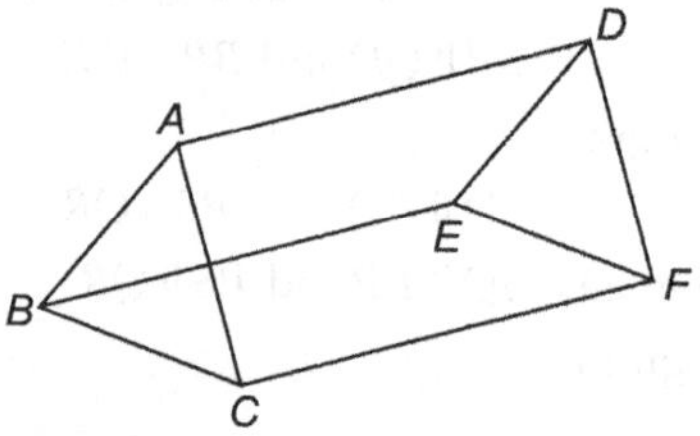

Ans. Given In figure, $AB \parallel DE$ and $AC \parallel DF$, also $AB = DE$ and $AC = DF$

To prove $BC \parallel EF$ and $BC = EF$

Proof In quadrilateral $ABED$,

$AB \parallel DE$ and $AB = DE$

So, $ABED$ is a parallelogram.

$\therefore$ $AD \parallel BE$ and $AD = BE$ ...(i)

Now, in quadrilateral $ACFD$,

$AC \parallel FD$ and $AC = FD$

Thus, $ACFD$ is a parallelogram.

$\therefore$ $AD \parallel CF$ and $AD = CF$ ...(ii)

From Eqs. (i) and (ii), we get

$AD = BE = CF$ and $CF \parallel BE$ ...(iii)

Now, in quadrilateral $BCFE$,

$BE = CF$

and $BE \parallel CF$ [from Eq. (iii)]

So, $BCFE$ is a parallelogram.

$\therefore$ $BC = EF$ and $BC \parallel EF$ **Hence proved.**

Q.10 E is the mid-point of a median AD of ΔABC and BE is produced to meet AC at F. Show that $AF = \frac{1}{3} AC$.

Ans. Given In a ΔABC, AD is a median and E is the mid-point of AD.

Construction Draw $DP \parallel EF$.

Proof In ΔADP, E is the mid-point of AD and $EF \parallel DP$.

So, F is mid-point of AP. [by converse of mid-point theorem]

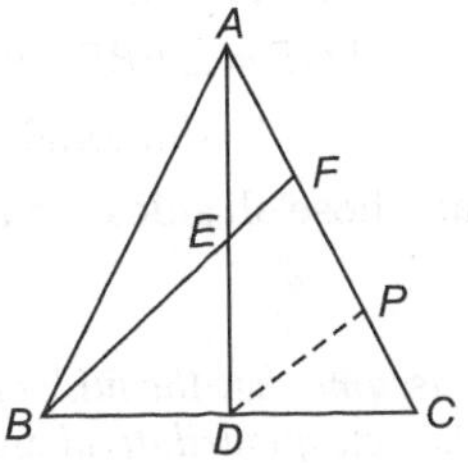

In ΔFBC, D is mid-point of BC and $DP \parallel BF$.

So, P is mid-point of FC. [by converse of mid-point theorem]

Thus, $AF = FP = PC$

$\therefore$ $AF = \frac{1}{3} AC$ **Hence proved.**

Q.11 Show that the quadrilateral formed by joining the mid-points of the consecutive sides of a square is also a square.

Ans. Given In a square $ABCD$, P, Q, R and S are the mid-points of AB, BC, CD and DA, respectively.

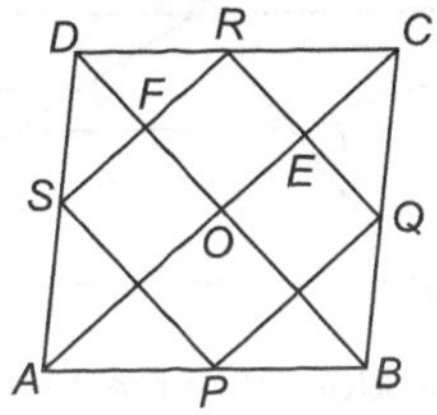

To show $PQRS$ is a square.

Construction Join AC and BD.

Proof Since, $ABCD$ is a square.

$\therefore$ $AB = BC = CD = AD$

Also, P, Q, R and S are the mid-points of AB, BC, CD and DA, respectively.

Then, in ΔADC, $SR \parallel AC$

and $SR = \frac{1}{2} AC$ [by mid-point theorem]...(i)

In ΔABC, $PQ \parallel AC$

and $PQ = \frac{1}{2} AC$ ...(ii)

From Eqs. (i) and (ii), we get

$SR \parallel PQ$ and $SR = PQ = \frac{1}{2} AC$ ...(iii)

Similarly, $SP \parallel BD$ and $BD \parallel RQ$

$\therefore$ $SP \parallel RQ$ and $SP = RQ = \frac{1}{2} BD$ ...(iv)

Also, $AC = BD$ [$\because$ $ABCD$ is a square] ...(v)

From Eqs. (iii) and (iv), we get

$SR = PQ = SP = RQ$

Now, in quadrilateral $OERF$, $OE \parallel FR$ and $OF \parallel ER$

$\therefore$ $$\angle EOF = \angle ERF = 90°$$

[$\because$ diagonals of square bisect each other at 90°]

Thus, $PQRS$ is a quadrilateral whose all sides are equal and an angle is equal to 90°.

Hence, $PQRS$ is a square. **Hence proved.**

Mistake Alert! *Students may assume that the midpoints directly form a square without properly proving the sides of the new quadrilateral are equal and angles are right angles.*

Q.12 E and F are respectively the mid-points of the non-parallel sides AD and BC of a trapezium $ABCD$. Prove that $EF \parallel AB$ and $EF = \frac{1}{2}(AB + CD)$.

- **Concept Insight** Use converse mid- point theorem: If a line drawn through the mid-point of one side of a triangle and is parallel to another side, then it will bisect the third side of the triangle.

Ans. **Given** $ABCD$ is a trapezium in which $AB \parallel CD$. Also, E and F are the mid-points of sides AD and BC, respectively.

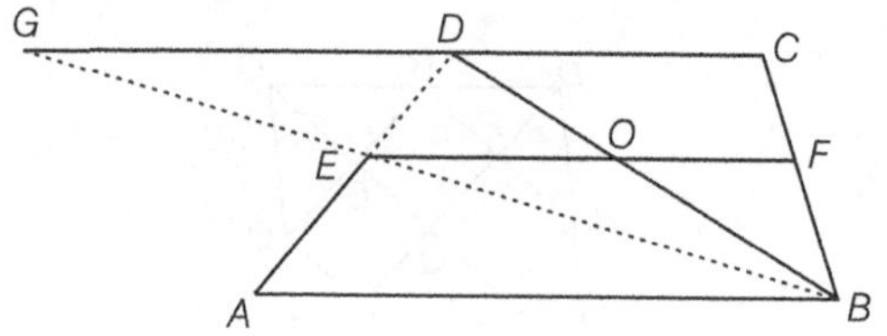

Construction Join BE and produce it to meet CD produced at G, also draw BD which intersects EF at O.

To prove $EF \parallel AB$ and $EF = \frac{1}{2}(AB + CD)$.

Proof Since, $\Delta GED \cong \Delta BEA \Rightarrow GE = BE$ [by CPCT]

Hence, E is also the mid-point of BG.

In ΔGCB, E and F are respectively the mid-points of BG and BC, then by mid-point theorem,

$$EF \parallel GC$$

But $GC \parallel AB$ or $CD \parallel AB$ [given]

$\therefore$ $$EF \parallel AB$$

In ΔADB, $AB \parallel EO$ and E is the mid-point of AD.

Therefore by converse of mid-point theorem, O is mid-point of BD.

Also, $$EO = \frac{1}{2}AB \quad \text{...(i)}$$

In ΔBDC, $OF \parallel CD$ and O is the mid-point of BD.

$\therefore$ $$OF = \frac{1}{2}CD$$ [by converse of mid-point theorem]...(ii)

On adding Eqs. (i) and (ii), we get

$$EO + OF = \frac{1}{2}AB + \frac{1}{2}CD$$

$\Rightarrow$ $$EF = \frac{1}{2}(AB + CD)$$ **Hence proved.**

Q.13 Prove that the quadrilateral formed by the bisectors of the angles of a parallelogram is a rectangle.

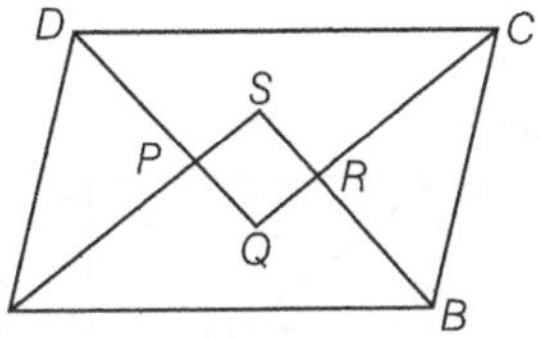

Ans. Given Let $ABCD$ be a parallelogram and AP, BR, CR, and DP are the bisectors of $\angle A$, $\angle B$, $\angle C$ and $\angle D$, respectively.

To prove Quadrilateral $PQRS$ is a rectangle.

Proof Since, $ABCD$ is a parallelogram, then $DC \parallel AB$ and DA is a transversal.

We have, $\angle A + \angle D = 180°$ [∵ sum of co-interior angles of a parallelogram is 180°]

⇒ $\frac{1}{2}\angle A + \frac{1}{2}\angle D = 90°$ [dividing both sides by 2]

⇒ $\angle PAD + \angle PDA = 90°$

⇒ $\angle APD = 90°$ [∵ sum of all angles of a triangle is 180°]

∴ $\angle SPQ = 90°$ [vertically opposite angles]

Similarly, $\angle PQR = 90°$

$\angle QRS = 90°$ and $\angle PSR = 90°$

Thus, $PQRS$ is a quadrilateral whose each angle is 90°.

Hence, $PQRS$ is a rectangle. **Hence proved.**

Q.14 P and Q are points on opposite sides AD and BC of a parallelogram $ABCD$ such that PQ passes through the point of intersection O of its diagonals AC and BD. Show that PQ is bisected at O.

Thinking Process Firstly, prove that ΔODP and ΔOBQ are congruent by ASA rule. Further, show the required result by $CPCT$ rule.

Ans. Given $ABCD$ is a parallelogram whose diagonals bisect each other at O.
To show PQ is bisected at O.

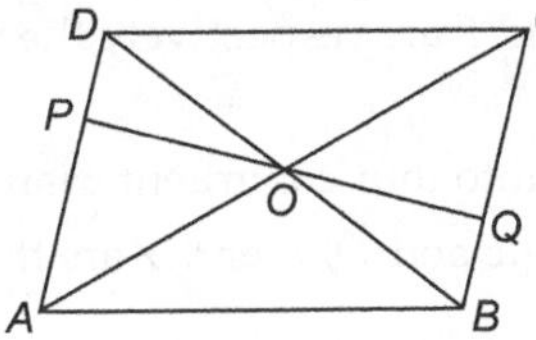

Proof Since, diagonals AC and BD bisect each other at O.

So, $OA = OC$ and $DB = OD$

In ΔODP and ΔOBQ, $\angle BOQ = \angle POD$ [vertically opposite angles]

$\angle OBQ = \angle ODP$ [alternate interior angles]

and $OB = OD$ [given]

∴ $\Delta ODP \cong \Delta OBQ$ [by ASA congruence rule]

∴ $OP = OQ$ [by CPCT]

So, PQ is bisected at O. **Hence proved.**

Q.15 *ABCD* is a rectangle in which diagonal *BD* bisects $\angle B$. Show that *ABCD* is a square.

Ans. Given In a rectangle *ABCD*, diagonal *BD* bisects $\angle B$.

Construction Join AC.

To show *ABCD* is a square.

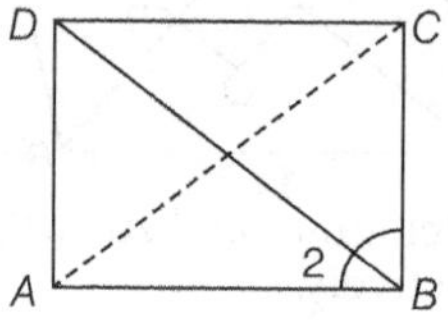

Proof

In ΔBAD and ΔBCD, $\angle ABD = \angle CBD$ [given]

$\angle A = \angle C$ [each 90°]

and $BD = BD$ [common side]

$\therefore$ $\Delta BAD \cong \Delta BCD$ [by AAS congruence rule]

$\Rightarrow$ $AB = BC$ [by CPCT rule]

and $AD = CD$ [by CPCT rule] ...(i)

Also, in rectangle *ABCD*, opposite sides are equal.

$\therefore$ $AB = CD$

and $BC = AD$ ...(ii)

From Eqs. (i) and (ii), we get

$$AB = BC = CD = DA.$$

So, *ABCD* is a square. **Hence proved.**

Q.16 *D*, *E* and *F* are respectively the mid-points of the sides *AB*, *BC* and *CA* of a ΔABC. Prove that by joining these mid-points *D*, *E* and *F*, the ΔABC is divided into four congruent triangles.

Thinking Process Use SSS congruence rule *i.e* if three sides of one triangle are equal to the three sides of the other triangle, then the two triangles are congruent. Further, shown the required result.

Ans. Given In a ΔABC, *D*, *E* and *F* are respectively the mid-points of the sides *AB*, *BC* and *CA*.

To prove ΔABC is divided into four congruent triangles.

Proof Since, *ABC* is a triangle and *D*, *E* and *F* are the mid-points of sides *AB*, *BC* and *CA*, respectively.

Then, $AD = BD = \frac{1}{2}AB,\ BE = EC = \frac{1}{2}BC$

and $AF = CF = \frac{1}{2}AC$

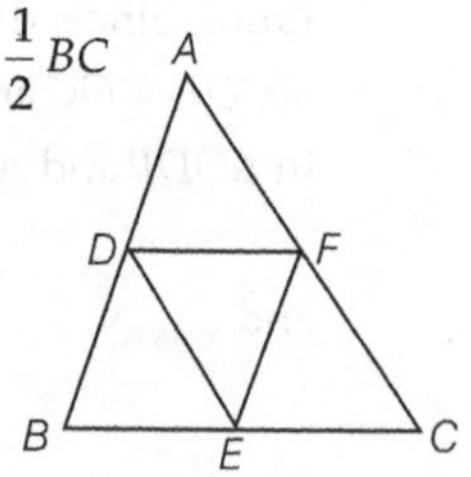

Now, on using the mid-point theorem,

$$EF \parallel AB \text{ and } EF = \frac{1}{2}AB = AD = BD$$

$$ED \parallel AC \text{ and } ED = \frac{1}{2}AC = AF = CF$$

and $$DF \parallel BC \text{ and } DF = \frac{1}{2}BC = BE = CE$$

In ΔADF and ΔEFD, $AD = EF$

$AF = DE$

and $DF = FD$ [common]

$\therefore$ $\Delta ADF \cong \Delta EFD$ [by SSS congruence rule]

Similarly, $\Delta DEF \cong \Delta EDB$

and $\Delta DEF \cong \Delta CFE$

Hence, ΔABC is divided into four congruent triangles. **Hence proved.**

Q.17 Prove that the line joining the mid-points of the diagonals of a trapezium is parallel to the parallel sides of the trapezium.

Ans. Given Let $ABCD$ be a trapezium in which $AB \parallel DC$ and let M and N be the mid-points of the diagonals AC and BD, respectively.

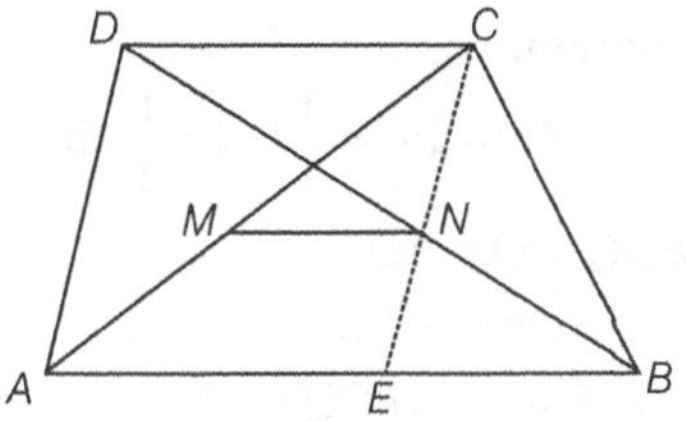

To prove $MN \parallel AB \parallel CD$

Construction Join CN and produce it to meet AB at E.

In ΔCDN and ΔEBN, we have

$DN = BN$ [$\because$ N is the mid-point of BD given]

$\angle DCN = \angle BEN$ [alternate interior angles]

and $\angle CDN = \angle EBN$ [alternate interior angles]

$\therefore$ $\Delta CDN \cong \Delta EBN$ [by AAS congruence rule]

$\therefore$ $DC = EB$ and $CN = NE$ [by CPCT rule]

Thus, in ΔCAE, the points M and N are the mid-points of AC and CE, respectively.

$\therefore$ $MN \parallel AE$ [by mid-point theorem]

$\Rightarrow$ $MN \parallel AB \parallel CD$ **Hence proved.**

Q.18 P is the mid-point of the side CD of a parallelogram $ABCD$. A line through C parallel to PA intersects AB at Q and DA produced at R. Prove that $DA = AR$ and $CQ = QR$.

Ans. Given In a parallelogram $ABCD$, P is the mid-point of DC.

To prove $DA = AR$ and $CQ = QR$

Proof $ABCD$ is a parallelogram.

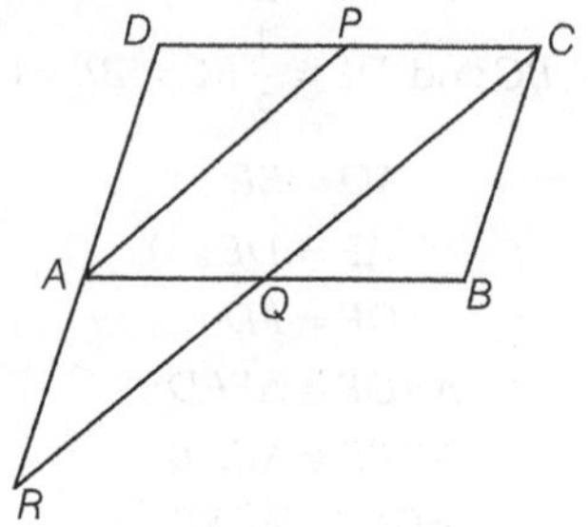

$\therefore$ $BC = AD$ and $BC \parallel AD$

Also, $DC = AB$ and $DC \parallel AB$

Since, P is the mid-point of DC.

$\therefore$ $DP = PC = \frac{1}{2} DC$

Now, $QC \parallel AP$ and $PC \parallel AQ$

So, $APCQ$ is a parallelogram.

$\therefore$ $AQ = PC = \frac{1}{2} DC = \frac{1}{2} AB = BQ$ [$\because DC = AB$] ...(i)

Now, in ΔAQR and ΔBQC, $AQ = BQ$ [from Eq. (i)]

$\angle AQR = \angle BQC$ [vertically opposite angles]

and $\angle ARQ = \angle BCQ$ [Alternate interior angles]

$\therefore$ $\Delta\ AQR \cong \Delta\ BQC$ [by AAS congruence rule]

$\therefore$ $AR = BC$ [by CPCT rule]

But $BC = DA$

$\therefore$ $AR = DA$

Also, $CQ = QR$ [by CPCT rule] **Hence proved.**

Mistake Alert! *Students may be place point P at some other wrong location or draw the parallel lines incorrectly.*

Chapter

09

Areas of Parallelograms and Triangles*

Multiple Choice Questions (MCQs)

Choose the correct answer from the given four options in the following questions:

Q.1 The median of a triangle divides it into two

(a) triangles of equal area
(b) congruent triangles
(c) right triangles
(d) isosceles triangles

Ans. *(a)* We know that a median of a triangle is a line segment joining a vertex to the mid-point of the opposite side. Thus, a median of a triangle divides it into two triangles of equal area.

Q.2 In which of the following figures, you find two polygons on the same base and between the same parallels?

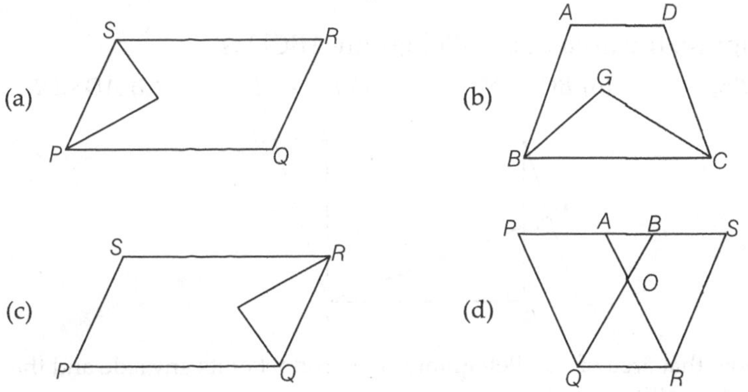

Ans. *(d)* In figures, (a), (b) and (c) there are two polygons on the same base but they are not between the same parallels.

In figure (d), there are two polygons ($PQRA$ and $BQRS$) on the same base and between the same parallels.

(*) This chapter has been deleted from latest NCERT.

Q.3 The figure obtained by joining the mid-points of the adjacent sides of a rectangle of sides 8 cm and 6 cm is

(a) a rectangle of area 24 cm^2 (b) a square of area 25 cm^2
(c) a trapezium of area 24 cm^2 (d) a rhombus of area 24 cm^2

Ans. *(d)* We know that on joining the mid-points of the adjacent sides of a rectangle, we get a rhombus.

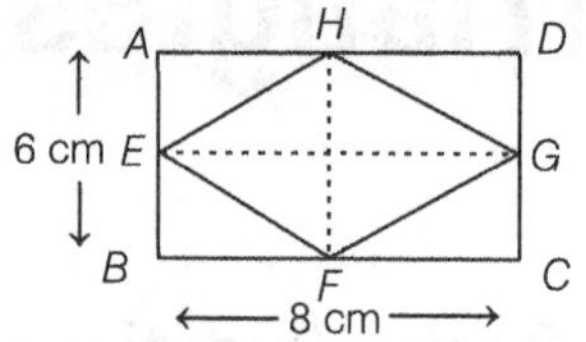

Here, length of rectangle $ABCD = 8$ cm
and breadth of rectangle $ABCD = 6$ cm

Let E, F, G and H are the mid-points of the sides of rectangle $ABCD$, then $EFGH$ is a rhombus.

Then, diagonal of rhombus $EFGH$ are EG and HF.

Here, $EG = BC = 8$ cm and $HF = AB = 6$ cm

$$\therefore \quad \text{Area of rhombus} = \frac{\text{Product of diagonals}}{2}$$

$$= \frac{8 \times 6}{2} = 4 \times 6 = 24 \text{ cm}^2$$

Hence, joining the mid-points of the adjacent sides of a rectangle forms a rhombus of area 24 cm^2.

Q.4 In the figure, the area of parallelogram $ABCD$ is

(a) $AB \times BM$ (b) $BC \times BN$ (c) $DC \times DL$ (d) $AD \times DL$

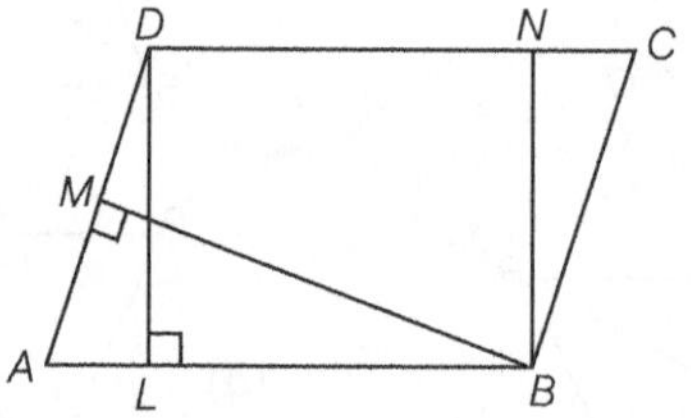

Ans. *(c)* We know that area of parallelogram is the product of its any side and the corresponding altitude or height.

Here, when AB is base, then height is DL.

$$\therefore \quad \text{Area of parallelogram} = AB \times DL$$

and when AD is base, then height is BM.

$$\therefore \quad \text{Area of parallelogram} = AD \times BM$$

When DC is base, then height is DL.

$$\therefore \quad \text{Area of parallelogram} = DC \times DL$$

and when BC is base, then height is not given.

Hence, option (c) is correct.

Mistake Alert! *Students may assume that any two sides as the base and height of a parallelogram without being sure that they are perpendicular.*

Q.5 In figure, if parallelogram $ABCD$ and rectangle $ABEM$ are of equal area, then:

(a) Perimeter of $ABCD$ = Perimeter of $ABEM$
(b) Perimeter of $ABCD$ < Perimeter of $ABEM$
(c) Perimeter of $ABCD$ > Perimeter of $ABEM$
(d) Perimeter of $ABCD = \frac{1}{2}$ (Perimeter of $ABEM$)

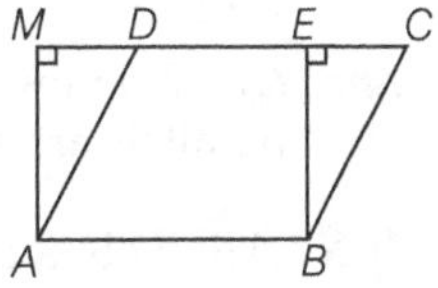

Ans. *(c)* In rectangle $ABEM$, $AB = EM$ [sides of rectangle] ...(i)
and in parallelogram $ABCD$, $CD = AB$ ...(ii)
From Eqs. (i) and (ii), we get

$$CD = AB = EM \quad \text{...(iii)}$$

We know that the perpendicular distance between two parallel sides of a parallelogram is always less than the length of the other parallel sides.

$\therefore$ $BE < BC$ and $AM < AD$

[since, in a right angled triangle, the hypotenuse is greater than the other side]

On adding both above inequalities, we get

$$BE + AM < BC + AD \text{ or } BC + AD > BE + AM$$

On adding $AB + CD$ both sides, we get

$$AB + CD + BC + AD > AB + CD + BE + AM$$

$\Rightarrow$ $AB + BC + CD + AD > AB + BE + EM + AM$ [$\because CD = AB = EM$]

$\therefore$ Perimeter of parallelogram $ABCD$ > perimeter of rectangle $ABEM$

Mistake Alert! *Students may think that if two shapes have the same area, they must also have the same perimeter.*

Q.6 The mid-point of the sides of a triangle along with any of the vertices as the fourth point make a parallelogram of area equal to

(a) $\frac{1}{2}$ ar(ABC) (b) $\frac{1}{3}$ ar(ABC) (c) $\frac{1}{4}$ ar(ABC) (d) ar(ABC)

Concept Insight If the four triangles formed by joining the pairs of mid-points of the sides of a triangle, then all the four triangles have equal area.

Ans. *(a)* We know that if D, E and F are respectively the mid-points of the sides BC, CA and AB of a ΔABC, then all the four triangles has equal area *i.e.,*

$$\text{ar}(\Delta AFE) = \text{ar}(\Delta BFD) = \text{ar}(\Delta EDC) = \text{ar}(\Delta DEF) \quad \text{...(i)}$$

$$\therefore \quad \text{Area of } \Delta DEF = \frac{1}{4} \text{ Area of } \Delta ABC \quad \text{...(ii)}$$

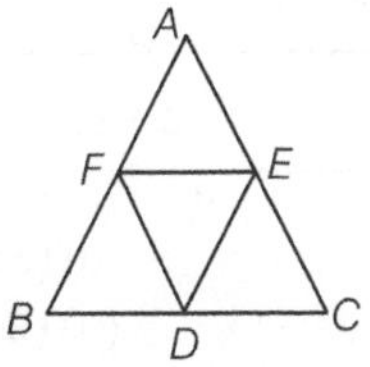

If we take D as the fourth vertex, then area of the parallelogram $AFDE$

= Area of ΔAFE + Area of ΔDEF
= Area of ΔDEF + Area of ΔDEF = 2 Area of ΔDEF [from Eq. (i)]
$= 2 \times \frac{1}{4}$ Area of $\Delta ABC = \frac{1}{2}$ Area of ΔABC [from Eq. (ii)]

Q.7 Two parallelograms are on equal bases and between the same parallels. The ratio of their areas is

(a) 1 : 2 (b) 1 : 1 (c) 2 : 1 (d) 3 : 1

Ans. *(b)* We know that parallelogram on the equal bases and between the same parallels are equal in area. So, ratio of their areas is 1 : 1.

Q.8 $ABCD$ is a quadrilateral whose diagonal AC divides it into two parts, equal in area, then $ABCD$

(a) is a rectangle (b) is always a rhombus

(c) is a parallelogram (d) need not be any of (a), (b) or (c)

Ans. *(d)* Here, $ABCD$ need not be any of rectangle, rhombus and parallelogram because all of these satisfy the given condition.

Q.9 If a triangle and a parallelogram are on the same base and between same parallels, then the ratio of the area of the triangle to the area of parallelogram is

(a) 1 : 3 (b) 1 : 2

(c) 3 : 1 (d) 1 : 4

Ans. *(b)* We know that if a parallelogram and a triangle are on the same base and between the same parallels, then area of the triangle is half the area of the parallelogram.

i.e., $$\text{Area of triangle} = \frac{1}{2}\text{Area of parallelogram}$$

$$\Rightarrow \quad \frac{\text{Area of triangle}}{\text{Area of parallelogram}} = \frac{1}{2}$$

$\therefore$ Area of triangle : Area of parallelogram = 1 : 2

Mistake Alert! *Students may assume that if a triangle and a parallelogram are on the same base and between the same parallels, then the area of triangle is equal to one-third of the area of parallelogram.*

Q.10 $ABCD$ is a trapezium with parallel sides $AB = a$ cm and $DC = b$ cm. E and F are the mid-points of the non-parallel sides. The ratio of ar$(ABFE)$ and ar$(EFCD)$ is

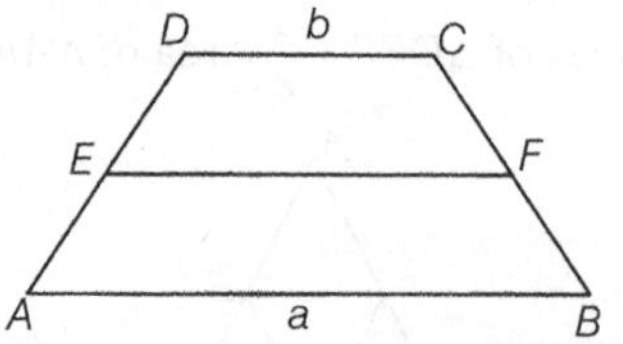

(a) $a : b$ (b) $(3a + b) : (a + 3b)$

(c) $(a + 3b) : (3a + b)$ (d) $(2a + b) : (3a + b)$

Concept Insight Use the mid-point theorem; the line segment in a triangle joining the mid-point of any two sides of the triangle is said to be parallel to its third side and also half of the length of the third side.

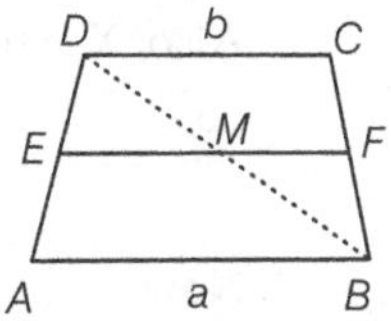

Ans. *(b)* Given, $AB = a$ cm, $DC = b$ cm and $AB \parallel DC$.

Also, E and F are mid-points of AD and BC, respectively.

So, distance between CD, EF and AB, EF will be same say h.

Join BD which intersect EF at M.

Now, in ΔABD, E is the mid-point of AD and $EM \parallel AB$

So, M is the mid-point of BD

and $$EM = \frac{1}{2}AB \quad \text{[by mid-point theorem] ...(i)}$$

Similarly in ΔCBD, $$MF = \frac{1}{2}CD \quad \text{...(ii)}$$

On adding, Eqs. (i) and (ii), we get

$$EM + MF = \frac{1}{2}AB + \frac{1}{2}CD \Rightarrow EF = \frac{1}{2}(AB + CD) = \frac{1}{2}(a + b)$$

Now, area of trapezium $ABFE = \frac{1}{2}$ (sum of parallel sides)

× (distance between parallel sides)

$$= \frac{1}{2}\left(a + \frac{1}{2}(a + b)\right) \times h = \frac{1}{4}(3a + b)\,h$$

Now, area of trapezium $EFCD = \frac{1}{2}\left[b + \frac{1}{2}(a + b)\right] \times h = \frac{1}{4}(3b + a)h$

$$\therefore \text{ Required ratio} = \frac{\text{Area of } ABFE}{\text{Area of } EFCD} = \frac{\frac{1}{4}(3a + b)h}{\frac{1}{4}(3b + a)h} = \frac{(3a + b)}{(a + 3b)} \text{ or } (3a + b) : (a + 3b)$$

Short Answer Questions with Reasoning

Write True or False and justify your answer in each questions.

Q.1 $ABCD$ is a parallelogram and X is the mid-point of AB. If ar $(AXCD) = 24 \text{ cm}^2$, then ar $(ABC) = 24 \text{ cm}^2$.

Concept Insight A diagonal divides a parallelogram into two triangles of equal area.

Ans. *False*

Given, $ABCD$ is a parallelogram and ar $(AXCD) = 24 \text{ cm}^2$

Let area of parallelogram $ABCD$ is $2y \text{ cm}^2$ and join AC.

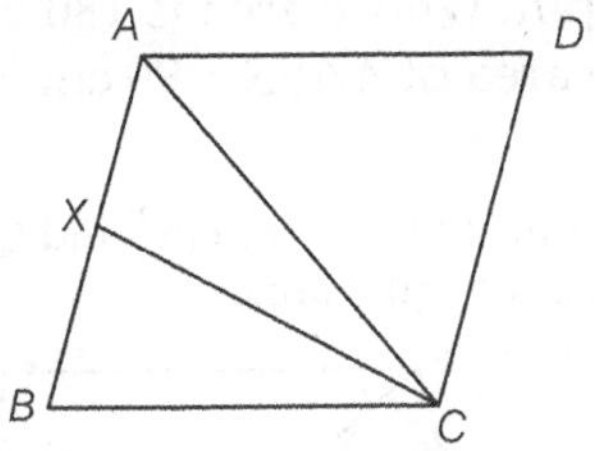

We know that a diagonal divides a parallelogram in two triangles of equal area.

$\therefore$ $$\text{ar}(\Delta ABC) = \text{ar}(ACD) = y \quad \text{(say)}$$

Also, X is the mid-point of AB.

So, $\text{ar}(\Delta ACX) = \text{ar}(BCX)$ [$\because X$ is median in ΔABC]

$$= \frac{1}{2}\text{ar}(ABC) = \frac{1}{2}y$$

Now, $\text{ar}(AXCD) = \text{ar}(\Delta ADC) + \text{ar}(ACX)$

$\Rightarrow$ $24 = y + \frac{y}{2}$ [given]

$\Rightarrow$ $24 = \frac{3y}{2} \Rightarrow y = \frac{24 \times 2}{3} = 16\text{ cm}^2$

Hence, $\text{ar}(\Delta ABC) = 16\text{ cm}^2$

Therefore, given statement is false.

Q.2 *PQRS* is a rectangle inscribed in a quadrant of a circle of radius 13 cm. *A* is any point on *PQ*. If $PS = 5$ cm, then $\text{ar}(\Delta PAS) = 30\text{ cm}^2$.

Ans. *False*

Given, $PS = 5\text{cm}$

and radius of circle $= SQ = 13\text{ cm}$

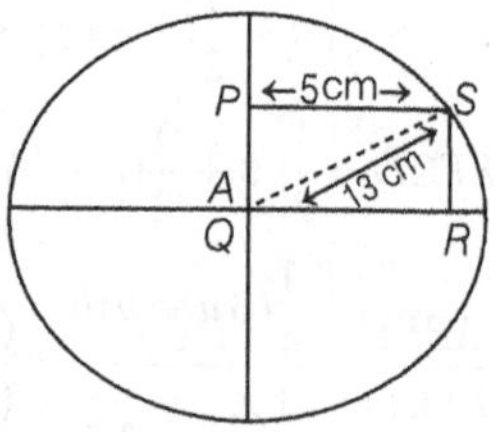

In right angled ΔSPQ, $SQ^2 = PQ^2 + PS^2$ [by Pythagoras theorem]

$$(13)^2 = PQ^2 + (5)^2 \Rightarrow PQ^2 = 169 - 25 = 144$$

$\Rightarrow$ $PQ = 12\text{ cm}$

[take positive square root, because length is always positive]

Now, area of $\Delta PQS = \frac{1}{2} \times \text{Base} \times \text{Height} = \frac{1}{2} \times PS \times PQ = \frac{1}{2} \times 5 \times 12 = 30\text{ cm}^2$

So, given statement is true, if *A* coincides *Q*.

But, *A* is point on *PQ*.

So, area of $\Delta PAS <$ area of ΔPQS.

Hence, area of ΔPAS will be less than 30 cm^2.

Q.3 *PQRS* is a parallelogram whose area is 180 cm^2 and *A* is any point on the diagonal *QS*. The area of $\Delta ASR = 90\text{ cm}^2$.

Ans. *False*

Given, area of parallelogram $PQRS = 180\text{ cm}^2$ and *QS* is its diagonal which divides it into two triangles of equal area.

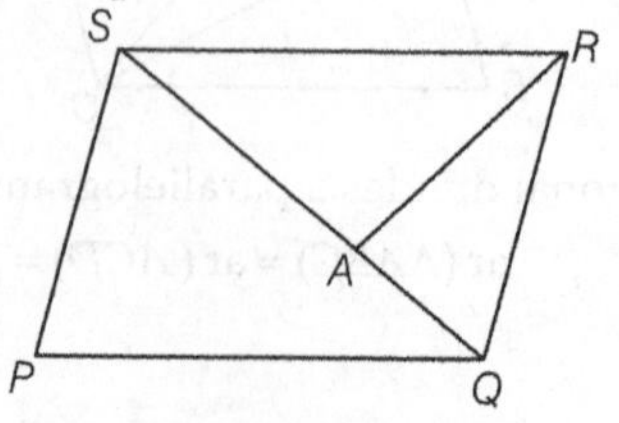

So, area of $\Delta SRQ = \frac{180}{2} = 90 \text{ cm}^2$

Now, A is any point on QS.

So, area of $\Delta ASR <$ area of ΔSRQ.

i.e., area of ΔASR cannot be 90 cm^2.

Q.4 *ABC* and *BDE* are two equilateral triangles such that *D* is the mid-point of *BC*. Then ar $(\Delta BDE) = \frac{1}{4}$ ar (ΔABC).

Ans. *True*

Given, ΔABC and ΔBDE are two equilateral triangles.

$\therefore$ Area of an equilateral $\Delta ABC = \frac{\sqrt{3}}{4} \times (\text{Side})^2 = \frac{\sqrt{3}}{4}(BC)^2$ ...(i)

[$\because$ in equilateral ΔABC, $AB = BC = AC$]

Also, given D is the mid-point of BC.

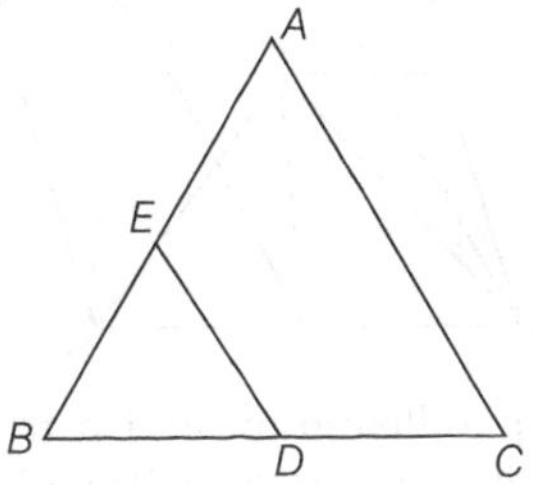

$\therefore$ $BD = DC = \frac{1}{2}BC$ ...(ii)

Now, area of an equilateral $\Delta BDE = \frac{\sqrt{3}}{4} \times (\text{Side})^2$

$= \frac{\sqrt{3}}{4} \times (BD)^2$ [$\because$ in equilateral ΔBDE, $BD = DE = BE$]

$= \frac{\sqrt{3}}{4} \times \left(\frac{1}{2}BC\right)^2$ [from Eq. (ii)]

$= \frac{\sqrt{3}}{4} \times \frac{1}{4}BC^2 = \frac{1}{4}\left(\frac{\sqrt{3}}{4}BC^2\right)$

$\therefore$ Area of $\Delta BDE = \frac{1}{4}$ (Area of ΔABC)

Mistake Alert! *Students may incorrectly use the area of an equilateral triangle as* $\frac{4}{\sqrt{3}}(\text{Side})^2$ *instead of* $\frac{\sqrt{3}}{4}(\text{Side})^2$.

Q.5 In the figure, $ABCD$ and $EFGD$ are two parallelograms and G is the mid-point of CD. Then ar $(\Delta DPC) = \frac{1}{2}$ ar $(EFGD)$.

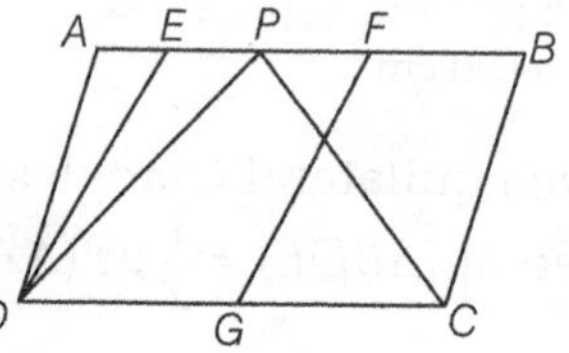

Concept Insight The median of a triangle divides it into two triangles of equal areas.

Ans. *False*

In the given figure, join PG. Since, G is the mid-point of CD.

Thus, PG is a median of ΔDPC and it divides the triangle into parts of equal areas.

Then, $$\text{ar}(\Delta DPG) = \text{ar}(\Delta GPC) = \frac{1}{2}\text{ar}(\Delta DPC) \quad \text{...(i)}$$

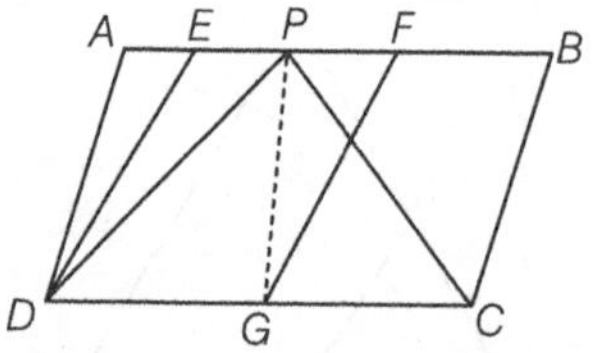

Also, we know that if a parallelogram and a triangle lie on the same base and between the same parallels, then area of triangle is equal to half of the area of parallelogram.

Here, parallelogram $EFGD$ and ΔDPG lie on the same base DG and between the same parallels DG and EF.

So, $$\text{ar}(\Delta DPG) = \frac{1}{2}\text{ar}(EFGD) \quad \text{...(ii)}$$

From Eqs. (i) and (ii), $\frac{1}{2}\text{ar}(\Delta DPC) = \frac{1}{2}\text{ar}(EFGD) \Rightarrow \text{ar}(\Delta DPC) = \text{ar}(EFGD)$

Short Answer Type Questions

Q.1 In the figure, $PSDA$ is a parallelogram. Points Q and R are taken on PS such that $PQ = QR = RS$ and $PA \parallel QB \parallel RC$. Prove that ar (PQE) = ar (CFD).

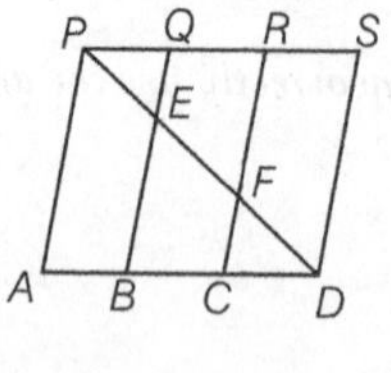

Thinking Process

(i) Firstly, prove that $PABQ$, $QBCR$ and $RCDS$ are parallelograms.

(ii) Further, prove that $\Delta PQE \cong \Delta DCF$, by ASA congruent rule.

(iii) At the end, use the property that congruent figures have same area.

Ans. **Given** In a parallelogram $PSDA$, points Q and R are on PS such that

$$PQ = QR = RS \text{ and } PA \parallel QB \parallel RC.$$

To prove $\text{ar}(PQE) = \text{ar}(CFD)$

Proof In parallelogram $PSDA$, $PS \parallel AD$

$\therefore$ $PQ \parallel AB$

and $PA \parallel QB$ [given]

So, $PABQ$ is a parallelogram.

$\therefore$ $PQ = AB$ ...(i)

Similarly, $QBCR$ is also a parallelogram.

$\therefore$ $QR = BC$ ...(ii)

and $RCDS$ is also a parallelogram.

$\therefore$ $RS = CD$ ...(iii)

Now, $PQ = QR = RS$ ...(iv)

From Eqs. (i), (ii) (iii) and (iv), we get

$$PQ = QR = RS = AB = BC = CD \quad \text{...(v)}$$

In ΔPQE and ΔDCF, $\angle QPE = \angle FDC$

[$\because$ $PS \parallel AD$ and PD is transversal, then alternate interior angles are equal]

$PQ = CD$ [from Eq. (v)]

and $\angle PQE = \angle FCD$

[$\because$ $\angle PQE = \angle PRC$ corresponding angles and $\angle PRC = \angle FCD$ alternate interior angles]

$\therefore$ $\Delta PQE \cong \Delta DCF$ [by ASA congruence rule]

$\therefore$ $\text{ar}(\Delta PQE) = \text{ar}(\Delta CFD)$ [$\because$ congruent figures have equal area]

Hence proved.

Q.2 X and Y are points on the side LN of the triangle LMN such that $LX = XY = YN$. Through X, a line is drawn parallel to LM to meet MN at Z (see figure). Prove that ar (LZY) = ar $(MZYX)$.

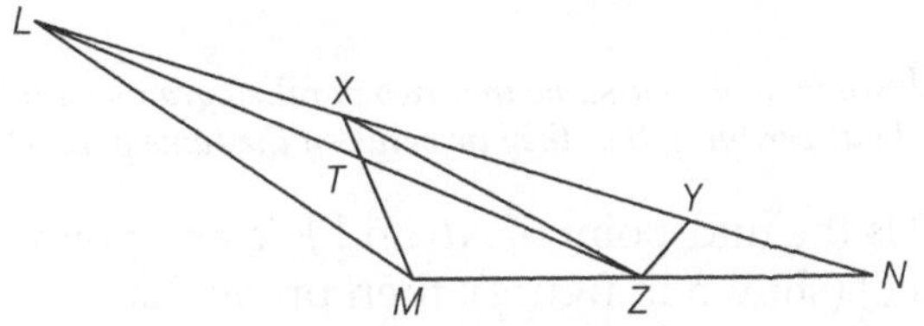

Thinking Process Use the property that the triangles on the same base and between the same two parallel lines are equal in area. Further, prove the required result.

Ans. **Given** X and Y are points on the side LN such that

$$LX = XY = YN \text{ and } XZ \parallel LM$$

To prove $\text{ar}(\Delta LZY) = \text{ar}(MZYX)$

Proof Since, ΔXMZ and ΔXLZ are on the same base XZ and between the same parallel lines LM and XZ.

Then, $\text{ar}(\Delta XMZ) = \text{ar}(\Delta XLZ)$ ...(i)

On adding $\text{ar}(\Delta XYZ)$ both sides of Eq. (i), we get

$\text{ar}(\Delta XMZ) + \text{ar}(\Delta XYZ) = \text{ar}(\Delta XLZ) + \text{ar}(\Delta XYZ) \Rightarrow \text{ar}(MZYX) = \text{ar}(\Delta LZY)$

Hence proved.

Q.3 The area of the parallelogram $ABCD$ is $90\ cm^2$. Find

(i) ar $(ABEF)$ (ii) ar (ABD) (iii) ar (BEF)

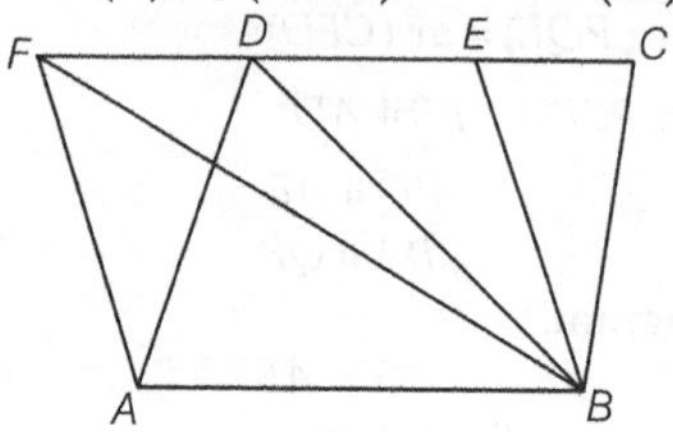

Ans. Given, area of parallelogram $ABCD = 90\ cm^2$.

(i) We know that parallelograms on the same base and between the same parallel are equal in areas.

Here, parallelograms $ABCD$ and $ABEF$ are on same base AB and between the same parallels AB and CF.

So, $$ar\ (ABEF) = ar\ (ABCD) = 90\ cm^2$$

(ii) We know that if a triangle and a parallelogram are on the same base and between the same parallels, then area of triangle is equal to half of the area of the parallelogram. Here, ΔABD and parallelogram $ABCD$ are on the same base AB and between the same parallels AB and CD.

So, $$ar\ (\Delta ABD) = \frac{1}{2} ar\ (ABCD)$$

$$= \frac{1}{2} \times 90 = 45\ cm^2 \quad [\because ar\ (ABCD) = 90\ cm^2]$$

(iii) Here, ΔBEF and parallelogram $ABEF$ are on the same base EF and between the same parallels AB and EF.

So, $$ar\ (\Delta BEF) = \frac{1}{2}\ ar\ (ABEF)$$

$$= \frac{1}{2} \times 90 = 45\ cm^2 \quad [\because ar\ (ABEF) = 90\ cm^2, \text{ from part (i)}]$$

Mistake Alert ! *Students may assume that two parallelograms with the same base have equal areas, without verifying that they lie between the same parallel lines.*

Q.4 In $\Delta\ ABC$, D is the mid-point of AB and P is any point on BC. If $CQ \parallel PD$ meets AB in Q (shown in figure), then prove that

$$ar\ (\Delta BPQ) = \frac{1}{2}\ ar\ (\Delta ABC).$$

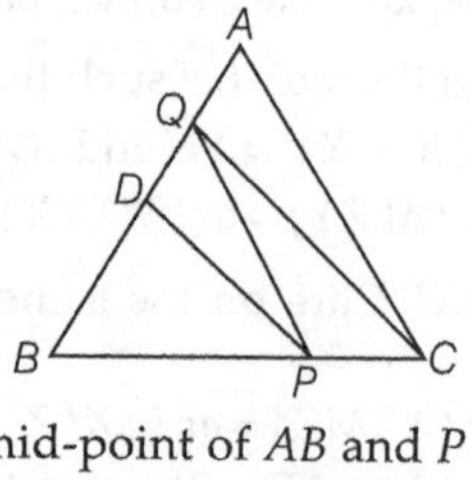

Ans. **Given** In ΔABC, D is the mid-point of AB and P is any point on BC.

$CQ \parallel PD$ meets AB in Q.

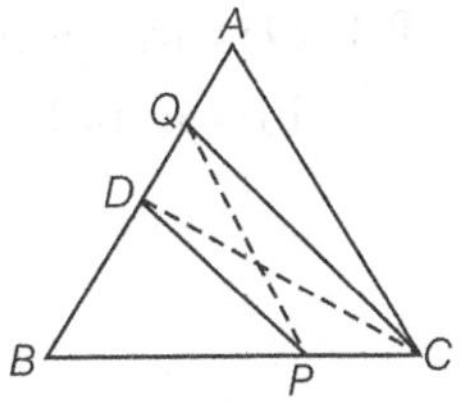

To prove $\text{ar}(\Delta BPQ) = \frac{1}{2}\text{ar}(\Delta ABC)$

Construction Join PQ and CD.

Proof Since, D is the mid-point of AB. So, CD is the median of ΔABC.

We know that, a median of a triangle divides it into two triangles of equal areas.

$\therefore \quad \text{ar}(\Delta BCD) = \frac{1}{2}\text{ar}(\Delta ABC)$

$\Rightarrow \quad \text{ar}(\Delta BPD) + \text{ar}(\Delta DPC) = \frac{1}{2}\text{ar}(\Delta ABC)$ ...(i)

Now, ΔDPQ and ΔDPC are on the same base DP and between the same parallel lines DP and CQ.

So, $\text{ar}(\Delta DPQ) = \text{ar}(\Delta DPC)$ ...(ii)

On putting the value from Eq. (ii) in Eq. (i), we get

$$\text{ar}(\Delta BPD) + \text{ar}(\Delta DPQ) = \frac{1}{2}\text{ar}(\Delta ABC)$$

$\Rightarrow \quad \text{ar}(\Delta BPQ) = \frac{1}{2}\text{ar}(\Delta ABC)$ **Hence proved.**

Q.5 *ABCD* is a square. *E* and *F* are respectively the mid-points of *BC* and *CD*. If *R* is the mid-point of *EF*, prove that $\text{ar}(\Delta AER) = \text{ar}(\Delta AFR)$.

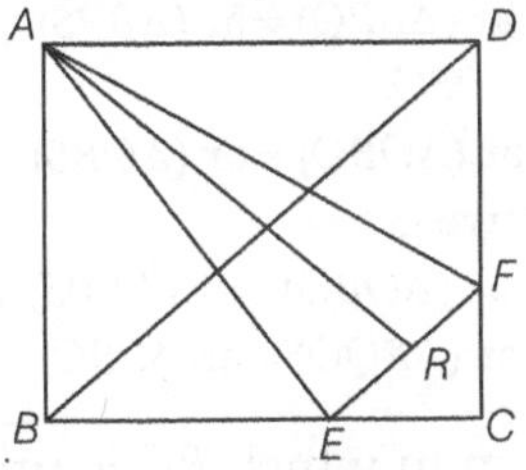

Concept Insight Area of triangle $= \frac{1}{2} \times \text{Base} \times \text{Height}$

Ans. **Given** In square $ABCD$, E and F are the mid-points of BC and CD respectively. Also, R is the mid-point of EF.

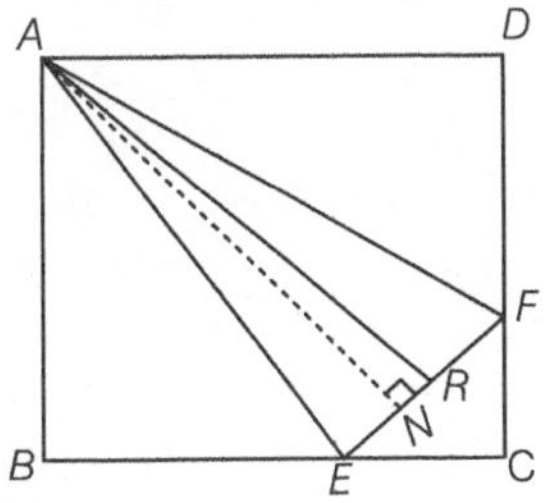

To prove $\text{ar}(\Delta AER) = \text{ar}(\Delta AFR)$

Construction Draw $AN \perp EF$.

Proof $\because \quad \text{ar}(\Delta AER) = \frac{1}{2} \times \text{Base} \times \text{Height}$

$$= \frac{1}{2} \times ER \times AN$$

$$= \frac{1}{2} \times FR \times AN$$

[$\because$ R is the mid-point of EF, so $ER = FR$]

$$= \text{ar}(\Delta AFR)$$

Hence proved.

Q.6 O is any point on the diagonal PR of a parallelogram $PQRS$ (see figure). Prove that ar(ΔPSO) = ar(ΔPQO).

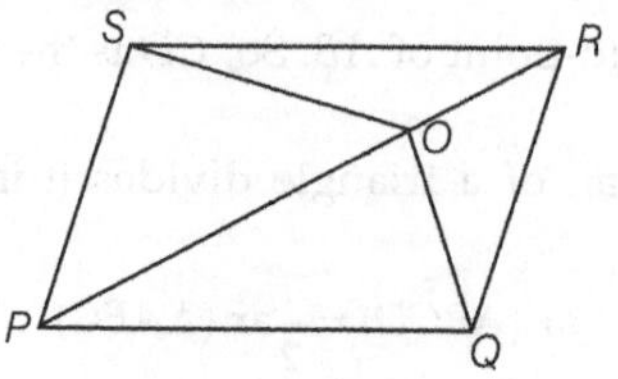

Ans. Given In a parallelogram $PQRS$, O is any point on the diagonal PR.

To prove ar (ΔPSO) = ar (ΔPQO)

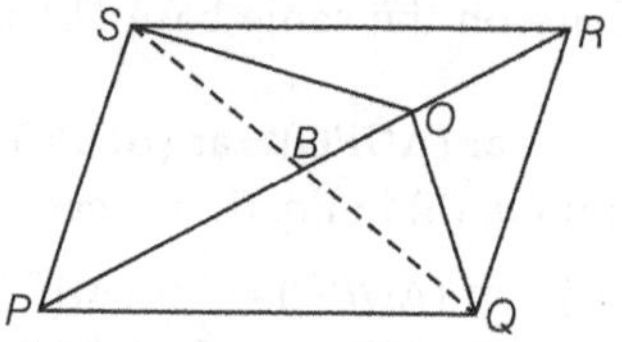

Construction Join SQ which intersects PR at B.

Proof We know that diagonals of a parallelogram bisect each other, so B is the mid-point of SQ.

Here, PB is a median of ΔQPS and we know that a median of a triangle divides it into two triangles of equal area.

$\therefore$ ar (ΔBPQ) = ar (ΔBPS) ...(i)

Also, OB is the median of ΔOSQ.

$\therefore$ ar (ΔOBQ) = ar (ΔOBS) ...(ii)

On adding Eqs. (i) and (ii), we get

ar (ΔBPQ) + ar (ΔOBQ) = ar (ΔBPS) + ar (ΔOBS)

$\Rightarrow$ ar (ΔPQO) = ar(ΔPSO) **Hence proved.**

Q.7 $ABCD$ is a parallelogram in which BC is produced to E such that $CE = BC$. AE intersects CD at F.

If ar $(\Delta DFB) = 3\text{ cm}^2$, then find the area of the parallelogram $ABCD$.

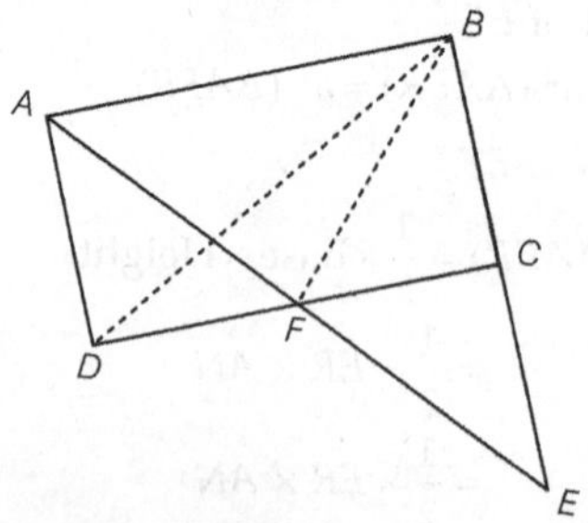

Ans. Given, $ABCD$ is a parallelogram and $CE = BC$ *i.e.*, C is the mid-point of BE.

Also, ar $(\Delta DFB) = 3\text{ cm}^2$

Now, ΔADF and ΔDFB are on the same base DF and between parallels CD and AB. Then,

ar (ΔADF) = ar $(\Delta DFB) = 3\text{ cm}^2$ ...(i)

In ΔABE, by the converse of mid-point theorem,

$EF = AF$ [$\because$ C is mid-point of BE]...(ii)

In ΔADF and ΔECF,

$\angle AFD = \angle CFE$ [vertically opposite angles]

$AF = EF$ [from Eq. (ii)]

and $\angle DAF = \angle CEF$

[since, $BE \parallel AD$ and AE is transversal, then alternate interior angles are equal]

$\therefore$ $\Delta ADF \cong \Delta ECF$ [by ASA congruence rule]

Then, ar (ΔADF) = ar (ΔCFE)

[$\because$ congruent figures have equal area]

$\therefore$ ar (ΔCFE) = ar $(\Delta ADF) = 3\text{ cm}^2$ [from Eq. (i)]...(iii)

Now, in ΔBFE, C is the mid-point of BE then CF is median of ΔBFE.

$\therefore$ ar (ΔCEF) = ar (ΔBFC)

[$\because$ median of a triangle divides it into two triangles of equal area]

$\Rightarrow$ ar $(\Delta BFC) = 3\text{ cm}^2$ ...(iv)

Now, ar (ΔBDC) = ar (ΔDFB) + ar (ΔBFC)

$= 3 + 3 = 6\text{ cm}^2$ [from Eqs. (i) and (iv)]

We know that, diagonal of a parallelogram divides it into two congruent triangles of equal areas.

$\therefore$ Area of parallelogram $ABCD = 2 \times$Area of $\Delta BDC = 2 \times 6 = 12\text{ cm}^2$

Hence, the area of parallelogram $ABCD$ is 12 cm^2.

Mistake Alert! *Students may assume that triangles with same base have the same area even, if they do not lie between the same parallels.*

Q.8 In trapezium $ABCD$, $AB \parallel DC$ and L is the mid-point of BC. Through L, a line $PQ \parallel AD$ has been drawn which meets AB in P and DC produced in Q. Prove that ar $(ABCD)$ = ar $(APQD)$.

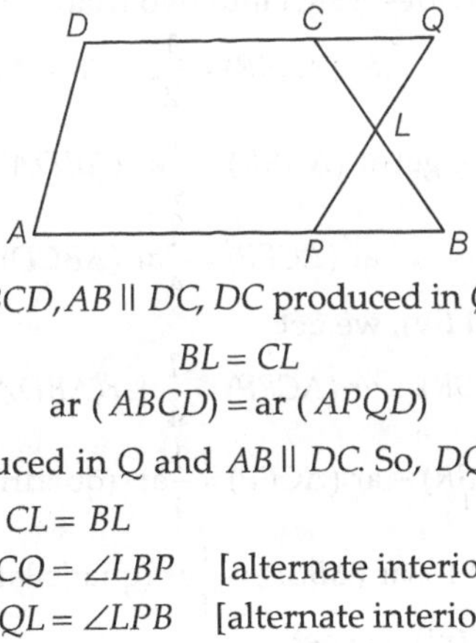

Ans. Given In trapezium $ABCD$, $AB \parallel DC$, DC produced in Q and L is the mid-point of BC.

$\therefore$ $BL = CL$

To prove ar $(ABCD)$ = ar $(APQD)$

Proof Since, DC produced in Q and $AB \parallel DC$. So, $DQ \parallel AB$

In ΔCLQ and ΔBLP, $CL = BL$ [$\because$ L is the mid-point of BC]

$\angle LCQ = \angle LBP$ [alternate interior angles as BC is a transversal]

$\angle CQL = \angle LPB$ [alternate interior angles as PQ is a transversal]

$\therefore$ $\Delta CLQ \cong \Delta BLP$ [by AAS congruence rule]

Then, ar (ΔCLQ) = ar (ΔBLP) ...(i)

[$\because$ congruent triangles have equal area]

Now, ar $(ABCD)$ = ar $(APQD)$ − ar (ΔCQL) + ar (ΔBLP)

= ar $(APQD)$ − ar (ΔBLP) + ar (ΔBLP) [from Eq. (i)]

$\Rightarrow$ ar $(ABCD)$ = ar $(APQD)$ **Hence proved.**

Q.9 If the mid-points of the sides of a quadrilateral are joined in order, prove that the area of the parallelogram, so formed will be half of the area of the given quadrilateral (see figure).

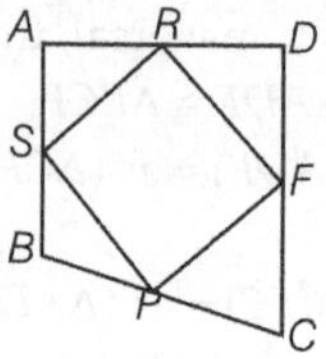

Ans. **Given** Let $ABCD$ is a quadrilateral and P, F, R and S are the mid-points of the sides BC, CD, AD and AB respectively and $PFRS$ is a parallelogram.

To prove ar (parallelogram $PFRS$) $= \frac{1}{2}$ ar (quadrilateral $ABCD$)

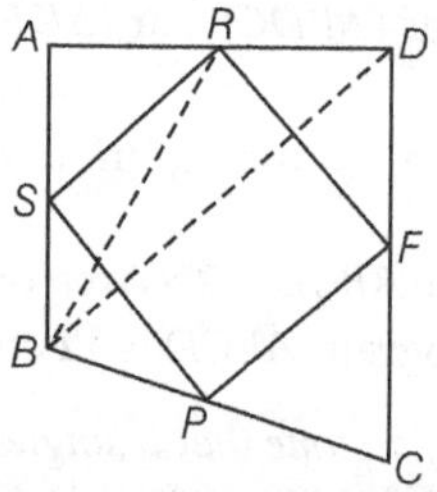

Construction Join BD and BR.

Proof Median BR divides ΔBDA into two triangles of equal area.

$$\therefore \quad \text{ar}(\Delta BRA) = \frac{1}{2}\text{ar}(\Delta BDA) \quad \text{...(i)}$$

Similarly, median RS divides ΔBRA into two triangles of equal area.

$$\therefore \quad \text{ar}(\Delta ASR) = \frac{1}{2}\text{ar}(\Delta BRA) \quad \text{..(ii)}$$

From Eqs. (i) and (ii), we get $\text{ar}(\Delta ASR) = \frac{1}{4}\text{ar}(\Delta BDA)$ ...(iii)

Similarly, $\text{ar}(\Delta CFP) = \frac{1}{4}\text{ar}(\Delta BCD)$ ...(iv)

On adding Eqs. (iii) and (iv), we get

$$\text{ar}(\Delta ASR) + \text{ar}(\Delta CFP) = \frac{1}{4}[\text{ar}(\Delta BDA) + \text{ar}(\Delta BCD)]$$

$$\Rightarrow \quad \text{ar}(\Delta ASR) + \text{ar}(\Delta CFP) = \frac{1}{4}\text{ar (quadrilateral } BCDA) \quad \text{...(v)}$$

Similarly, $\text{ar}(\Delta DRF) + \text{ar}(\Delta BSP) = \frac{1}{4}\text{ar (quadrilateral } BCDA)$ ...(vi)

On adding Eqs. (v) and (vi), we get

$$\text{ar}(\Delta ASR) + \text{ar}(\Delta CFP) + \text{ar}(\Delta DRF) + \text{ar}(\Delta BSP) = \frac{1}{2}\text{ar (quadrilateral } BCDA) \quad \text{...(vii)}$$

But $\text{ar}(\Delta ASR) + \text{ar}(\Delta CFP) + \text{ar}(\Delta DRF) + \text{ar}(\Delta BSP) + \text{ar (parallelogram } PFRS) = \text{ar (quadrilateral } BCDA)$ ...(viii)

On subtracting Eq. (vii) from Eq. (viii), we get

$$\text{ar (parallelogram } PFRS) = \frac{1}{2}\text{ar (quadrilateral } BCDA)$$ **Hence proved.**

Long Answer Type Questions

Q. 1 *A point E is taken on the side BC of a parallelogram ABCD. AE and DC are produced to meet at F. Prove that* ar (ΔADF) = ar ($ABFC$).

Ans. **Given** $ABCD$ is a parallelogram and E is a point on BC. AE and DC are produced to meet at F.

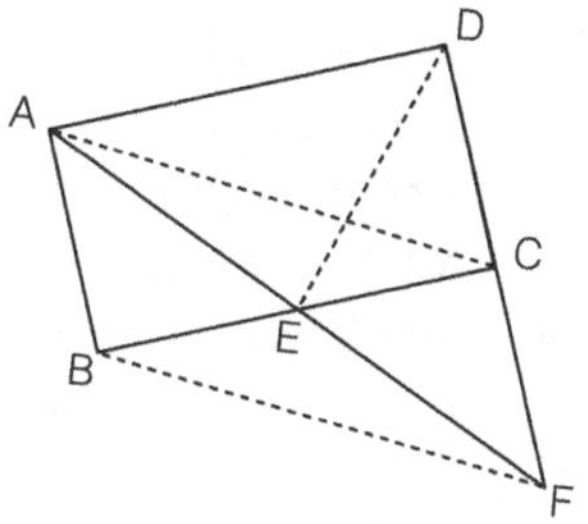

$\therefore$ $AB \parallel CD$ and $BC \parallel AD$ ...(i)

To prove ar (ΔADF) = ar ($ABFC$)

Construction Join AC, BF and DE.

Proof Since, AC is a diagonal of parallelogram $ABCD$.

So, ar (ΔABC) = ar (ΔACD) ...(ii)

Since, ΔABF and ΔABC are on the same base AB and between the same parallels AB and DF. [$\because AB \parallel DC$ and DC produced to F]

$\therefore$ ar (ΔABF) = ar (ΔABC) ...(iii)

From Eqs. (ii) and (iii), we get

$$\text{ar}(\Delta ABC) = \text{ar}(\Delta ACD) = \text{ar}(\Delta ABF)$$

On subtracting ar (ΔABE) from both sides of Eq. (iii), we get

$$\text{ar}(\Delta ABF) - \text{ar}(\Delta ABE) = \text{ar}(\Delta ABC) - \text{ar}(\Delta ABE)$$

$\Rightarrow$ ar (ΔBEF) = ar (ΔAEC) ...(iv)

Now, ar ($AECD$) = ar (ACD) + ar (AEC)

= ar (ΔABC) + ar (ΔBEF) [from Eqs. (ii) and (iv)]

On adding ar (ΔCEF) both sides, we get

$$\text{ar}(AECD) + \text{ar}(\Delta CEF) = \text{ar}(\Delta ABC) + \text{ar}(\Delta BEF) + \text{ar}(\Delta CEF)$$

$\Rightarrow$ ar (ΔADF) = ar ($ABFC$) **Hence proved.**

Q.2 The diagonals of a parallelogram $ABCD$ intersect at a point O. Through O, a line is drawn to intersect AD at P and BC at Q. Show that PQ divides the parallelogram into two parts of equal area.

Concept Insight Diagonals of a parallel ogram bisect each other and congruent figures have equal areas.

Ans. **Given** In a parallelogram $ABCD$, diagonals interect at O and draw a line PQ, which intersects AD and BC.

To prove PQ divides the parallelogram $ABCD$ into two parts of equal area.

i.e., ar ($ABQP$) = ar ($CDPQ$)

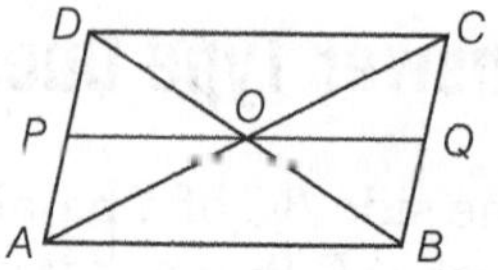

Proof We know that, diagonals of a parallelogram bisect each other.

$\therefore$ $OA = OC$ and $OB = OD$ ...(i)

In ΔAOB and ΔCOD,

$OA = OC$

$OB = OD$ [from Eq. (i)]

and $\angle AOB = \angle COD$ [vertically opposite angles]

$\therefore$ $\Delta AOB \cong \Delta COD$ [by SAS congruence rule]

Then, ar (ΔAOB) = ar (ΔCOD) ...(ii)

[$\because$ congruent figures have equal area]

Now, in ΔAOP and ΔCOQ,

$\angle PAO = \angle OCQ$ [alternate interior angles]

$OA = OC$ [from Eq. (i)]

and $\angle AOP = \angle COQ$ [vertically opposite angles]

$\therefore$ $\Delta AOP \cong \Delta COQ$ [by ASA congruence rule]

$\therefore$ ar (ΔAOP) = ar (ΔCOQ) ...(iii)

[$\because$ congruent figures have equal areas]

Similarly, ar (ΔPOD) = ar (ΔBOQ) ...(iv)

Now, ar($CDPQ$) = ar (ΔCOQ) + ar (ΔCOD) + ar (ΔPOD)

= ar (ΔAOP) + ar (ΔAOB) + ar (ΔBOQ)

= ar ($ABQP$) [from Eqs. (ii), (iii) and (iv)]

$\therefore$ ar ($ABQP$) = ar ($CDPQ$) **Hence proved.**

Q.3 The median BE and CF of a triangle ABC intersect at G. Prove that the area of ΔGBC = Area of the quadrilateral $AFGE$.

Ans. **Given** In ΔABC, medians BE and CF intersect each other at G.

To prove ar (ΔGBC) = ar ($AFGE$)

Proof Since, BE is the median of ΔABC and we know that a median of a triangle divides it into two parts of equal area.

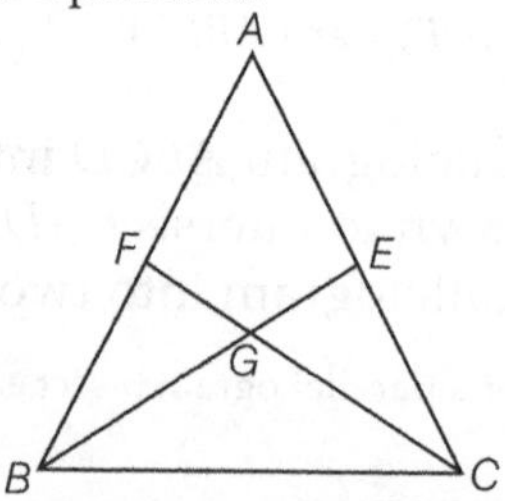

So, ar (ΔABE) = ar (ΔCBE)

$\Rightarrow$ ar (ΔABE) = $\frac{1}{2}$ar (ΔABC) ...(i)

Similarly, CF is the median of ΔABC.

Then, $\text{ar}(\Delta ACF) = \text{ar}(\Delta BCF)$

$\Rightarrow \quad \text{ar}(\Delta BCF) = \frac{1}{2}\text{ar}(\Delta ABC)$ ...(ii)

From Eqs. (i) and (ii), we get

$\text{ar}(\Delta ABE) = \text{ar}(\Delta BCF)$ ...(iii)

On subtracting ar (ΔGBF) from both sides of Eq. (iii), we get

$$\text{ar}(\Delta ABE) - \text{ar}(\Delta GBF) = \text{ar}(\Delta BCF) - \text{ar}(\Delta GBF)$$

$\Rightarrow \quad \text{ar}(AFGE) = \text{ar}(GBC)$ **Hence proved.**

Q.4 In figure, $CD \parallel AE$ and $CY \parallel BA$. Prove that ar (CBX) = ar (AXY).

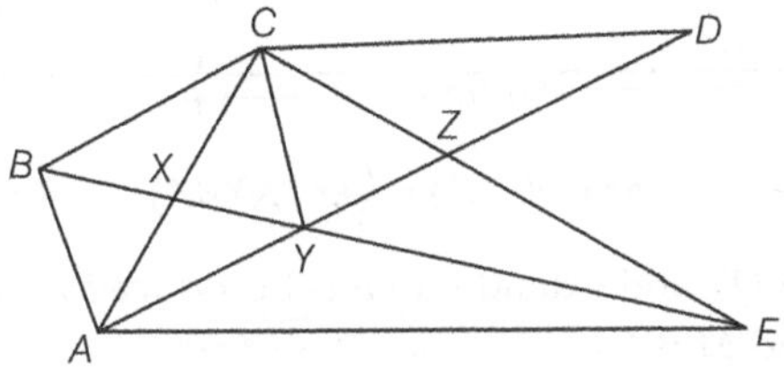

Ans. **Given** In figure, $CD \parallel AE$

and $CY \parallel BA$

To prove $\text{ar}(\Delta CBX) = \text{ar}(\Delta AXY)$

Proof We know that triangles on the same base and between the same parallel lines are equal in areas.

Here, ΔABY and ΔABC both lie on the same base AB and between the same parallel lines CY and BA.

$\therefore \quad \text{ar}(\Delta ABY) = \text{ar}(\Delta ABC)$

$\Rightarrow \quad \text{ar}(\Delta ABX) + \text{ar}(\Delta AXY) = \text{ar}(\Delta ABX) + \text{ar}(\Delta CBX)$

$\Rightarrow \quad \text{ar}(\Delta AXY) = \text{ar}(\Delta CBX)$ [eliminating ar (ΔABX) from both sides]

Hence proved.

Q.5 $ABCD$ is trapezium in which $AB \parallel DC$, $DC = 30$ cm and $AB = 50$ cm. If X and Y are, respectively the mid-points of AD and BC, prove that

$$\text{ar}(DCYX) = \frac{7}{9}\text{ar}(XYBA).$$

Thinking Process First, use the mid-point theorem to find the length of XY, then use area of trapezium as $\frac{1}{2}$ (sum of parallel sides) × Distance between parallel sides to get the required result.

Ans. **Given** In a trapezium $ABCD$, $AB \parallel DC$, $DC = 30$ cm and $AB = 50$ cm.

Also, X and Y are respectively the mid-points of AD and BC.

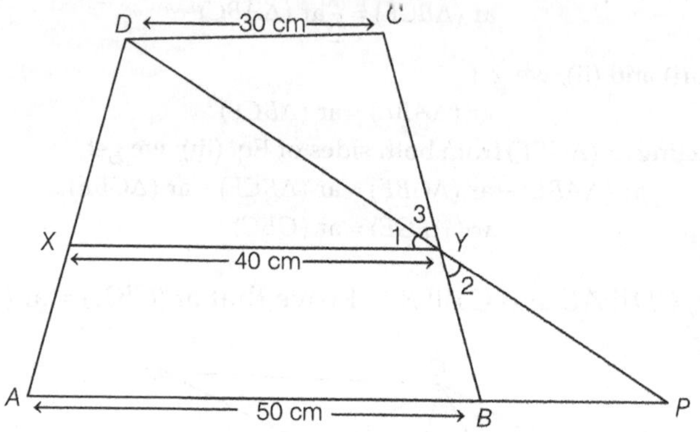

To prove $$\text{ar}(DCYX) = \frac{7}{9}\text{ar}(XYBA)$$

Construction Join DY and extend it to meet produced AB at P.

Proof In ΔDCY and ΔPBY,

$CY = BY$ [$\because$ Y is the mid-point of BC]

$\angle DCY = \angle PBY$ [alternate interior angles]

and $\angle 2 = \angle 3$ [vertically opposite angles]

$\therefore$ $\Delta DCY \cong \Delta PBY$ [by ASA congruence rule]

Then, $DC = BP$ [by CPCT]

But $DC = 30$ cm [given]

$\therefore$ $DC = BP = 30$ cm

Now, $AP = AB + BP = 50 + 30 = 80$ cm

In ΔADP, by mid-point theorem,

$$XY = \frac{1}{2}AP = \frac{1}{2} \times 80 = 40 \text{ cm}$$

Let distance between AB, XY and XY, DC be h cm.

Now, area of trapezium $DCYX = \frac{1}{2}h(30 + 40)$

[$\because$ area of trapezium $= \frac{1}{2}$ sum of parallel sides $\times$ distance between them]

$$= \frac{1}{2}h(70) = 35\,h \text{ cm}^2$$

Similarly, area of trapezium $XYBA = \frac{1}{2}h(40 + 50) = \frac{1}{2}h \times 90 = 45h \text{ cm}^2$

$$\therefore \quad \frac{\text{ar}(DCYX)}{\text{ar}(XYBA)} = \frac{35h}{45h} = \frac{7}{9}$$

$$\Rightarrow \quad \text{ar}(DCYX) = \frac{7}{9}\text{ar}(XYBA)$$

Hence proved.

Q.6 In ΔABC, if L and M are the points on AB and AC, respectively such that $LM \parallel BC$. Prove that ar (ΔLOB) = ar (ΔMOC).

Ans. **Given** In ΔABC, L and M are points on AB and AC respectively such that $LM \parallel BC$.

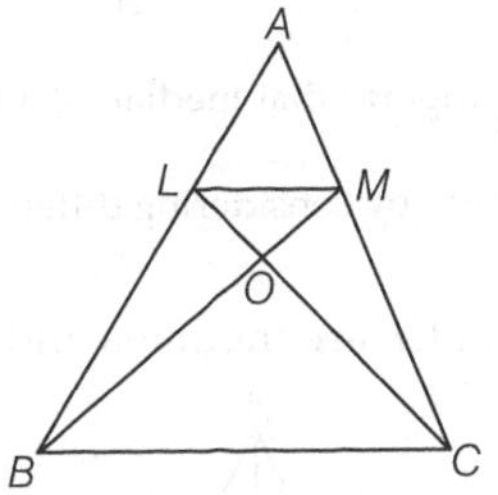

To prove ar (ΔLOB) = ar (ΔMOC)

Proof We know that triangles on the same base and between the same parallels are equal in area.

Hence, ΔLBC and ΔMBC lie on the same base BC and between the same parallels BC and LM.

So, ar (ΔLBC) = ar (ΔMBC)

$\Rightarrow$ ar (ΔLOB) + ar (ΔBOC) = ar (ΔMOC) + ar (ΔBOC)

On eliminating ar (ΔBOC) from both sides, we get

ar (ΔLOB) = ar (ΔMOC) **Hence proved.**

Q.7 In figure, $ABCDE$ is any pentagon. BP drawn parallel to AC meets DC produced at P and EQ drawn parallel to AD meets CD produced at Q. Prove that ar ($ABCDE$) = ar (ΔAPQ).

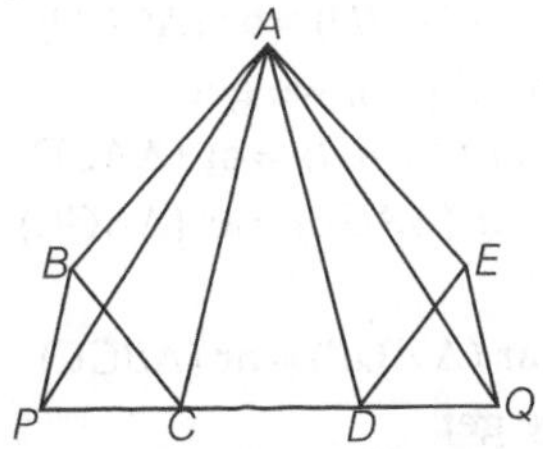

Ans. **Given** $ABCDE$ is a pentagon. $BP \parallel AC$ and $EQ \parallel AD$.

To prove ar ($ABCDE$) = ar (APQ)

Proof We know that triangles on the same base and between the same parallels are equal in area.

Here, ΔADQ and ΔADE lie on the same base AD and between the same parallels AD and EQ.

So, ar (ΔADQ) = ar (ΔADE) ...(i)

Similarly, ΔACP and ΔACB lie on the same base AC and between the same parallels AC and BP.

So, ar (ΔACP) = ar (ΔACB) ...(ii)

On adding Eqs. (i) and (ii), we get

ar (ΔADQ) + ar (ΔACP) = ar (ΔADE) + ar (ΔACB)

On adding ar (ΔACD) both sides, we get

ar (ΔADQ) + ar (ΔACP) + ar (ΔACD) = ar (ΔADE) + ar (ΔACB) + ar (ΔACD)

$\Rightarrow$ ar (ΔAPQ) = ar ($ABCDE$) **Hence proved.**

Q. 8 If the medians of a ΔABC intersect at G, then show that

$$\text{ar}(\Delta AGB) = \text{ar}(\Delta AGC) = \text{ar}(\Delta BGC) = \frac{1}{3}\text{ar}(\Delta ABC).$$

Thinking Process Use the property that median of a triangle divides it into two triangles of equal area.
Further, apply above property by considering different triangles and prove the required result.

Ans. Given In ΔABC, AD, BE and CF are medians and intersect at G.

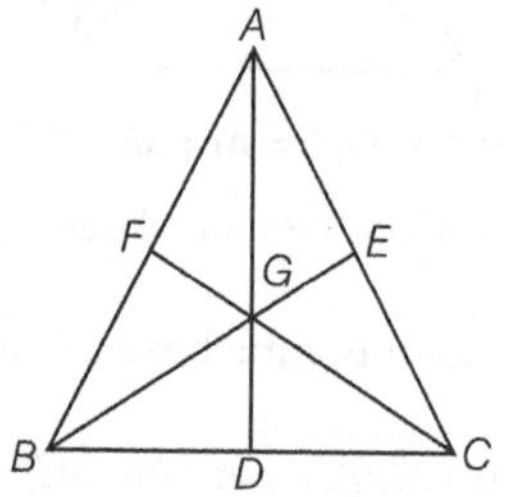

To prove $\text{ar}(\Delta AGB) = \text{ar}(\Delta AGC) = \text{ar}(\Delta BGC) = \frac{1}{3}\text{ar}(\Delta ABC)$

Proof We know that a median of a triangle divides it into two triangles of equal area.

In ΔABC, AD is a median.

$\therefore \quad \text{ar}(\Delta ABD) = \text{ar}(\Delta ACD)$ ...(i)

In ΔBGC, GD is a median.

$\therefore \quad \text{ar}(\Delta GBD) = \text{ar}(\Delta GCD)$ ...(ii)

On subtracting Eq. (ii) from Eq. (i), we get

$$\text{ar}(\Delta ABD) - \text{ar}(\Delta GBD) = \text{ar}(\Delta ACD) - \text{ar}(\Delta GCD)$$

$\Rightarrow \quad \text{ar}(\Delta AGB) = \text{ar}(\Delta AGC)$ ...(iii)

Similarly,

$\text{ar}(\Delta AGB) = \text{ar}(\Delta BGC)$ ...(iv)

From Eqs. (iii) and (iv), we get

$\text{ar}(\Delta AGB) = \text{ar}(\Delta BGC) = \text{ar}(\Delta AGC)$ ...(v)

Now,

$$\text{ar}(\Delta ABC) = \text{ar}(\Delta AGB) + \text{ar}(\Delta BGC) + \text{ar}(\Delta AGC)$$

$\Rightarrow \quad \text{ar}(\Delta ABC) = \text{ar}(\Delta AGB) + \text{ar}(\Delta AGB) + \text{ar}(\Delta AGB)$ [from Eq. (v)]

$\Rightarrow \quad \text{ar}(\Delta ABC) = 3\,\text{ar}(\Delta AGB)$

$\Rightarrow \quad \text{ar}(\Delta AGB) = \frac{1}{3}\text{ar}(\Delta ABC)$ ...(vi)

From Eqs. (v) and (vi), we get

$$\text{ar}(\Delta BGC) = \frac{1}{3}\text{ar}(\Delta ABC)$$

and $\quad \text{ar}(\Delta AGC) = \frac{1}{3}\text{ar}(\Delta ABC)$ **Hence proved.**

Q. 9 In figure, X and Y are the mid-points of AC and AB respectively, $QP \parallel BC$ and CYQ and BXP are straight lines. Prove that ar (ΔABP) = ar (ΔACQ).

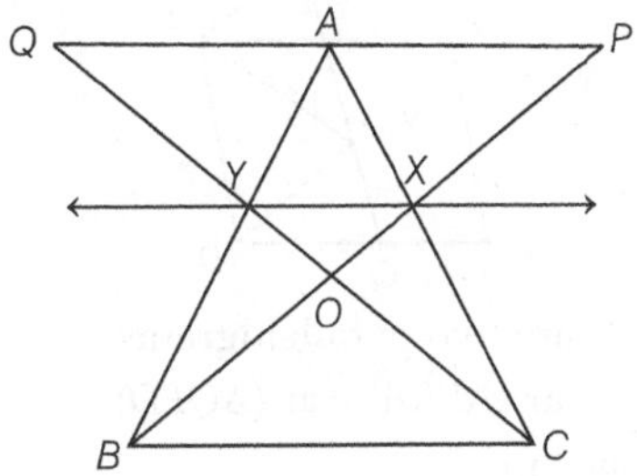

Thinking Process

(i) Firstly, use the theorem that joining the mid-points of the two sides of a triangle is parallel to the third side.

(ii) Further, use the theorem that triangles on the same base and between the same parallels are equal in area. Use this theorem by considering different triangles and prove the required result.

Ans. **Given** X and Y are the mid-points of AC and AB respectively. Also, $QP \parallel BC$ and CYQ, BXP are straight lines.

To prove ar (ΔABP) = ar (ΔACQ)

Proof Since, X and Y are the mid-points of AC and AB respectively.

So, $XY \parallel BC$

We know that triangles on the same base and between the same parallels are equal in area.

Here, ΔBYC and ΔBXC lie on same base BC and between the same parallels BC and XY.

So, ar (ΔBYC) = ar (ΔBXC)

On subtracting *ar* (ΔBOC) from both sides, we get

$$\text{ar}(\Delta BYC) - \text{ar}(\Delta BOC) = \text{ar}(\Delta BXC) - \text{ar}(\Delta BOC)$$

$$\Rightarrow \quad \text{ar}(\Delta BOY) = \text{ar}(\Delta COX)$$

On adding *ar* (ΔXOY) both sides, we get

$$\text{ar}(\Delta BOY) + \text{ar}(\Delta XOY) = \text{ar}(\Delta COX) + \text{ar}(\Delta XOY)$$

$$\Rightarrow \quad \text{ar}(\Delta BYX) = \text{ar}(\Delta CXY) \quad \text{...(i)}$$

Hence, we observe that quadrilaterals $XYAP$ and $YXAQ$ are on the same base XY and between the same parallels XY and PQ.

$$\therefore \quad \text{ar}(XYAP) = \text{ar}(YXAQ) \quad \text{...(ii)}$$

On adding Eqs. (i) and (ii), we get

$$\text{ar}(\Delta BYX) + \text{ar}(XYAP) = \text{ar}(\Delta CXY) + \text{ar}(YXAQ)$$

$$\Rightarrow \quad \text{ar}(\Delta ABP) = \text{ar}(\Delta ACQ)$$

Hence proved.

Q. 10 In figure, $ABCD$ and $AEFD$ are two parallelograms. Prove that ar (ΔPEA) = ar (ΔQFD). [**Hint** : Join PD]

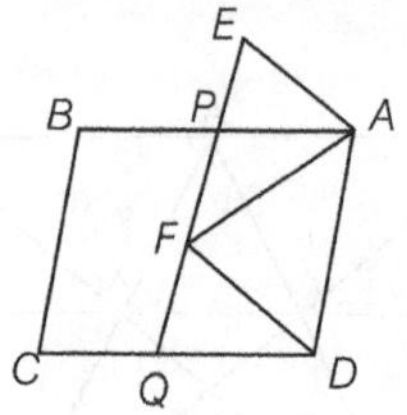

Ans. **Given**, $ABCD$ and $AEFD$ are two parallelograms.

To prove ar (ΔPEA) = ar (ΔQFD)

Proof In quadrilateral $PQDA$,

$AP \parallel DQ$ [since, in parallelogram $ABCD$, $AB \parallel CD$]

and $PQ \parallel AD$ [since, in parallelogram $AEFD$, $FE \parallel AD$]

Then, quadrilateral $PQDA$ is a parallelogram.

Also, parallelogram $PQDA$ and $AEFD$ are on the same base AD and between the same parallels AD and EQ.

$\therefore$ ar (parallelogram $PQDA$) = ar (parallelogram $AEFD$)

On subtracting ar (quadrilateral $APFD$) from both sides, we get

ar (parallelogram $PQDA$) − ar (quadrilateral $APFD$)

= ar (parallelogram $AEFD$) − ar (quadrilateral $APFD$)

$\Rightarrow$ ar (ΔQFD) = ar (ΔPEA) **Hence proved.**

Chapter

10 Circles

Multiple Choice Questions (MCQs)

Choose the correct answer from the given four options in the following questions:

Q.1 AD is a diameter of a circle and AB is a chord. If $AD = 34$ cm, $AB = 30$ cm, the distance of AB from the centre of the circle is

(a) 17 cm (b) 15 cm

(c) 4 cm (d) 8 cm

- **Concept Insight** In this problem, we will use the concept; the perpendicular from the centre of a circle to a chord bisects the chord. Also, use the Pythagoras theorem, $(\text{Hypotenuse})^2 = (\text{Base})^2 + (\text{Perpendicular})^2$.

Ans. *(d)* Given, $AD = 34$ cm and $AB = 30$ cm

In figure, draw $OL \perp AB$.

Since, the perpendicular from the centre of a circle to a chord bisects the chord.

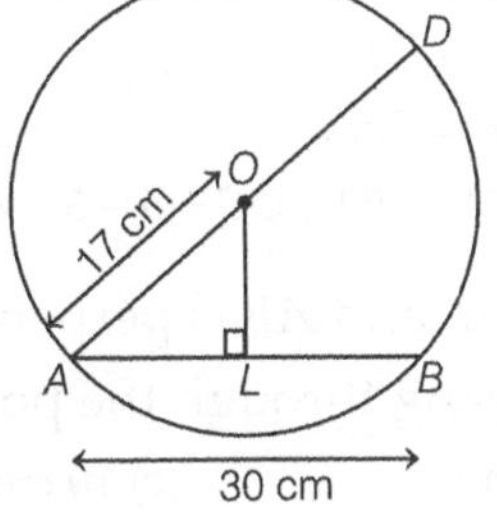

$\therefore$ $AL = LB = \frac{1}{2} AB = 15$ cm

and $OA = \frac{1}{2} AD = 17$ cm

In right angled ΔOLA, $OA^2 = OL^2 + AL^2$ [by Pythagoras theorem]

$\therefore$ $(17)^2 = OL^2 + (15)^2$

$\Rightarrow$ $289 = OL^2 + 225$

$\Rightarrow$ $OL^2 = 289 - 225 = 64$

$\therefore$ $OL = 8$ cm

[take positive square root because length is always positive]

Hence, the distance of the chord from the centre is 8 cm.

Q.2 In figure, if $OA = 5$ cm, $AB = 8$ cm and OD is perpendicular to AB, then CD is equal to

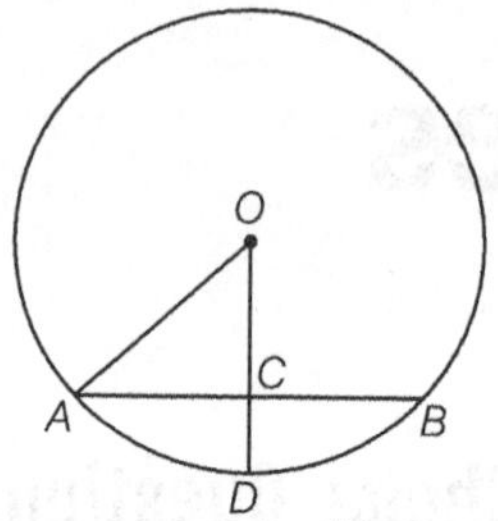

(a) 2 cm (b) 3 cm (c) 4 cm (d) 5 cm

- **Concept Insight** The perpendicular from the centre of a clock to a chord bisects the chord.

Ans. *(a)* We know that the perpendicular from the centre of a circle to a chord bisects the chord.

$\therefore \quad AC = CB = \frac{1}{2} AB = \frac{1}{2} \times 8 = 4\text{cm}$ $\quad$ [$\because AB = 8\text{ cm}$, given]

$\because \quad OA = 5\text{cm}$ $\quad$ [given]

In right angled ΔOCA, $AO^2 = AC^2 + OC^2$ $\quad$ [by Pythagoras theorem]

$\Rightarrow \quad (5)^2 = (4)^2 + OC^2$

$\Rightarrow \quad 25 = 16 + OC^2$

$\Rightarrow \quad OC^2 = 25 - 16 = 9$

$\Rightarrow \quad OC = 3\text{ cm}$

[take positive square root because length is always positive]

$\because \quad OA = OD$ $\quad$ [radii of same circle]

$\Rightarrow \quad OD = 5\text{cm}$

$\therefore \quad CD = OD - OC = 5 - 3 = 2\text{cm}$

Q.3 If $AB = 12$ cm, $BC = 16$ cm and AB is perpendicular to BC, then the radius of the circle passing through the points A, B and C is

(a) 6 cm (b) 8 cm (c) 10 cm (d) 12 cm

Thinking Process Firstly, use the concept that the diameter of a circle subtends a right angle at any point on the circumference of the circle and then use Pythagoras theorem *i.e.*, $(\text{Hypotenuse})^2 = (\text{Base})^2 + (\text{Perpendicular})^2$ to get the required result

Ans. *(c)* Given, $AB = 12$ cm and $BC = 16$ cm

In a circle, $BC \perp AB$, it means that AC will be a diameter of circle.

[diameter of a circle subtends a right angle to the circle]

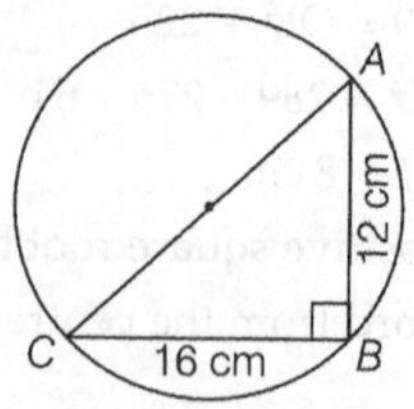

Using Pythagoras theorem in right angled ΔABC,

$$AC^2 = AB^2 + BC^2$$

$\Rightarrow$ $$AC^2 = (12)^2 + (16)^2$$

$\Rightarrow$ $$AC^2 = 144 + 256 \Rightarrow AC^2 = 400$$

$\Rightarrow$ $$AC = \sqrt{400} = 20 \text{ cm}$$

[take positive square root because length is always positive]

$\therefore$ Radius of circle $= \frac{1}{2}(AC) = \frac{1}{2} \times 20 = 10$ cm

Hence, the radius of circle is 10 cm.

Q.4 In figure, if $\angle ABC = 20°$, then $\angle AOC$ is equal to

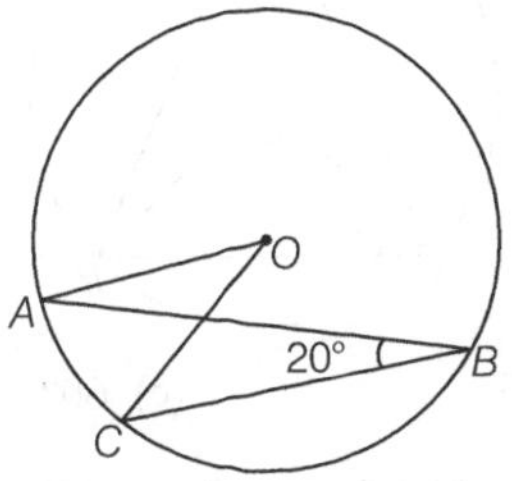

(a) 20° (b) 40° (c) 60° (d) 10°

Thinking Process Use the theorem that in a circle, the angle subtended by an arc at the centre is twice the angle subtended by it at any point on the remaining part of the circle and further simplify it.

Ans. *(b)* Given, $\angle ABC = 20°$

We know that angle subtended by an arc at the centre is twice the angle subtended by it at any point on the remaining part of circle.

$\therefore$ $$\angle AOC = 2\angle ABC = 2 \times 20° = 40°$$

Q.5 In figure, if AOB is a diameter of the circle and $AC = BC$, then $\angle CAB$ is equal to

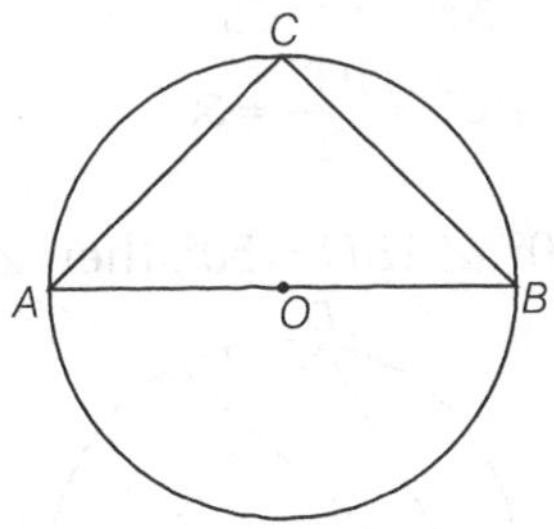

(a) 30° (b) 60° (c) 90° (d) 45°

Ans. *(d)* Since, angle in a semi-circle is a right angle.

$\therefore$ $$\angle BCA = 90° \quad \ldots(i)$$

Given, $$AC = BC$$

$\Rightarrow$ $$\angle ABC = \angle CAB \quad \ldots(ii)$$

[$\because$ angles opposite to equal sides are equal]

In ΔABC, $\angle CAB + \angle ABC + \angle BCA = 180°$ [by angle sum property of a triangle]

$\Rightarrow \angle CAB + \angle CAB + \angle 90° = 180°$ [from Eqs. (i) and (ii)]

$\Rightarrow 2\angle CAB = 180° - 90°$

$\Rightarrow \angle CAB = \frac{90°}{2}$

$\therefore \angle CAB = 45°$

Q.6 In figure, if $\angle OAB = 40°$, then $\angle ACB$ is equal to

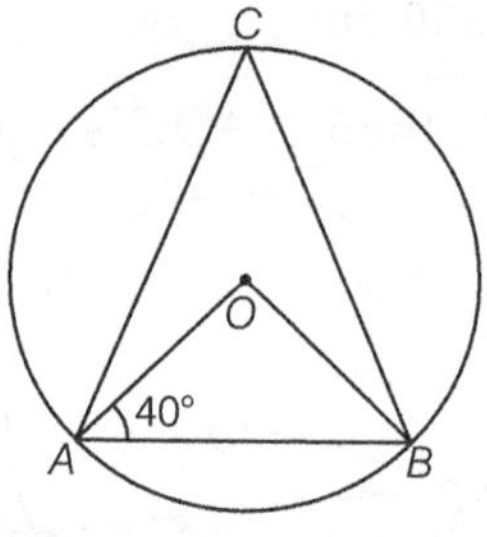

(a) 50° (b) 40° (c) 60° (d) 70°

- **Concept Insight** The angle subtended by an arc at the centre is double the angle subtended by it at any point on the remaining part of the circle.

Ans. *(a)* In ΔOAB, $OA = OB$ [radii of same circle]

$\therefore \angle OAB = \angle OBA \Rightarrow \angle OBA = 40°$

[$\because$ angles opposite to equal sides are equal]

Also, $\angle AOB + \angle OBA + \angle BAO = 180°$ [by angle sum property of a triangle]

$\therefore \angle AOB + 40° + 40° = 180°$

$\Rightarrow \angle AOB = 180° - 80° = 100°$

We know that, in a circle, the angle subtended by an arc at the centre is twice the angle subtended by it at any point on the remaining part of the circle.

$\therefore \angle AOB = 2\angle ACB$

$\Rightarrow 100° = 2\angle ACB$

$\therefore \angle ACB = \frac{100°}{2} = 50°$

Q.7 In figure, if $\angle DAB = 60°, \angle ABD = 50°$, then $\angle ACB$ is equal to

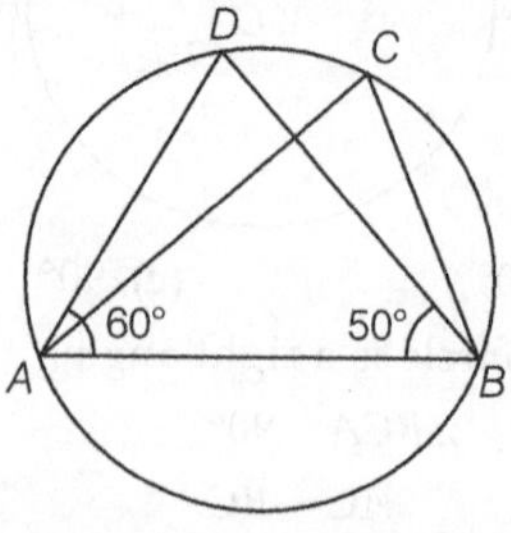

(a) 60° (b) 50° (c) 70° (d) 80°

Thinking Process Use the theorem that angles in the same segment of a circle are equal and further simplify it.

Ans. *(c)* Given, $\angle DAB = 60°$, $\angle ABD = 50°$

Since, $\angle ADB = \angle ACB$ ...(i)

[$\because$ angles in same segment of a circle are equal]

In ΔABD, $\angle ABD + \angle ADB + \angle DAB = 180°$ [by angle sum property of a triangle]

$\therefore$ $50° + \angle ADB + 60° = 180°$

$\Rightarrow$ $\angle ADB = 180° - 110° = 70°$

From Eq. (i), $\angle ACB = \angle ADB = 70°$

Q.8 $ABCD$ is a cyclic quadrilateral such that AB is a diameter of the circle circumscribing it and $\angle ADC = 140°$, then $\angle BAC$ is equal to

(a) 80° (b) 50° (c) 40° (d) 30°

- **Concept Insight** The sum of the opposite angles of a cyclic quadrilateral is 180°.

Ans. *(b)* Given, $ABCD$ is a cyclic quadrilateral and $\angle ADC = 140°$.

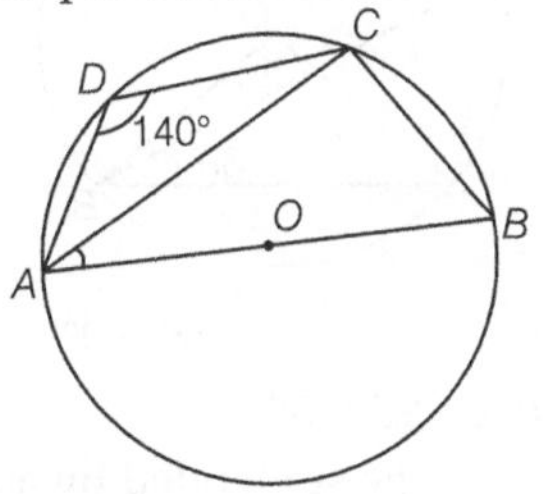

We know that, sum of the opposite angles in a cyclic quadrilateral is 180°.

$\angle ADC + \angle ABC = 180°$

$\Rightarrow$ $140° + \angle ABC = 180°$

$\Rightarrow$ $\angle ABC = 180° - 140°$

$\therefore$ $\angle ABC = 40°$

Since, $\angle ACB$ is an angle in a semi-circle.

$\therefore$ $\angle ACB = 90°$

In ΔABC, $\angle BAC + \angle ACB + \angle ABC = 180°$ [by angle sum property of a triangle]

$\Rightarrow$ $\angle BAC + 90° + 40° = 180°$

$\Rightarrow$ $\angle BAC = 180° - 130° = 50°$

Q.9 In figure, BC is a diameter of the circle and $\angle BAO = 60°$. Then, $\angle ADC$ is equal to

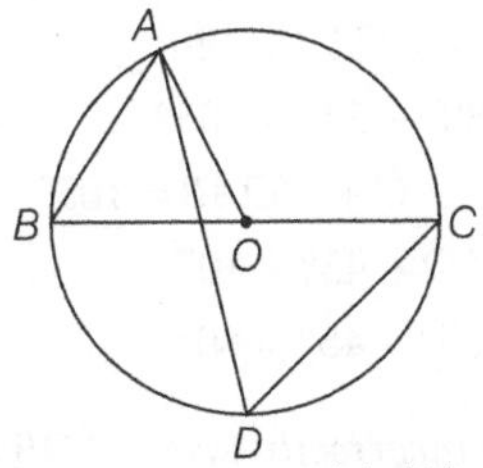

(a) 30° (b) 45° (c) 60° (d) 120°

Thinking Process First, use the property, angles opposite to equal sides are equal then, use the theorem, angles in the same segment of a circle are equal.

Ans. *(c)* In ΔAOB,

$OA = OB$ [radii of same circle]

$\Rightarrow \angle OBA = \angle BAO$ [$\because$ angles opposite to equal sides are equal]

$\Rightarrow \angle OBA = 60°$ [$\because \angle BAO = 60°$, given]

We know that $\angle ABC = \angle ADC$

[$\because$ angles in the same segment are equal]

$\therefore \angle ADC = 60°$

Q.10 In figure, if $\angle AOB = 90°$ and $\angle ABC = 30°$, then $\angle CAO$ is equal to:

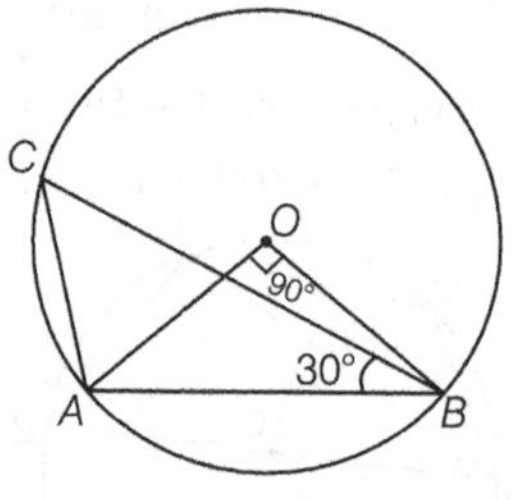

(a) 30° (b) 45° (c) 90° (d) 60°

Ans. *(d)* Given, $\angle AOB = 90°$ and $\angle ABC = 30°$

We know that in a circle, the angle subtended by an arc at the centre is twice the angle subtended by it at any point on the remaining part of the circle.

$\therefore \angle AOB = 2\angle ACB$

$\Rightarrow 90° = 2\angle ACB$ [$\because \angle AOB = 90°$, given]

$\Rightarrow \angle ACB = 45°$

Also, $AO = OB$ [radii of same circle]

$\Rightarrow \angle ABO = \angle OAB$ ...(i)

[$\because$ angles opposite to equal sides are equal]

In ΔOAB, $\angle OAB + \angle ABO + \angle BOA = 180°$ [by angle sum property of a triangle]

$\angle OAB + \angle OAB + 90° = 180°$ [from Eq. (i)]

$\Rightarrow 2\angle OAB = 180° - 90°$

$\Rightarrow \angle OAB = \frac{90°}{2} = 45°$ ...(ii)

In ΔACB, $\angle ACB + \angle CBA + \angle CAB = 180°$ [by angle sum property of a triangle]

$\therefore 45° + 30° + \angle CAB = 180°$

$\Rightarrow \angle CAB = 180° - 75° = 105°$

$\because \angle CAB = \angle CAO + \angle OAB = 105°$

$\Rightarrow \angle CAO + 45° = 105°$ [from Eq. (ii)]

$\therefore \angle CAO = 105° - 45° = 60°$

Mistake Alert! *Students may incorrectly take* $\angle AOB = \frac{1}{2}\angle ACB$ *instead of* $\angle AOB = 2\angle ACB$

Short Answer Questions with reasoning

Write True or False and justify your answer in each of the following

Q.1 Two chords AB and CD of a circle are each at distances 4 cm from the centre. Then $AB = CD$.

- **Concept Insight** Chords equidistant from the centre of a circle are equal in length.

Ans. *True*

Because, the chords equidistant from the centre of a circle are equal in length.

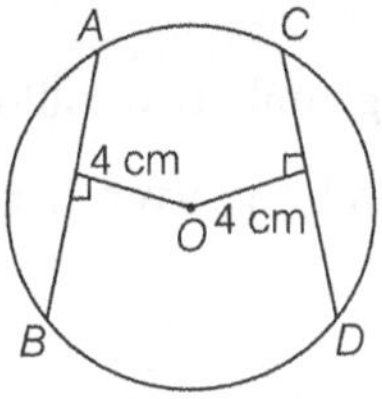

Q.2 Two chords AB and AC of a circle with centre O are on the opposite sides of OA. Then $\angle OAB = \angle OAC$.

Ans. *False*

In figure, AB and AC are two chords of a circle.

Join OB and OC.

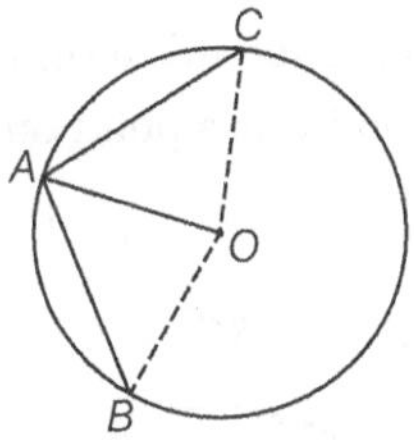

In ΔOAB and ΔOAC,

$$OA = OA \quad \text{[common side]}$$

$$OB = OC \quad \text{[radii of same circle]}$$

Here, we are not able to show that either any angle or third side is equal and thus ΔOAB is not congruent to ΔOAC.

$$\therefore \quad \angle OAB \neq \angle OAC.$$

Q.3 Two congruent circles with centres O and O' intersect at two points A and B. Then, $\angle AOB = \angle AO'B$.

Ans. *True*

Two congruent circles means that their radii are equal.

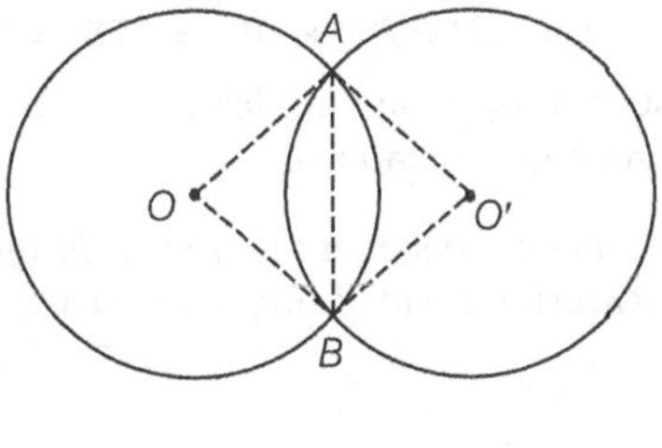

Join AB, OA, OB, $O'A$ and $O'B$.

In ΔAOB and $\Delta AO'B$,

$$OA = AO' \quad [\because \text{ both circles have same radius}]$$

$$OB = BO' \quad [\because \text{ both circles have same radius}]$$

and $$AB = AB \quad [\text{common chord}]$$

$\therefore$ $$\Delta AOB \cong \Delta AOB' \quad [\text{by SSS congruence rule}]$$

$\Rightarrow$ $$\angle AOB = \angle AOB' \quad [\text{by CPCT}]$$

Q.4 Through three collinear points a circle can be drawn.

Ans. *False*

Because, circle can pass through only two collinear points.

Q.5 A circle of radius 3 cm can be drawn through two points A, B such that $AB = 6$ cm.

Ans. *True*

Suppose, we consider diameter of a circle is $AB = 6$ cm.

Then, radius of a circle $= \frac{AB}{2} = \frac{6}{2} = 3$ cm, which is true.

Q.6 If AOB is a diameter of a circle and C is a point on the circle, then $AC^2 + BC^2 = AB^2$.

Ans. *True*

Since, any diameter of the circle subtends a right angle to any point on the circle.

If AB is a diameter of a circle and C is a point on the circle, then ΔACB is right angled at C.

In right angled ΔACB,

$$AC^2 + BC^2 = AB^2 \quad [\text{by Pythagoras theorem}]$$

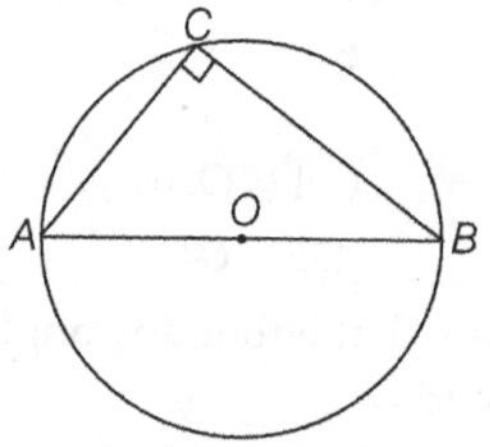

Q.7 $ABCD$ is a cyclic quadrilateral such that $\angle A = 90°$, $\angle B = 70°$, $\angle C = 95°$ and $\angle D = 105°$.

Ans. *False*

In a cyclic quadrilateral, the sum of opposite angles is 180°.

Now, $$\angle A + \angle C = 90° + 95° = 185° \neq 180°$$

and $$\angle B + \angle D = 70° + 105° = 175° \neq 180°$$

Here, we see that the sum of opposite angles in a cyclic quadrilateral is not equal to 180°. So, it is not a cyclic quadrilateral.

Mistake Alert ! *Students may assume that the sum of the opposite angles of a cyclic quadrilateral is complementary instead of supplementary.*

Q.8 If A, B, C and D are four points such that $\angle BAC = 30°$ and $\angle BDC = 60°$, then D is the centre of the circle through A, B and C.

Ans. *False*

Because, there can be many points D such that $\angle BDC = 60°$ and each such point cannot be the centre of the circle through A, B and C.

Q.9 If A, B, C and D are four points such that $\angle BAC = 45°$ and $\angle BDC = 45°$, then A, B, C and D are concyclic.

Ans. *True*

Since, $\angle BAC = 45°$ and $\angle BDC = 45°$

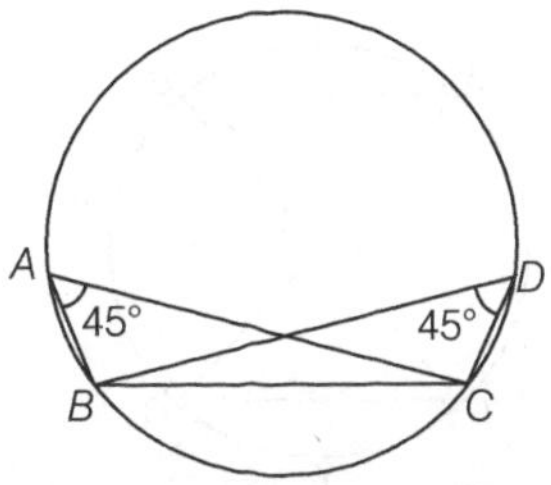

As we know that angles in the same segment of a circle are equal.

Hence, A, B, C and D are concyclic.

Q.10 In figure, if AOB is a diameter and $\angle ADC = 120°$, then $\angle CAB = 30°$.

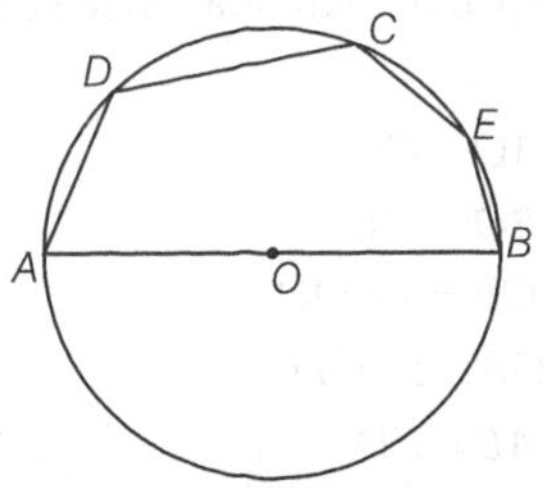

● **Concept Insight** The sum of opposite angles of a cyclic quadrilateral is 180°.

Ans. *True*

Join CA and CB.

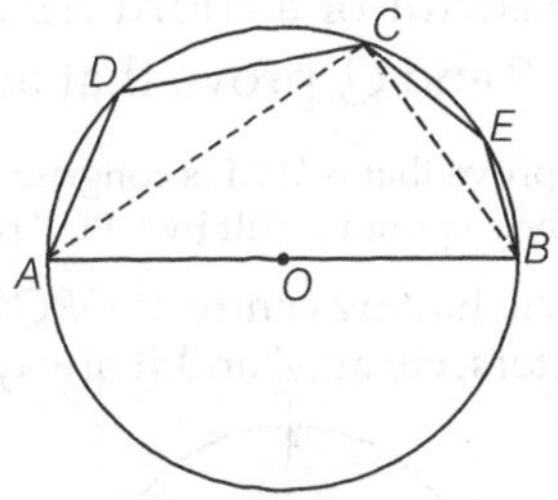

Since, $ADCB$ is a cyclic quadrilateral.

$\therefore \qquad \angle ADC + \angle CBA = 180°$.

[$\because$ sum of opposite angles of a cyclic quadrilateral is 180°]

$\Rightarrow \quad \angle CBA = 180° - 120° = 60° \quad [\because \angle ADC = 120°]$

In ΔACB, $\angle CAB + \angle CBA + \angle ACB = 180°$ [by angle sum property of a triangle]

$\therefore \quad \angle CAB + 60° + 90° = 180°$

[angle in a semi-circle is a right angle *i.e.*, $\angle ACB = 90°$]

$\Rightarrow \quad \angle CAB = 180° - 150° = 30°$

Short Answer Type Questions

Q.1 If arcs AXB and CYD of a circle are congruent, find the ratio of AB and CD.

Ans. Let AXB and CYD are arcs of circle whose centre and radius are O and r, respectively.

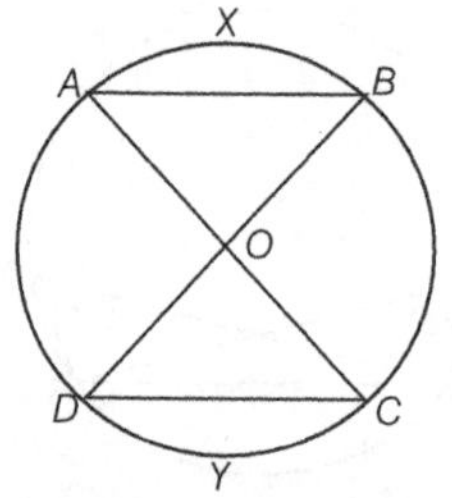

So, $\quad OA = OB = OC = OD = r$ [radii of same circle] ...(i)

$\because \quad$ arc $AXB \cong$ arc CYD

$\therefore \quad \angle AOB = \angle COD$ ...(ii)

[$\because$ congruent arcs of a circle subtend equal angles at the centre]

In ΔAOB and ΔCOD,

$AO = CO$ [from Eq. (i)]

$BO = DO$ [from Eq. (i)]

$\angle AOB = \angle COD$ [from Eq. (ii)]

$\therefore \quad \Delta AOB \cong \Delta COD$ [by SAS congruence rule]

$\Rightarrow \quad AB = CD$ [by CPCT]

$\Rightarrow \quad \dfrac{AB}{CD} = 1$

Hence, the ratio of AB and CD is 1:1.

Q.2 If the perpendicular bisector of a chord AB of a circle $PXAQBY$ intersects the circle at P and Q, prove that arc $PXA \cong$ arc PYB.

Thinking Process Firstly, prove that ΔAPM is congruent to ΔBPM by SAS congruence rule, then further prove the required result by CPCT rule.

Ans. Let AB be a chord of a circle having centre at OPQ be the perpendicular bisector of the chord AB, which intersects at M and it always passes through O.

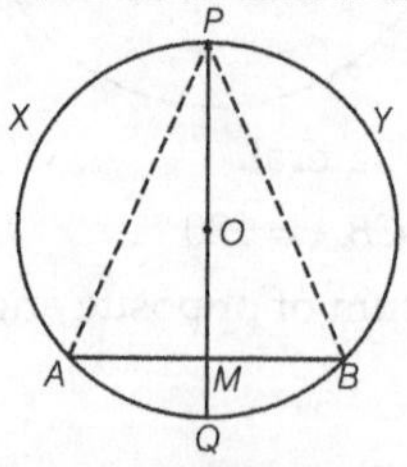

To prove arc $PXA \cong$ arc PYB

Construction Join AP and BP.

Proof In ΔAPM and ΔBPM,

	$AM = MB$	[$\because PM$ bisects AB]
	$\angle PMA = \angle PMB$	[$\because PM \perp AB$]
	$PM = PM$	[common side]
$\therefore$	$\Delta APM \cong \Delta BPM$	[by SAS congruence rule]
$\therefore$	$PA = PB$	[by CPCT]
$\Rightarrow$	arc $PXA \cong$ arc PYB	**Hence proved.**

Q.3 A, B and C are three points on a circle. Prove that the perpendicular bisectors of AB, BC and CA are concurrent.

Thinking Process

(i) Firstly, inscribe a ΔABC in a circle, then draw the perpendicular bisecters of any two sides of a triangle.

(ii) Secondly, prove that ΔOEA and ΔOEB are congruent by SAS congruence rule and also ΔOMB and ΔOMC are congruent by RHS congruence rule. Further, prove the required result.

Ans. Given A circle passing through three points A, B and C.

Construction Draw perpendicular bisectors of AB and AC and they meet at a point O. Join OA, OB, OC and OM.

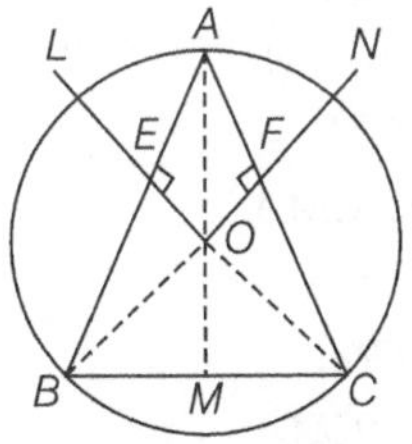

To prove Perpendicular bisector of BC, also passes through O *i.e.*, LO, ON and OM are concurrent.

Proof In ΔOEA and ΔOEB,

	$AE = BE$	[OL is the perpendicular bisector of AB]
	$\angle AEO = \angle BEO$	[each 90°]
and	$OE = OE$	[common side]
$\therefore$	$\Delta OEA \cong \Delta OEB$	[by SAS congruence rule]
$\therefore$	$OA = OB$	[by CPCT]
Similarly,	$\Delta OFA \cong \Delta OFC$	[by SAS congruence rule]
$\therefore$	$OA = OC$	[by CPCT]
$\therefore$	$OA = OB = OC = r$	[say]

Now, we draw a perpendicular from O to the BC and join them.

In ΔOMB and ΔOMC,

	$OB = OC$	[proved above]
	$OM = OM$	[common side]

and $\angle OMB = \angle OMC$ [each 90°]

$\therefore$ $\Delta OMB \cong \Delta OMC$ [by RHS congruence rule]

$\Rightarrow$ $BM = MC$ [by CPCT]

Hence, OM is the perpendicular bisector of BC.

Hence, OL, ON and OM are concurrent. **Hence proved.**

Q.4 *AB* and *AC* are two equal chords of a circle. Prove that the bisector of the angle *BAC* passes through the centre of the circle.

Ans. **Given** AB and AC are two equal chords whose centre is O.

To prove Centre O lies on the bisector of $\angle BAC$.

Construction Draw the bisector AM of the angle BAC. Join BM and CM.

Proof In ΔBAM and ΔCAM,

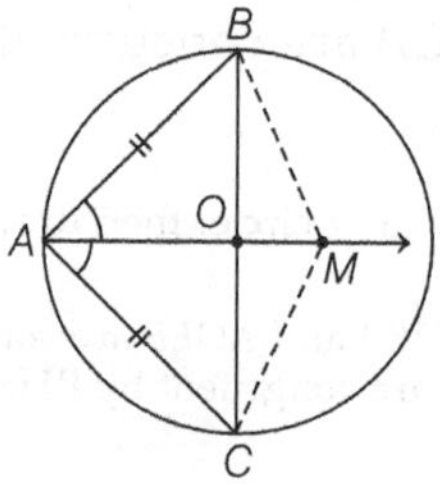

$AB = AC$ [given]

$\angle BAM = \angle CAM$ [given]

and $AM = AM$ [common side]

$\therefore$ $\Delta BAM \cong \Delta CAM$ [by SAS congruence rule]

$\Rightarrow$ $BM = CM$ [by CPCT]...(i)

and $\angle BMA = \angle CMA$ [by CPCT]...(ii)

In ΔBOM and ΔCOM,

$BM = CM$ [from Eq. (i)]

$\angle BMA = \angle CMA$ [from Eq. (ii)]

$OM = OM$ [common side]

$\therefore$ $\Delta BOM \cong \Delta COM$ [by SAS congruence rule]

$\therefore$ $\angle BOM = \angle COM$ [by CPCT]...(iii)

$\because$ $\angle BOM + \angle COM = 180°$ [linear pair axiom]

$\Rightarrow$ $\angle BOM + \angle BOM = 180°$ [from Eq (iii)]

$\Rightarrow$ $\angle BOM = 90° = \angle COM$

So, AM is the perpendicular bisector of the chord BC.

Hence, bisector of $\angle BAC$ *i.e.*, AM passes through the centre O. **Hence proved.**

Q.5 If a line segment joining mid-points of two chords of a circle passes through the centre of the circle, prove that the two chords are parallel.

Ans. **Given** AB and CD are two chords of a circle whose centre is O and PQ is a diameter bisecting the chord AB and CD at L and M, respectively and the the line segment LM passes through the centre O of the circle.

To prove $AB \parallel CD$

Proof Since, L is the mid-point of AB.

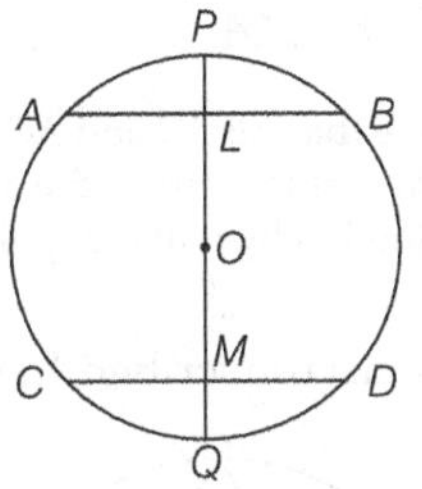

$\therefore$ $OL \perp AB$

[since, the line joining the centre of a circle to the mid-point of a chord is perpendicular to the chord]

$\Rightarrow$ $\angle ALO = 90°$ ...(i)

Similarly, $OM \perp CD$

$\therefore$ $\angle OMD = 90°$ ...(ii)

From Eqs. (i) and (ii), we get $\angle ALO = \angle OMD = 90°$

Since, the above two angles are alternate interior angles.

So, $AB \parallel CD$ **Hence proved.**

Q.6 $ABCD$ is such a quadrilateral that A is the centre of the circle passing through B, C and D. Prove that $\angle CBD + \angle CDB = \frac{1}{2} \angle BAD$.

- **Concept Insight** Use the theorem that in a circle, the angle subtended by an arc at the centre is twice the angle subtended by it any point on at the remaining part of circle.

Ans. **Given** In a circle, $ABCD$ is a quadrilateral having centre A.

To prove $\angle CBD + \angle CDB = \frac{1}{2} \angle BAD$

Construction Join AC and BD.

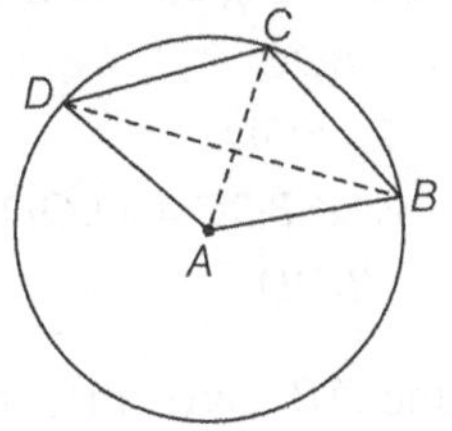

Proof Since, arc DC subtends $\angle DAC$ at the centre and $\angle CBD$ at a point B in the remaining part of the circle.

$\therefore$ $\angle DAC = 2\angle CBD$ ...(i)

Similarly, arc BC subtends $\angle CAB$ at the centre and $\angle CDB$ at a point D at the remaining part of the circle.

$\therefore$ $\angle CAB = 2\angle CDB$ ...(ii)

On adding Eqs. (i) and (ii), we get

$$\angle DAC + \angle CAB = 2\angle CBD + 2\angle CDB$$

$\Rightarrow$ $\angle BAD = 2(\angle CBD + \angle CDB)$

$\Rightarrow$ $\angle CDB + \angle CBD = \frac{1}{2} \angle BAD$ **Hence proved.**

Q.7 O is the circumcentre of the triangle ABC and D is the mid-point of the base BC. Prove that $\angle BOD = \angle A$.

Thinking Process Firstly, prove that ΔBOD and ΔCOD are congruent by SSS congruence rule. Further, use the theorem that in a circle, the angle subtended by an arc at the centre is twice the angle subtended by it at any point on the remaining part of the circle and prove the required result.

Ans. Given In a ΔABC a circle is circumscribed having centre O.

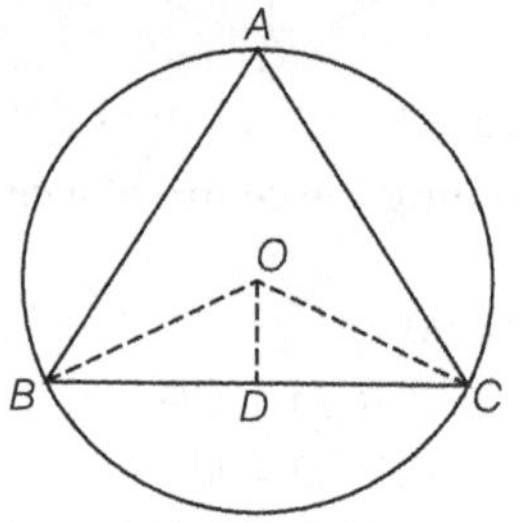

Also, D is the mid-point of BC.

To prove $\angle BOD = \angle A$ or $\angle BOD = \angle BAC$

Construction Join OB, OD and OC.

Proof In ΔBOD and ΔCOD,

$OB = OC$ [radii of same circle]

$BD = DC$ [$\because$ D is the mid-point of BC]

and $OD = OD$ [common side]

$\therefore$ $\Delta BOD \cong \Delta COD$ [by SSS congruence rule]

$\therefore$ $\angle BOD = \angle COD$ [by CPCT]...(i)

We know that in a circle, the angle subtended by an arc at the centre is twice the angle subtended by it at the remaining part of the circle.

$\therefore$ $2\angle BAC = \angle BOC$

$\Rightarrow$ $2\angle BAC = 2\angle BOD$

[$\because \angle BOC = \angle BOD + \angle COD = 2\angle BOD$] [from Eq. (i)]

$\Rightarrow$ $\angle BAC = \angle BOD$ **Hence proved.**

Q.8 On a common hypotenuse AB, two right angled triangles, ACB and ADB are situated on opposite sides. Prove that $\angle BAC = \angle BDC$.

Ans. Given, ΔACB and ΔADB are two right angled triangles with common hypotenuse AB.

To prove $\angle BAC = \angle BDC$

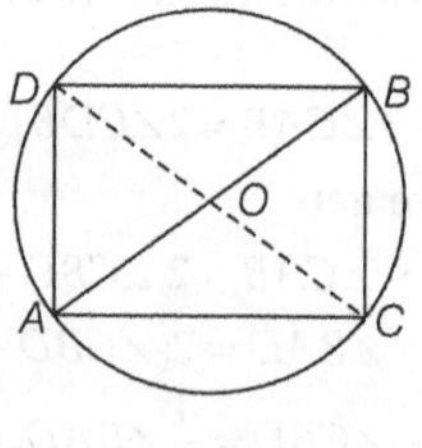

Construction Join CD.

Proof Let O be the mid-point of AB.

Since, mid-point of the hypotenuse of a right triangle is equidistant from its vertices.

Then, $OA = OB = OC = OD$

Now, draw a circle to pass through the points A, B, C and D with O as centre and radius equal to OA.

We know that angles in the same segment of a circle are equal. From the figure, $\angle BAC$ and $\angle BDC$ are angles in same segment BC.

$\therefore$ $\angle BAC = \angle BDC$ **Hence proved.**

Q.9 Two chords AB and AC of a circle subtends angles equal to 90° and 150°, respectively at the centre. Find $\angle BAC$, if AB and AC lie on the opposite sides of the centre.

Ans. In ΔBOA, $OB = OA$ [radii of same circle]

$\therefore$ $\angle OAB = \angle OBA$ ...(i)

[$\because$ angles opposite to equal sides are equal]

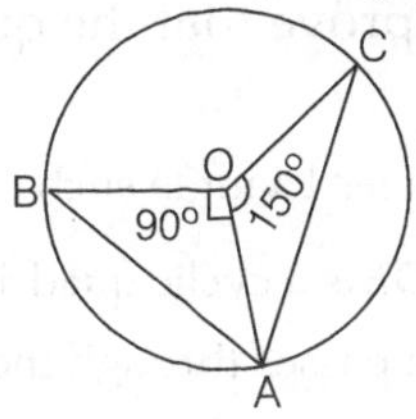

Also, $\angle OBA + \angle OAB + \angle AOB = 180°$ [by angle sum property of a triangle]

$\Rightarrow$ $\angle OAB + \angle OAB + 90° = 180°$ [from Eq. (i)]

$\Rightarrow$ $2\angle OAB = 180° - 90°$

$\Rightarrow$ $\angle OAB = \frac{90°}{2} = 45°$

Now, in ΔAOC, $AO = OC$ [radii of same circle]

$\therefore$ $\angle OCA = \angle OAC$ ...(ii)

[angles opposite to equal sides are equal]

Also, $\angle AOC + \angle OAC + \angle OCA = 180°$ [by angle sum property of a triangle]

$\Rightarrow$ $150° + 2\angle OAC = 180°$ [from Eq. (ii)]

$\Rightarrow$ $2\angle OAC = 180° - 150°$

$\Rightarrow$ $2\angle OAC = 30°$

$\Rightarrow$ $\angle OAC = 15°$

$\therefore$ $\angle BAC = \angle OAB + \angle OAC = 45° + 15° = 60°$

Q.10 If BM and CN are the perpendiculars drawn on the sides AC and AB of the triangle ABC, prove that the points B, C, M and N are concyclic.

Ans. **Given** In ΔABC, $BM \perp AC$ and $CN \perp AB$.

To prove Points B, C, M and N are concyclic.

Construction Draw a circle passing through the points B, C, M and N. Join MN.

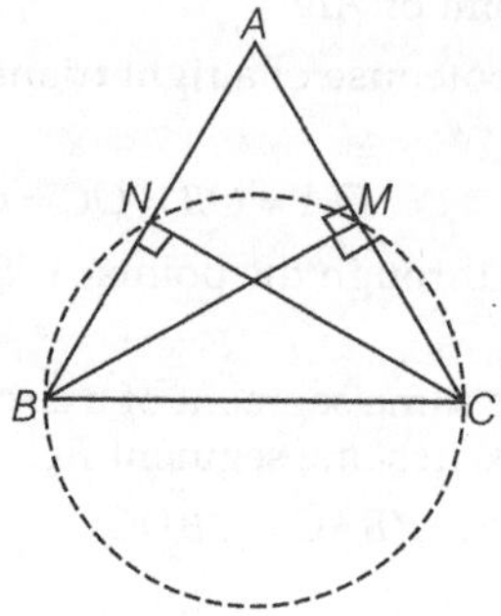

Proof Suppose, we consider BC as a diameter of the circle. Also, we know that BC subtends a right angle to the circle.

So, the points M and N should be lie on a circle.

Hence, the points B, C, M and N form a concyclic. **Hence proved.**

Q.11 If a line is drawn parallel to the base of an isosceles triangle to intersect its equal sides, prove that the quadrilateral, so formed is cyclic.

Ans. **Given** Let ΔABC be an isosceles triangle such that $AB = AC$ and also $DE \parallel BC$.

To prove Quadrilateral $BCDE$ is a cyclic quadrilateral.

Construction Draw a circle passes through the points B, C, D and E.

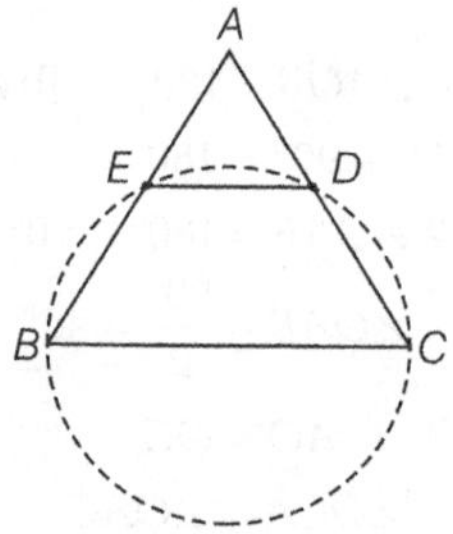

Proof In ΔABC, $AB = AC$ [equal sides of an isosceles triangle]

$\Rightarrow$ $\angle ACB = \angle ABC$ ...(i)

[$\because$ angles opposite to the equal sides are equal]

Since, $DE \parallel BC$

$\Rightarrow$ $\angle ADE = \angle ACB$ [corresponding angles] ...(ii)

On adding $\angle EDC$ both sides in Eq. (ii), we get

$$\angle ADE + \angle EDC = \angle ACB + \angle EDC$$

$\Rightarrow$ $180° = \angle ACB + \angle EDC$

[$\angle ADE$ and $\angle EDC$ form linear pair]

$\Rightarrow$ $\angle EDC + \angle ABC = 180°$ [from Eq. (i)]

Hence, $BCDE$ is a cyclic quadrilateral because sum of the opposite angles is 180°.

Q.12 If a pair of opposite sides of a cyclic quadrilateral are equal, prove that its diagonals are also equal.

Thinking Process Firstly, prove that ΔAOD is congruent to ΔBOC by ASA congruence rule then add ΔDOC on both sides to prove that ΔACD is congruent to ΔBDC by congruence rule and then further, prove the required result.

Ans. **Given** Let $ABCD$ be a cyclic quadrilateral and $AD = BC$.

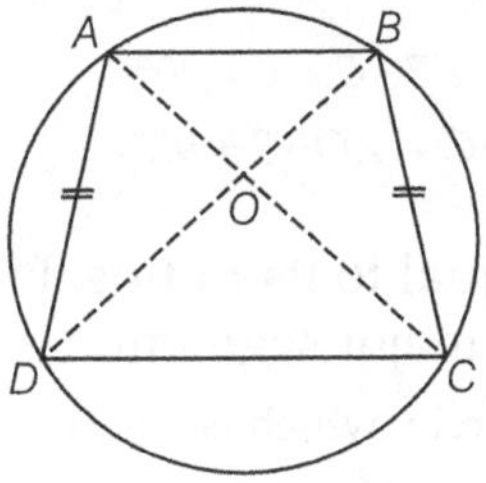

Construction Join AC and BD.

To prove $AC = BD$

Proof In ΔAOD and ΔBOC,

$$\angle OAD = \angle OBC$$

and $$\angle ODA = \angle OCB$$

[since, angles on the same segment of a circle]

$$AD = BC \quad \text{[given]}$$

$\therefore$ $$\Delta AOD \cong \Delta BOC \quad \text{[by ASA congruence rule]}$$

Adding ΔDOC on both sides, we get

$$\Delta AOD + \Delta DOC \cong \Delta BOC + \Delta DOC$$

$\Rightarrow$ $$\Delta ADC \cong \Delta BCD$$

$\therefore$ $$AC = BD$$ [by CPCT] **Hence proved.**

Q.13 The circumcentre of the ΔABC is O. Prove that $\angle OBC + \angle BAC = 90°$.

Ans. **Given** A circle is circumscribed on a ΔABC having centre O.

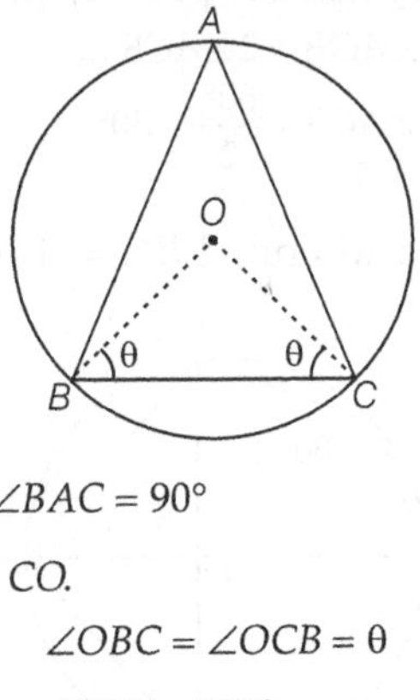

To prove $\angle OBC + \angle BAC = 90°$

Construction Join BO and CO.

Proof Let $$\angle OBC = \angle OCB = \theta \quad \text{...(i)}$$

In ΔOBC, $\angle BOC + \angle OCB + \angle CBO = 180°$

[by angle sum property of a triangle]

$\Rightarrow \quad \angle BOC + \theta + \theta = 180°$

$\Rightarrow \quad \angle BOC = 180° - 2\theta$

We know that in a circle, the angle subtended by an arc at the centre is twice the angle subtended by it at any point on the remaining part of the circle.

$\therefore \quad \angle BOC = 2\angle BAC$

$\Rightarrow \quad \angle BAC = \frac{\angle BOC}{2} = \frac{180° - 2\theta}{2} = 90° - \theta$

$\Rightarrow \quad \angle BAC + \theta = 90°$

$\therefore \quad \angle BAC + \angle OBC = 90°$ [from Eq. (i)] **Hence proved.**

Q.14 A chord of a circle is equal to its radius. Find the angle subtended by this chord at a point in major segment.

Ans. Given, *AB* is a chord of a circle, which is equal to the radius of the circle *i.e.,*

$$AB = BO \quad \text{...(i)}$$

Let *C* be a point on the circle.

Join *OA*, *AC* and *BC*.

Since, $OA = OB$ = Radii of same circle

$\therefore \quad OA = AB = BO$ [from Eq. (i)]

Thus, ΔOAB is an equilateral triangle.

$\Rightarrow \quad \angle AOB = 60°$ [$\because$ each angle of an equilateral triangle is 60°]

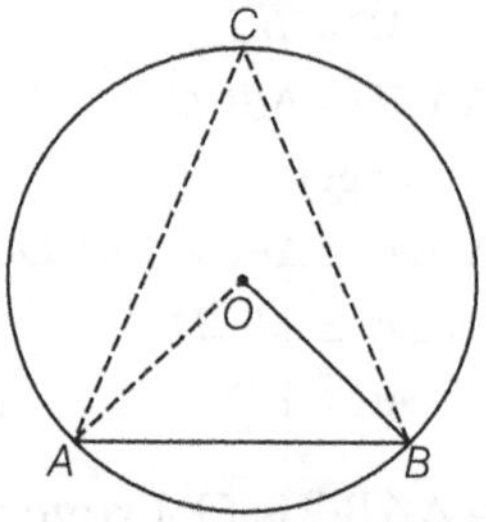

By using the theorem, in a circle, the angle subtended by an arc at the centre is twice the angle subtended by it at any point on the remaining part of the circle.

i.e., $\quad \angle AOB = 2\angle ACB$

$\Rightarrow \quad \angle ACB = \frac{60°}{2} = 30°$

Q.15 In figure, $\angle ADC = 130°$ and chord BC = chord BE. Find $\angle CBE$.

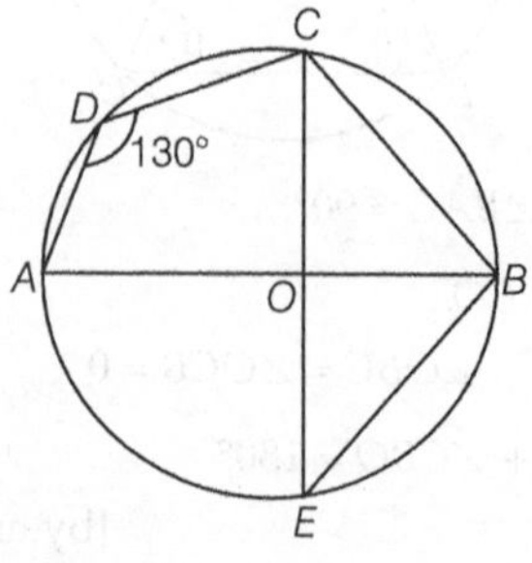

Ans. Let us assume, O is the mid-point of CE

$\therefore \quad OE = OC \quad \ldots(i)$

We have, $\angle ADC = 130°$ and chord BC = chord BE. Since, the points A, B, C and D lie on the circumference of a circle. So, they form a cyclic quadrilateral.

Since, the sum of opposite angles of a cyclic quadrilateral $ABCD$ is 180°.

$\therefore \quad \angle ADC + \angle OBC = 180°$

$\Rightarrow \quad 130° + \angle OBC = 180°$

$\Rightarrow \quad \angle OBC = 180° - 130° = 50°$

In ΔBOC and ΔBOE,

$BC = BE$ [given]

$OC = OE$ [from Eq (i)]

and $OB = OB$ [common side]

$\therefore \quad \Delta BOC \cong \Delta BOE$ [by SSS congruence rule]

$\Rightarrow \quad \angle OBC = \angle OBE = 50°$ [by CPCT]

Now, $\angle CBE = \angle CBO + \angle EBO$

$= 50° + 50° = 100°$

Mistake Alert! *Student may incorrectly assume that inside a circle all quadrilaterals are cyclic quadrilateral.*

Q.16 In figure, $\angle ACB = 40°$. Find $\angle OAB$.

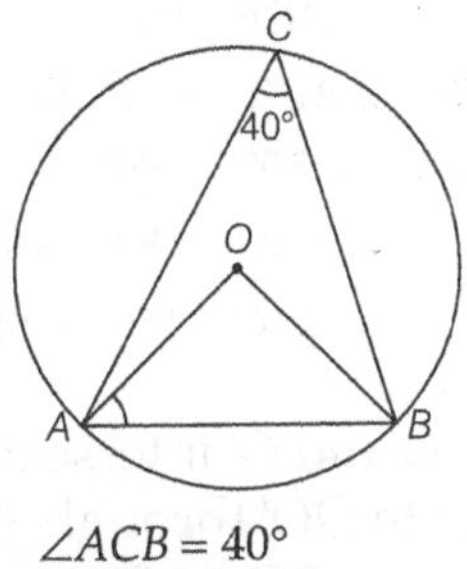

Ans. Given, $\angle ACB = 40°$

We know that in a circle, the angle subtended by an arc at the centre is twice the angle subtended by it at any point on the remaining part of the circle.

$\therefore \quad \angle AOB = 2\angle ACB$

$\Rightarrow \quad \angle AOB = 2 \times 40°$

$\Rightarrow \quad \angle AOB = 80° \quad \ldots(i)$

In ΔAOB, $AO = BO$ [radii of same circle]

$\Rightarrow \quad \angle OBA = \angle OAB \quad \ldots(ii)$

[$\because$ angles opposite to the equal sides are equal]

We know that the sum of all three angles in a triangle is 180°.

$\therefore \quad \angle AOB + \angle OBA + \angle OAB = 180°$

$\Rightarrow \quad 80° + \angle OAB + \angle OAB = 180°$ [from Eqs. (i) and (ii)]

$\Rightarrow \quad 2\angle OAB = 180° - 80°$

$\Rightarrow \quad 2\angle OAB = 100°$

$\therefore \quad \angle OAB = \dfrac{100°}{2} = 50°$

Q.17 A quadrilateral $ABCD$ is inscribed in a circle such that AB is a diameter and $\angle ADC = 130°$. Find $\angle BAC$.

Ans. Let $ABCD$ be a quadrilateral inscribed in a circle having centre O. Given, $\angle ADC = 130°$

Since, $ABCD$ is a quadrilateral inscribed in a circle therefore, $ABCD$ becomes a cyclic quadrilateral.

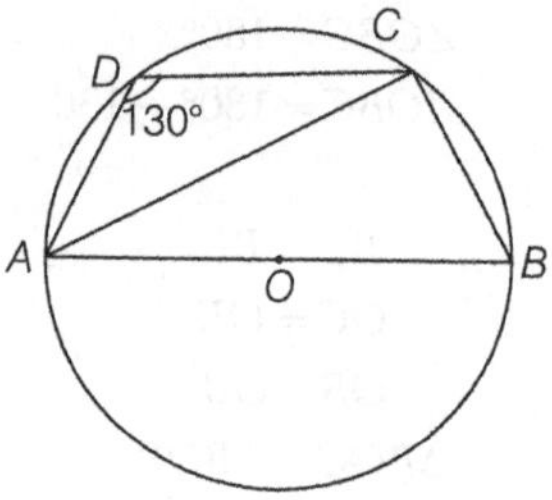

$\because$ The sum of opposite angles of a cyclic quadrilateral is 180°.

$\therefore \quad \angle ADC + \angle ABC = 180°$

$\Rightarrow \quad 130° + \angle ABC = 180°$

$\Rightarrow \quad \angle ABC = 50°$

Since, AB is a diameter of a circle. Then, AB subtends an angle to the circle is right angle.

$\therefore \quad \angle ACB = 90°$

In ΔABC, $\quad \angle BAC + \angle ACB + \angle ABC = 180°$ [by angle sum property of a triangle]

$\Rightarrow \quad \angle BAC + 90° + 50° = 180°$

$\Rightarrow \quad \angle BAC = 180° - (90° + 50°)$

$\Rightarrow \quad \angle BAC = 180° - 140° = 40°$

Q.18 Two circles with centres O and O' intersect at two points A and B. A line PQ is drawn parallel to OO' through A (or B) intersecting the circles at P and Q. Prove that $PQ = 2OO'$.

Ans. **Given,** two circles having centres O and O' intersect at two points A and B. Also, the line PQ parallel to OO'.

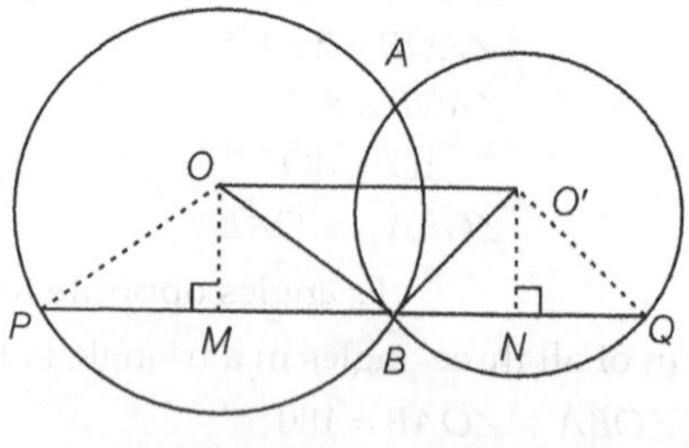

Construction Draw OM and $O'N$, the perpendicular bisectors of PB and BQ respectively. Also, join OP and $O'Q$.

To prove $\quad PQ = 2OO'$

Proof In ΔOPB, $\quad BM = MP \quad$ [OM is the perpendicular bisector of PB]

and in $\Delta O'BQ$, $\quad BN = NQ \quad$ [$O'N$ is the perpendicular bisector of BQ]

On adding above two equations, we get

$\therefore \quad BM + BN = PM + NQ$

$\Rightarrow \quad 2(BM + BN) = BM + BN + PM + NQ \quad$ [adding both sides $BM + BN$]

$\Rightarrow \quad 2OO' = (BM + MP) + (BN + NQ) \quad [\because OO' = MN = MB + BN]$

$= BP + BQ = PQ$

$\Rightarrow \quad 2OO' = PQ$ **Hence proved.**

Q.19 In figure, AOB is a diameter of the circle and C, D, E are any three points on the semi-circle. Find the value of $\angle ACD + \angle BED$.

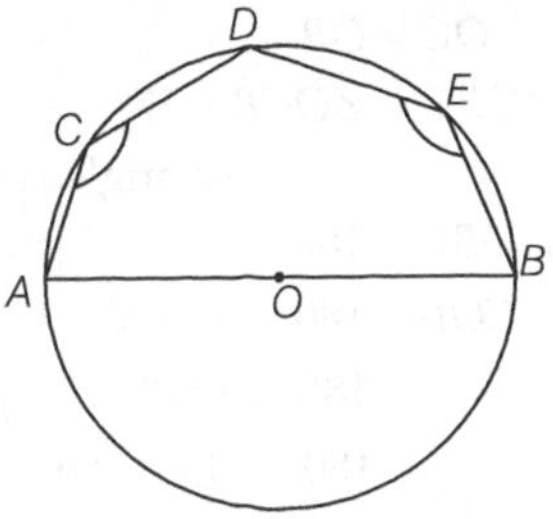

Ans. In the given figure, join AE.

Since, A, C, D and E are four point on a circle. Then, $ACDE$ is a cyclic quadrilateral.

$\therefore \quad \angle ACD + \angle AED = 180° \quad$ ...(i)

[$\because$ sum of opposite angles in a cyclic quadrilateral is 180°]

We know that diameter subtends a right angle to the circle.

$\therefore \quad \angle AEB = 90° \quad$ ...(ii)

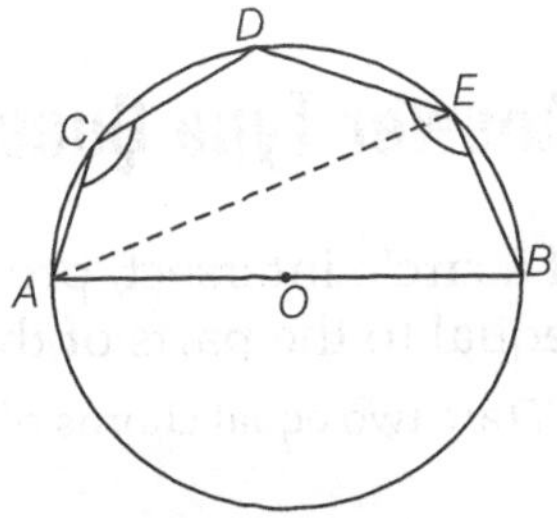

On adding Eqs. (i) and (ii), we get

$(\angle ACD + \angle AED) + \angle AEB = 180° + 90° = 270° \Rightarrow \angle ACD + \angle BED = 270°$

Mistake Alert ! *Students may incorrectly assume that quadrilaterals ODEB and ODCA are cyclic quadrilateral.*

Q.20 In figure, $\angle OAB = 30°$ and $\angle OCB = 57°$. Find $\angle BOC$ and $\angle AOC$.

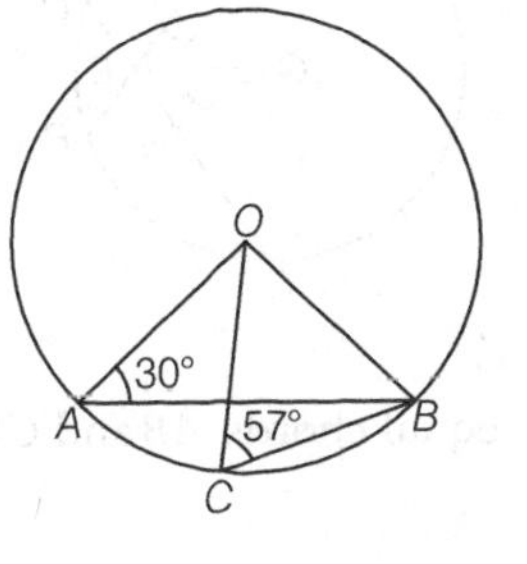

Ans. Given, $\angle OAB = 30°$ and $\angle OCB = 57°$

In ΔAOB, $AO = OB$ [radii of same circle]

$\Rightarrow$ $\angle OBA = \angle BAO = 30°$

[$\because$ angles opposite to equal sides are equal]

Also, $\angle AOB + \angle OBA + \angle BAO = 180°$ [by angle sum property of a triangle]

$\Rightarrow$ $\angle AOB + 30° + 30° = 180°$

$\Rightarrow$ $\angle AOB = 180° - (30° + 30°)$

$= 180° - 60° = 120°$ ...(i)

Now, in ΔOCB,

$OC = OB$ [radii of same circle]

$\Rightarrow$ $\angle OBC = \angle OCB = 57°$

[$\because$ angles opposite to equal sides are equal]

Also, $\angle COB + \angle OCB + \angle OBC = 180°$ [by angle sum property of triangle]

$\therefore$ $\angle COB = 180° - (\angle OCB + \angle OBC)$

$= 180° - (57° + 57°)$

$= 180 - 114° = 66°$ ...(ii)

From Eq. (i), we get $\angle AOB = 120°$

$\Rightarrow$ $\angle AOC + \angle COB = 120°$

$\Rightarrow$ $\angle AOC + 66° = 120°$ [from Eq. (ii)]

$\Rightarrow$ $\angle AOC = 120° - 66° = 54°$

$\Rightarrow$ $\angle BOC = 66°$ and $\angle AOC = 54°$

Long Answer Type Questions

Q.1 If two equal chords of a circle intersect, prove that the parts of one chord are separately equal to the parts of the other chord.

Ans. Given Consider AB and CD are two equal chords of a circle, which intersect at point E.

To prove $AE = CE$ and $BE = DE$

Construction Draw $OM \perp AB$ and $ON \perp CD$ and join OE, where O is the centre of circle.

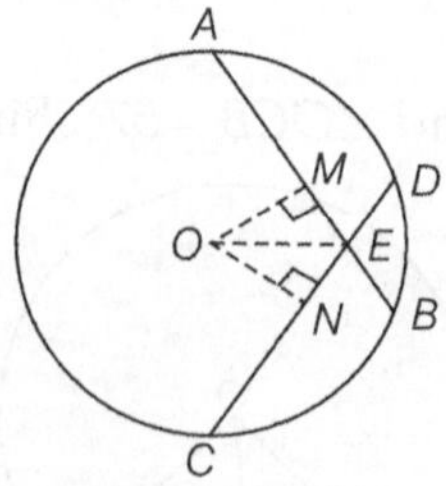

Proof In ΔOME and ΔONE,

$OM = ON$ [$\because$ equal chords AB and CD are equidistant from the centre]

$OE = OE$ [common side]

and $\angle OME = \angle ONE$ [each 90°]

$\therefore$ $\Delta OME \cong \Delta ONE$ [by RHS congruence rule]

$\Rightarrow$ $EM = EN$ [by CPCT]...(i)

Now, $AB = CD$ [given]

On dividing both sides by 2, we get

$$\frac{AB}{2} = \frac{CD}{2} \Rightarrow AM = CN \quad ...(ii)$$

[since, perpendicular from the centre of circle to a chord bisects the chord *i.e.*, $AM = MB$ and $CN = ND$]

On adding Eqs. (i) and (ii), we get

$$EM + AM = EN + CN \Rightarrow AE = CE \quad ...(iii)$$

Now, $AB = CD$ [given]

On subtracting AE from both sides, we get

$$AB - AE = CD - AE \Rightarrow BE = CD - CE \quad \text{[from Eq. (iii)]}$$

$\Rightarrow$ $BE = DE$ **Hence proved.**

Q.2 If non-parallel sides of a trapezium are equal, prove that it is cyclic.

Ans. Given $ABCD$ is a trapezium whose non-parallel sides AD and BC are equal.

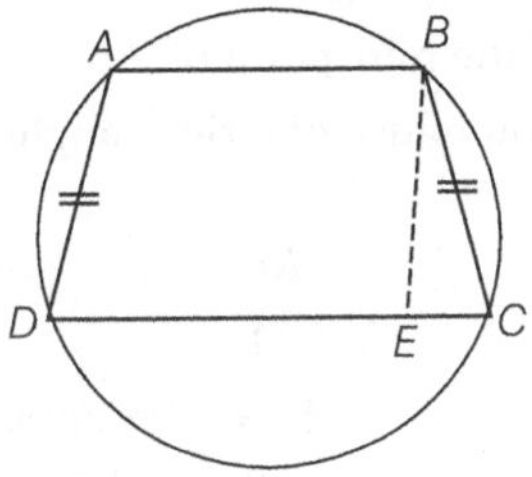

To prove Trapezium $ABCD$ is a cyclic.

Construction Join BE, where $BE \parallel AD$.

Proof Since, $AB \parallel DE$ and $AD \parallel BE$

So, the quadrilateral $ABED$ is a parallelogram.

$\therefore$ $\angle BAD = \angle BED$ ...(i)

[$\because$ opposite angles of a parallelogram are equal]

and $AD = BE$ ...(ii)

[$\because$ opposite sides of a parallelogram are equal]

But $AD = BC$ [given] ...(iii)

From Eqs. (ii) and (iii), we get $BC = BE$

$\Rightarrow$ $\angle BEC = \angle BCE$ ...(iv)

[$\because$ angles opposite to the equal sides are equal]

Also, $\angle BEC + \angle BED = 180°$ [linear pair axiom]

$\therefore$ $\angle BCE + \angle BAD = 180°$ [from Eqs. (i) and (iv)]

If sum of the opposite angles of a quadrilateral is 180°, then quadrilateral is cyclic.

Hence, trapezium $ABCD$ is a cyclic. **Hence proved.**

Mistake Alert! *If non-parallel sides of a trapezium are equal, then students may incorrectly assume that it is a parallelogram.*

Q.3 If P, Q and R are the mid-points of the sides, BC, CA and AB of a triangle and AD is the perpendicular from A on BC, prove that P, Q, R and D are concyclic.

- **Concept Insight** If a line segment adjoins the mid-point of any two sides of a triangle, then the line segment is said to be parallel to the remaining third side.

Ans. **Given** In ΔABC, P, Q and R are the mid-points of the sides BC, CA and AB, respectively. Also, $AD \perp BC$.

To prove P, Q, R and D are concyclic.

Construction Join DR, RQ and QP

Proof

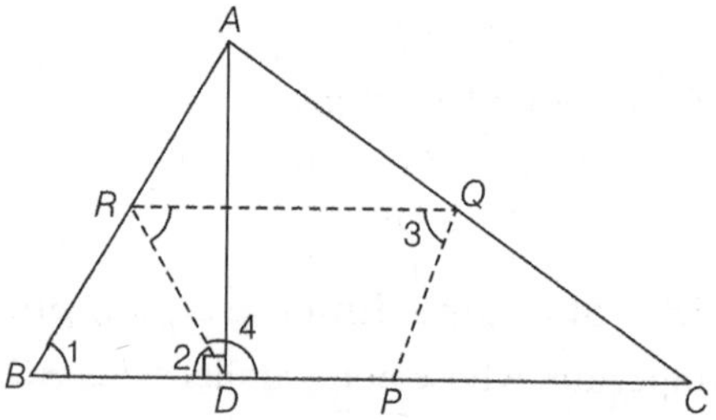

In right angled ΔADB, R is the mid-point of AB.

Since, mid-point of the hypotenuse of a right angled triangle in equidistant from the vertices.

$\therefore \quad RB = RD$

$\Rightarrow \quad \angle 2 = \angle 1 \quad \ldots$(i)

[$\because$ angles opposite to the equal sides are equal]

Since, R and Q are the mid-points of AB and AC, respectively, then

$RQ \parallel BC$ [by mid-point theorem]

or $\quad RQ \parallel BP$

Since, $QP \parallel RB$, then quadrilateral $BPQR$ is a parallelogram.

$\Rightarrow \quad \angle 1 = \angle 3 \quad \ldots$(ii)

[$\because$ opposite angles of parallelogram are equal]

From Eqs. (i) and (ii), we get $\angle 2 = \angle 3$

But $\quad \angle 2 + \angle 4 = 180°$ [linear pair axiom]

$\therefore \quad \angle 3 + \angle 4 = 180°$ [$\because \angle 2 = \angle 3$]

Hence, the quadrilateral $PQRD$ is a cyclic quadrilateral.

So, points P, Q, R and D are con-cyclic. **Hence proved.**

Q.4 $ABCD$ is a parallelogram. A circle through A, B is so drawn that it intersects AD at P and BC at Q. Prove that P, Q, C and D are concyclic.

Ans. **Given** $ABCD$ is a parallelogram. A circle whose centre O, passes through A, B is so drawn that it intersect AD at P and BC at Q

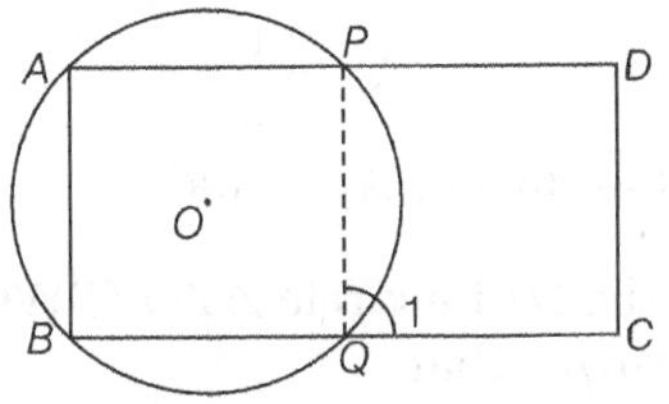

To prove Points P, Q, C and D are concyclic.

Construction Join PQ.

Proof A, P, Q and B are four points lying on a circle, then $APQB$ is a cyclic quadrilateral.

$\angle 1 = \angle A$ [exterior angle property of cyclic quadrilateral]

But $\angle A = \angle C$ [opposite angles of a parallelogram]

$\therefore$ $\angle 1 = \angle C$ ...(i)

But $\angle C + \angle D = 180°$ [sum of co-interior angles is 180°]

$\Rightarrow$ $\angle 1 + \angle D = 180°$ [from Eq. (i)]

Thus, the quadrilateral $QCDP$ is cyclic.

So, the points P, Q, C and D are concyclic. **Hence proved.**

Q.5 Prove that angle bisector of any angle of a triangle and perpendicular bisector of the opposite side, if intersect they will intersect on the circumcircle of the triangle.

- **Concept Insight** Equal chords of circle subtend equal angles at the centre.

Ans. Given, ΔABC with O as centre of its circumcircle. The perpendicular bisector of BC passes through O.

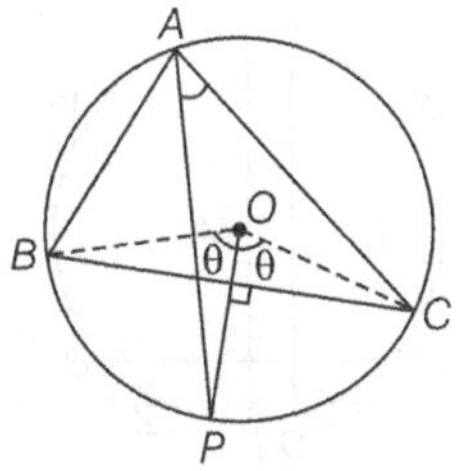

Construction Join OB and OC. Suppose it cuts circumcircle at P.

To prove In order to prove that the perpendicular bisector of BC and bisector of angle A of ΔABC intersect at P, it is sufficient to show that AP is bisector of $\angle A$ of ΔABC.

Arc BC makes angle θ on the circumference

$\therefore$ $\angle BOC = 2\theta$

[Angle at centre is double the angle made by an arc at circumference]

Also, in ΔBOC, $OB = OC$ and OP is the perpendicular bisector of BC.

So, $\angle BOP = \angle COP = \theta$

Arc CP makes angle θ at O, so it will make angle $\frac{\theta}{2}$ at circumference.

So, $\angle CAP = \frac{\theta}{2}$

Hence, AP is the angle bisector of $\angle A$ of ΔABC.

Q.6 If two chords AB and CD of a circle $AYDZBWCX$ intersect at right angles (see figure), prove that
arc CXA + arc DZB = arc AYD + arc BWC = semi-circle.

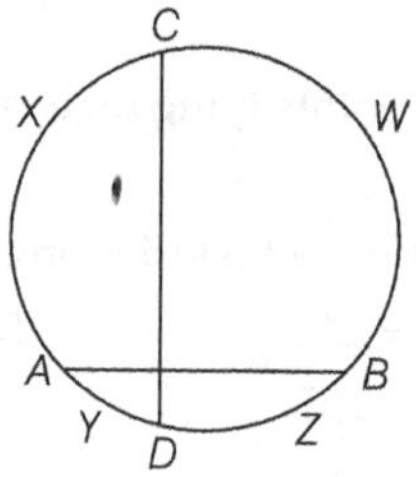

Ans. **Given** In a circle $AYDZBWCX$, two chords AB and CD intersect at right angles.

To prove arc CXA + arc DZB = arc AYD + arc BWC = Semi-circle.

Construction Draw a diameter EF parallel to CD having centre M.

Proof Since, $CD \parallel EF$

$\therefore$ arc EC = arc FD ...(i)

Also, arc $ECXA$ = arc EWB

[symmetrical about diameter of a circle]

and arc AF = arc BF ...(ii)

We know that arc $ECXAYDF$ = Semi-circle

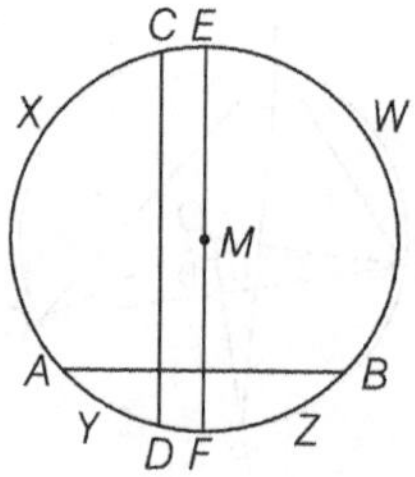

Now, arc EA + arc AF = Semi-circle

$\Rightarrow$ arc EC + arc CXA + arc FB = Semi-circle [from Eq. (ii)]

$\Rightarrow$ arc DF + arc CXA + arc FB = Semi-circle [from Eq. (i)]

$\Rightarrow$ arc DF + arc FB + arc CXA = Semi-circle

$\Rightarrow$ arc DZB + arc CXA = Semi-circle

We know that circle divides itself in two semi-circles, therefore the remaining portion of the circle is also equal to the semi-circle.

$\therefore$ arc AYD + arc BWC = Semi-circle **Hence proved.**

Q.7 If ABC is an equilateral triangle inscribed in a circle and P be any point on the minor arc BC which does not coincide with B or C, prove that PA is angle bisector of $\angle BPC$.

Ans. **Given** ΔABC is an equilateral triangle inscribed in a circle and P be any point on the minor arc BC which does not coincide with B or C.

To prove PA is an angle bisector of $\angle BPC$.

Construction Join PB and PC.

Proof

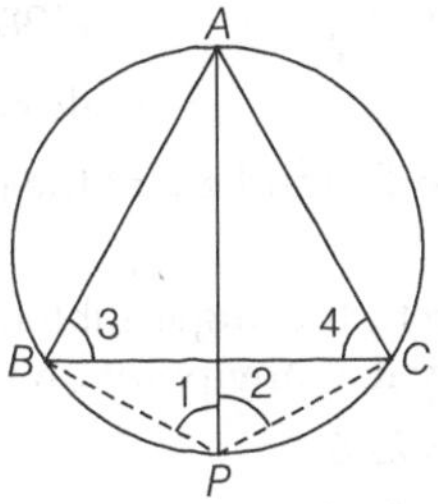

Since, ΔABC is an equilateral triangle.

$$\angle 3 = \angle 4 = 60°$$

Now, $\angle 1 = \angle 4 = 60°$ ...(i)

[angles in the same segment AB]

$\angle 2 = \angle 3 = 60°$ ...(ii)

[angles in the same segment AC]

$\therefore$ $\angle 1 = \angle 2 = 60°$ [from Eqs. (i) and (ii)]

Hence, PA is the angle bisector of $\angle BPC$. **Hence proved.**

Q.8 In figure, AB and CD are two chords of a circle intersecting each other at point E. Prove that $\angle AEC = \frac{1}{2}$ (angle subtended by arc CXA at centre + angle subtended by arc DYB at the centre).

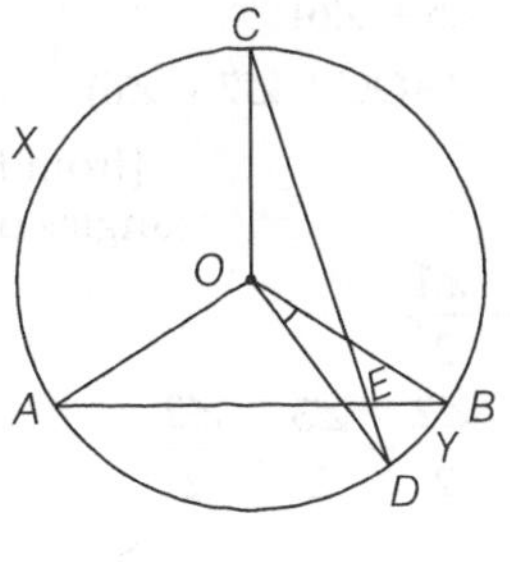

Ans. **Given** In a figure, two chords AB and CD intersecting each other at point E.

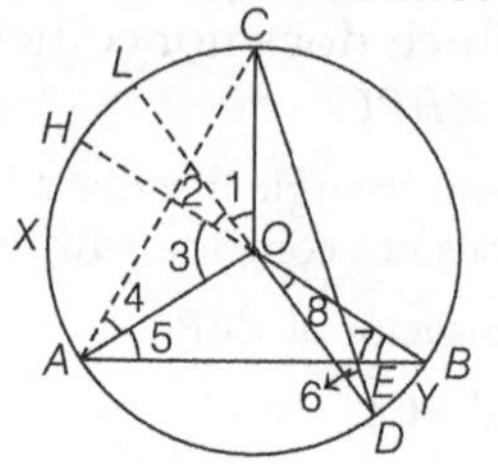

To prove $\angle AEC = \frac{1}{2}$ [angle subtended by arc CXA at centre + angle subtended by arc DYB at the centre]

Construction Extend the line DO and BO at the points L and H on the circle respectively. Also, join AC.

Proof We know that in a circle, the angle subtended by an arc at the centre is twice the angle subtended by it at any point on the remaining part of the circle.

$\therefore$ $\angle 1 = 2\angle 6$ ...(i)

and $\angle 3 = 2\angle 7$ ...(ii)

In ΔAOC, $OC = OA$ [radii of same circle]

$\angle OCA = \angle 4$ [$\because$ angles opposite to equal sides are equal]

Also, $\angle AOC + \angle OCA + \angle 4 = 180°$ [by angle sum property of triangle]

$\Rightarrow$ $\angle AOC + \angle 4 + \angle 4 = 180°$

$\Rightarrow$ $\angle AOC = 180° - 2\angle 4$ ...(iii)

Now, in ΔAEC, $\angle AEC + \angle ECA + \angle CAE = 180°$

[by angle property sum of a triangle]

$\Rightarrow$ $\angle AEC = 180° - (\angle ECA + \angle CAE)$

$\Rightarrow$ $\angle AEC = 180° - [(\angle ECO + \angle OCA) + (\angle CAO + \angle OAE)]$

$= 180° - (\angle 6 + \angle 4 + \angle 4 + \angle 5)$

[in ΔOCD, $\angle 6 = \angle ECO$ and in ΔOCA, $\angle 4 = \angle OCA$; angles opposite to equal sides are equal]

$= 180° - (2\angle 4 + \angle 5 + \angle 6)$

$= 180° - (180° - \angle AOC + \angle 7 + \angle 6)$

[from Eq. (iii) and in ΔAOB, $\angle 5 = \angle 7$, as (angles opposite to equal sides are equal)]

$= \angle AOC - \frac{\angle 3}{2} - \frac{\angle 1}{2}$ [from Eqs. (i) and (ii)]

$= \angle AOC - \frac{\angle 1}{2} - \frac{\angle 2}{2} - \frac{\angle 3}{2} + \frac{\angle 2}{2}$ $\left[\text{adding and subtracting } \frac{\angle 2}{2}\right]$

$= \angle AOC - \frac{1}{2}(\angle 1 + \angle 2 + \angle 3) + \frac{\angle 8}{2}$

[$\because$ $\angle 2 = \angle 8$ (vertically opposite angles)]

$= \angle AOC - \frac{\angle AOC}{2} + \frac{\angle DOB}{2}$

$$\Rightarrow \quad \angle AEC = \frac{1}{2}(\angle AOC + \angle DOB)$$

$= \frac{1}{2}$ [angle subtended by arc CXA at the centre + angle subtended by arc DYB at the centre] **Hence Proved.**

Q.9 If bisectors of opposite angles of a cyclic quadrilateral $ABCD$ intersect the circle, circumscribing it at the points P and Q, prove that PQ is a diameter of the circle.

Thinking Process Use the property of cyclic quardrilateral, the sum of opposite angles of cyclic quadrilateral is supplementary. Further, simplify it to prove the required result.

Ans. **Given** $ABCD$ is a cyclic quadrilateral, where DP and QB are the bisectors of $\angle D$ and $\angle B$, respectively.

To prove PQ is the diameter of a circle.

Construction Join QD and QC.

Proof

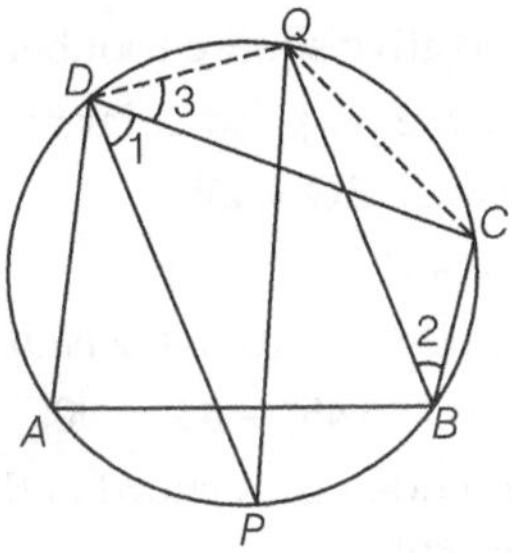

Since, $ABCD$ is a cyclic quadrilateral.

$$\therefore \quad \angle CDA + \angle CBA = 180°$$

[$\because$ sum of opposite angles of cyclic quadrilateral is 180°]

On dividing both sides by 2, we get

$$\frac{1}{2}\angle CDA + \frac{1}{2}\angle CBA = \frac{1}{2} \times 180° = 90°$$

$$\Rightarrow \quad \angle 1 + \angle 2 = 90° \quad \text{...(i)}$$

$$\left[\because \angle 1 = \frac{1}{2}\angle CDA \text{ and } \angle 2 = \frac{1}{2}\angle CBA\right]$$

But $\angle 2 = \angle 3$ [$\because$ angles in the same segment QC are equal]...(ii)

From Eqs. (i) and (ii), we get

$$\angle 1 + \angle 3 = 90°$$

$$\Rightarrow \quad \angle PDQ = 90°$$

Hence, PQ is a diameter of a circle because diameter of the circle subtends a right angle at the circumference.

Q.10 A circle has radius $\sqrt{2}$ cm. It is divided into two segments by a chord of length 2 cm. Prove that the angle subtended by the chord at a point in major segment is 45°.

Ans. Given A circle having centre O. Let $AB = 2$ cm be a chord of a circle.

To prove $\angle APB = 45°$

Construction Draw a perpendicular bisector OM on AB which bisects AB at N.

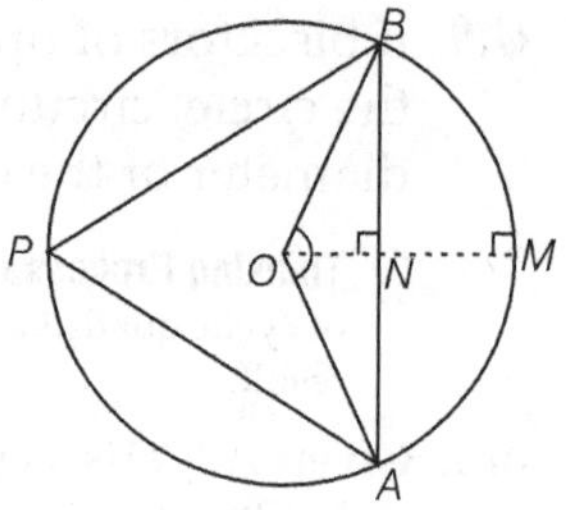

Proof

Here, $AN = NB = \frac{AB}{2} = 1\,\text{cm}$

and $OB = \sqrt{2}$ cm

In ΔONB, $OB^2 = ON^2 + NB^2$ [by Pythagoras theorem]

$\Rightarrow (\sqrt{2})^2 = ON^2 + (1)^2$

$\Rightarrow ON^2 = 2 - 1 = 1$

$\Rightarrow ON = 1\,\text{cm}$

[take positive square root because distance is always positive]

Also, $\angle ONB = 90°$ [ON is the perpendicular bisector of the chord AB]

$\therefore \angle NOB = \angle NBO = 45°$ [$\because NB = ON$]

Similarly, $\angle AON = 45°$

Now, $\angle AOB = \angle AON + \angle NOB$

$= 45° + 45° = 90°$

We know that the angle subtended by a chord at the circumference is half the angle subtended by it at the centre.

$\therefore \angle APB = \frac{1}{2}\angle AOB$

$= \frac{90°}{2} = 45°$ **Hence proved.**

Q.11 Two equal chords AB and CD of a circle when produced intersect at a point P. Prove that $PB = PD$.

Thinking Process First, use the theorem, equal chords of a circle are equidistant from the centre and then use the theorem, the perpendicular from the centre of a circle to a chord bisects the chord, to show the required result.

Ans. Given Two equal chords AB and CD of a circle intersecting at a point P.

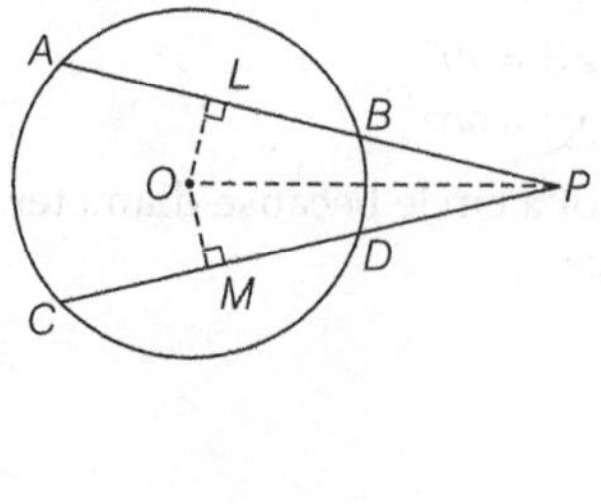

To prove $PB = PD$

Construction Join OP, draw $OL \perp AB$ and $OM \perp CD$

Proof

We have, $AB = CD$

$\Rightarrow$ $OL = OM$

[$\because$ equal chords of a circle are equidistant from the centre]

In ΔOLP and ΔOMP, $OL = OM$ [proved above]

$\angle OLP = \angle OMP$ [each 90°]

and $OP = OP$ [common side]

$\therefore$ $\Delta OLP \cong \Delta OMP$ [by RHS congruence rule]

$\Rightarrow$ $LP = MP$ [by CPCT] ...(i)

Now, $AB = CD$

$\Rightarrow$ $\frac{1}{2}(AB) = \frac{1}{2}(CD)$ [dividing both sides by 2]

$\Rightarrow$ $BL = DM$ ...(ii)

[$\because$ the perpendicular from the centre of a circle to a chord bisects the chord *i.e.*, $AL = LB$ and $CM = MD$]

On subtracting Eq. (ii) from Eq. (i), we get

$$LP - BL = MP - DM$$

$\Rightarrow$ $PB = PD$ **Hence proved.**

Q.12 AB and AC are two chords of a circle of radius r such that $AB = 2AC$. If p and q are the distances of AB and AC from the centre, prove that $4q^2 = p^2 + 3r^2$.

Thinking Process Firstly, use the Pythagoras theorem in ΔOAM and ΔOAN and further adjust them to prove the required result.

Ans. **Given** In a circle of radius r, there are two chords AB and AC such that $AB = 2AC$. Also, the distance of AB and AC from the centre are p and q, respectively.

To prove $4q^2 = p^2 + 3r^2$

Proof Let $AC = a$, then $AB = 2a$

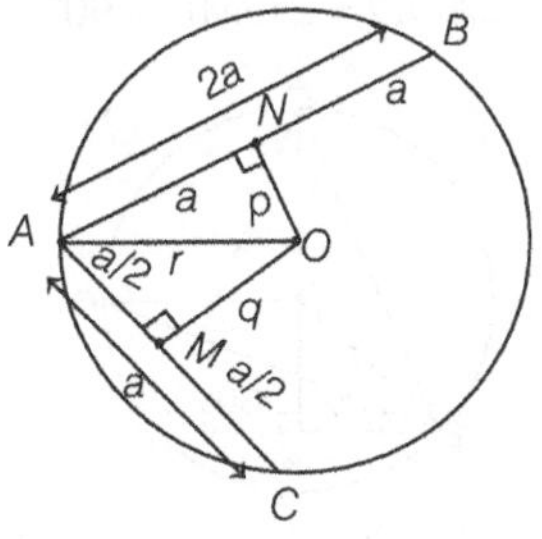

From centre O, perpendicular is drawn to the chords AC and AB at M and N, respectively.

$\therefore$ $$AM = MC = \frac{a}{2}$$

$$AN = NB = a$$

In ΔOAM $$AO^2 = AM^2 + MO^2$$ [by Pythagoras theorem]

$\Rightarrow$ $$r^2 = \left(\frac{a}{2}\right)^2 + q^2$$ [$\because AO = r$] ...(i)

In ΔOAN, by Pythagoras theorem,

$$AO^2 = (AN)^2 + (NO)^2$$

$\Rightarrow$ $$r^2 = (a)^2 + p^2$$ ...(ii)

From Eqs. (i) and (ii), we get

$$\left(\frac{a}{2}\right)^2 + q^2 = a^2 + p^2$$

$\Rightarrow$ $$\frac{a^2}{4} + q^2 = a^2 + p^2$$

$\Rightarrow$ $$a^2 + 4q^2 = 4a^2 + 4p^2$$ [multiplying both sides by 4]

$\Rightarrow$ $$4q^2 = 3a^2 + 4p^2 = 3a^2 + 3p^2 + p^2$$

$\Rightarrow$ $$4q^2 = p^2 + 3(a^2 + p^2)$$

$\Rightarrow$ $$4q^2 = p^2 + 3r^2$$ [from Eq. (ii)]

Hence proved.

Q.13 In figure, O is the centre of the circle, $\angle BCO = 30°$. Find x and y.

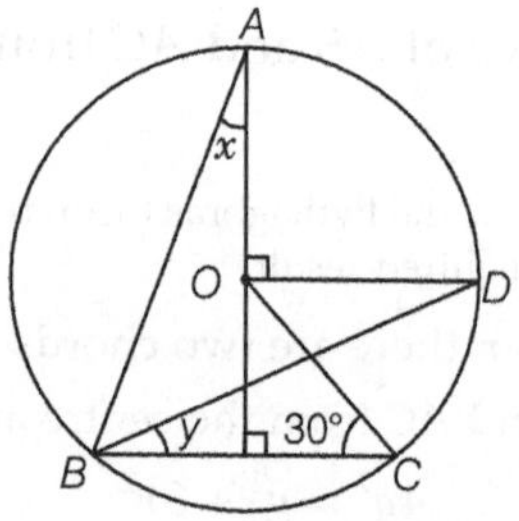

Ans. We have, O is the centre of a circle and $\angle BCO = 30°$

$$\angle AOD = \angle OMC = 90°$$

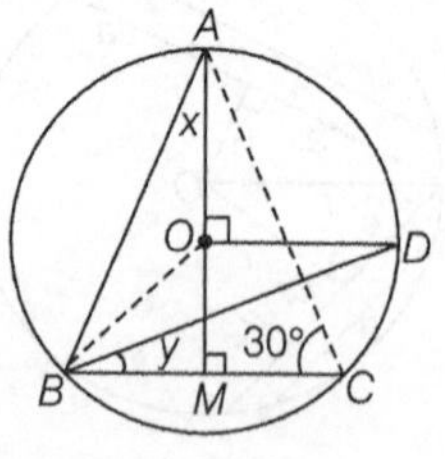

And $\angle AOD$ and $\angle OMC$ form a pair of corresponding angles.

$\therefore$ $$OD \parallel BC$$

Since, $OD \parallel BC$ and OC is a transversal.

$\therefore \quad \angle COD = \angle OCB = 30°$ [Alternate interior angles] ...(i)

Now, $\angle DBC = \frac{1}{2}(\angle DOC) = \frac{30°}{2} = 15°$ [from Eq. (i)] ...(ii)

[The angle subtended by the arc at the circle is half the angle subtended by it at the centre]

$\therefore \quad y = 15°$

And $\angle ABD = \frac{1}{2}(AOD) = \frac{90°}{2} = 45°$ ...(iii)

[The angle subtended by the arc at the circle is half the angle subtended by it at the centre]

Now, in ΔABM,

$$\angle ABM + \angle AMB + \angle BAM = 180°$$

[Sum of all angles of a triangle is 180°]

$\Rightarrow \quad \angle ABD + \angle DBC + 90° + x = 180°$ [$\because \angle AMB = 90°$]

$\Rightarrow \quad 45° + 15° + 90° + x = 180°$ [From (ii) and (iii)]

$\Rightarrow \quad x = 180° - 150° = 30°$

Thus, $x = 30°$ and $y = 15°$.

Q.14 In figure, O is the centre of the circle, $BD = OD$ and $CD \perp AB$. Find $\angle CAB$.

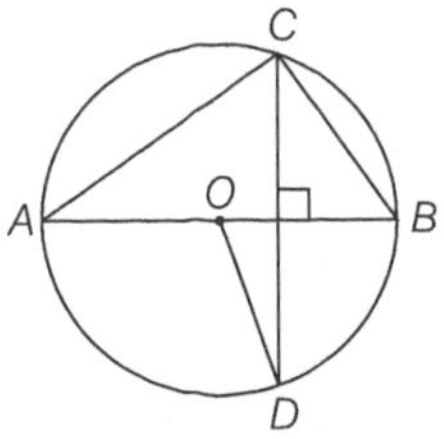

Ans. Given, $BD = OD$, $CD \perp AB$. In the given figure join BD.

In ΔOBD, $\quad BD = OD$ [given] ...(i)

$OD = OB$ [radii of same circle] ...(ii)

$\therefore \quad OB = OD = BD$ [from Eqs. (i) and (iii)]

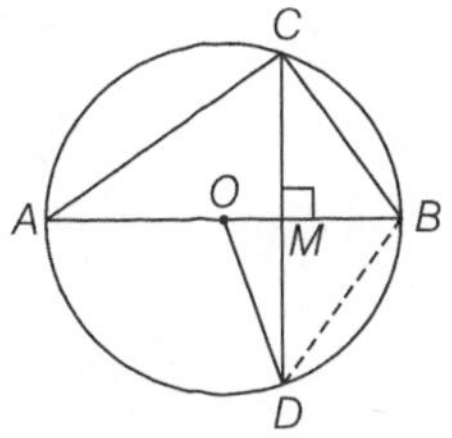

Thus, ΔODB is an equilateral triangle.

$\therefore \quad \angle BOD = \angle OBD = \angle ODB = 60°$

In ΔMBC and ΔMBD, $MB = MB$ [common side]

$\angle CMB = \angle BMD = 90°$ [each 90°]

and $CM = MD$

[in a circle, any perpendicular drawn from the centre on a chord bisects the chord]

$\therefore$ $\Delta MBC \cong \Delta MBD$ [by SAS congruence rule)

$\therefore$ $\angle MBC = \angle MBD$ [by CPCT]

$\Rightarrow$ $\angle MBC = \angle OBD = 60°$ [$\because$ $\angle OBD = 60°$]

Since, AB is a diameter of the circle.

$\therefore$ $\angle ACB = 90°$

In ΔACB, $\angle CAB + \angle CBA + \angle ACB = 180°$

[by angle sum property of a triangle]

$\Rightarrow$ $\angle CAB + 60° + 90° = 180°$

$\Rightarrow$ $\angle CAB = 180° - (60° + 90°) = 180° - 150° = 30°$

Chapter

11

Construction*

Multiple Choice Questions (MCQs)

Choose the correct answer from the given four options in the following questions:

Q.1 With the help of a ruler and a compass it is not possible to construct an angle of

(a) 37.5° (b) 40° (c) 22.5° (d) 67.5°

Ans. ***(b)*** With the help of a ruler and a compass, we can construct the angels, 90°, 60°, 45°, 22.5°, 30° etc., and its bisector of an angle. So, it is not possible to construct an angle of 40°.

Q.2 The construction of ΔABC, given that $BC = 6\text{cm}$, $\angle B = 45°$ is not possible when difference of AB and AC is equal to :

(a) 6.9 cm (b) 5.2 cm (c) 5.0 cm (d) 4.0 cm

● **Concept Insight** The sum of the lengths of any two sides of a triangle is always greater than the length of the third side.

Ans. ***(a)*** Given, $BC = 6\text{ cm}$ and $\angle B = 45°$

We know that the construction of a triangle is not possible, if the sum of two sides is less than or equal to the third side of the triangle.

i.e., $$AB + BC \le AC$$

$$\Rightarrow \quad BC \le AC - AB \Rightarrow 6 \le AC - AB$$

So, if $AC - AB = 6.9\text{ cm}$, then construction of ΔABC with given conditions is not possible.

Q.3 The construction of a ΔABC, given that $BC = 3\text{ cm}$, $\angle C = 60°$ is possible when difference of AB and AC is equal to:

(a) 3.2 cm (b) 3.1 cm (c) 3 cm (d) 2.8 cm

Ans. ***(d)*** Given, $BC = 3\text{ cm}$ and $\angle C = 60°$

We know that the construction of a triangle is possible, if the sum of two sides is greater than the third side of the triangle *i.e.,*

$$AB + BC > AC \Rightarrow BC > AC - AB \Rightarrow 3 > AC - AB$$

So, if $AC - AB = 2.8\text{ cm}$, then construction of ΔABC with given conditions is possible.

Mistake Alert ! *While constructing a triangle, students are misinterpreting whether to use the sum or difference.*

(*) This chapter has been deleted from latest NCERT.

Short Answer Questions with Reasoning

Write True or False in each of the following. Give reason for your answer

Q.1 An angle of 52.5° can be constructed.

Ans. *True*

To construct an angle of 52.5°, firstly construct an angle of 90°, then construct an angle of 120° and then plot an angle bisector of 120° and 90° to get an angle 105° (60° + 45°). Now, bisect this angle to get an angle of 52.5°.

Q.2 An angle of 42.5° can be constructed.

Ans. *False*

We know that $42.5° = \frac{1}{2} \times 85°$ and an angle of 85° cannot be constructed with the help of ruler and compass.

Q.3 A triangle ABC can be constructed in which $AB = 5\text{ cm}$, $\angle A = 45°$ and $BC + AC = 5\text{ cm}$.

Ans. *False*

We know that a triangle can be constructed, if the sum of its two sides is greater than third side.

Here, $BC + AC = AB = 5$ cm

So, ΔABC cannot be constructed.

Q.4 A triangle ABC can be constructed in which $BC = 6\text{ cm}$, $\angle C = 30°$ and $AC - AB = 4$ cm.

- **Concept Insight** A triangle can be constructed, if the sum of any two sides of the triangle is greater than the third side.

Ans. *True*

We know that a triangle can be constructed if the sum of its two sides is greater than the third side.

i.e., in ΔABC, $AB + BC > AC$

$\Rightarrow$ $BC > AC - AB$

$\Rightarrow 6 > 4$, which is true, so ΔABC with given conditions can be constructed.

Q.5 A triangle ABC can be constructed in which $\angle B = 105°$, $\angle C = 90°$ and $AB + BC + CA = 10$ cm.

- **Concept Insight** The sum of all the angles of a triangle is 180°.

Ans. *False*

Here, $\angle B = 105°, \angle C = 90°$

and $AB + BC + CA = 10$ cm

We know that sum of angles of a triangle is 180°.

$\therefore$ $\angle A + \angle B + \angle C = 180°$

Here, $\angle B + \angle C = 105° + 90° = 195° > 180°$, which is not true.

Thus, ΔABC with given conditions cannot be constructed.

Q.6 A triangle ABC can be constructed in which $\angle B = 60°$, $\angle C = 45°$, and $AB + BC + CA = 12$ cm.

- **Concept Insight** The sum of all angles of a triangle is 180°.

Ans. *True*

We know that, sum of angles of a triangle is 180°.

$\therefore \quad \angle A + \angle B + \angle C = 180°$

Here, $\angle B + \angle C = 60° + 45° = 105° < 180°$, which is true.

Thus, ΔABC with given conditions can be constructed.

Short Answer Type Questions

Q.1 Draw an angle of 110° with the help of a protractor and bisect it. Measure each angle.

Ans. Draw $\angle BXA = 110°$ with the help of a protractor. Now, we use the following steps for required construction

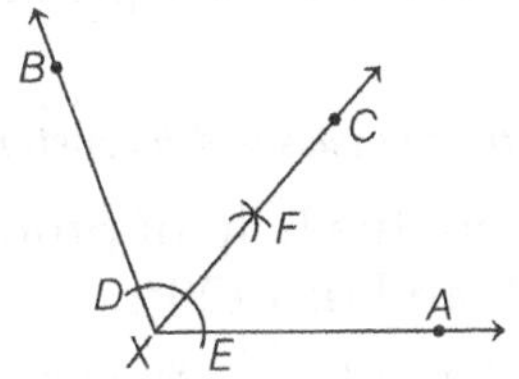

(i) Taking X as centre and any radius daw an arc to intersect the rays XA and XB, say at E and D, respectively.

(ii) Taking D and E as centres and with the radius more than $\frac{1}{2}DE$, draw arcs to intersect each other, say at F.

(iii) Draw the ray XF.

Thus, ray XF is the required bisector of the angle BXA.

On measuring each angle, we get

$$\angle BXC = \angle AXC = 55° \quad \left[\because \angle BXC = \angle AXC = \frac{1}{2}\angle BXA = \frac{1}{2} \times 110° = 55°\right]$$

Q.2 Draw a line segment AB of 4 cm in length. Draw a line perpendicular to AB through A and B, respectively. Are these lines parallel?

Ans. To draw a line perpendicular to AB through A and B, respectively. Use the following steps of construction.

(i) Draw a line segment $AB = 4$ cm.

(ii) Taking A as centre and radius more than $\frac{1}{2}AB$ (*i.e.*, 2 cm), draw an arc say it intersect AB at E.

(iii) Taking E as centre and with same radius as above, draw an arc which intersect previous arc at F.

(iv) Again, taking F as centre and with same radius as above, draw an arc which intersect previous arc (obtained in step ii) at G.

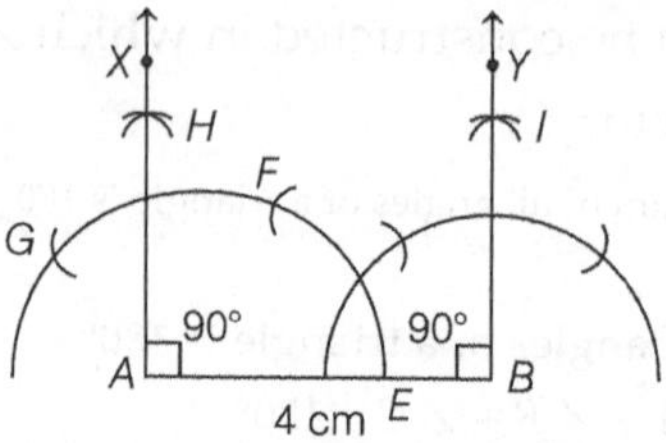

(v) Taking G and F are centres, draw arcs which intersect each other at H.

(vi) Join AH. Thus, AX is perpendicular to AB at A. Similarly, draw $BY \perp AB$ at B.

Now, we know that if two lines are parallel, then the angle between them will be 0° or 180°.

Here, $\angle XAB = 90°$ [$\because XA \perp AB$]

and $\angle YBA = 90°$ [$\because YB \perp AB$]

$\therefore$ $\angle XAB + \angle YBA = 90° + 90° = 180°$

So, the lines XA and YB are parallel.

[since, it sum of interior angle on same side of transversal is 180°, then the two lines are parallel]

Mistake Alert! *Not keeping the compass width constant while marking arcs.*

Q. 3 Draw an angle of 80° with the help of protractor. Then, construct angles of (i) 40° (ii) 160° and (iii) 120°.

Ans. First, draw an angle of 80° (say $\angle QOA = 80°$) with the help of protractor. Now, use the following steps to construct angles of

(i) 40° (ii) 160° (iii) 120°

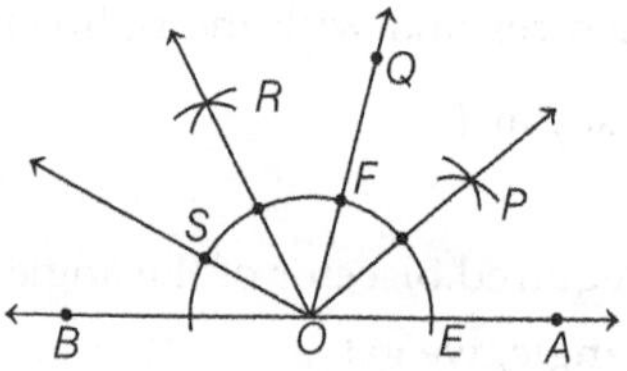

(i) Taking O as centre and any radius, draw an arc which intersect OA at E and OQ at F.

(ii) Taking E and F as centres and radius more than $\frac{1}{2}EF$, draw arcs which intersect each other at P.

(iii) Join OP. Thus, $\angle POA = \frac{1}{2}(\angle QOA) = 40°$

(iv) Now, taking F as centre and radius equal to EF, draw an arc which intersect previous arc (obtained in step ii) at S.

(v) Join OS. Thus, $\angle SOA = 2 \times \angle QOA = 160°$

(vi) Taking S and F as centre and radius more than $\frac{1}{2}SF$, draw arcs which intersect each other at R.

(vii) Join OR. Thus, $\angle ROA = \angle ROQ + \angle QOA = 40° + 80° = 120°$

Mistake Alert! *Misplacing the compass while marking arcs on either side of the line segment.*

Q.4 Construct a triangle whose sides are 3.6 cm , 3.0 cm and 4. 8 cm. Bisect the smallest angle and measure each part.

- **Concept Insight** Angle opposite to smallest side is smallest.

Ans. To construct a triangle ABC in which $AB = 3.6$ cm, $AC = 3.0$ cm and $BC = 4.8$ cm, use the following steps.

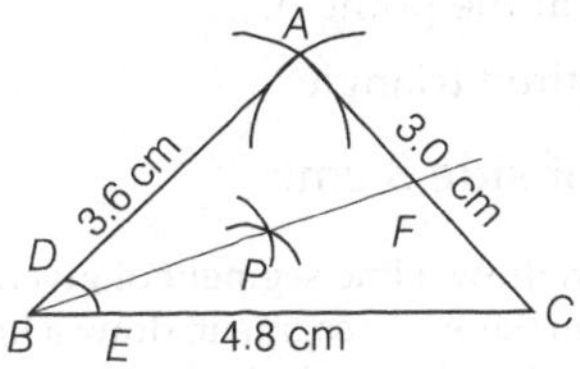

(i) Draw a line segment BC of length 4.8 cm.

(ii) From the point B, point A is at a distance of 3.6 cm. So, having B as centre, draw an arc of radius 3.6 cm.

(iii) From the point C, point A is at a distance of 3 cm. So, having C as centre, draw an arc of radius 3 cm which intersect previous arc at A.

(iv) Join AB and AC. Thus, ΔABC is the required triangle.

Here, angle B is smallest, as AC is the smallest side. To bisect angle B, we use the following steps.

(i) Taking B as centre, we draw an arc intersecting AB and BC at the points D and E, respectively.

(ii) Taking D and E as centres we draw arcs intersecting at P.

(iii) Joining BP, we obtain angle bisector of $\angle B$.

(iv) Here, $\angle ABC = 39°$

Thus, $\angle ABF = \angle FBC = \frac{1}{2} \times 39° = 19.5°$

Q.5 Construct a triangle ABC in which $BC = 5$ cm, $\angle B = 60°$ and $AC + AB = 7.5$ cm.

Ans. Given, in ΔABC, $BC = 5$cm, $\angle B = 60°$ and $AC + AB = 7.5$ cm. To construct the triangle ABC, use the following steps.

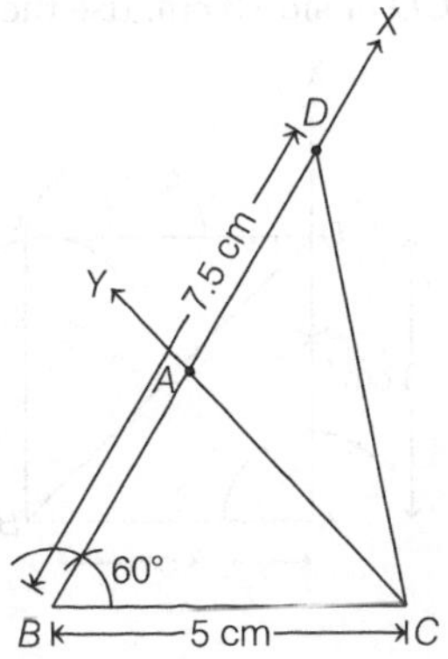

(i) Draw the base $BC = 5$ cm.

(ii) At the point B make an $\angle XBC = 60°$.

(iii) Cut a line segment BD which is equal to $AB + AC = 7.5$ cm from the ray BX.

(iv) Join DC.

(v) Make an $\angle DCY = \angle BDC$.

(vi) Let CY intersect BX at the point A.

So, ΔABC is the required triangle.

Q.6 Construct a square of side 3 cm.

Thinking Process Firstly, draw a line segment of given length. In both ends of segment, draw an angle of 90° from these line segment, draw a line upto the given length. Further, draw an angle of 90° from these line and join the other line to get the required construction.

Ans. We know that, each angle of a square is a right angle (*i.e.*, 90°).

To construct a square of side 3 cm, use the following steps.

(i) Draw a line segment AB of length 3 cm.

(ii) Now, generate an angle of 90° at points A and B of the line segment and plot the parallel lines AX and BY at these points.

(iii) Cut AD and BC of length 3 cm from AX and BY, respectively.

(iv) Draw an angle of 90° at any one of the point C or D and join both points by a line segment CD of length 3 cm.

Thus, $ABCD$ is the required square of side 3 cm.

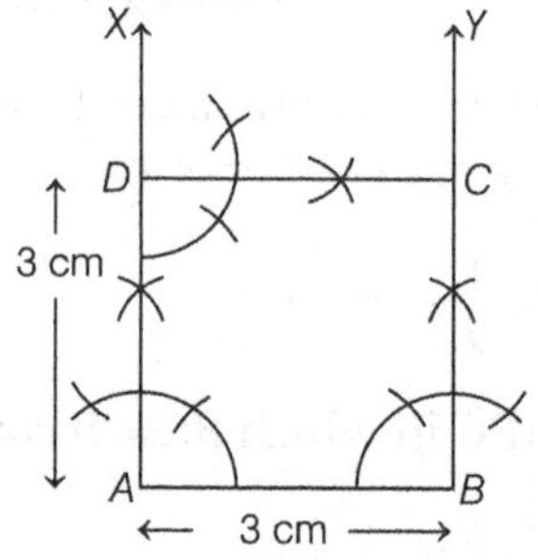

Alternate Method

To construct a square $ABCD$ of side 3 cm, use the following steps

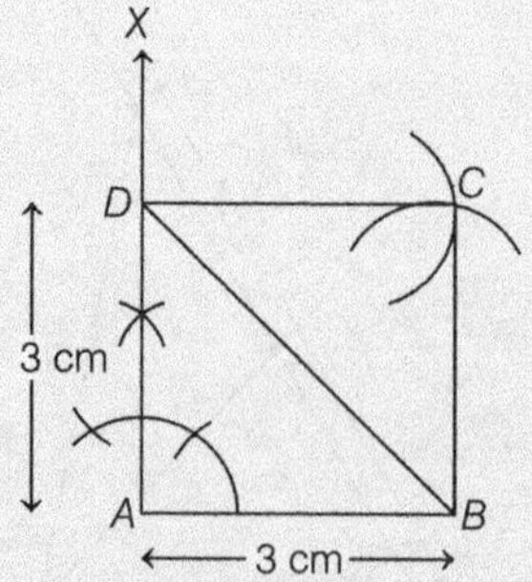

(i) Draw a line segment AB of length 3 cm.
(ii) Now, draw an angle $XAB = 90°$ at point A of line segment AB.
(iii) Cut a line segment $AD = 3$ cm from the ray AX and join BD.
(iv) Now, from point D, point C is at a distance of 3 cm. So, having D as centre, draw an arc of radius 3 cm.
(v) From B, point C is at a distance of 3 cm. So, having B as centre, draw an arc of radius 3 cm which intersect previous arc (obtained in step iv) at C.
(vi) Join DC and BC. Thus, $ABCD$ is the required square of side 3 cm.

Q.7 Construct a rectangle whose adjacent sides are of lengths 5 cm and 3.5 cm.

Ans. We know that, each angle of a rectangle is a right angle (*i.e.*, 90°) and its opposite sides are equal and parallel.

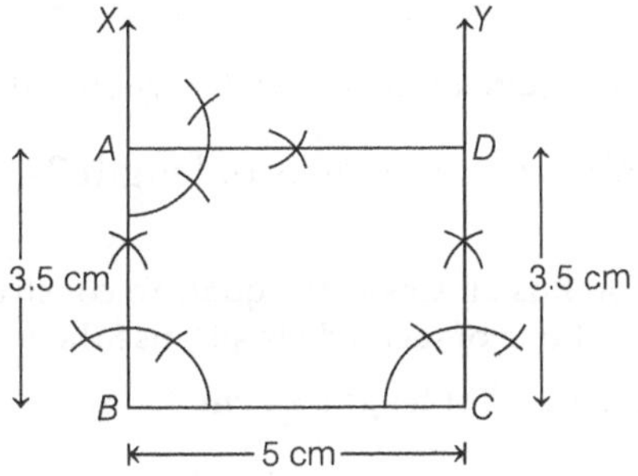

To construct a rectangle whose adjacent sides are of lengths 5 cm and 3.5 cm, use the following steps

(i) Draw a line segment BC of length 5 cm.
(ii) Now, generate an angle of 90° at points B and C of the line segment BC and plot the parallel lines BX and CY at these points.
(iii) Cut AB and CD of length 3.5 cm from BX and CY, respectively.
(iv) Draw an angle 90° at one of the point A or D and join both points by a line segment AD of length 5 cm.

Thus, $ABCD$ is the required rectangle with adjacent sides of length 5 cm and 3.5 cm.

Alternate Method

To construct a rectangle $ABCD$ whose adjacent sides are of lengths 5 cm and 3.5 cm, use the following steps

(i) Draw a line segment BC of length 5 cm.
(ii) Now, draw an $\angle XBC = 90°$ at point B of line segment BC.
(iii) Cut a line segment $AB = 3.5$ cm from the ray BX and join AC.
(iv) Now, from A, point D is at a distance of 5 cm. So, having A as centre draw an arc of radius 5 cm.

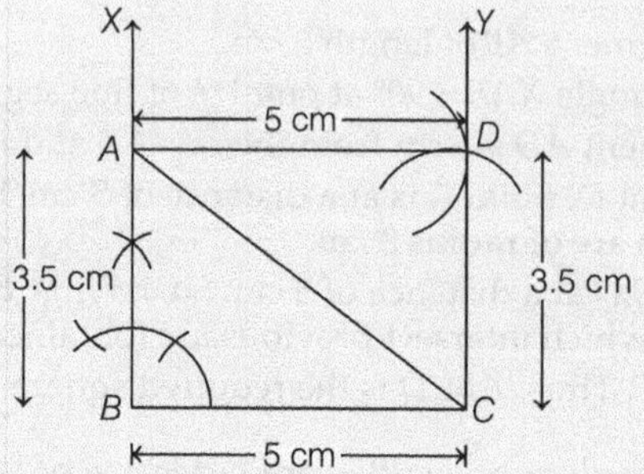

(v) From point *C*, point *D* is at a distance of 3.5 cm. So, having *C* as centre draw an arc of radius 3.5 cm which intersect previous arc (obtained in step iv) at *D*.

(vi) Join *AD* and *CD*.

Thus, *ABCD* is the required rectangle with adjacent sides of length 5 cm and 3.5 cm.

Q.8 Construct a rhombus whose side is of length 3.4 cm and one of its angles is 45°.

Ans. We know that in rhombus all sides are equal. To construct a rhombus whose side is of length 3.4 cm and one of its angle is 45°, use the following steps

(i) Draw a line segment *AB* of length 3.4 cm.

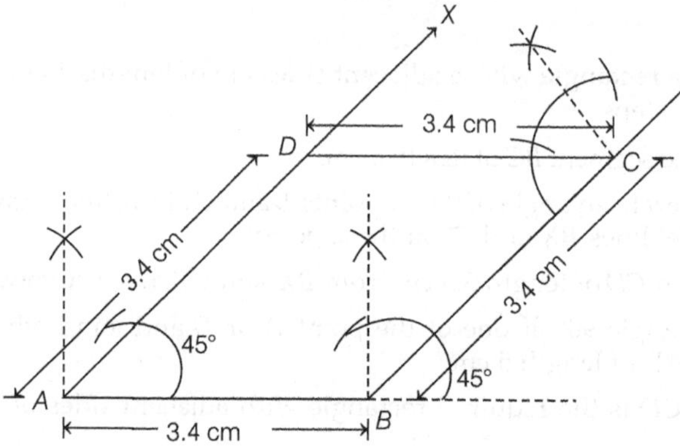

(ii) Now, generate an angle 45° at both ends *A* and *B* of line segment *AB* and plot the parallel lines *AX* and *BY*.

(iii) Cut *AD* and *BC* of length 3.4 cm from *AX* and *BY*, respectively.

(iv) Draw an angle of 45° at one of the point *D* or *C* and join both points by a line segment *DC* of length 3.4 cm and parallel to *AB*.

Thus, *ABCD* is the required rhombus whose side is of length 3.4 cm and one of its angle is 45°.

Alternate Method

To construct a rhombus whose side is of length 3.4 cm and one of its angle is 45°, use the following steps.

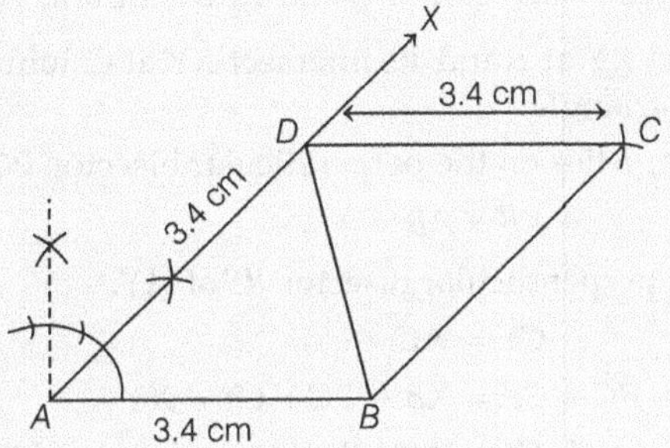

(i) Draw a line segment *AB* of length 3.4 cm.
(ii) Now, draw an angle $XAB = 45°$ at point *A* of line segment *AB*.
(iii) Cut a line segment $AD = 3.4$ cm from the ray *AX* and join *BD*.
(iv) Now, from point *D*, point *C* is at a distance of 3.4 cm. So, having *D* as centre draw an arc of radius 3.4 cm.
(v) From point *B*, point *C* is at distance of 3.4 cm. So, having *B* as centre draw an arc of radius 3.4 cm which intersect previous arc (obtained in step iv) at *C*.
(vi) Join *CD* and *BC*.

Thus, *ABCD* is required rhombus whose side is of length 3.4 cm and one of its angle is 45°.

Long Answer Type Questions

Construct each of the following and give justification

Q.1 A triangle if its perimeter is 10.4 cm and two angles are 45° and 120°.

Ans. Let *ABC* be a triangle. Then, given perimeter = 10.4 cm *i.e.*, $AB + BC + CA = 10.4$ cm and two angles are 45° and 120°. Let $\angle B = 45°$ and $\angle C = 120°$

Now, to construct the ΔABC use the following steps.

(i) Draw a line segment say *XY* and equal to perimeter *i.e.*, $AB + BC + CA = 10.4$ cm.

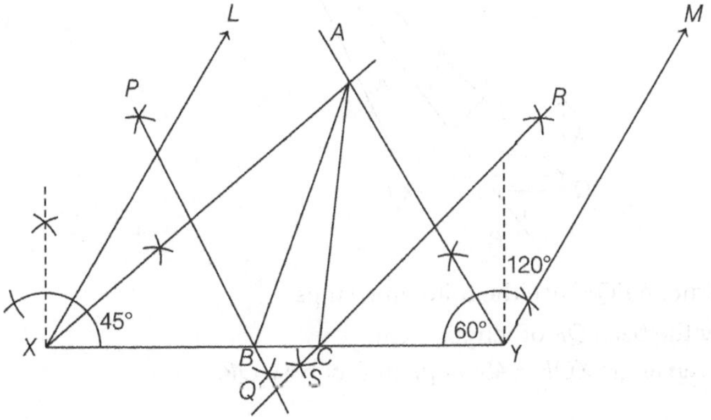

(ii) Make angle $\angle LXY = \angle B = 45°$ and $\angle MYX = \angle C = 120°$.

(iii) Bisect $\angle LXY$ and $\angle MYX$ and let these bisectors intersect at a point A (say).

(iv) Draw perpendicular bisectors PQ and RS of AX and AY, respectively.

(v) Let PQ intersect XY at B and RS intersect XY at C. Join AB and AC. Thus, ΔABC is the required triangle.

Justification Since, B lies on the perpendicular bisector PQ of AX.

$\therefore \quad XB = AB$

Since, C lies on the perpendicular bisector RS of AY.

$\therefore \quad CY = AC$

Thus, $AB + BC + CA = XB + BC + CY = XY$

Again, $\angle BAX = \angle AXB$ $\quad$ [$\because$ in ΔAXB, $AB = XB$] ...(i)

Also, $\angle ABC = \angle BAX + \angle AXB$

[$\because \angle ABC$ is an exterior angle of ΔAXB]

$= \angle AXB + \angle AXB$ $\quad$ [from Eq. (i)]

$= 2\angle AXB = \angle LXY$ $\quad$ [$\because$ AX is a bisector of $\angle LXB$]

Also, $\angle CAY = \angle AYC$ $\quad$ [$\because$ in ΔAYC, $AC = CY$]

$\therefore \quad \angle ACB = \angle CAY + \angle AYC$

[$\because \angle ACB$ is an exterior angle of ΔAYC]

$= \angle CAY + \angle CAY$

$= 2\angle CAY = \angle MYX$ $\quad$ [$\because$ AY is a bisector of $\angle MYX$]

Thus, our construction is justified.

Q.2 A triangle PQR, given that $QR = 3$ cm, $\angle PQR = 45°$ and $QP - PR = 2$ cm.

Ans. Given, in ΔPQR, $QR = 3$cm,

$$\angle PQR = 45° \text{ and } QP - PR = 2 \text{ cm}$$

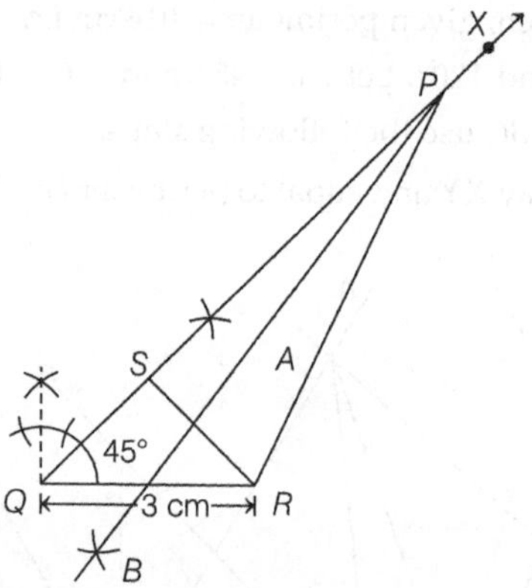

To construct ΔPQR, use the following steps.

(i) Draw the base QR of length 3 cm.

(ii) Make an angle $XQR = 45°$ at point Q of base QR.

(iii) Cut the line segment $QS = QP - PR = 2$ cm from the ray QX.

(iv) Join SR and draw the perpendicular bisector of SR, say AB.

(v) Let bisector AB intersect QX at P. Join PR

Thus, ΔPQR is the required triangle.

Justification

Base QR and $\angle PQR$ are drawn as given.

Since, the point P lies on the perpendicular bisector of SR.

$\therefore \quad PS = PR$

Now, $\quad QS = PQ - PS = PQ - PR$

Thus, our construction is justified.

Q.3 **A right triangle when one side is 3.5 cm and sum of other sides and the hypotenuse is 5.5 cm.**

Ans. Let given right triangle be ABC.

Then, given $BC = 3.5$ cm, $\angle B = 90°$ and sum of other side and hypotenuse *i.e.*, $AB + AC = 5.5$ cm.

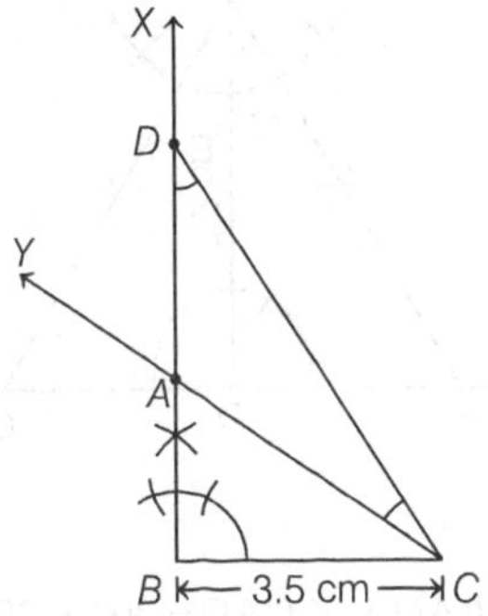

To construct ΔABC use the following steps

(i) Draw the base $BC = 3.5$ cm

(ii) Make an angle $XBC = 90°$ at the point B of base BC.

(iii) Cut the line segment BD equal to $AB + AC$ *i.e.*, 5.5 cm from the ray XB.

(iv) Join DC and make an $\angle DCY$ equal to $\angle BDC$.

(v) Let Y intersect BX at A.

Thus, ΔABC is the required triangle.

Justification

Base BC and $\angle B$ are drawn as given.

In ΔACD, $\quad \angle ACD = \angle ADC$ [by construction]

$\therefore \quad AD = AC$ ...(i)

[$\because$ sides opposite to equal angles are equal]

Now, $\quad AB = BD - AD = BD - AC$ [from Eq. (i)]

$\Rightarrow \quad BD = AB + AC$

Thus, our construction is justified.

Q.4 An equilateral triangle, if its altitude is 3.2 cm.

Ans. We know that in an equilateral triangle all sides are equal and all angles are equal *i.e.*, each angle is of 60°.

Given, altitude of an equilateral triangle say ABC is 3.2 cm. To construct the ΔABC use the following steps.

(i) Draw a line PQ.
(ii) Take a point D on PQ and draw a ray $DE \perp PQ$.
(iii) Cut the line segment AD of length 3.2 cm from DE.
(iv) Make angles equal to 30° at A on both sides of AD say $\angle CAD$ and $\angle BAD$, where B and C lie on PQ.
(v) Cut the line segment DC from PQ such that $DC = BD$
(vi) Join AC.

Thus, ΔABC is the required triangle.

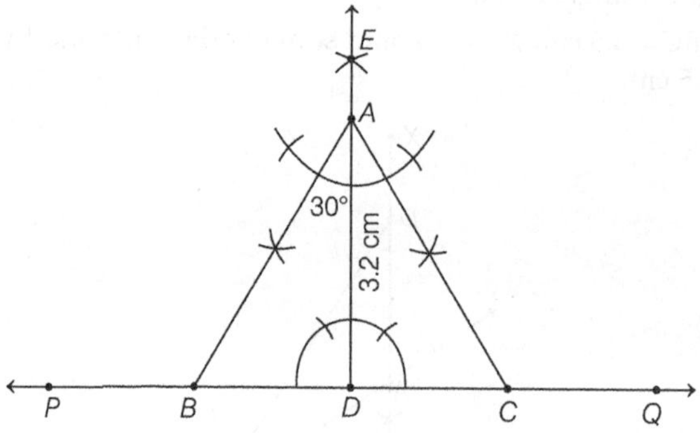

Justification

Here, $\angle A = \angle BAD + \angle CAD = 30° + 30° = 60°$.

Also, $AD \perp BC$

$\therefore$ $\angle ADB = 90°$.

In ΔABD, $\angle BAD + \angle DBA + \angle BDA = 180°$ [angle sum property]

$30° + 90° + \angle DBA = 180°$ [$\angle BAD = 30°$, by construction]

$\angle DBA = 60°$

Similary, $\angle DCA = 60°$

Thus, $\angle A = \angle B = \angle C = 60°$

Hence, ΔABC is an equilateral triangle.

Q.5 A rhombus whose diagonals are 4 cm and 6 cm in lengths.

Ans. We know that all sides of a rhombus are equal and the diagonals of a rhombus are perpendicular bisectors of one another. So, to construct a rhombus whose diagonals are 4 cm and 6 cm use the following steps.

(i) Draw the diagonal say $AC = 4$ cm
(ii) Taking A and C as centres and radius more than $\frac{1}{2}AC$ draw arcs on both sides of the line segment AC which intersect each other.

(iii) Cut both arcs intersect each other at P and Q, then join PQ.
(iv) Let PQ intersect AC at the point O. Thus, PQ is perpendicular bisector of AC.
(v) Cut off 3 cm lengths from OP and OQ, then we get points B and D.
(vi) Now, join AB, BC, CD, and DA.

Thus, $ABCD$ is the required rhombus.

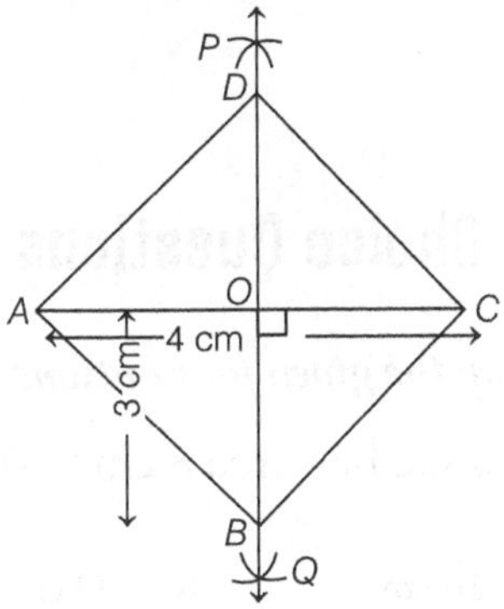

Justification

Since, D and B lie on perpendicular bisector of AC.

$$DA = DC \text{ and } BA = BC \quad \text{...(i)}$$

[∵ every point on perpendicular bisector of line segment is equidistant from end points of line segment]

Now, $\angle DOC = 90°$

Also, $OD = OB = 3$ cm

Thus, AC is perpendicular bisector of BD.

$$CD = CB \quad \text{...(ii)}$$

From Eqs. (i) and (ii), we get $AB = BC = CD = DA$

Hence, $ABCD$ is a rhombus.

Chapter

12 Heron's Formula

Multiple Choice Questions (MCQs)

Choose the correct answer from the given four options in the following questions:

***Q.1** An isosceles right triangle has area 8 cm^2. The length of its hypotenuse is

(a) $\sqrt{32}$ cm (b) $\sqrt{16}$ cm (c) $\sqrt{48}$ cm (d) $\sqrt{24}$ cm

Ans. *(a)* Given, area of an isosceles right triangle = 8cm^2

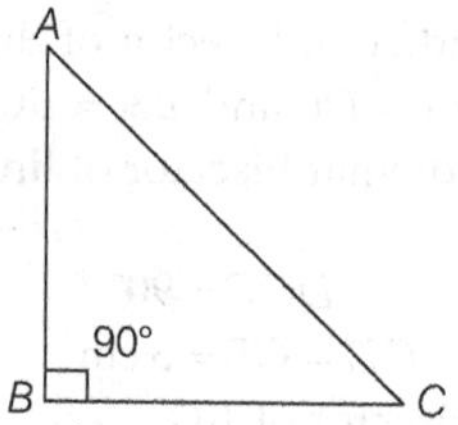

Area of an isosceles triangle $= \frac{1}{2}$ (Base × Height)

$\Rightarrow \quad 8 = \frac{1}{2}$ (Base × Base)

[∵ base = height, as the triangle is an isosceles triangle]

$\Rightarrow \quad (\text{Base})^2 = 16 \Rightarrow \text{Base} = 4$ cm

$\Rightarrow \quad AB = BC = 4$ cm

In ΔABC, using Pythagoras theorem,

$$AC^2 = AB^2 + BC^2 = 4^2 + 4^2 = 16 + 16$$

$\Rightarrow \quad AC^2 = 32 \Rightarrow AC = \sqrt{32}$ cm

[take positive square root because length is always positive]

Hence, the length of its hypotenuse is $\sqrt{32}$ cm .

Q.2 The perimeter of an equilateral triangle is 60 m. The area is

(a) $10\sqrt{3}$ m^2 (b) $15\sqrt{3}$ m^2 (c) $20\sqrt{3}$ m^2 (d) $100\sqrt{3}$ m^2

Thinking Process

(i) First, determine the side of an equilateral triangle by using formula, perimeter = 3 × side .

(ii) Further, find the semi-perimeter of the triangle and then determine the area of the triangle by using Heron's formula.

(*) Topics related to these question have been removed from latest NCERT.

Ans. *(d)* Let each side of an equilateral triangle be x.

$\because$ Perimeter of an equilateral triangle = 60 m

$$\Rightarrow \quad 3x = 60 \Rightarrow x = 20 \text{ m}$$

Semi-perimeter of triangle $= \frac{60}{2} = 30$ m

$\therefore$ Area of triangle $= \sqrt{s(s-a)(s-b)(s-c)}$ [by Heron's formula]

$$= \sqrt{30\,(30-20)\,(30-20)\,(30-20)}$$
$$= \sqrt{30 \times 10 \times 10 \times 10} = \sqrt{10 \times 3 \times 10 \times 10 \times 10} = 100\sqrt{3} \text{ m}^2$$

Alternate Method

Let each side of an equilateral triangle be x.

Then, perimeter of an equilateral triangle = 60 m

$$\therefore \quad 3x = 60 \Rightarrow x = \frac{60}{3} = 20 \text{ m}$$

$\therefore$ Area of an equilateral triangle $= \frac{\sqrt{3}}{4}(\text{Side})^2 = \frac{\sqrt{3}}{4} \times 20 \times 20 = 100\sqrt{3} \text{ m}^2$

Thus, the area of triangle is $100\sqrt{3}$ m^2.

Q.3 The sides of a triangle are 56 cm, 60 cm and 52 cm long. Then, the area of the triangle is

(a) 1322 cm^2 (b) 1311 cm^2 (c) 1344 cm^2 (d) 1392 cm^2

Thinking Process

(i) First, determine the semi-perimeter of a triangle by using the formula, $s = \frac{a+b+c}{2}$.

(ii) Further, determine the area of triangle by using Heron's formula, as $\sqrt{s(s-a)(s-b)(s-c)}$.

Ans. *(c)* Let the three sides of a triangle are $a = 56$ cm, $b = 60$ cm and $c = 52$ cm.

Then, semi-perimeter of a triangle, $s = \frac{a+b+c}{2} = \frac{56+60+52}{2} = \frac{168}{2} = 84$ cm

$\therefore$ Area of a triangle $= \sqrt{s(s-a)(s-b)(s-c)}$ [by Heron's formula]

$$= \sqrt{84\,(84-56)\,(84-60)\,(84-52)} = \sqrt{84 \times 28 \times 24 \times 32}$$
$$= \sqrt{(4 \times 7 \times 3) \times (4 \times 7) \times (4 \times 2 \times 3) \times (4 \times 4 \times 2)}$$
$$= \sqrt{(4)^6 \times (7)^2 \times (3)^2} = (4)^3 \times 7 \times 3 = 1344 \text{ cm}^2$$

Hence, the area of the triangle is 1344 cm^2.

Q.4 The area of an equilateral triangle with side $2\sqrt{3}$ cm is

(a) 5.196 cm^2 (b) 0.866 cm^2 (c) 3.496 cm^2 (d) 1.732 cm^2

Ans. *(a)* Given, side of an equilateral triangle = $2\sqrt{3}$ cm

Semi-perimeter of triangle $= \frac{2\sqrt{3} + 2\sqrt{3} + 2\sqrt{3}}{2} = \frac{6\sqrt{3}}{2} = 3\sqrt{3}$ cm

$\therefore$ Area of triangle $= \sqrt{3\sqrt{3}\,(3\sqrt{3} - 2\sqrt{3})\,(3\sqrt{3} - 2\sqrt{3})\,(3\sqrt{3} - 2\sqrt{3})}$

[by Heron's formula]

$$= \sqrt{3\sqrt{3} \times \sqrt{3} \times \sqrt{3} \times \sqrt{3}} = 3\sqrt{3} = 3 \times 1.732 = 5.196 \text{ cm}^2$$

Alternate Method

Given, side of an equilateral triangle is $2\sqrt{3}$ cm.

$\therefore$ Area of an equilateral triangle $= \frac{\sqrt{3}}{4}(\text{Side})^2$

$$= \frac{\sqrt{3}}{4}(2\sqrt{3})^2 = \frac{\sqrt{3}}{4} \times 4 \times 3$$

$$= 3\sqrt{3} = 3 \times 1.732 = 5.196 \text{ cm}^2$$

Hence, the area of an equilateral triangle is 5.196 cm^2.

Mistake Alert! *Students may incorrectly use formula, area of an equilateral triangle as* $\frac{4}{\sqrt{3}}(\textit{Side})^2$ *instead of* $\frac{\sqrt{3}}{4}(\textit{Side})^2$.

Q.5 The length of each side of an equilateral triangle having an area of $9\sqrt{3}$ cm^2 is

(a) 8 cm (b) 36 cm (c) 4 cm (d) 6 cm

Ans. *(d)* Let 'a' be the length of each side of the equilateral triangle.

$\therefore$ Semi-perimeter of triangle $= \frac{a+a+a}{2} = \frac{3a}{2}$

$\because$ Area of triangle $= 9\sqrt{3}$ cm^2 [Given]

$$\Rightarrow \sqrt{\frac{3a}{2}\left(\frac{3a}{2}-a\right)\left(\frac{3a}{2}-a\right)\left(\frac{3a}{2}-a\right)} = 9\sqrt{3} \quad \text{[by Heron's formula]}$$

$$\Rightarrow \sqrt{\frac{3a}{2} \times \frac{a}{2} \times \frac{a}{2} \times \frac{a}{2}} = 9\sqrt{3} \Rightarrow \frac{\sqrt{3}}{4}a^2 = 9\sqrt{3}$$

$$\Rightarrow a^2 = 36 \Rightarrow a = 6 \text{ cm}$$

Alternate Method

Given, area of an equilateral triangle $= 9\sqrt{3}$ cm^2

$\because$ Area of an equilateral triangle $= \frac{\sqrt{3}}{4}(\text{Side})^2$

$$\Rightarrow \frac{\sqrt{3}}{4}(\text{Side})^2 = 9\sqrt{3}$$

$$\Rightarrow (\text{Side})^2 = 36$$

$$\therefore \text{Side} = 6 \text{ cm}$$

[take positive square root because length is always positive]

Hence, the length of an equilateral triangle is 6 cm.

Q.6 If the area of an equilateral triangle is $16\sqrt{3}$ cm^2, then the perimeter of the triangle is

(a) 48 cm (b) 24 cm (c) 12 cm (d) 36 cm

Ans. *(b)* Let 'a' be the length of each side of the equilateral triangle.

Semi-perimeter of triangle $= \frac{a+a+a}{2} = \frac{3a}{2}$

$\because$ Area of triangle $= 16\sqrt{3}$ cm^2

$$\Rightarrow \quad \sqrt{\frac{3a}{2}\left(\frac{3a}{2}-a\right)\left(\frac{3a}{2}-a\right)\left(\frac{3a}{2}-a\right)} = 16\sqrt{3} \quad \text{[by Heron's formula]}$$

$$\Rightarrow \quad \sqrt{\frac{3a}{2} \times \frac{a}{2} \times \frac{a}{2} \times \frac{a}{2}} = 16\sqrt{3}$$

$$\Rightarrow \quad \frac{\sqrt{3}}{4} a^2 = 16\sqrt{3}$$

$$\Rightarrow \quad a^2 = 64 \Rightarrow a = 8 \text{ cm}$$

$\therefore$ Perimeter of equilateral triangle $= 3a = 3 \times 8 = 24$ cm

Q.7 The sides of a triangle are 35 cm, 54 cm and 61 cm, respectively. The length of its longest altitude

(a) $16\sqrt{5}$ cm (b) $10\sqrt{5}$ cm (c) $24\sqrt{5}$ cm (d) 28 cm

Thinking Process

(i) First, determine the semi-perimeter, s and then determine the area of triangle by using Heron's formula.

(ii) For the longest altitude, take base as the smallest side. Apply the formula, Area $= \frac{1}{2} \times$ Base $\times$ Altitude

(iii) Equate the area obtained by using the two formulae and obtain the required altitude.

Ans. *(c)* Let ABC be a triangle in which sides are $AB = a = 35$ cm, $BC = b = 54$ cm, $CA = c = 61$ cm and CD is the altitude.

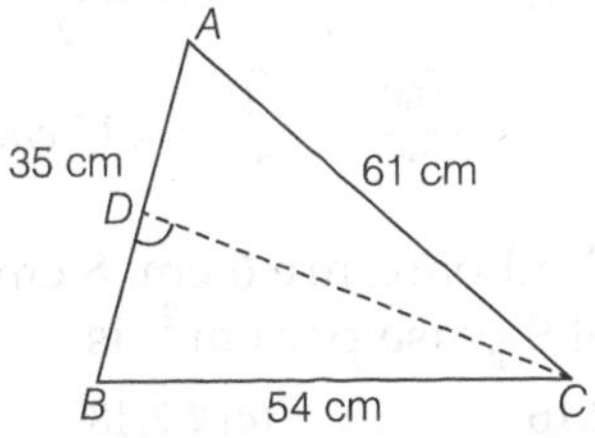

Now, semi-perimeter of a triangle,

$$s = \frac{a+b+c}{2} = \frac{35+54+61}{2} = \frac{150}{2} = 75 \text{ cm}$$

$$\left[\because \text{semi-perimeter}, s = \frac{a+b+c}{2}\right]$$

$\because$ Area of $\Delta ABC = \sqrt{s(s-a)(s-b)(s-c)}$ [by Heron's formula]

$$= \sqrt{75(75-35)(75-54)(75-61)} = \sqrt{75 \times 40 \times 21 \times 14}$$

$$= \sqrt{25 \times 3 \times 4 \times 2 \times 5 \times 7 \times 3 \times 7 \times 2}$$

$$= 5 \times 2 \times 2 \times 3 \times 7\sqrt{5} = 420\sqrt{5} \text{ cm}^2$$

Also, area of $\Delta ABC = \frac{1}{2} \times AB \times CD$

[Since, the smallest side is AB will. So, longest altitude will be CD]

$$\Rightarrow \quad \frac{1}{2} \times 35 \times CD = 420\sqrt{5} \Rightarrow CD = \frac{420 \times 2\sqrt{5}}{35}$$

$$\therefore \quad CD = 24\sqrt{5}$$

Hence, the length of altitude is $24\sqrt{5}$ cm.

Q.8 The area of an isosceles triangle having base 2 cm and the length of one of the equal sides 4 cm, is

(a) $\sqrt{15}\text{ cm}^2$ (b) $\sqrt{\frac{15}{2}}\text{ cm}^2$

(c) $2\sqrt{15}\text{ cm}^2$ (d) $4\sqrt{15}\text{ cm}^2$

Ans. *(a)* Let the sides of an isosceles triangle be

$$a = 2\text{ cm},\ b = 4\text{ cm and } c = 4\text{ cm}$$

Semi-perimeter of triangle,

$$s = \frac{a+b+c}{2} = \frac{2+4+4}{2} = \frac{10}{2} = 5\text{ cm}$$

$\therefore$ Area of triangle $= \sqrt{s(s-a)(s-b)(s-c)}$ [by Heron's formula]

$$= \sqrt{5(5-2)(5-4)(5-4)}$$

$$= \sqrt{5 \times 3 \times 1 \times 1} = \sqrt{15}\text{ cm}^2$$

Alternate Method

We know that area of an isosceles triangle $= \frac{a}{4}\sqrt{4b^2 - a^2}$

Where, b is the length of equal sides and a is the length of the base.

Let the length of sides of the triangle be $b = 4$ cm and $a = 2$ cm

$\therefore$ Area of an isosceles triangle $= \frac{2\sqrt{4(4)^2 - 4}}{4} = \frac{\sqrt{64-4}}{2}$

$$= \frac{\sqrt{60}}{2} = \frac{2\sqrt{15}}{2} = \sqrt{15}\text{ cm}^2$$

Q.9 The edges of a triangular board are 6 cm, 8 cm and 10 cm. The cost of painting it at the rate of 9 paise per cm^2 is

(a) ₹ 2.00 (b) ₹ 2.16 (c) ₹ 2.48 (d) ₹ 3.00

Ans. *(b)* Let the edges of a triangular board are $a = 6$ cm, $b = 8$ cm and $c = 10$ cm.
Now, semi-perimeter of a triangular board,

$$s = \frac{a+b+c}{2} = \frac{6+8+10}{2} = \frac{24}{2} = 12\text{ cm}$$

Now, area of a triangular board $= \sqrt{s(s-a)(s-b)(s-c)}$ [by Heron's formula]

$$= \sqrt{12(12-6)(12-8)(12-10)}$$

$$= \sqrt{12 \times 6 \times 4 \times 2}$$

$$= \sqrt{(12)^2 \times (2)^2} = 12 \times 2 = 24\text{ cm}^2$$

Since, the cost of painting for area 1 cm^2 = ₹ 0.09

$\therefore$ Cost of painting for area 24 cm^2 = 0.09 × 24 = ₹ 2.16

Hence, the cost of painting a triangular board is ₹ 2.16.

Mistake Alert! *If students use Heron's formula, they may incorrectly assume the semi-perimeter to be* $\frac{a+b+c}{3}$ *instead of* $\frac{a+b+c}{2}$.

Short Answer Questions with Reasoning

Write True or False and justify your answer in each questions.

***Q.1** The area of a triangle with base 4 cm and height 6 cm is 24 cm^2.

Ans. *False*

We know that, area of a triangle $= \frac{1}{2}$ (Base × Height)

Here, base = 4 cm and height = 6 cm

$\therefore$ Area of a triangle $= \frac{1}{2} \times 4 \times 6 = 12 \text{ cm}^2$

Q.2 The area of a ΔABC is 8 cm^2 in which $AB = AC = 4$ cm and $\angle A = 90°$.

Ans. *True*

We have, ABC is a right angled triangle at A whose sides are given $AB = AC = 4$ cm.

In ΔABC,

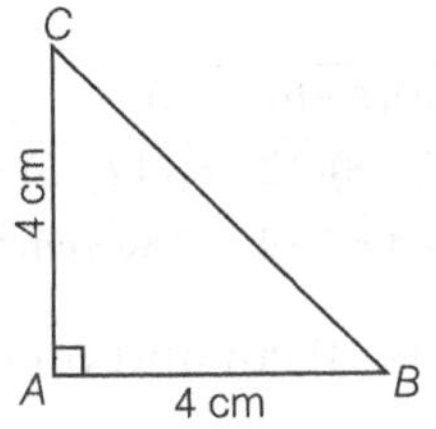

$$BC^2 = AB^2 + AC^2 \quad \text{[by Pythagorus theorem]}$$
$$= 4^2 + 4^2 = 16 + 16 = 32$$
$$\Rightarrow \quad BC = 4\sqrt{2} \text{ cm}$$

Now, semi-perimeter of triangle

$$= \frac{4 + 4 + 4\sqrt{2}}{2} = \frac{8 + 4\sqrt{2}}{2} = 4 + 2\sqrt{2}$$

$$\therefore \text{Area of triangle} = \sqrt{(4 + 2\sqrt{2})(4 + 2\sqrt{2} - 4)(4 + 2\sqrt{2} - 4)(4 + 2\sqrt{2} - 4\sqrt{2})}$$

[by Heron's formula]

$$= \sqrt{(4 + 2\sqrt{2}) \times 2\sqrt{2} \times 2\sqrt{2} \times (4 - 2\sqrt{2})}$$
$$= 2\sqrt{2 \times [(4)^2 - (2\sqrt{2})^2]} = 2\sqrt{16} = 2 \times 4 = 8 \text{ cm}^2$$

Q.3 The area of the isosceles triangle is $\frac{5}{4}\sqrt{11}$ cm^2, if the perimeter is 11 cm and the base is 5 cm.

- **Concept Insight** If a, b and c be the sides of a triangle, then area of triangle is $\sqrt{s(s-a)(s-b)(s-c)}$, where s is semi-perimeter of the triangle.

Ans. *True*

Let equal sides of an isosceles triangle be b.

$\therefore$ Perimeter of a triangle $= b + b + 5$

(*) Topics related to these question have been removed from latest NCERT.

$\therefore \quad 11 = 2b + 5$

$\Rightarrow \quad 2b = 11 - 5 \Rightarrow 2b = 6$

$\Rightarrow \quad b = \frac{6}{2} = 3$ cm

Now, semi-perimeter of triangle $= \frac{11}{2} = 5.5$ cm

$\therefore$ Area of triangle $= \sqrt{5.5\,(5.5-5)\,(5.5-3)\,(5.5-3)}$ [by Heron's formula]

$$= \sqrt{5.5 \times 0.5 \times 2.5 \times 2.5}$$

$$= 2.5\sqrt{\frac{55}{10} \times \frac{5}{10}} = \frac{25}{10}\sqrt{\frac{11}{4}} = \frac{5\sqrt{11}}{4} \text{ cm}^2$$

Q.4 The area of the equilateral triangle is $20\sqrt{3}$ cm^2 whose each side is 8 cm.

Ans. *False*

Given, side of an equilateral triangle is 8 cm *i.e.*, $a = 8, b = 8$ and $c = 8$.

$\therefore$ Semi-perimeter, $s = \frac{a+b+c}{2} = \frac{8+8+8}{2} = \frac{24}{2} = 12$ cm

Now, area of triangle

$$= \sqrt{s(s-a)(s-b)(s-c)}$$ [by Heron's formula]

$$= \sqrt{12(12-8)(12-8)(12-8)} = \sqrt{12 \times 4 \times 4 \times 4}$$

$$= \sqrt{4 \times 3 \times 4 \times 4 \times 4} = 16\sqrt{3} \text{ cm}^2$$

*** Q.5** If the side of a rhombus is 10 cm and one diagonal is 16 cm, the area of the rhombus is 96 cm^2.

● **Concept Insight** Area of rhombus $= \frac{1}{2} \times$ Product of diagonals.

Ans. *True*

Given, side of a rhombus *PQRS* is 10 cm and one of the diagonal is 16 cm.

i.e., $PQ = QR = RS = SP = 10$ cm and $PR = 16$ cm

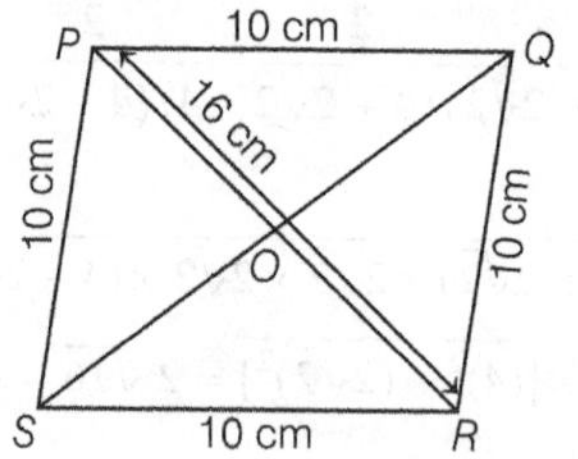

In ΔPOQ, $PQ^2 = OP^2 + OQ^2$ [by Pythagoras theorem]

[since, the diagonals of rhombus bisect each other at 90°]

$\Rightarrow \quad OQ^2 = PQ^2 - OP^2 = (10)^2 - (8)^2$

$\Rightarrow \quad OQ^2 = 100 - 64 = 36$

$\Rightarrow \quad OQ = 6$ cm

[take positive square root because length is always positive]

$\therefore \quad SQ = 2 \times OP = 2 \times 6 = 12$ cm

(*) Topics related to these question have been removed from latest NCERT.

Thus, area of the rhombus $= \frac{1}{2}$ (Product of diagonals)

$$= \frac{1}{2}(QS \times PR) = \frac{1}{2} \times 12 \times 16 = 96 \text{ cm}^2$$

*** Q.6** The base and the corresponding altitude of a parallelogram are 10 cm and 3.5 cm, respectively. The area of the parallelogram is 30 cm^2.

Ans. *False*

Given, parallelogram in which base = 10 cm and altitude = 3.5 cm

$\therefore$ Area of a parallelogram = Base × Altitude = $10 \times 3.5 = 35 \text{ cm}^2$

*** Q.7** The area of a regular hexagon of side a is the sum of the areas of the five equilateral triangles with side a.

Ans. *False*

We know that regular hexagon is divided into six equilateral triangles.

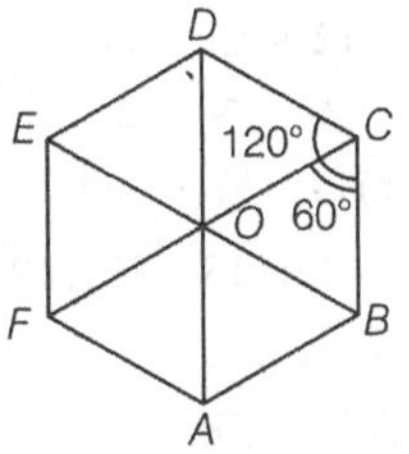

$\therefore$ Area of regular hexagon of side a = Sum of area of the six equilateral triangles

Q.8 The cost of levelling the ground in the form of a triangle having the sides 51 m, 37m and 20 m at the rate of ₹ 3 per m^2 is ₹ 918.

Ans. *True*

Let sides of a triangle be $a = 51$ m, $b = 37$ m and $c = 20$ m

Now, semi-perimeter of triangle,

$$s = \frac{a+b+c}{2} = \frac{51+37+20}{2} = \frac{108}{2} = 54 \text{ m}$$

$\therefore$ Area of a triangle $= \sqrt{s(s-a)(s-b)(s-c)}$ [by Heron's formula]

$$= \sqrt{54(54-51)(54-37)(54-20)}$$

$$= \sqrt{54 \times 3 \times 17 \times 34}$$

$$= \sqrt{9 \times 3 \times 2 \times 3 \times 17 \times 17 \times 2}$$

$$= 3 \times 3 \times 2 \times 17 = 306 \text{ m}^2$$

$\because$ Cost of levelling the ground of area 1 m^2 = ₹ 3

$\therefore$ Cost of levelling the ground of area 306 m^2 = 3×306 = ₹ 918

Mistake Alert! *After computing $s(s-a)(s-b)(s-c)$, students sometimes forget to take the square root.*

(*) Topics related to these question have been removed from latest NCERT.

Q.9 In a triangle, the sides are given as 11 cm, 12 cm and 13 cm. The length of the altitude is 10.25 cm corresponding to the side having 12 cm.

Ans. *True*

Let the sides of a triangle be $a = 11\text{cm}, b = 12\text{ cm}$ and $c = 13\text{ cm}$.

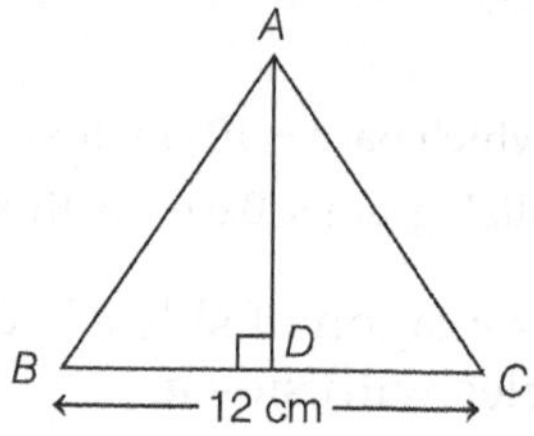

Now, semi-perimeter, $s = \dfrac{a+b+c}{2}$

$= \dfrac{11+12+13}{2} = \dfrac{36}{2} = 18\text{ cm}$

$\therefore$ Area of a triangle $= \sqrt{s(s-a)(s-b)(s-c)}$ [by Heron's formula]

$= \sqrt{18(18-11)(18-12)(18-13)}$

$= \sqrt{18 \times 7 \times 6 \times 5}$

$= \sqrt{3 \times 6 \times 7 \times 6 \times 5}$

$= 6\sqrt{3 \times 7 \times 5}$

$= 6\sqrt{105} = 6 \times 10.25$

$= 61.5\text{ cm}^2$

Also, area of $\Delta ABC = \dfrac{1}{2} \times BC \times AD$ $\left[\because \text{area of triangle} = \dfrac{1}{2}(\text{base} \times \text{height})\right]$

$\Rightarrow \quad 61.5 = \dfrac{1}{2} \times 12 \times AD$

$\Rightarrow \quad AD = 10.25\text{ cm}$

Thus, length of altitude is 10.25 cm.

Short Answer Type Questions

Q.1. Find the cost of laying grass in a triangular field of sides 50 m, 65 m and 65 m at the rate of ₹ 7 per m^2.

Thinking Process

(i) First, determine the semi-perimeter's by using formula $s = \dfrac{a+b+c}{2}$ and then, determine the area of a triangle by using Heron's formula $\sqrt{s(s-a)(s-b)(s-c)}$

(ii) Cost of laying grass = Area of field (in m^2)× (Cost of laying grass per 1 m^2)

Ans. Let ABC is a triangular field of sides

$$AB = a = 50 \text{ m}, \; BC = b = 65 \text{ m} \text{ and } CA = c = 65 \text{ m}.$$

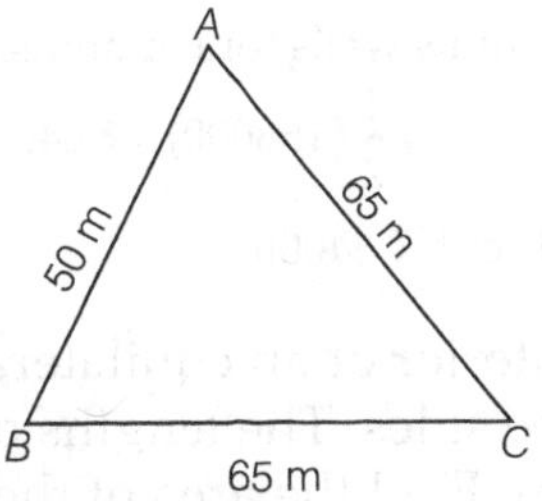

$\therefore$ Semi-perimeter of triangular field,

$$s = \frac{a+b+c}{2} = \frac{50+65+65}{2} = \frac{180}{2}$$

$\Rightarrow$ $s = 90$ m

$\therefore$ Area of a triangular field

$$= \sqrt{s(s-a)(s-b)(s-c)} \quad \text{[by Heron's formula]}$$
$$= \sqrt{90(90-50)(90-65)(90-65)}$$
$$= \sqrt{90 \times 40 \times 25 \times 25}$$
$$= 3 \times 2 \times 10 \times 25$$
$$= 1500 \text{ m}^2$$

$\because$ Cost of laying grass of area 1 m^2 = ₹ 7

$\therefore$ Cost of laying grass of area 1500 m^2 = 7×1500 = ₹ 10500

Hence, the cost of laying grass in a triangular field is ₹ 10500.

Q.2 The triangular side walls of a flyover have been used for advertisements. The sides of the walls are 13m, 14m and 15m. The advertisements yield an earning of ₹ 2000 per m^2 a year. A company hired one of its walls for 6 months. How much rent did it pay?

- **Concept Insight** Total advertisements yield earning in 1 year = Total area × Rate of advertisements yield

  $\therefore$ Rent paid by company for 6 months = $\dfrac{\text{Total advertisement yield earning in 1 year}}{2}$

Ans. Let the sides of a triangular walls are $a = 13$ m, $b = 14$ m and $c = 15$ m

$\therefore$ Semi-perimeter of triangular side wall, $s = \dfrac{a+b+c}{2} = \dfrac{13+14+15}{2} = \dfrac{42}{2} = 21$ m

$\therefore$ Area of triangular side wall $= \sqrt{s(s-a)(s-b)(s-c)}$ [by Heron's formula]

$$= \sqrt{21(21-13)(21-14)(21-15)}$$
$$= \sqrt{21 \times 8 \times 7 \times 6}$$
$$= \sqrt{21 \times 4 \times 2 \times 7 \times 3 \times 2}$$
$$= \sqrt{(21)^2 \times (4)^2}$$
$$= 21 \times 4 = 84 \text{ m}^2$$

Since, the advertisement yield earning in 1 year for area $1 m^2 = ₹\ 2000$

$\therefore$ Advertisement yield earning per year for area $84\ m^2 = 2000 \times 84 = ₹\ 168000$

As the company hired one of its walls for 6 months, therefore company pay the rent

$$= \frac{1}{2}(168000) = ₹\ 84000$$

Hence, the company paid rent ₹ 84000.

Q.3 From a point in the interior of an equilateral triangle, perpendiculars are drawn on the three sides. The lengths of the perpendiculars are 14 cm, 10 cm and 6 cm. Find the area of the triangle.

Thinking Process

(i) From an interior point of a triangle, three triangle will be formed. Determine area of each triangle by using the formula $\frac{1}{2}$ (Base $\times$ Height).

(ii) Determine the area of an equilateral triangle by using the Heron's formula *i.e.*, $\sqrt{s(s-a)(s-b)(s-c)}$.

(iii) Further, equate the area of triangle by Heron's formula and the sum of areas of all three triangles. Simplify it to get the side of the triangle. Hence, find area of the triangle.

Ans. Let ABC be an equilateral triangle, O be the interior point and AQ, BR and PC are the perpendicular drawn from point O.

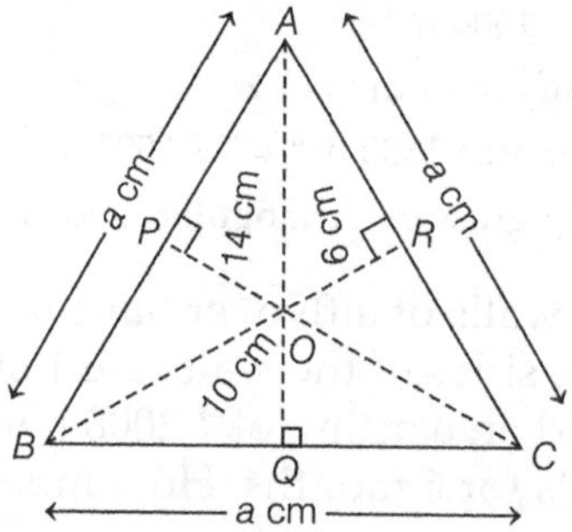

Let sides of an equilateral triangle be a cm.

Area of $\Delta OAB = \frac{1}{2} \times AB \times OP$ $\left[\because \text{area of a triangle} = \frac{1}{2}(\text{base} \times \text{height})\right]$

$= \frac{1}{2} \times a \times 14 = 7a\ cm^2$ ...(i)

Area of $\Delta OBC = \frac{1}{2} \times BC \times OQ$

$= \frac{1}{2} \times a \times 10 = 5a\ cm^2$ ...(ii)

Area of $\Delta OAC = \frac{1}{2} \times AC \times OR$

$= \frac{1}{2} \times a \times 6 = 3a\ cm^2$ ...(iii)

$\therefore$ Area of an equilateral ΔABC = Area of ($\Delta OAB + \Delta OBC + \Delta OAC$)

$= (7a + 5a + 3a) = 15\ a\ cm^2$ ...(iv)

Now, semi-perimeter $(s) = \frac{a + a + a}{2} \Rightarrow s = \frac{3a}{2}$ cm

$$\left[\because \text{semi-perimeter's} = \frac{a+b+c}{2}\right]$$

$\therefore$ Area of an equilateral $\Delta ABC = \sqrt{s(s-a)(s-b)(s-c)}$ [by Heron's formula]

$$= \sqrt{\frac{3a}{2}\left(\frac{3a}{2} - a\right)\left(\frac{3a}{2} - a\right)\left(\frac{3a}{2} - a\right)}$$

$$= \sqrt{\frac{3a}{2} \times \frac{a}{2} \times \frac{a}{2} \times \frac{a}{2}} = \frac{\sqrt{3}}{4} a^2 \quad \ldots(\text{v})$$

From Eqs. (iv) and (v), we get

$$\frac{\sqrt{3}}{4} a^2 = 15a$$

$$\Rightarrow \quad a = \frac{15 \times 4}{\sqrt{3}} \times \frac{\sqrt{3}}{\sqrt{3}} = \frac{60\sqrt{3}}{3} = 20\sqrt{3} \text{ cm}$$

On putting $a = 20\sqrt{3}$ in Eq. (v), we get

$$\therefore \quad \text{Area of } \Delta ABC = \frac{\sqrt{3}}{4}(20\sqrt{3})^2$$

$$= \frac{\sqrt{3}}{4} \times 400 \times 3$$

$$= 300\sqrt{3} \text{ cm}^2$$

Hence, the area of an equilateral triangle is $300\sqrt{3}$ cm^2.

Q.4 The perimeter of an isosceles triangle is 32 cm. The ratio of the equal side to its base is 3 : 2. Find the area of the triangle.

Ans. Let ABC be an isosceles triangle with perimeter 32 cm.

We have, ratio of equal side to its base is 3 : 2.

Let sides of a triangle be $AB = BC = 3x$ and $AC = 2x$

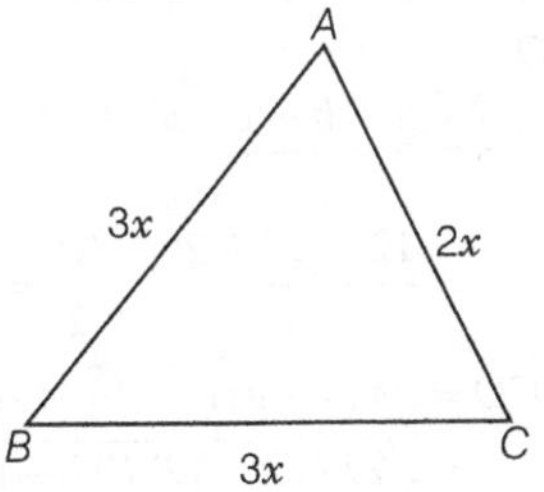

$\because$ Perimeter of a triangle = 32 m

$\Rightarrow \quad 3x + 3x + 2x = 32$

$\Rightarrow \quad 8x = 32$

$\Rightarrow \quad x = 4$

$\therefore \quad AB = BC = 3 \times 4 = 12$ cm

and $\quad AC = 2 \times 4 = 8$ cm

$\therefore$ The sides of triangle are $a = 12$ cm, $b = 12$ cm and $c = 8$ cm

Now, semi-perimeter of an isosceles triangle,

$$s = \frac{a+b+c}{2}$$

$$= \frac{12+12+8}{2} = \frac{32}{2} = 16 \text{ cm}$$

$\therefore$ Area of an isosceles $\Delta ABC = \sqrt{s(s-a)(s-b)(s-c)}$ [by Heron's formula]

$$= \sqrt{16(16-12)(16-12)(16-8)}$$

$$= \sqrt{16 \times 4 \times 4 \times 8}$$

$\Rightarrow$ $= 4 \times 4 \times 2\sqrt{2} = 32\sqrt{2} \text{ cm}^2$

Hence, the area of an isosceles triangle is $32\sqrt{2}$ cm^2.

*** Q.5** Find the area of a parallelogram given in the figure. Also, find the length of the altitude from vertex A on the side DC.

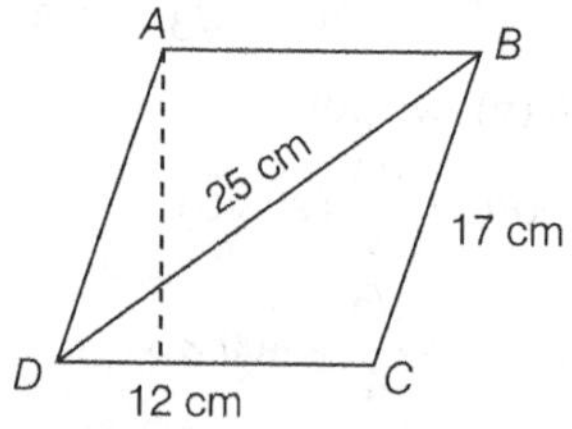

Thinking Process

(i) Determine the area of ΔBCD by using Heron's formula.

(ii) Using relation, area of parallelogram $ABCD = 2$ (Area of ΔBCD)

(iii) Also, determine the area of parallelogram by using the formula Base $\times$ Altitude.

(iv) Further, equate the area of parallelogram in (ii) and (iii). Obtain the required length of the altitude.

Ans. Given, $ABCD$ is a parallelogram

Let, the sides of a ΔBCD are $a = 12$ cm, $b = 17$ cm and $c = 25$ cm .

$\therefore$ Semi-perimeter of ΔBCD,

$$s = \frac{a+b+c}{2}$$

$$= \frac{12+17+25}{2} = \frac{54}{2} = 27 \text{ cm}$$

$\therefore$ Area of $\Delta BCD = \sqrt{s(s-a)(s-b)(s-c)}$ [by Heron's formula]

$$= \sqrt{27(27-12)(27-17)(27-25)}$$

$$= \sqrt{27 \times 15 \times 10 \times 2}$$

$$= \sqrt{9 \times 3 \times 3 \times 5 \times 5 \times 2 \times 2}$$

$$= 3 \times 3 \times 5 \times 2 = 90 \text{ cm}^2 \quad \text{...(i)}$$

Now, area of parallelogram $ABCD = 2 \times$ (Area of ΔBCD)

$$= 2 \times 90 = 180 \text{ cm}^2 \quad \text{...(ii)}$$

Let altitude of a parallelogram be h cm.

(*) Topics related to these question have been removed from latest NCERT.

Also, area of parallelogram $ABCD = \text{Base} \times \text{Altitude}$

$$\Rightarrow \quad 180 = DC \times h \quad \text{[from Eq. (ii)]}$$

$$\Rightarrow \quad 180 = 12 \times h$$

$$\therefore \quad h = \frac{180}{12} = 15 \text{ cm}$$

Hence, the area of parallelogram is 180 cm^2 and the length of altitude is 15 cm.

*** Q.6 A field in the form of a parallelogram has sides 60 m and 40 m and one of its diagonals is 80 m long. Find the area of the parallelogram.**

Ans. Let $ABCD$ be a parallelogram field with sides $AB = CD = 60$ m, $BC = DA = 40$ m and diagonal $BD = 80$ m.

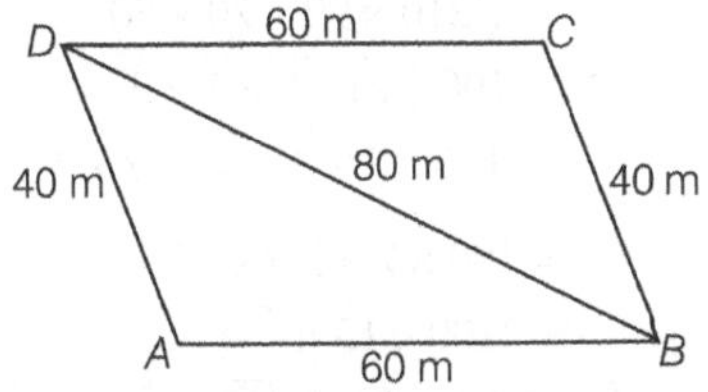

In ΔABD, let $a = AB = 60$ m, $b = BD = 80$ cm

and $C = DA = 40$ cm

Semi-perimeter of a ΔABD,

$$s = \frac{a+b+c}{2}$$

$$= \frac{60+80+40}{2} = \frac{180}{2}$$

$$= 90 \text{ m}$$

$$\therefore \quad \text{Area of } \Delta ABD = \sqrt{s(s-a)(s-b)(s-c)} \quad \text{[by Heron's formula]}$$

$$= \sqrt{90(90-60)(90-80)(90-40)}$$

$$= \sqrt{90 \times 30 \times 10 \times 50}$$

$$= 100 \times 3\sqrt{15} = 300\sqrt{15} \text{ m}^2$$

$\therefore$ Area of Parallelogram $ABCD = 2(\text{Area of } \Delta ABD) = 2 \times 300\sqrt{15} = 600\sqrt{15} \text{ m}^2$

Hence, the area of the parallelogram is $600\sqrt{15}$ m^2.

Q.7 The perimeter of a triangular field is 420 m and its sides are in the ratio 6 : 7 : 8. Find the area of the triangular field.

Thinking Process First, find the sides of the triangle by using the given ratio and perimeter, then find area of triangle by using Heron's formula as $\sqrt{s(s-a)(s-b)(s-c)}$.

Ans. Given, perimeter of a triangular field is 420 m and its sides are in the ratio 6 : 7 : 8.

Let sides of a triangular field be $a = 6x$, $b = 7x$ and $c = 8x$.

$\therefore$ Perimeter of a triangular field $= a + b + c$

$$\Rightarrow \quad 420 = 6x + 7x + 8x$$

$$\Rightarrow \quad 420 = 21x$$

$\Rightarrow \qquad x = \frac{420}{21} = 20\,\text{m}$

$\therefore$ Sides of a triangular field are

$$a = 6 \times 20 = 120\,\text{m}$$
$$b = 7 \times 20 = 140\,\text{m}$$
and $$c = 8 \times 20 = 160\,\text{m}.$$

Now, semi-perimeter, $s = \frac{420}{2} = 210\,\text{m}$

$\therefore$ Area of a triangular field $= \sqrt{s(s-a)(s-b)(s-c)}$ [by Heron's formula]

$$= \sqrt{210(210-120)(210-140)(210-160)}$$
$$= \sqrt{210 \times 90 \times 70 \times 50}$$
$$= 100\sqrt{21 \times 9 \times 7 \times 5}$$
$$= 100\sqrt{7 \times 3 \times 3^2 \times 7 \times 5}$$
$$= 100 \times 7 \times 3 \times \sqrt{15}$$
$$= 2100\sqrt{15}\,\text{m}^2$$

Hence, the area of triangular field is $2100\sqrt{15}\,\text{m}^2$.

***Q.8** The sides of a quadrilateral $ABCD$ are 6cm, 8cm, 12cm and 14cm (taken in order) respectively, and the angle between the first two sides is a right angle. Find its area.

Ans. Given, $ABCD$ is a quadrilateral with sides $AB = 6\text{cm}$, $BC = 8\text{cm}$, $CD = 12\text{cm}$ and $DA = 14\,\text{cm}$. Now, join AC.

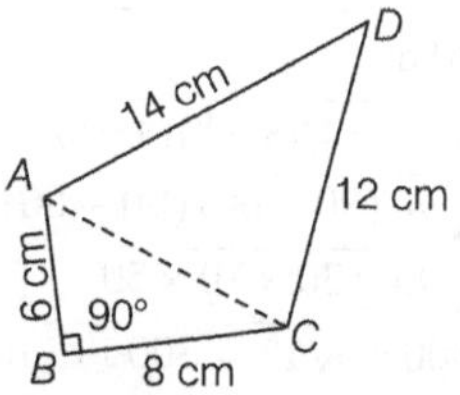

We have, ABC is a right angled triangle at B.

Now, $AC^2 = AB^2 + BC^2$ [by Pythagoras theorem]

$$= 6^2 + 8^2 = 36 + 64 = 100$$

$\Rightarrow \qquad AC = 10\,\text{cm}$

[take positive square root because length is always positive]

Now, area of $\Delta ABC = \frac{1}{2} \times AB \times BC$ [$\because$ area of triangle $= \frac{1}{2}$ (base $\times$ height)]

$$= \frac{1}{2} \times 6 \times 8 = 24\,\text{cm}^2$$

In ΔACD, let $AC = a = 10\,\text{cm}$, $CD = b = 12\,\text{cm}$

and $DA = c = 14\,\text{cm}$

Now, semi-perimeter of ΔACD, $s = \frac{a+b+c}{2} = \frac{10+12+14}{2}$

(*) Topics related to these question have been removed from latest NCERT.

$$= \frac{36}{2} = 18 \text{ cm}$$

$\therefore$ Area of $\Delta ACD = \sqrt{s(s-a)(s-b)(s-c)}$ [by Heron's formula]

$$= \sqrt{18(18-10)(18-12)(18-14)}$$

$$= \sqrt{18 \times 8 \times 6 \times 4}$$

$$= \sqrt{(3)^2 \times 2 \times 4 \times 2 \times 3 \times 2 \times 4}$$

$$= 3 \times 4 \times 2\sqrt{3 \times 2} = 24\sqrt{6} \text{ cm}^2$$

$\therefore$ Area of quadrilateral $ABCD$ = Area of ΔABC + Area of ΔACD

$$= 24 + 24\sqrt{6} = 24(1+\sqrt{6}) \text{ cm}^2$$

Hence, the area of quadrilateral is $24(1+\sqrt{6})$ cm^2.

***Q.9** A rhombus shaped sheet with perimeter 40 cm and one diagonal 12 cm, is painted on both sides at the rate of ₹ 5 per cm^2. Find the cost of painting.

Ans. Let $ABCD$ be a rhombus having each side equal to x cm.

i.e., $AB = BC = CD = DA = x$ cm

Given, perimeter of a rhombus = 40 cm

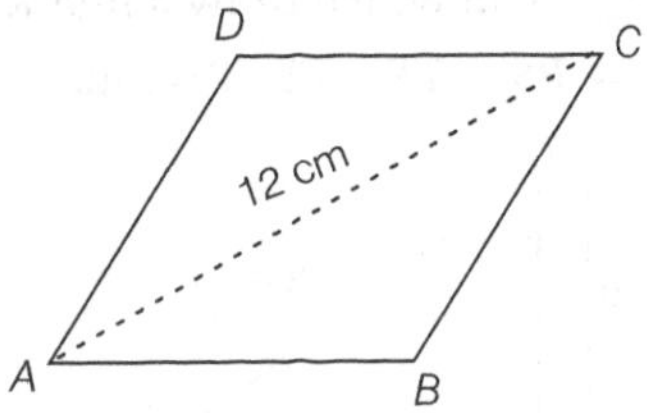

$\therefore$ $AB + BC + CD + DA = 40$

$\Rightarrow$ $x + x + x + x = 40$

$\Rightarrow$ $4x = 40$

$\Rightarrow$ $x = 10$ cm

In ΔABC, let $a = AB = 10$ cm, $b = BC = 10$ cm

and $c = AC = 12$ cm

Now, semi-perimeter of a ΔABC, $s = \frac{a+b+c}{2}$

$$= \frac{10+10+12}{2} = \frac{32}{2} = 16 \text{ cm}$$

$\therefore$ Area of $\Delta ABC = \sqrt{s(s-a)(s-b)(s-c)}$ [by Heron's formula]

$$= \sqrt{16(16-10)(16-10)(16-12)}$$

$$= \sqrt{16 \times 6 \times 6 \times 4} = 4 \times 6 \times 2 = 48 \text{cm}^2$$

Now, area of the rhombus = 2 (Area of ΔABC) = 2×48

$$= 96 \text{cm}^2$$

(*) Topics related to these question have been removed from latest NCERT.

∵ Cost of painting of the sheet of area 1 cm^2 = ₹ 5

∴ Cost of painting of the sheet of area 96 cm^2 = 96×5 = ₹ 480

Hence, the cost of the painting of the sheet on both sides = 2×480 = ₹ 960

***Q.10** Find the area of the trapezium *PQRS* with height *PQ* given in the figure

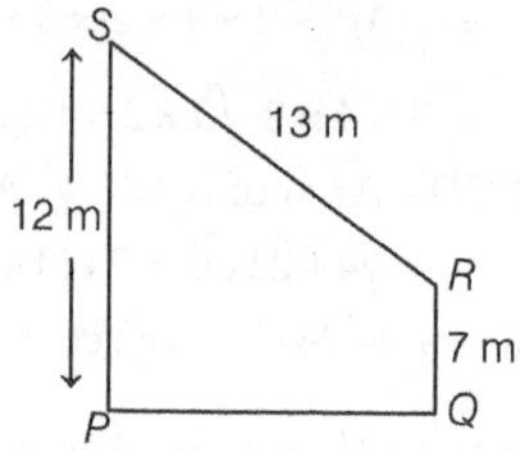

Thinking Process

(i) Draw a line *RT* perpendicular to *PS*. Determine area of ΔSTR by using the formula, $\frac{1}{2}$ (Base × Height) and also, determine the area of rectangle *PQRT* by using the formula, length × breadth.

(ii) The area of trapezium is equal to the sum of areas of ΔSTR and rectangle *PQRT*.

Ans. We have, a trapezium *PQRS*, in which draw a line *RT* perpendicular to *PS*.

∴ $ST = PS - TP = 12 - 7 = 5\,\text{m}$. [∵ $TP = RQ = 7\,\text{m}$]

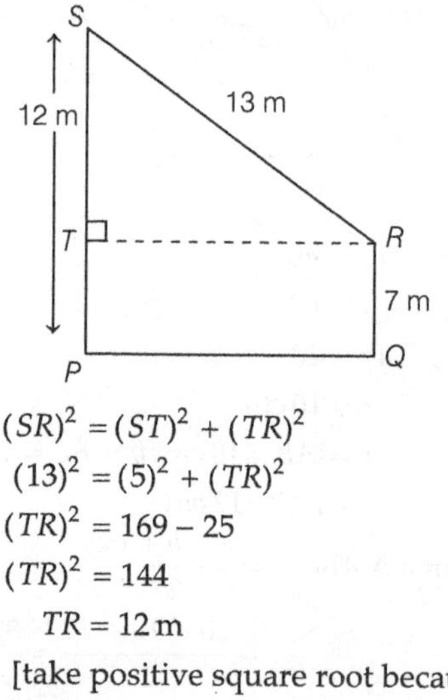

In right angled ΔSTR, $(SR)^2 = (ST)^2 + (TR)^2$ [by Pythagoras theorem]

$\Rightarrow \quad (13)^2 = (5)^2 + (TR)^2$

$\Rightarrow \quad (TR)^2 = 169 - 25$

$\Rightarrow \quad (TR)^2 = 144$

$\therefore \quad TR = 12\,\text{m}$

[take positive square root because length is always positive]

Now, area of $\Delta STR = \frac{1}{2} \times TR \times TS$ [∵ area of triangle $= \frac{1}{2}$ (base × height)]

$= \frac{1}{2} \times 12 \times 5 = 30\ \text{m}^2$

Now, area of rectangle $PQRT = PQ \times RQ = 12 \times 7$

[∵ area of a rectangle = length × breadth]

[∵ $PQ = TR = 12\,\text{m}$]

$= 84\ \text{m}^2$

$\therefore$ Area of trapezium $PQRS$ = Area of ΔSTR + Area of rectangle $PQRT$

$$= 30 + 84 = 114 \text{ m}^2$$

Hence, the area of trapezium is 114 m^2.

Alternate Method

Find TR as in above method

$\therefore$ Area of a trapezium $= \frac{1}{2}$ (Sum of parallel sides) × Distance between two points

$$= \frac{1}{2}(PS + QR) \times TR = \frac{1}{2} \times (12 + 7) \times 12$$

$$= \frac{1}{2} \times 19 \times 12 = 114 \text{ m}^2$$

Hence, the area of trapezium is 114 m^2.

Long Answer Type Questions

***Q.1** How much paper of each shade is needed to make a kite given in figure, in which $ABCD$ is a square with diagonal 44 cm.

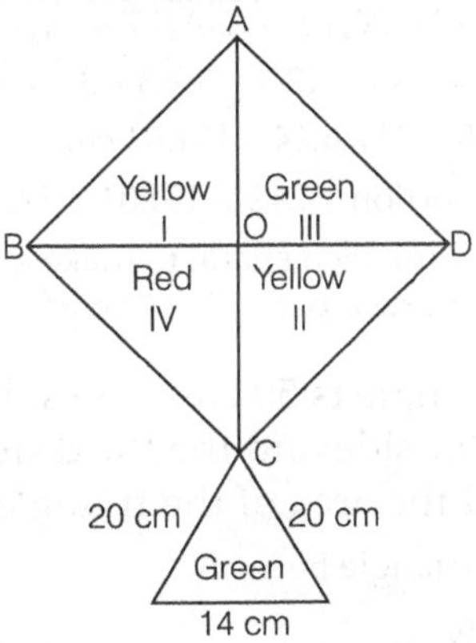

Ans. Given, $ABCD$ is a square,

We know that all the sides of a square are always equal.

i.e., $AB = BC = CD = DA$

In ΔACD, $AC = 44$ cm, $\angle D = 90°$

In ΔACD,

$$AC^2 = AD^2 + DC^2 \quad \text{[by Pythagorus theorem]}$$

$$\Rightarrow 44^2 = AD^2 + AD^2 \quad [\because DC = AD]$$

$$\Rightarrow 2AD^2 = 44 \times 44$$

$$\Rightarrow AD^2 = 22 \times 44 \Rightarrow AD = \sqrt{22 \times 44}$$

[take positive square root because length is always positive]

$$\Rightarrow AD = \sqrt{2 \times 11 \times 4 \times 11}$$

$$\Rightarrow AD = 22\sqrt{2} \text{ cm}$$

(*) Topics related to these question have been removed from latest NCERT.

So, $AB = BC = CD = DA = 22\sqrt{2}$ cm

Now, area of square $ABCD$ = Side × Side = $22\sqrt{2} \times 22\sqrt{2} = 968\ \text{cm}^2$

∴ Area of the red portion $= \frac{968}{4} = 242\ \text{cm}^2$

[∵ area of square is divided into four parts]

Now, area of the green portion $= \frac{968}{4} = 242\ \text{cm}^2$

Area of the yellow portion $= \frac{968}{2} = 484\ \text{cm}^2$

Now, consider a triangle

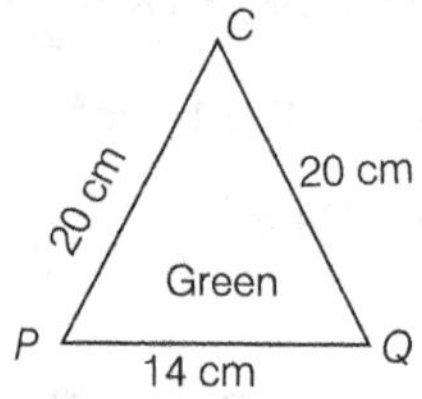

In ΔPCQ, let $PC = a = 20$ cm, $CQ = b = 20$ cm and $PQ = c = 14$ cm

∴ Semi-perimeter, $s = \frac{a+b+c}{2} = \frac{20+20+14}{2} = \frac{54}{2} = 27$ cm

∴ Area of $\Delta PCQ = \sqrt{s(s-a)(s-b)(s-c)}$ [by Heron's formula]

$= \sqrt{27(27-20)(27-20)(27-14)}$

$= \sqrt{27 \times 7 \times 7 \times 13} = \sqrt{3 \times 3 \times 3 \times 7 \times 7 \times 13}$

$= 21\sqrt{39} = 21 \times 6.24 = 131.04\ \text{cm}^2$

∴ Total area of the green portion $= 242 + 131.04 = 373.04\ \text{cm}^2$

Hence, the paper required for each shade to make a kite is red paper $242\ \text{cm}^2$, yellow paper $484\ \text{cm}^2$ and green paper $373.04\ \text{cm}^2$.

Q.2 The perimeter of a triangle is 50 cm. One side of a triangle is 4 cm longer than the smaller side and the third side is 6 cm less than twice the smaller side. Find the area of the triangle.

Ans. Let the smaller side of a triangle be x cm.

According to the question,

Second side $= (x + 4)$ cm

Third side $= (2x - 6)$ cm

∵ Perimeter of a triangle = 50 cm

⇒ $x + x + 4 + 2x - 6 = 50 \Rightarrow 4x - 2 = 50$

⇒ $4x = 52 \Rightarrow x = \frac{52}{4}$

⇒ $x = 13$ cm

Let smaller side, $a = 13$ cm

second side, $b = 13 + 4 = 17$ cm

and third side, $c = 2 \times 13 - 6 = 26 - 6 = 20$ cm

(✱) Topics related to these question have been removed from latest NCERT.

Now, semi-perimeter, $s = \dfrac{a+b+c}{2} = \dfrac{13+17+20}{2} = \dfrac{50}{2} = 25$ cm

$\therefore$ Area of a triangle $= \sqrt{s(s-a)(s-b)(s-c)}$ [by Heron's formula]

$= \sqrt{25(25-13)(25-17)(25-20)}$

$= \sqrt{25 \times 12 \times 8 \times 5}$

$= \sqrt{5 \times 5 \times 2 \times 2 \times 3 \times 2 \times 2 \times 2 \times 5}$

$= 5 \times 2 \times 2\sqrt{30} = 20\sqrt{30}$

Hence, the area of triangle is $20\sqrt{30}$ cm^2.

***Q.3** The area of a trapezium is 475 cm^2 and the height is 19 cm. Find the lengths of its two parallel sides if one side is 4 cm greater than the other.

Ans. Let one side of a trapezium, $DC = x$ cm

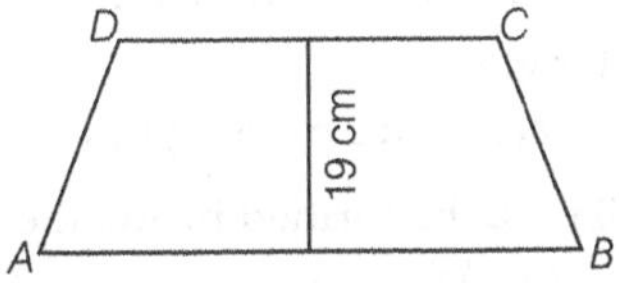

According to the question,

Other side, $AB = (x + 4)$ cm

As we know,

Area of a trapezium $= \dfrac{1}{2}$ (Sum of parallel sides) $\times$ Distance between parallel sides

$\Rightarrow \quad 475 = \dfrac{1}{2}(x + x + 4) \times 19$

$\Rightarrow \quad 475 = \dfrac{(2x+4) \times 19}{2}$

$\Rightarrow \quad \dfrac{(2x+4)}{2} = \dfrac{475}{19}$

$\Rightarrow \quad \dfrac{2(x+2)}{2} = 25$

$\Rightarrow \quad x + 2 = 25$

$\Rightarrow \quad x = 23$

$\therefore$ Other side $= x + 4 = 23 + 4 = 27$ cm

Hence, the two parallel sides of trapezium are 23 cm and 27 cm.

***Q.4** A rectangular plot is given for constructing a house; having a measurement of 40 m long and 15 m in the front. According to the laws, a minimum of 3 m, wide space should be left in the front and back each and 2 m wide space on each of other sides. Find the largest area where house can be constructed.

(*) Topics related to these question have been removed from latest NCERT.

Ans. Let $ABCD$ is a rectangular plot having a measurement of 40 m long and 15 m front.

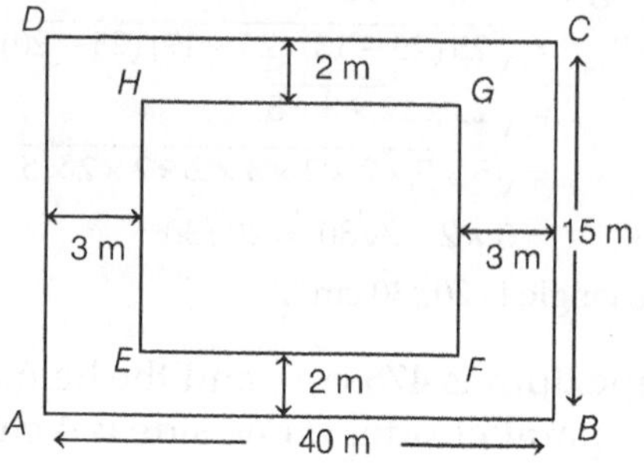

$\therefore$ Length of inner-rectangle,

$$EF = 40 - 3 - 3 = 34 \text{ m}$$

and breadth of inner-rectangle,

$$FG = 15 - 2 - 2 = 11 \text{ m}$$

$\therefore$ Another rectangle EFGH will be formed inside the rectangle $ABCD$.

$\therefore$ Area of inner rectangle, $EFGH$ = Length × Breadth

$$= EF \times FG = 34 \times 11 = 374 \text{ m}^2$$

[$\because$ area of a rectangle = length × breadth]

Hence, the largest area where the house can be constructed in 374 m^2.

*** Q.5** A field is in the shape of a trapezium having parallel sides 90 m and 30 m. These sides meet the third side at right angles. The length of the fourth side is 100 m. If it costs ₹ 4 to plough 1 m^2 of the field, find the total cost of ploughing the field.

Ans. Consider a trapezium $ABCD$ with $AB \parallel DC$ we draw a perpendicular line CE to the line AB.

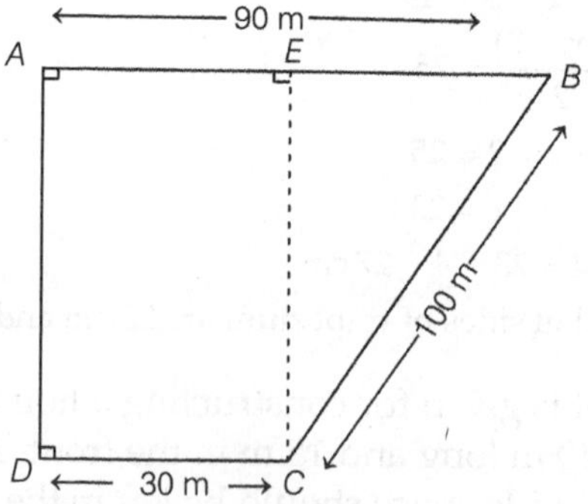

We have, $DC = AE = 30$ m

Now, $BE = AB - AE = 90 - 30 = 60$ m

(✱) Topics related to these question have been removed from latest NCERT.

In right angled Δ *BEC*, $(BC)^2 = (BE)^2 + (EC)^2$ [by Pythagoras theorem]

$\Rightarrow$ $(100)^2 = (60)^2 + (EC)^2$

$\Rightarrow$ $(EC)^2 = 10000 - 3600$

$\Rightarrow$ $(EC)^2 = 6400$

$\therefore$ $EC = \sqrt{6400} = 80\text{ m}$

[take positive square root because length is always positive]

$\therefore$ Area of trapezium *ABCD*

$= \frac{1}{2}$ (Sum of parallel sides) × Distance between parallel sides

$= \frac{1}{2}(AB + CD) \times EC = \frac{1}{2}(90 + 30) \times 80$

$= \frac{1}{2} \times (120) \times 80 = 4800\text{ m}^2$

$\because$ Cost of ploughing the field of area 1 m^2 = ₹ 4

$\therefore$ Cost of ploughing the field of area 4800 m^2 = 4800 × 4 = ₹ 19200

Hence, the total cost of ploughing the field is ₹ 19200.

***Q.6** In figure, Δ *ABC* has sides *AB* = 7.5 cm, *AC* = 6.5 cm and *BC* = 7 cm. On base *BC* a parallelogram *DBCE* of same area as that of Δ *ABC* is constructed. Find the height *DF* of the parallelogram.

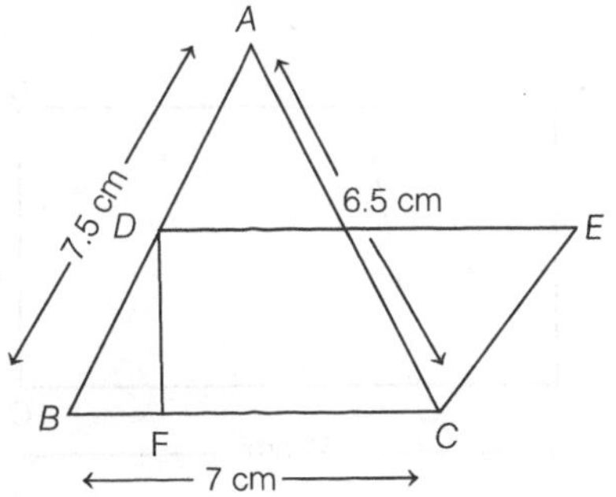

Thinking Process

(i) Firstly, determine the area of ΔABC by using Heron's formula *i.e.*, $\sqrt{s(s-a)(s-b)(s-c)}$.

(ii) Secondly, determine the area of parallelogram *BCED* by using the formula, Base × Height.

(iii) Further, equate the area of triangle and area of parallelogram to get the height of the parallelogram.

Ans. In ΔABC, let $AB = a = 7.5$ cm, $BC = b = 7$ cm

and $CA = c = 6.5$ cm

Now, semi-perimeter of a ΔABC,

$$s = \frac{a+b+c}{2} = \frac{7.5 + 7 + 6.5}{2}$$

(*) Topics related to these question have been removed from latest NCERT.

$$= \frac{21}{2} = 10.5 \text{ cm}$$

$\therefore$ Area of $\Delta ABC = \sqrt{s(s-a)(s-b)(s-c)}$ [by Heron's formula]

$$= \sqrt{10.5(10.5-7.5)(10.5-7)(10.5-6.5)}$$
$$= \sqrt{10.5 \times 3 \times 3.5 \times 4}$$
$$= \sqrt{441} = 21 \text{ cm}^2 \quad \text{... (i)}$$

Now, area of parallelogram $BCED$ = Base × Height

$$= BC \times DF = 7 \times DF \quad \text{... (ii)}$$

According to the question,

Area of ΔABC = Area of parallelogram $BCED$

$\Rightarrow$ $21 = 7 \times DF$ [from Eqs. (i) and (ii)]

$\Rightarrow$ $DF = \frac{21}{7} = 3 \text{cm}$

Hence, the height of parallelogram is 3 cm.

*** Q.7** The dimensions of a rectangle $ABCD$ are 51 cm × 25 cm. A trapezium $PQCD$ with its parallel sides QC and PD in the ratio 9 : 8, is cut off from the rectangle as shown in the figure. If the area of the trapezium $PQCD$ is $\frac{5}{6}$th part of the area of the rectangle, find the lengths QC and PD.

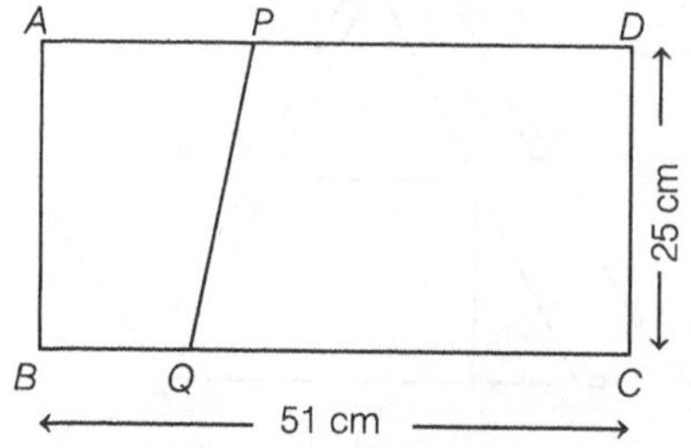

Ans. We have, dimensions of a rectangle $ABCD$ are 51 cm ×25 cm. Also, in trapezium $PQCD$, parallel sides QC and PD are in the ratio 9 : 8.

i.e., $QC : PD = 9 : 8$

Let $QC = 9x$

and $PD = 8x$

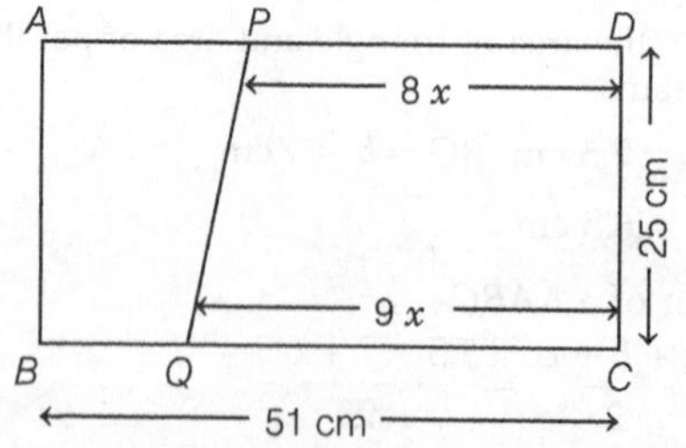

(✱) Topics related to these question have been removed from latest NCERT.

According to the question,

Area of trapezium $PQCD = \frac{5}{6}$ (Area of rectangle $ABCD$)

$\Rightarrow \frac{1}{2}$ (Sum of parallel sides) $\times$ Distance between parallel sides

$$= \frac{5}{6} \times (BC \times CD)$$

$$\Rightarrow \quad \frac{1}{2}(8x + 9x) \times 25 = \frac{5}{6} \times 51 \times 25$$

$$\Rightarrow \quad \frac{1}{2} \times 17x \times 25 = \frac{5}{6} \times 51 \times 25$$

$$\Rightarrow \quad x = \frac{5 \times 51 \times 25 \times 2}{25 \times 17 \times 6}$$

$$\Rightarrow \quad x = 5$$

$\therefore$ Lengths of trapezium are

$$QC = 9 \times 5 = 45 \text{ cm}$$

and $\quad PD = 8 \times 5 = 40$ cm.

***Q.8** A design is made on a rectangular tile of dimensions 50 cm $\times$ 70 cm as shown in figure. The design shows 8 triangle, each of sides 26 cm, 17 cm and 25 cm. Find the total area of the design and the remaining area of the tiles.

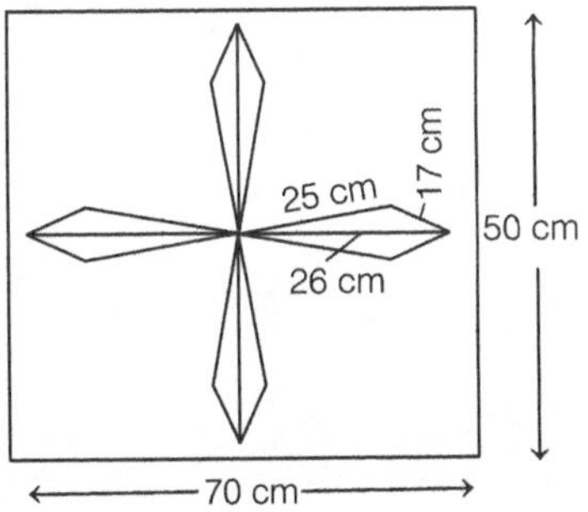

Ans. Given, the dimensions of rectangular tile are 50 cm $\times$ 70 cm.

$\therefore$ Area of rectangular tile $= 50 \times 70 = 3500 \text{ cm}^2$

The sides of one triangle of the design be

$$a = 25 \text{ cm}, \ b = 17 \text{ cm}$$

and $\quad c = 26$ cm.

Now, semi-perimeter,

$$s = \frac{a + b + c}{2}$$

$$= \frac{25 + 17 + 26}{2}$$

(*) Topics related to these question have been removed from latest NCERT.

$$= \frac{68}{2} = 34 \text{ cm}$$

$\therefore$ Area of one triangle $= \sqrt{s(s-a)(s-b)(s-c)}$ [by Heron's formula]

$$= \sqrt{34(34-25)(34-17)(34-26)}$$
$$= \sqrt{34 \times 9 \times 17 \times 8}$$
$$= \sqrt{17 \times 2 \times 3 \times 3 \times 17 \times 2 \times 2 \times 2}$$
$$= 17 \times 3 \times 2 \times 2$$
$$= 204 \text{ cm}^2$$

$\therefore$ Total area of eight triangles $= 204 \times 8 = 1632 \text{ cm}^2$

Now, area of the design = Total area of eight triangles

$$= 1632 \text{ cm}^2$$

Also, remaining area of the tile = Area of the rectangle – Area of the design

$$= 3500 - 1632$$
$$= 1868 \text{ cm}^2$$

Hence, the total area of the design is 1632 cm^2 and the remaining area of the tile is 1868 cm^2.

Chapter 13

Surface Area and Volumes

Multiple Choice Questions (MCQs)

Choose the correct answer from the given four options in the following questions:

Q.1 The radius of a sphere is $2r$, then its volume will be

(a) $\frac{4}{3}\pi r^3$ (b) $4\pi r^3$ (c) $\frac{8\pi r^3}{3}$ (d) $\frac{32}{3}\pi r^3$

Ans. *(d)* Given, radius of a sphere = $2r$

As we known, volume of a sphere $= \frac{4}{3}\pi\,(\text{Radius})^3$

$$= \frac{4}{3}\pi(2r)^3 = \frac{4}{3}\pi \cdot 8r^3 \quad [\because \text{radius} = 2r]$$

$$= \frac{32\pi r^3}{3} \text{ Cu units}$$

Hence, the volume of a sphere is $\frac{32\pi r^3}{3}$ cu units.

***Q.2** The total surface area of a cube is 96 cm^2. The volume of the cube is

(a) 8cm^3 (b) 512cm^3 (c) 64cm^3 (d) 27cm^3

Ans. *(c)* Given, the total surface area of a cube = 96 cm^2

$\therefore$ Surface area of a cube $= 6\,(\text{Side})^2 = 96$ $[\because \text{surface area of a cube} = 6a^2]$

$\Rightarrow$ $(\text{Side})^2 = 16$

$\Rightarrow$ Side = 4 cm

[take positive square root because side is always a positive quantity]

$\therefore$ Volume of cube= $(\text{Side})^3 = (4)^3 = 64\text{ cm}^3$

Hence, the volume of the cube is 64 cm^3.

Q.3 A cone is 8.4 cm high and the radius of its base is 2.1 cm. It is melted and recast into a sphere. The radius of the sphere is

(a) 4.2 cm (b) 2.1 cm (c) 2.4 cm (d) 1.6 cm

(*) Topics related to these question have been removed from latest NCERT.

Thinking Process

(i) Firstly, determine the volume of a cone and volume of a sphere using the formulae, volume of sphere $= \frac{4}{3}\pi r^3$ and volume of cone $= \frac{1}{3}\pi r^2 h$, respectively.

(ii) Further, equate volume of a cone and volume of sphere, so that we get the radius of sphere.

Ans. *(b)* Given, height of a cone $= 8.4$ cm

Radius of base of a cone $= 2.1$ cm

Volume of a cone $= \frac{1}{3}\pi r^2 h = \frac{1}{3} \times \pi \times (2.1)^2 \times 8.4$

$$= \frac{1}{3} \times \pi \times 2.1 \times 2.1 \times 8.4 = \pi \times 4.41 \times 2.8 \text{ cm}^3$$

Since, cone is melted and recast into a sphere.

Let the radius of a sphere be R.

Then, volume of a sphere = Volume of a cone

$$\Rightarrow \quad \frac{4}{3}\pi R^3 = \pi \times 4.41 \times 2.8 \Rightarrow R^3 = \frac{4.41 \times 2.8 \times 3}{4}$$

$$\Rightarrow \quad R^3 = 4.41 \times 0.7 \times 3$$

$$\Rightarrow \quad R^3 = 4.41 \times 2.1 = 2.1 \times 2.1 \times 2.1$$

$$\therefore \quad R = 2.1$$

Hence, the radius of the sphere is 2.1 cm.

***Q.4** In a cylinder, radius is doubled and height is halved, then curved surface area will be

(a) halved
(b) doubled
(c) same
(d) four times

Ans. *(c)* Let r and h be the radius and height of a cylinder, respectively

$\therefore$ Curved surface area of cylinder $= 2\pi rh$

Let new radius $= 2r$ and new height $= \frac{h}{2}$

$\therefore$ New curved surface area $= 2\pi (2r) \times \frac{h}{2} = 2\pi rh$

Hence, the curved surface area will be same.

Q.5 The total surface area of a cone whose radius is $\frac{r}{2}$ and slant height $2l$ is

(a) $2\pi r(l + r)$
(b) $\pi r\left(l + \frac{r}{4}\right)$
(c) $\pi r(l + r)$
(d) $2\pi rl$

Ans. *(b)* Let radius, $R = \frac{r}{2}$ and slant height, $L = 2l$

$\therefore$ Total surface area of a cone

$$= \pi R(L + R) = \pi \times \frac{r}{2}\left(2l + \frac{r}{2}\right) = \pi r\left(l + \frac{r}{4}\right).$$

(✱) Topics related to these question have been removed from latest NCERT.

***Q.6** The radii of two cylinders are in the ratio of 2 : 3 and their heights are in the ratio of 5 : 3. The ratio of their volumes is

(a) 10 : 17 (b) 20 : 27 (c) 17 : 27 (d) 20 : 37

Thinking Process Use the concept, the volume of cylinder = $\pi r^2 h$

Ans. ***(b)*** Let the radii of two cylinders be r_1 and r_2 and heights of the cylinder be h_1 and h_2.

Given, $\frac{r_1}{r_2} = \frac{2}{3}$ and $\frac{h_1}{h_2} = \frac{5}{3}$

$$\therefore \text{ Ratio of volumes} = \frac{\pi r_1^2 h_1}{\pi r_2^2 h_2} = \left(\frac{r_1}{r_2}\right)^2 \left(\frac{h_1}{h_2}\right)$$

$$= \left(\frac{2}{3}\right)^2 \left(\frac{5}{3}\right) = \frac{4}{9} \times \frac{5}{3} = 20 : 27$$

Hence, the ratio of their volumes is 20 : 27.

***Q.7.** The lateral surface area of a cube is 256 m^2. The volume of the cube is

(a) 512 m^3 (b) 64 m^3 (c) 216 m^3 (d) 256 m^3

Ans. ***(a)*** Given, lateral surface area of a cube = 256 m^2

We know that lateral surface area of a cube = $4 \times (\text{Side})^2$

$$\Rightarrow \quad 256 = 4 \times (\text{Side})^2$$

$$\Rightarrow \quad (\text{Side})^2 = \frac{256}{4} = 64$$

$$\Rightarrow \quad \text{Side} = \sqrt{64} = 8 \text{ m}$$

[take positive square root because side is always a positive quantity]

Now, volume of a cube = $(\text{Side})^3 = (8)^3 = 8 \times 8 \times 8 = 512 \text{ m}^3$

Hence, the volume of the cube is 512 m^3.

***Q.8** The number of planks of dimensions (4 m × 50 cm × 20 cm) that can be stored in a pit which is 16 m long, 12 m wide and 4 m deep is

(a) 1900 (b) 1920 (c) 1800 (d) 1840

Thinking Process

(i) Firstly, determine the volume of plank and volume of pit by using the formula. $l \times b \times h$.

(ii) Further, find the quotient of the volume of pit to the volume of the plank to get the number of planks.

Ans. ***(b)*** Given, dimensions of the plank are

$$l = 4 \text{ m}, b = 50 \text{ cm} = \frac{50}{100} \text{ m} = 0.5 \text{ m}$$

and $$h = 20 \text{ cm} = \frac{20}{100} \text{ m} = 0.2 \text{ m}$$

$\therefore$ Volume of the plank $= l \times b \times h = 4 \times 0.5 \times 0.2 = 0.4 \text{ m}^3$

Also, given dimensions of the pit are

$$l = 16 \text{ m}, \; b = 12 \text{ m and } h = 4 \text{ m}$$

(*) Topics related to these question have been removed from latest NCERT.

$\therefore$ Volume of a pit $= l \times b \times h = (16 \times 12 \times 4)\, m^3$

$$\therefore \quad \text{Number of planks} = \frac{\text{Volume of the pit}}{\text{Volume of the plank}} = \frac{16 \times 12 \times 4}{0.4}$$

$$= 16 \times 12 \times 10 = 1920$$

Hence, the number of planks is 1920.

*** Q.9** The length of the longest pole that can be put in a room of dimensions (10 m× 10 m× 5 m) is

(a) 15 m (b) 16 m
(c) 10 m (d) 12 m

Thinking Process Length of the longest pole = Diagonal of a cuboid (room).

Ans. *(a)* Given, dimensions of a room, $l = 10$ m, $b = 10$ m, $h = 5$ m

$\therefore$ Length of the longest pole = Diagonal of a cuboid (room)

$$= \sqrt{l^2 + b^2 + h^2} = \sqrt{(10)^2 + (10)^2 + (5)^2}$$

$$= \sqrt{100 + 100 + 25} = \sqrt{225} = 15 \text{ m}$$

Hence, the length of the longest pole is 15 m.

Q.10 The radius of a hemispherical balloon increases from 6 cm to 12 cm as air is being pumped into it. The ratios of the surface areas of the balloon in the two cases is

(a) 1 : 4 (b) 1 : 3 (c) 2 : 3 (d) 2 : 1

Ans. *(a)* Let radius of a hemispherical balloon, $r_1 = 6$ cm

Since, air is pumped into balloon. Then, radius of a hemispherical balloon, $r_2 = 12$ cm

$\therefore$ Ratio of the surface areas of the balloon in two cases $= \dfrac{3\pi r_1^2}{3\pi r_2^2}$

$$\Rightarrow \quad = \frac{r_1^2}{r_2^2} = \frac{(6)^2}{(12)^2} = \frac{36}{144} = \frac{1}{4} = 1:4$$

Hence, ratio of the surface areas of the balloon in the two cases in 1 : 4.

Short Answer Questions with Reasoning

Write True or False and justify your answer in each of the following questions.

Q.1 The volume of a sphere is equal to two-third of the volume of a cylinder whose height and diameter are equal to the diameter of the sphere.

Ans. *True*

Let r be the radius of the sphere and cylinder.

Given, height of the cylinder = Diameter of the base

$$\Rightarrow \quad h = 2r$$

(*) Topics related to these question have been removed from latest NCERT.

According to the given condition,

Volume of sphere $= \frac{2}{3} \times$ Volume of cylinder

$$\Rightarrow \quad \frac{4}{3}\pi r^3 = \frac{2}{3} \times \pi r^2 \times 2r$$

$$\Rightarrow \quad \frac{4}{3}\pi r^3 = \frac{4}{3}\pi r^3$$

Hence, the volume of the sphere is equal to two-third of the volume of the cylinder.

Q.2 If the radius of a right circular cone is halved and height is doubled, then volume will remain unchanged.

Ans. *False*

Let r and h be the radius and height of a right circular cone, respectively.

Then, the volume of a right circular cone $= \frac{1}{3}\pi r^2 h$

According to the condition,

Let new radius, $R = \frac{r}{2}$ and new height, $H = 2h$

New volume of a right circular cone $= \frac{1}{3}\pi R^2 H = \frac{1}{3}\pi\left(\frac{r}{2}\right)^2 \times 2h = \frac{1}{3}\pi \times \frac{r^2}{4} \times 2h$

$$= \frac{1}{3}\pi \times \frac{r^2}{2}h = \frac{1}{2}\left(\frac{1}{3}\pi r^2 h\right)$$

Hence, the new volume of the right circular cone becomes half of original volume of the right circular cone.

Q.3 In a right circular cone, height, radius and slant height do not always be sides of a right triangle.

Ans. *True*

On rotating a right-angled triangular lamina AOB about OA, it generates a cone. The point A is the vertex of a cone. Its base is a circle with centre O and radius OB. The length OA is the height of the cone and the length AB is called its slant height.

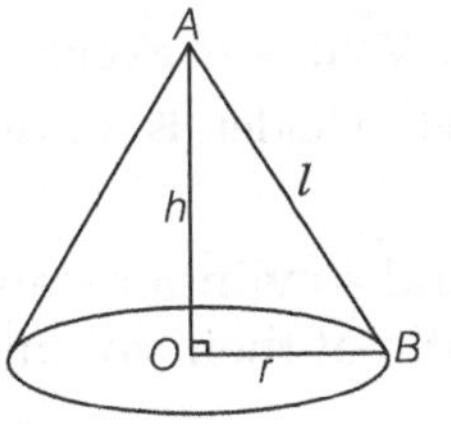

Clearly, $\angle AOB = 90°$

Let the radius of the base $= r$ units, height $= h$ units

and slant height $= l$ units, then

$$l^2 = h^2 + r^2 \Rightarrow l = \sqrt{h^2 + r^2}$$

Hence, in a right circular cone, height, radius and slant height are always the sides of a right triangle.

***Q.4** If the radius of a cylinder is doubled and its curved surface area is not changed, the height must be halved.

Ans. *True*

Let the radius of a cylinder be r and height be h.

Curved surface area of a cylinder $= 2\pi rh$

Again, let the radius of a cylinder be $R = 2r$ and height be H.

Since, curved surface of a cylinder is not changed, therefore

$$2\pi rh = 2\pi RH$$

$$2\pi rh = 2\pi(2r) \times H$$

$$\Rightarrow \quad 2\pi rh = 4\pi rH$$

$$\Rightarrow \quad H = \frac{2\pi rh}{4\pi r} \Rightarrow H = \frac{h}{2}$$

Hence, the height must be halved.

Q.5 The volume of the largest right circular cone that can be fitted in a cube whose edge is $2r$ equals to the volume of a hemisphere radius r.

Ans. *True*

Given, edge of a cube $= 2r$, then height of cube becomes $h = 2r$.

$$\text{Volume of a cone} = \frac{1}{3}\pi r^2 h = \frac{1}{3}\pi r^2(2r) = \frac{2}{3}\pi r^3$$

$$\text{Volume of a hemisphere} = \frac{2}{3}\pi r^3$$

Hence, the volume of the cone is equal to the volume of the hemisphere.

Q.6 A cylinder and a right circular cone are having the same base and same height. The volume of the cylinder is three times the volume of the cone.

Ans. *True*

Let the radius and height of a cylinder and a right circular cone be r and h, respectively. Then, as we know

Volume of a cylinder $= \pi r^2 h$ and volume of a cone $= \frac{1}{3}\pi r^2 h$

$\therefore$ Volume of a cylinder $= 3 \times$ Volume of a cone

Hence, the volume of the cylinder is three times the volume of the right circular cone.

Q.7 A cone, a hemisphere and a cylinder stand on equal bases and have the same height. The ratio of their volumes is 1 : 2 : 3.

Ans. *True*

Let r be the radius of a cone, a hemisphere and a cylinder.

$$\text{Volume of a cone, } V_1 = \frac{1}{3}\pi r^2 h$$

$$V_1 = \frac{1}{3}\pi r^2 (r) \qquad [\because h = r]$$

(*) Topics related to these question have been removed from latest NCERT.

$\Rightarrow \quad = \frac{1}{3}\pi r^3$

Now, volume of a hemisphere, $V_2 = \frac{2}{3}\pi r^3$

and volume of cylinder, $V_3 = \pi r^2 h = \pi r^2 \times r = \pi r^3$ $[\because h = r]$

$\therefore \quad V_1 : V_2 : V_3 = \frac{1}{3}\pi r^3 : \frac{2}{3}\pi r^3 : \pi r^3 = 1 : 2 : 3$

Hence, the ratio of their volumes is 1 : 2 : 3.

***Q.8** If the length of the diagonal of a cube is $6\sqrt{3}$ cm, then the length of the edge of the cube is 3 cm.

Ans. *False*

Given, the length of the diagonal of a cube = $6\sqrt{3}$ cm

Let the edge (side) of a cube be a cm.

We know that diagonal of a cube = $a\sqrt{3}$

$\therefore \quad 6\sqrt{3} = a\sqrt{3}$

$\Rightarrow \quad a = 6$ cm

Hence, the edge of the cube is 6 cm.

Q.9 If a sphere is inscribed in a cube, then the ratio of the volume of the cube to the volume of the sphere will be $6:\pi$.

Ans. *True*

We known that volume of cube $(V_1) = (\text{Side})^3$

And radius of sphere$(r) = \frac{\text{Side}}{2}$

Now, Volume of sphere $(V_2) = \frac{4}{3}\pi(r^3) = \frac{4}{3}\pi\left(\frac{\text{Side}}{2}\right)^3 = \frac{4}{3}\pi \times \frac{(\text{Side})^3}{8}$

$$\therefore \quad \frac{V_1}{V_2} = \frac{(\text{Side})^3}{\frac{4}{3}\pi\frac{(\text{Side})^3}{8}} = \frac{6}{\pi} \text{ or } 6 : \pi$$

Hence, the ratio of the volume of the cube to the volume of the sphere is $6 : \pi$.

***Q.10** If the radius of a cylinder is doubled and height is halved, the volume will be doubled.

Ans. *True*

Let the radius and height of a cylinder be r and h.

Then, volume of a cylinder, $V_1 = \pi r^2 h$

Again, let radius of a cylinder, $R = 2r$ and height of a cylinder, $H = \frac{h}{2}$

$\therefore$ The new volume of a cylinder, $\pi R^2 H = \pi(2r)^2 \frac{h}{2} = 2\pi r^2 h = 2 \times V_1$

Hence, if the radius of a cylinder is doubled and height is halved, then volume of a cylinder is doubled.

(*) Topics related to these question have been removed from latest NCERT.

Short Answer Type Questions

Q.1 Metal spheres, each of radius 2 cm, are packed into a rectangular box of internal dimensions 16 cm× 8 cm× 8 cm. When 16 spheres are packed the box is filled with preservative liquid. Find the volume of this liquid. Give your answer to the nearest integer. [use $\pi = 3.14$]

Thinking Process

(i) Firstly, determine the volume of metallic sphere by using formula, $\frac{4}{3}\pi r^3$ and then multiply it by number of spheres.

(ii) Secondly, determine the volume of rectangular box by using the formula, $l \times b \times h$.

(iii) Finally, subtract the volume of all metallic spheres from volume of internal rectangular box to get volume of preservative liquid.

Ans. Given, radius of each metal sphere = 2 cm

Internal dimensions of a rectangular box,

$$l = 16 \text{ cm}, b = 8 \text{ cm and } h = 8 \text{ cm}$$

$\therefore$ Volume of a metallic sphere $= \frac{4}{3}\pi r^3 = \frac{4}{3} \times 3.14 \times (2)^3$

$$= \frac{4}{3} \times 3.14 \times 8$$

Now, volume of 16 metallic spheres $= \frac{4 \times 3.14 \times 8 \times 16}{3} = \frac{100.48 \times 16}{3}$

$$= \frac{1607.68}{3} = 535.89 \text{ cm}^3$$

And internal volume of a rectangular box

$$= l \times b \times h = 16 \times 8 \times 8$$

$$= 1024 \text{ cm}^3$$

$\therefore$ Volume of preservative liquid $= 1024 - 535.89 = 488.11 \text{ cm}^3 \approx 488 \text{ cm}^3$

Hence, the volume of preservative liquid when 16 metallic spheres are backed in rectangular box is 488 cm^3.

***Q.2** A storage tank is in the form of a cube. When it is full of water, the volume of water is 15.625 m^3. If the present depth of water is 1.3 m, then find the volume of water already used from the tank.

Ans. Let side of a cube be x m.

Given, volume of cubical tank = 15.625 m^3

$\Rightarrow \quad x^3 = 15.625 \text{ m}^3 \quad$ [$\because$ volume of cube = $(\text{side})^3$]

$\Rightarrow \quad x = 2.5$ m

And present depth of water in cubical tank = 1.3 m [given]

$\therefore$ Height of water used = 2.5 – 1.3 m = 1.2 m

Now, volume of water already used $= 1.2 \times 2.5 \times 2.5 = 7.5 \text{ m}^3$

$= 7.5 \times 1000 = 7500$ L $\quad$ [$\because 1 \text{ m}^3 = 1000$ L]

Hence, the volume of water already used from the tank is 7500 L.

(*) Topics related to these question have been removed from latest NCERT.

Q.3 Find the amount of water displaced by a solid spherical ball of diameter 4.2 cm, when it is completely immersed in water.

Thinking Process Amount of water displaced by solid spherical ball = Volume of solid spherical ball $= \frac{4}{3}\pi r^3$.

Ans. Given, diameter of a solid spherical ball = 4.2 cm

$\therefore$ Radius of a solid spherical ball, $r = \frac{4.2}{2} = 2.1\text{ cm}$

Now, volume of water displaced by a solid spherical ball when it is completely immersed in water = Volume of a solid spherical ball

$$= \frac{4}{3}\pi r^3 = \frac{4}{3} \times \frac{22}{7} \times (2.1)^3$$

$$= \frac{4}{3} \times \frac{22}{7} \times 2.1 \times 2.1 \times 2.1$$

$$= \frac{814.968}{21} = 38.808 = 38.81\text{ cm}^3$$

Hence, the amount of water displaced by a solid spherical ball, when it is completely immersed in water is 38.81 cm^3.

Q.4 How many square metres of canvas is required for a conical tent whose height is 3.5 m and the radius of the base is 12 m?

Thinking Process

(i) Firstly, determine the slant height of conical tent by using the formula, $l = \sqrt{h^2 + r^2}$

(ii) Further, use the formula, curved surface area of cone $= \pi r l$, which will give us the area of the canvas we need.

Ans. Given, height of a conical tent, $h = 3.5$ m and radius of the base of a conical tent, $r = 12$ m

Slant height, $l = \sqrt{h^2 + r^2} = \sqrt{(3.5)^2 + (12)^2}$

$$= \sqrt{12.25 + 144}$$

$$= \sqrt{156.25} = 12.5\text{ m}$$

$\therefore$ Required canvas for a conical tent = Curved surface area of the cone (conical tent)

$$= \pi r l = \frac{22}{7} \times 12 \times 12.5 = 471.42\text{ m}^2$$

Hence, the canvas required to make a conical tent is 471.42 m^2.

Q.5 Two solid spheres made of the same metal have weights 5920 g and 740 g, respectively. Determine the radius of the larger sphere, if the diameter of the smaller one is 5 cm.

Thinking Process

(i) Firstly, determine the volume of each solid sphere by using the formula,

$$V = \frac{\text{Mass}}{\text{Density}} = \frac{4}{3}\pi r^3$$

(ii) Secondly, use the ratio $\frac{V_1}{V_2}$ to get the radius.

Ans. Given, weight of one solid sphere, $m_1 = 5920$ g

and weight of another solid sphere, $m_2 = 740$ g

Diameter of the smaller sphere = 5 cm

$\therefore$ Radius of the smaller sphere, $r_2 = \frac{5}{2}$, $m_2 = 740$ g

Let radius of larger circle be r_1.

We know that $\text{Density} = \frac{\text{Mass }(M)}{\text{Volume }(V)}$

$$\Rightarrow \quad \text{Volume, } V = \frac{M}{D}$$

$$\Rightarrow \quad V_1 = \frac{5920}{D} \text{ cm}^3 \quad \text{...(i)}$$

$$\text{and} \quad V_2 = \frac{740}{D} \text{ cm}^3 \quad \text{..(ii)}$$

On dividing Eq. (i) by Eq. (ii), we get

$$\frac{V_1}{V_2} = \frac{\frac{5920}{D}}{\frac{740}{D}}$$

$$\Rightarrow \quad \frac{V_1}{V_2} = \frac{5920}{740} = \frac{8}{1}$$

$$\frac{\frac{4}{3}\pi r_1^3}{\frac{4}{3}\pi r_2^3} = \frac{8}{1} \Rightarrow \left(\frac{r_1}{r_2}\right)^3 = \frac{8}{1} \quad \left[\because \text{volume of a sphere} = \frac{4}{3}\pi r^3\right]$$

$$\Rightarrow \quad \left(\frac{r_1}{5/2}\right)^3 = \frac{8}{1} \quad \left[\because r_2 = \frac{5}{2}\text{ cm}\right]$$

$$\Rightarrow \quad \frac{r_1^3}{\frac{125}{8}} = \frac{8}{1} \Rightarrow \frac{8r_1^3}{125} = \frac{8}{1}$$

$$\Rightarrow \quad r_1^3 = \frac{8}{1} \times \frac{125}{8} = 125$$

$$\therefore \quad r_1 = 5 \text{ cm}$$

Hence, the radius of larger sphere is 5 cm.

***Q.6** A school provides milk to the students daily in a cylindrical glasses of diameter 7 cm. If the glass is filled with milk upto an height of 12 cm, find how many litres of milk is needed to serve 1600 students.

Ans. Given, diameter of a glass = 7cm

Radius of a glass, $r = \frac{7}{2}$ cm

$\therefore$ Milk contained in the cylindrical glass = Volume of cylindrical glass

$$= \pi r^2 h = \frac{22}{7} \times \frac{7}{2} \times \frac{7}{2} \times 12 = 462 \text{cm}^3$$

(✱) Topics related to these question have been removed from latest NCERT.

Now, milk required for 1600 students $= 462 \times 1600 = 739200\ \text{cm}^3$

$$= \frac{739200}{1000} = 739.2\ \text{L} \qquad \left[\because 1\ \text{cm}^3 = \frac{1}{1000}\ \text{L}\right]$$

Hence, 739.2 L of milk is needed to serve 1600 students.

*** Q.7** A cylindrical roller 2.5 m in length, 1.75 m in radius when rolled on a road was found to cover the area of $5500\ \text{m}^2$. How many revolutions did it make?

Thinking Process

(i) Curved surface area of cylindrical roller = Area covered in one revolution by roller.

(ii) Divide total area covered by area covered in one revolution to get the number of revolutions.

Ans. Given, length of a cylindrical roller, $h = 2.5$ m

Radius of a cylindrical roller, $r = 1.75$ m

and total area rolled on a road by cylindrical roller $= 5500\ \text{m}^2$

$\therefore$ Area rolled to cover in one revolution = Curved surface area of a cylindrical roller

$$= 2\pi rh = 2 \times \frac{22}{7} \times 1.75 \times 2.5 = \frac{44 \times 4.375}{7} = \frac{192.5}{7} = 27.5\ \text{m}^2$$

$\therefore$ Number of revolutions rolled by a cylindrical roller

$$= \frac{\text{Total area rolled by a cylindrical roller}}{\text{Area rolled to cover by a cylindrical roller in one revolution}}$$

$$= \frac{5500}{27.5} = 200\ \text{revolutions}$$

Hence, the number of revolutions rolled by a cylindrical roller on a road is 200.

*** Q.8** A small village, having a population of 5000, requires 75 L of water per head per day. The village has got an overhead tank of measurement 40 m × 25 m × 15 m. For how many days will the water of this tank last?

Ans. Given, total population of a small village = 5000

Water required per head per day = 75 L

Volume of water required for a small village per day $= 5000 \times 75 = 375000$ L

$$= \frac{375000}{1000}\ \text{m}^3 = 375\ \text{m}^3 \qquad [\because 1\ \text{m}^3 = 1000\ \text{L}]$$

Now, total capacity of water in overhead tank = Volume of overhead tank

$$= 40 \times 25 \times 15 = 15000\ \text{m}^3$$

$$\therefore \text{Number of days} = \frac{\text{Total capacity of water in overhead tank}}{\text{Volume of water required for a small village per day}}$$

$$= \frac{15000}{375} = 40\ \text{days}$$

Hence, water of the tank will be last in 40 days.

(*) Topics related to these question have been removed from latest NCERT.

Q.9 A shopkeeper has one spherical laddoo of radius 5 cm. With the same amount of material, how many laddoos of radius 2.5 cm can be made?

Thinking Process

(i) Firstly, determine the volumes of spherical laddoo and small laddoo by using the formula $\frac{4}{3}\pi r^3$.

(ii) Further, find the quotient of volume of laddoo to the volume of small laddoo to get the number of small laddoos.

Ans. Given, radius of a spherical laddoo, $r = 5$ cm

$\therefore$ Volume of a spherical laddoo $= \frac{4}{3}\pi r^3 = \frac{4}{3}\pi (5)^3$

$$= \frac{4}{3} \times 125\pi = \frac{500}{3}\pi \text{ cm}^3$$

Now, radius of a small laddoo = 2.5 cm

So, volume of a small laddoo $= \frac{4}{3}\pi \times (2.5)^3 = \frac{62.5}{3}\pi \text{ cm}^3$

$$\therefore \quad \text{Number of laddoos} = \frac{\text{Volume of laddoo}}{\text{Volume of small laddoo}} = \frac{\frac{500\pi}{3}}{\frac{62.5\pi}{3}} = \frac{500}{62.5} = 8$$

Hence, the number of small laddoos is 8.

Q.10 A right triangle with sides 6 cm, 8 cm and 10 cm is revolved about the side 8 cm. Find the volume and the curved surface of the solid so formed.

Ans. When a right triangle with sides 6 cm, 8 cm and 10 cm is revolved about the side 8 cm, then solid formed is a cone whose height of a cone, $h = 8$ cm and radius of a cone, $r = 6$ cm.

Slant height of a cone, $l = 10$ cm

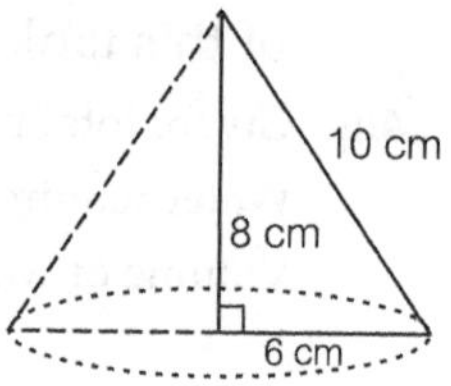

$\therefore$ Volume of a cone $= \frac{1}{3}\pi r^2 h$

$$= \frac{1}{3} \times \frac{22}{7} \times 6 \times 6 \times 8$$

$$= \frac{6336}{21} = 301.7 \text{ cm}^3$$

And curved surface area of a cone $= \pi r l$

$$= \frac{22}{7} \times 6 \times 10 = \frac{1320}{7}$$

$$= 188.5 \text{ cm}^2$$

Hence, the volume and surface area of a cone are 301.7 cm^3 and 188.5 cm^2, respectively.

Long Answer Type Questions

***Q.1** A cylindrical tube opened at both the ends is made of iron sheet which is 2 cm thick. If the outer diameter is 16 cm and its length is 100 cm, find how many cubic centimetres of iron has been used in making the tube?

Thinking Proces Quantity of iron used in making cylindrical tube = Outer volume of tube – Inner volume of tube = $\pi(r_1^2 - r_2^2)h$.

Ans. Given, outer diameter of a cylindrical tube, $d = 16$ cm

$\Rightarrow$ Let r_1 = outer radius of a cylindrical tube = 8 cm [$\because d = 16$ cm]

r_2 = inner radius of a cylindrical tube = Outer radius of tube – thickness of the iron sheet

$= 8 - 2 = 6$ cm

and height of a cylindrical tube, $h = 100$ cm

$\therefore$ Volume of metal used in making cylindrical tube

= Outer volume of cylindrical tube – Inner volume of tube

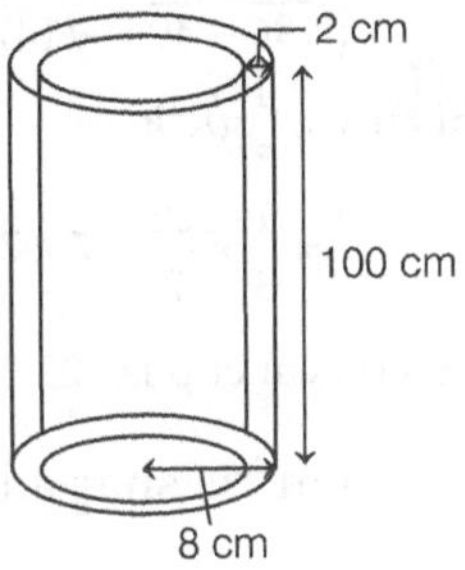

$$= \pi r_1^2 h - \pi r_2^2 h = \pi h(r_1^2 - r_2^2)$$
$$= \frac{22}{7} \times 100(8^2 - 6^2) = \frac{22}{7} \times 100(8+6)(8-6)$$
$$= \frac{22}{7} \times 100 \times 14 \times 2$$
$$= 2200 \times 4 = 8800 \text{ cm}^3$$

Hence, 8800 cm^3 of iron has been used in making a cylindrical tube.

Q.2 A semi-circular sheet of metal of diameter 28 cm is bent to form an open conical cup. Find the capacity of the cup.

Thinking Process

(i) Firstly, determine the circumference of cone by using the formula $2\pi R$ and circumference of semi-circle by using the formula, πr and equate them to get the radius of cone.

(ii) Secondly, determine the height of cone by using the formula, $h = \sqrt{l^2 - R^2}$.

(iii) Further, determine the capacity of conical cup by using the formula,

Capacity of cup = Volume of cup = $\frac{1}{3}\pi R^2 h$.

(*) Topics related to these question have been removed from latest NCERT.

Ans. Given, diameter of a semi-circular sheet = 28 cm

$\therefore$ Radius of a semi-circular sheet, $r = \frac{28}{2} = 14$ cm

Since, a semi-circular sheet of metal is bent to form an open conical cup. Let the radius of a conical cup be R.

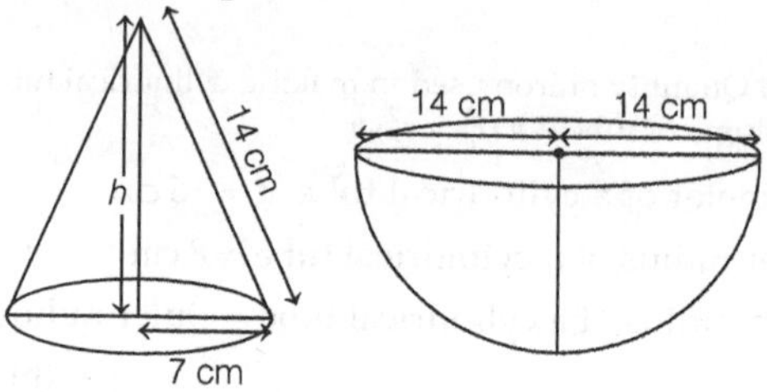

$\therefore$ Circumference of base of cone = Circumference of semi-circle

$$2\pi R = \pi r$$

$$\Rightarrow \quad 2\pi R = \pi \times 14 \Rightarrow R = 7\text{cm}$$

Now, $$h = \sqrt{l^2 - R^2} = \sqrt{14^2 - 7^2} \qquad [\because l^2 = h^2 + R^2]$$

$$= \sqrt{196 - 49} = \sqrt{147} = 12.1243 \text{ cm}$$

$\therefore$ Volume (capacity) of conical cup $= \frac{1}{3}\pi R^2 h$

$$= \frac{1}{3} \times \frac{22}{7} \times 7 \times 7 \times 12.1243 = 622.38 \text{ cm}^3$$

Hence, the capacity of an open conical cup is 622.38 cm^3.

Q.3 A cloth having an area of 165 m^2 is shaped into the form of a conical tent of radius 5 m.

(i) How many students can sit in the tent if a student, on an average, occupies $\frac{5}{7}$ m^2 on the ground?

(ii) Find the volume of the cone.

Ans. (i) Given, radius of the base of a conical tent = 5 m

and area required for a student to sit on the ground $= \frac{5}{7}$ m^2

$\therefore$ Area of the base of a conical tent $= \pi r^2 = \frac{22}{7} \times 5 \times 5$ m^2

Now, number of students $= \dfrac{\text{Area of the base of a conical tent}}{\text{Area required for a student to sit on the ground}}$

$$= \frac{\frac{22 \times 5 \times 5}{7}}{\frac{5}{7}} = \frac{22}{7} \times 5 \times 5 \times \frac{7}{5} = 110$$

Hence, 110 students can sit in the conical tent.

(ii) Given, area of the cloth to form a conical tent = 165 m^2

Radius of the base of a conical tent, $r = 5$ m

Curved surface area of a conical tent = Area of cloth to form a conical tent

$$\Rightarrow \quad \pi rl = 165$$

$$\Rightarrow \quad \frac{22}{7} \times 5 \times l = 165$$

$$\therefore \quad l = \frac{165 \times 7}{22 \times 5} = \frac{33 \times 7}{22} = 10.5 \text{ m}$$

Now, height of a conical tent $= \sqrt{l^2 - r^2} = \sqrt{(10.5)^2 - (5)^2}$

$$= \sqrt{110.25 - 25} = \sqrt{85.25} = 9.23 \text{ m}$$

Volume of a cone (conical tent) $= \frac{1}{3}\pi r^2 h = \frac{1}{3} \times \frac{22}{7} \times 5 \times 5 \times 9.23$

$$= \frac{1}{3} \times \frac{1550 \times 9.23}{7} = \frac{5076.5}{7 \times 3} = 241.7 \text{ m}^3$$

Hence, the volume of the cone (conical tent) is 241.7 m^3.

Q.4 The water for a factory is stored in a hemispherical tank whose internal diameter is 14 m. The tank contains 50 kL of water. Water is pumped into the tank to fill to its capacity. Calculate the volume of water pumped into the tank.

Ans. Given, internal diameter of a hemispherical tank = 14m

Then, internal radius of a hemispherical tank, $r = 7$m

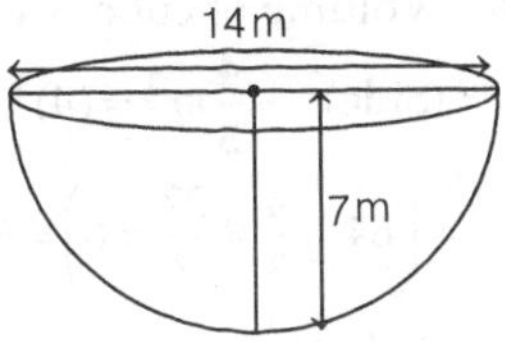

Quantity of water in the hemispherical tank = 50 kL = 50 × 1000 L = 50000 L

[∵ 1 kL = 1000L]

$= 50 \text{ m}^3$ [∵ $1 \text{ m}^3 = 1000$ L]

$\therefore$ Volume of the hemispherical tank $= \frac{2}{3}\pi r^3 = \frac{2}{3} \times \frac{22}{7} \times (7)^3$

$$= \frac{2}{3} \times \frac{22}{7} \times 7 \times 7 \times 7 = 718.66 \text{ m}^3$$

Now, volume of water pumped into the hemispherical tank = 718.66 – 50

$$= 668.66 \text{ m}^3$$

Hence, the volume of water pumped into the tank is 668.66 m^3.

Q.5 The volumes of the two spheres are in the ratio 64 : 27. Find the ratio of their surface areas.

Ans. Let the radius of two spheres be r_1 and r_2.

Given, the ratio of the volumes of two spheres = 64 : 27

$$\frac{V_1}{V_2} = \frac{64}{27} \Rightarrow \frac{\frac{4}{3}\pi r_1^3}{\frac{4}{3}\pi r_2^3} = \frac{64}{27} \qquad \left[\because \text{volume of sphere} = \frac{4}{3}\pi r^3\right]$$

$$\Rightarrow \quad \left(\frac{r_1}{r_2}\right)^3 = \left(\frac{4}{3}\right)^3$$

$$\Rightarrow \quad \frac{r_1}{r_2} = \frac{4}{3}$$

Let the surface areas of the two spheres be S_1 and S_2.

$$\therefore \quad \frac{S_1}{S_2} = \frac{4\pi r_1^2}{4\pi r_2^2} = \left(\frac{r_1}{r_2}\right)^2 \Rightarrow \frac{S_1}{S_2} = \left(\frac{4}{3}\right)^2 = \frac{16}{9}$$

[$\because$ surface area of sphere $= 4\pi r^2$]

$$\Rightarrow \quad S_1 : S_2 = 16 : 9$$

Hence, the ratio of the their surface areas is 16 : 9.

Q.6 A cube of side 4 cm contains a sphere touching its sides. Find the volume of the gap in between.

Ans. Given, side of a cube = 4 cm

Side of a cube = Diameter of a sphere

4 = Diameter of a sphere

$\therefore$ Radius of a sphere, $r = \frac{4}{2} = 2$ cm

Volume of the gap = Volume of cube – Volume of sphere

$$= (\text{Side})^3 - \frac{4}{3}\pi r^3 = (4)^3 - \frac{4}{3}\pi(2)^3$$

$$= \left(64 - \frac{4}{3} \times \frac{22}{7} \times 8\right) = 64 - 33.52 = 30.48 \text{ cm}^3$$

Hence, the volume of the gap in between a cube and a sphere is 30.48 cm^3.

Q.7 A sphere and a right circular cylinder of the same radius have equal volumes. By what percentage does the diameter of the cylinder exceed its height?

Ans. Let r be the radius of a sphere and a cylinder

According to the question,

Volume of cylinder = Volume of a sphere

$$\Rightarrow \quad \pi r^2 h = \frac{4}{3}\pi r^3 \Rightarrow h = \frac{4}{3} r$$

$$\left[\because \text{volume of cylinder} = \pi r^2 h \text{ and volume of sphere} = \frac{4}{3}\pi r^3\right]$$

$\because$ Diameter of the cylinder $= 2r$

$\therefore$ Increase in diameter from height of the cylinder $= 2r - \frac{4r}{3} = \frac{2r}{3}$

Now, percentage increase in diameter of the cylinder $= \dfrac{\frac{2r}{3} \times 100}{\frac{4}{3} r} = 50\%$

Hence, the diameter of the cylinder exceeds its height by 50%.

***Q.8** 30 circular plates, each of radius 14 cm and thickness 3 cm are placed one above the another to form a cylindrical solid. Find

(i) the total surface area.

(ii) volume of the cylinder so formed.

Thinking Process Height of the solid cylinder = Total thickness of 30 circular plates

Ans. Given, radius of a circular plate, $r = 14$ cm

Thickness of a circular plate = 3 cm

Thickness of 30 circular plates = $30 \times 3 = 90$ cm

Since, 30 circular plates are placed one above the another to form a cylindrical solid. Then,

Height of the cylindrical solid, h = Thickness of 30 circular plates = 90 cm

(i) Total surface area of the cylindrical solid so formed

$$= 2\pi r(h + r) = 2 \times \frac{22}{7} \times 14(90 + 14)$$

$$= 44 \times 2 \times 104 = 9152 \text{ cm}^2$$

Hence, the total surface area of the cylindrical solid is 9152 cm^2.

(ii) Volume of the cylinder so formed = $\pi r^2 h$

$$= \frac{22}{7}(14)^2 \times 90 = \frac{22}{7} \times 14 \times 14 \times 90$$

$$= 22 \times 28 \times 90 = 55440 \text{ cm}^3$$

Hence, the volume of the cylinder so formed is 55440 cm^3.

(*) Topics related to these question have been removed from latest NCERT.

Chapter 14

Statistics and Probability*

Multiple Choice Questions (MCQs)

Choose the correct answer from the given four options in the following questions:

Q.1 The class mark of the class 90-120 is

(a) 90 (b) 105 (c) 115 (d) 120

Ans. *(b)* In a given class 90-120, upper class limit = 120

and lower class limit = 90

We know that class mark $= \dfrac{\text{Upper class limit} + \text{Lower class limit}}{2}$

$$= \frac{120 + 90}{2} = \frac{210}{2} = 105$$

Q.2 The range of the data 25, 18, 20, 22, 16, 6, 17, 15, 12, 30, 32, 10, 19, 8, 11 and 20 is

(a) 10 (b) 15 (c) 18 (d) 26

Ans. *(d)* In a given data, maximum value = 32

and minimum value = 6

As we know, range of the data = Maximum value − Minimum value

$$= 32 - 6 = 26$$

Hence, the range of the given data is 26.

Q.3 In a frequency distribution, the mid value of a class is 10 and the width of the class is 6. The lower limit of the class is

(a) 6 (b) 7 (c) 8 (d) 12

Ans. *(b)* Let x and y be the upper and lower class limit in a frequency distribution, respectively.

Now, mid value of a class $= \dfrac{x + y}{2} = 10$ [given]

$\Rightarrow$ $x + y = 20$ ...(i)

Also, given that width of class = 6

$\Rightarrow$ $x - y = 6$ ...(ii)

Note (*) Topic probability has been deleted from latest NCERT.

On adding Eqs. (i) and (ii), we get

$$2x = 20 + 6$$

$$\Rightarrow \quad 2x = 26 \Rightarrow x = 13$$

On putting $x = 13$ in Eq. (i), we get

$$13 + y = 20 \Rightarrow y = 7$$

Hence, the lower limit of the class is 7.

Q.4 The width of each of five continuous classes in a frequency distribution is 5 and the lower class limit of the lowest class is 10. The upper class limit of the highest class is

(a) 15 (b) 25 (c) 35 (d) 40

Ans. *(c)* Let x and y be the upper and lower class limit of the lowest class in frequency distribution respectively.

Given, width of the class = 5

$$\Rightarrow \quad x - y = 5 \quad \ldots(i)$$

and lower class limit $(y) = 10$

On putting $y = 10$ in Eq. (i), we get

$$x - 10 = 5 \Rightarrow x = 15$$

So, the upper class limit of the lowest class is 15.

We know that the upper class limit of the highest class

= (Number of continuous classes × Class width + Lower class limit of the lowest class)

$$= 5 \times 5 + 10 = 25 + 10 = 35$$

Hence, the upper class limit of the highest class is 35.

Alternate Method

After finding the upper class limit of the lowest class, the five continuous classes in a frequency distribution with width 5 are 10-15, 15-20, 20-25, 25-30 and 30-35.

Thus, the highest class is 30-35,

Hence, the upper limit of this class is 35.

Q.5 Let m be the mid-point and l be the upper class limit of a class in a continuous frequency distribution. The lower class limit of the class is

(a) $2m + l$ (b) $2m - l$ (c) $m - l$ (d) $m - 2l$

Ans. *(b)* Let x and y be the lower and upper class limit of a continuous frequency distribution, respectively.

Now, mid-point of a class $= \dfrac{x + y}{2} = m$ [given]

$$\Rightarrow \quad x + y = 2m \Rightarrow x + l = 2m$$

[$\because$ $y = l$ = upper class limit (given)]

$$\Rightarrow \quad x = 2m - l$$

Hence, the lower class limit of the class is $2m - l$.

Q.6 The class marks of a frequency distribution are given as follows 15, 20, 25, ... The class corresponding to the class mark 20 is

(a) 12.5 - 17.5 (b) 17.5 - 22.5 (c) 18.5 - 21.5 (d) 19.5 - 20.5

Ans. ***(b)*** Width of class = 20 − 15 = 5

Class marks = 20

$$\therefore \quad \text{lower limit} = 20 - \frac{5}{2} = \frac{40-5}{2} = \frac{35}{2} = 17.5$$

$$\text{and upper limit} = 20 + \frac{5}{2} = \frac{40+5}{2} = \frac{45}{2} = 22.5$$

Therefore, the class corresponding to the class mark 20 is 17.5-22.5.

Q.7 In the class intervals 10-20, 20-30, the number 20 is included in

(a) 10-20 (b) 20-30

(c) Both the intervals (d) None of these

Ans. ***(b)*** Since, the class interval 10-20 is the first interval of frequency distribution and 20-30 is the next one but the number 20 is present in both intervals. We know that the number is always included in the lower limit of the class interval. So, 20 is included in 20-30.

***Q.8** A grouped frequency table with class intervals of equal sizes using 250-270 (270 not included in this interval) as one of the class interval is constructed for the following data

268, 220, 368, 258, 242, 310, 272, 342, 310, 290, 300, 320, 319, 304, 402, 318, 406, 292, 354, 278, 210, 240, 330, 316, 406, 215, 258, 236.

The frequency of the class 310-330 is

(a) 4 (b) 5 (c) 6 (d) 7

Ans. ***(c)*** Here, we arrange the given data into groups like 210-230, 230-250, ..., 390-410. (since, our data is from 210 to 406). The class width in this case is 20.

Now, the given data can be arrange in tabular form as follows

Class interval	Tally marks	Frequency
210 - 230	III	3
230 - 250	III	3
250 - 270	III	3
270 - 290	II	2
290 - 310	IIII	4
310 - 330	IIII I	6
330 - 350	II	2
350 - 370	II	2
370 - 390	-	0
390 - 410	III	3

Thus, the frequency of the class 310-330 is 6.

(*) Topics related to these question have been removed from latest NCERT.

***Q.9** A grouped frequency distribution table with classes of equal sizes using 63-72 (72 included) as one of the class is constructed for the following data.
30, 32, 45, 54, 74, 78, 108, 112, 66, 76, 88,
40, 14, 20, 15, 35, 44, 66, 75, 84, 95, 96,
102, 110, 88, 74, 112, 14, 34, 44.
The number of classes in the distribution will be

(a) 9 (b) 10 (c) 11 (d) 12

Ans. *(b)* We arrange the given data into groups like 13-22, 23-32,..., 103-112. (since, our data is from 14 to 112). The class width in this case is 9.

Now, the given data can be arranged in tabular form as follows

Class interval	Tally marks	Frequency
13 - 22	||||	4
23 - 32	||	2
33 - 42	|||	3
43 - 52	|||	3
53 - 62	|	1
63 - 72	||	2
73 - 82	~~||||~~	5
83 - 92	|||	3
93 - 102	|||	3
103 - 112	||||	4

Hence, the number of classes in distribution will be 10.

Mistake Alert ! *Students be careful to arrange the data to their respective intervals.*

Q.10 To draw a histogram to represent the following frequency distribution.

Class interval	5 - 10	10 - 15	15 - 25	25 - 45	45 - 75
Frequency	6	12	10	8	15

The adjusted frequency for the class 25-45 is

(a) 6 (b) 5 (c) 3 (d) 2

Thinking Process

Use the formula,

$$\text{Adjusted frequency} = \frac{\text{Frequency}}{\text{Class width}} \times \text{Minimum class width}$$

Ans. *(d)* Here, minimum class width = 5

Corresponding frequency in the interval (25-45) = 8

and the width of the interval 25-45 = 20

(*) Topics related to these question have been removed from latest NCERT.

$\therefore$ Adjusted frequency $= \dfrac{\text{Frequency}}{\text{Class width of (25 - 45)}} \times \text{Minimum class width}$

$$= \frac{8}{20} \times 5 = \frac{8}{4} = 2$$

Hence, the adjusted frequency for the class 25-45 is 2.

***Q.11** The mean of five numbers is 30. If one number is excluded, their mean becomes 28. The excluded number is

(a) 28 (b) 30

(c) 35 (d) 38

Ans. *(d)* Let x_1, x_2, x_3, x_4 and x_5 be five numbers and the excluded number be x_5.

Given, mean of the five numbers = 30

$$\Rightarrow \quad \frac{x_1 + x_2 + x_3 + x_4 + x_5}{5} = 30$$

$$\Rightarrow \quad x_1 + x_2 + x_3 + x_4 + x_5 = 150$$

$$\Rightarrow \quad x_1 + x_2 + x_3 + x_4 = 150 - x_5$$

On dividing both sides by 4, we get

$$\frac{x_1 + x_2 + x_3 + x_4}{4} = \frac{150 - x_5}{4} \quad \text{...(i)}$$

Given, mean of the four numbers = 28

$$\therefore \quad \frac{150 - x_5}{4} = 28 \quad \text{[from Eq. (i)]}$$

$$\Rightarrow \quad 150 - x_5 = 112$$

$$\Rightarrow \quad x_5 = 150 - 112$$

$$\Rightarrow \quad x_5 = 38$$

Hence, the excluded number is 38.

***Q.12** If the mean of the observations $x, x+3, x+5, x+7$ and $x+10$ is 9, then mean of the last three observations is

(a) $10\frac{1}{3}$ (b) $10\frac{2}{3}$

(c) $11\frac{1}{3}$ (d) $11\frac{2}{3}$

● **Concept Insight** Use the formula for mean of ungrouped data, $\bar{x} = \dfrac{x_1 + x_2 + \ldots + x_n}{n}$.

Ans. *(c)* Given that the mean of the observations $x, x + 3, x + 5, x + 7$ and $x + 10$ is 9.

$$\therefore \quad \frac{x + x + 3 + x + 5 + x + 7 + x + 10}{5} = 9$$

$$\Rightarrow \quad 5x + 25 = 45$$

$$\Rightarrow \quad 5x = 20$$

$$\Rightarrow \quad x = 4$$

$\therefore$ Last three observations are $x + 5 = 4 + 5 = 9$, $x + 7 = 4 + 7 = 11$

and $x + 10 = 4 + 10 = 14$

(*) Topics related to these question have been removed from latest NCERT.

So, the mean of last three observations $= \dfrac{9+11+14}{3}$

$$= \frac{34}{3} = 11\frac{1}{3}$$

Hence, the mean of last three observations is $11\frac{1}{3}$.

***Q.13** If $\bar{x}$ represents the mean of n observations $x_1, x_2, \ldots, x_n$, then value of $\sum_{i=1}^{n} (x_i - \bar{x})$ is

(a) -1 (b) 0
(c) 1 (d) $n-1$

Ans. *(b)* Given, $\bar{x} = \dfrac{\sum_{i=1}^{n} x_i}{n}$

$$\Rightarrow \quad \sum_{i=1}^{n} x_i = n\bar{x} \quad \ldots\text{(i)}$$

Now, $\sum_{i=1}^{n}(x_i - \bar{x}) = \sum_{i=1}^{n} x_i - \sum_{i=1}^{n} \bar{x}$

$$= n\bar{x} - \bar{x}\sum_{i=1}^{n} 1 \quad \text{[from Eq. (i)]}$$

$$= n\bar{x} - \bar{x}\cdot n \quad \left[\because \sum_{i=1}^{n}(1) = n\right]$$

$$= 0$$

***Q.14** If each observation of the data is increased by 5, then their mean

(a) remains the same (b) becomes 5 times the original mean
(c) is decreased by 5 (d) is increased by 5

Thinking Process First, add 5 on each observation of the data, then use the formula, mean $= \dfrac{\text{Sum of all observations}}{\text{Number of observations}}$. Further, simplify it to get the required result.

Ans. *(d)* Let $x_1, x_2, \ldots, x_n$ be the n observations.

Then, old mean $\bar{x}_{\text{old}} = \dfrac{\sum_{i=1}^{n} x_i}{n}$ ...(i)

Now, adding 5 in each observation, the new mean,

$$\bar{x}_{\text{new}} = \frac{(x_1+5)+(x_2+5)+\cdots+(x_n+5)}{n}$$

$$\Rightarrow \quad \bar{x}_{\text{new}} = \frac{(x_1+x_2+\cdots+x_n)+5n}{n}$$

(*) Topics related to these question have been removed from latest NCERT.

$$\Rightarrow \quad \bar{x}_{\text{new}} = \frac{\sum_{i=1}^{n} x_i}{n} + 5$$

$$\Rightarrow \quad \bar{x}_{\text{new}} = \bar{x}_{\text{old}} + 5 \qquad \text{[from Eq. (i)]}$$

Hence, the new mean is increased by 5.

***Q.15** Let $\bar{x}$ be the mean of $x_1, x_2, \ldots, x_n$ and $\bar{y}$ be the mean of $y_1, y_2, \ldots, y_n$. If $\bar{z}$ is the mean of $x_1, x_2, \ldots, x_n, y_1, y_2, \ldots, y_n$, then $\bar{z}$ is equal to

(a) $\bar{x} + \bar{y}$ (b) $\frac{\bar{x} + \bar{y}}{2}$ (c) $\frac{\bar{x} + \bar{y}}{n}$ (d) $\frac{\bar{x} + \bar{y}}{2n}$

Ans. ***(b)*** Given, $\sum_{i=1}^{n} x_i = n\bar{x}$ and $\sum_{j=1}^{n} y_j = n\bar{y}$ ...(i) $\left[\because \bar{x} = \frac{\sum_{i=1}^{n} x_i}{n}\right]$

Now,

$$\bar{z} = \frac{(x_1 + x_2 + \cdots + x_n) + (y_1 + y_2 + \cdots + y_n)}{n + n}$$

$$= \frac{\sum_{i=1}^{n} x_i + \sum_{j=1}^{n} y_j}{2n}$$

$$= \frac{n\bar{x} + n\bar{y}}{2n} = \frac{\bar{x} + \bar{y}}{2} \qquad \text{[from Eq. (i)]}$$

Mistake Alert! *Do not forget to divide* $\sum x_i$ *by* n.

***Q.16** If $\bar{x}$ is the mean of $x_1, x_2, \ldots, x_n$, then for $a \neq 0$, the mean of $ax_1, ax_2, \ldots, ax_n, \frac{x_1}{a}, \frac{x_2}{a}, \ldots, \frac{x_n}{a}$ is

(a) $\left(a + \frac{1}{a}\right)\bar{x}$ (b) $\left(a + \frac{1}{a}\right)\frac{\bar{x}}{2}$ (c) $\left(a + \frac{1}{a}\right)\frac{\bar{x}}{n}$ (d) $\frac{\left(a + \frac{1}{a}\right)\bar{x}}{2n}$

Ans. ***(b)*** Given, the mean of $x_1, x_2, \ldots, x_n$ is $\bar{x}$.

$$\therefore \quad \sum_{i=1}^{n} x_i = n\bar{x} \qquad \text{...(i)}$$

Now, let the mean of $\left(ax_1, ax_2, \ldots, ax_n, \frac{x_1}{a}, \frac{x_2}{a}, \ldots, \frac{x_n}{a}\right)$ be $\bar{z}$.

Then,

$$\bar{z} = \frac{(ax_1 + ax_2 + \cdots + ax_n) + \left(\frac{x_1}{a} + \frac{x_2}{a} + \cdots + \frac{x_n}{a}\right)}{n + n}$$

$$= \frac{a(x_1 + x_2 + \cdots + x_n) + \frac{1}{a}(x_1 + x_2 + \cdots + x_n)}{2n}$$

(*) Topics related to these question have been removed from latest NCERT.

$$= \frac{\left(a+\frac{1}{a}\right)(x_1+x_2+\cdots+x_n)}{2n}$$

$$= \frac{\left(a+\frac{1}{2}\right)(x_1+x_2+\ldots+x_n)}{2n} = \frac{\left(a+\frac{1}{1}\right)\sum_{i=1}^{n} x_i}{2n}$$

$$= \frac{\left(a+\frac{1}{a}\right)\cdot n\bar{x}}{2n} \qquad \text{[from Eq. (i)]}$$

$$= \frac{\left(a+\frac{1}{a}\right)\bar{x}}{2}$$

***Q.17** If $\bar{x}_1, \bar{x}_2, \bar{x}_3, \ldots, \bar{x}_n$ are the means of n groups with $n_1, n_2, \ldots, n_n$ number of observations, respectively, then the mean $\bar{x}$ of all the groups taken together is given by

(a) $\sum_{i=1}^{n} n_i \bar{x}_i$ (b) $\frac{\sum_{i=1}^{n} n_i \bar{x}_i}{n^2}$ (c) $\frac{\sum_{i=1}^{n} n_i \bar{x}_i}{\sum_{i=1}^{n} n_i}$ (d) $\frac{\sum_{i=1}^{n} n_i \bar{x}_i}{2n}$

Ans. *(c)* Given, $\bar{x}_1, \bar{x}_2, \bar{x}_3, \ldots, \bar{x}_n$ are the means of n groups having number of observations $n_1, n_2, \ldots, n_n$, respectively.

Then, $n_1\bar{x}_1 = \sum_{i=1}^{n_1} x_i,\ n_2\bar{x}_2 = \sum_{j=1}^{n_2} x_j,\ n_3\bar{x}_3 = \sum_{k=1}^{n_3} x_k, \ldots,\ n_n\bar{x}_n = \sum_{p=1}^{n_n} x_p$

Now, the mean $\bar{x}$ of all the groups taken together is given by

$$\bar{x} = \frac{\sum_{i=1}^{n_1} x_i + \sum_{j=1}^{n_2} x_j + \sum_{k=1}^{n_3} x_k + \cdots + \sum_{p=1}^{n_n} x_p}{n_1+n_2+\cdots+n_n}$$

$$= \frac{n_1\bar{x}_1 + n_2\bar{x}_2 + n_3\bar{x}_3 + \cdots + n_n\bar{x}_n}{n_1+n_2+\cdots+n_n} = \frac{\sum_{i=1}^{n} n_i \bar{x}_i}{\sum_{i=1}^{n} n_i}$$

Hence, the mean of all the groups taken together is given by $\bar{x} = \frac{\sum_{i=1}^{n} n_i \bar{x}_i}{\sum_{i=1}^{n} n_i}$.

***Q.18** The mean of 100 observations is 50. If one of the observation which was 50 is replaced by 150, the resulting mean will be

(a) 50.5 (b) 51
(c) 51.5 (d) 52

(*) Topics related to these question have been removed from latest NCERT.

Ans. ***(b)*** Given, mean of 100 observations is 50.

Here, $n = 100$ and $\bar{x} = 50$

Then, $$\text{mean} = \frac{\sum_{i=1}^{n} x_i}{n}$$

$$\therefore \quad \frac{1}{100} \times \sum_{i=1}^{100} x_i = 50 \Rightarrow \sum_{i=1}^{100} x_i = 5000 \quad \ldots\text{(i)}$$

Now, the observation 50 is replaced by 150, then Eq. (i) becomes,

$$\sum_{i=1}^{100} x_i = 5000 - 50 + 150 = 5100$$

$$\therefore \quad \text{Resulting mean} = \frac{\sum_{i=1}^{100} x_i}{100} = \frac{5100}{100} = 51$$

Hence, the resulting mean is 51.

***Q.19** There are 50 numbers. Each number is subtracted from 53 and the mean of the numbers so obtained is found to be – 3.5. The mean of the given numbers is

(a) 46.5 (b) 49.5 (c) 53.5 (d) 56.5

Ans. ***(d)*** Given, $n = 50$, then mean $(\bar{x}) = \frac{\sum_{i=1}^{n} x_i}{n}$

Then, $$\bar{x} = \frac{1}{50} \times \sum_{i=1}^{50} x_i \quad \ldots\text{(i)}$$

$$\Rightarrow \quad \sum_{i=1}^{50} x_i = 50\,\bar{x}$$

Now, subtract each observation from 53, we get a new mean, say $\bar{x}_{new}$.

$$\therefore \quad \bar{x}_{new} = \frac{(53 - x_1) + (53 - x_2) + \cdots + (53 - x_{50})}{50}$$

$$\Rightarrow \quad -3.5 = \frac{-(x_1 + x_2 + \cdots + x_{50}) + (53 + 53 + \cdots + 50 \text{ times})}{50}$$

$$\Rightarrow \quad -3.5 \times 50 = -(x_1 + x_2 + \cdots + x_{50}) + 53 \times 50$$

$$\Rightarrow \quad \sum_{i=1}^{50} x_i = 2650 + 175 = 2825$$

$$\therefore \text{ Mean of 50 observations} = \frac{1}{50} \sum_{i=1}^{50} x_i = \frac{1}{50} \times 2825 = 56.5 \qquad \left[\because \text{mean} = \frac{\sum_{i=1}^{n} x_i}{n}\right]$$

Hence, the mean of given number is 56.5.

(*) Topics related to these question have been removed from latest NCERT.

***Q.20** The mean of 25 observations is 36. Out of these observations if the mean of first 13 observations is 32 and that of the last 13 observations is 40, the 13th observation is

(a) 23 (b) 36 (c) 38 (d) 40

Ans. *(b)* Given, mean of 25 observations = 36

$\therefore$ Sum of 25 observations = $36 \times 25 = 900$

Now, the mean of first 13 observations = 32

$\therefore$ Sum of first 13 observations = $13 \times 32 = 416$

and the mean of last 13 observations = 40

$\therefore$ Sum of last 13 observations = $40 \times 13 = 520$

So, 13th observation = (Sum of last 13 observations + Sum of first 13 observations) – (Sum of 25 observations)

$$= (520 + 416) - 900 = 936 - 900 = 36$$

Hence, the 13th observation is 36.

***Q.21** The median of the data 78, 56, 22, 34, 45, 54, 39, 68, 54 and 84 is

(a) 45 (b) 49.5 (c) 54 (d) 56

Thinking Process First, arrange the given data in ascending order. Then, use the following formula for median.

(i) If, n is odd, then median = $\left(\frac{n+1}{2}\right)$th observation.

(ii) If n is even, then median = $\dfrac{\left(\frac{n}{2}\right)\text{th} + \left(\frac{n}{2}+1\right)\text{th}}{2}$ observation.

Ans. *(c)* First, we arrange the given observations in ascending order as follows

22, 34, 39, 45, 54, 54, 56, 68, 78, 84

Here, total number of observations, $n = 10$

Since, n is even, so we use the formula for median,

$$\text{Median} = \frac{\left(\frac{n}{2}\right)\text{th observation} + \left(\frac{n}{2}+1\right)\text{th observation}}{2}$$

$$= \frac{\left(\frac{10}{2}\right)\text{th observation} + \left(\frac{10}{2}+1\right)\text{th observation}}{2} \quad [\text{put, } n = 10]$$

$$= \frac{5\text{ th observation} + 6\text{th observation}}{2} = \frac{54+54}{2} = \frac{108}{2} = 54$$

Hence, the median of given data is 54.

Q.22 For drawing a frequency polygon of a continuous frequency distribution, we plot the points whose ordinates are the frequencies of the respective classes and abcissae are respectively.

(a) upper limits of the classes (b) lower limits of the classes

(c) class marks of the classes (d) upper limits of preceding classes

(*) Topics related to these question have been removed from latest NCERT.

Ans. *(c)* For drawing a frequency polygon of continuous frequency distribution, we draw the class marks of the classes on abcissae and frequencies of the respective classes on ordinates.

***Q.23** Median of the following numbers 4, 4, 5, 7, 6, 7, 7, 12, 3 is

(a) 4 (b) 5 (c) 6 (d) 7

Ans. *(c)* First, we arrange the given numbers in ascending order as follows

3, 4, 4, 5, 6, 7, 7, 7, 12

Here, $n = 9$

Since, n is odd, so we use the formula for median,

$$\text{Median} = \left(\frac{n+1}{2}\right)\text{th observation}$$

$$= \left(\frac{9+1}{2}\right)\text{th observation} \qquad [\text{put } n = 9]$$

$$= \left(\frac{10}{2}\right)\text{th observation} = 5\text{th observation} = 6$$

Hence, median of the given number is 6.

***Q.24** Mode of data 15, 14, 19, 20, 14, 15, 16, 14, 15, 18, 14, 19, 15, 17, 15 is

(a) 14 (b) 15 (c) 16 (d) 17

Thinking Process Find the maximum number of repeated observation to get the value of mode.

Ans. *(b)* First, we arrange the given data in ascending order as follows

14, 14, 14, 14, 15, 15, 15, 15, 15, 16, 17, 18, 19, 19, 20

From above, we see that 15 occurs most frequently *i.e.,* 5 times.

Hence, the mode of the given data is 15.

***Q.25** In a sample study of 642 people, it was found that 514 people have a high school certificate. If a person is selected at random, the probability that the person has a high school certificate is

(a) 0.5 (b) 0.6 (c) 0.7 (d) 0.8

Ans. *(d)* The total number of people in sample study = 642

The number of people who have high school certificate = 514

So, the probability that the person selected has a high school certificate

$$= \frac{\text{Number of favourable outcomes}}{\text{Total number of outcomes}} = \frac{514}{642} = 0.8$$

Hence, the probability that the person has a high school certificate is 0.8.

***Q.26** In a survey of 364 children aged 19-36 months, it was found that 91 liked to eat potato chips. If a child is selected at random, the probability that he/she does not like to eat potato chips is

(a) 0.25 (b) 0.50

(c) 0.75 (d) 0.80

(*) Topics related to these question have been removed from latest NCERT.

Ans. *(c)* Total number of children aged 19-36 month in the survey = 364
Since, 91 out of them like to eat potato chips.
∴ Number of children who do not like to eat potato chips = 364 − 91 = 273
∴ Probability that he/she does not like to eat potato chips

$$= \frac{\text{Number of favourable outcomes}}{\text{Total number of outcomes}}$$

$$= \frac{273}{364} = 0.75$$

Hence, the probability that he/she does not like to eat potato chips is 0.75.

***Q.27** In a medical examination of students of a class, the following blood groups are recorded.

Blood group	A	AB	B	O
Number of students	10	13	12	5

A student is selected at random from the class. The probability that he/she has blood group *B*, is

(a) $\frac{1}{4}$ (b) $\frac{13}{40}$

(c) $\frac{3}{10}$ (d) $\frac{1}{8}$

Ans. *(c)* Total number of students in a medical examination = 10 + 13 + 12 + 5 = 40
Number of persons who have *B* blood group = 12
∴ Probability that he/she has blood group $B = \frac{\text{Number of favourable outcomes}}{\text{Total number of outcomes}}$

$$= \frac{12}{40} = \frac{3}{10}$$

Hence, the probability that he/she has blood group *B* is $\frac{3}{10}$.

***Q.28** Two coins are tossed 1000 times and the outcomes are recorded as below

Number of heads	2	1	0
Frequency	200	550	250

Based on this information, the probability for atmost one head is

(a) $\frac{1}{5}$ (b) $\frac{1}{4}$

(c) $\frac{4}{5}$ (d) $\frac{3}{4}$

Ans. *(c)* The total number of times coins are tossed = 1000
Number of outcomes in which getting atmost one head = 550 + 250 = 800
∴ Probability for atmost one head $= \frac{800}{1000} = \frac{4}{5}$

(*) Topics related to these question have been removed from latest NCERT.

***Q.29** 80 bulbs are selected at random from a lot and their life time (in hours) is recorded in the form of a frequency table given below

Life time (in hours)	300	500	700	900	1100
Frequency	10	12	23	25	10

One bulb is selected at random from the lot. The probability that its life is 1150 hours is

(a) $\frac{1}{80}$ (b) $\frac{7}{16}$ (c) 0 (d) 1

Ans. ***(c)*** Total number of bulbs in a lot = 80

Number of bulbs whose life time is 1150 hours = 0

$\therefore$ Probability that its life time is 1150 hours $= \frac{0}{80} = 0$

Hence, the probability that its life time is 1150 is 0.

***Q.30** Refer to Q. 29. The probability that bulbs selected randomly from the lot has life less than 900 hours is

(a) $\frac{11}{40}$ (b) $\frac{5}{16}$ (c) $\frac{7}{16}$ (d) $\frac{9}{16}$

Ans. ***(d)*** Total number of bulbs in a lot = 80

Number of bulbs whose life time is less than 900 hours = 10 + 12 + 23 = 45

$\therefore$ Probability that bulbs has life time less than 900 hours $= \frac{45}{80} = \frac{9}{16}$

Hence, the probability that bulb has life time less than 900 hours is $\frac{9}{16}$.

Short Answer Questions with Reasoning

Q. 1 The frequency distribution has been represented graphically as follows.

Marks	0-20	20-40	40-60	60-100
Number of students	10	15	20	25

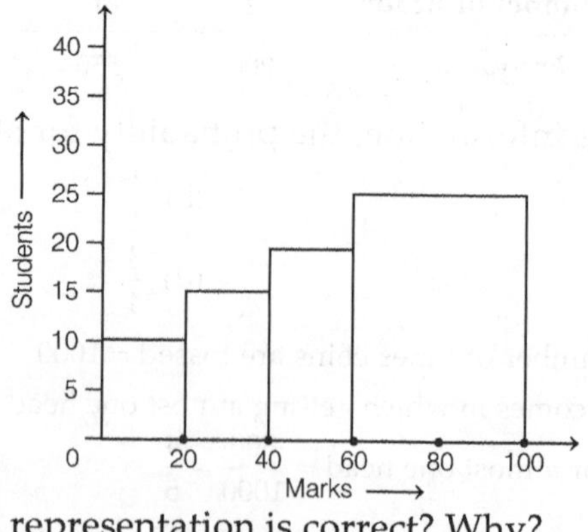

Do you think this representation is correct? Why?

(*) Topics related to these question have been removed from latest NCERT.

Ans. No, here the widths of the rectangles are varying, so we need to make certain modifications in the length of the rectangles so that the areas are proportional to the frequencies. We proceed as follows

1. Select a class interval with the minimum class size. Here, the minimum class size is 20.
2. Then, the length of the rectangles are modified to be proportionate to the class size 20 by using the formula, length of rectangle

$$= \left[\frac{\text{Minimum class size}}{\text{Class size}} \times \text{Frequency}\right]$$

Now, we get the following modified table

Marks	Number of students (Frequency)	Width of the class	Length of the rectangle
0-20	10	20	$\frac{10}{20} \times 20 = 10$
20-40	15	20	$\frac{15}{20} \times 20 = 15$
40-60	20	20	$\frac{20}{20} \times 20 = 20$
60-100	25	40	$\frac{25}{40} \times 20 = 12.5$

So, the correct histogram with varying width is given below

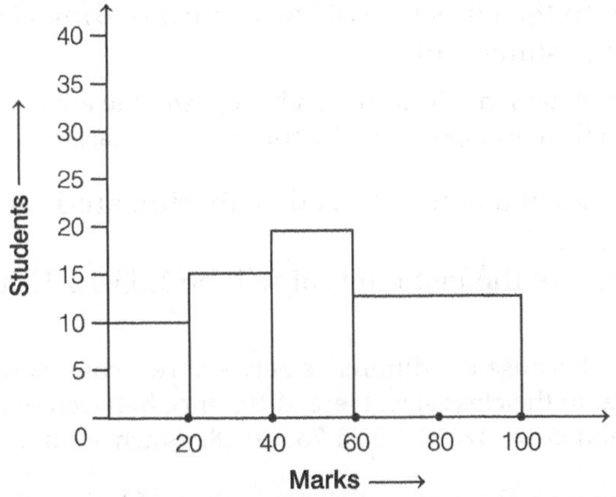

***Q.2** In a diagnostic test in Mathematics given to students, the following marks (out of 100) are recorded 46, 52, 48, 11, 41, 62, 54, 53, 96, 40, 98 and 44. Which average will be a good representative of the above data and why?

Ans. Median will be a good representative of the data, because

(i) Each value occurs once. (ii) The data is influenced by extreme values.

***Q.3** A child says that the median of 3, 14, 18, 20 and 5 is 18. What does not the child understand about finding the median?

Ans. The child does not understand, that data has to be arranged in ascending or descending order before finding the median.

(*****) Topics related to these question have been removed from latest NCERT.

*** Q.4** A football player scored the following number of goals in the 10 matches 1, 3, 2, 5, 8, 6, 1, 4, 7 and 9.

Since, the number of matches is 10 (an even number), therefore

$$\text{Median} = \frac{\text{5th observation} + \text{6th observation}}{2} = \frac{8+6}{2} = 7$$

Is it the correct answer and why?

Ans. *No*, It is not the correct answer, because the data have to be arranged in ascending or descending order before finding the median.

Arranging the data in ascending order 1, 1, 2, 3, 4, 5, 6, 7, 8, 9.

Here, number of observations is 10, which is even.

So, $$\text{median} = \frac{\left(\frac{n}{2}\right)\text{th observaton} + \left(\frac{n}{2}+1\right)\text{th observation}}{2}$$

$$= \frac{\left(\frac{10}{2}\right)\text{th observaton} + \left(\frac{10}{2}+1\right)\text{th observation}}{2}$$

$$= \frac{\text{5 th observation} + \text{6 th observation}}{2} = \frac{4+5}{2} = \frac{9}{2} = 4.5$$

Q.5 Is it correct to say that in a histogram, the area of each rectangle is proportional to the class size of the corresponding class interval? If not, correct the statement.

Ans. It is not correct statement. Because in a histogram, the area of each rectangle is proportional to the corresponding frequency of its class.

Q.6 The class marks of a continuous distribution are 1.04, 1.14, 1.24, 1.34, 1.44, 1.54 and 1.64.

Is it correct to say the last interval will be 1.55-1.73? Justify your answer.

Ans. It is not correct. Because the difference between two consecutive class marks should be equal to the class size. Here, difference between two consecutive class marks is 0.10 and class size of 1.55-1.73 is 0.18, which are not equal.

Q.7 30 children were asked about the number of hours they watched TV programmes last week. The result are recorded as under

Number of hours	0-5	5-10	10-15	15-20
Frequency	8	16	4	2

Can we say that the number of children who watched TV for 10 or more hours in a week is 22? Justify your answer.

Ans. *No*, the number of children who watched TV for 10 or more hours in a week is 4 + 2 *i.e.*, 6.

(*) Topics related to these question have been removed from latest NCERT.

***Q.8** Can the experimental probability of an event be a negative number? If not, why?

Ans. No, since the number of trials in which the event can happen cannot be negative and the total number of trials is always positive.

***Q.9** Can the experimental probability of an event be greater than 1? Justify your answer.

Ans. No, since the number of trials in which the event can happen cannot be greater than the total number of trials.

***Q.10** As the number of tosses of a coin increases, the ratio of the number of heads to the total number of tosses will be $\frac{1}{2}$. Is it correct? If not, write the correct one.

Ans. No, as the number tosses of coin increases, the ratio of the number of heads to the total number of tosses will be nearer to $\frac{1}{2}$ but not exactly $\frac{1}{2}$.

Short Answer Type Questions

* **Q.1** The blood groups of 30 students are recorded as follows
A, B, O, A, AB, O, A, O, B, A, O, B, A, AB, B, A, AB, B, A, A, O, A, AB, B, A, O, B, A, B, A
Prepare a frequency distribution table for the data.

Ans. The number of students who have a certain type of blood group is called the frequency of those blood groups. The required frequency distribution table for the given data is given below

Blood group	Tally marks	Number of students (Frequency)
A	~~IIII~~ ~~IIII~~ II	12
B	~~IIII~~ III	8
AB	IIII	4
O	~~IIII~~ I	6
Total		30

***Q.2** The value of π upto 35 decimal places is given below.
3.14159265358979323846264338327950288
Make a frequency distribution of the digits 0 to 9 after the decimal point.

Ans. The number of repeated digit is called the frequency of those digits. The required frequency distribution table for the given data is given below.

Digit	0	1	2	3	4	5	6	7	8	9	**Total**
Tally marks	I	II	~~IIII~~	~~IIII~~ I	III	IIII	III	II	~~IIII~~	IIII	
Frequency	1	2	5	6	3	4	3	2	5	4	35

(*) Topics related to these question have been removed from latest NCERT.

***Q.3** The scores (out of 100) obtained by 33 students in a Mathematics test are as follows: 69, 48, 84, 58, 48, 73, 83, 48, 66, 58, 84, 66, 64, 71, 64, 66, 69, 66, 83, 66, 69, 71, 81, 71, 73, 69, 66, 66, 64, 58, 64, 69, 69.
Represent this data in the form of a frequency distribution.

Ans. The number of students who have the same marks in mathematics is called the frequency of that mark. The required frequency distribution table for the given data is given below

Scores	Tally marks	Frequency
48	III	3
58	III	3
64	IIII	4
66	~~IIII~~ II	7
69	IIII I	6
71	III	3
73	II	2
81	I	1
83	II	2
84	II	2
Total		33

Q.4 Prepare a continuous grouped frequency distribution from the following data

Mid-point	Frequency
5	4
15	8
25	13
35	12
45	6

Also, find the size of class intervals.

Thinking Process

(i) Firstly, find the difference between two mid-points. Then, using the mid-point formula $= \frac{a + (a + 10)}{2}$, a is lower limit of the class and 10 is the difference between the two mid-points.

(ii) Further, prepare a continuous grouped frequency distribution table.

Ans. Here, the difference between two mid-points is $15 - 5 = 10$.
It means the width of the class interval is 10.
Let the lower limit of the first class interval be a.
Then, its upper limit $= a + 10$
Now, mid value of the first class interval = 5

We know, Mid value $= \frac{\text{Lower limit} + \text{Upper limit}}{2}$

$$\Rightarrow \quad 5 = \frac{a + a + 10}{2} \Rightarrow 2a + 10 = 10 \Rightarrow 2a = 0 \Rightarrow a = 0$$

(*) Topics related to these question have been removed from latest NCERT.

So, the first class interval is 0-10.

Now, we prepare a continuous grouped frequency distribution table is given below

Mid-point	Class interval	Frequency
5	0 - 10	4
15	10 - 20	8
25	20 - 30	13
35	30 - 40	12
45	40 - 50	6

Hence, the size of the class interval is 10 *i.e.*, $10 - 0$.

Q.5 Convert the given frequency distribution into a continuous grouped frequency distribution

Class interval	Frequency
150 - 153	7
154 - 157	7
158 - 161	15
162 - 165	10
166 - 169	5
170 - 173	6

In which intervals would 153.5 and 157.5 be included?

Ans. We can see that the given table has discontinuous frequency distribution. So, we first convert it into continuous frequency distribution.

Now, consider the classes 150-153, 154-157.

$\therefore$ Lower limit of 154-157 =154

and upper limit of 150-153=153

$\therefore$ Required difference $= 154 - 153 = 1$

So, half the difference $= \frac{1}{2} = 0.5$

So, we subtract 0.5 from each lower limit and add 0.5 to each upper limit.

The table for continuous grouped frequency distribution is given below

Class interval	Frequency
149.5 - 153.5	7
153.5 - 157.5	7
157.5 - 161.5	15
161.5 - 165.5	10
165.5 - 169.5	5
169.5 - 173.5	6

Thus, 153.5 and 157.5 are included in the class intervals 153.5-157.5 and 157.5-161.5, respectively.

Q.6 The expenditure of a family of different heads in a month is given below

Head	Food	Education	Clothing	House rent	Others	Savings
Expenditure (₹)	4000	2500	1000	3500	2500	1500

Draw a bar graph to represent the data above.

Ans. We draw a bar graph of this data in the following steps.

***Step* I** We represent the heads (variable) on the horizontal axis choosing any scale, as the width of the bar is not important. But for clarity, we take equal widths for all bars and maintain equal gaps in between them. Let one head be represented by one unit.

***Step* II** We represent the expenditure on the vertical axis. Since, the maximum expenditure is ₹ 4000, we can choose the scale as 1 unit = ₹ 500.

***Step* III** To represent our first head *i.e.*,food, we draw a rectangular bar with width 1 unit and height 8 units.

***Step* IV** Similarly, other heads are represented by leaving a gap of 1 unit in between two consecutive bars.

The bar graph for given data is shown below

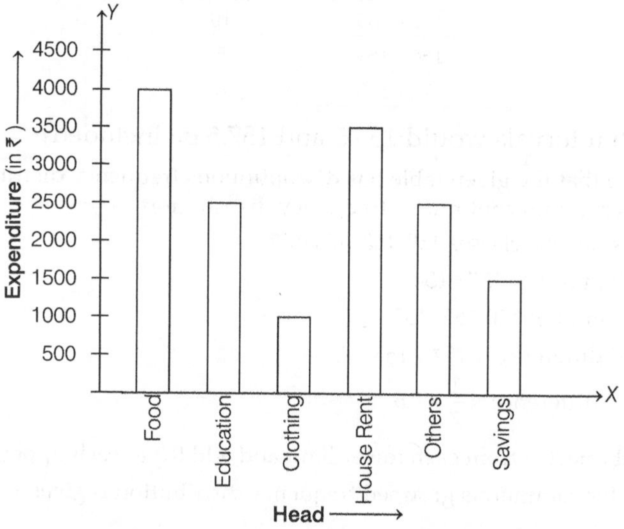

Q.7 Expenditure on education of a country during a five years period (2002-2006), in crore of rupees, is given below

Elementary Education	240
Secondary Education	120
University Education	190
Teacher's Training	20
Social Education	10
Other Educational Programmes	115
Cultural Programmes	25
Technical Education	125

Represent the information above by a bar graph.

Ans. We draw bar graph of this data in the following steps

***Step* I** We represent the education of a country (variable) on the horizontal axis choosing any scale, as the width of the bar is not important. But for clarity, we take equal widths for all bars and maintain equal gaps in between them. Let one head be represented by one unit.

***Step* II** We represent the expenditure on the vertical axis. Since, the maximum expenditure is ₹ 240 crore, we can choose the scale as 1 unit = ₹ 25 crore.

***Step* III** To represent our first education of a country *i.e.*,elementary education, we draw a rectangular bar with width 1 unit and height 9.6 units.

***Step* IV** Similarly, other variables are represented by leaving gap of 1 unit in between two consecutive bars.

The bar graph for given data is shown below

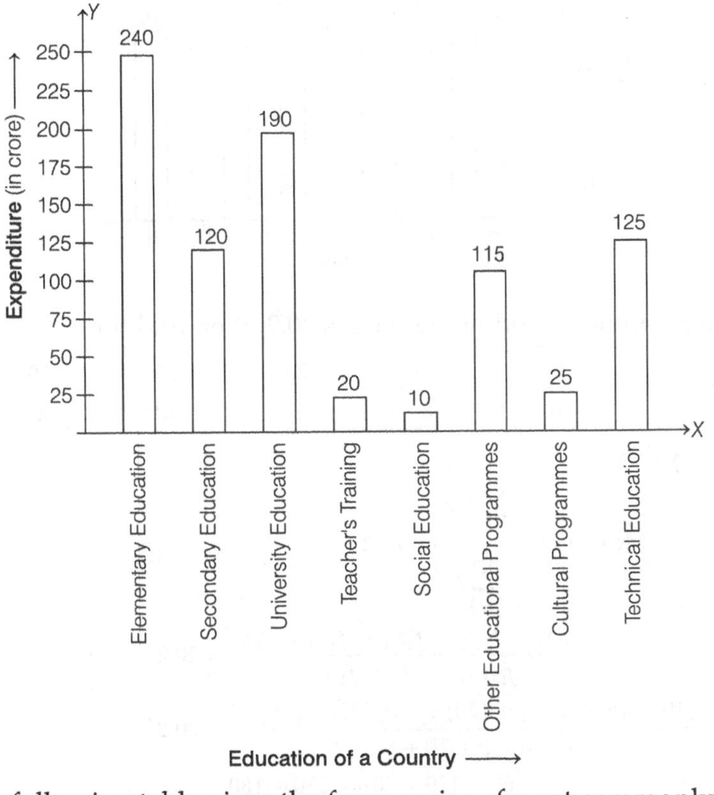

Q.8. The following table gives the frequencies of most commonly used letters *a, e, i, o, r, t, u,* from a page of a book :

Letters	*a*	*e*	*i*	*o*	*r*	*t*	*u*
Frequency	75	125	80	70	80	95	75

Represent the information above by a bar graph.

Ans. We draw bar graph of this data in the following steps

***Step* I** We represent the letters (variable) on the horizontal axis choosing any scale, as the width of the bar is not important. But for clarity, we take equal widths for all bars and maintain equal gaps in between them. Let one letter be represented by one unit.

Step **II** We represent the frequency on the vertical axis. Since, the maximum frequency is 125, we can choose the scale as 1 unit = 15 frequency.

Step **III** To represent our first letter *i.e.*, *a*, we draw a rectangular bar with width 1 unit and height 5 units.

Step **IV** Similarly, other letters are represented by leaving a gap of 1 unit in between two consecutive bars.

The bar graph for given data is shown below

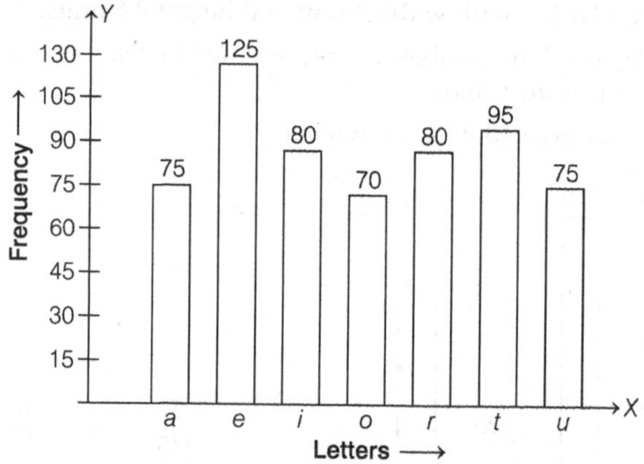

***Q.9** If the mean of the following data is 20.2, then find the value of p.

x	10	15	20	25	30
f	6	8	p	10	6

Ans. We know that,

$$\text{Mean } (\bar{x}) = \frac{\sum_{i=1}^{5} f_i x_i}{\sum_{i=1}^{5} f_i} = 20.2 \quad \text{[given]}$$

$$\Rightarrow \quad \frac{f_1x_1 + f_2x_2 + f_3x_3 + f_4x_4 + f_5x_5}{f_1 + f_2 + f_3 + f_4 + f_5} = 20.2$$

$$\Rightarrow \quad \frac{(6)(10) + (8)(15) + (p)(20) + (10)(25) + (6)(30)}{6 + 8 + p + 10 + 6} = 20.2$$

$$\Rightarrow \quad \frac{60 + 120 + 20p + 250 + 180}{30 + p} = 20.2$$

$$\Rightarrow \quad 20p + 610 = 606 + 20.2p$$

$$\Rightarrow \quad 610 - 606 = 0.2p \Rightarrow \frac{2p}{10} = 4$$

$$\therefore \quad p = 10 \times 2 = 20$$

Hence, the value of p is 20.

(*) Topics related to these question have been removed from latest NCERT.

***Q.10** Obtain the mean of the following distribution.

Frequency (f_i)	Variable (x_i)
4	4
8	6
14	8
11	10
3	12

Ans. We know that

$$\text{Mean } (\bar{x}) = \frac{\sum_{i=1}^{5} f_i x_i}{\sum_{i=1}^{5} f_i} = \frac{f_1x_1 + f_2x_2 + f_3x_3 + f_4x_4 + f_5x_5}{f_1 + f_2 + f_3 + f_4 + f_5}$$

$$= \frac{4 \times 4 + 8 \times 6 + 14 \times 8 + 11 \times 10 + 3 \times 12}{4 + 8 + 14 + 11 + 3}$$

$$= \frac{16 + 48 + 112 + 110 + 36}{40} = \frac{322}{40} = 8.05$$

Hence, the mean of the given data is 8.05.

***Q.11** A class consists of 50 students out of which 30 are girls. The mean of marks scored by girls in a test is 73 (out of 100) and that of boys is 71. Determine the mean score of the whole class.

Ans. Given, the number of girls out of 50 students = 30

∴ The number of boys out of 50 students = 50 − 30 = 20

Now, the marks obtained by 30 girls = 30 × 73 = 2190

and the marks obtained by 20 boys = 20 × 71 = 1420

[∵ mean of marks scored by girls in a test is 73 and that of boys is 71]

∴ Mean score of the whole class

$$= \frac{\text{Marks obtained by 30 girls} + \text{Marks obtained by 20 boys}}{\text{Number of girls} + \text{Number of boys}}$$

$$= \frac{2190 + 1420}{20 + 30}$$

$$= \frac{3610}{50} = 72.2$$

Hence, the mean score of the whole class is 72.2.

***Q.12** Mean of 50 observations was found to be 80.4. But later on, it was discovered that 96 was misread as 69 at one place. Find the correct mean.

Ans. Given, the mean of 50 observations = 80.4

∴ Sum of 50 observations = 80.4 × 50 = 4020

But later, we observe that 96 was misread as 69 at one place.

(*) Topics related to these question have been removed from latest NCERT.

Then, the correct mean $= \dfrac{(\text{Sum of 50 observations}) - 69 + 96}{50}$

$$= \frac{4020 - 69 + 96}{50} = \frac{4047}{50} = 80.94$$

Hence, the correct mean is 80.94.

***Q.13** Ten observations 6, 14, 15, 17, $x+1$, $2x-13$, 30, 32, 34 and 43 are written in an ascending order. The median of the data is 24. Find the value of x.

Ans. Given observations are 6, 14, 15, 17, $x + 1$, $2x - 13$, 30, 32, 34, 43

Here, total number of given observations, $n = 10$ (even)

Since, n is even.

$$\therefore \quad \text{Median} = \frac{\left(\frac{n}{2}\right)\text{th observation} + \left(\frac{n}{2}+1\right)\text{th observation}}{2}$$

$$= \frac{\left(\frac{10}{2}\right)\text{th observation} + \left(\frac{10}{2}+1\right)\text{th observation}}{2} \quad [\text{put } n = 10]$$

$$= \frac{\text{5th observation} + \text{6th observation}}{2}$$

$$\Rightarrow \quad 24 = \frac{(x+1) + (2x-13)}{2} \quad [\text{median} = 24 \text{ (given)}]$$

$$\Rightarrow \quad 3x - 12 = 48$$

$$\Rightarrow \quad 3x = 60$$

$$\Rightarrow \quad x = 20$$

Hence, the value of x is 20.

***Q.14** The points scored by a basket ball team in a series of matches are as follows

17, 2, 7, 27, 25, 5, 14, 18, 10, 24, 48, 10, 8, 7, 10, 28

Find the median and mode for the data.

Ans. First, arrange the given points scored in ascending order

2, 5, 7, 7, 8, 10, 10, 10, 14, 17, 18, 24, 25, 27, 28, 48

Here, number of given observations, $n = 16$ (even)

Since, n is even.

$$\therefore \quad \text{Median} = \frac{\left(\frac{n}{2}\right)\text{th observation} + \left(\frac{n}{2}+1\right)\text{th observation}}{2}$$

$$= \frac{\left(\frac{16}{2}\right)\text{th observation} + \left(\frac{16}{2}+1\right)\text{th observation}}{2} \quad [\text{put } n = 16]$$

$$= \frac{\text{8th observation} + \text{9th observation}}{2} = \frac{10 + 14}{2} = \frac{24}{2} = 12$$

We know that mode is the observation which is repeated maximum number of times. Here, we see in the given data, 10 is repeated 3 times. So, mode of a given data is 10. Hence, median and mode for the given data are 12 and 10, respectively.

(*) Topics related to these question have been removed from latest NCERT.

Q.15 In the figure, there is a histogram depicting daily wages of workers in a factory. Construct the frequency distribution table.

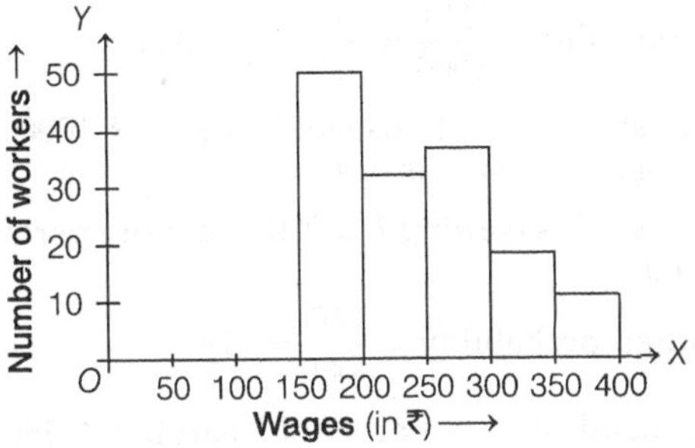

Ans. It is clear from the histogram that class intervals start from 150-200, 200-250, having width 50.

The frequency distribution table is given below.

Wage (in ₹)	Number of workers
150-200	50
200-250	30
250-300	35
300-350	20
350-400	10
Total	145

***Q.16** A company selected 4000 households at random and surveyed them to find out a relationship between income level and the number of television sets in a home. The information, so obtained is listed in the following table

Monthly income (in ₹)	Number of televisions/households			
	0	1	2	Above 2
< 10000	20	80	10	0
10000-14999	10	240	60	0
15000-19999	0	380	120	30
20000-24999	0	520	370	80
25000 and above	0	1100	760	220

Find the probability

(i) of a household earning ₹ 10000-₹ 14999 per year and having exactly one television.

(ii) of a household earning ₹ 25000 and more per year owning 2 televisions.

(iii) of a household not having any television.

(*) Topics related to these question have been removed from latest NCERT.

Ans. The total number of the households selected by the company = 4000

(i) Number of households earning ₹ 10000 - ₹ 14999 per year and having exactly one television = 240

$\therefore$ Required probability $= \frac{240}{4000} = \frac{6}{100} = \frac{3}{50} = 0.06$

Hence, the probability of a household earning ₹ 10000 - ₹ 14999 per year and having exactly one television is 0.06.

(ii) Number of households earning ₹ 25000 and more per year owning 2 televisions = 760

$\therefore$ Required probability $= \frac{760}{4000} = 0.19$

Hence, the probability of a household earning ₹ 25000 and more per year owning 2 televisions is 0.19.

(iii) Number of households not having any television = 20 + 10 = 30

$\therefore$ Required probability $= \frac{30}{4000} = \frac{3}{400}$

Hence, the probability of a household not having any television is $\frac{3}{400}$.

***Q.17** Two dice are thrown simultaneously 500 times. Each time the sum of two numbers appearing on their tops is noted and recorded as given in the following table

Sum	Frequency
2	14
3	30
4	42
5	55
6	72
7	75
8	70
9	53
10	46
11	28
12	15

If the dice are thrown once more, then what is the probability of getting a sum

(i) 3? (ii) more than 10?

(iii) less than or equal to 5? (iv) between 8 and 12?

Ans. Total number of times, when two dice are thrown simultaneously = 500

(i) Number of times of getting a sum 3 = 30

$\therefore$ Probability of getting a sum 3 $= \frac{30}{500} = \frac{3}{50} = 0.06$

Hence, the probability of getting a sum 3 is 0.06.

(*) Topics related to these question have been removed from latest NCERT.

(ii) Number of times of getting a sum more than 10 = 28 + 15 = 43

$\therefore$ Probability of getting sum more than 10 = $\frac{43}{500}$ = 0.086

Hence, the probability of getting a sum more than 10 is 0.086

(iii) Number of times of getting a sum less than or equal to 5

= 55 + 42 + 30 + 14 = 141

$\therefore$ Probability of getting a sum less than or equal to 5 = $\frac{141}{500}$ = 0.282

Hence, the probability of getting a sum less than or equal to 5 is 0.282.

(iv) The number of times of getting a sum between 8 and 12

= 53 + 46 + 28 = 127

$\therefore$ Required probability = $\frac{127}{500}$ = 0.254

Hence, the probability of getting a sum between 8 and 12 is 0.254.

***Q.18** Bulbs are packed in cartons each containing 40 bulbs. Seven hundred cartons were examined for defective bulbs and the results are given in the following table

Number of defective bulbs	0	1	2	3	4	5	6	More than 6
Frequency	400	180	48	41	18	8	3	2

One carton was selected at random. What is the probability that it has

(i) no defective bulb? (ii) defective bulbs from 2-6?

(iii) defective bulbs less than 4?

Ans. Total number of cartons, = 400 + 180 + 48 + 41 + 18 + 8 + 3 + 2 = 700

(i) Number of cartons which have no defective bulb, = 400

$\therefore$ Probability that carton has no defective bulb = $\frac{400}{700} = \frac{4}{7}$

Hence, the probability that no defective bulb is $\frac{4}{7}$.

(ii) Number of cartons which have defective bulbs from 2 to 6

= 48 + 41 + 18 + 8 + 3 = 118

$\therefore$ Probability that the carton has defective bulbs from 2 to 6 = $\frac{118}{700} = \frac{59}{350}$

Hence, the probability that the defective bulbs from 2 to 6 is $\frac{59}{350}$.

(iii) Number of cartons which have defective bulbs less than 4

= 400 + 180 + 48 + 41 = 669

$\therefore$ The probability that the carton has defective bulbs less than 4 = $\frac{669}{700}$

Hence, the probability that the defective bulb less than 4 is $\frac{669}{700}$.

(*) Topics related to these question have been removed from latest NCERT.

***Q.19** Over the past 200 working days, the number of defective parts produced by a machine is given in the following table

Number of defective parts	0	1	2	3	4	5	6	7	8	9	10	11	12	13
Days	50	32	22	18	12	12	10	10	10	8	6	6	2	2

Determine the probability that tomorrow's output will have

(i) no defective part. (ii) atleast one defective part.

(iii) not more than 5 defective parts. (iv) more than 13 defective parts.

- **Concept Insight**

$$\text{Probability } P(E) = \frac{\text{Number of trials in which the event has happened}}{\text{Total number of trials}}$$

Ans. Total number of working days = 200

(i) Number of days in which no defective part is produced = 50

∴ Probability that tomorrow's output will have no defective part

$$= \frac{50}{200} = \frac{1}{4} = 0.25$$

Hence, the probability that no defective part is 0.25.

(ii) Number of days in which atleast one defective part produced

$$= 32 + 22 + 18 + 12 + 12 + 10 + 10 + 10 + 8 + 6 + 6 + 2 + 2 = 150$$

∴ Probability that tomorrow's output will have atleast one defective part

$$= \frac{150}{200} = \frac{3}{4} = 0.75$$

Hence, the probability that atleast one defective part is 0.75.

(iii) Number of days in which not more than 5 defective parts are produced

$$= 50 + 32 + 22 + 18 + 12 + 12 = 146$$

∴ Probability that tomorrow's output will not have more than 5 defective parts

$$= \frac{146}{200} = 0.73$$

Hence, the probability that not more than 5 defective parts is 0.73.

(iv) Number of days in which more than 13 defective parts are produced = 0

∴ Probability that tomorrow's output will have more than 13 defective parts

$$= \frac{0}{200} = 0$$

Hence, the probability that more than 13 defective parts is 0.

***Q.20** A recent survey found that the ages of workers in a factory is distributed as follows.

Age (in years)	20-29	30-39	40-49	50-59	60 and above
Number of workers	38	27	86	46	3

(*) Topics related to these question have been removed from latest NCERT.

If a person is selected at random, find the probability that the person is

(i) 40 years or more. (ii) under 40 years.

(iii) having age from 30 to 39 years.

(iv) under 60 but over 39 years.

Ans. Total number of workers in a factory = 38 + 27 + 86 + 46 + 3 = 200

(i) Number of persons having the age of 40 years or more = 86 + 46 + 3 = 135

∴ Probability that the person selected is of 40 years or more = $\frac{135}{200} = 0.675$

Hence, the probability that the person selected at the age of 40 years or more is 0.675.

(ii) Number of persons having the age under 40 years = 38 + 27 = 65

∴ Probability that the person selected is under the age of 40 years = $\frac{65}{200} = 0.325$

Hence, the probability that the persons selected under the age of 40 years is 0.325.

(iii) Number of persons having age from 30 to 39 years = 27

∴ Probability that the person selected is having age from 30 to 39 years

$$= \frac{27}{200} = 0.135$$

Hence, the probability that the persons selected having age from 30 to 39 years is 0.135.

(iv) Number of persons selected having age under 60 but over 39 years

$$= 86 + 46 = 132$$

∴Probability that the persons selected is having age under 60 but over 39 years

$$= \frac{132}{200} = 0.66$$

Hence, the probability that the persons, selected having age under 60 but over 39 years is 0.66.

Long Answer Type Questions

* **Q.1** The following are the marks (out of 100) of 60 students in Mathematics.

16, 13, 5, 80, 86, 7, 51, 48, 24, 56, 70, 19, 61, 17, 16, 36, 34, 42, 34, 35, 72, 55, 75, 31, 52, 28, 72, 97, 74, 45, 62, 68, 86, 35, 85, 36, 81, 75, 55, 26, 95, 31, 7, 78, 92, 62, 52, 56, 15, 63, 25, 36, 54, 44, 47, 27, 72, 17, 4, 30.

Construct a grouped frequency distribution table with width 10 of each class starting from 0-9.

Ans. First, arranging the given data in ascending order.

4, 5, 7, 7, 13, 15, 16, 16, 17, 17, 19, 24, 25, 26, 27, 28, 30, 31, 31, 34, 34, 35, 35, 36, 36, 36, 42, 44, 45, 47, 48, 51, 52, 52, 54, 55, 55, 56, 56, 61, 62, 62, 63, 68, 70, 72, 72, 72, 74, 75, 75, 78, 80, 81, 85, 86, 86, 92, 95, 97.

(*) Topics related to these question have been removed from latest NCERT.

We arrange the given data into groups like 0-9, 10-19, 20-29, ... The class width in each case is 10.

The frequency distribution of the given data is given below

Class interval	Tally marks	Frequency
0-9	||||	4
10-19	~~||||~~ ||	7
20-29	~~||||~~	5
30-39	~~||||~~ ~~||||~~	10
40-49	~~||||~~	5
50-59	~~||||~~ |||	8
60-69	~~||||~~	5
70-79	~~||||~~ |||	8
80-89	~~||||~~	5
90-99	|||	3

***Q.2** Refer to Q.1 above. Construct a grouped frequency distribution table with width 10 of each class, in such a way that one of the class is 10-20 (20 not included).

Ans. We arrange the given data into groups like 0-10, 10-20, 20-30, ... in which upper class limit is not included in that class. The class width of each case is 10.
The frequency distribution of the given data is given below

Class interval	Tally marks	Frequency
0-10	||||	4
10-20	~~||||~~ ||	7
20-30	~~||||~~	5
30-40	~~||||~~ ~~||||~~	10
40-50	~~||||~~	5
50-60	~~||||~~ |||	8
60-70	~~||||~~	5
70-80	~~||||~~ |||	8
80-90	~~||||~~	5
90-100	|||	3

Q.3 Draw a histogram of the following distribution

Height (in cm)	Number of students
150-153	7
153-156	8
156-159	14
159-162	10
162-165	6
165-168	5

Ans. Clearly, the given frequency distribution is in exclusive form. Along the horizontal axis, we represent the class intervals of heights on some suitable scale.

(✱) Topics related to these question have been removed from latest NCERT.

The corresponding frequencies of number of students are represented along the vertical axis on a suitable scale.

Given the intervals start with 150-153. It means that there is some break (〰) indicated near the origin to signify the graph is drawn with a scale beginning at 150.

A histogram of the given distribution is given below.

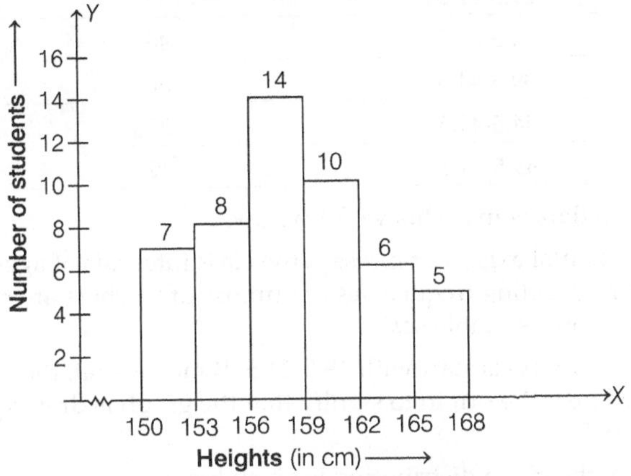

Q.4 Draw a histogram to represent the following grouped frequency distribution

Age (in years)	Number of teachers
20-24	10
25-29	28
30-34	32
35-39	48
40-44	50
45-49	35
50-54	12

Thinking Process

(i) Firstly, convert the given data into continuous form by adjusting minus 0.5 in lower limit and plus 0.5 in upper limit.

(ii) Further, we take age in horizontal axis and frequency in vertical axis. Corresponding frequencies of the height are plotted in the form of rectangle and get the required histogram.

Ans. The given frequency distribution is in inclusive form. So, first we convert it into exclusive form.

Now, consider the class 20-24, 25-29.

Lower limit of 25-29 is 25.

Upper limit of 20-24 is 24.

Thus, the half of the difference is $\frac{25-24}{2} = \frac{1}{2} = 0.5$

So, we subtract 0.5 from each lower limit and add 0.5 to each upper limit.

The table for continuous grouped frequency distribution is given below

Age (in years)	Number of teachers
19.5-24.5	10
24.5-29.5	28
29.5-34.5	32
34.5-39.5	48
39.5-44.5	50
44.5-49.5	35
49.5-54.5	12

Thus, the given data is in exclusive form now.

Along the horizontal axis, we represent the class intervals of ages on some suitable scale. The corresponding frequencies of number of teachers are represented along the vertical axis on a suitable scale.

Since, the given intervals start with 19.5-24.5. It means that, there is some break (⩘⩘) indicated near the origin to signify that the graph is drawn with a scale beginning at 19.5.

A histogram of the given distribution is given below

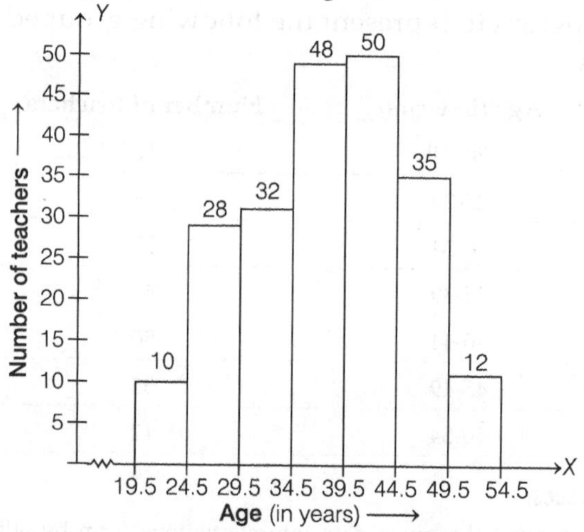

Q.5 The lengths of 62 leaves of a plant are measured in millimetres and the data is represented in the following table

Length (in mm)	Number of leaves
118-126	8
127-135	10
136-144	12
145-153	17
154-162	7
163-171	5
172-180	3

Draw a histogram to represent the data above.

Thinking Process

(i) Firstly, convert the given distribution into exclusive form by using adjusting factor

$$= \frac{127 - 126}{2} = 0.5.$$

(ii) Further, we subtract 0.5 from each lower limit and add 0.5 to each upper limit.

(iii) Finally, draw a histogram using the modified data.

Ans. The given frequency distribution is in inclusive form. So, first we convert it into exclusive form.

Now, adjusting factor $= \frac{127 - 126}{2} = \frac{1}{2} = 0.5$

So, we subtract 0.5 from each lower limit and add 0.5 to each upper limit.

The table for continuous grouped frequency distribution is given below.

Length (in mm)	**Number of leaves**
117.5-126.5	8
126.5-135.5	10
135.5-144.5	12
144.5-153.5	17
153.5-162.5	7
162.5-171.5	5
171.5-180.5	3

Thus, the given data is in exclusive form now.

Along the horizontal axis, we represent the class intervals of length on some suitable scale. The corresponding frequencies of number of leaves are represented along the Y-axis on a suitable scale.

Since, the given intervals start with 117.5-126.5. It means that, there is some break (⩘) indicated near the origin to signify that the graph is drawn with a scale beginning at 117.5.

A histogram of the given distribution is given below

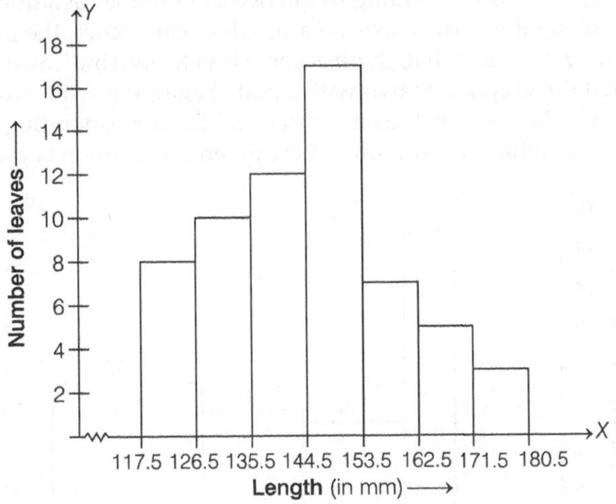

Q.6 The marks obtained (out of 100) by a class of 80 students are given below

Marks	Number of students
10-20	6
20-30	17
30-50	15
50-70	16
70-100	26

Construct a histogram to represent the data above.

Ans. In the given frequency distribution, class sizes are different. So, we calculate the adjusted frequency for each class.

Here, minimum size = 20 − 10 = 10

We use the formula,

$$\text{Adjusted frequency of a class} = \frac{\text{Minimum class size}}{\text{Class size of this class}} \times \text{Its frequency}$$

The modified table for frequency distribution is given below.

Marks	Number of students (Frequency)	Adjusted frequency
10-20	6	$\frac{10}{10} \times 6 = 6$
20-30	17	$\frac{10}{10} \times 17 = 17$
30-50	15	$\frac{10}{20} \times 15 = \frac{15}{2} = 7.5$
50-70	16	$\frac{10}{20} \times 16 = \frac{16}{2} = 8$
70-100	26	$\frac{10}{30} \times 26 = \frac{26}{3} = 8.67$

Along the horizontal axis, we represent the class intervals of marks on some suitable scales. The corresponding frequencies of number of students are represented along the vertical axis on a suitable scale. Since, the given intervals start with 10-20. It means that, there is some break (⩘) indicated near the origin to signify that the graph is drawn with a scale beginning at 10. Now, we draw rectangles with class intervals as the bases and the corresponding adjusted frequencies as heights. A histogram of the given distribution is given below

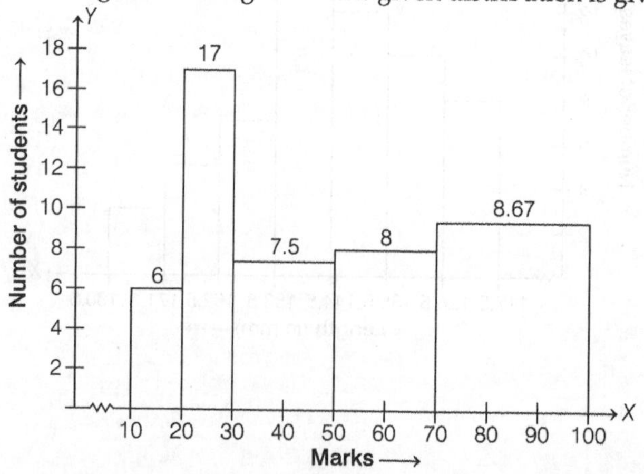

Q.7 Following table shows a frequency distribution for the speed of cars passing through at a particular spot on a high way.

Class interval (km/h)	Frequency
30-40	3
40-50	6
50-60	25
60-70	65
70-80	50
80-90	28
90-100	14

Draw a histogram and frequency polygon representing the data above.

Ans. Clearly, the given frequency distribution is in exclusive form.
Along the horizontal axis, we represent the class intervals on some suitable scale.
The corresponding frequencies are represented along the vertical axis on a suitable scale.
We construct rectangles with class intervals as the bases and the respective frequencies as the heights.

Let us draw a histogram for this data and mark the mid-points of the top of the rectangles as *B, C, D, E, F, G* and *H*, respectively. Here, the first class is 30-40 and the last class is 90-100.
Also, consider the imagined classes 20-30 and 100-110 each with frequency 0. The class marks of these classes are 25 and 105 at the points *A* and *I*, respectively.

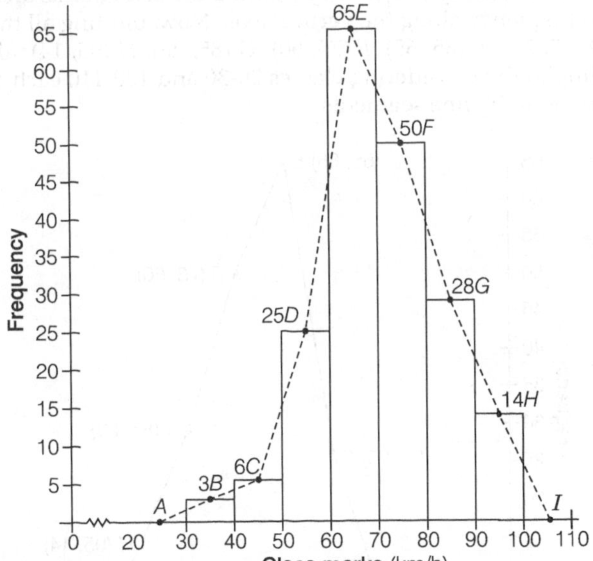

Join all these points by dotted line.
Then, the curve *ABCDEFGHI* is the required frequency polygon.

Q.8 Refer to Q. 7. Draw the frequency polygon representing the above data without drawing the histogram.

- **Concept Insight** Use the formula of class-mark = $\frac{\text{Upper limit + lower limit}}{2}$

Ans. We have to draw a frequency polygon without a histogram.
Firstly, we find the class marks of the classes given that is 30-40, 40-50, 50-60, 60-70 ...

$$\therefore \quad \text{The class mark} = \frac{30+40}{2}$$

$$= \frac{70}{2} = 35$$

Similarly, we can determine the class marks of the other classes.
So, table for class marks is shown below

Class interval (km/h)	Class marks	Frequency
30-40	35	3
40-50	45	6
50-60	55	25
60-70	65	65
70-80	75	50
80-90	85	28
90-100	95	14

We can draw a frequency polygon by plotting the class marks along the horizontal axis and the frequency along the vertical axis. Now, plotting all the points *B* (35, 3), *C* (45, 6), *D* (55, 25), *E* (65, 65), *F* (75, 50), *G* (85, 28), *H* (95, 14), also plot the point corresponding to the considering classes 20-30 and 100-110 each with frequency 0. Join all these point by line segments.

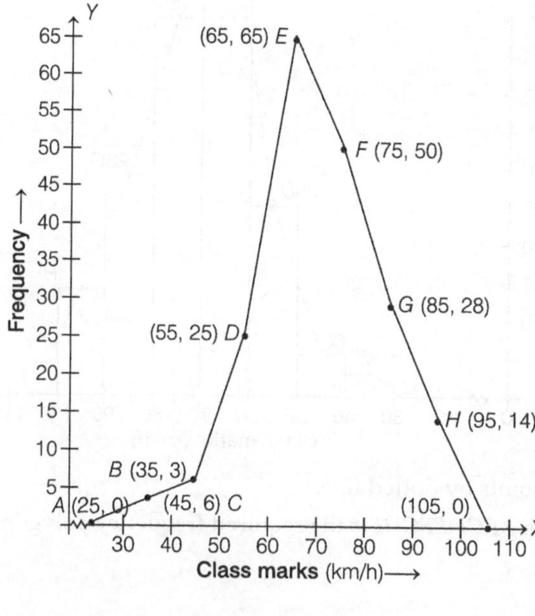

Q.9 Following table gives the distribution of students of sections A and B *of a class according to the marks obtained by them.*

Section A		Section B	
Marks	**Frequency**	**Marks**	**Frequency**
0-15	5	0-15	3
15-30	12	15-30	16
30-45	28	30-45	25
45-60	30	45-60	27
60-75	35	60-75	40
75-90	13	75-90	10

Represent the marks of the students of both the sections on the same graph by two frequency polygons. What do you observe?

Ans. Firstly, we find the mid marks of the given sections A and B by using the formula

$$\text{Class mark} = \frac{\text{Lower limit} + \text{Upper limit}}{2}$$

So, the new table for section A and section B is shown below

Section A			Section B		
Marks	**Mid marks**	**Frequency**	**Marks**	**Mid marks**	**Frequency**
0-15	7.5	5	0-15	7.5	3
15-30	22.5	12	15-30	22.5	16
30-45	37.5	28	30-45	37.5	25
45-60	52.5	30	45-60	52.5	27
60-75	67.5	35	60-75	67.5	40
75-90	82.5	13	75-90	82.5	10

We can draw a frequency polygon by plotting the class marks along the horizontal axis and the frequency along the vertical axis.

Now, plotting all the points A (7.5, 5), B (22.5, 12), C (37.5, 28), D (52.5, 30), E (67.5, 35), F(82.5, 13) for section A.

Also, plotting all the points H (7.5, 3), I (22.5, 16), J (37.5, 25), K (52.5, 27), L (67.5, 40) and M (82.5, 10) for section B.

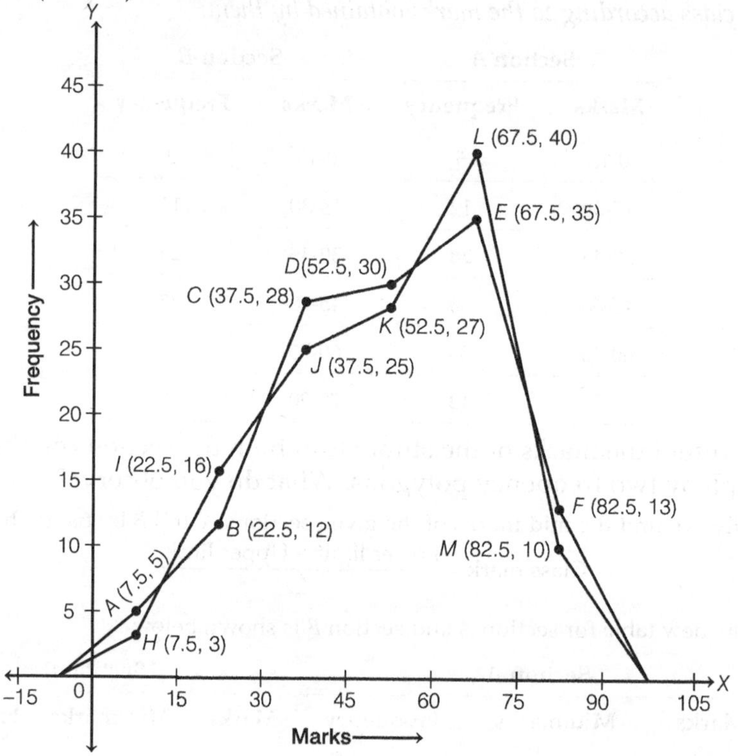

It is clear from the graph that maximum marks 67.5 score by 40 students in section B.

***Q.10** The mean of the following distribution is 50.

x	10	30	50	70	90
f	17	$5a + 3$	32	$7a - 11$	19

Find the value of a and hence the frequencies of 30 and 70.

Ans. We know that,

$$\text{Mean of the distribution } (\overline{x}) = \frac{\sum_{i=1}^{5} f_i x_i}{\sum_{i=1}^{5} f_i} = 50 \quad \text{[given]}$$

$$\Rightarrow \quad \frac{f_1x_1 + f_2x_2 + f_3x_3 + f_4x_4 + f_5x_5}{f_1 + f_2 + f_3 + f_4 + f_5} = 50$$

$$\Rightarrow \quad \frac{(17)(10) + (5a+3)(30) + (32)(50) + (7a-11)(70) + (19)(90)}{17 + 5a + 3 + 32 + 7a - 11 + 19} = 50$$

$$\Rightarrow \quad \frac{170 + 150a + 90 + 1600 + 490a - 770 + 1710}{12a + 60} = 50$$

(*) Topics related to these question have been removed from latest NCERT.

$$\Rightarrow \quad \frac{3570 - 770 + 640a}{12a + 60} = 50$$

$$\Rightarrow \quad 2800 + 640a = 600a + 3000$$

$$\Rightarrow \quad 40a = 200 \Rightarrow a = 5$$

$\therefore$ Frequency of 30 $= 5a + 3 = 5(5) + 3$ $[\because a = 5]$

$= 25 + 3 = 28$

and frequency of 70 $= 7a - 11 = 7(5) - 11$ $[\because a = 5]$

$= 35 - 11 = 24$

Hence, the frequencies of 30 and 70 are respectively, 28 and 24.

***Q.11** The mean marks (out of 100) of boys and girls in an examination are 70 and 73, respectively. If the mean marks of all the students in that examination is 71, find the ratio of the number of boys to the number of girls.

Ans. Let n_1 and n_2 be the number of boys and girls, respectively.

Given, mean marks (out of 100) of boys $(\bar{x}_1) = 70$

and mean marks (out of 100) of girls $(\bar{x}_2) = 73$

Also, given that, mean marks of all the students in the examination $(\bar{x}_{12}) = 71$

Now, using the formula,

Combined mean, $(\bar{x}_{12}) = \dfrac{\bar{x}_1 n_1 + \bar{x}_2 n_2}{n_1 + n_2} = 71$ [given]

$$\therefore \quad \frac{70n_1 + 73n_2}{n_1 + n_2} = 71$$

$$\Rightarrow \quad 70n_1 + 73n_2 = 71n_1 + 71n_2$$

$$\Rightarrow \quad 73n_2 - 71n_2 = 71n_1 - 70n_1$$

$$\Rightarrow \quad 2n_2 = n_1$$

$$\Rightarrow \quad \frac{n_1}{n_2} = \frac{2}{1} \text{ or } n_1 : n_2 = 2 : 1$$

Hence, the ratio of number of boys to the number of girls is 2 : 1.

***Q.12** A total of 25 patients admitted to a hospital are tested for levels of blood sugar, (mg/dl) and the results obtained were as follows.

87	71	83	67	85
77	69	76	65	85
85	54	70	68	80
73	78	68	85	73
81	78	81	77	75

Find mean, median and mode (mg/dl) of the above data.

Ans. Firstly, arrange the give table in ascending order, which is shown below

54, 65, 67, 68, 68, 69, 70, 71, 73, 73, 75, 76, 77, 77, 78, 78, 80, 81, 81, 83, 85, 85, 85, 85, 87

Here, number of observations, $n = 25$

(*) Topics related to these question have been removed from latest NCERT.

Sum of all observations

$$= 54 + 65 + 67 + 68 + 68 + 69 + 70 + 71 + 73 + 73 + 75 + 76 + 77 + 77 + 78 + 78 + 80 + 81 + 81 + 83 + 85 + 85 + 85 + 85 + 87$$

$$= 1891$$

∴ Mean of blood sugar testing

$$= \frac{\text{Sum of all observations}}{\text{Total number of observations}} = \frac{1891}{25} = 75.64$$

Here, $n = 25$ which is odd.

So, $\text{median} = \left(\frac{n+1}{2}\right)\text{th observation} = \left(\frac{25+1}{2}\right)\text{th observation}$

$$= 13\text{th observation} = 77$$

We know that, mode is the highest frequency of an observation.
In the given data, we see that maximum repeated number is 85.
Hence, mode of the given data is 85.